MCSE Guide to

Designing a Microsoft® Windows® 2000 Directory Service

By Michael J. Palmer

COURSE
TECHNOLOGY
TM
THOMSON LEARNING

Australia • Canada • Mexico • Singapore • Spain • United Kingdom • United States

MCSE Guide to Designing a Microsoft Windows 2000 Directory Service

By Michael J. Palmer

Managing Editor:
Stephen Solomon

Senior Product Manager:
Dave George

Developmental Editor:
Deb Kaufmann

Marketing Manager:
Toby Shelton

Production Editor:
Debbie Masi

Associate Product Manager:
Elizabeth Wessen

Editorial Assistant:
Janet Aras

Quality Assurance Manager:
John Bosco

Cover Design:
Joseph Lee, Black Fish Design

Text Design:
GEX Publishing Services

Composition House:
GEX Publishing Services

Disclaimer
Course Technology reserves the right to revise this publication and make changes from time to time in its content without notice.

ISBN 0-619-01689-2

Contents

TABLE OF

Contents

CHAPTER THREE
Analyzing Information Technology Structures   103

Preface

Microsoft Active Directory is the central nervous system of a Windows 2000 server network because users and servers depend on it for managed access to network resources. The vital role that Active Directory plays means that information technology organizations are constantly looking for people qualified in designing Active Directory services. This book provides you with the knowledge and practical experience needed to jumpstart your career as an Active Directory services designer.

If you are preparing for Microsoft certification as a Microsoft Certified Professional (MCP) or as a Microsoft Certified Systems Engineer (MCSE), this book supplies the knowledge you need to get ready for certification exam # 70-219, *Designing a Microsoft Windows 2000 Directory Services Infrastructure*. If you already have experience in Active Directory design, the book will help in broadening that experience to make you a better designer.

The book is written to take the mystery out of Active Directory design through using clear language and step-by-step examples, while giving you confidence to handle all kinds of design situations. You learn to apply design principles to small regional organizations, national organizations, and international organizations. You begin by learning how to analyze different kinds of organizations, including information technology departments, so that you can tailor a design to an organization's needs. Next, you learn how to create an Active Directory design to match your analysis of an organization.

Every chapter of the book is filled with information and features that are geared to maximize your learning and prepare you for certification exam # 70-219, *Designing a Microsoft Windows 2000 Directory Services Infrastructure*. Analysis concepts and design principles are presented in a basic and understandable fashion. Useful notes and tips are included throughout the book to provide valuable information for certification and to help you become a solid designer. The chapters include review questions that enable you to test your knowledge in a particular area and prepare you for certification. Because the Microsoft certification examination uses a case format, Chapters 2 through 11 provide review questions that enable you to practice using this format. The chapters also include longer case projects and optional team case projects for certification preparation and to help lock in what you have learned through practice. Hands-on experience is another important way to learn and so each chapter contains a variety of hands-on projects to give you direct experience. Appendix A includes a mapping grid to show you where each certification objective is presented in the book. Appendix B provides a listing of the main Active Directory management tools.

The book is divided into 12 chapters. Three sample companies are followed throughout to provide realistic examples of regional, national, and international organizations. The beginning chapters focus on the certification objectives that relate to analyzing business and technical requirements. After you master the analysis techniques the second half of the book stresses the design objectives for certification, showing you how to set up Active Directory services by applying your analyses. The last chapter offers a review of the key analysis and design concepts. The following is a summary of each chapter:

- *Chapter 1: Introduction to Directory Services* gives you an overview of the directory services that are part of Active Directory. The chapter introduces key elements, such as forests, trees, domains, organizational units, sites, group policies, and security.

- *Chapter 2: Analyzing Business Requirements* shows you how to analyze organizational structures, management models, business strategies, and business processes that affect Active Directory design.

- *Chapter 3: Analyzing Information Technology Structures* enables you to analyze information technology groups or departments in terms of organization, decision making, strategies, funding, and other factors. Information technology change management is introduced to show how Windows 2000 operating systems can be used to minimize operations costs.

- *Chapter 4: Analyzing Software Requirements* gives you a solid foundation in the analysis of software that is used by an organization. You will learn to analyze client operating systems, user access, software resources, software security needs, and technical support needs. One of the analysis tools that you use is Microsoft Network Monitor.

- *Chapter 5: Analyzing Hardware and Network Requirements* focuses on analyzing technical requirements such as hardware, network bandwidth, LANs, WANs, the Internet, network management, and network security.

- *Chapter 6: Designing Forests, Trees, and Domains* shows you how to design principle Active Directory elements on the basis of your business and technical requirements analyses. You will learn how to design forests, trees, domains, and the Active Directory schema for different kinds of organizations.

- *Chapter 7: Designing Organizational Units, Sites, and DNS Implementation* enables you to design the organizational unit and site structures in Active Directory. Also, you will learn how to design and implement DNS services to complement your Active Directory design. This chapter builds on the design concepts presented in Chapter 6.

- *Chapter 8: Security Group and Group Policy Design* presents how to design Active Directory services for using security groups, delegating authority, and implementing group policies. Your mastery of group policies opens the way to strengthen network security and to reduce client desktop management costs.

- *Chapter 9: Planning Active Directory Security and Coexistence* gives you grounding in how to set up security for Active Directory administrators and how to protect critical Active Directory elements, such as domains. Also, you will learn how to enable Active Directory to coexist with other directory services, such as Novell Directory Services and with specialized databases, such as the Microsoft Exchange database.

- *Chapter 10: Designing for Operations Masters and Global Catalog Servers* shows you how to create an operations master and global catalog server design architecture for different kinds of organizations. You will learn how different organizational analyses influence where you place operations masters and global catalog servers on networks.

- *Chapter 11: Designing Replication and Disaster Recovery* focuses on how to establish an Active Directory replication design for fault tolerance and disaster recovery. Two key elements that you will learn are how the Knowledge Consistency Checker is used for replication and how to strategically locate domain controllers.

- *Chapter 12: Analysis and Design Review* provides a review of the key Active Directory elements, analysis techniques, design techniques, and how to plan an Active Directory implementation. Use this chapter as review just before you take the certification examination and as a refresher when you are starting an Active Directory design project.

Features

To aid you in fully understanding Windows 2000 concepts, there are many features in this book designed to match the ways in which you learn.

- **Chapter Objectives.** Each chapter in this book begins with a detailed list of the concepts to be mastered within that chapter. This list provides you with a quick reference to the contents of that chapter, as well as a useful study aid.

- **Illustrations and Tables.** Numerous illustrations of server screens and components aid you in the visualization of common setup steps, theories, and concepts. In addition, many tables provide details and comparisons of both practical and theoretical information and can be used for a quick review of topics.

- **Chapter Summaries.** Each chapter's text is followed by a summary of the concepts it has introduced. These summaries provide a helpful way to recap and revisit the ideas covered in each chapter.

- **Review Questions.** The end-of-chapter assessments begin with a set of review questions that reinforce the ideas introduced in each chapter. These questions not only ensure that you have mastered the concepts, but are written to help you become familiar with the types of questions used in Microsoft certification examinations.

- **Hands-on Projects.** Although it is important to understand the theory behind server and networking technology, nothing can improve upon real-world experience. To this end, along with theoretical explanations, each chapter provides numerous hands-on projects aimed at providing you with real-world implementation experience.

- **Case Project.** Located at the end of each chapter is a multi-part case project. In this extensive case example, as a consultant at the fictitious Aspen Consulting, you implement the skills and knowledge gained in the chapter through real-world Active Directory setup and administration scenarios.

- **Team Case Projects.** Each chapter concludes with two optional team case projects that enable you to work in a small group of students to solve a real-world problem or to extensively research a topic. These projects give you experience working as a team member, which is a common format used by many businesses and corporations.

Text and Graphic Conventions

Wherever appropriate, additional information and exercises have been added to this book to help you better understand what is being discussed in the chapter. Icons throughout the text alert you to additional materials. The icons used in this textbook are described below.

The Note icon is used to present additional helpful material related to the subject being described.

Tips are included from the author's experience that provide extra information about how to attack a problem, how to set up Active Directory for a particular need, or what to do to in certain real-world situations.

The cautions are provided to help you anticipate potential mistakes or problems so you can prevent them from happening.

Each Hands-on Project in this book is preceded by the Hands-on icon and a description of the exercise that follows.

Case project icons mark the case project. These are more involved, scenario-based assignments. In each extensive case example, you are asked to implement independently what you have learned.

Optional case project icons indicate special projects that students can tackle as a group and that often require extra research and group decision making, which simulates the project team environment stressed in many organizations.

Instructor's Materials

The following supplemental materials are available when this book is used in a classroom setting. All of the supplements available with this book are provided to the instructor on a single CD-ROM.

Electronic Instructor's Manual. The Instructor's Manual that accompanies this textbook includes:

- Additional instructional material to assist in class preparation, including suggestions for lecture topics, class discussion topics, suggested lab activities, tips on setting up a lab for the hands-on assignments, and alternative lab setup ideas in situations where lab resources are limited.
- Quick quizzes to help reinforce learning at key junctures.
- Solutions to all end-of-chapter materials, including the Review Questions, Hands-on Projects, Case and Optional Team Case assignments.
- A list of key terms and concepts used in each chapter.

ExamView® This textbook is accompanied by ExamView, a powerful testing software package that allows instructors to create and administer printed, computer (LAN-based), and Internet exams. ExamView includes hundreds of questions that correspond to the topics covered in this text, enabling students to generate detailed study guides that include page references for further review. The computer-based and Internet testing components allow students to take exams at their computers, and also save the instructor time by grading each exam automatically.

PowerPoint Presentations. This book comes with Microsoft PowerPoint slides for each chapter. These are included as a teaching aid for classroom presentation, to make available to students on the network for chapter review, or to be printed for classroom distribution. Instructors, please feel at liberty to add your own slides for additional topics you introduce to the class.

About your CertPack

The CertPack envelope bound into this book contains additional training tools designed to prepare you for MCSE certification. On the CD-ROM you will find CoursePrep exam preparation software, which provides 50 sample MCSE exam questions mirroring the look and feel of the MCSE exams, and CourseSim simulation software, which allows you to perform tasks in a simulated Windows 2000 environment. Accompanying the CD-ROM is a coupon for a discount on your MCSE exam at any Prometric testing center.

STUDENT'S MATERIALS

Student Case Assignment Files. The instructor's CD-ROM comes with student case assignment files for each chapter. These files contain the end-of-chapter Case and Optional Team Case assignments in electronic format so that students can enter their answers and submit them through e-mail, to a shared network folder, or print them for submission to the instructor.

Electronic Glossary. An electronic glossary with hyperlinks is provided on the instructor's CD-ROM for distribution to each student, such as through a Web page or a shared network folder.

Windows 2000 Server Command Summary. A summary of the Windows 2000 Server Command Prompt window commands is provided for distribution to students in electronic format.

ACKNOWLEDGMENTS

Writing a book is really a great expedition into the realm of ideas and crafting words. One of the best parts of the expedition is the opportunity to work with many talented and supportive people. This project is made possible through the efforts of Managing Editor Stephen Solomon and Publisher Kristen Duerr. Product Manager Dave George has skillfully provided a guiding hand from start to finish to make sure that all of the disparate parts of the process become the reality of a finished book. The words and thoughts that you read on every page are wisely influenced by Deb Kaufmann, an incredibly talented developmental editor, who is always reassuring that there is light at the end of the expedition. My thanks also go to Elizabeth Wessen, the associate product manager, for the production of quality instructors and students materials; and to Debbie Masi for her work as production editor.

Nicole Ashton and John Freitas, who provide quality assurance, have carefully reviewed each word and tested each keystroke to ensure accuracy in every chapter. I am also indebted to Lorna St. George and Fred Bisel, the technical reviewers for the book, and to other fine people at Course Technology who include Marketing Manager Toby Shelton and Editorial Assistant Janet Aras.

DEDICATION

To Shawn and Kristy

Read This Before You Begin

To the Student

This book gives you a foundation in designing and implementing Microsoft Active Directory. Every chapter is designed to present you with easy-to-understand information about Active Directory so that you can become a capable directory services designer. Each chapter of the book ends with review questions, hands-on projects, case assignments, and team case assignments that are written to be as realistic as the work you will soon be performing. Your instructor can provide you with answers to the review questions and additional information about the hands-on projects. When you complete the case and optional team case assignments, you can submit them electronically or in written form. The student project files provided by your instructor consist of Microsoft Word files for each end-of-chapter case and optional team case project. You can enter your answers in the space provided within the file and submit them to your instructor by disk, by printing out your answers, through the network, or through e-mail.

To the Instructor (Please refer to the Instructor's Resource Kit that accompanies this text for more details.)

Setting up the Classroom or Lab File Server. To complete the projects and assignments in the book, the students will need access to a computer running Windows 2000 Server or higher. To maximize the learning experience, it is recommended that you have one or more servers which can be dedicated for classroom use. Each server need not be an expensive model, but should be on Microsoft's Hardware Compatibility List. There is an advantage in having several servers for student projects so that the students have more flexibility in their practice. Every server should be equipped with Microsoft Windows 2000 Server or higher and there should be enough licenses as appropriate for your laboratory or practice setup. The Instructor's Resource Kit contains many suggestions about how to set up a lab, including how to equip and manage a lab in which there are limited resources. It also contains alternative projects and assignments for students. *The Hands-on Projects in the text require that students have Administrator privileges or accounts with Administrator privileges.*

Internet Assignments. A few projects require Internet access for information searches. These projects are not mandatory, however, the projects will help train the student in using this resource as a prospective server administrator.

CHAPTER 1

INTRODUCTION TO DIRECTORY SERVICES

After reading this chapter and completing the exercises, you will be able to:

♦ Explain Windows 2000 directory services and Windows 2000 Server Active Directory structure

♦ Explain the use of organizational units, domains, trees, forests, and sites in Active Directory

♦ Discuss the use of group policies in Windows 2000 directory services

♦ Discuss the advantages of using Active Directory and TCP/IP together on a network

Networks are like vibrant communities that are filled with resources. In a community, the resources are its people, businesses, schools, libraries, recreation centers, and parks. A network's resources are its client users, workstations, servers, shared files, shared printers, fax devices, and shared disk storage. Neither the resources in a community nor the resources in a network attain their full potential until their existence is advertised to those who want to use them. In a community, resources can be found by consulting a community directory or telephone book. The resources of a network are located through its directory services.

In this chapter, you will learn about the Windows 2000 Active Directory services, which house the resources of the smallest to the largest network so that those resources can be accessed by network users. You will learn the basics of how Active Directory turns a potentially chaotic and formidable range of users, computers, servers, printers, and different networks into an orderly set of known resources that can be easily accessed and managed. You will also learn about Active Directory functions, including directory services, directory service components, security, and group policies.

WINDOWS 2000 DIRECTORY SERVICES

A directory on a computer is a container for files and subdirectories. On a network, a directory contains the resources of the network, such as computers, printers, user accounts, and user groups. A network **directory service** does more than a directory alone because it combines three vital functions. It provides:

- A central listing of resources
- Ways to quickly find specific resources
- Ways to access and manage resources

The Windows 2000 Server directory services compose Active Directory, which is a directory service that acts as a container for resources called objects. An **object** can be a physical resource, such as a computer or printer, or an object can be a logical resource, such as a user account or a group of user accounts. In Active Directory, the resource objects include the following (as shown in Figure 1-1):

- Servers
- Workstations
- Printers
- Shared folders
- Shared storage
- User accounts
- Groups of users and resources
- Network fax devices
- Network divisions, such as subnetworks (subnets)

Each object can have a set of characteristics, or attributes, that distinguish it from other kinds of objects. For example, a network printer has attributes such as a printer name and a description of that particular printer. A user account has attributes that include the logon name of the user and the user's full name.

Publishing and Finding an Object

One reason for having Active Directory is to enable certain objects to be "published" so that users can find and access those objects quickly. **Publishing** an object means that it is made available for users to access when they view Active Directory contents and that the data associated with the object can be replicated. For example, a shared folder or a shared printer can be published in Active Directory for clients to access. Publishing an object also makes it easier to find when a user searches for that object—for example, by using

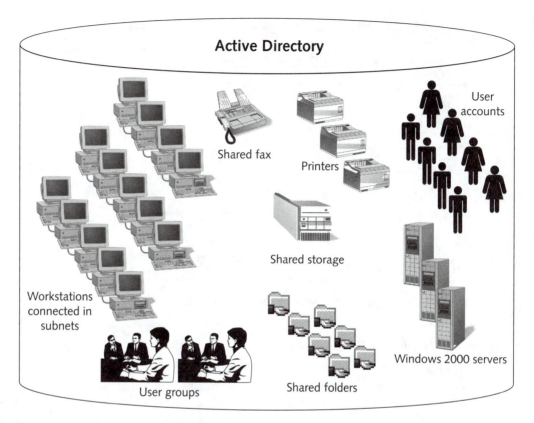

Figure 1-1   Active Directory objects

My Network Places in Windows 2000 Professional or Server (see Figure 1-2). Once an object has been published, information associated with that object is duplicated in the copies of Active Directory that are kept when there are multiple servers on a network, enabling a published object to be accessed even when one server is down.

Active Directory search capabilities are automatically built into all Windows 2000 operating systems (try Hands-on Projects 1-1 and 1-2). Non-Windows 2000 operating systems, such as Windows 95 and Windows 98, are able to search Active Directory when the **Directory Service Client (DSClient)** software is installed on those systems. The Directory Service Client software is available as the program Dsclient.exe, which is located on the Windows 2000 Server CD-ROM in the folder \Clients\WIN9X. Try Hands-on Project 1-3 to install the Directory Service Client software on a Windows 95 or Windows 98 client.

The Directory Service Client software installs Active Directory search features at the client, such as the ability to search Active Directory for a printer, even if the client does not know the specific name of the printer. To search for a printer using Windows 98 for example, click Start, point to Find, and click Printers. (Printers is a new option added by the Directory Service Client.)

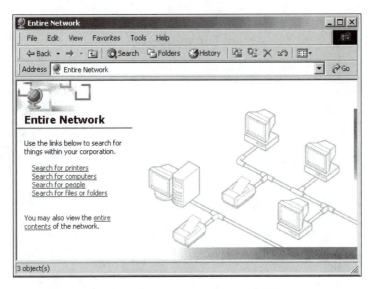

Figure 1-2   Searching by using My Network Places

Managing Resources

Windows 2000 Active Directory provides several functions that enable you to manage and maintain the directory services, as well as to publish and locate objects. For example, there must be ways to specify which users can access objects, such as shared folders, and the level of access given to users, such as giving some users the ability to modify files while giving other users access only to read the contents of a folder. Also, there needs to be methods to enable object management to be either centralized or decentralized. For example, some organizations like to centralize management of user accounts with their information technology (IT) department. Other organizations prefer to decentralize user account management by giving this responsibility to managers or administrative assistants in the departments within those organizations. Another important function is to ensure that Active Directory contents are not lost when a disk drive or server fails.

The management functions built into Active Directory include:

- Maintenance of a schema of attributes for objects

- Distribution of directory services among servers

- Automatic replication of Active Directory among servers

- Security management of objects

- Ability to delegate management of specific objects

- Ability to store a large number of objects and to scale Active Directory as an organization grows

- Division of objects into a hierarchical tree structure of main objects and child objects within main objects

- Compatibility with directory service standards and name formats

- Use of a namespace for network and Internet hierarchical domain naming

Active Directory Schema

Every type of object in Active Directory is defined through a schema. A **schema** is a database consisting of the definitions of all objects in Active Directory, and reflects the skeletal structure and rules of Active Directory. The principal contents of the Active Directory schema are object classes and the attributes associated with each object class. You can think of a schema in terms of the characteristics associated with a network. First, there are object classes of network resources, such as computers, printers, and user accounts. An **object class** is a unit designating a group of resources that have the same characteristics—computers represent an object class and so do user accounts, for example. Also, each object class has a set of attributes. An **attribute** is a characteristic, quality, or property that helps define an object class. For a computer, the attributes include the name of the computer, a description, and the domain or workgroup to which the computer belongs. Some attributes must be defined, such as the computer's name, and others are optionally defined, such as the computer's description.

When you install Active Directory for the first time on a network server, you create several object classes automatically. The default object classes include:

- Domain

- User account

- Group

- Shared drive

- Shared folder

- Computer

- Printer

Most objects have the following attributes within the object class:

- A unique object name

- A **globally unique identifier (GUID)**, which is a unique 128-bit hexadecimal number associated with the object name

- Required attributes (those that must be defined with each object)

- Optional attributes (those that are defined only if and as you choose)

- A syntax (format) to determine how attributes are defined

- Pointers to parent entities (for a shared printer, this might be the computer to which that printer is attached)

For example, the user account object class has the following required attributes, which must be set up for each account (see Figure 1-3):

- Logon name
- User's full name
- Password
- Domain (discussed later in this chapter)

The optional attributes for a user account include:

- Account description
- Account holder's office number or address
- Account holder's telephone number
- Account holder's e-mail address

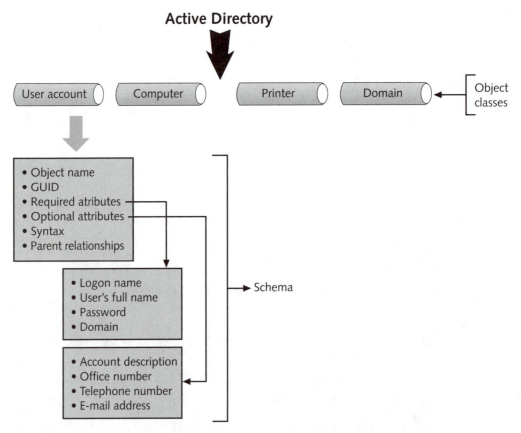

Figure 1-3   Sample schema information for user accounts

In some instances, the attributes that are required and those that are optional can be influenced by the security policies that the server administrator sets in Active Directory for a class of objects. Also, each attribute is automatically given a version number and date when it is created or changed. This information enables Active Directory to know when an attribute value, such as a password, is changed and to update only that value on all servers that maintain Active Directory data.

Distributing Active Directory Services

Several Windows 2000 servers can be set up to maintain information using Active Directory, and these servers are called **domain controllers (DCs)**. In Active Directory, a **domain** is a high-level component or container that holds information about all network objects that are grouped under it—servers, printers, network devices, user accounts, and user groups. An important function of a domain is to create a security boundary around the objects held within it and to provide a means to administer those objects as a unit. A DC is a Windows 2000 server that contains a copy of Active Directory domain information (an Active Directory partition).

In Windows 2000 Server, each DC is equal to every other DC in that it contains the full range of information that composes Active Directory for the domain. For example, when you create a new user account, the information associated with that account can be created on any Windows 2000 Server DC. This differs from the Windows NT Server method of creating accounts only on a primary domain controller (PDC) and then making a backup copy on one or more backup domain controllers (BDCs). In Windows 2000 Server, all DCs are equal in status. This technique significantly improves network performance because registration of new objects and Active Directory replication can be distributed among DCs so that the network load is also distributed. In the previous Windows NT PDC/BDC architecture, the portion of the network containing the PDC could become congested because of the centralization of the process of creating new objects and replicating them from a main server. Another advantage of the Windows 2000 Server DC architecture is that the authentication of access to the network and network resources can be handled by the DC closest to the client. Try Hands-on Project 1-4 to view the DCs on a network.

Active Directory Replication

The replication of DCs on a Windows 2000 Server network is called **multimaster replication**. When an account is created, the full information about that account is replicated on every other DC in the domain. The advantage of this approach is that if one DC fails, Active Directory is fully intact on all other DCs, and there is no visible network interruption because there is no pause to manually promote a server to take over as the master database.

Because each DC contains a mirror image of Active Directory, Microsoft recommends that networks that deploy two or more Windows 2000 servers
also deploy at least two DCs for fault tolerance.

In multimaster replication, Windows 2000 Server can determine how much of Active
Directory is replicated each time it is copied from one DC to another. Also, replication of
Active Directory information can be adjusted to occur at a preset interval instead of as soon as
an update occurs. For example, Active Directory can improve network performance by:

- Replicating individual attributes of an object instead of all attributes—for example,
  updating only a change in an account's password instead of updating all of that
  account's attributes when the password is changed

- Replicating Active Directory on the basis of the speed of the network link—
  for example, replicating more frequently over a local area network (LAN)
  than over a wide area network (WAN) link

Security Management of Objects

Each object in Active Directory can be protected through a collection of security properties that are cumulatively called a **security descriptor** and that control how that object
may be accessed. For example, a shared folder in Active Directory can be associated with
a set of accounts and information about the level of access each account is allowed. A security descriptor for a server can control which accounts have access to the server, or
whether that server can even be accessed over the network. A security descriptor is also
referred to as an **access control list (ACL)**, which contains all information about access
to a particular object.

There are two components to an ACL or security descriptor in Active Directory: a discretionary access control list and a system access control list. A **discretionary access control
list (DACL)** is a partial access control list of users, groups, and computers that are allowed
or denied some form of permission to access an object. For example, a shared folder on a
server called Payroll can have a DACL that specifies only the accounts RBrown, LMason,
AGonzales, and MKlein have full access to that folder, in an organization of 275 employees,
while another folder called Paypolicies has a DACL that includes read-only access for everyone in the organization. A **system access control list (SACL)** is a partial access control
list that determines which, if any, events associated with an object are to be audited. For
example, the Payroll folder can have an SACL as part of its security descriptor that specifies
a security event be recorded each time any user writes to that folder.

Each ACL for an object typically contains four categories of information:

- The user accounts (or account groups) that can access the object

- The rights and permissions that determine the level of access

- The ownership of the object (the default owner of an object is its creator; ownership can be taken by another user account if that account has sufficient permission)

- An indication of whether specific events associated with an object are to be audited

Each user account or group of accounts is assigned a type of access to an object, called a right or permission. A **right** is an access privilege for high-level activities such as logging on to a server from the network, shutting down a server, and the ability to log on locally.

A **permission** involves privileges to access and manipulate resource objects, such as folders and printers, as in the privilege to read a file, or to create a new file. There are standard permissions and special permissions available through the NT File System (NTFS). A standard permission is most frequently used and consists of the object permissions that are available by default. The permissions available relate to the nature of the object and the appropriate security that applies to the object. The typical standard permissions that are available for objects in Active Directory are as follows:

- *Deny* or *No Access:* No permission to access the object in any way

- *Allow:* Permit access on the basis of a specific permission

- *Read:* Permission for viewing an object, reading its contents (for folders and files), and determining properties or attributes of the object

- *Write:* Permission to change object properties or the contents of an object (for folders and files)

- *Delete All Child Objects:* Permission to remove an object, such as removing a user account from a domain

- *Create All Child Objects:* Permission to add an object, such as creating a new user account in a domain

- *Full Control:* Permission to access the object for nearly any purpose, including to take ownership of the object or to change the permissions associated with that object

Figure 1-4 shows an example of the standard permissions associated with the domain TheFirm.com in Active Directory. Try Hands-on Project 1-5 to view the permissions for a domain.

An NTFS special permission is used in situations where a standard permission must be more finely tuned for a particular kind of access. For example, you may need to give applications developers in the organization specialized access to a domain to list all of the domain contents and to create child objects, but not to delete child objects. Figure 1-5 shows the special permissions for the domain TheFirm.com.

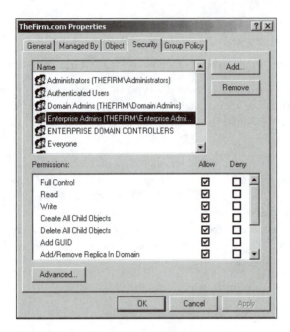

Figure 1-4 Standard permissions

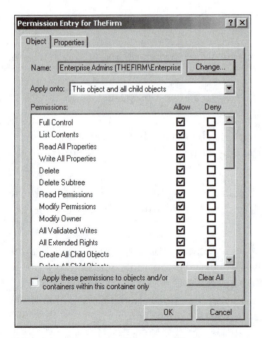

Figure 1-5 Special permissions

Delegating Management of Objects

Active Directory enables management of objects to be delegated to reflect the lines of authority in an organization. This means that objects can be managed centrally, or object management can be decentralized among several individuals. For example, the management style of a university might be to give only the server administrators authority to create user accounts. In a tax accounting firm, the firm's financial auditors may require that only one security administrator have the ability to create user accounts and manage all security. Both of these represent centralized security management.

In a decentralized management structure, such as for an organization that develops computer software, the creation of user accounts and the management of security associated with those accounts might be delegated to each project team leader. Similarly, a community college that maintains server-based instructional labs might delegate authority over user accounts to instructors who use those labs.

Active Directory permits as much or as little delegation of management as is needed for an organization. In some organizations, the delegation of management can increase productivity and enable those organizations to exercise rapid response to security needs. For example, a department head in a company can immediately create a new account and assign security to that account just minutes after hiring a new employee. When the employee reports for work, even if it is the same day as she or he is hired, that employee can start accessing network resources. Similarly, if an employee's responsibilities change, the same department head can adjust security access to match the change in responsibilities.

Windows 2000 Server has a Delegation of Control Wizard that customizes the delegation options to the type of object (see Figure 1-6). Try Hands-on Project 1-6 to practice delegating control of an Active Directory object.

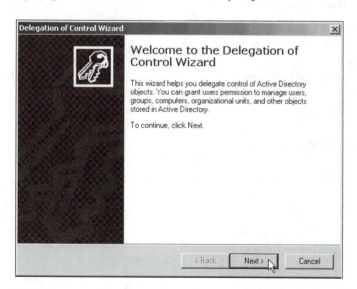

Figure 1-6   Delegation of Control Wizard

Scaling Active Directory

The database that stores Active Directory object information is called the **Extensible Storage Engine (ESE)**. This database engine is the same one that is used in Microsoft Exchange and has a proven history of scaling beyond 90 GB. For Active Directory implementations, this means that server administrators can start with just a few hundred objects and scale to millions of objects as an organization grows.

 ESE is contained in the file \%SystemRoot%\System32\Esent.dll, and new entries into the file are protected by transaction tracking, which keeps a log from which data can be restored or backed out. For example, if a Windows 2000 DC system goes down in the middle of an Active Directory entry or during replication, the log provides a way to restore or back out transactions in order to retain the integrity of Active Directory data. Also, for the sake of reference, note that in this book \%SystemRoot% is the directory in which Windows 2000 Server operating system files are stored, which in default installations is \Winnt.

Another way that Active Directory can be scaled is by distributing DCs across the same network and across different networks. The ability to distribute DCs enables the total object capacity for an organization to be expanded using multiple Active Directory domains and databases. For example, a multinational corporation might have DCs for one network in Brazil, DCs for a different network in France, DCs for a third network in Mexico, and DCs for a fourth network in Canada. Using this network architecture, the total database capacity is increased at least four times and possibly more, depending on how the DCs are deployed in each country.

Hierarchical Tree Structure

Active Directory objects are grouped into a hierarchical tree structure. The tree structure is similar to a folder structure in which a folder can have subfolders and each subfolder can have subfolders under it. Instead of folders, Active Directory uses containers. A **container** is a **parent object,** which is a logical grouping of **child objects**. For example, a domain is a high-level parent container within Active Directory that can hold child objects consisting of computers, domain controllers, user accounts, and user groups. A child object can also be a container that holds lower-level child objects, for example the domain child object called Domain Controllers contains its own child objects, which are the individual computers that are DCs (see Figure 1-7).

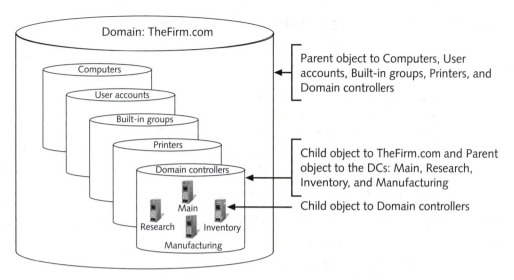

Figure 1-7   Parent and child objects in a domain

The hierarchical tree structure of Active Directory enables you to organize and manage objects in hundreds of ways. For example, it can be used to reflect:

- Countries, states, or cities in which an organization operates
- Business divisions and subdivisions
- Departments
- Network topologies and geographic locations
- Branch offices
- Department head and supervisor responsibilities
- Team structures
- Security requirements
- Auditing requirements
- Project divisions
- Company mergers
- Company partnerships

The hierarchical structure of Active Directory is also dynamic. For example, a hierarchy might first be set up to reflect each college, such as the Business College; and then each college's departments, such as Accounting, Economics, Management, and Marketing in a large university. If a college is reorganized, and the composition of its departments changes, the Active Directory hierarchy of containers can be rearranged to mirror the new organizational structure.

Directory Service Standards and Name Formats

Active Directory is compatible with common directory service standards and name formats. One of those standards is the **Domain Name System (DNS)**. DNS is an application and directory service that is part of the Transmission Control Protocol/Internet Protocol (TCP/IP) suite. The primary function of DNS is to translate domain and computer names, such as *microsoft.com*, to an IP address, such as 207.46.130.45. It also translates an IP address to a domain or computer name. The DNS software typically runs on one or more DNS servers in a network, and Windows 2000 Server can be installed to provide the Microsoft DNS service. The process of translating names to addresses is called name resolution, or just resolution.

The DNS translation information is stored in database tables called zones. Generally, name-to-IP-address lookups are performed using data in a forward lookup zone, and IP-address-to-name resolution occurs via a reverse lookup zone. DNS database information is stored in a tree structure that reflects domains and child or subdomains.

The resolution of names takes place in a designated logical area of a network called a **namespace**, which is set up for this purpose. The namespace contains a domain name, such as *microsoft.com*. On a network consisting of Windows 2000 servers, namespace logic is composed of two key elements: (1) Active Directory, which contains named objects, and (2) one or more DNS servers that can resolve names. These services can be on a single computer, such as a Windows 2000 server set up as both a DC and a DNS server in a small network. Or, these functions can be distributed across several servers on a large network that might have two servers set up as DNS servers and 22 servers set up as DCs. When you install Active Directory, the installation process automatically checks for a DNS server on the local network. If there is no DNS server, Active Directory installation provides an option to install Microsoft DNS.

Active Directory recognizes two kinds of namespaces: contiguous and disjointed. A **contiguous namespace** is one in which every child object contains the name of the parent object, such as in the example of the child domain *msdn.microsoft.com* and its parent domain *microsoft.com*. When the child name does not resemble the name of its parent object, this is called a **disjointed namespace**—for example, when the parent domain for a university is *uni.edu* and a child domain is *bio.ethicsresearch.org*.

Modern versions of DNS include **Dynamic DNS (DDNS)**, which enables clients to automatically register their IP addresses in DNS, saving network administrators from having to perform this as a manual task. Microsoft DDNS offers two important capabilities. One is that it enables client operating systems that have the ability to perform DNS updates, such as Windows 2000, to register directly with a DNS server. The second is that it enables client operating systems that do not have the ability to register their IP addresses, such as Windows 95, to have a proxy server that assigns IP addresses to perform the automated registration. A server that can assign IP addresses is called a **Dynamic Host Configuration Protocol (DHCP)** server, because it uses DHCP and DHCP services to lease IP addresses for a designated period of time. Microsoft DHCP can be configured to enable its clients to dynamically update a DNS server or to perform the dynamic DNS updates as a DNS proxy server.

You can find out more about DNS by reading the Internet Engineering Task Force (IETF) Request for Comment (RFC) document numbers 1034, 1035, and 1123. Many network and Internet standards are presented through RFCs. To research a particular RFC, access the IETF's Internet site at www.ietf.org. Try Hands-on Project 1-8 to practice finding an RFC.

Another standard that Active Directory supports is the **Lightweight Directory Access Protocol (LDAP)**. LDAP is implemented in Active Directory to provide fast access to all objects. LDAP treats each DC as a **directory system agent** that contains a **directory information tree** of objects, such as computers, printers, user accounts, associated ACLs, and other resources. The directory information tree consists of the hierarchy of parent and child objects. LDAP interacts with the directory information tree in Active Directory to enable management of objects, and to provide for object searches and fast access to objects. For example, when a client logs on to a user account in Active Directory, the logon process uses LDAP to quickly track down that account in Active Directory for access. Active Directory supports LDAP versions 2 and 3 (V2 and V3), which enable it to interact with other standard directory services that use LDAP, such as Novell Directory Services (NDS).

LDAP was first developed in the early 1990s as a way to realistically implement portions of the International Telecommunications Union (ITU) X.500 standard for e-mail and information services. The X.500 standard introduced the client-to-directory access protocol (DAP) and directory-to-directory system protocol (DSP), both of which provide the basis for LDAP. You can read more about LDAP in RFC 1777.

Active Directory also supports the Internet standard protocol for accessing and displaying Web-formatted documents, **Hypertext Transfer Protocol (HTTP)**. This protocol enables the transport of Hypertext Markup Language (HTML) documents over the Internet. These are the documents that you read through an HTTP-compliant browser, such as Microsoft Internet Explorer and Netscape Communicator, providing access to text and embedded audio, video, and graphics files.

Using standardized naming formats, such as LDAP and HTTP naming, has several advantages. One advantage is that it enables data in one directory service, Active Directory for example, to be more easily translated into a different directory service, such as Novell Directory Services (NDS, see Chapter 9). Another advantage is that standardized naming permits a directory service to communicate with Internet and e-mail services. If you send e-mail over the Internet or access Web sites, then you already use two forms of common naming. The standardized naming formats that are supported by Active Directory are:

- *LDAP Uniform Resource Locator (URL):* A common name convention that is defined in the LDAP RFC 1779 for common directory service naming and that is in the format *ldap://domain name/common name/organizational unit name/domain component name*

- *HTTP Uniform Resource Locator (URL):* A common name convention used to locate Internet sites in the format *http://Internet domain name/Web page name*

- *Universal Naming Convention (UNC):* A common name convention that designates network servers, computers, and shared resources using the format *\\servername (or computername)\sharename\folder\file*

- *User Principal Name (UPN):* Specified in RFC 822, a common name convention used for Internet e-mail traffic using the format *username@domain name*

Refer to RFCs 1945, 2068, 2616, and 2817 for more information about HTTP.

LDAP URL Naming Used in Active Directory

Each Active Directory object has an LDAP URL that is in the form of a **common name (CN)** and a **distinguished name (DN)**. The CN is the most basic and unique name for an object, which may be HPLaserMain for a printer or the combination first name and last name for a user account, Heather Chen for example. The DN of an object gives more information; it contains the name of the object (CN), the object class name (CN), and the name of any higher-level entities to which the object belongs, such as a domain (DC) and an organizational unit (OU) within a domain (organizational units are discussed later in this chapter). When an Active Directory client needs to access an object, such as a user account or printer, that client can use the DN for unmistakable identification of the object. For example, the DN of Heather Chen, who belongs to the domain *tracksports.org* and the organizational unit *events*, would be: /DC=org/DC=tracksports/OU=events/CN=Users/CN=Heather Chen

Notice in this example, that there are two CNs: one is Users, which identifies the Users folder that contains accounts, and the other is Heather Chen, which identities one of the users within the Users folder. Also, there are two DCs (org and tracksports), which are domain component names that equate to the namespace, tracksports.org.

This DN is also an example of a **relative distinguished name (RDN)**, a DN in which part of the name is a reference to another part of the name or an attribute that is a reference to its own object. In this case, Users is a higher-level or parent object (accounts in a domain), and Heather Chen is an attribute (one user name) of that parent object. Both are linked in a two-way relationship. If you would search for Heather Chen as an account, your search route would follow the database structure from domain (tracksports.org), through Users, to Heather Chen. If you were the user Heather Chen and you wanted to change your password, you would go from the account Heather Chen through the parent object Users to update the information associated with the Heather Chen account. The RDN relationship enables users to quickly find an object, such as a specific account, by going from the domain level to the accounts object level and finally to the specific account. Consider how much longer it would take to perform a search for an account in a structure that did not divide objects into groupings, so that you had to search every object (printers, domains, group names, accounts, etc.) until you found the single account you wanted to locate.

To ensure that there is no confusion when attempting to find a common name object, such as a user account, all RDNs within an OU must be unique. Thus in this example, there cannot be two Heather Chens in the events OU.

Essential Directory Service Components

Overall, the guidelines for implementing a directory service include several general components:

- *Database model:* The database model that involves creating a structure for a schema and for the hierarchical arrangement of objects in the directory service.

- *Database:* A robust database and engine consisting of tables, records, and indexes for quickly accessing and sorting information. The Active Directory database, called the directory store, is found in two places: \%SystemRoot%\NTDS\ Ntds.dit, which is the live version that is currently used by the DC; and \%SystemRoot%\System32\Ntds.dit, which is the default data that is used when you first promote a Windows 2000 server to a DC (copied to \%SystemRoot%\ NTDS\Ntds.dit when you configure a DC). As discussed earlier, the ESE engine is found in \%SystemRoot%\System32\Esent.dll. The Active Directory transaction log files are found in \%SystemRoot%\NTDS (or can be placed on a separate volume other than \%SystemRoot%\NTDS for protection in case of a disk failure) and are the files Edb.chk (checkpoint file), Edb.log (transaction log),and Res1.log and Res2.log (reserved logs).

- *Server:* The server, such as a Windows 2000 Server DC, that acts as a directory system agent and that contains a directory information tree of objects that are stored in a database.

- *Program interfaces:* Application program interfaces (APIs) that act as links between the operating system, such as Windows 2000 Server, and the directory service, such as Active Directory.

The Active Directory APIs in Windows 2000 Server are called Active Directory Service Interfaces (ADSIs). Active Directory also uses the Java Naming and Directory Interface (JNDI) and a specialized LDAP API.

- *Replication:* A server replication service and a replication protocol that enable the directory services database to be copied to other directory system agent servers as a backup and for fault tolerance.

- *Security:* Measures that control access, such as user account passwords, permissions, and rights, coupled with network security, such as Kerberos and certificate security.

- *Directory service protocols:* Protocols (LDAP, for example) that enable the directory service contents to be accessed, protocols that enable directory replication, and protocols that enable directory service agent servers to mutually communicate (called chaining protocols).

- *Name resolution service:* A service that can resolve computer names and IP addresses, such as DNS.

- *Directory management tools:* Tools that can be used to configure and manage the directory service and the database contents.

- *Clients:* Although listed last, clients are the reason for having a directory service and must have software, such as Microsoft's DSClient, that enable them to access directory services.

 Kerberos, which is the main logon security for Windows 2000 servers, is a security system developed by the Massachusetts Institute of Technology to enable two parties on an open network to communicate without interception by an intruder, by creating a unique encryption key for each communication session. Kerberos enables the authentication of a user or computer, which gives that user or computer access to server and network services for the duration of a communication session. At this writing, Active Directory uses Kerberos version 5 (V5), which is supported by all Windows 2000 operating systems, including Windows 2000 Professional. When Windows 2000 servers also have MS-DOS, Windows 3.x, Windows 95, Windows 98, and Windows NT clients, LAN Manager (LM) and NT LAN Manager (NTLM) can be used for logon security with those clients. NTLM uses a challenge/response technique for authentication and is much slower than Kerberos. By default, three versions of NTLM are installed in Windows 2000 Server for mixed mode operations: LAN Manager (least secure), NTLM version 1 (more secure), and NTLM version 2 (most secure version of NTLM).

HIERARCHICAL ELEMENTS OF MICROSOFT ACTIVE DIRECTORY

The hierarchical tree structure of Active Directory is generally organized into a series of containers that are in parent and child object relationships. These objects are (see Figure 1-8):

- Organizational units
- Domains
- Trees
- Forests
- Sites

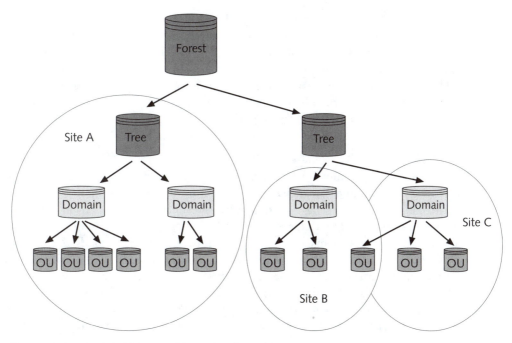

Figure 1-8   Active Directory hierarchical containers

Organizational Unit

An **organizational unit (OU)** offers a way to achieve flexibility in Active Directory for managing the resources associated with a business unit, department, or division in an organization. The functions of an OU include:

- Grouping user accounts, user account groups, shared printers, and shared folders into smaller containers within a domain

- Reflecting the internal structure of an organization

- Reflecting how authority is delegated in an organization, such as in manager, supervisor, and team leader relationships

- Enabling security and management of resources to be customized

An OU is a grouping of related objects within a domain (its immediate parent container), similar to the idea of having subfolders within a folder. OUs can be used to reflect the structure of the organization without having to completely restructure the domain(s) when that structure changes.

In Windows 2000 Server environments, OUs allow the grouping of objects so that they can be administered using the same policies such as security and desktop setup. OUs also make it possible for server administration to be delegated or decentralized. For example, in a software company in which the employees are divided into 15 project teams, the user accounts, shared folders, shared printers, and other shared resources of each team can be defined as objects in separate OUs. There would be one domain for the entire company and 15 OUs within that domain, all defined in Active Directory. With this arrangement, file and folder objects can be defined to specific OUs for security, and the management of user accounts, account setup policies, and file and folder permissions can be delegated to each group leader (OU administrator).

Consider another example that consists of a larger network and organization, which is a grocery chain that has three separate divisions: manufacturing, distribution, and retail. In this scenario, the manufacturing unit consists of five sites that are networked into a WAN, and the computer resources of that unit are managed by their own IT group of server administrators and programmers. The manufacturing unit provides prepared foods that include canned items, frozen foods, bakery goods, soft drinks, and other foods. The distribution unit transports all food items to the retail stores and has its own independent IT group and network. Finally, the retail unit provides central management of hundreds of grocery stores throughout 20 states, and it networks each store into a central site through a WAN, with computer resources managed by a third independent IT group. In this situation, there are three separate administrative units, each with its own IT group and unique management policies. Each administrative group can be incorporated into an individual OU, as in Figure 1-9.

OUs can be nested within other OUs, as subfolders are nested in other subfolders, so that you can create them several layers deep. In the grocery chain example, you might have one OU under the retail OU for the accounting department, an OU under the accounting OU for the accounts receivable group, and an OU under accounts receivable for the cashiers—creating four layers of OUs. The problem with this approach is that creating OUs many layers deep can get as confusing as creating subfolders several layers deep. It is confusing for the server administrator to track layered OUs, and it is laborious for Active Directory to search through each layer.

When you plan to create OUs, keep three concerns in mind:

- Microsoft recommends that you limit OUs to 10 levels or fewer (3 or 4 levels deep is an even more efficient design).

- Active Directory works more efficiently (using less CPU resources) when OUs are set up horizontally instead of vertically. Using the grocery chain example, it is more efficient to create the manufacturing, distribution, and retail OUs all on the same level, so that there is only one level of OUs for the CPU to negotiate. This is more efficient than nesting distribution under manufacturing, and manufacturing under retail, resulting in three levels for the CPU to traverse.

- The creation of OUs involves more processing resources because each request through an OU—for example, to determine a permission on a folder—requires CPU time. When that request must go several layers deep through nested OUs, even more CPU time is needed.

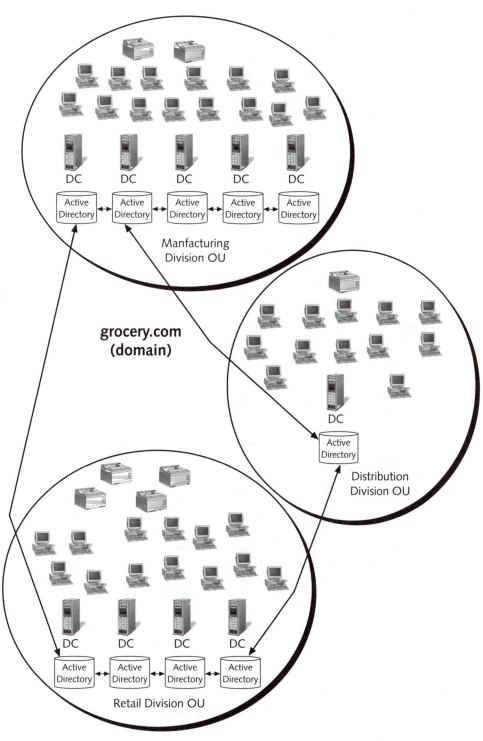

grocery.com
(domain)

Figure 1-9   OUs used to reflect the divisional structure of a company

Domain

A domain is a logical grouping of computers and other network devices that are administered as a unit, and it functions as a security boundary around that unit of computers and devices. A domain typically exists as a primary Active Directory container, just as a country is a primary division for a continent. Within a domain there exist OUs, user accounts, printers, shared folders, and other resources within Active Directory—all of which must be anchored to a domain. Thus, every Active Directory implementation must have at least one domain and can have more. A domain is a parent object to an OU. The basic functions of a domain are as follows:

- To provide a security boundary around objects that have a common relationship
- To establish a set of Active Directory information to be replicated from one DC to another
- To expedite management of a set of objects

Domains can also be set up in Windows NT Server, but without the use of hierarchical containers or Active Directory.

If you are planning to use Active Directory for a small business of 34 employees who have workstations connected to a network that also has one or two Windows 2000 servers, then one domain is sufficient for that business. The domain functions as a security boundary within which are grouped all of the network resource objects, consisting of servers, user accounts, shared printers, and shared folders and files. If there is Internet connectivity and one or more intranets, then the domain provides a security boundary to keep information within intranets secure from outside access via the Internet. The boundary establishes the capability to manage what information comes into the network from the Internet and what information goes out (see Figure 1-10).

In a medium or large business, you might use more than one domain—for example, when business units are separated by great distances and you want to limit the amount of DC replication over expensive WAN links as well as to establish tight security boundaries for each location. Consider a company that builds tractors in South Carolina and that has a parts manufacturing division in Japan. Each site has a large enterprise network of Windows 2000 servers, and the sites are linked together in a WAN by an expensive satellite connection. When you calculate the cost of replicating DCs over the satellite WAN link, you cannot justify it in terms of the increased traffic that will delay other vital daily business communications. In this situation, it makes sense to create two separate domains, one for each site, as shown in Figure 1-11.

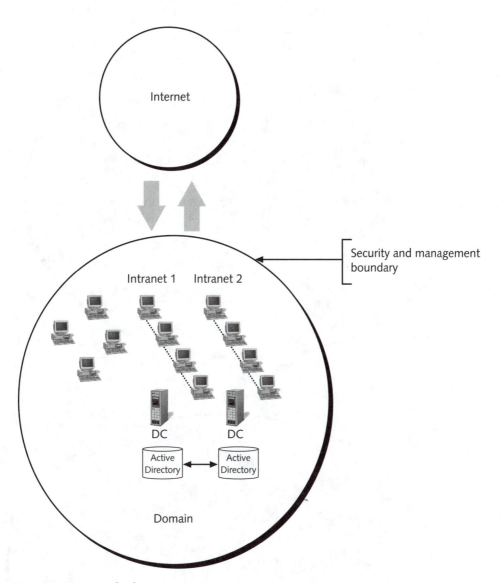

Figure 1-10   Single domain

Typically the most efficient maximum size for a domain is about 1 million objects when considered in terms of server and database performance, even though a domain can actually hold up to about 10 million objects.

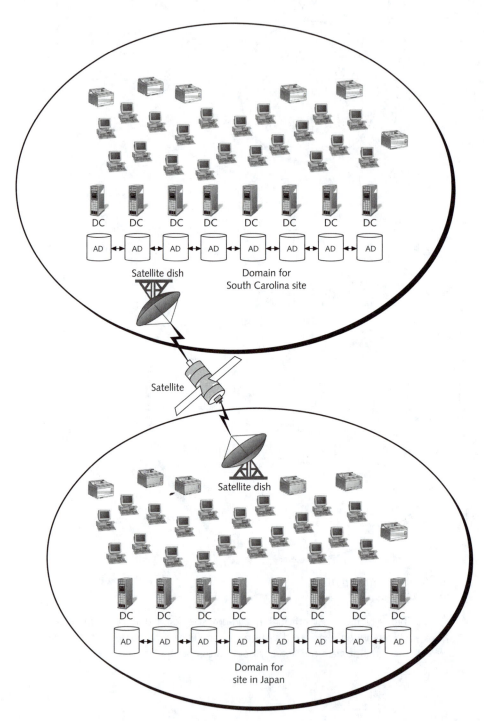

Figure 1-11   Using multiple domains

Tree

A **tree** contains one or (usually) more domains that are in a common relationship, and it has the following characteristics:

- Domains are represented in a contiguous namespace and can be in a hierarchy.
- Two-way security trust relationships exist between domains, in which each domain can access the resources of the other.
- Member domains use the same schema for all types of common objects.
- Member domains use the same global catalog (a global catalog is something like an encyclopedia of information about objects and their attributes in all domains).

The domains in a tree typically have a hierarchical structure, such as a root domain at the top and other domains under the root. In the *tracksports.org* example, *tracksports.org* might be the root domain and have four domains under the root to form one tree: *east.tracksports.org*, *west.tracksports.org*, *north.tracksports.org*, and *south.tracksports.org*, as shown in Figure 1-12. These domains use the contiguous namespace format in that the child domains each contain the name of the parent domain.

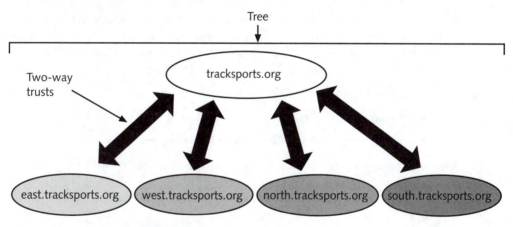

Figure 1-12   Tree with hierarchical domains

The domains within a tree are in what is called a Kerberos **transitive trust** relationship, which consists of two-way trusts between all domains (see Figure 1-12). This is similar to the universal trust relationship among domains in Windows NT Server. In a **two-way trust**, each domain is trusting and trusted. A **trusted domain** is one that is granted access to resources, whereas a **trusting domain** is the one granting access. In a two-way trust, members of each domain can have access to the resources of the other.

Because all domains have a two-way trust relationship, any one domain can have access to the resources of all others. The security in the two-way trust relationships is based on Kerberos V5 specifications, using a combination of protocol-based and encryption-based security techniques between clients and servers. A new domain joining a tree has an instant trust relationship with all other member domains, which makes all objects in the other domains available to the new one. Also, all trees in the same forest (see the next section) automatically have two-way transitive trust relationships.

All domains in a tree share the same schema, which means that they share the same object classes and attributes. This provides an important advantage in terms of security. For example, if the first domain in the tree requires password restrictions, such as a minimum password length, then all others will have the same restriction by default.

The **global catalog** is a single storehouse of information about every object in every domain within a tree or forest. As a storehouse, the global catalog contains a copy of the most used attributes for each object, such as the actual user's name that is associated with a user account. The global catalog also provides services to users, such as the ability to find an object or information about an object without already knowing the domain or OU in which the object is held. This enables one user to find another, even though they are in different domains. All member domains in a tree or forest share the same global catalog. The global catalog is a subset of Active Directory because it contains information about selected attributes for all objects in all domains in the same forest. The value of the global catalog is that DCs in one domain do not have to replicate their information to DCs in another domain. The global catalog serves the following purposes:

- Authenticating users when they log on

- Providing lookup and access to all resources in all domains

- Providing replication of key Active Directory elements

- Keeping a copy of the most used attributes for each object for quick access

 The first DC created in a domain is by default a global catalog server.

Each tree must have at least one DC that is also configured to operate as a global catalog server. When you plan a tree, also plan the location of global catalog servers so that users are quickly authenticated for access in the tree. In the *tracksports.org* example, observe that each domain is separated by many miles—for example, the parent domain is in Washington, D.C. and the child domains are located in Boston, Los Angeles, Chicago, and Atlanta. In this situation, it makes sense to locate a global catalog server in each location because authentication over WAN links is likely to be slow. If there is only one global catalog server, in Washington, then users in the other four cities will have to wait longer to log on than users in Washington. If there is a global catalog server in each of the five cities, then logon response will be faster, and the WAN links will be freed to give priority to other types of communications.

Forest

A **forest** consists of one or more trees or domains that are in a common relationship and that have the following characteristics:

- The trees use a disjointed namespace.

- All domains and trees use the same schema.

- All domains and trees use the same global catalog.

- Domains and trees have transitive trust relationships.

A forest provides a means to relate trees that use a contiguous namespace in domains within each tree but that have disjointed namespaces in relationship to each other. Consider, for example, an international automotive parts company that is really a conglomerate of separate companies, each having a different brand name. The parent company is PartsPlus, located in Toronto. PartsPlus manufactures alternators, coils, and other electrical parts at plants in Toronto, Montreal, and Detroit and has a tree structure for domains that are part of *partsplus.com*. Another company that they own, Marty and Mike's (*2m.com*), makes radiators in two South Carolina cities, Florence and Greenville, and radiator fluid in Atlanta. A third member company, Chelos (*chelos.com*), makes engine parts and starters in Mexico City, Oaxaca, Monterrey, and Puebla, all in Mexico. In this situation, it makes sense to have a contiguous tree structure for each of the three related companies and to join the trees in a forest of disjointed namespaces, as shown in Figure 1-13.

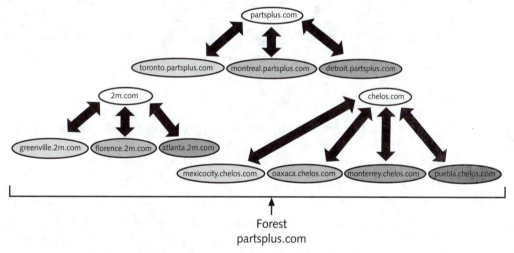

Figure 1-13   A forest

The advantage of joining trees into a forest is that all domains share the same schema and global catalog. A schema is set up in the root domain, which is *partsplus.com* in our example, and the root domain is home to the schema master server (see Chapter 10). At least one DC functions as a global catalog server in each tree, but in our example, it is likely that you would plan to have a global catalog server located at each geographic site (domain).

Kerberos trusts are transitive between trees in a forest, but they cannot be transitive between two or more forests. The Active Directory structure in Figure 1-13 is also called a **single forest** model by Microsoft. It is possible to join two or more forests for common communication in a model that Microsoft calls a **separate forest** (see Figure 1-14). In a separate forest, there cannot be transitive trusts between forests, which is a critical consideration when you plan Active Directory. Establishing a separate forest means that replication cannot take place between forests, that there are different schema and different global catalogs, and that the forests cannot be blended into a single forest in the future.

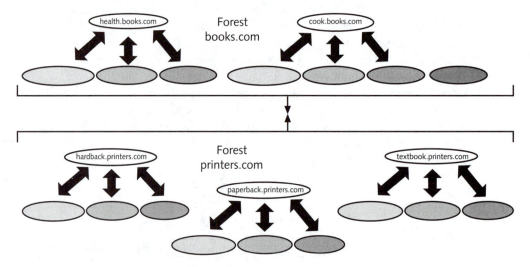

Figure 1-14   Separate forest model

 Typically, the reason for creating two or more forests is to have two or more different namespaces—one for each forest.

Site

Microsoft defines a **site** as a collection of TCP/IP-based subnets that are connected by links which are relatively *fast*, at 512 Kbps or faster, and that are relatively *reliable* in terms of always being on or accessible. A site has the following characteristics:

- Consists of one or more interconnected IP subnets (IP subnets are covered in Chapter 5)
- Often reflects the same boundaries as the LAN it represents
- Is used for efficient Active Directory replication among DCs

- Is used to enable a client to access the DC that is physically closest
- Is composed of two types of objects, servers and configuration objects

Sites are based on connectivity and replication functions and so they do not have a visible entry in Active Directory or a namespace name. You might think of sites as a way of grouping Active Directory objects by physical location so that Active Directory can identify the fastest communications paths between clients and servers, and between DCs. The physical representation of the network to Active Directory is accomplished by defining subnets that are interconnected. A single domain can contain multiple sites; a single site can span multiple domains. The most typical boundary for a site consists of the LAN topology and subnet boundaries rather than the domain and OU boundaries.

There are two important reasons to define a site. First is that by defining site locations based on IP subnets, you enable a client to access network servers using the most efficient physical route. In the PartsPlus example, it is faster for a client in Toronto to be authenticated by a Toronto global catalog server than for the client to go through Detroit or Mexico City. Second, DC replication is most efficient when Active Directory has information about which DCs are in which locations.

Within a site, each DC replicates forest, tree, domain, and OU naming structures, configuration naming elements, such as computers and printers, and schema information. One advantage of creating a site is that it sets up redundant paths between DCs, so that if one path is down there is a second path that can be used for replication. This redundancy is in a logical ring format, which means that replication goes from DC to DC around a ring until each DC is replicated. If a DC is down along the main route, then Active Directory uses site information to send replication information in the opposite direction around the ring. Whenever a new DC is added or an old one removed, Active Directory reconfigures the ring to make sure there are two replication paths available from each DC.

The Windows 2000 Server feature that automatically adds or removes DCs is called the **Knowledge Consistency Checker (KCC)**. The KCC is a Windows 2000 service that runs by default on every domain controller. Using Active Directory information about sites, the KCC sets up domain controller replication connections within and between sites and determines the most efficient replication routes between domain controllers. Also by default, the KCC runs every 15 minutes.

When information is replicated within a site, the information is sent from DC to DC uncompressed so there is less demand placed on each DC's CPU. Replication information that is sent between different sites is compressed so it goes over WAN links more quickly and creates less interference with other WAN communications. Intersite compression is in a ratio of up to 10 to 1.

 In terms of replication, keep in mind two general goals. One is to minimize the time between when changes are made in Active Directory and when those changes are replicated to DCs within the same site. A second goal is to configure Active Directory replication between sites to minimize the use of bandwidth, saving valuable bandwidth for other work functions.

If you are new to IP communication, the concept of sites may at first be confusing. As you plan for a site, keep in mind two factors. First, a site is simply a grouping of subnets and is really independent of OUs, domains, trees, and forests (although one site might contain multiple domains or OUs). Second, the purpose of creating a site is to enable network traffic to go along the most efficient route on a medium or large network. Whereas OUs, domains, trees, and forests are used to manage computer, printer, and user resources, sites are used to speed communications between resources.

Consider a state university's network that might take advantage of sites. The university has three domains, *students.uni.edu, faculty.uni.edu*, and *staffadmin.uni.edu*, organized under a single tree root domain, *uni.edu*. Also, there are three campuses, each in different cities. The domains span each campus location. Thus *students.uni.edu* contains accounts and printers on DCs at all locations. Each domain contains OUs that are appropriate to that domain, for instance *students.uni.edu* has an OU for students at each campus for a total of three OUs all at the same level. The campuses are relatively large with 7000 students, 10,000 students, and 18,000 students, and have networks that are physically divided into subnets. In this situation, you can designate each campus network as a site in Active Directory, which enables it to find the fastest routes for traffic that is on-campus and for traffic that goes between campuses. For example, when a student logs on to *students.uni.edu*, Active Directory can help that student find the nearest DC and avoid the chance that the logon authentication is performed over a WAN link at a different campus location. Another advantage is that the DC replication for each domain between sites (over WAN links) can be set to occur less frequently than replication within a site.

 Designing and implementing Active Directory OUs, domains, trees, forests, and sites is covered in depth in Chapters 6 and 7.

AN OVERVIEW OF GROUP POLICIES

When sites, domains, and OUs are created, it is possible to establish group policies that apply to those Active Directory elements. For example, in your organization there might be a need to limit access to network resources to user accounts in a specific OU by limiting what options appear on the desktops of the corresponding client workstations, including eliminating the My Network Places icon in Windows 2000 Professional. Network access by these users might be limited to a menu that automatically appears when they log on to the network. In another situation, you might decide to eliminate access for users in a domain to the Registry editors in Windows 95, Windows 98, Windows ME, Windows NT, and Windows 2000, or you might remove the Run option from the Start button.

Technically, a **group policy** is a single policy that is applied to users and computers, such as requiring that logon passwords are over a certain length or removing the My Network Places icon from the desktop of specific users. Group policies cover areas such as account security, network security, logon and logoff scripts, folder redirection, software installation, and desktop settings. A **group policy object (GPO)** is a set of group policies that is applied to users and computers in a site, domain, or OU.

Security access is one of the most critical applications of group policies. Through group policies, you can establish account policies that govern the length of passwords and how long a password can be used before it expires. Another security policy might be to audit an accounting or sales file each time it is accessed or modified. Group policies can also be established to set up specialized network authentication and encryption.

Some of the resources that can be managed through setting group policies include:

- Software settings and software access
- Account and Active Directory logon security
- Active Directory access and activity auditing
- Access and management of Windows 2000 Server software components
- Access and management of Windows 2000 Server system components
- Security access
- Local area and remote network connectivity options
- Network encryption and authentication techniques
- Shared printer and shared folder access
- Use of scripts
- Client desktop settings
- Customization of administrative templates for server and client management

Try Hands-on Project 1-7 to view the default GPO for a domain.

AN OVERVIEW OF TCP/IP AND ACTIVE DIRECTORY

Microsoft Active Directory and TCP/IP have an important interrelationship on a network because when they are used together they provide significant advantages:

- Both are well suited for networks of all sizes and particularly for medium-sized to very large networks.
- Both are vital in making possible efficient Internet, intranet, and virtual private network designs. A **virtual private network (VPN)** is a private network that uses encapsulation, encryption, and authentication to create a "tunnel" through a larger network, such as the Internet, but that is restricted to only designated member clients.

- In a Windows 2000 Server network, both can be used to reduce the total cost of operation (TCO) for computer resources in an organization.

- Both enable networks that deploy diverse server and client operating systems on the same and on different networks.

As you learned earlier in this chapter, Active Directory depends on the TCP/IP-based DNS service for network address resolution, which alone is one important reason for using TCP/IP. Also, since networks often are a perpetual area of growth in an organization, using Active Directory and TCP/IP together is a key strategy for handling growth, because both provide functions that enable server and network performance to keep up with rapid growth. In Active Directory, scalability is made possible by an efficient database engine, and in TCP/IP scalability is made possible by dividing networks into subnets. Used together, both offer complementary features such as the ability to set up sites dynamically in Active Directory to take advantage of TCP/IP subnets.

The security that is provided through TCP/IP is yet another reason why it is a good match with Active Directory. TCP/IP enables network administrators to implement **IP security (IPSec)**, which is a set of IP-based secure communications and encryption standards created through the Internet Engineering Task Force. IPSec works in the following ways:

- When an IPSec communication begins between two computers, the computers exchange certificates to authenticate the receiver and sender.

- Data is encrypted at the network interface card of the sending computer as it is formatted into an IP packet.

- IPSec provides security for all TCP/IP-based application and communications protocols, including the TCP/IP-based File Transfer Protocol (FTP) and HTTP, both of which are used in Internet transmissions.

IPSec communications in Windows 2000 Server function in any of three roles:

- *Client (Respond Only):* When Windows 2000 Server is contacted by a client using IPSec, it will respond by using IPSec communications. This mode is also called responder.

- *Server (Request Security):* When Windows 2000 Server is first contacted or when it initiates a communication, it will use IPSec by default. If the responding client does not support IPSec, Windows 2000 Server will switch to the clear mode which does not employ IPSec. This role is also called the initiator.

- *Secure Server (Require Security):* Also called the lockdown role, Windows 2000 Server will respond only using IPSec communications, which means that communications sent by any account and with any client are secured through strict IPSec enforcement.

After IPSec is enabled, it can be managed through group policies, which consist of the security methods to use for client and server communications, the IP filters to apply to communications, and the customized IPSec group policies that apply to specified Active Directory containers.

1

Chapter Summary

❏ Directory services are used by network server operating systems to enable vast access to and coordination of resources, which include user accounts, servers, shared printers, and shared folders. The directory services in Windows 2000 Server are incorporated into Windows 2000 Active Directory.

❏ Windows 2000 Active Directory incorporates a database engine, a database, application programming interfaces, security techniques, directory service protocols, and management tools to provide a full range of directory services.

❏ One of the main ways in which Active Directory enables resources to be managed is by creating a hierarchy of containers, such as organizational units, domains, trees, and forests. Each of these containers is a logical grouping of network resources. Another way to group resources is by creating sites, which reflect the network resources by using physical IP subnet groupings.

❏ After containers are created, different security and management polices can be applied by creating specific group policies. For example, group policies can be set to manage security for all accounts in a domain.

❏ Active Directory relies on many features enabled through the use of TCP/IP. The TCP/IP-based DNS service is used by Active Directory to resolve computer names and IP addresses. Other TCP/IP features are used with Active Directory to enable networks to experience smooth performance and growth as a network expands.

In the next chapter, you will learn how to analyze the business process requirements of different kinds of organizations. You are introduced to different models of business operation and how particular goals and strategies affect business. The chapter sets a foundation on which to analyze how directory services can be set up to match the needs of different business models.

Key Terms

access control list (ACL) — A list of all security properties that have been set up for a particular object, such as for a shared folder or a shared printer.

attribute — A characteristic, quality, or property associated with an Active Directory object class, such as the name of the object and a security list of who can access that object.

child object — In the hierarchical structure of Active Directory, an object that is layered under a higher-level object, such as the server Accounting that is a domain controller (child object) in the Domain Controllers parent object container. A child object is an object that is contained in another object.

common name (CN) — The most basic name of an object in Active Directory, such as the name of a printer.

container — An element of Active Directory that holds a grouping of related objects, such as the Domain Controllers container, which holds all of the computers that are set up as domain controllers.

contiguous namespace — A namespace in which every child object contains the name of its parent object.

directory information tree — A hierarchy of directory service objects, such as organizational units, domains, computers, printers, user accounts, ACLs, and other resources.

directory service — A large container of network data and resources, such as computers, printers, user accounts, and user groups that (1) provides a central listing of resources and ways to quickly find specific resources and (2) provides a way to access and manage network resources.

Directory Service Client (DSClient) — Microsoft software for non–Windows 2000 clients that connects to Windows 2000 Server and that enables those clients to use Kerberos authentication security, and to view information published in Windows 2000 Active Directory, such as all network printers.

directory system agent — A server, such as one running Windows 2000 Server, that houses a directory service's database, has directory service APIs, and communicates with clients and other directory system agents.

discretionary access control list (DACL) — A portion of an access control list (ACL) consisting of users, groups, and computers that are allowed or denied some form of permission to access an object.

disjointed namespace — A namespace in which the child object name does not resemble the name of its parent object.

distinguished name (DN) — A name in Active Directory that contains all hierarchical components of an object, such as that object's organizational unit and domain, in addition to the object's common name. The distinguished name is used by an Active Directory client to access a particular object, such as a printer.

domain — A grouping of resource objects, computers, printers, network devices, user accounts, and user groups, for example, that can be managed as a unit or partition in Active Directory in Windows 2000 Server. A domain usually is a higher-level representation of how a business, government, or school is organized—for example, reflecting a geographical site or major division of that organization. An important function of a domain is to create a security boundary around the objects held within it.

domain controller (DC) — A Windows 2000 server that contains a copy of Active Directory domain information (an Active Directory partition), that is used to add a new object to Active Directory and to modify an object, and that replicates all changes made to Active Directory so those changes are updated on every DC in the same domain. Domain controllers also help manage user account and computer account access to a domain, including logon access and access to resources such as shared folders.

Domain Name System (DNS) — A TCP/IP application service that resolves domain and computer names to IP addresses, or IP addresses to domain and computer names. In Active Directory implementations, DNS is also used to enable clients to find domain controllers.

Dynamic DNS (DDNS) — A modern DNS application that enables client computers to automatically register their IP addresses without intervention by a user or network administrator.

Dynamic Host Configuration Protocol (DHCP) — A TCP/IP-based network protocol that provides a way for a server running DHCP services to automatically assign (through a lease) an IP address to a workstation or client computer on its network.

Extensible Storage Engine (ESE) — The database engine that stores Active Directory object information in a database system.

forest — A grouping of trees that each have contiguous namespaces within their own domain structure, but that have disjointed namespaces between trees. The trees and domains in a forest use the same schema and global catalog, and are related through transitive trusts.

global catalog — A single storehouse of information about every object in every domain within a tree or forest. As a storehouse, the global catalog contains a copy of the most-used attributes for each object, such as the actual user's name that is associated with a user account. The global catalog also provides services to users, such as the ability to find an object or information about an object, without already knowing the domain or OU in which the object is held.

globally unique identifier (GUID) — A unique number, up to 16 characters long (128 bits), that is associated with an Active Directory object.

group policy — A single policy that is applied to specific users or computers in an Active Directory site, domain, or OU container, such as requiring that logon passwords be over a certain length or removing the My Network Places icon from the desktop of specific users. Group policies cover areas such as account security, network security, logon and logoff scripts, folder redirection, software installation, and desktop settings.

group policy object (GPO) — A set of group policies that is applied to users and computers in a site, domain, or OU. Each GPO is identified in Active Directory by a unique name and a unique GUID.

Hypertext Transfer Protocol (HTTP) — A protocol in the TCP/IP suite that transports HTML documents over the Internet (and over intranets) for access by Web-compliant browsers.

implicit two-way transitive trust — *See* transitive trust.

IP security (IPSec) — A set of IP-based secure communications and encryption standards created through the Internet Engineering Task Force (IETF).

Kerberos — The main logon security for Windows 2000 Server; a security system developed by the Massachusetts Institute of Technology to enable two parties on an open network to communicate without interception by an intruder, by creating a unique encryption key per each communication session. Kerberos enables the authentication of a user or computer. At this writing, Active Directory uses Kerberos version 5 (V5), which is supported by all Windows 2000 operating systems, including Windows 2000 Professional.

Knowledge Consistency Checker (KCC) — A Windows 2000 service that runs by default on all domain controllers. It sets up domain controller replication connections within and between sites and determines the most efficient replication routes between domain controllers.

Lightweight Directory Access Protocol (LDAP) — A standard directory access protocol that is used to help access and manage objects in a directory service.

multimaster replication — In Windows 2000 Server, there can be multiple servers, called domain controllers (DCs), that store the Active Directory contents for the domain, including all objects, and replicate the contents to one another. Because each DC acts as a master, replication does not stop when one is down and updates to Active Directory continue, for example, when new accounts are created.

namespace — A logical area on a network that contains directory services and named objects, and that has the ability to perform name resolution.

object — A network resource, such as a server or a user account, that has distinct attributes or properties, that is usually defined in a forest, tree, domain, OU, or site, and that exists in the Windows 2000 Active Directory.

object class — A type or grouping of network resources that is tracked by Active Directory. User accounts, groups, and computers are examples of different object classes. Each object class has attributes associated with it.

organizational unit (OU) — A grouping of objects, usually within a domain, used as a means to establish specific policies for governing those objects and to enable object management to be delegated. An OU contains objects such as user accounts, computers, printers, groups, shared folders, and nested OUs, and it is the smallest container for which to delegate authority or to apply a GPO.

parent object — A hierarchical Active Directory container that holds objects under it.

permission — In Windows 2000, privilege to access and manipulate resource objects, such as folders and printers; for example, the privilege to read a file, or to create a new file.

publish — To make an object, such as a printer or shared folder, available for users to access when they view Active Directory contents and to allow the data associated with the object to be replicated.

relative distinguished name (RDN) — An object name in Active Directory that has two or more related components, such as the RDN of a user account name that consists of User and the first and last name of the actual user. In an RDN, part of the DN name is a reference to another part of the object's name.

right — In Windows 2000, an access privilege for high-level activities such as logging on to a server from the network, shutting down a server, and logging on locally.

schema — A database that consists of the definitions of all objects in Active Directory, and that reflects the skeletal structure and rules of Active Directory. The principal elements of the Active Directory schema are object classes and attributes.

security descriptor — A collection of security properties that are associated with an Active Directory object, such as granting permission for the Managers group of user accounts to read the contents of a folder and auditing that group each time one of its members accesses the folder.

separate forest — An Active Directory model that links two or more forests in a partnership; however, the forests do not have Kerberos two-way transitive trusts and do not use the same schema.

single forest — An Active Directory model in which there is only one forest, with interconnected trees and domains that use the same schema and global catalog.

1

site — One or more TCP/IP-based subnets that are aggregated into a logical Active Directory container object (a site). The links between subnets in a site are relatively fast (512 Kbps or faster) and reliable.

system access control list (SACL) — A portion of an access control list that determines which events associated with an object are to be audited for user and user group activity.

transitive trust — A trust relationship between two or more domains in a tree, between domains and a tree, or between two or more trees in the same forest, in which each domain or tree has access to objects in the others. When a new domain or tree is created in a forest, a transitive trust is automatically established. In Active Directory, a transitive trust is also called an *implicit two-way transitive trust*.

tree – Related domains that use a contiguous namespace, share the same schema, and have two-way, transitive trust relationships. The domains in a tree, in general, have a common configuration and employ the same global catalog.

trusted domain — A domain that has been granted security access to resources in another domain.

trusting domain — A domain that allows another domain security access to its resources and objects, such as to servers.

two-way trust — A domain relationship in which both domains are trusted and trusting, enabling one to have access to objects in the other.

virtual private network (VPN) — A private network that uses encapsulation, authentication, and encryption to create a tunnel through a larger network—such as the Internet, an enterprise network, or both—that is restricted to only designated member clients.

REVIEW QUESTIONS

Every chapter in this book contains 25 review questions to help you review Active Directory design concepts and to prepare for the Microsoft 70-219 examination. Because the information covered in this chapter is an introduction to Active Directory, the review questions are in a typical multiple-choice format. In Chapters 2 through 11, you learn how to apply Active Directory analysis and design concepts to different kinds of realistic situations. In these chapters, the review questions are presented in a combined multiple-choice and small case-study format to provide additional help in preparing for the format used in the 70-219 examination.

1. Which of the following is(are) necessary to have a directory service?

   a. a database

   b. directory service protocols

   c. application programming interfaces

   d. all of the above

   e. none of the above are absolutely necessary

   f. only a and c

   g. only b and c

2. Which of the following characteristics of Active Directory replication are used in Windows 2000 Server for optimum performance and fault tolerance?

a. multimaster

b. full replication of the entire Active Directory contents each time any portion of an object is updated, such as the security for a shared printer

c. full replication only to global catalog servers

d. all of the above

e. only a and b

f. only a and c

3. You are training a new Windows 2000 Server administrator about Active Directory. When you open Active Directory to view a domain and then to view the Domain Controllers container in the domain, what would you expect to show your trainee in that container?

a. user accounts

b. child domains

c. computers

d. all of the above

e. only a and b

f. only b and c

4. In Question 3 above, the domain is an example of a(n) _____, and the Domain Controllers container is an example of a(n) _____.

a. main container and subsidiary container

b. folder container and file container

c. primary object and tertiary object

d. parent object and child object

e. all of the above

f. none of the above

g. only a and b

h. only a and c

5. In Windows 2000 Professional, to search for a published Active Directory object on a network...

   a. You must install DSClient when you install network connectivity.

   b. You do not have to first install any special software because the ability to search Active Directory for an object, such as a printer, is built in by default.

   c. You must install a full copy of Active Directory in Windows 2000 Professional.

   d. all of the above

   e. none of the above

   f. only a and c

6. You are looking at information about an object in Active Directory that shows the name /DC=com/DC=handtools/OU=sales/CN=Printers/CN=OuterOfficeLaser. What are the components in this name and what type of name is it?

   a. This is a common name that has the components folder, object class, and printer name.

   b. This is a distinguished name that has the components domain, relative domain, printer organizational unit, and user account ownership name.

   c. This is a universal name that has the components domain name, organizational name, and printer name.

   d. This is a distinguished name that has the components domain name, domain name, organizational unit name, organizational unit name, and printer name.

7. In what protocol is a DC treated as a directory system agent?

   a. LDAP

   b. TCP

   c. IP

   d. PPTP

   e. all of the above

   f. none of the above

8. One of the shared printers on your network is called CorpOneLaser. This is an example of a(n) _____ of that printer in Active Directory.

   a. schema

   b. table

   c. attribute

   d. engine

9. Which of the following might be in an ACL associated with a shared printer?

   a. permission for an account to send a print job to that printer

   b. ownership of the printer by an account

   c. denial of access to the printer for a specific account group

   d. all of the above

   e. only a and c

   f. only b and c

10. You are setting up Active Directory for your college, which has 35 departments. Which of the following containers would you most likely use to reflect the departmental structure?

    a. sites

    b. organizational units

    c. domains

    d. trees

    e. None of the above can be used to reflect department structure.

11. You are in an executive council meeting for your company, and one of the vice presidents wants to know if your Active Directory administrative duties can be shared with other members of the organization. Which of the following might you suggest?

    a. It is a security breach for anyone but you to handle any Active Directory maintenance.

    b. Active Directory security can be decentralized only if you give certain other accounts Full Control access to the domain.

    c. Only account management can be delegated to specified supervisor accounts.

    d. There are several Active Directory tasks that can be delegated, such as managing shared printers, shared folders, and user accounts through a delegated OU.

12. Your network contains many CD-ROM "jukeboxes" that consist of from 4 to 10 CD-ROM drives per jukebox and that enable users to access CD-ROM software. For the sake of Active Directory management, you might consider making CD-ROM jukeboxes a:

    a. new object class

    b. new schema

    c. new domain

    d. all of the above

    e. only a and b

    f. only b and c

13. You are planning a network that will support 474 clients through five Windows 2000 servers and Active Directory. What is the minimum number of DCs that you should plan to use for this network, for optimum accessibility? Also, is a DNS server needed for a network that is this small?

    a. Plan for a minimum of two DCs and plan to implement DNS.

    b. All five servers must be DCs and DNS servers.

    c. Plan to implement only one DC and no DNS services for best performance.

    d. DC replication requires at least three DCs and three DNS servers.

14. Your organization is installing its first Windows 2000 server and Active Directory. Which of the following containers must be defined in Active Directory?

    a. one primary OU for user account groups

    b. two trees

    c. one disjointed namespace

    d. one domain

    e. all of the above

    f. none of the above

15. You have just created an account for a new department head and have also assigned permissions to that account. When the department head tries her new account to take ownership of the folder containing her department's budget information, Windows 2000 Server refuses to let her take ownership. What regular permission to that folder should you give her account?

    a. Write

    b. Read

    c. Ownership

    d. Full Control

16. You are troubleshooting a DC that seems to operate slowly when multiple users access resources such as shared printers and folders. Which of the following might be the problem?

    a. All user accounts are in only one OU.

    b. Some user accounts are located in OUs that are nested 20 layers deep.

    c. The shared folders use ACLs for security instead of Kerberos.

    d. Too many special permissions are defined to security groups, and the DC is having a hard time calculating the actual permissions.

17. When sites are set up to help with DC replication, the advantage(s) is (are) that:

    a. There can be redundancy in DC replication so that if one subnet is down, replication can take place over an alternate route.

    b. The DC replication service can automatically create a new domain or tree when it senses one is needed for more efficient replication or better security.

    c. IPSec is automatically set up on all global catalog servers, when there is more than one global catalog.

    d. all of the above

    e. none of the above

    f. only a and b

    g. only b and c

18. Your college has just converted manual cash registers to an automated cash register system that enables the cashiers' new workstations to function as cash registers that automatically update the accounts receivable program. To help the cashiers make the conversion, you want to enable them all to use a very basic Windows 2000 Professional desktop that is identical on all of the cashier's workstations. What can you do?

    a. Create a Cashiers OU.

    b. Use special permissions for each cashier's account.

    c. Create a GPO for the cashiers that limits the desktop options.

    d. all of the above

    e. both a and b

    f. both a and c

19. Assume that a network client changes his password, but forgets that password shortly after making the change. He calls you, as the network administrator, and asks you to change the password so he will be able to access his account. Just after you change the password, you call him and ask him to log on and then change the password again so you won't know the password. How does Active Directory know which is the most recent password to use for replication to other servers?

    a. It queries you as network administrator before replicating that information.

    b. It queries the user before replicating the information.

    c. It checks the date and version number associated with the password attribute.

    d. all of the above

    e. only a and b

    f. only b and c

1

20. In your organization, the chief financial officer (CFO) is also functioning as the interim chief information officer (CIO) until a new CIO is hired. He has been informed by the former CIO that one of the limitations of using Active Directory is that when there are multiple domains in a tree, you must create a new and separate schema for each domain. The CFO is concerned that this is a lot of work. What is your response as the team leader for all server and network administrators?

    a. This information is true, but there are many server and network administrators who can set up the schemas quickly.

    b. This information is true, which is why you plan to limit the number of domains to one.

    c. This information is false, because all domains in a tree use the same schema.

    d. This information is false because Active Directory does not use a schema; instead it uses a combination of flat files and network file relationships in its database.

21. Which of the following is not an example of a default object class that is created when Active Directory is created?

    a. computer

    b. user account

    c. shared subnet

    d. shared folder

22. Active Directory data is stored and managed using the:

    a. Windows 2000 Server Registry

    b. Extensible Storage Engine

    c. page file

    d. Microsoft Access data view finder

23. You are demonstrating the forward and reverse lookup zones of data that are needed for Active Directory use on your company's network. What standard(s) are these zones a part of?

    a. DNS

    b. DAP

    c. SAP

    d. all of the above

    e. only a and b

    f. only a and c

24. You are setting up a new network that has 32 Windows 2000 servers, two of which are to be set up as Web servers for connection to an Internet service provider. When you set up Active Directory, which of the following will you use as the security boundary between the 32 servers and the Internet?

  a. a forest

  b. an OU

  c. two OUs, one for each Web server

  d. a domain

25. You are analyzing the Active Directory structure of an organization and find that not all domains share the same schema, that there are different global catalogs, and that some domains use disjointed namespaces in relation to one another. This means there is (are):

  a. at least two levels of OUs

  b. two trees in one forest

  c. a single forest model

  d. a separate forest model

HANDS-ON PROJECTS

Each chapter of this book contains hands-on projects that enable you to practice procedures, concepts, and techniques and learn additional information related to the main body of the text. These projects are intended to give you direct experience and practice each step along the way and to reinforce your learning. Plan to create a lab journal or a running word-processed document so that you can record your findings as you perform each project. The lab journal or word-processed document will be a valuable study aid.

 To complete many of the Hands-on Projects in this book, you will need Administrator privileges in Windows 2000 Server.

 ## Project 1-1

In this project you use the Search option in Windows 2000 Server or Professional to find a particular user in Active Directory. Ask your instructor for a user name to locate, search for your own account, or search for the Administrator account to complete this assignment. (Administrator privileges are not required for this project.)

To search Active Directory for an account:

  1. Log on to Windows 2000 Server or Professional.

  2. Click **Start**, point to **Search**, and click **For People**.

  3. Click the list arrow in the Look in box.

4. What are some examples of places in which you can look for a person?

5. Click **Active Directory**.

6. Enter the last name of the person you want to find, such as Brown, in the Name box. Click **Find Now.**

7. How does the Find People dialog box change to report the results of the search?

8. Can you find a person by entering their user account name, if it is different from their last name?

9. How would you locate a person by using her or his e-mail address?

10. Record your findings in a lab journal or in a word-processed document.

11. Close the Find People dialog box.

Project 1-2

In this project, you practice searching Active Directory in an alternate way by using My Network Places in Windows 2000 Server or Professional.

To search Active Directory using My Network Places:

1. Double-click **My Network Places** on the Windows 2000 Server or Professional desktop.

2. Double-click **Entire Network**.

3. Click the **entire contents** hyperlink.

4. What are the options displayed in the right-hand pane of the Entire Network window? Record your observations.

5. Double-click **Directory**. What is displayed?

6. Double-click a domain (if there are more than one).

7. What is displayed now?

8. Double-click the **Users** folder.

9. What is displayed? How would you find the user that you located in Hands-on Project 1-1?

10. Record your observations and then close the Users window.

Project 1-3

This project enables you to install the Directory Service Client software on a computer running Windows 95 or Windows 98. You will need the Windows 2000 Server CD-ROM. Before you start, create a shared folder called DSClient on a Windows 2000 server, or use a folder that is specified by your instructor.

The prerequisites for using the Directory Service Client software are that the client must have Internet Explorer 4.0 or higher, and 10 MB of free disk space.

To install the Directory Service Client software:

1. Log on to Windows 2000 Server using administrator privileges.

2. Insert the Windows 2000 Server CD-ROM.

3. Click **Browse This CD** after the Microsoft Windows 2000 CD dialog box is displayed.

4. Double-click the **CLIENTS** folder. Next, double-click the **WIN9X** folder.

5. Copy the **DSCLIENT** (dsclient.exe) program to the shared folder that you created in advance, such as DSClient, so that clients can access the dsclient.exe program over the network.

6. Click **Exit** to close the Microsoft Windows CD dialog box.

7. Log on to the domain from the client, such as from Windows 98. Double-click **Network Neighborhood** on the client's desktop, find the host Windows 2000 server, double-click the server, and then double-click the shared folder containing the dsclient.exe program.

8. Double-click the **dsclient.exe** file and wait for the installation software components to be extracted into the client operating system.

9. The Directory Service Client Setup Wizard starts automatically. Click **Next**.

10. Click **Next** so that the Wizard can detect the system setup and copy the Directory Service Client files.

11. Click **Finish** and then click **Yes** to restart the client computer.

12. Record your observations about the installation process in your lab journal or in a word-processed document.

Project 1-4

In this project, you use the Active Directory Users and Computers tool to view the DCs on a network. You should be logged on with Administrator privileges.

To view the DCs:

1. Click **Start**, point to **Programs**, point to **Administrative Tools,** and click **Active Directory Users and Computers**.

2. What objects do you see listed under the top domain in the left-hand pane? (If no objects are listed, double-click the domain so that the child objects appear under it in the left-hand pane.) Record your observations.

3. Click **Domain Controllers** under the top domain.

4. Record the names of domain controllers that are displayed in the right-hand pane.

5. Double-click one of the domain controllers. What information is displayed? Record your observations.

6. Click the **Object** tab. What is the purpose of the USN?

7. Close the **Properties** dialog box.

8. Leave the Active Directory Users and Computers tool open for the next project.

Project 1-5

In this activity you view the permissions associated with a domain.

To view the permissions:

1. Make sure that the Active Directory Users and Computers tool is open and if not, open it.

2. Locate the top domain in the left-hand pane and then right-click that domain, such as TheFirm.com.

3. What options are displayed on the shortcut menu? What option would you use to give management control of the domain to a specific user account or group of accounts? Record your observations.

4. Click **Properties**.

5. Click the **Security** tab.

6. What permissions are given to the Domain Admins group? What permissions are given to the Everyone group? Record your observations.

7. Close the Properties dialog box.

8. Leave the Active Directory Users and Computers tool open for the next project.

Project 1-6

In this project, you practice creating an OU and delegating control of the OU. You will need Administrator privileges for this project.

To create an OU and delegate control:

1. Make sure that the Active Directory Users and Computers tool is open and if not, open it.

2. Right-click the top domain in the left-hand pane, such as TheFirm.com, point to **New** and click **Organizational Unit**.

3. Enter OU and then with your initials appended, such as OUMJP. Click **OK**.

4. Find the OU you created (now displayed in the left-hand pane under the domain) and right-click it.

5. What options are available in the shortcut menu? Record your observations.

6. Click **Delegate Control**.

7. Click **Next** when the Delegation of Control Wizard starts.

8. Click **Add**. How would you enable a specific account holder to have control of this OU?

9. Double-click **Account Operators** and then click **OK**.

10. Click **Next**.

11. Make sure that **Delegate the following common tasks** is selected.

12. What tasks can be delegated to the Account Operators group? Record your observations.

13. Check the boxes for: **Create**, **delete**, **and manage user accounts**, and **Reset passwords on user accounts**. Click **Next**.

14. Click **Finish**.

15. Leave the Active Directory Users and Computers tool open for Hands-on Project 1-7.

Project 1-7

In this project, you access the default group policy object for a domain.

To access the default group policy object:

1. Make sure that the Active Directory Users and Computers tool is open, and if not, open it.

2. Right-click the top domain, such as TheFirm.com and then click **Properties**.

3. Click the **Group Policy** tab.

4. What group policies are listed?

5. Make sure that **Default Domain Policy** is highlighted and then click **Edit**.

6. Click or double-click the objects listed under Default Domain Policy in the left-hand pane. Record several examples of policies that can be set, such as security settings.

7. Close the Group Policy window, close the Properties dialog box, and close the Active Directory Users and Computers tool.

Project 1-8

In this project, you practice finding an RFC in the Internet Engineering Task Force's Web site. You need Internet access to perform the project.

To find the contents of an RFC:

1. Connect to the Internet with your Web browser.

2. Access the Web site **www.ietf.org**.

3. Click the link for RFCs (at this writing the link is a bullet on the home page titled **RFC Pages**).

4. In the RFC number box, enter the RFC for domain name system (DNS), which is **1034**.

5. Click the **go** button.

6. When was this RFC written and by whom? Record your observations.

7. Take a few moments to read the RFC.

8. How would you look up another RFC?

9. Exit the browser when you are finished.

Sometimes Web sites change; thus to perform this project you may have to try somewhat different steps.

CASE PROJECT

Aspen Consulting Project: Active Directory Overview for a Client

In each chapter of this book, you work on a variety of Microsoft Active Directory and network projects as a business process analyst and Windows 2000 Server networking consultant for Aspen Consulting. Your boss at Aspen Consulting is Mark Arnez, who manages the consultants and consultant teams that work with organizations using Windows 2000 Server. Your group specializes in business processes analysis, networking, computer operating systems, and Microsoft computer systems support. Your client base includes national and international organizations on every continent, such as multinational corporations, small and large businesses, universities and colleges, telecommunications companies, and government organizations.

Your current assignment is as a consulting team member for the newly formed Pensions Institute in the Czech Republic. The Pensions Institute is working with economists, sociologists, political scientists, health care professionals, and information technology specialists to develop a new retirement system for the citizens of the Czech Republic. This week, you are meeting with the Pensions Institute Information Technology team to plan a Windows 2000 Server network for the retirement system. You are the member of the team who has Active Directory experience.

1. The other members of the Information Technology team do not have much experience with Windows 2000 Server Active Directory. They ask you to give a short executive presentation of the important elements of Active Directory. Create a presentation using any tools that you think will help make it effective, such as tables, slides, overheads, and so on.

2. The Information Technology team has already been discussing the initial purchase of 21 Windows 2000 Servers to store a national database of information on each citizen, to enable fast reporting from the national database, to provide Web services, to run software applications, and to generate monthly retirement checks. Ten of the servers will be located in the main server computer room of the central government's IT operations in Prague, and 11 servers will be housed in the new Pensions Institute IT computer operations facility that is located across town. The networks in the two locations will be connected initially by a high-speed telecommunications line transmitting at 44.736 Mbps, and this line is anticipated to have heavy network traffic. Four of

the servers in the Pensions Institute IT facility will be Web servers for access by remote offices. You have been asked to discuss in very general terms the following issues:

❑ What questions should be asked to determine how to set up OUs, domains, trees, forests, and sites?

❑ What are some sample options for setting up OUs, domains, trees, forests, and sites?

❑ How might Active Directory replication work in your examples of setup options?

❑ How might the global directory setup work in your sample options?

3. After completing your discussion of the issues in Assignment 2, the chair of the team asks if Active Directory should be solely managed by a few network administrators or if management should be decentralized. Discuss the options regarding centralized versus decentralized management, including the pros and cons of each.

4. The chair of the Pensions Institute Information Technology team is very concerned about following standards so that the new network will be positioned to easily grow as future needs grow. Make a presentation about the standards that are incorporated into Active Directory.

OPTIONAL CASE PROJECTS FOR TEAMS

Team Case One

Currently, the central government network in the Czech Republic has been using a mix of two protocols, IPX/SPX for some older NetWare servers, and TCP/IP for other computers. Form a special research team to study and report on the differences between IPX/SPX and TCP/IP. In your report, address why TCP/IP is a sound alternative for the pension system network.

Team Case Two

The chair of the Pensions Institute Information Technology team asks your special research team to make a presentation on another issue in addition to the one described in Team Case One. This time she would like a report comparing the Windows 2000 Server Active Directory hierarchical structure to the domain-based structure of Windows NT Server 4.0. What are the advantages and disadvantages of each?

2

ANALYZING BUSINESS REQUIREMENTS

> **After reading this chapter and completing the exercises, you will be able to:**
> - Analyze business organizational structures
> - Analyze business management models
> - Analyze business goals and strategies
> - Analyze business processes and information flow
> - Analyze legal requirements and company policies
> - Analyze outside relationships, acquisition plans, and risk tolerance

Every organization has a unique social personality and effect on the community it serves. When you begin designing Active Directory services for an organization, your job is to understand that organization's personality, because the Active Directory design is a reflection of the organization's inner workings. Some organizations have multiple personalities that correspond to the different kinds of products they make for markets throughout the world. Other organizations that are smaller, or that focus on producing only one product or providing one service, may have simpler personalities.

The focus of this and the next four chapters (Chapters 3–5) is primarily on how to analyze the inner workings of different kinds of organizations, which is the first step that you must take before starting Active Directory design. These chapters teach you how to thoroughly analyze an organization and prepare you to meet the Microsoft 70-219 certification objectives that address:

- Analyzing business requirements
- Analyzing technical requirements

Chapters 6 through 11 show you how to apply different aspects of your organizational analysis skills to Active Directory design and cover the remaining two groups of Microsoft 70-219 certification objectives:

- Designing a directory service architecture
- Designing service locations

Three fictitious organizations are introduced in this chapter that will be used as examples throughout this book: Jefferson Philately, a small company providing products and services for stamp collectors; Interstate Security Bank, a large banking business that spans five states; and York Industries, a multinational company that operates in seven countries on four continents. You will learn how to analyze vital business features of these and other organizations, such as the organizational models used, the way the organizations are managed, organizational goals, business processes, legal and policy issues, and the way the organizations interact with outside forces.

ANALYZING ORGANIZATIONAL MODELS

One of the first places to start when conceptualizing Active Directory structure for a company, educational institution, or governmental institution is to analyze the organizational structure. There are many different organizational models that can be followed, but typically the models are organized on the basis of at least one, and often a combination, of the following categories:

- Geography
- Functional unit
- Department, division, or business unit
- Product or service
- Project-based unit
- Cost center

2

Organization by Geography

Some companies or institutions may be organized on a geographical model. As you analyze an organization for information about how to structure Active Directory services, determine all of its geographical locations, including the locations of network devices, servers, and clients. There are several models that reflect geographic scope:

- *Regional:* A **regional geographic organization** is one in which all network and computer resources are located in relatively close proximity, such as in a single building, on a business or school campus, in multiple locations within the same city, or in different cities that are relatively close—for example, in a large city and its suburbs. In a regional scope, the company activities are particularly influenced by local and state laws. Also, the communications connectivity between separate locations is usually dependent on the services of one or more *regional Bell operating companies (RBOCs)*, which are telecommunications companies that provide telephone and network services to a designated region. Bell South and Qwest (formerly U.S. West and Quest) are examples of RBOCs.

- *National:* A **national geographic organization** is one that covers multiple states, provinces, or other major boundaries within the same country. State and federal laws are particularly important in influencing the activities of an organization that has a national scope. Also, the connectivity between locations is influenced by a combination of RBOCs and long-distance carriers. Two examples of long-distance carriers are AT&T and MCI.

- *International:* An **international geographic organization** spans multiple countries and can span different continents. In an international scope, an organization is especially influenced by national and international laws. Another factor that affects an organization with international scope is that different locations may use different languages. The communications connectivity can be a very complex mixture of regional, national, long-distance, and international telecommunications carriers, including satellite communications (see Chapter 5).

Each of these models can also include subsidiary and branch offices. A **subsidiary office** is one that is owned by the main company or organization, but that has relative decision-making autonomy. For example, a subsidiary may be a company that has been purchased by another company, but that retains a portion or all of its original identity. A book publishing company may own radio, television, and Internet companies, for instance, each of which retains its own name and has its own management. The electronics industry is another example, in which electrical appliances are manufactured under a parent company's name, and specific electrical parts are made by separate companies that have been purchased by the parent company. A **branch office** is one that is relatively dependent on a higher-level office or corporate headquarters, because it is not an autonomous organizational entity. You are probably already familiar with branch banks that are in communities throughout a state or that are in multiple states; the branch banks have the same name as the parent bank and are controlled by the organizational policies established by the parent.

Consider, for example, our three fictitious companies, which illustrate the different geo-graphic models. The regional model, which is also the simplest, is the fictitious company Jefferson Philately located in Cleveland, Ohio. This company, which manufactures and sells collectable stamps, plates, and art, is entirely housed in one building that contains Administrative, Marketing, Human Resources, Information Technology, and Manufacturing Departments for a company of 295 employees.

An example of the national model, which is more complex, is the fictitious bank, Interstate Security Bank, headquartered in Seattle, Washington, and that has regional and branch offices in Idaho, Montana, Oregon, Washington (separate from the headquarters), and Wyoming. The regional offices house the main business processing functions for each state and report to the headquarters office in Seattle. The branch offices offer direct banking services to the cus-tomers in their communities and report to the regional offices. Interstate Security Bank has 2100 employees. Because the geography of Interstate Security Bank spans several states, it is useful to create a flow chart of the organization's geography from which to start your orga-nizational analysis and gradually build in more details about the organization as the details are revealed (see Figure 2-1).

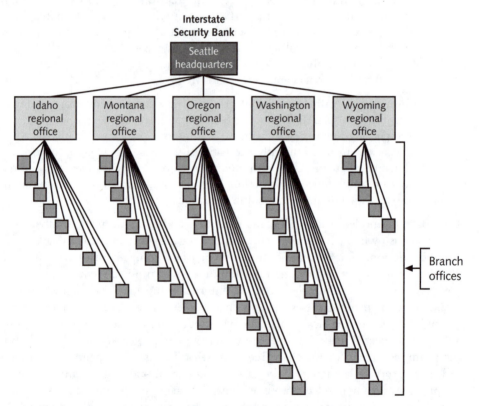

Figure 2-1   Organizational structure of a multistate organization

2

One advantage of developing a geographic representation of the organization is that you can later expand the representation to include more detail, such as the city locations and information about the network connection speeds between locations. For example, Figure 2-2 shows an expansion of the geographic organizational structure that exists between the main office in Seattle and the regional and branch offices in Wyoming. Included in this diagram are the connection speeds of each geographic link. The following information can be used in planning the following Active Directory elements:

- Domain divisions
- Sites
- Placement of DC servers
- Placement of global catalog servers
- Placement of DNS and DHCP servers

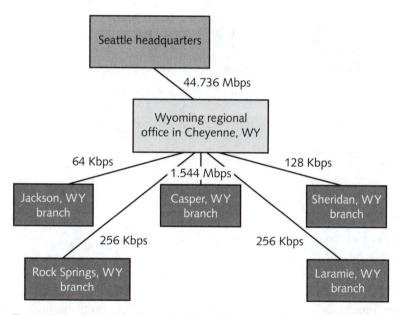

Figure 2-2   Expanded organizational structure for one portion of an organization

A third model is a company that has an international scope, York Industries, which makes appliances under different brand names. This company has 21,400 employees spread throughout Canada, England, France, Japan, Argentina, Poland, and the United States. The company has fewer geographic sites than Interstate Security Bank, but there are greater distances between sites and more employees. Creating a geographic diagram of this organization provides a way to understand the physical layout of the organization and the ways the physical layout might influence the Active Directory design. Figure 2-3 is a representation of the large-scale international geographic organization.

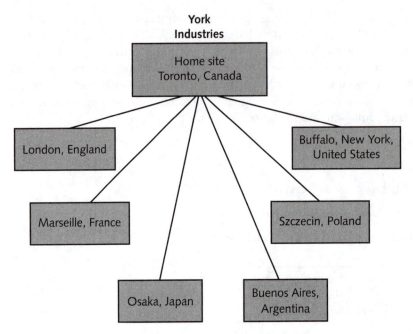

Figure 2-3   Organizational structure of an international company

As you learn later in this chapter, York Industries is also a conglomerate of subsidiary companies, which are:

- B & E Electronics
- Nantes Appliances
- Kanazawa
- Pampas Fixtures
- Sudeten Motors
- Palisades Corporation

Try Hands-on Project 2-1 to practice creating a diagram of a company on the basis of its geographic organization.

Organization by Function

Another way to analyze an organization is by determining its functional units, another step you can take in gathering information about how to set up elements in Active Directory, such as security groups, group policies, and containers. For example, when Jefferson

Philately is analyzed by functional units, the following groups can be diagrammed in a flow chart (see Figure 2-4):

- Board of directors
- Management
- Accounting and payroll
- Cashiers
- Human resources
- Marketing and subscriptions

- Manufacturing
- Journeyman printer operators
- Customer service
- Information technology
- Inventory, warehouse, and distribution
- Physical plant

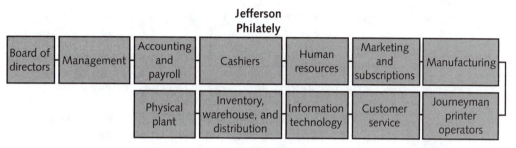

Jefferson Philately

Figure 2-4   Organizational structure by function

For example, by studying the functional groups, you may find that it makes sense to set up security or distribution groups of accounts based on these groups. Active Directory employs two general types of groups, those used for security and those used for e-mail lists. **Security groups** are groups of users that are created as a way to reduce the amount of work involved in administering security. For example, if you are managing Active Directory for an organization of 295 users, it is much easier to divide the users into logical groupings on the basis of the type of security they will need and then assign security to each group. It is much faster to assign security to 12 groups than to assign security individually to 295 users. This principle is even more important as the number of users grows larger—for example as for the 2100 users at Interstate Security Bank and the 21,400 users employed by York Industries. Security groups exist primarily to control access to resources and services. The other type of group is called a **distribution group** and is intended strictly for use as an e-mail distribution list. An e-mail distribution list is a list of users created so that an e-mail message can be sent one time to all users on the list, for example via Microsoft Exchange. Figure 2-5 shows how security groups might be set up in Active Directory for Jefferson Philately.

Figure 2-5   Linking functional groups to Active Directory security groups

Because Active Directory is scalable to a very large size, you can add more groups as your organization grows. This ability accommodates small companies that experience rapid growth, company reorganizations, and mergers.

Organization by Department, Division, or Business Unit

Larger organizations can be analyzed on the basis of department, division, or business unit, or a combination of all three, which Microsoft groups under the *departmental business model*. In a university, for example, there are different academic colleges, such as the college of arts and sciences, the business college, the law school, the medical school, and the engineering school. Within each college there are departments, such as anthropology, biology, chemistry, math, psychology, and so on, in the college of arts and sciences. Also, on the administrative side of the university, there are different divisions and departments within each division, such as the executive, financial services, information technology, and student services divisions. In the student services division, for example, there are departments that include Admissions, Financial Aid, Cashiers, and Registration and Records. (Try Hands-on Project 2-2 to practice such an analysis of your school.)

Both Interstate Security Bank and York Industries are examples of companies that can be analyzed in terms of department, division, and business unit. Interstate Security Bank, for instance, can be analyzed by business unit, by dividing it into the headquarters office, the regional offices, and the branch offices. Within the headquarters and regional offices the departments consist of Executive, Business, Marketing, Customer Service, Loans, Investments, and Information Technology. Also, the headquarters office has a board of directors. Each branch office has Business, Loans, Investments, Customer Service, and Tellers departments. In addition to these business units and departments, the bank also outsources regular auditing services to a private external auditing firm, R.D. Hutton. Further, federal auditors check the headquarters, regional, and branch offices twice each year. The relationship with companies that handle outsourced services is also important to analyze for Active Directory design, because you may need to create an organizational unit (OU), create a group, or link a domain to handle the security needs for access by those outside companies.

In addition to creating a diagram of the geographic organization, plan to create a diagram of the department, divisional, and business unit organization of a company. Figures 2-6 and 2-7 illustrate how to diagram Interstate Security Bank in this way.

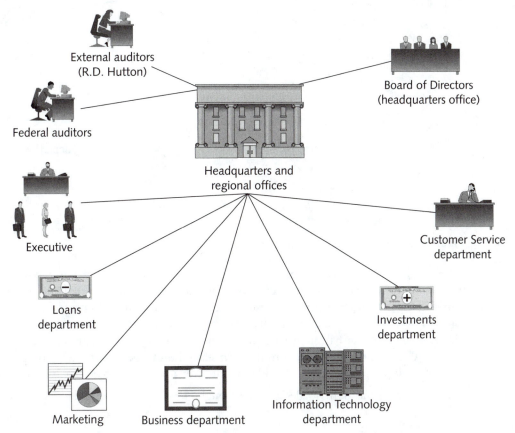

Figure 2-6   Headquarters and regional office departments and business units

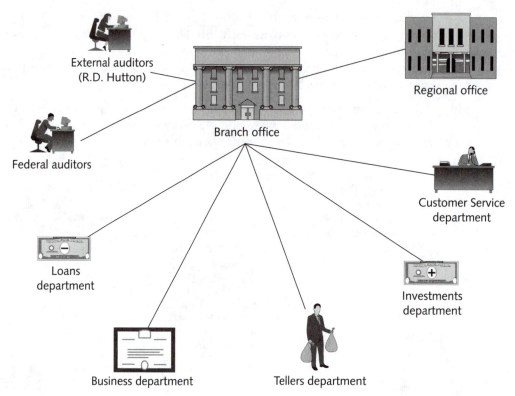

Figure 2-7   Branch office departments

These diagrams are valuable when it comes to planning OUs and domains. For example, one way to apply the analysis of the geographic and business unit organizational structure is to propose a parent domain for the headquarters office and child domains for each regional office. This structure creates a security boundary around each domain, a practice that both the federal and external auditors may require to provide added protection for banking records. Creating the child domains for each state also can be used to help comply with the laws of some states that require banking records for its residents to reside only in that state.

Supplementing the domain design, there might be OUs in the parent domain for each department:

- Executive
- Business
- Marketing
- Customer Service
- Loans
- Investments
- Information Technology

The OUs for the child domains might be set up on the basis of the branch office organization, the branch department organization, or a combination of both. For example, the Idaho child domain might have nine OUs, each named for the city of the corresponding branch office. Departments in each branch office might be OUs under that branch. For instance, in the Idaho regional office, the Boise branch OU would contain child OUs for the Business, Loans, Investments, Tellers, and Customer Service departments.

Organization by Product or Service

Some organizations can be analyzed in terms of the product they make or the particular service that specific groups of people in the company perform. For example, one way to analyze Jefferson Philately is in terms of the products that it makes. In this type of analysis, you might analyze the company in terms of three general groupings of products: stamps, plates, and art. A broader way to analyze the same company is to combine general services and products so that you have five groupings (see Figure 2-8):

- Business and accounting
- Customer service
- Stamps
- Plates
- Art

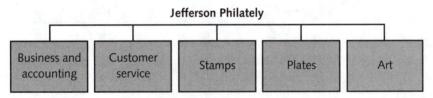

Figure 2-8   Organization by product and service

For some organizations, the management may prefer to recognize different units primarily by the services that they perform, which often follows the line-and-staff organization. The line-and-staff organization consists of the chain of command—for example, from president to vice presidents to department heads and down the hierarchy.

Analysis by product, service, or a combination of these can provide information for setting up account groups, group policies, OUs, and domains. For example, if you perform an analysis of Jefferson Philately on the basis of the line-and-staff service organization, you would show business functions that are under specific service-based units. This type of organizational analysis is illustrated in Figure 2-9.

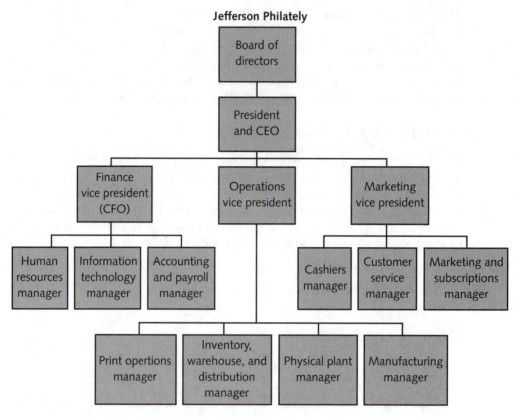

Figure 2-9   Organization by service within the company

Using the service organizational analysis in Figure 2-9, Active Directory structure might focus on using OUs to reflect the line-and-staff structure, instead of simply creating groups, as previously illustrated in Figure 2-5. The approach of using OUs to reflect the organizational hierarchy would include creating three levels of OUs. The top level would be President and would contain three OUs: VPFinance, VPOperations, and VPMarketing. Under these OUs there would be a third level for managers. For example, under the VPFinance second level OU there would be the OUs: HRManager, ITManager, and AccountingManager.

 Another way to structure the OUs in this example for Jefferson Philately is to use only two levels of OUs by collapsing the first and second levels into one executive level consisting of Pres, VPFinance, VPOperations, and VPMarketing. The advantage of eliminating a level is that you reduce the load on the CPU because there is one less OU level to search in order to perform a specific task (see Chapter 1).

Organization by Project

A relatively new model is one that consists of project teams. This might reflect the structure of an entire organization or only a portion of an organization. For instance, there are firms that exist solely to contract with other companies for developing new product ideas. One example is a "new idea" company that was contracted to develop a more user-friendly shopping cart than exists currently. Some of the development goals included child safety, easier loading and unloading, and better maneuverability. Company employees were divided into four teams that competed to come up with the best idea. The project-based structure of this company consists of one president, team leaders, and team members. Although the president does not change positions, the team leaders change by project and so do the team members.

A more typical example of project-based organization is one in which certain departments or functional areas set up in teams. This applies to York Industries' IT department at the main location in Toronto. The IT department has a mix of user support personnel, application development programmers, systems development programmers, quality assurance testers, systems administrators, database administrators, Web developers, operations personnel, and technical support personnel. For new projects and system installations, project teams are formed under the leadership of a project manager. There are 10 permanently assigned project managers who manage projects such as installing a new server and accounting system, developing a new time-clock system, setting up a Web site for a new product, upgrading a manufacturing system, and so on. Each time there is a new project, one of the project managers is assigned to that project, and team members are selected on the basis of matching their area of expertise to the needs of the particular project. The composition of teams changes as each new project is started. For example, a team that is installing a new accounting system might consist of a project manager, two systems development programmers, one systems administrator, eight applications development programmers, a database administrator, a Web developer, and an operations scheduler (plus members of the Accounting department). After the project is tested, completed, and brought to live production, that particular team disbands and its members go on to other teams and projects. An IT employee might be on only one team or might be a member of two or three teams simultaneously, depending on the demands of each project.

Active Directory design for an organization or department that uses a project-based model of organization must be flexible enough to change as the teams change. In this type of organization, an OU might be used to reflect each team, and management of accounts and groups within an OU might be delegated to the team leader. Once a team project is finished, accounts and groups can be shifted to other OUs and the OU for the disbanded team can be deleted.

Organization by Cost Center

Some organizations focus particularly on **cost centers**, which are areas in the organization that are connected with the cost of doing business or the *cost of operations*. Any of the organizational models that have already been discussed can be associated with the cost of operations. For example, if you analyze Jefferson Philately on the basis of the products that it makes, then each product area can be a cost center. This type of analysis might show that the operations to make collectable stamp products cost $4.2 million, plate production costs $5.4 million, and art products cost $2.8 million to make. In another example, if you analyze the headquarters at Interstate Security Bank on the basis of department and business units, each department might be considered a cost center, because it costs a specific amount of money for that department to function in a given calendar or fiscal year (see Figure 2-10). A fiscal year is typically a business accounting period of 12 months, and depending on a particular state's laws, incorporated organizations, partnerships, and sole proprietorships are required to report fiscal year accounting data.

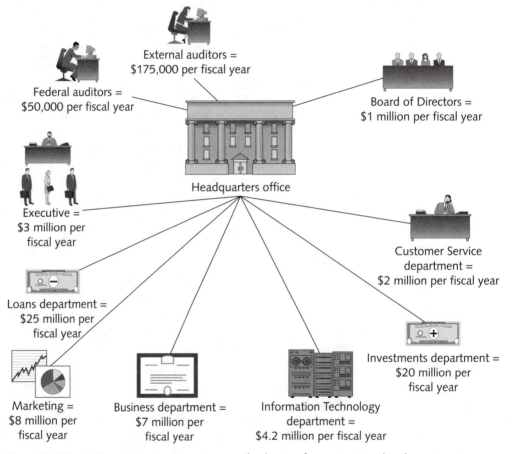

Figure 2-10   Determining cost centers on the basis of organization by department

When you analyze an organization, one way to determine cost centers is by viewing the amount that is budgeted to departments or that is budgeted for specific functions within an organization, such as computer support, telecommunications, accounting, creating a specific product, and so on. Also, a cost centered organization is indicated when one group in an organization charges another group for its services. The Accounting department might charge each department a fee for tracking that department's budget and expenditures (refer to the Operating Plan and the Cost of Operations section later in this chapter). The IT department might charge each department in the organization for the use of computer resources and computer support, such as charging for the amount of time each department spends using the resources of servers or charging every time a user consultant helps a new user set up his or her computer.

Typically, an analysis of cost centers can be used in the design of forests, trees, domains, OUs, and groups in an organization. For example, in an organization such as York Industries, the cost centers might be connected to the individual subsidiaries in that company or to the cost of producing certain products. For instance, if York Industries prefers to use the analysis by subsidiary as a cost center, then there are two basic design scenarios. In one design scenario, the analysis shows that all subsidiaries work in an atmosphere of trust and are therefore able to use the same schema. In this scenario, York Industries uses different trees for each subsidiary/cost center (see Chapter 6 for more on this design scenario). A second scenario is that the subsidiaries do not fully trust one another in terms of cost accounting and Active Directory management and thus want a separate schema for each subsidiary/cost center. In this scenario, you would create a separate forest for each subsidiary/cost center, which enables each to have its own secure schema.

The different scenarios for York Industries point to the importance of offering two or more design plans from which an organization can choose. This is possible because you can analyze an organization to emphasize different factors or a combination of factors—for example, emphasizing geographical organization or emphasizing a combination of product-based and cost center organization. For instance, if you use geographical organization to analyze Jefferson Philately, the design plan may be to keep Active Directory simple by using one domain and the default OUs (see Chapters 6 and 7). If you use product-based and cost center analysis, the design plan may be to create OUs for each product/cost center, or even to create separate domains if you need to create special security boundaries around each product/cost center.

Try Hands-on Project 2-3 to practice using information from Active Directory to help in your analysis of the organizational model or models that apply to a business or institution.

Analyzing Business Management Models

In addition to analyzing organizational structure, the management style in an organization affects Active Directory design in terms of establishing group policies, security, and delegation of control. Before designing Active Directory containers and relationships, it is valuable to analyze how an organization is managed. Also, in any organization there can be many different management styles used in different departments or divisions. For example, in York Industries, the management model in the Toronto-based IT department is relatively decentralized among project leaders and teams. But the management style in the Finance department is centralized, with the CFO delegating authority to her managers, because there are no teams to share management decisions.

There are several general management models that an organization or a department in an organization can follow:

- Centralized
- Decentralized
- Formal-informal
- Path-goal
- Situational

Try Hands-on Project 2-4 to practice analyzing the decision-making style of a department or organization.

Centralized Decision Model

The **centralized decision model** is perhaps the oldest model. In this model, the decision making is held in the top positions of an organization—for example, with the officers of the organization (the board, chief executive officer, chief financial officer, chief information officer, etc.) and managers. When management centralization is combined with an authoritative management style, then decisions are made with little input from nonmanagement staff. Less authoritative management means that staff can provide input into decisions, but the final decisions are still made by officers and managers.

Centralized and authoritative managements are characterized by little delegation. Upper-level management retains tight control of decisions, which typically results in nonmanagement staff members taking little initiative. The advantage of this type of management is that some critical operations, such as those involving financial matters, are watched closely. In other areas, such as marketing which requires broad creativity, this management style can be a disadvantage.

Often a centralized management model is very obvious because there is a large number of managers in relation to the number of nonmanagement staff. Another characteristic of this management model is that change happens relatively slowly.

 From the Active Directory designer's standpoint, the centralized management model that uses little delegation can be a plus for CPU performance, because it often results in fewer OU levels.

Decentralized Decision Model

In a **decentralized decision model**, decision-making responsibilities are spread beyond traditional managers, to nonmanagerial staff. The decentralized style is often accompanied by a less authoritative environment, which means that staff members have more direct input into the decision-making process. Often this management style accompanies the project-based organizational model. For example, the York Industries' Toronto-based IT department, which uses a project-based organizational style, employs a decentralized decision model because it uses teams and project leaders who coordinate the teams. Decisions on project timelines, personnel assignments to specific tasks, quality assurance methods, and even the censuring of team members who are not producing are typically made by the teams. When a new team is formed, the members of the team determine their own operating and decision-making rules, the frequency of meetings, and the ways new input will be brought to the team, for example.

The characteristics of decentralized management are:

- Greater delegation

- Fewer managers

- Faster response to change

- Lower operational costs

- Greater participation from employees

- More communication about company and project goals

Although decentralized management has significant advantages, such as more employee participation and interest, some significant problems can develop. One common problem is that decisions can vastly differ from the goals of the organization, or can slow progress toward completing a task or project. Misdirected decisions can take a group of employees far down the wrong path before the problem is detected. Another difficulty with decentralized management, when combined with a project-based organization, is that conflicting personalities or approaches among team members can significantly delay decision making. For example, in one college a team that was working to decide on a new student services computer system had a major disagreement about which database to use for that system. The disagreement went on for months, significantly delaying the selection and implementation of the system.

 When an organization uses decentralized management and teams, design Active Directory structures to be as fluid as the decisions and the teams that make those decisions. Start by using security groups and OUs, which can be restructured most easily. Also, use the Windows 2000 Server System Security and Analysis tool frequently to check security for holes each time you reconfigure groups and OUs.

Formal and Informal Decision-making Structures

Organizations have both formal and informal decision-making structures. For example, the **formal decision making** structure in a department may be officially centralized with the director or manager of that department. In reality, the director or manager may be reluctant to make decisions, and the **informal decision making** may be handled by one or two people in the department who are not in a formal management role. The classic example is the department head whose job duties include a wide range of decision-making tasks, but who hands off many of those tasks to an administrative assistant.

When you set up an OU and an associated group policy for a department, analyze the formal and informal decision-making structures first. This task is often much simpler than it sounds. For example, in one university, the formally stated guideline for managing accounts and security on a physical plant server was that the plant director would handle these duties. The reality was that the director was not comfortable with computer technology and did not want to follow this guideline. The plant director's division head gave the director unofficial latitude to delegate this task to the physical plant's business manager. The Active Directory designer who was setting up the server simply had to ask the plant director who would be creating accounts and managing security before setting up Active Directory.

Learn as much as possible about the informal decision-making structures of an organization before you design and implement Active Directory. Often there is more informal decision control than formal decision control. As you learn about the informal lines of decision control, investigate whether any of these are in conflict with legal or auditing requirements and request that the organization settle the conflicts prior to Active Directory implementation. In most instances, the organization will be grateful that you helped them clarify a possible conflict of which they were unaware.

Path-Goal Decision Model

The **path-goal decision model** focuses on defining the goal that is to be achieved and the steps that must be completed along the path to achieve the goal. The path-goal model often is indicated by use of project management software and project management techniques that involve:

- A listing of tasks that must be completed along the way to achieving a goal and milestones that represent a group of completed tasks at critical junctures

- Associating each task or milestone with one or more staff or management participants who are responsible for it

- Associating a start and completion date with each task and a completion date with each milestone

- Creating a timeline showing the relationship of start and completion dates for all tasks and milestones

The decisions that are made are directly related to the nature of the tasks and the final goal. For example, the goal may be defined as completing the design and implementation of Active Directory by the end of the fiscal year or calendar year. The general tasks, task assignments, and timeline for this project are illustrated in Table 2-1.

A fiscal year is a one-year period of financial activity for a company, and a company's budget is usually calculated on the basis of the fiscal year. The fiscal year may or may not follow the calendar year. For example, a typical fiscal year is July 1st to June 30th.

2

Table 2-1 Project Tasks

Task	Milestone	Assigned To	Start Date	Completion Date
Plan the Windows 2000 Server installation		P. Candelaria R. Chen	September 4th	September 21st
Plan the Active Directory structure		J. Anderson, P. Candelaria, A. Goldsmith, T. Brown, F. Lucus	September 11th	November 3rd
Purchase new server hardware and software		R. Chen	September 25th	September 29th
Install Windows 2000 Server on new servers		P. Candelaria	November 7th	November 7th
	Planning for server installa-tion and actual installation are completed			November 7th
Distribute Active Directory plan for review by management		A. Goldsmith	November 7th	November 8th
Present Active Directory plan to management for feedback and approval		J. Anderson, P. Candelaria, A. Goldsmith, T. Brown, F. Lucus	November 14th	November 14th
	Active Directory design plan completed and approved by management			November 14th
Create step-by-step Active Directory implementation script of actions		J. Anderson, P. Candelaria	November 20th	November 22nd
Establish an Active Directory implementation date with management and users		J. Anderson, P. Candelaria	November 27th	November 30th

Table 2-1   Project Tasks (continued)

Task	Milestone	Assigned To	Start Date	Completion Date
Install Active Directory and its components per the design plan		J. Anderson, P. Candelaria	December 30th	December 31st
Test Active Directory installation		J. Anderson, P. Candelaria	December 31st	December 31st
	Project completed			December 31st

 Tip Most task lists in a project can be broken down into many subtasks for more accurate division of labor and precise planning. Project management software, such as Microsoft Project, is available to help in creating the task list.

The path–goal decision model can be used along with a centralized decision model or a decentralized decision model. When it is used with the centralized decision model, a manager determines the specific tasks, task assignments, and task dates. If it is used with the decentralized model, then a team or a group of staff members develop the tasks, task assignments, and task dates. There are also two middle-ground models used with the path–goal decision model that are in between the centralized and decentralized approaches:

- *Participatory,* which places more responsibility with the manager, but in which the manager seeks and uses suggestions from her or his staff

- *Supportive,* which places more responsibility with the staff, but in which the manager actively coaches and supports her or his staff in making the decisions

In the path–goal model, Active Directory design typically focuses on matching the group and OU structures to the defined goals and those who are responsible for completing the goals. For example, each project associated with a goal may have its own OU, and the individuals responsible for completing selected tasks may be assigned to specific Active Directory security groups. Consider, for example, Jefferson Philately, which is in the process of creating a new inventory system on the basis of a path–goal decision model. Because the company also has a centralized decision structure, the company management has designated the IT manager to oversee the project. The steps they might take in the Active Directory design to prepare for the project are:

- Create an OU, called Inventory Design, which will contain information for the project participants, such as project management software that includes project tasks and guidelines.

- Delegate authority over the Inventory Design OU to the IT manager, who will control which user accounts and computers can access the Inventory Design OU.

- Have the IT manager create a nested OU, called Development, inside the Inventory Design OU, for use as an applications development area for programmers and a database administrator. This area would initially be secured by the IT manager to give the programmers and database administrator Read and Write access while they develop the software. Later, it would be opened to inventory and warehouse personnel for access to test the inventory applications before going into production.

■ After the project is completed, applications and database structures would be moved to the appropriate folder areas for production programs (and a regular test area would be created for future development and modifications).

■ Also upon completion of the project, the Development and Inventory Design OUs would be deleted by the IT manager.

Situational Decision Model

The **situational decision model** means that decision making is related to specific socio-logical factors or situations. Each situation can be thought of as on a continuum in which the situational factors vary in the following ways (see Figure 2-11):

■ *Loyalty:* Is this an organization that fosters loyalty among employees?

■ *Trust in management:* Do the employees trust management?

■ *Management authority:* How much power does management have to execute rewards, such as raises and promotions, and punishment, such as terminating employment?

■ *Complexity of the work:* Is the work creative, challenging, and thought provoking, or is the work mundane, simple, and repetitive?

Figure 2-11   Situational factors

An organization that fosters loyalty and trust in management, in which managers have power to use rewards and punishments, and in which the work is relatively complex is likely to be focused on completing tasks and goals, or *task-oriented*. In contrast, an organization in which loyalty and trust in management are low, in which managers have little authority, and where the work is repetitive, is likely to be focused on relationships among people, or *relationship-oriented*. The latter type of organization often makes decisions on the basis of political concerns.

An example of a task-oriented organization is a software business in which employees perform the complex work of writing and testing code. In this business, employees are highly valued and have developed a strong sense of dedication to the company. Also, those who are high achievers can be rewarded quickly with raises and promotions. An example of a relationship-oriented organization might be a Physical Plant department in a state university. In this organization, the managers and supervisors are most concerned about university politics, such as budget struggles. There are no tangible promotion paths for the staff employees, because the difference between their salaries and those of their supervisors is only a few hundred dollars a year. After a new employee has been on the job six months, he or she is made a permanent employee, and it is difficult to fire a permanent employee, except for extreme negligence or illegal behavior. The work is very repetitive and there is little loyalty to this job. More attention is given to the relationships among the individual staff members than to their actual work performance.

The Active Directory structure used for the situational model depends on whether the organization is task-oriented or relationship-oriented. If the organization is task-oriented, there are likely to be many OUs that reflect both management authority and specific tasks. In the software company example, each manager might have control over an OU, and there might be additional OUs under each manager's OU to reflect specific projects or project teams. In the physical plant example, the Active Directory structure is likely to be a reflection of the political divisions in that department or even in the university as a whole. For example, the physical plant may have its own domain, domain administrator, and separate OUs for each department (painters, custodians, electricians, plumbers, and carpenters).

Try Hands-on Project 2-5 to use information that is already in Active Directory to help analyze the decision-making model or models used by a company or institution.

ANALYZING BUSINESS GOALS AND STRATEGIES

When you perform an analysis of an organization, use a discovery process to learn about the purpose of the organization. Some examples of general questions you might ask about an organization include:

- What is the main business of the organization?
- Does the organization consist of different business units, companies, or divisions that make different products?
- Does the organization use a planning process or establish business objectives?
- Does the organization have any merger or reorganization plans?

Developing a broad understanding of an organization, such as understanding broad and specific organizational boundaries, security needs, and interaction with other organizations, will help you plan Active Directory components. For example, York Industries, the multinational corporation introduced earlier in this chapter, can be analyzed by establishing the subsidiary companies in this conglomerate. The main company, York Industries, manufactures refrigerators, freezers, electric ranges, and electric ovens at the Toronto location, selling them in

North America under the York brand name. The London-based company within the York Industries conglomerate, B & E Electronics, makes electrical timers, relay switches, motors, and other electronic components for kitchen appliances. Another York Industries company is Nantes Appliances, which makes refrigerators and freezers in Marseille, France for use in Europe and Asia. These appliances are sold under the Nantes brand name. A subsidiary company in Osaka, Japan makes blenders, microwave ovens, toasters, and toaster ovens under the brand name Kanazawa. In Buenos Aires, Argentina, the York Industries company called Pampas Fixtures makes plastic parts for appliances, such as knobs, handles, and levers. In Szczecin, Poland, the member company Sudeten Motors makes electrical parts, capacitors, compressors, and electric motors. The Palisades Corporation in Buffalo, New York manufactures dishwashers, stoves, and ovens under the York brand name. Figure 2-12 illustrates how to diagram the different companies within York Industries.

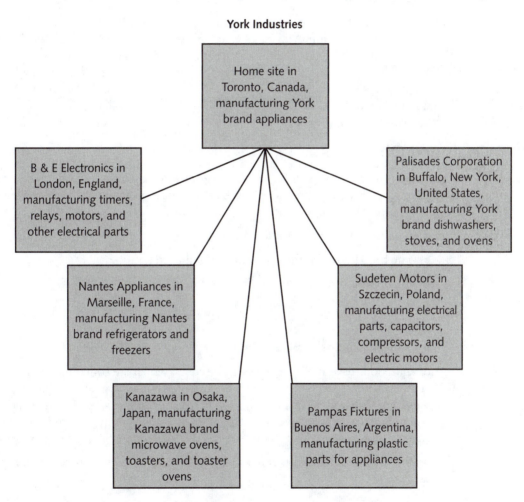

Figure 2-12   The York Industries companies

Besides understanding the companies and products of York Industries, your analysis should include a grasp of the following elements for York Industries as a whole and for each company within York Industries:

- Mission statement
- Organizational goals or business objectives
- Strategic plan
- Operating plan
- Project plans

Mission Statement

Most organizations have a **mission statement** that gives a broad-brush overview of the purpose of the organization. A mission statement provides information about the products or services that are provided and about the recipients of those products or services. For example, the mission statement for York Industries is: "We will manufacture the highest quality kitchen appliances for customers in countries throughout the world." The mission statement for one subsidiary of York Industries, Sudeten Motors, is: "We will produce the finest motors, electrical parts, and compressors that give York Industries appliances years of flawless service."

Goals and Objectives

Organizations usually have statements of their **goals** or **objectives**. Goals or objectives that are used by an organization are more specific than a mission statement because they contain quantifiable elements such as:

- A general or specific task to be completed
- The time by which the task will be completed
- An amount of money or profit to be attained
- A percentage increase in a service, in the number of customers, or in the amount of business
- A marketing or sales accomplishment

Most organizations have multiple goals or objectives, which are sometimes ranked in terms of priority from most important to least important. Also, most goals or objectives contain some elements that can be quantified, by a percentage, for example. In general, goals or objectives indicate what is to be completed, when it will be completed, and how much will be completed. For example, York Industries has the following goals (in order of priority):

1. Increase worldwide sales revenues by 35 percent by the end of the next fiscal year.

2. Increase the refrigerator and freezer sales by 17 percent by the end of the next fiscal year.

3. Develop 5000 new distributors and sales partners within six months.

4. Increase the worldwide marketing staff by 7 percent in the next four months.

5. Create within one year a new department for recycling the parts in defective units.

6. Over the next two years, decentralize warehouse management and implement "just-in-time" parts inventory practices in all manufacturing plants.

7. Within four years, phase out the unprofitable blender business and phase in coffee makers and coffee bean grinders as new products.

The goals for York Industries are valuable to know when you're designing Active Directory services because they signal some changes that the Active Directory designer should take into account. For instance, does the increase in new distributors or sales partners mean there will be a need for groups, OUs, or domains to handle these new associates? Will the increased marketing staff work out of one location or different locations? Will there be new departments or divisions growing out of marketing? How will the decentralization of warehouse management affect network security and the delegation of computer-related tasks? What organizational changes will accompany the phasing out of blenders and the phasing in of coffee makers and coffee bean grinders?

As you ask an organization about its goals or objectives, often you will find that there are multiple levels of goals or objectives. Each member company of York Industries and each department in a company will have its own goals or objectives. Some goals and objectives will be very broadly written and some will be extremely specific.

Strategic Plan

The **strategic plan** of an organization is usually a detailed long-range game plan that is related to the mission statement. Many strategic plans are written to encompass a period of three, five, or more years. The characteristics of a strategic plan are:

- Written for the board of directors, officers, and upper management of an organization as a guiding document for their decision making

- Comprehensive, including all companies, divisions, departments, and units in an organization

- Includes the mission statement and selected goals or objectives of the organization

- Specific, showing how aspects of the company will change and grow over the next several years

- Targeted to address different organizational areas such as human resources, accounting, purchasing, marketing, manufacturing, customer services, and distribution

- Establishes or modifies procedures, rules, and regulations of a company

- Includes sales, growth, cost, and budget projections

As an Active Directory designer, the strategic plan helps you understand how the organization perceives growth and change in the long run. *It can be the best single way to anticipate how growth will affect the Active Directory structure.* Although the organization may not follow everything that is written in the strategic plan, the plan can be invaluable in helping you initially design Active Directory services to anticipate how changes will occur. Your ability to anticipate the nature of the changes will reduce the difficulties in adapting or reorganizing Active Directory services in the long run. This is particularly important in deciding whether to use OUs or domains, because domains are much harder to restructure than OUs, to reflect a company reorganization, for example.

Operating Plan and the Cost of Operations

An **operating plan** is usually written on a yearly basis to reflect relatively short-term actions, particularly in terms of the cost of operations. The short-term actions contained in the operating plan are:

- Personnel and labor costs
- Materials costs and acquisitions
- Equipment needs and costs
- Building needs and costs
- Production needs and costs

For some organizations, the operating plan goes no further than projecting the budget for the next fiscal year. Other organizations include more detailed planning in the operating plan to correspond with immediate goals or objectives. Sometimes the operating plan is an addition to or appendix of the strategic plan to take into account changes in a market or in the financial situation of the organization.

For Active Directory planning, the value of reviewing the operating plan is that you can see immediate trends, such as the creation of a new department or the hiring of new employees. Because the operating plan usually contains the next year's budget, you also can determine how budget expenses are projected to affect information technology plans. This enables you to see how much will be expended on network equipment, new servers, and new applications, so there are no surprises.

Some organizations, such as public colleges and universities, are mandated by law or legislative action to spend only certain budgeted monies on specific areas of operations, such as only on building improvements, on a specific academic program, or for faculty and staff raises. These organizations often have accounting systems that enable them to *encumber* funds, which means that the accounting systems allow only those budgeted funds to be spent for the intended purpose. Your Active Directory design in this situation might, for example, treat the encumbered fund areas as individual cost centers and allocate specific OUs in which to perform specialized accounting for each cost center.

Project Plans

Project-based and path-goal organizations have specific projects that are in some stage of completion and that are explained in project plans. A **project plan** is a specific-purpose plan, such as a plan that outlines the addition of a new wing in a hospital for a maternity unit, or a plan for reorganizing a Finance department into two new departments, Accounting and Human Resources. Ask to review examples of project plans to gain an understanding of how to create groups and OUs for an organization. Project plans also provide information about the decision-making style of an organization and about how the organization addresses new tasks.

 When studied as a whole, the mission statement, goals and objectives, strategic plan, operating plan, and project plans enable you to determine a company's true priorities, including anticipated areas of growth and growth strategies.

ANALYZING BUSINESS FLOW AND BUSINESS PROCESSES

Every organization contains many levels of business flow and business processes. These are the day-to-day processes that organizations use to get work done. Every organization uses processes that may be formalized as policies or that may follow informal decision-making structures. One effective way to approach the analysis of business processes is to divide your analysis into the following categories:

- Business processes
- Information and communication flow
- Business cycles
- Service and product life cycles

Analyzing Business Processes

Some examples of business processes that you might analyze are:

- Hiring
- Payroll
- Product design
- Inventory

- Budget
- Marketing
- Production
- Distribution

To find out about a business process, you may be able to obtain a flow diagram of the process from a manager. In other situations, you may have to briefly interview employees and build your own basic business process flow diagram. Consider, for example, how a new CIO is hired by Interstate Security Bank. The first step in the process is for the director of Human Resources to meet with the bank's CEO and vice presidents to decide how they want to advertise for the position and to discuss the qualities needed. Next, the director of Human

Resources has an assistant prepare an advertisement and place that advertisement in specific newspapers and on the Internet. While the advertisement is running, a selection committee is chosen by the director of Human Resources and the CEO. The selection committee reviews the applicants and narrows the applicant pool to five people, all of whom are brought to the Seattle headquarters for an interview. Members of the selection committee also call the references provided by the five applicants and report this information to the entire selection committee. The travel arrangements and expenses of the applicants are handled by an assistant in the Human Resources department. After the interview, the selection committee narrows the applicant pool to three people, all of whom are brought back for interviews with the CEO and vice presidents. Following these interviews, the CEO, vice presidents, and selection committee meet to rank the three finalists. After reviewing the three finalists' resumes, references, and interview results, and talking with key people on the board of directors, the CEO makes the final selection. Once the decision is made, the director of Human Resources contacts the finalist to negotiate the salary. After the finalist accepts the job, the Human Resources department processes multiple computer-generated hiring forms, such as payroll forms, benefits forms, and federal equal opportunity forms. Figure 2-13 illustrates how you might diagram the hiring process via a flow chart, using squares or rectangles to show a process step and diamonds to show a decision step.

Another common business process is the one used to generate a budget. In a large organization, such as Interstate Security Bank, there is a budget officer who starts the budget process. The budget officer works with the heads of the regional offices, who work with each branch office head. Thus, the budget process begins with the branch office heads developing a budget and submitting their budgets to the regional office heads. The regional office heads compile the branch office budgets and integrate their own regional office budgets, which include budget requests from each department within the regional offices. Once the budgets are developed at the regional offices, they are sent to the budget officer in the Seattle headquarters office, who compiles the regional office budgets and integrates them with the headquarters budget. The headquarters budget includes budget requests for each department in the headquarters office. Finally, the budget officer presents the entire budget to the CEO and vice presidents of Interstate Security Bank. This group makes budget changes to accommodate factors such as the business objectives and strategic plan. Finally, the budget is presented to the board of directors for any changes and final approval.

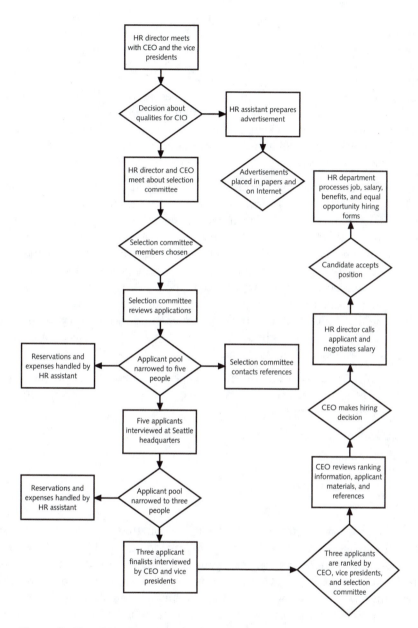

Figure 2-13   Diagramming the hiring process

Information and Communication Flow

The analysis of information and communication flow in an organization can be performed from several angles. First, information and communication follows the organizational and management models that have been discussed earlier in this chapter. Communication follows a top-down path in the centralized model—for example, as from a top manager to a middle manager to a supervisor to a line employee. In the centralized model, the director of finance in an organization may take the position that all accounting processes must balance to the penny at the close of each working day. She may communicate this instruction to the accounting manager by sending a memo via e-mail. After receiving the message, the accounting manager might hold a meeting with the accounts receivable, accounts payable, and payroll supervisors to pass along this instruction and discuss how to implement it. Last, each of these supervisors might discuss how to implement balancing to the penny with the assistants and clerks who work under them.

In a decentralized decision-making model, the same type of decision may be communicated in a combination of: (1) peer-to-peer horizontal communications that are transmitted from the line staff to team leaders and (2) vertical communications from the team leaders to upper management. Using the example of balancing to the penny, several payroll, accounts receivable, and accounts payable clerks may find themselves in a team meeting discussing the need to balance to the penny. Their discussion might focus on the problems of having to manually recalculate accounting data because the computer programs with which they work have rounding problems and do not always balance to the penny. As a team, they might decide to initiate a policy to balance to the penny as a way to reduce unnecessary work. The team leader might invite the CFO to attend their next meeting, at which they strongly recommend the new policy. The result might be that the CFO would then meet with the CIO to formalize the policy as specified by the team.

When you perform an analysis of the information and communication flow, start by understanding the decision-making model used. Next, study the tools that are used in the process. The commonly used tools include a combination of:

- E-mail and e-mail memos
- Hard-copy memos
- Telephone conversations
- Meetings

Often there is a paper or electronic trail of information that you can examine, such as archived e-mail messages or meeting minutes. Understanding how decisions are made and the tools that are used can be important in your Active Directory design. For example, if e-mail is used, then you may need to create security and distribution groups to match the particular communication flow of e-mail. The communication flow by e-mail may also influence what software applications or shared folders are published in the Active Directory. For instance, if spreadsheets are e-mailed, then a spreadsheet program with e-mail capabilities may need to be published.

The information flow in modern organizations is rapidly moving from the exchange and storage of paper to electronic methods. Employees use electronic methods to communicate with the organizations for which they work, and the organizations use electronic methods to communicate with them. Your analysis for Active Directory design should include documenting the forms of electronic information flow and the types of paper information flow.

For example, Interstate Security Bank uses both printed and electronic means for information flow. When a customer uses a branch office's Internet site to transfer $1,000 from savings to checking, the customer's monthly paper-based statement reflects that transfer.

York Industries has made electronic communication a priority for nearly all aspects of the company as a way to save money. When an employee applies for a job, she or he uses a form on the Internet or submits an electronic form on floppy disk. After an employee is hired, she or he again uses electronic Internet forms to specify health care selections, retirement options, worker compensation information, company investment options, and federal deduction information. At each country site, there is a Human Resources OU established to enable employees to provide this information.

Some examples of the electronic flow of information are:

- Making decisions through e-mail
- Scheduling meetings through electronic calendar schedulers and e-mail
- Completing an application for a job or for school
- Providing human resources information
- Sending memos and communicating company policies
- Sending a word-processed document, a spreadsheet, or a database
- Holding meetings electronically, for example, through NetMeeting
- Completing purchase orders
- Replenishing inventories

Business Cycles

Most organizations have business cycles that can be identified and that may influence the structure of Active Directory. One of the most common business cycles is the fiscal year, which can be important to Active Directory design because some organizations start new projects, install new software, hire more people, change accounting practices, implement raises, and purchase new computers to correspond with the fiscal year. Any of these changes can mean changes in Active Directory, such as creating an OU for a new project team that starts when the fiscal year starts. If a new accounting system is implemented at the beginning of the fiscal year, this may mean restructuring Active Directory design so that there are new elements created for the new system and elements for the old system are deleted.

The fiscal year is just one example of many kinds of business cycles that can affect Active Directory design. Some other examples are:

- Printing bank statements at the end of each month at all of the Interstate Security Bank branch offices
- Preparing a larger than normal on-hand inventory of York Industries appliances for the Christmas season
- Preparing a quarterly catalog mailing at Jefferson Philately

For instance, the Christmas preparations on the part of York Industries may necessitate creating special OUs just for the Christmas inventories or for special Christmas promotions. As an example, one OU might be created at Kanazawa for a Christmas promotion in which a free toaster is packaged with each microwave oven.

Product and Service Life Cycles

In business, new products and services are introduced and old products and services are removed from the market. Consider, for example, the microwave industry, in which older, less powerful 300-watt ovens are retired from production as newer, more powerful products are introduced. The introduction of new products and the elimination of old ones can result in corresponding changes that must be made in the Active Directory design. Some examples of new product life cycles include:

- Retooling machinery for new products, such as a new stove line produced by York Industries

- Introduction of a new product or product line, such as introducing new investment services at Interstate Security Bank

- Starting a new subscription program, as is common at Jefferson Philately

In the example of Jefferson Philately, consider the impact when the company decides to introduce a new subscription service program in which customers can purchase each first day of issue cover that commemorates every United States president from Dwight Eisenhower to the present one. A first day cover consists of an envelope with the new stamp affixed and a U.S. Postal Service cancellation on the date that the stamp is officially made available. The collectable value of the first day of issue cover is increased when a cache (pronounced *cash-a*) that is representative of the stamp is printed on the envelope. The cache is artwork that is sometimes created by the artist commissioned to create the stamp. The new subscription program involves many teams that include: (1) the marketing team to set up the new product program and advertise it, (2) the creative team that hires artists to create cache art for new issue envelopes, (3) the copywriters to create advertising, (4) manufacturing teams to create notebooks to hold the collection, (5) information technology teams to set up programs for the new subscription product, and (6) printing press operators to print cache art on new issue envelopes. Each of these groups affects OU Active Directory design—for example, by creating a need for a new OU for the new product, and OUs within it for the groups of employees who will participate.

ANALYZING LEGAL REQUIREMENTS AND COMPANY POLICIES

All organizations are bound by legal requirements and by policies that fall into categories as follows:

- Policies set by the governing board, such as the board of directors

- Policies set by company officers, such as the CEO, CFO, CIO, and COO

- Policies set by the Human Resources department, like those in the employee handbook

- Policies set by individual departments, such as pay periods set by the payroll department

- Policies set by state government, such as those requiring an end-of-fiscal-year financial report and report of company operations to the secretary of state or other state office

- Policies set by local and state governments and by the federal government for taxing income

- Policies set by the federal government for hiring practices, retirement contributions, health care contributions, and social security

Many policies become the responsibility of one or more departments, such as the Human Resources and Payroll departments handling health and retirement benefits. Another example is a policy in which each company vice president must make public to the employees an annual report about the finances and activities of her or his department through a shared folder or through a company intranet.

Income tax withholding is one example of a common legal requirement with which a company must comply. Another example is to have a regular audit performed by an external auditing firm. For some companies, the audit is a legal requirement in the articles of incorporation of the state in which the company resides. For a bank, such as Interstate Security Bank, the audit also is a federal requirement.

There are many resources you can use to become familiar with the policies and legal requirements that are followed by an organization:

- Interview officers of the company

- Obtain company policy manuals

- Obtain employee policy manuals

- Interview the Payroll and Accounting department heads

- Interview the Human Resources department head

- Interview the organization's legal staff

- Obtain state and federal tax codes (usually available on the Internet)

State and federal tax laws change yearly, and new changes can be confusing. Encourage your organization to contact a tax accountant or tax lawyer to help interpret changing tax laws, if it doesn't already do so.

ANALYZING OUTSIDE RELATIONSHIPS

Many organizations maintain outside relationships as a part of doing business; these include vendor, partner, and customer relationships. One of the most typical outside relationships involves obtaining materials from vendors for manufacturing goods. In the example of Jefferson Philately, the company makes regular purchases of vinyl, plastic, and cardboard for the notebooks that they manufacture to hold stamps and first day issue covers. Interstate Security Bank has a relationship with a printing company and prints its forms and prints checks for customers. Interstate Security Bank also operates as an electronic payroll clearinghouse for other banks. In its function as a payroll clearinghouse, the bank has customer relationships with public organizations and private companies that send their payroll information to a special department of the bank. Once the payroll information is received, Interstate Security Bank transmits it to all other banks used by a company's employees. For example, Pacific Technical College (a fictional college) in Bend, Oregon has a payroll of 2245 employees who have automatic deposit with all 20 banks and credit unions in Bend. On the last working day of each month, Pacific Technical College transmits its payroll to the Interstate Security Bank clearinghouse in Seattle. On the same day, the clearinghouse processes the information and transmits the automatic deposits to the Bend, Oregon banks so that each employee's pay is automatically deposited in the right bank.

In another example, York, Nantes Appliances, Kanazawa, and Palisades Corporation all purchase premade aluminum, plastic, and steel forms for appliances from 10 different suppliers of those products. The vendor relationships between these companies include automated ordering and order payment through the Internet.

Another example is from Microsoft, which has relationships with hardware and software solution partners. Three examples of Microsoft partner programs are Direct Access, Microsoft Certified Solution Providers, and Microsoft OEM System Builders. Airline companies are another example of partnerships in which domestic airlines work with international airline partners in regions where they have limited or no access. Companies that have partnerships can customize Active Directory access for their partners by creating specialized domain, OU, group, and security access rights.

All of these examples are important to analyze for their effect on the Active Directory design, particularly in terms of:

- Security and security groups
- Remote access
- Internet and virtual private network access
- Distribution groups
- OUs
- Domains

Some typical outside relationships to look for in your analysis of an organization are:

- Purchasing relationships for raw materials and office products
- Relationships with credit card and lending companies
- Outsourcing financial services functions such as accounting and payroll
- Outsourcing information technology functions
- Outsourcing food and custodial services
- Fleet services with car companies
- Outsourcing medical services, such as medical lab services
- Financial services, such as a bank outsourcing investment services
- Relationships with Internet service providers and telecommunications providers

Another type of outside relationship is the relationship with customers. For example, Jefferson Philately, Interstate Security Bank, and York Industries all have Web sites for customers. Customers of Jefferson Philately can purchase products and check on the status of their orders through the company's Web servers. Interstate Security Bank enables customers to check their accounts and make electronic transfers via the Web, while York Industries advertises products, offers customer service assistance, and sells all of its products over the Web. Making a Web server available to customers entails planning security and a domain structure in Active Directory.

ANALYZING ACQUISITION PLANS

The business world is a changing environment in which one business acquires another to diversify its interests or to consolidate its position in a particular market. Telecommunication, networking, and computer software companies are good examples of the frequency of business acquisitions. The long-distance and high-speed network carrier Quest Communications purchased the RBOC U.S. West to become Qwest and broaden its share of the telecommunications market. Microsoft purchased the company Zoomit to be able to expand its directory services capabilities, and Compaq purchased Digital Equipment Corporation (DEC) to be able to offer UNIX-based Alpha processor computers.

When you analyze the acquisition plans of a company, determine how its newly acquired company or companies will fit in. There are two common acquisition models: (1) to integrate the new company into the company that purchases it and (2) to leave the newly acquired company as a separate organization with its own management, IT department, and organizational structure.

In the first model, when the new company is integrated with its parent company, then the approach is typically to design new trees, domains, or OUs in Active Directory. In the second acquisition model, the newly acquired company retains its original name and has a separate management structure. In this approach, you would likely use separate forests, if there is a need to keep the company operations entirely separate—or you would use trees and domains, if it is possible for the new company to use the same schema as its parent company. For example, the companies acquired by York Industries have retained their original names and have a decentralized management structure, but they are willing to use the same schema. The approach for their Active Directory design proposals presented in Chapter 6 stresses using trees and domains.

ANALYZING RISK TOLERANCE

Companies have different tolerances for risk. Interstate Security Bank, for example, has a low tolerance for risk because it must guarantee the safety of its customers' money. For an organization that has low risk tolerance, your Active Directory design planning would incorporate the following:

- A slow and methodical implementation of Active Directory

- Emphasis on security capabilities, such as using domains to create security boundaries and using other Active Directory security measures, such as IPSec, encryption, and authentication

- Emphasis on network fault-tolerance measures, such as redundant LAN and WAN links and reflecting those links in the design of Active Directory sites

- Emphasis on Active Directory fault-tolerance measures, such as implementing extra domain controllers for Active Directory replication and placing domain controllers in specific locations to ensure reliable replication

- Emphasis on thorough Active Directory planning and testing before going live

Sometimes smaller companies, such as Jefferson Philately, have a greater tolerance for risk because they have to maintain a competitive edge by reacting quickly to opportunities and changes in their particular market. They may work to implement a particular product or IT strategy so that they beat their competition to the same idea. For companies that have a higher tolerance for risk, Active Directory planning incorporates:

- Faster implementation of Active Directory

- Emphasis on flexibility in changing Active Directory structure through using OUs and security groups

- Less emphasis on methodical Active Directory planning and testing before going live, which often leads to keeping the Active Directory implementation as simple as possible

- Less emphasis on using fault-tolerance precautions and more emphasis on rapid software implementation to achieve organizational goals and strategies

Try Hands-on Project 2-6 to analyze a company for its level of risk tolerance.

Chapter Summary

2

❐ The first step in planning an Active Directory structure is to perform an analysis of the organization for which Active Directory will be implemented. There are many dimensions to analyzing an organization, but plan to start by analyzing the organizational model. Organizations can be analyzed by using one or more organizational models: geographic organization, organization by function, organization by department, organization by product or service, project-based organization, and cost center organization.

❐ Another tool you can use when analyzing an organization is the management model. For example, some organizations use the more traditional centralized model for management while other organizations use a decentralized model.

❐ All organizations exist to accomplish specific goals and objectives. Plan to analyze an organization's reason for existence as a way to set a foundation for planning Active Directory services. The first place to start in this analysis is to review the mission statement and next to study the formal business goals or objectives. Use the strategic plan to identify growth patterns.

❐ The organizational and management structures of an organization are reflected in the business processes and business flow. Business processes and business flow often directly affect Active Directory services design because access to resources and the delegation of resources typically reflect the business processes and flow.

❐ Other areas that affect how you design Active Directory are legal/policy requirements, outside relationships, acquisition plans, and risk tolerance. All organizations must follow legal requirements and policies, such as filing fiscal year reports and tax information. Important among outside relationships for an organization are the relationships with its customers, business partners, and suppliers, for example through a Web site. Corporate acquisitions are a common occurrence in business, and can affect the Active Directory elements that you use to integrate a new business or to keep its original identity. Finally, companies respond to risk tolerance in different ways, which can affect the timeline in which you design Active Directory and the fault-tolerance measures that you implement.

In the next chapter you will learn to analyze information technology departments in different kinds of organizations.

Key Terms

branch office — A portion of an organization that is relatively dependent on a higher level office, or corporate headquarters because it is not an autonomous organizational entity, such as a branch bank in a community.

centralized decision model — A decision-making management model in which the locus of decision making is held in the top positions of an organization. When applied to network and computer resources, the centralized decision model often means that management of those resources is performed by a limited group of people in a central location.

cost centers — Areas or groups in an organization that are connected with the cost of operations. Cost center analysis enables an organization to understand the cost of producing a product or providing a service, such as computer operations. To help determine the cost of operations, one group, department, division, or unit may charge others within the organization for its services.

decentralized decision model — A decision-making model in which the decision-making responsibilities are spread through more than traditional top-level managers—for example, to midlevel managers, nonmanagerial staff, and project teams. When compared to the centralized decision management model, the decentralized model stresses placing management and decision making in hands that are closer to those who make the products or provide the services.

distribution group — A list of Windows 2000 users that enables one e-mail message to be sent to all users on the list. A distribution group is not used for security and thus cannot appear in an ACL.

formal decision making — A decision-making model in which decisions follow the formally defined management lines.

goals — Specific and quantifiable tasks that an organization plans to accomplish, particularly within a certain time. Goals are also referred to as objectives or business objectives.

informal decision making — A decision-making model in which decisions follow the informal lines of authority—for example, when an administrative assistant really makes the decisions for a manager.

international geographic organization — An organization that spans multiple countries and that can also span different continents.

mission statement — A general statement from an organization that describes its purpose, such as the products it makes and the constituents or customers that are reached.

national geographic organization — An organization that covers multiple states, provinces, or other major boundaries within the same country.

objectives — Also called business objectives, *see* goals.

operating plan — A plan that is written approximately once a year to reflect relatively short-term actions, and that normally includes an organization's immediate budget projections.

path-goal decision model — A decision-making model that focuses on defining the goal that is to be achieved and the steps that must be completed along the path to achieve the goal.

project plan — A specific-purpose plan that describes in detail a new project, such as a plan that outlines the addition of a new wing on a hospital.

regional geographic organization — An organization in which company sites and resources are located in relatively close proximity, such as in a single building, on a business or school campus, in multiple locations within the same city, or in different cities that are relatively close—a large city and its suburbs, for example.

security group — A grouping of Windows 2000 user accounts, computers, and other security groups that is used to assign access privileges—rights and permissions—to objects and services. Security groups appear in ACLs. Although not technically a distribution group, a security group can also be used to send an e-mail message to all members of the group.

situational decision model — A model in which decision making is related to specific sociological factors or situations that exist in an organization.

strategic plan — A long-range planning document that is usually linked to the mission statement of an organization.

subsidiary office — A portion of an organization that is owned by a parent company or organization, but that has relative decision-making autonomy and often does business under a different name from the parent.

REVIEW QUESTIONS

Answer questions 1–9 using this case information:

Fine Furniture Warehouse is a family-owned business that sells discounted furniture at 10 different locations in Minnesota. They have a three-year plan that they follow for growth and to introduce new product lines, which is revised every year. They also create a one-year budget each year. The founder of the business, Jason Brown, runs the company with an iron hand. All employees receive a handbook that contains rules and regulations they must follow. He employs managers at each store, but the managers have little decision-making authority other than to hire the store employees. However, the managers do seem to vie with one another for more influence with Jason Brown. There are no real departments, just the store managers and individuals who do specific jobs, such as the store accountants, the floor sales staff, delivery drivers, and cashiers.

1. Which management model(s) would apply to this organization?
   a. centralized
   b. decentralized
   c. manager-oriented
   d. all of the above
   e. none of the above
   f. only a and c
   g. only b and c

2. The three-year plan is an example of:
   a. an operating goal
   b. an Active Directory plan
   c. a strategic plan
   d. all of the above
   e. none of the above
   f. only a and c
   g. only b and c

3. Which of the following would you most likely find in the three-year plan?

   a. mission statement

   b. goals or objectives

   c. sales projections

   d. all of the above

   e. none of the above

   f. only a and b

   g. only b and c

4. What organization model(s) would apply to this business?

   a. organization by project

   b. organization by geography

   c. organization by department

   d. all of the above

   e. none of the above

   f. only a and b

   g. only a and c

5. On the wall in Jason Brown's office there is a sign for all employees to view that says, "We exist to offer customers the best value in furniture and the best selection." You might equate this to:

   a. a business objective

   b. a mission statement

   c. a strategic plan

   d. employee orientation

6. Which of the following would be something you would analyze for information about company policies?

   a. the store managers' business philosophies

   b. the employee handbook

   c. the three-year plan

   d. all of the above

   e. none of the above

   f. only a and c

   g. only b and c

7. As you are performing your analysis, you examine the issue of employee loyalty in terms of planning security in the Active Directory design. Which of the following is (are) likely to be true?

a. This is an example of a task-oriented management model.

b. This is an example of a relationship-oriented management model.

c. Employees are likely to show relatively weak loyalty.

d. Managers are likely to be trusted by employees.

e. all of the above

f. none of the above

g. only a, c, and d

h. only b and c

8. The one-year budget can be of value to analyze as a(n):

a. influence on the tree structure

b. operating plan

c. goal

d. business objective

9. Each time Jason Brown starts to carry a new brand or product line, he personally writes an objective and sends it to each store manager. What elements would you expect to find in an objective?

a. a sales goal

b. a time range

c. a statement of penalty if the new brand or product line fails

d. the total cost of the new project

e. all of the above

f. none of the above

g. only a and b

h. only a, c, and d

Answer questions 10–19 using this case information:

Olive Grinder is a company that makes submarine sandwiches with Italian sausages, cheeses, and specialty sauces. The sandwiches are produced, frozen, and shipped from a single business location in Chicago to convenience stores in the midwestern states of the United States. Olive Grinder is an employee owned and run company. As a business, Olive Grinder is divided into several departments: Finance and Accounting, Marketing, Human Resources, Food Preparation, Information Technology, and Shipping. Each department is run by a director who functions as a business coach—and the real work is performed by employee teams in the departments. For example, the Food Preparation department consists of the bakers, sandwich builders, and wrapper and freezers teams. Every team has a team leader. Every employee team has its own set of guidelines developed by that team, which include a written statement about how the team functions, how decisions are made, and what work tasks are that team's responsibilities. Each team also writes a new "productivity statement" every three months to one year. For example, one of the bakers' team productivity statements currently is: "To design a 10% lighter sandwich loaf for white bread and a 5% lighter sandwich loaf for whole wheat bread within six months." Along with the productivity statement, each team develops a step-by-step project plan that specifies each task required for the outcome in the productivity statement and the team members responsible for each task. Also, each team prepares a yearly budget and tracks its own cost of operations.

10. What organization model(s) would apply to this business?

    a. organization by project

    b. organization by geography, because this is a regional company

    c. organization by department

    d. all of the above

    e. none of the above

    f. only a and b

    g. only a and c

11. How would you characterize the communication flow in Olive Grinder?

    a. horizontal peer-to-peer communication

    b. top-down vertical communication

    c. disorganized communication

    d. board of directors to line-staff communication

    e. all of the above

    f. none of the above

    g. only a, b, and d

    h. only b and d

12. Which management model(s) would apply to this organization?

    a. centralized

    b. decentralized

    c. project-based

    d. situational

    e. all of the above

    f. none of the above

    g. only a and c

    h. only b and c

13. In addition to your answer for Question 12, because each team tracks its cost of oper-ations, the _____ model can be applied.

    a. cost center

    b. middle-ground participatory

    c. authoritative decision-making model

    d. manager–matrix model

    e. all of the above

    f. none of the above

    g. only a and c

    h. only b and d

14. The bakers' team productivity statement is an example of a(n):

    a. operating plan

    b. strategic plan

    c. business objective

    d. mission statement

    e. all of the above

    f. none of the above

    g. only a and c

    h. only b, c, and d

15. Your analysis of this organization would most likely lead to an Active Directory design that includes:

    a. OUs for departments

    b. separate domains for departments, but one tree

    c. distribution groups but no security groups

    d. OUs for teams

    e. all of the above

    f. none of the above

    g. only a and b

    h. only a and d

2

16. As you create the Active Directory design, you are likely to recommend:

    a. using sites to correspond with each team

    b. delegating control over some Active Directory objects—for example, delegating the creation of accounts to the directors or team leaders

    c. centralizing shared folder management with the Information Technology Department

    d. giving additional authority to managers as a way to create additional trust in the company and better security for Active Directory elements

    e. all of the above

    f. none of the above

    g. only a and b

    h. only a, c, and d

17. What legal aspects would you expect to analyze in relation to this company?

    a. laws governing food preparation

    b. state and federal tax laws

    c. laws relating to company audits

    d. all of the above

    e. none of the above

    f. only a and b

    g. only b and c

18. Which of the following would you expect to have the most effect on company policies and would provide you with the best information about the reasons for certain policies?

    a. individual employees

    b. the department directors

    c. the teams

    d. the board of directors

19. What general business cycle(s) is the Olive Grinder mostly likely to have in common with most other companies?

    a. the time frame for completing a policy

    b. a fiscal year designation

    c. introduction of a new product or service

    d. all of the above

    e. only a and b

    f. only b and c

Answer questions 20-25 using this case information:

Martindale Community College services all communities in Martindale county. The main college campus is in Dexter, and there are small branch campuses in the cities of Northridge, Brighten, Albany, and Westchester. One distinguishing characteristic of this college is that although it has a traditional administrative structure with the board of trustees and the president at the top, it is really run by the vice presidents of each academic division, which are: General Studies, Occupational and Technical Studies, and Community Outreach Studies. Although the state legislature and the college policies specify that the president is the highest college officer, the sitting president does very little decision making and waits for major decisions to come from the vice presidents. The vice presidents are very strong on long- and short-range planning and management by objectives.

20. Which management model(s) best apply to this organization?

　　a. cost center

　　b. formal decision making

　　c. informal decision making

　　d. all of the above

　　e. none of the above

　　f. only a and b

21. Which of the following would you expect to find in this organization?

　　a. strategic plan

　　b. operating plan

　　c. policy statements

　　d. mission statement

　　e. all of the above

　　f. none of the above

　　g. only a and c

　　h. only a, b, and d

22. What organization model(s) would apply to this college?

　　a. organization by project

　　b. organization by geography

　　c. organization by division

　　d. organization by product or service

　　e. all of the above

　　f. none of the above

　　g. only a, b, and c

　　h. only b, c, and d

23. Martindale Community College has a fall and spring semester plus two summer sessions. These are an example of:

a. a policy

b. a business cycle

c. a communication flow

d. a business process

24. The manager of the Information Technology department, who reports to the vice president of General Studies, is a strong manager who instills a sense of trust and loyalty among Information Technology staff. Also, she has broad powers to promote employees and to reward employees with time off when they have worked unusually long hours. The result is that this department accomplishes most of its tasks on time or early. This is an example of:

a. situational decision making

b. informal decision making

c. project-based decision making

d. autocratic decision making

e. all of the above

f. none of the above

g. only a, b, and c

h. only b and d

25. When the Information Technology department takes on a large task, such as installing a new segment of network cable in a building or setting up a new computer lab, they plan the task by scripting it into a series of smaller tasks. This is an example of a(n):

a. project plan

b. operating plan

c. goal

d. functional management

HANDS-ON PROJECTS

Project 2-1

In this project you practice creating a simple diagram of the geographic organization of Anderson Chemicals, a tri-state company that makes liquid and pill-based antacids. You will need access to a computer running Windows 95, Windows 98, Windows NT, or Windows 2000 and to diagramming software such as Visio or Microsoft Paint.

2

To create the diagram:

1. Start the diagramming software available at your school, such as AutoCad, Visio, or Microsoft Paint.

2. Open a clear drawing area.

3. If a flow chart stencil is available in the drawing package, drag a box to the left side of the drawing area about halfway between the top and the bottom of the area. If no stencil is available, use a box- or line-drawing tool to create a box.

4. Label the box **Irvine, CA**, either on the inside or underneath.

5. Drag or copy a second box to the right of the first box so that they line up horizontally. Label that box **Boulder, CO**.

6. Drag or copy a third box so that it is to the right of the second box and so that they line up horizontally. Label that box **Lincoln, NE**.

7. Use the line drawing tool to draw a line from the leftmost box to the box in the middle.

8. Put a label under the line that says **44.736 Mbps**.

9. Use the drawing tool to draw a line from the box in the middle to the rightmost box, and label that line **1.544 Mbps**.

10. Place a title at the top of your diagram that says **Geographic Organization of Anderson Chemicals**. Your final diagram should look similar to Figure 2-14.

11. In your lab journal or in a word-processed document, note how you might expand on this diagram to make it even more useful for your analysis of Anderson Chemicals.

12. Also, record what Active Directory elements might be affected by the geographic organization of Anderson Chemicals.

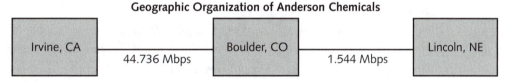

Geographic Organization of Anderson Chemicals

Figure 2-14   Geographic organization model

Project 2-2

In this project, you practice analyzing your school on the basis of department, division, and business unit organization. Ask your instructor for a flow chart of the school's organization divided into academic departments. (Often a flow chart or a description of the academic departments, divisions, or units is available in your school's catalog, phone and e-mail directory, or Web page. If you don't have a copy of the school catalog or directory, check in the school's library.)

To perform an analysis by department, division, and business unit:

1. Obtain the organizational chart from your instructor, or consult your school catalog, school directory, or school Web page.

2. Are there any divisions represented?

3. What departments are represented?

4. In what division or department is the class you are taking?

5. Does this flow chart give you any clues about the products or services of the school? Does it provide any clues about the management model used at the school?

6. Are there any branch offices or campuses represented in the chart?

7. How might this chart be of value to you in planning an Active Directory structure for your school?

8. Record your observations in your lab journal or in a word-processed document.

Project 2-3

Sometimes you will perform an analysis of an organization that already has an Active Directory set up, but that wants to examine ways in which to redesign the Active Directory structure. In this situation, you can use information that is already in Active Directory to help you analyze the organization. This project enables you to use Active Directory to help gain an understanding of the organizational model or models used by an organization. You will need access to a computer running Windows 2000 Server (or Advanced Server or Datacenter) via an account that has Administrator privileges.

To use Active Directory to perform an analysis of the organization of a company or institution:

1. Click **Start**, point to **Programs**, point to **Administrative Tools**, and click **Active Directory Users and Computers**.

2. What domains are already set up? How might the examination of existing domains provide you with clues about the organizational model? Record your observations.

3. What OUs are set up under each domain? How might the examination of the OUs give you information about the organizational model? Record your observations.

4. Open each folder or OU and observe the user accounts, computers, groups, and OUs that are in each one. How might this provide information about the organizational model? Record your observations.

5. Close the Active Directory Users and Computers tool.

6. Click **Start**, point to **Programs**, point to **Administrative Tools**, and click **Active Directory Sites and Services**.

7. Double-click the sites folder to display its child objects, if they are not displayed.

8. What sites are already set up? How can you use site information to help in your analysis of an organizational model? Record your observations.

9. Close the Active Directory Sites and Services tool.

Project 2-4

In this project, you analyze the decision-making style used at a business or in a department in your school. You instructor will invite a department head from a local business or from your school who will make a presentation in class about the decision-making style in her or his department or organization.

To analyze the decision-making style:

1. Create several general questions to ask about the decision-making style she or he will discuss before the department head visits your class. Some example questions will include:

   ❐ How does your department or organization make decisions, such as to offer a new service, product, or course?

   ❐ Does your department or organization hold regular meetings? Who leads the meetings and how are decisions made in the meetings?

   ❐ Does your department or organization have any committees or subgroups that are used to help in decision making? If so, what are some examples?

   ❐ Does your department or organization use project or special task force teams?

   ❐ How is a department head selected in your department? How are other officers of the organization selected?

   ❐ What kind of authority is granted to department heads?

   ❐ How do department heads and other officers solicit input from others in the department or organization?

   ❐ What authority is given to a department head or officer in your organization?

2. Take notes in your lab journal or your word-processed document during the presentation.

3. On the basis of what you have learned in the presentation, analyze the decision-making style of the department, organization, or both. How might this decision-making style affect the Active Directory design for a server used by the department or organization?

An alternative for this assignment is to visit a department head at a business in which you work, or to analyze how decisions are made in a study group to which you belong.

Project 2-5

An existing Active Directory setup can provide you with information about the decision-making model of an organization by observing how authority is delegated to domains and OUs. This project allows you to use the Active Directory Users and Computers tool to view who has what kind of control over a domain and an OU. You will need access to a computer running Windows 2000 Server (or Advanced Server or Datacenter) and use of an account that has Administrator privileges.

To use Active Directory information to help analyze the decision-making model:

1. Click **Start**, point to **Programs**, point to **Administrative Tools**, and click **Active Directory Users and Computers**.

2. Click the **View** menu and click **Advanced Features**, if a checkmark is not already in front of that option.

3. Find a domain in the tree, such as TheFirm.com, and right-click it.

4. Click **Properties**.

5. Click the **Security** tab.

6. One at a time, click each group or user in the Name box. Notice the permissions that each has. Are there any that have Full Control permissions (you will learn more about domain permissions in Chapter 9)? Which ones have permissions to Write, Create All Child Objects, and Delete All Child Objects? How might this kind of information enable you to determine the delegation of control for the domain?

7. Close the domain Properties box.

8. Right-click an OU (designated by an icon of a folder with a folder inside it) and click **Properties**.

9. Click the **Security** tab.

10. One at a time, click each group or user in the Name box. Notice the permissions that each has. Are there any that have Full Control permissions? Which ones have permissions to Write, Create All Child Objects, and Delete All Child Objects? How might this information enable you to determine the delegation of control for an OU?

11. Close the OU Properties box.

12. Record your observations in your lab journal or in a word-processed document.

13. Leave the Active Directory Users and Computers tool open for the next project.

Project 2-6

In this project, you use the Active Directory setup to gather information about the risk tolerance of an organization.

To gather information about risk tolerance:

1. Open the Active Directory Users and Computers tool, if it is not already open.

2. Click the **Domain Controllers** OU under a domain in the tree.

3. How many computers are listed as domain controllers? If there is only one domain controller for a regional company, what would that say about the company's risk tolerance? Record your observations.

4. Right-click a domain in the tree, such as TheFirm.com.

5. Click **Properties**.

6. Click the **Group Policy** tab.

7. Click **Default Domain Policy**, if it is not already selected, and then click **Edit**.

8. Double-click **Windows Settings** in the tree under Computer Configuration.

9. Click **Security Settings** in the tree.

10. Notice the types of security settings displayed in the right-hand pane. Note that you can gain clues about a company's risk tolerance by studying how the company has set up domain security settings (you will learn more about default domain policy in Chapter 8).

11. Close the Group Policy window. Close the domain Properties dialog box, and then close the Active Directory Users and Computers tool.

CASE PROJECT

Aspen Consulting Project: Analyzing Business Requirements

All Team Sports manufactures sporting goods at three locations:

❐ Atlanta, Georgia, which makes baseball gloves, bats, balls, and field equipment and is also the headquarters for the company

❐ Jacksonville, Florida, which makes basketballs, footballs, and soccer balls

❐ Greenville, South Carolina which makes customized uniforms for team sports

Their products are sold in sporting goods, department, and variety stores throughout the United States. Customers also can access the All Team Sports Web site to order products. The Atlanta location houses the Executive, Business, Marketing, and Information Systems units. Further, all three sites have Customer Service, Manufacturing, Inventory, and Distribution units. The Web site is maintained as a team-based cooperative effort by the Marketing, Customer Service, and Information Systems departments at the Atlanta site. All three sites use managers to head each department and project teams within the departments. You have been assigned to work with All Team Sports because they are converting from legacy mainframe systems to Windows 2000 Server systems. At this stage in your work with the company, you are helping to analyze business processes for background information in designing Active Directory services.

1. Based on what you know now, what type of decision-making model is used by All Team Sports? What questions would you develop to ask for additional information about the decision-making model that is used?

2. How would you diagram the organizational structure of All Team Sports? What additional information would you gather to better determine all aspects of the organizational structure?

3. As you are gathering information about the management structure, you learn that this company uses projects and management by objectives very extensively. For example, they have a project to introduce a new baseball catcher's glove design. A team has been formed at the Atlanta site for this project that includes members of

the Marketing, Manufacturing, Customer Service, and Information Systems departments. The job of the team is to establish specific objectives for this project, to develop a project management plan, and to execute the plan. Given this information, how would you analyze the management model used? What questions would you ask to better determine the model? How might you diagram the model for better understanding?

4. Your next task is to analyze the business processes used at each site by this company. Explain four business processes you would expect to find. What would you do to analyze these business processes and how might they affect your Active Directory design analysis?

5. What might be an example of a product cycle you would expect to find for this company?

6. What outside relationships would you expect to find?

7. What other business analysis information would you seek as an aid to designing Active Directory services?

OPTIONAL CASE PROJECTS FOR TEAMS

Team Case One

Mark Arnez asks you to be a member of a team that is designing Active Directory services for the United States House of Representatives. What organizational and management models are used by this organization? Create a diagram to illustrate your analysis. What outside relationships should you consider in your analysis?

Team Case Two

Mark asks you to build on your analysis in Team Case One by performing an analysis of the goals and strategies of the United States House of Representatives. What elements should you take into account for this analysis?

3

ANALYZING INFORMATION TECHNOLOGY STRUCTURES

After reading this chapter and completing the exercises, you will be able to:

♦ Analyze IT organizational structures

♦ Analyze IT decision flow

♦ Analyze the relationships between a company and its IT organization

♦ Analyze how IT strategies map to an organization's goals and objectives

♦ Analyze IT funding and cost issues

♦ Analyze change management and user productivity issues

♦ Analyze the effect of outsourcing on Active Directory design

Information technology (IT) departments within companies and organizations have become increasingly important because they are a central focus of strategic initiatives, such as creating Web sites for e-commerce. When you design Active Directory services, it is vital to analyze the structure of the IT department, because its members play a central role in managing and maintaining server and network resources.

In this chapter, you will learn to analyze how information technology departments are organized and how decisions are made within them. You will learn to assess how IT departments work with other departments and with outsourcing vendors. Also, you will learn about IT management models, funding issues, and how computer system changes are managed to increase user productivity.

ANALYZING THE IT ORGANIZATION

The information technology responsibilities in an organization are typically assigned to an IT department or computer support group, depending on the size of the organization. A small organization, such as a law office consisting of 30 attorneys and support staff, may have a two- or three-person computer support group that works under the office manager. Larger organizations of over 200 employees, which are the focus of this book, typically have an IT department. In very large organizations, all IT functions may be centralized in the IT department, or some functions may be decentralized to computer professionals in specific departments. Consider two different approaches to IT responsibilities, one used by Jefferson Philately and another used by Interstate Security Bank.

Centralized IT Organization

At Jefferson Philately, there is an IT department under the Vice President of Finance, which is led by the IT manager. The information technology functions are centralized in this department, which has responsibilities that include managing all servers, managing the network, installing new software, setting up workstations, and assisting Jefferson Philately employees with their computer support needs. When a computer user has a computer-related problem, he or she calls the IT department. If a new server is purchased—for example, to handle new marketing and subscription functions—the IT department sets up the server and administers it.

When designing Active Directory services for Jefferson Philately, much of the security and control of computer resources will be with the IT department. One way to manage security is to set up security groups for each administrative function, such as a security group for server management, a security group to manage shared folders that contain software, and a security group to manage Microsoft Remote Installation Service (RIS) for installing operating systems on workstations.

Decentralized IT Organization

Interstate Security Bank provides a more decentralized model, in which some computer-related responsibilities are handled by computer professionals who work for departments other than IT. The IT department manages the network, mainframe computers, most of the servers, and other key computer-related activities. Many of the departments, however, employ their own computer support professionals who provide support for workstation users and printer services, and in some instances manage a server. For example, the Loans, Investments, Business, Marketing, and Customer Service departments each have from one to three computer professionals who support users with workstation or printing problems. The computer professionals provide advice when a new computer is purchased for an employee. Also, each branch office has from one to five computer professionals who support computer users and maintain a server that is set up at each branch location. The computer professionals report to the managers of their respective departments and not to the IT department.

Managing resources through Active Directory in the Interstate Security Bank situation will mean creating a more complex Active Directory structure than for Jefferson Philately. For example, one approach is to create an OU for each department and then to establish security groups within each OU. There might be an OU for the Marketing department and security groups under that OU, for example, to enable managing shared folders.

Sometimes the decentralized model of computer support responsibilities yields a level of tension between the IT department and the departments that have their own computer professionals. The IT department may want a reorganization in which the departmental computer professionals are under it, whereas the departments may vigorously defend their need to have computer professionals who understand their needs and support only those needs. When you design Active Directory in this situation, recognize that there can be tension and the possibility of a reorganization to further centralize computer responsibilities or to further decentralize computer responsibilities. Attempt to use OUs and not domains to reflect departmental boundaries, so that it is easy to change the design as the politics change.

The internal workings of IT departments are typically organized via a combination of organization by function and project-based organization. Organization by function is the older traditional model of organization, and project-based organization is relatively new. Both of these organizational models (introduced in Chapter 2) are discussed in the sections that follow. A third model, organization by federation, is one in which departments have some or all IT functions, similar to the Interstate Security Bank example. Finally, cost center organization is a model that is often used along with any of the three other models and is intended to help an organization determine the actual costs of running IT services.

IT Departments Organized by Function

Some IT departments are organized on the basis of the functions they perform, which can include some or all of the following:

- *Applications development and programming:* Writing, testing, and implementing software and Web applications

- *Database programming:* Designing, installing, managing, tuning, and testing database applications, plus creating and optimizing database queries (people who perform these functions work closely with applications and systems development groups)

- *Network development and administration:* Designing, installing, managing, and tuning LANs and WANs

- *Operations:* Operating computer systems on a day-to-day basis, including performing backups, mounting tapes and CD-ROMs, maintaining printer pools, and performing routine maintenance

- *Security:* Overseeing security for software applications, databases, and user access

- *Systems development and programming:* Installing, integrating, tuning, and managing computer operating systems such as Windows 2000 Server, UNIX, open MVS (an IBM mainframe operating system), NetWare, and other systems

- *Telecommunications:* Installing and managing local telecommunications services and integrating those services with regional telephone companies (regional Bell operating companies, RBOCs) and long-distance carriers

- *User support:* Providing computer support for users, such as providing hardware and software support for users' desktop systems and offering user training

Typically, IT departments are divided into groups that are responsible for performing the computer functions needed by an organization. At the relatively small Jefferson Philately, there are only three groups within the IT Department: Applications and Systems Programming, Operations, and User Support, as shown in Figure 3-1.

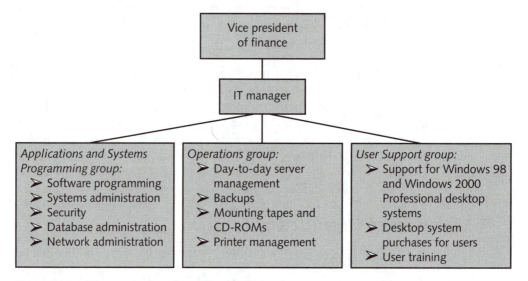

Figure 3-1 IT organization for Jefferson Philately

The analysis of Jefferson Philately's IT department by function can lead to at least two approaches to Active Directory design. One approach, which is the simplest, is to:

1. Use the default Active Directory Users folder in Jefferson Philately's domain (see Chapter 7) in which to create users and security groups.

2. Create user accounts in the Users folder for each member of the IT department.

3. Create global security groups (see Chapter 8) in the Users folder so that those groups contain the appropriate IT Department user accounts. The global security groups might be called Applications and Systems, Operations, and User Support. Figure 3-2 shows the Applications and Systems group created in the Users folder (there are too many users and other groups in the Users folder to view the Applications and Systems, Operations, and User Support groups at the same time).

4. Join the global security groups as appropriate to other groups (such as domain local or universal groups that have access to resources, see Chapter 8) and to the security descriptors (see Chapter 1) of resources, such as shared folders. For example, there might be a security group called Servers, which has the Applications and Systems and the Operations security groups as members.

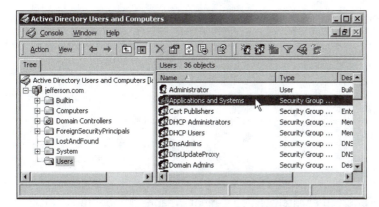

Figure 3-2   The Jefferson Philately IT Department's Applications and Systems group created in the Users folder

An alternate approach for the Active Directory design for Jefferson Philately is to:

1. Create an OU in the domain called IT.

2. Delegate authority over the IT OU to the IT manager.

3. Have the IT manager create the user accounts in the IT OU for all members of the IT department.

4. Have the IT manager create global security groups in the IT OU, called Applications and Systems, Operations, and User Support, and join the appropriate user accounts to each group (see Figure 3-3).

5. Give the three global groups access to the resources that they need by joining each group, as appropriate, to other groups (such as domain local or universal groups that have access to resources) and to the security descriptors of resources, such as shared folders.

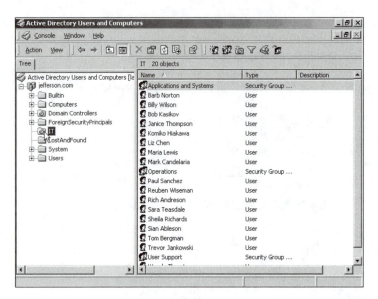

Figure 3-3   The Jefferson Philately IT department organized under the IT OU

IT Departments Organized by Department and by Function

Some mid- and large-sized organizations divide the IT organization into departments or a combination of departments and functions. This arrangement is particularly common for companies that are composed of subsidiaries, such as York Industries. The York Industries IT organization is more complex than at Jefferson Philately, because each of the York Industries subsidiaries has its own IT department. All of the IT departments report to the York Industries chief information officer (CIO) and vice president of information technology. Under the CIO there are separate IT departments at each of the seven country locations, with each IT department managed by a director and by managers for each IT functional group. Also, under each director, there are project managers who are responsible for putting together and managing project teams. The IT departments in each country have a different makeup that is related to the needs of each location. For example, Nantes Appliances in Marseille, France has an IT department divided into the groups: Applications Development, Networking, Security, Telecommunications, Quality Assurance, Systems, and User Support, as shown in Figure 3-4.

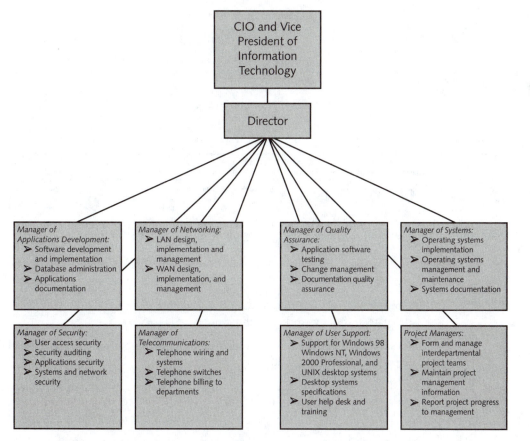

Figure 3-4   IT organization for Nantes Appliances

An effective way to reflect the IT Department's structure for Nantes Appliances is the following:

1. Create an IT OU in the domain that is designated for Nantes Appliances.

2. Create user accounts in the IT OU for the Nantes Appliances IT employees.

3. Create global groups in the IT OU to reflect each of the functional groups in the IT department: Applications Development, Networking, Security, Telecommunications, Quality Assurance, Systems, and User Support.

4. Create a global group for each project that is managed by a project manager (see Figure 3-5).

5. Give the global groups access to the resources that they need by joining each group, as appropriate, to other domain local and universal groups and to the security descriptors of resources, such as shared folders.

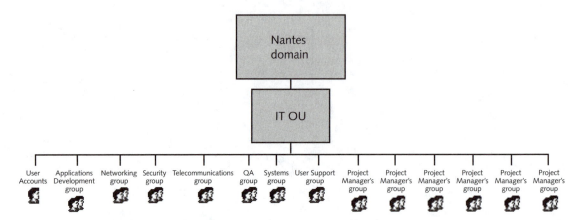

Figure 3-5   Reflecting the Nantes Appliances IT Department through groups

An alternate way to set up Active Directory to reflect the Nantes Appliances IT organization is as follows:

1. Create an IT OU in the domain that is designated for Nantes Appliances and delegate authority to the IT director.

2. Nest an OU under the IT OU for each of the functional groups in the IT department. Delegate authority for each of these OUs to the respective manager for that functional group.

3. Nest an OU under the IT OU for each of the project managers and delegate authority for each of these OUs to the respective project manager (see Figure 3-6).

4. Have each manager of each functional group create user accounts in his or her OU for his or her functional area. Also, have each manager create security groups to reflect the areas of responsibilities under him or her. For example, the Manager of Applications development might create groups called Software Development, Database Admins, and Documentation.

IT Departments Organized by Project

Some IT departments use a project-based structure within the functional or departmental organizational structure. In this arrangement there are groups or departments within IT, as illustrated in the example of Nantes Appliances (see Figure 3-4). Members of each department also serve on one or more project teams, which means each employee is permanently assigned to a department and also temporarily assigned to teams on the basis of the specific expertise needed for a team. At Nantes Appliances, this means that a system programmer who works under the manager of systems will have regular systems duties, such as administering Windows 2000 servers, and will also be assigned to one or more project teams under one or more project managers.

3

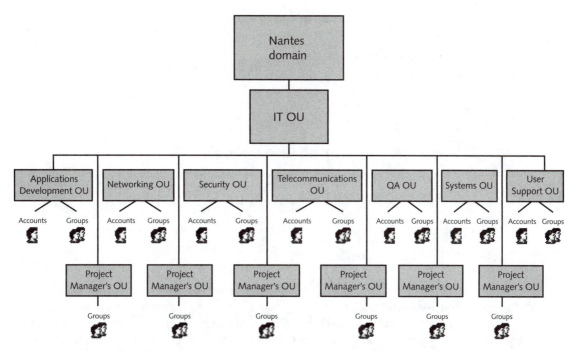

Figure 3-6   Reflecting the Nantes Appliances IT department through nested OUs

Consider, for example, a project in which the goal is to create a data warehouse on a Windows 2000 server from data originally stored in a legacy mainframe database. The data consists of parts inventories, and managers need a way to quickly create reports from the database on an ad hoc basis. Currently, reports are written by programmers in an older mainframe language called Culprit, a process that may take several days. To start this new project, a request is sent to the IT director who assigns the project to one of the project managers.

The project manager selects a team consisting of two database programmers from the Applications Development group, a systems programmer from the Systems group, a security analyst from the Security group, and a network analyst from the Networking group. In addition to the IT members, the project team has an inventory specialist from warehousing, and a member of the management group who originally requested the project (see Figure 3-7). The purpose of the team is to set up a system on a Windows 2000 server using an Oracle database. Data is to be imported from the mainframe's database to the Windows 2000 server Oracle database twice each day. The job of the team is to set up the Windows 2000 server, set up and design the Oracle database, and develop a way to import the data from the mainframe database to Oracle. Once that job is finished, the team will select a report-writing tool that can be used to create ad hoc reports from the Oracle database and that is easy for managers to use. To help get the managers started, the team will also create a set of sample reports that provide a basis on which to design other reports.

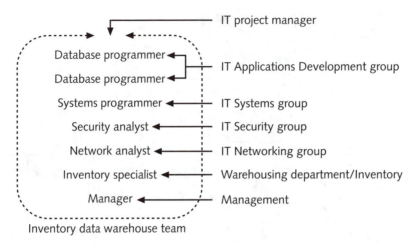

Figure 3-7   Project team composition

In the models discussed in the last section, Active Directory might be set up to handle the project in one of two ways. In the first model (see Figure 3-5), a new security group consisting of the team members would be created and given access to the resources, such as the database and specific server folders. In this model the project manager has limited control over managing Active Directory containers for her or his project.

Through the second model (see Figure 3-6), the project manager has more control because she or he has been delegated authority to manage an OU nested under the IT OU. With this authority, the project manager can create specialized security groups, such as one for planning, one for database management, one for programming, and one for managing specific server resources. The project manager also has the ability to establish nested OUs and shared folders within her or his project management OU to match the needs of each project she or he is managing. For example, the project manager might create a Warehouse Project OU for this particular project and then set up groups and publish shared folders under the Warehouse Project OU (see Figure 3-8).

IT Departments Organized by Federation

In some organizations, there are two or more separate IT departments or units that are organized to fulfill specific functions and that are under a parent division or department. This model is called a **federated IT organization** because the discrete IT organizations have the following characteristics that are similar to a country that is composed of federated states:

- Each IT organization has delineated areas of responsibility and autonomy.

- All IT organizations have areas in which they must work cooperatively.

- All IT organizations are part of a larger whole, such as a university or multinational corporation.

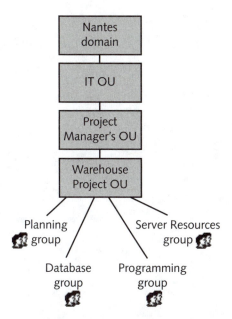

Figure 3-8   Using nested OUs and groups to match the data warehouse project

Community colleges and liberal arts colleges often have two federated IT groups, one for academic computing and one for administrative computing. The academic computing group reports to the dean of instruction, dean of faculty, or vice president of academic affairs, for example. The objectives of this group are to provide support for computer labs, computer-related instructional technologies, class Web pages, and training faculty in new technologies. The administrative IT group may report to the business manager, dean of instruction, or vice president of administrative services. This IT group is often responsible for all administrative and financial computer-related activities, such as accounting, budget, payroll, human resources, registration and records, and the college foundation.

Universities often provide an example of a more diverse number of federated IT groups. One university can have autonomous IT groups for administrative computing, library services, the bookstore, the physical plant, and for each college within the university, such as Arts and Sciences, Business, Engineering, and Law (see Figure 3-9). Even though these groups have different objectives, they still have structures, such as committees (discussed later in this chapter), that enable them to work cooperatively in areas that affect them all, such as networking and telecommunications services.

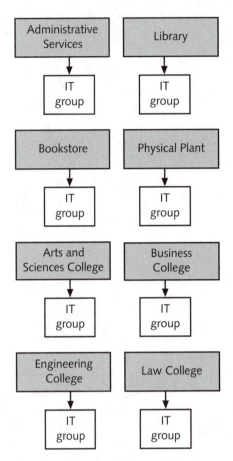

Figure 3-9   Federated IT organization in a university

When you analyze an organization, there are several clues you can use to determine if it is divided into federated IT groups:

- Different departments or divisions have their own IT groups that report to the department or division head.

- The IT groups have different objectives.

- The IT groups create separate strategic plans tailored to the needs of their parent department or division.

- The IT groups create separate operating plans or budgets.

Try Hands-on Project 3-1 to practice analyzing an IT organization.

Of the organizational models, organization by federation can be the most complex for Active Directory planning. This is because the politics of the situation may require separate domains and trees or a combination of child and parent domains, so that each group can enforce the autonomy it wants to retain. Also, tailoring group policies for each domain will entail careful research about the needs of each group. You will learn more in the chapters that follow about how to design domains, child domains, and group policies in this situation.

IT Departments Organized by Cost Center

In some organizations, part or all of the functions performed by the IT department are viewed as cost centers. This means that IT services are treated as a single cost of operations or charged out to other departments. When IT services are treated as a single cost, then the operating plan or budget may lump all of the cost of IT operations into one large budgeted item. State legislatures, for example, sometimes treat the IT operations of the state government or of a state college as a single budgeted item. When the IT department is viewed as a single cost center, then you can reflect this in the Active Directory design by creating a single IT OU, which is used to manage IT user accounts and functional groups, for example. The OU may also house programs and databases that are used to calculate and track the cost of operations for IT activities.

In other cost center IT department or organizational models, specific services are broken down into cost centers and are charged to each department in the company or institution. Some examples of services that may be charged to other departments are:

- User support and training

- Network support

- User accounts

- Amount of time, such as in minutes, logged on to specific servers or mainframe computers

- PC maintenance

- Application program development and maintenance

- Database development and maintenance

- Disk storage

- Equipment costs that are associated with certain products or operations

- Network equipment costs that are associated with certain departmental or geographic locations

- Telecommunications costs, including monthly telephone fees and long-distance fees (for organizations that have their own telephone systems)

One way to reflect the cost center IT organizational model is to:

1. Create an IT Cost Center OU.

2. Nest the individual IT cost centers under the IT Cost Center OU (see Figure 3-10).

3. Place the statistical accounting of each cost center under its respective OU. For example, some organizations charge other departments for the total time that users from those departments are logged on to servers. In this Active Directory design, there might be a Server Use Time OU nested under the IT Cost Center OU in a domain. Cost accounting and database information about each department's use of servers would be kept in shared folders contained in the Server Use Time OU.

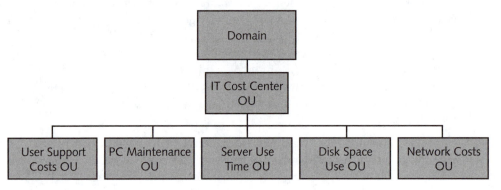

Figure 3-10   Using OUs to reflect cost center IT organization

ANALYZING IT DECISION FLOW

Decision-making models in IT departments include centralized, decentralized, formal-informal, path-goal, situational, and federated. The traditional model for IT departments is centralized, but the continuous introduction of new technologies and advancements in rapid application development (RAD) have ushered in other models in modern IT departments. The sections that follow show how to analyze an IT department using each of the business management decision models.

As you study these models, keep in mind that an IT department can have elements of several models, such as a combination of decentralized and path-goal decision flow or a combination of centralized and formal-informal.

Centralized Decision Flow

Traditional models for IT departments have followed the centralized decision flow structure. In this model, the top IT manager makes decisions that flow down through middle managers, supervisors, and line staff, as shown in Figure 3-11. Consider, for example, the implementation of a new accounting system. Using this model, the top IT manager or CIO assigns a middle IT manager to work with the accounting manager in selecting an accounting package. After the package is purchased, the IT middle manager determines which of his or her staff will install the package, sets timelines for the installation, and may even decide when the installation will begin (without consulting the accounting manager). When any problem arises, the IT middle manager or the top IT manager decides how to resolve it. There is little to no input from the line staff throughout the installation process other than to execute the project. If there is a question about the specifics in setting up tables, the chart of accounts, or designing reports, those questions are directed to the middle manager, who may consult the accounting manager.

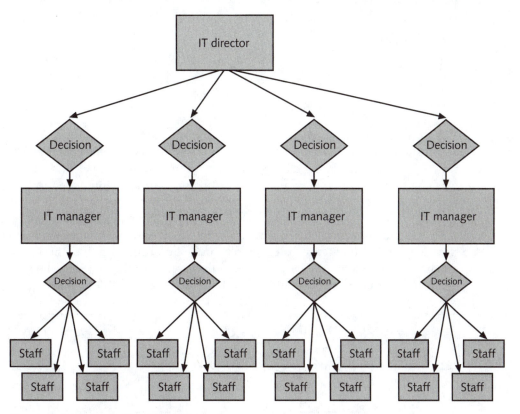

Figure 3-11   Centralized IT decision flow

 A centralized IT decision flow structure is often accompanied by a centralized IT organizational model, which means that IT decisions come from the top down, and IT resources are geographically centralized in the IT department.

When the IT decision flow is centralized, the result is that the Active Directory design is simpler. Instead of having multiple forests and domains controlled by different groups in a large organization, for example, there are likely to be fewer forests and domains, with centralized decision-making and control in the IT department. Because control is centralized, an organization is more likely to have only one forest and one schema. The centralized decision-making structure is more likely to be reflected in the Active Directory design through the use of OUs and will have relatively less nesting of OUs. Typically, departments other than IT have less flexibility in the management of computer and network resources, but there is more consistency and management costs are lower.

Decentralized Decision Flow

In the decentralized model of IT decision flow, the decision making can come from several directions, which include:

- Managers
- Supervisors
- Line staff
- Customers

When a decision is required, it is often made by the individual or group that has the most information about the situation. Customers in this instance are those who directly use systems, such as the accounting manager, accountants, and accounting clerks in the example of installing a new accounting system. For instance, the decision about when to bring the system to live production would be made by the accounting manager, to time live production with the new fiscal year. Decisions about how to set up vendor tables would be made by accountants and accounting clerks (see Figure 3-12). Decisions about how to optimize data storage in the accounting database would be made by a combination of the accountants and the database administrator. The start time of the project would be a mutual decision among the managers, supervisors, and line staff in both the IT and accounting departments.

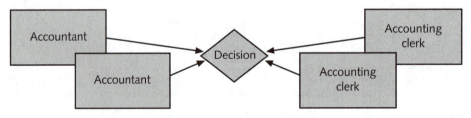

Figure 3-12   Decentralized IT decision flow

 Decentralized decision flow typically accompanies IT departments that have decentralized, project-based, or federated organizational models—or a combination of these.

Active Directory design is usually more complex when there is a decentralized decision flow structure. Decentralization typically means that there is a need for different forests and domains, often with different groups in control of these containers. This is particularly true if there is some distrust or a strong need for autonomy between factions in an organization. For example, a university that has a decentralized decision flow model for IT operations and that uses a federated IT structure is very likely to have multiple domains and more than one forest. The use of different forests enables each faction at the university to customize and secure different schemas from those used by other factions—for example, having one forest and schema for the academic departments and a different forest and schema for the administrative departments.

At the very least, a decentralized decision flow structure means there are likely to be multiple OUs, frequent delegation of OUs, and widespread nesting of OUs. Also, there is likely to be a need for more domains than in a centralized decision flow model, with different group policies associated with domains and with OUs (see Chapters 6, 7, and 8 for design methods).

Formal-Informal Decision Flow

IT departments can be analyzed in terms of their formal versus informal decision flow patterns. The formal structure may mandate that a particular manager or staff member make a decision. The reality is that the formal structure may be followed or it may be bypassed. For example, if IP addresses are assigned statically (manually), then the formal structure may dictate that new IP addresses be assigned by the manager of the Networking group in the IT department. In an organization where the formal structure is followed precisely, the network manager keeps a database of IP addresses and assigns them. If an informal structure is followed, then users may know that they should call a particular network analyst for new IP addresses, because the network manager is usually in meetings and is difficult to reach, and he normally depends on that network analyst to assign IP addresses anyway.

Using the example of installing a new accounting system, the formal decision-making structure may be that the manager of the applications development group has the responsibility for establishing the timelines for tasks in the project. But the reality is that the timelines are set by a lead applications programmer (see Figure 3-13).

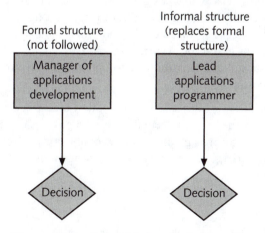

Figure 3-13   Formal-informal decision flow

Two of the best Active Directory tools for accommodating formal-informal decision flow situations are security groups and the ability to delegate authority over OUs. In the IP address management example, where the network analyst really assigns the addresses, the IT department might create a security group consisting of the manager of the networking staff and the network analyst, giving that security group privileges to manage the database. If the database is contained in an OU that is delegated to the manager, the manager can also delegate certain OU tasks to the network analyst—or the tasks can be delegated to the security group to which both belong.

Groups and OU delegation can also be used in the second example in which timelines are really established by the lead applications programmer and not by the manager of applications development. Since the timelines are most likely to be set up in project management software, the software might be located in a shared folder contained within an OU. Along with the manager of applications development, the lead applications programmer can belong to a security group that has privileges to make changes in the timeline data that is managed by the software. The same security group might be given authority over the OU that contains the shared folder.

Path-Goal Decision Flow

IT departments that operate using project managers often use the path-goal decision flow model, which focuses on a goal and the tasks necessary to accomplish that goal. When the path-goal decision model is employed, tasks are assigned to specific individuals, and those individuals are able to make decisions about the best way to accomplish the tasks. A manager is available to provide advice when questions arise or to coach the individual in making the best decision, as shown in Figure 3-14.

In the accounting installation example, the goal is to install the accounting package. The installation process is divided into tasks, such as installing the database, installing individual pieces of the accounting software, configuring tables in the software, configuring security, setting up beginning balances, and so on. The individual who is assigned the task has decision-making ability for that task. For example, the security specialist has the authority to set up security, but must decide how to set security for the special accounts used by auditors. She may have prior experience in making this decision from setting up security on another system or she may consult with her manager for advice or for coaching on how to obtain the necessary advice from someone in the Accounting department.

Rights, permissions, group policies, security groups, and OUs are often used to enable individual users or a group of users to perform the tasks needed to reach a goal. In the example of the security specialist, she may decide to manage the special accounts for the auditors in an Auditors OU for which she has been delegated authority to create accounts and to manage the group policies linked to that OU.

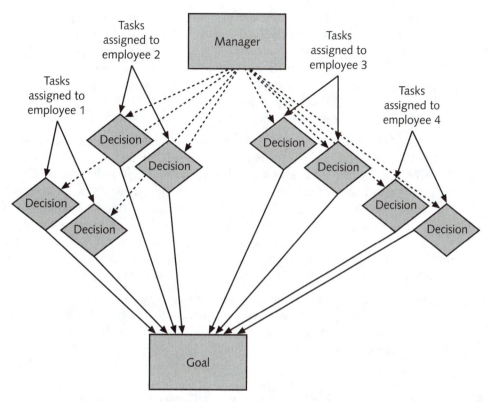

Figure 3-14   Path-goal decision flow

Situational Decision Flow

The situational decision flow model is unique when applied to an IT department because these departments often use a combination of task-oriented and people-oriented approaches. The complexity of the work provides a task-oriented element, as in the path-goal decision model (see Figure 3-14), but with managers influencing decisions in a participatory (more influential) fashion instead of a supportive or coaching (less influential) fashion. At the other end of the spectrum, the high market demand for IT professionals often makes them less loyal to the organizations for which they work, creating a people-oriented element. In a people-oriented organization, there are likely to be complex and shifting political divisions that may represent coalitions of different groups. For example, consider a large IT division in a university that has different departments for applications development, operations, security, systems, telecommunications, and user support. Each of these departments is in competition with the other departments over budget issues and for control of the overall direction of the IT division. Politically, the departments have formed three people-oriented coalitions: (1) applications development and security, (2) operations and systems, and (3) telecommunications and user support. In this situation, decision making can be very conflicted, and decisions sometimes shift suddenly, depending on which coalition has the most influence at the time. One example of a change in decision might be a large project involving all of these groups to set up a new student information and advising system. At the beginning of the project planning stage, the applications development and security coalition has the most influence, which results in the decision to use one vendor's database system. However, when the implementation starts and the funds for purchasing hardware and the database are transferred to the Operations department, this department along with the Systems department decides that a different vendor's database is easier to use and influences the decision to purchase that database instead.

Creating an Active Directory structure for task-oriented IT organizations and for people-oriented IT organizations involves frequent change, but for different reasons. The Active Directory structure for the task-oriented IT organization will likely include OUs and security groups that represent existing projects. These will change as projects and goals change. The Active Directory structure for the people-oriented IT organization will use OUs and security groups to represent political alignments or coalitions. These will change as the politics change. In the university example, a strong coalition may result in two departments merging, such as Systems and Operations; or a change in power at the CIO level may result in a different merging, such as Applications Development with Operations and Security.

Organizations that have the ability to match market salaries, to offer training, and to offer promotion paths are more likely to be task-oriented. Medium- to large-sized businesses and corporations typically fall into this category. Organizations such as educational institutions and government sometimes have fewer financial resources for salaries and more limited promotion paths and thus are more likely to have people-oriented IT departments.

Federated IT Organization Decision Flow

The decision flow in a federated IT organization typically comes from two directions. The first and main direction is from the head of the department or division in which each IT group resides. In the earlier example of the university federated IT organization structure (see Figure 3-9), decisions flow from the division or college head to the IT manager in each IT group. In the Arts and Sciences College, for example, this means that decisions about the strategic plan, objectives, and operating plan flow from the Arts and Sciences dean to the IT manager under the dean. This represents a top-down or vertical decision flow.

The second decision-making flow is horizontal among the federated IT groups. Often there are one or more committees that exist for the purpose of coordinating the efforts among groups. In the example of the university, there may be one information technology steering committee that consists of either the division and college heads or the IT managers. This committee makes decisions about areas of mutual interest, such as what networking technologies to deploy, how to share server resources, how to coordinate e-mail services, and what computer and domain naming conventions to use (see Figure 3-15).

Try Hands-on Project 3-2 to perform an analysis of the decision flow in an IT department.

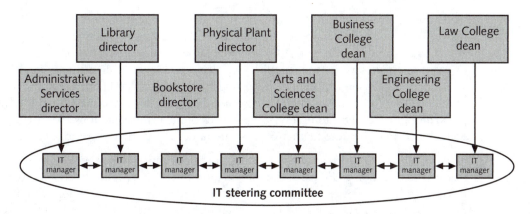

Figure 3-15   Federated IT organization decision flow in a university

The Active Directory structure for federated decision flow typically consists of using a combination of domains, OUs, and security groups. In the example shown in Figure 3-15, Active Directory might contain OUs for each of the IT managers in each of the eight areas. Also, there might be an OU for the steering committee, with authority for that OU delegated to the steering committee's chairperson. Within the OU for the steering committee, the chairperson can establish a security group containing the user accounts of each member and establish shared folders for access by members of that security group.

ANALYZING COMPANY AND IT RELATIONSHIPS

When you analyze an IT department, consider the following aspects of its relationship to the organization that it serves:

- Location in the company hierarchy
- IT governing groups
- Role in the organization
- Relationship to users

The location of an IT department within a company is a reflection of the amount of autonomy of that department. In the example of Interstate Security Bank, the IT department at the headquarters office is run by a CIO who reports to the CEO of the company. Because the CIO has direct access to the company president, this structure gives the IT department relatively more autonomy to make its own decisions about developing objectives, strategic plans, and operating plans.

Instead of reporting directly to the company president, the IT department at Jefferson Philately is one of three departments—IT, Human Resources, and Accounting—under the vice president of finance. In this structure, the IT department has less autonomy and must vie with two other departments for the vice president's attention and for their share of the budget. The IT department's business objectives, strategic plan, and operating plan must be approved by the vice president of finance. The same is true for major equipment purchases, such as expensive servers, and for all hiring decisions. Another element to consider when analyzing the Jefferson Philately IT department structure is that IT services are first tailored to the needs of the financial side of the business, because this is the main interest of the vice president of finance. The computer-related needs of the plant operations and marketing areas will be secondary, because neither of these are under the vice president of finance.

Some organizations, particularly in education and government, have governing committees that set the direction of IT, particularly in relation to the short-range goals and objectives of the IT department. For example, one community college has an IT Steering Committee that decides on the priority given to each IT project and determines what desktop computer brands are to be purchased. The committee consists of the dean of instruction, the dean of administration, the business officer, two faculty members, the head of the library, the head of the physical plant, and the information technology director. The committee meets twice a month to hear a progress report on all IT projects, to determine what new projects will be accepted, and to rerank projects when new ones are added. The committee also approves the IT director's goals and strategic plan. The Active Directory design reflects the structure of this decision-making group because it contains a special security group, consisting of the committee members, that gives them access to shared folders containing reports, the strategic plan, committee minutes, and the agenda for the next meeting.

When you analyze an IT department, study the role of that department in its parent organization. In some organizations the IT department plays a central role, particularly in organizations that have centralized IT functions within the IT department. In organizations that have extensively decentralized IT functions or that use a federated structure, the IT department is more likely to play a secondary role. For example, consider how one university uses the strength of its centralized IT department and computer facilities as a recruiting tool to attract new students who want to have access to the latest technologies. Because that IT department is central to the school's recruiting and student retention, it is well funded and relatively powerful in the organization. In another example, consider the IT department in a large law firm. In this firm the IT functions are very secondary to the courtroom successes of its attorneys. The IT department is in a support role on the same level as legal assistants and secretarial staff.

The role of the IT department is important in terms of designing Active Directory structures and determining the delegation of authority. When there is a strong, centralized IT department that plays a central role in an organization, the IT department is likely to maintain control over domains and OUs, resulting in fewer of each. When the IT department is in a less influential, secondary role, and IT functions are more decentralized, then there will likely be more domains and OUs created in Active Directory. Also, authority over some domains and OUs is likely to be delegated to other departments or groups in an organization.

Another factor to analyze is the relationship that the IT department has to specific groups of users. The nature of the relationship can be classified on a continuum from strong partnership at one end to adversarial at the other. Also, the placement on the continuum can vary from department to department. For instance, the IT department might work as a partnership with the Research department, but in an adversarial relationship with the manufacturing plant. When the relationship is a strong partnership, members of the IT department are likely to work closely with those they serve. Working closely means that the customers are brought into decisions and there is an emphasis on tailoring systems to meet customer needs. The partnership model includes frequent communication between the IT line staff and those who they serve. There is also frequent communication between the IT department head and the heads of other departments. When a partnership relationship exists, the IT department is likely to complete a high number of projects for the reciprocating departments.

At the opposite end of the spectrum, the relationship between the IT department and some other departments may be adversarial or typified by mutual suspicion. In these situations, the IT department may complete fewer projects for such departments, and projects are more likely to miss deadlines and budget projections. Security account groups are of greater concern because of the suspicion. The IT department is more likely to make decisions on its own without consulting the other departments, even though the decisions affect those departments. For example, in one business, the Electrical Engineering department was at odds with the IT department over how to network its area. The adversarial relationship resulted in delays of the network installation in that area.

MATCHING BUSINESS GOALS AND STRATEGIES TO IT STRATEGIES

One of the most important business analysis tasks is to map IT strategies to the business goals and objectives of an organization, because achieving the goals and objectives of the organization is the fundamental reason for having computer resources. In many organizations, the IT strategies can be mapped directly to one or more business goals or objectives. Consider York Industries, which has the business objective: "Develop 5000 new distributors and sales partners within six months." The IT strategies to help in achieving this objective are the following:

- Purchase and deploy within six months five new Windows 2000 intranet servers to support the distributor and sales network.

- Purchase and deploy within four months a Windows 2000 Datacenter server for the distributor database.

- Increase the WAN bandwidth within six months for more users and faster access.

- Develop an enhanced version of the distributor software within six to eight months.

- Develop a distributor and sales partner help desk system within nine months.

In another example, the business objectives of Interstate Security Bank for this year involve improving the existing backup techniques used at each branch office per the auditor's requirements. The auditor has reported that the server backup techniques used at many branch offices and even at some of the regional offices are not standardized or sufficiently fault tolerant. The resulting business objective of the bank is: "Develop and implement within four months a new tape rotation system and automated backups for each branch and regional office with the ability to restore the last business day's data." For this business objective, the IT strategies are:

- Purchase and install automated tape changers for each branch office.

- Develop a standardized Tower of Hanoi tape rotation system to provide alternatives when a backup tape is damaged.

- Develop a fail-safe combination of full and partial tape backups.

- Develop a standardized tape library system.

- Establish both on-site and off-site backup tape storage.

- Develop a standardized security system governing who can perform tape backups.

- Ensure that all system state data, including the Registry and Active Directory, are regularly backed up.

When you analyze a company's goals and objectives, create a diagram to show the IT strategies designed to empower those goals and objectives. One place to begin looking is in the IT department's strategic plan. If you cannot find it there, consult with the IT director and other officers of the organization. Figure 3-16 illustrates how IT strategies might be mapped to Interstate Security Bank's objective to create more comprehensive backups.

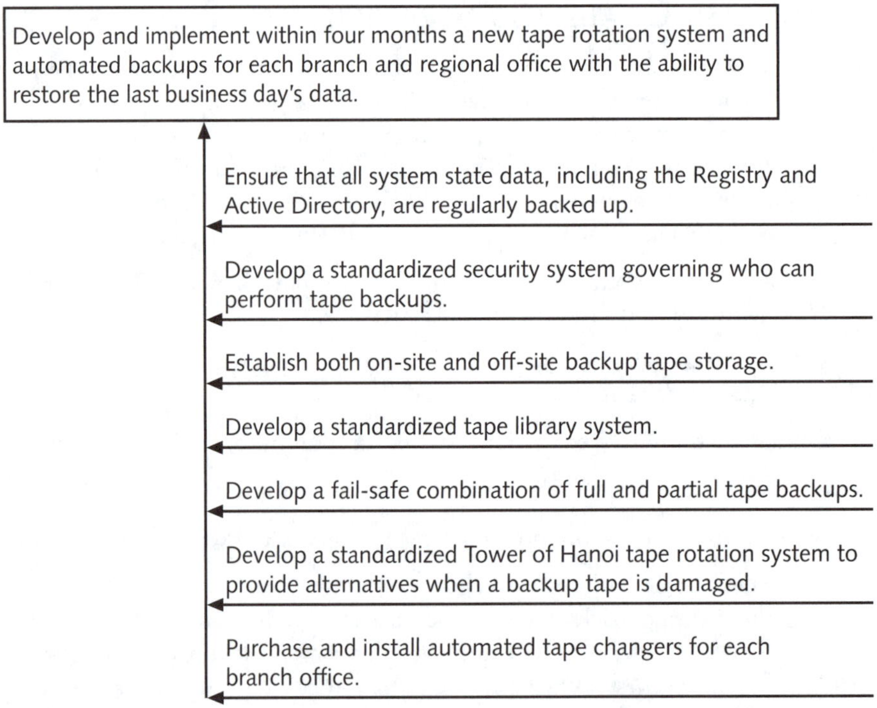

Develop and implement within four months a new tape rotation system and automated backups for each branch and regional office with the ability to restore the last business day's data.

Ensure that all system state data, including the Registry and Active Directory, are regularly backed up.

Develop a standardized security system governing who can perform tape backups.

Establish both on-site and off-site backup tape storage.

Develop a standardized tape library system.

Develop a fail-safe combination of full and partial tape backups.

Develop a standardized Tower of Hanoi tape rotation system to provide alternatives when a backup tape is damaged.

Purchase and install automated tape changers for each branch office.

Figure 3-16   Mapping IT strategies to a business objective

Sometimes an IT strategy is intended to map to several goals, which is particularly true when a new server is planned or when LAN and WAN access is enhanced. For example, a new server for an academic department in a college may be intended to enable professors to conduct research, allow an administrative assistant to track the department's budget and expenditures, and provide access to a CD-ROM array for professors and students.

ANALYZING FUNDING AND COST ISSUES

All organizations are concerned about funding and cost issues, which affect what they can accomplish currently and what can be proposed in strategic planning. The most direct way to analyze funding issues is by studying the IT operating plan or budget.

Sometimes funding is divided into one-time costs and ongoing costs. **One-time costs** are costs initially incurred for specific items, such as the cost of purchasing a new server or network router. **Ongoing costs** are continuous expenditures such as:

- Staffing
- Hardware and software vendor support agreements
- Software updates
- Yearly software licensing charges
- Training
- User support
- Equipment leases
- WAN access costs
- LAN maintenance costs

Both the one-time and ongoing costs can be combined to determine the **total cost of ownership (TCO)**. For example, the TCO for supporting one user on one workstation in a typical organization can range from $10,000 to $12,000 per year. The TCO can be reduced by up to two-thirds by using tools to consolidate and simplify network, server, and workstation management. Windows 2000 Active Directory is one step in that direction, because centralized directory services avoid duplication of effort across many servers.

Combining the use of Windows 2000 Server and Windows 2000 Professional is another way to significantly reduce TCO. Microsoft's long-term objective is to encourage organizations to convert workstation operating systems on a network to Windows 2000 Professional, because the cost of configuring and maintaining Windows 2000 Professional workstations on the network is less than for Windows 95, Windows 98, or Windows ME workstations. The TCO is less because Windows 2000 Professional is able to tap directly into automated configuration and software features designed for it in Windows 2000 Server. For example, network connectivity, desktop setup, and fast installation of standardized software can be automated from Windows 2000 Server to Windows 2000 Professional so that the user can set up a workstation with practically no technical knowledge or assistance.

Many organizations focus on the one-time costs of computer and network equipment and are reluctant to take new initiatives because the costs seem high. They fail to fully assess their growing ongoing costs, particularly for staffing and support. You can provide an invaluable service by showing an organization how to reduce their long-range TCO through implementing new tools, such as Active Directory and other Windows 2000 capabilities:

- *IntelliMirror:* The combined use of Windows 2000 Server and Windows 2000 Professional offers some built-in capabilities. IntelliMirror is intended to enable Windows 2000 Professional clients to access the same desktop settings, applications, and data from wherever they access the network or even if they are not on the network. IntelliMirror also uses information in Active Directory to ensure that consistent security and group policies apply to the client and that the client's software is upgraded or removed on the basis of a central management scheme. User data can be managed so that it is available when the user is logged on to the network or not connected to the network.

- *Web-Based Enterprise Management (WBEM):* Web-Based Enterprise Management (WBEM) is intended as a means to make life easier for network and server administrators. WBEM is an attempt to standardize the tools and interfaces used by administrators to gain a total picture of the relationship between their networks and the physical devices connected to their networks, servers, and workstations. WBEM uses the Common Information Model (CIM), which is a proposed standard to obtain consistent tracking and management information about a network and its attached devices. The CIM implementation in Windows 2000 Server is an extensible schema to enable WBEM management of software applications, databases, devices, operating system objects, and network objects.

- *Terminal Services:* These are services that reduce hardware costs by using thin-client computers, which have a minimal operating system and that work similarly to terminals, by running applications on a server.

- *Remote Installation Services (RIS):* These are services that can be installed on a Windows 2000 server and enable Windows 2000 Professional to be installed over the network. One advantage in using RIS is that a standard installation image can be used for a set of workstations.

- *Distributed File System (Dfs):* Dfs is a file system in which folders are shared across multiple computers, but are published in Active Directory as one shared resource or tree of folders. Dfs contributes to a lower TCO by providing fault tolerance and enabling users to find resources faster.

- *System State Data and Driver Signing:* These two options provide redundant storage of operating system files and registering of critical operating system files in case they are inadvertently overwritten or deleted.

- *Zero Administration for Windows (ZAW):* This is a combination of Windows 2000 management techniques that are designed to reduce TCO, such as the tools that are used to manage Active Directory services.

3

Consider two examples of how the TCO can be lowered in an organization and how user productivity can be increased. The first example is a phone-based customer service representative at Jefferson Philately who is using a non–Windows 2000 workstation operating system. This customer service representative comes to work half an hour early one morning so that he can delete some unneeded files. He unintentionally deletes an operating system file or driver and is unable to launch the customer service program he needs to use while taking orders from customers. His next step is to spend an unproductive hour trying to fix the problem. Next, he calls a user support person from the IT department, who spends an hour and a half working on the problem and finally decides to reinstall the operating system, which takes another hour. The result is that the customer service representative is paid for three and a half hours of unproductive time, and the user support person is paid for two and a half hours to fix the problem. Also, the phone lines are backed up because the company is short one customer service representative, which means the company is losing money. The total loss in dollars is about $5000, totaling the salaries of the employees plus the value of the orders lost because of the overloaded telephone lines. If that customer service representative had been using Windows 2000 Professional, he could have instantly restored the deleted operating system files from the \Winnt\repair\regback folder, with a five-minute phone call to a user support person. The total cost would be a one-time cost of about $200 for Windows 2000 Professional plus about $3 in staff salaries.

The second example is York Industries, which at one time spent an average of $102,000 on staff salaries every two years to upgrade workstation operating systems. An operating system upgrade required a user support person to make an appointment with each user to upgrade a system. The upgrade took from one to two hours and incurred costs for two staff salaries during that time. York Industries was able to reduce their TCO by migrating to Windows 2000 Server Remote Installation Services (RIS) servers. The involvement of user support is now to make RIS disks, provide online documentation about how to use RIS, and to offer occasional telephone support. There are no additional server costs because the company uses existing servers to provide RIS. The staff salary costs are reduced to about $35,000 dollars for the time an employee spends performing her or his own installation over the network and for the occasional calls to user support—representing a total savings of $67,000.

Try Hands-on Project 3-3 to practice an analysis of an IT department's budget.

CHANGE MANAGEMENT AND USER PRODUCTIVITY

Monitoring and standardizing computer-related changes has long been a difficult process for organizations. The changes that organizations experience include:

- Creating desktop setups to match the business needs
- Installing new software
- Changing from one software package to another, such as changing office suites
- Upgrading old versions of software to the new versions
- Offering new shared folders

Computer users and organizations depend on having a stable environment that enables users to be as productive as possible. Changes in software, the desktop, and operating systems can introduce a period of instability that makes users less productive. **Change management** is the implementation of processes and capabilities that enable organizations to control how changes are made and whom they affect. When you analyze a company, determine how changes are currently implemented and how change management can help that company. For many organizations, you will find that change is a random process and some element of chaos reigns.

One example of a chaotic situation occurs in York Industries, whose users prefer having the ability to customize their own desktops and who like to choose which version of Microsoft Office software to use. The companies of York Industries enable users to decide whether to use the Office software in the 95, 97, or 2000 versions. All three versions are maintained for users, which means that user consultants must spend time staying current on all three versions. This creates a problem, for example, when a manager creates Excel spreadsheets in a shared folder for her employees to view. Consider a situation in which that manager visits an employee's office and asks that employee to open one of her Excel spreadsheets prepared using the 2000 version, but the employee is still using the Excel 95 version. The time of both people is wasted, because the manager has to go back to her office, convert the spreadsheet to the 95 version, e-mail it to the employee—or print a copy of the 2000 version—and then go back to that employee's office to complete their original meeting.

Another example is the problem of having vastly different desktop settings. When one employee's hard drive fails while that employee is working on an important report for an executive meeting, he asks to temporarily use another employee's workstation. He wastes time determining how to work on that report while trying to navigate an unfamiliar desktop—and once he finds the report software on the desktop, it may be a different version than he is used to operating. This is just the surface of the confusion and lack of productivity in the York Industries environment that is frustrating to computer users and to the user support staff. A small list of the problems includes:

- Use of different software versions
- Use of different software to perform the same functions
- Wasted time and frustration in the user support departments at each location because there are so many different versions of software, types of software, and desktop settings in use
- Storing important files in inconsistent locations
- Frequent loss of important files
- Wasted time spent converting files
- Different desktop configurations
- Different printer configurations
- Users who unintentionally delete critical operating system files and software

York Industries represents a situation in which change management can make a significant difference and lower the TCO. In this situation the IT departments at each subsidiary company can use the software components of IntelliMirror to help manage change and lower TCO:

1. To start, the IT departments in each subsidiary company can set up users in Active Directory to reflect their natural work groupings using security groups, OUs, and domains.

2. IT should consult with each group and management to develop group policies that standardize desktop settings and what software is accessed by these groups on the basis of using OUs and domains (see Chapter 8).

3. IT can set up roaming profiles so that users access their own desktop settings from any computer, particularly if different desktop settings are established for different groups via group policies. **Roaming profiles** are desktop and other settings that are associated with an account so that the same settings are employed no matter what computer is used to access the account (the profile is downloaded to the client from a server).

4. IT can help standardize software use by deploying a combination of terminal services, assigned software, and published software. Terminal services enable IT to set up one standard version of software that all users run on a Terminal Services server. **Publishing applications** (or publishing software) involves setting it up through an Active Directory group policy so that users install the software from a central place using the Add/Remove Programs applet in Control Panel. **Assigning applications** (or assigning software) entails setting up a group policy so that a particular version of software is automatically started through a desktop shortcut, through a menu selection, or by clicking a file that has a specific file extension (such as starting Excel 2000 when the user opens a file with the .xls extension). Try Hands-on Project 3-4 to learn how to create a group policy to publish or assign applications.

 When software is assigned, it remains assigned each time the user logs on to the network. For example, if the user deletes the shortcut icon to that software on the desktop, the icon will automatically be restored the next time that user logs on. Assigning software (see Chapter 8), which is an IntelliMirror feature, is a better alternative offered via a Windows 2000 group policy than the older technique of creating mandatory profiles or system policies via Windows NT 4.0, because it is more secure. Group policies cannot be temporarily or permanently changed by users, as is possible for mandatory profiles or system policies (such as through users editing the Registry).

5. Dfs can be set up so that user files and folders are shared in a consistent way on the network and so that fault tolerance is employed to ensure that if a folder or file is deleted, it is automatically restored from a member Dfs server. Try Hands-on Project 3-5 to practice installing a new Dfs root folder.

6. IT can use one or more RIS servers to create standardized Windows 2000 Professional installation images. When an employee receives a new computer or when an employee's hard drive fails, Windows 2000 Professional can be installed or restored using a standardized image. Also, through using Dfs, important files can be copied or restored to that employee's computer.

7. Once operating system setups are standardized, such as through RIS and group policies, IT can save system state data in a central place so that critical operating system files are easily restored from the network.

8. Driver signing can be turned on for Windows 2000 Professional users through a group policy, which means that if an operating system file, such as a .dll file, is inadvertently deleted or overwritten, it is automatically restored. **Driver signing** is a digital signature that Microsoft incorporates into driver and system files as a way to verify the files and to ensure that they are not inappropriately overwritten. Try Hands-on Projects 3-6 and 3-7 to practice setting up driver signing and making driver signing a group policy.

All of these are steps that the York Industries IT departments can set up in each location by employing the IntelliMirror components. These are concrete examples of how to implement change management and enable users to be more productive.

Change management can significantly reduce TCO, but it is a capability that comes with political consequences. Users who have become accustomed to certain software and desktop features may feel that the IT department is interfering with their work autonomy. You can address this problem by educating the users about the positive consequences of change management that enable them to complete their work faster and with less frustration—which in some cases means they spend fewer overtime hours at work. Another way to successfully introduce change management is by enabling users to have input into how change management will be used.

OUTSOURCING

It is common for a company, educational institution, or government organization to outsource some or even all IT functions. **Outsourcing** means that a separate company performs specific IT tasks, which might be manufacturing plant applications, accounting applications, payroll applications, network implementation, or other specialized services. Outsourcing is an operating plan or budgetary approach to saving money. For example, a federal agency may find that it is less expensive to outsource all payroll functions because a private company that specializes in handling payrolls can perform this service at less cost than the agency's own IT organization.

3

One of the most common reasons for outsourcing is to enable an organization to accomplish a specific objective without hiring additional staff on a permanent basis. For example, consider York Industries' goal: "Over the next two years, decentralize warehouse management and implement 'just-in-time' parts inventory practices in all manufacturing plants." Part of this goal is to standardize inventory practices across all of the York companies by using the same inventory software. Because all of York's IT departments are already swamped with projects, the company decides to outsource the development of the new inventory system. This enables York to meet the goal of having the inventory system in place within two years, while avoiding the need to permanently hire extra IT staff.

Outsourcing affects Active Directory design in one of two ways: (1) the Active Directory structure will reflect one of the organizational and decision flow models already discussed, or (2) the Active Directory structure will focus on special delegation of objects. The first instance reflects the situation in which all IT services are outsourced. Often when an organization decides to outsource all IT functions, the outsourcing vendor simply hires most of the existing IT employees and retains the existing organizational structure, or reorganizes the structure to one that the vendor is accustomed to using.

The second instance applies to situations in which some, but not all IT functions are outsourced. In this instance, the IT department typically retains full control over Active Directory services, but delegates some responsibility for Active Directory objects to the outsourcing group. In the example of the new inventory system, York Industries might create a separate development domain for the company that is writing the new inventory system and delegate control of the domain to that company. After the project is fully implemented in each production domain, the York IT departments would simply take back control of the development domain and eventually delete it.

CHAPTER SUMMARY

- Many IT departments are organized either by function, by department, by project, or by using a federated organizational structure. In addition to these organizational models, an IT department also may divide its services into cost centers. These organizational structures involve decision flow models such as centralized, decentralized, formal-informal, path-goal, situational, or federated. Plan to use your analysis of these structures to help design Active Directory elements that include security groups, OUs, domains, trees, and forests.

- When you analyze an IT department, determine how that department fits into the overall structure of the organization and what relationships it has with other departments. One way to study both aspects is to determine how the goals of the IT department can be mapped to the goals of the parent organization and of specific departments.

◻ Focus your analysis of an IT department on the ways in which the TCO of the department can be reduced along with the ways in which the department can reduce the TCO of supporting computer resources for other departments. IntelliMirror in Windows 2000 offers many components that can significantly reduce TCO. Often when TCO is reduced, the productivity of IT and other employees goes up.

◻ Organizations sometimes outsource part or all of their IT functions. The amount of outsourcing affects Active Directory design in terms of how control of objects is delegated.

In the next chapter you will learn how to analyze the software requirements of an organization for the Active Directory design.

KEY TERMS

assigning applications — Also called assigning software, an IntelliMirror feature that enables the setting up of a group policy so that a particular version of software is automatically started through a desktop shortcut, through a menu selection, or by clicking a file that has a specific file extension.

change management — The implementation of processes and capabilities that enables organizations to control how changes are made and whom they affect.

driver signing — A digital signature that Microsoft incorporates into driver and system files as a way to verify the files and to ensure that they are not inappropriately overwritten.

federated IT organization — A set of IT groups or departments that have their own separate areas of responsibility, that exists to perform specific business functions, and that have different objectives, but that all exist within one parent organization.

ongoing costs — Continuous expenditures that involve costs for items such as staffing, user support, equipment and software leases, and hardware and software vendor support agreements.

one-time costs — Costs that an organization pays initially for specific items, such as the cost of purchasing a new server or network router.

outsourcing — When a separate individual or company performs specific tasks for an organization—for example, IT tasks that are not provided by a department or employee in that organization, such as supporting that company's payroll software applications or network implementation.

publishing applications — Also called publishing software, setting up software through Active Directory services so that users install the software from a central place using the Add/Remove Programs applet in Control Panel.

roaming profile — Also called a roaming user profile, desktop and other settings that are associated with an account so that the same settings are employed no matter what computer is used to access the account (the profile is downloaded to the client from a server).

total cost of ownership (TCO) — The cost of installing and maintaining computers and equipment on a network, which includes hardware, software, maintenance, and support costs.

REVIEW QUESTIONS

Answer questions 1–9 using this case information:

Out West Gear is a company that manufactures cowboy hats and western shirts. The IT responsibilities in this company are shared among different IT groups that are housed in the Business, Customer Service, Plant Operations, and Warehousing departments. There is no CIO for the company. The company outsources all software application development activities.

1. Since there is no CIO, what means is this company likely to use to help the different IT groups work together?

   a. presidential edict

   b. a committee

   c. the CFO

   d. all of the above

   e. none of the above

   f. only a and b

   g. only b and c

2. In this company, employees can purchase their own software of preference for word processing and spreadsheets. The problem is that a lot of time is wasted converting documents from one format to another. How might they solve this problem?

   a. Decide on a software standard and publish that software in Active Directory.

   b. Use driver signing.

   c. Obtain more conversion software that can handle additional file formats and then assign that conversion software.

   d. all of the above

   e. none of the above

   f. only a and c

3. What type of IT organizational structure is used by Out West Gear?

   a. centralized

   b. territorial

   c. federated

   d. situational

   e. none of the above

4. What technique(s) could be useful to give full control over Active Directory resources to the outsourcing company?

   a. Use hard-copy change control.

   b. Delegate control to the outsourcing company over specific Active Directory objects.

   c. Create a domain for each IT group in each department.

   d. Give the outsourcing company permission to take ownership of any resource as needed.

   e. all of the above

   f. only b and c

   g. only b, c, and d

5. Compared to some other companies, the IT portion of this company is best described as:

   a. centralized

   b. situational

   c. primary

   d. secondary

6. One problem that employees face is that there are literally dozens of disorganized shared folders on the network, and information is difficult to locate. What can they do?

   a. Use FTP more extensively.

   b. Hire an employee to keep track of what is contained in the shared folders, and have the employee publish this information as a file.

   c. Employ Dfs.

   d. all of the above

   e. none of the above

   f. only a and b

   g. only a and c

7. In a company like this that does not currently use IntelliMirror features, you would expect the TCO to be:

   a. relatively high

   b. relatively low

   c. impossible to calculate

   d. immaterial

8. In the Business department, all employees use a specialized business software application that was developed by the outsourcing company. Unfortunately, employees sometimes delete their icons or shortcuts to the software and have to be shown how to reinstall it. How might this be solved?

   a. Develop an automated accounting system to show the number of times software has been installed, and increase the support fees for those clients who reinstall more than once.

   b. Assign the software.

   c. Publish the software.

   d. Create an installation team from the outsourcing company because they can help users reinstall software more quickly than the company's own computer support staff.

9. Each department has a set of business objectives. What might you do to help analyze the relationship between Active Directory and a department's objectives?

   a. Map that department's IT strategies to the business objectives.

   b. Use situational analysis for each objective.

   c. Encourage each department to convert objectives to goals for more concrete analysis.

   d. all of the above

   e. none of the above

   f. only b and c

Answer questions 10–19 using this case information:

The Lawnery manufactures parts for sprinkler systems, and has one IT department that consists of small groups who specialize in software maintenance, systems maintenance, network maintenance, and user support. All of these groups report to the manager of IT services who makes the decisions about the direction of the department, task assignments, the budget, and who interfaces with the users. The manager of IT services is a strong and respected leader who reports directly to the company president. The Lawnery has three general types of users, some who use an old DOS-based word processor, some who use Microsoft Word 95, and some who use Microsoft Word 2000. There are also three databases employed by users: an old version of dBase, Microsoft Access 2000, and FoxPro.

10. Which organizational model(s) would apply to the IT department in this business?

    a. organization by project

    b. organization function

    c. organization by department

    d. all of the above

    e. none of the above

    f. only a and b

    g. only a and c

3

11. The IT manager has decided that it is best to encourage users to gradually move to using Microsoft Word 2000 and FoxPro. Which of the following actions will help most?

    a. publishing software

    b. assigning software

    c. having the IT manager work with user-based committees to promote the transition

    d. immediately ending support for anything but Word 2000 and FoxPro

    e. all of the above

    f. none of the above

    g. only b, c, and d

    h. only a and c

12. Workstation users at The Lawnery have Windows 2000 Professional. Occasionally users install their own device drivers—for example, when installing a tape system. How can the IT department best help prevent situations in which users overwrite critical drivers that are already installed?

    a. Enforce a new company-wide policy that prevents users from installing their own devices.

    b. Set up Dfs.

    c. Employ driver signing at the workstations.

    d. Disable sharing the system files at the server.

    e. all of the above

    f. none of the above

    g. only a and b

13. The IT decision flow in this organization is best characterized as:

    a. decentralized

    b. centralized

    c. situational

    d. federated

    e. all of the above

    f. a combination of a, c, and d

    g. a combination of b, c, and d

    h. only b and d

14. The manager of IT services has never liked keeping track of budgetary information such as how monies are spent for items throughout the year, although by company policy it is her responsibility. She delegates this to a senior programmer analyst. This is an example of:

    a. formal–informal decision flow

    b. path–goal decision flow

    c. decentralized decision flow

    d. optional decision flow

    e. all of the above

    f. none of the above

    g. a combination of b, c, and d

15. In the IT department's budget, which of the following types of costs would you expect to be included and tracked?

    a. vendor support agreements

    b. staffing

    c. training

    d. equipment leases

    e. all of the above

    f. only a and d

    g. only a, b, and d

16. Considering the chain of command, which would most likely be true of this IT department?

    a. It has little autonomy.

    b. It has a high level of autonomy.

    c. It plays an important strategic role for the company.

    d. It plays a minor role in the company.

    e. none of the above

    f. only a and d

    g. only b and c

17. While you are developing an analysis of this IT organization, the manager of IT services leaves to take a higher paying job. The company president decides that the manager's respected leadership role will be hard to duplicate; he decides to hire a project manager and define all IT functions in terms of goals, with different teams set up to carry out the tasks necessary to complete the goals. This is an example of:

    a. project-based organization and path–goal decision making

    b. federated organization and path–goal decision making

    c. federated organization and federated decision making

    d. situational organization and centralized decision making

    e. none of the above

    f. a combination of b and d

18. Users in the warehouse often have to log on to the network using different computers. What IntelliMirror function can help them most?

    a. hardware profiles

    b. roaming profiles and group policies

    c. team assignments

    d. publishing software

19. After the reorganization, described in Question 17, the president of the company decides to have the project manager report to the comptroller (business accountant), who is under the CFO. Which of the following is most likely affected by this decision?

    a. the autonomy of the IT department

    b. the strategic position of the IT department

    c. the amount of work performed by the IT department

    d. the complexity of work performed by the IT department

    e. none of the above

    f. only a and b

    g. only b, c, and d

Answer questions 20–25 using this case information:

Auto Deals is a chain of automobile dealerships in Arizona, California, and Colorado. The main headquarters is in San Diego, which is also the location of the IT department that supports all of the chain dealerships. The IT department is loosely organized into groups of computer professionals who each have responsibilities based on their job positions. For example, there are four system administrators who maintain the Windows 2000 servers and the network, five programmer analysts who work on specific software systems, and so on. These employees work in groups whose memberships change as the types of projects change. Each of the 10 senior employees rotate responsibilities as project managers. Decisions are made by the current project managers and their teams, based on consensus. When a new team forms, it makes its own rules about how to operate and achieve goals.

20. Which organizational model(s) best applies to this IT department?

    a. organization by federation

    b. organization by function

    c. organization by project

    d. all of the above

    e. none of the above

    f. a combination of a and b

21. How would you classify the decision flow in this IT department?

    a. situational

    b. centralized

    c. decentralized

    d. path–goal

    e. all of the above

    f. a combination of a and d

    g. a combination of c and d

22. Where would you look to map IT strategies to business goals in this organization?

    a. to the teams and individual IT professionals

    b. to company managers

    c. to the board of directors

    d. all of the above

    e. none of the above

23. One of the senior IT employees makes up the budget every year. What kinds of costs would you expect this company to have for IT activities?

    a. ongoing costs

    b. one-time costs

    c. marketing costs

    d. all of the above

    e. only a and b

    f. only b and c

24. One of the greatest costs to the company is the installation of new operating systems. Currently all dealerships are using Windows 98, but the plan is to upgrade all users to Windows 2000 Professional. In the past, the company has used IT staff members from the San Diego office to visit each dealership and upgrade the operating systems. What is the best alternative to save travel time, but still provide the functionality of a full-fledged operating system?

    a. implementing terminal services

    b. implementing Dfs

    c. implementing RIS

    d. implementing a shared folder with signed drivers

    e. none of the above

    f. only a and b

    g. only a and d

25. When an IT project team working on a project makes a decision that affects all of the users, which of the following would provide input?

    a. employees

    b. managers

    c. the dealerships

    d. all of the above

    e. none of the above because the decision would be made only by the team

    f. only b and c

HANDS-ON PROJECTS

Project 3-1

In this project, you practice performing an analysis of the IT organization at your school or a local business. Ask your instructor for a flow chart of the organization and answer the following questions.

To perform the analysis:

1. What computer-related functions are performed by the IT organization?

2. Does the IT organization employ teams, and if so, how?

3. Do any departments or divisions have their own IT organizations?

4. What would you do to this diagram to make it even more useful for designing Active Directory services?

5. In your lab journal, or in a word-processed document, describe what organizational model or models best describe this organization.

Project 3-2

In this project, you practice analyzing your school's IT department, or the IT department at a local business to assess its decision flow.

To analyze the IT department in terms of decision flow:

1. Arrange a time to interview the head of the IT department.

2. Create in advance a series of questions for the IT head, using the following as examples:

    ❏ How does your department make decisions about which projects to tackle?

    ❏ How are decisions made about who will handle a project or a project task?

    ❏ How are decisions made about a project or task after it is started?

3. Take notes in your lab journal or for your word-processed document during the interview.

3

4. On the basis of the interview, analyze the decision-making style of the department. How might this decision-making style affect the Active Directory design?

An alternative to all students performing interviews one at a time is to have the IT head make a presentation to the class.

Project 3-3

In this project, you practice analyzing the budget of the IT department at your school. Ask your instructor for an example of the budget.

To analyze the budget:

1. What portion of the budget is for one-time costs?
2. What are two examples of one-time costs?
3. What portion of the budget is for ongoing costs?
4. What are four examples of ongoing costs?
5. Can any cost centers be identified from the budget and, if so, what are they?
6. What is the portion of the budget that is spent on staffing?
7. What portion of the budget is spent on equipment?
8. What elements of the budget might be influenced most by Windows 2000 IntelliMirror?
9. Record your results in your lab journal or in a word-processed document.

Project 3-4

This project enables you to view where to assign or publish an application through the default domain policy for all users in a domain. You will need to be logged on to a computer running Windows 2000 Server using an account that has Administrator privileges.

To view where to assign or publish an application:

1. Click **Start**, point to **Programs**, point to **Administrative Tools**, and click **Active Directory Users and Computers**.
2. Right-click a domain in the tree, such as TheFirm.com and click **Properties**.
3. Click the **Group Policy** tab.
4. Make sure that **Default Domain Policy** is selected and then click the **Edit** button.
5. Under User Configuration in the tree, double-click **Software Settings** (to create a group policy for user accounts).
6. In the tree under Software Settings, right-click **Software Installation**, and then click **Properties**.
7. Make sure that the General tab is displayed.

8. How can you create a group policy to assign or publish software? What other options are available? Record your observations.

9. How can you specify to remove a software package from a client when that client is no longer in the domain (or in an OU)?

10. Click **Cancel**.

11. Close the Group Policy window.

12. Click **Cancel** to exit the domain Properties dialog box, and then close the Active Directory Users and Computers tool.

Project 3-5

In this project you practice creating a Dfs root using the domain-based model. (From this root you can later build pointers to shared folders on other computers, so that they appear to only be on the computer containing the root folder.) Make sure that the server on which you create the root has no other Dfs root. Before you start, check with your instructor about which drive path to use for the Dfs root.

To create a Dfs root:

1. Log on to Windows 2000 Server as Administrator or with Administrator privileges.

2. Click **Start**, point to **Programs**, point to **Administrative Tools**, and click **Distributed File System**.

3. Click **Distributed File System** in the console tree, if it is not already selected.

4. Click the **Action** menu, click **New Dfs root**, and click **Next** after the New Dfs Root Wizard starts.

5. Click **Create a domain Dfs root**, if it is not already selected. Click **Next**.

6. Make sure the domain name is displayed in the Domain name box, or use a different domain per your instructor's permission. What other information is displayed in the dialog box? Click **Next**.

7. Click the **Browse** button to find the server. What information is displayed in the Find Computers window that can help you locate a server, such as a domain controller? Double-click the server on where the Dfs root will reside, and then click **Next**.

8. Click **Create a new share**. Enter the path specified by your instructor, such as C:\Inventory, and enter **Inventory** as the share name. Click **Next** and then click **Yes**.

9. Use the default Dfs root name, **Inventory**, and enter the comment, **On-hand parts inventory**. Click **Next**.

10. Review the summary of information for the Dfs root creation. How can you reenter information if you find that you made a mistake earlier? Record the summary information in your lab journal or in a word-processed document. Click **Finish**.

11. Look for the new root in the console tree under Distributed File System.

12. Close the Distributed File System tool.

Project 3-6

In this project you practice setting up the block mode for driver signing. One of the IntelliMirror features of Windows 2000 is the ability to choose to ignore whether or not a driver is signed, to be warned that a driver is not signed, or to have the operating system prevent you from installing a driver that is not signed. The block mode enables you to make sure that unsigned driver and system files cannot overwrite ones that are signed.

To set the block mode:

1. Log on to Windows 2000 Server as Administrator or with Administrator privileges, if you are not already logged on.

2. Click **Start**, point to **Settings**, and click **Control Panel**.

3. Double-click the **System** applet.

4. Click the **Hardware** tab and click **Driver Signing**.

5. Notice the three options under *File signature verification*. Record these options.

6. What option is set as the default?

7. Click **Block – Prevent installation of unsigned files**.

8. Make sure that **Apply setting as system default** is checked. When you check this option, this means that Windows 2000 Server will apply signature verification to users who log on to Windows 2000 Server and attempt to install any software.

9. Click **OK** to save your settings in the Driver Signing Options dialog box.

10. Click **OK** to exit the System Properties dialog box.

11. Close Control Panel.

When you configure driver signing, you configure it to apply to all new software installations, as well as to device drivers. Each time you install a word processor or spreadsheet application, the drivers used in that application are also verified. Further, when you select the Block option, this means that drivers and operating system files cannot be modified or overwritten by files that do not have the appropriate digital signature. No software installation can inadvertently install a driver or system file that is inappropriate for your version of Windows 2000 Server.

Project 3-7

In this project, you set up the block mode driver signing capability as a default domain group policy for Windows 2000 Professional clients who access a Windows 2000 Server network.

To apply block mode driver signing to Windows 2000 Professional clients:

1. Click **Start**, point to **Programs**, point to **Administrative Tools**, and click **Active Directory Users and Computers**.

2. Right-click a domain in the tree, such as TheFirm.com, and click **Properties**.

3. Click the **Group Policy** tab.

4. Select **Default Domain Policy**, if it is not already selected.

5. Click **Edit**.

6. Double-click **Administrative Templates** in the tree under User Configuration.

7. Click **System** in the tree.

8. Double-click **Code signing for device drivers** in the right-hand pane.

9. Click **Enabled**.

10. Click the down-arrow to view the options in the text box. Record the options that are available.

11. Select **Block** in the text box. What does this option do?

12. Click **OK**.

13. Close the Group Policy window, and then click **OK** in the domain Properties window.

14. Close the Active Directory Users and Computers tool.

CASE PROJECT

Aspen Consulting Project: Analysis of a Company's IT Structure

Buck's Shoes is an international shoemaking company that produces dress, causal, and work shoes. The main offices of Buck's are located in New York City. The manufacturing plants are located in:

❐ Chicago, which makes casual shoes

❐ Mexico City, which makes dress shoes

❐ London, which makes work boots

❐ Sydney, which makes work boots

Each location has its own IT department that is run by an IT director, and each IT director reports to the CIO whose office is in New York City. The CIO gives each director great latitude in running her or his IT department. You have been hired to help provide an analysis of the IT departments for Active Directory design.

3

1. The Chicago location has the following groups in the IT department, each run by a manager:

   ❏ Applications development

   ❏ Systems development

   ❏ Network administration

   ❏ Telecommunications

   ❏ User consulting

   ❏ Web development

   What type of organizational structure does this IT department have? Create a diagram of the organizational structure.

2. In the Chicago IT department, there is an executive committee consisting of the IT director and the IT managers who make the decisions. The IT director has the most influence on decisions, but does solicit the opinions of the managers. Once a decision is made that affects a particular manager's group, that manager takes the decision to the line staff so that it is followed per the executive committee's decision. How would you analyze and diagram the decision flow in this IT organization?

3. The IT department in Sydney is divided into teams of IT professionals, and each team tackles specific projects. The work of the teams is coordinated by a team leader who is elected by each team and who reports to the IT director. What kind of IT organizational structure is used by this department? Create a conceptual diagram to show how this organization works. What type of decision flow is this IT organization likely to have?

4. At the New York site, there is a small IT department that is responsible for maintaining all of the Windows 2000 Servers, the network, and software applications that are used company-wide. However, each of the Business, Marketing, Planning, Quality Assurance, and Customer Care departments has its own IT group that reports to the department director. How would you analyze this IT organization and decision flow structure? Create a diagram to illustrate your analysis.

5. As part of your analysis, you study all locations to determine the single greatest source of nonproductive time spent by employees in relation to computer systems. You find that there is really a tie among the causes for the greatest source of problems: (1) employees and computer support personnel spend much unproductive time dealing with desktop operating systems because critical files often are deleted or overwritten, and (2) employees spend unproductive time searching for company-wide shared folders (each user is responsible for creating his or her own shared folders, as necessary, for others to use). What change management and productivity options in Windows 2000 can help in this situation?

OPTIONAL CASE PROJECTS FOR TEAMS

Team Case One

Mark Arnez asks you to form a team and work to achieve a consensus about the best decision flow structure for an IT organization in terms of helping the line staff to be most productive. Create a report to discuss and justify your ideas about the most ideal structure.

Team Case Two

Mark is interested in compiling a list of all of the factors that influence the cost of supporting one user and workstation on a network in a business. He asks you to form a team to develop this list and to report on research about typical per workstation costs.

4

ANALYZING SOFTWARE REQUIREMENTS

After reading this chapter and completing the exercises, you will be able to:

♦ Analyze an organization's user base, resources, user access, and user productivity

♦ Analyze an organization's existing software systems and databases

♦ Analyze corporate culture and software implementation

♦ Analyze system performance and security issues

♦ Analyze backup and disaster recovery methods

♦ Analyze technical support, user help, and training

Most companies have a significant investment in software and want to leverage these resources into the future. Your analysis in preparation for the Active Directory design must take into account the current software resources of an organization, such as workstation operating systems, business software, Web-based software, databases, and many kinds of specialty software. There is some software that you will publish or assign via Active Directory and other software that does not involve Active Directory, such as software offered through networked mainframe computers.

In this chapter you will learn to evaluate the software currently in use by an organization and the number of users associated with certain kinds of software. You will also learn about software performance and security issues. Finally, you will learn to analyze software security needs, fault tolerance methods, and disaster recovery plans.

EVALUATING THE COMPANY USER BASE AND RESOURCES

The software resource that will affect your Active Directory design the most is the user base of operating systems. Users in an organization may have a wide range of operating systems running on their workstations, from MS-DOS to Windows 2000 to UNIX. The sections that follow provide a summary of many of the operating systems you will encounter.

MS-DOS

In some cases, network clients will be running different versions of MS-DOS, such as MS-DOS 6.22 to support older 16-bit software. Some organizations still use customized and homegrown MS-DOS programs that were written to accomplish certain functions for those organizations. One example is a popular address correction program that is used for mass postal mailings. The program is unreliable when run from an MS-DOS window and so must be run using native MS-DOS. Another example is a specialized program written for a firm that tracks auto and truck fleet operations. Unfortunately, MS-DOS has many disadvantages for networking, and it is not designed to take full advantage of the features of a network operating system like Windows 2000 Server and Active Directory. For example, an MS-DOS client can not take advantage of published Active Directory resources such as shared folders, printers, and Dfs. Also, MS-DOS has limited network protocol support.

MS-DOS versions 3.2 and higher can connect to a Windows 2000 Server. The best connectivity solution is to upgrade to a later version of MS-DOS such as version 6.22 for the most connectivity options, including the NET command. The NET command enables the client to connect to start network services, connect to a server, use network printing, access a shared drive, and bind a protocol to a NIC.

 To enable MS-DOS to work with Microsoft Windows 2000 DHCP, MS-DOS should be installed with Microsoft Network Client version 3.0 for MS-DOS and with the real-mode TCP/IP driver.

Windows 3.1 and 3.11

With its GUI interface, Windows 3.1 is a step up from MS-DOS, but its networking abilities are almost as limited (except in later enhancements). With Windows 3.11 or Windows for Workgroups (WFW), Microsoft added significant network capabilities to Windows, such as options to have workgroups and set up a shared folder. WFW represents Windows' true first step into networking. It is a peer-to-peer network operating system, which means each computer on a network can communicate as an equal with other computers on the same network. Peer-to-peer communication capability opens the way for sharing resources such as files, folders, and printers. For example, the File Manager application in Windows 3.1 was upgraded in WFW to include icons to share directories with others.

Although WFW is a network operating system, it still has several limitations compared to a full-fledged network-capable operating system like Windows 95 or Windows 98. As is true for Windows 3.1, WFW is designed to run 16-bit applications and has a 640 KB conventional memory limitation. Applications from virtually all software vendors are now written for 32-bit operating systems without the 640 KB memory limit. For instance, Windows 3.1 and 3.11 are not compatible with most modern office software, such as Microsoft Office. Also, Microsoft support for Windows 3.11 is not as comprehensive as it is for later Microsoft operating systems. This is particularly important for obtaining specialized network software drivers, such as NIC drivers. As is true of MS-DOS, Windows 3.1 and 3.11 have significant limitations in two respects. First, they can not search for and view objects in Active Directory. Second, both operating systems are slow which can result in network bottlenecks along with lower user productivity.

 As you analyze the network operating systems used on a network, document those that are currently offering shared folders and printers. Next, discuss with the organization for which you are working whether it is more effective to share those resources from individual workstations or to centralize resource sharing through Active Directory, such as through published Dfs shared folders (see Chapter 3).

 To work with Microsoft Windows 2000 DHCP, Windows 3.1 and 3.11 should have the Microsoft 32-bit TCP/IP VxD installed.

Windows 95 and Windows 98

Windows 95 and Windows 98 are more solid clients for Windows 2000 Server-based networks because they have full peer-to-peer and network communication features. Both Windows 95 and Windows 98 have a greater capacity for folder sharing, printer sharing, network communication, workgroup activities, and other network operations than earlier versions of Windows. Both support TCP/IP, NetBEUI, and NWLink (Microsoft's IPX/SPX emulation protocol). Windows 95 introduces a GUI interface that is an improvement over previous versions of Windows, with new utilities such as Windows Explorer. Windows 98 adds more networking capabilities than Windows 95, such as connectivity for high-speed networks.

Because they are 32-bit operating systems, Windows 95 and Windows 98 can run 16-bit and 32-bit software applications. This makes them compatible with the newer 32-bit software that prevails on the market such as Microsoft Office, e-mail systems, and Web browsers.

Another advantage of Windows 95 and Windows 98 is their Plug and Play (PnP) capability, so that when you add hardware to a computer, the hardware is instantly recognized. This is handy when you install a NIC or an additional disk drive. Once the new component is installed, a computer running Windows 95/98 detects the presence of the component, as long as that component is designed for Plug and Play.

Although we take it for granted today, PnP represents a major step forward in making users, managers, and user support people more productive because they spend less time struggling to configure devices.

Microsoft Directory Service Client for Windows 95 and Windows 98

Microsoft offers the Directory Service Client (DSClient, see Chapter 1) software for Windows 95 and Windows 98 clients that connect to a Windows 2000 server. Directory Service Client does not provide the complete Active Directory client features that are built into Windows 2000 operating systems, but it does enable these non–Windows 2000 clients to profit from three important capabilities:

- Ability to use Kerberos authentication security

- Ability to view information published in Windows 2000 Active Directory, such as all network printers

- Enhanced domain logon performance

Windows 95 does not include the distributed file system client software, while Windows 98 and Windows NT 4.0 have the Dfs client software already installed. When you install DSClient in Windows 95, it installs the Dfs client software along with the Directory Service Client software. Dfs enables you to set up shared folders so that the client only needs to query the Dfs services for a hierarchy of shared folder locations, without knowing which server contains the folder.

Windows NT Workstation

Windows NT Workstation has all the peer-to-peer and network communication advantages of Windows 95 and Windows 98, and with version 4.0, Windows NT Workstation uses nearly the same GUI interface as used in Windows 95 and Windows 98. As is true for Windows 2000 operating systems, the Windows NT Workstation operating system runs in a privileged mode to insulate it from "crashes" caused by software applications. This characteristic has given it a reputation as a reliable workstation operating system for business applications. A disadvantage is that some 16-bit programs have trouble running under Windows NT Workstation because they attempt to directly access hardware components, an activity not permitted in the privileged mode. Early versions of Windows NT Workstation 4.0 that do not have service pack updates may lack some drivers that are needed for printers, NICs, pointing devices, sound devices, and other devices. Later versions of Windows NT Workstation and early versions that have service pack updates installed have a full range of drivers.

A unique advantage of Windows NT Workstation (as well as Windows 2000 Professional) is that it can act as a small server on a network. Up to 10 computers can effectively access Windows NT Workstation for network file services, such as running software or storing data files. Another advantage of Windows NT Workstation is that if users have installed service pack 3 or higher, it supports Dfs and Active Directory access to find network objects, such as computers, printers, and software.

Windows 2000 Professional

Windows 2000 Professional is an upgrade of Windows NT Workstation 4.0 with millions of lines of new code. Windows 2000 Professional has even more networking capabilities than Windows NT Workstation, support for new peripheral devices, and full PnP and energy-saving capabilities that are not available in Windows NT.

There are several advantages to using Windows 2000 Professional on a Windows 2000 Server network. The most obvious advantage is that Windows 2000 Professional is written to be fully compatible with Windows 2000 Server and Active Directory services. Another advantage is that Windows 2000 Professional is up to 25 percent faster than Windows NT Workstation. This translates into faster network response, because other workstations spend less time waiting for Windows 2000 Professional to complete its work, compared with earlier Windows versions.

 Slow operating systems and slow workstation hardware have a higher TCO because they make networks slower and contribute to network bottlenecks. Consider this effect on user productivity when you analyze an organization's needs.

Possibly the most important advantage of Windows 2000 Professional is its IntelliMirror features, which help users to be more productive through fast installation, automated configuration, versatile data handling, and recovery from problem situations.

Windows Millennium Edition

Developed after Windows 2000 Professional and targeted for the home computer market, Windows Millennium Edition (ME) is a Windows operating system offered as the next step in the Windows 95/98 track. New features in Windows ME include more capabilities for handling home movies, videos, music reproduction, and home photos. The operating system also includes more protection from inadvertently erasing or overwriting system files, a feature modeled after the capabilities of Windows 2000.

In addition to home entertainment, Windows ME offers better handling of PnP devices, including anticipated enhancements to enable the control of home appliances, such as thermostat settings. Also, there are enhancements to support broader networking and Internet connectivity, including new options for using high-speed Internet connections. Windows ME provides automated setup of home-based networks, and includes built-in DSClient capabilities for access to Active Directory on business and professional networks.

Because Windows ME is targeted for home use, it is less suited for business and professional use on enterprise networks. This is because Windows ME does not have Windows 2000 Professional's industrial-strength focus on business use of the Internet, protected system operation from crashes, reliability, power, and mobile business computing capabilities.

Macintosh

The Mac OS was developed for the Macintosh computer, which has long offered many GUI-based features to make computing easier to learn and execute. Macintosh computers connect to Windows 2000 Server-based networks by using the AppleTalk protocol or through TCP/IP. When AppleTalk is used for communication, Macintosh computers are linked to the network by setting up the Windows 2000 Server Services for Macintosh, which include the following components:

- File Server for Macintosh (MacFile)
- Print Server for Macintosh (MacPrint)
- AppleTalk Protocol

Using MacFile, a Windows 2000 server becomes a file server for Macintosh computers, as well as for computers running Microsoft operating systems. Through MacPrint and AppleTalk, Macintosh clients can print documents on network printers that are managed by a Windows 2000 server, and non-Macintosh clients can print files on printers shared by Macintosh computers. The Services for Macintosh also include the ability to route AppleTalk and to set up remote access for Macintosh computers via modem and telephone lines.

UNIX

There are several versions of UNIX operating systems that you may find on a network. All versions have the capability to act as host computers, and they can access resources on other computers that support the **Network File System (NFS) protocol**, which provides file transfer capabilities. For Windows NT Server, support for UNIX clients involves implementing third-party disk-sharing software that employs the NFS protocol, such as Intergraph DiskShare. In Windows 2000 Server, UNIX computers are supported by installing the Windows 2000 component for UNIX file and print services.

Analyzing Workstation Operating System Upgrades

Some organizations regularly upgrade their users' operating systems when an upgrade becomes available. Upgrades are often made following an assessment of how the upgrade will benefit the company in terms of new capabilities, increased user productivity, and lower TCO. Other factors in assessing whether to upgrade are the one-time purchase cost, the cost in terms of employee hours to perform the upgrade, and the ongoing support costs.

When you analyze an organization's user base and its workstation operating systems, consider how upgrades and rollouts of software are performed, and how the upgrades and rollouts will affect Active Directory design. Some organizations use a rollout period during which operating system upgrades are performed. For a school or college, the upgrades may be rolled out during the summer when there are few or no classes. This avoids interruptions when the school year is in full swing, in the fall and spring. The workstations in labs and in teachers' offices can be upgraded while teachers and students are on vacation. Active Directory services, such as publishing new software and creating accounts for new teachers, can be performed at the same time. Also, new services may be introduced that correspond to the updated capabilities of the operating system upgrades, such as additional printer or software access through the network.

Consider, for example, Interstate Security Bank, which has decided to upgrade workstations from Windows 98 to Windows 2000 Professional in all of the regional offices. This upgrade involves several steps:

1. Setting up group policies that affect the installations and the way employees use Windows 2000.

2. Setting up security restrictions in the group policies.

3. Creating roaming profiles for users.

4. Installing RIS on the regional office servers so that employees can perform their own upgrades.

5. Developing training documentation.

6. Setting a time range for employees to perform the installations, such as during a specific month.

Another consideration for the workstation upgrades and accompanying changes to Active Directory is to avoid performing them during busy IT and business cycle periods. For Interstate Security Bank, which is typical of many organizations, these are:

- Month's end, when the branch and regional offices perform reconciliation and posting. Posting is a process in which certain accounting records are tallied and committed to, so they cannot be changed.

- Year's end, when the branch, regional, and national offices perform reconciliation and posting of accounting records for year-to-date statements to customers.

- Year's end, when the branch, regional, and national offices prepare W2 income tax statements for employees and 1099 interest statements for customers, according to the requirements of the Internal Revenue Service.

- Fiscal year end (often different from the calendar year end), when the branch, regional, and national offices perform a final reconciliation and posting of all records, and initialize accounting systems for the new fiscal year.

- Twice-a-year auditing periods, when the auditors examine the records at the branch, regional, and national offices. Most bank auditors keep accounting and IT personnel busy providing information about computer processes and security.

Determining the User Base

Analyzing the types of operating systems in use by an organization involves determining the following information about the user base:

- The number of users

- The operating systems running on those users' computers

- The locations of the users

For example, Jefferson Philately has 295 users all in one location. Interstate Security Bank has 2100 users spread out in many locations including the main office, the regional offices, and the branch offices in five states. The user base for York Industries is even more complex because it spans seven countries: Canada, England, France, Japan, Argentina, Poland, and the United States. One way to assess the user base is to create a table of this information, such as Table 4-1 for York Industries.

Table 4-1   User Base Form

Operating System	Number of Users	Country Location	Future Upgrade Plans
Windows 2000			
Windows NT			
Windows 98			
Windows 95			
UNIX			
Mac OS			

One way to determine the operating system that is used by a networked computer via Windows 2000 Server is to double-click My Network Places, double-click Entire Network, click the Search for computers link, click the Search Now button to display the computers in the domain, right-click the computer, and click Properties to view the dialog box shown in Figure 4-1.

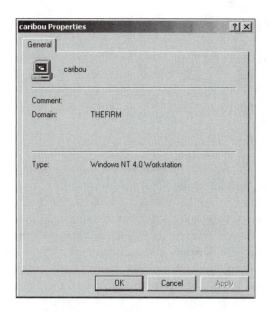

Figure 4-1   Determining the operating system of a networked computer

Besides determining the total number of users, it is valuable to analyze the typical number of users who are logged on at any one time, and the amount of network traffic that they create. This information is valuable for the following purposes:

- To help size Active Directory
- To determine where to locate DCs and global catalog servers
- To optimize performance by creating sites

To view the number of users from a Windows NT 4.0 server, start the Server Manager from the Administrative Tools (Common) menu, click the Computer menu, and click Properties. Alternately, you can go to the Control Panel and double-click the Server icon to view information about connections to the server. The Server dialog box shows the number of active sessions, as in Figure 4-2. The dialog box also shows the number of open files, file locks, and named pipes. The open file information shows if a file is in use. A **file lock** means that no one else can update or access a specified file because someone (or the operating system) has it open and can update information, and **named pipes** are open communication links. The buttons at the bottom of the screen are used to view information about connections in use, or to set service parameters. For example, when you click Users, a list appears of all users currently connected to the server along with a list of resources in use by each user, such as shared folders and printers (try viewing users and resources in Hands-on Project 4-1). The Shares button enables you to view the same information, but by resource instead of by user. For example, you can view users who are accessing a shared folder or printers. This can be a source of information about which software resources are typically accessed by users. The In Use button provides information about all resources, such as printers, that are currently being used.

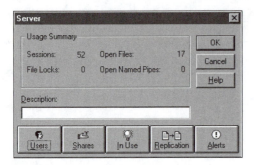

Figure 4-2   Viewing server resource use in Windows NT 4.0

On a Windows 2000 server, you can view logged-on users by starting the Computer Management tool from the Administrative Tools menu, double-clicking Shared Folders under System Tools in the tree, and clicking Sessions. The right pane shows the users who are connected with active sessions, the computer names of the clients, the operating systems used by the clients, the number of files each user has open, the connected time, the idle time, and whether users are logged on as guests. Depending on how the client is connected, one client may have two or more connections, such as a network connection for the computer and a connection for the user account.

 Some database connections take up two user sessions, one to connect to the server and one to connect to the database.

You can also view information about which shared folders are being accessed by users when you double-click Shares instead of Sessions in the tree under Shared Folders (see Figure 4-3). The # *Client Redirections* column shows the number of clients using shares. Notice in Figure 4-3 that some shares, such as C$ and print$, are set up by default as hidden ($ after the share name hides the share on the network). The print$ share enables you to view the number of clients currently using the server as a print server. You can view which files are in use by clicking Open Files under Shared Folders. The right pane shows the open file name, who is accessing the file, the operating system of the client, file locks, and permissions mode, such as Read+Write. The open file information shows if a file is in use (try Hands-on Project 4-2).

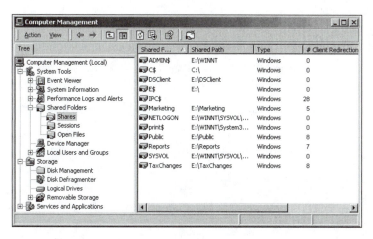

Figure 4-3   Viewing server resource use in Windows 2000

Using Network Monitor to Study User-based Network Traffic

You can obtain additional information about the user base and number of connections on a network by employing Microsoft Network Monitor. To use Network Monitor, install both Network Monitor Driver and Network Monitor as Windows components. The **Network Monitor Driver** is a protocol that works along with Network Monitor to enable you to monitor a network. **Network Monitor** is a Microsoft tool that captures and distills network performance information.

The Network Monitor Driver is installed in Windows 2000 Server by using the Network and Dial-up Connections tool. Click Start, point to Settings, click Network and Dial-up Connections, right-click Local Area Connection, click Properties, click Install, double-click Protocol, and double-click Network Monitor Driver (see Figure 4-4).

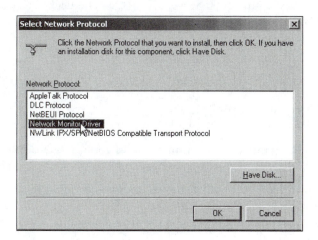

Figure 4-4   Installing Network Monitor Driver

The steps for installing Network Monitor are:

1. Open the Control Panel Add/Remove Programs tool.

2. Click Add/Remove Windows Components. If the Windows Components Wizard dialog box is not automatically started, click the Components button to start it.

3. Double-click Management and Monitoring Tools in the Windows Components dialog box.

4. Check the box for Network Monitor Tools, as in Figure 4-5, and click OK.

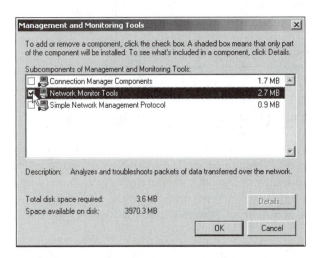

Figure 4-5   Installing Network Monitor

5. Click Next.

6. If requested, insert the Windows 2000 Server CD-ROM and click OK. (If a second dialog box is displayed, provide the path to the \I386 folder on the CD-ROM and click OK again.)

7. Click Finish.

8. Close the Add/Remove Programs window, and then close Control Panel.

Once Network Monitor Driver and Network Monitor are installed, you are ready to begin monitoring the traffic on a network. To start Network Monitor:

1. Click Start, point to Programs, point to Administrative Tools, and click Network Monitor.

2. Click OK if there is an information box that reminds you to select the network to monitor, or to use the local area network as the default; and then click the network you want to monitor in the Select a network dialog box. Click OK to close the Select a network dialog box.

3. Maximize one or both Network Monitor screens, if the display is not maximized.

4. Click the Start Capture button on the button bar to start capturing network performance data.

5. View the data displayed on the screen, such as % Network Utilization or the Network Statistics information (see Figure 4-6).

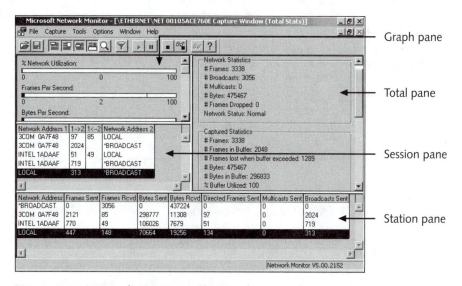

Figure 4-6   Network Monitor capturing data

6. Use the scroll bars in each of the four windows to view the information they offer.

7. If you want to pause data capturing, click the Pause button on the button bar and click it again later to resume capturing. When you are finished, click the Stop Capture button on the button bar.

8. Close Network Monitor.

Table 4-2 summarizes the general information about user and network activity that can be obtained through the four Network Monitor panes (see Figure 4-6).

Table 4-2   Network Monitor Panes

Pane	Information Provided in the Pane
Graph	Provides horizontal bar graphs of the following: % Network Utilization, Frames Per Second, Bytes Per Second, Broadcasts Per Second, and Multicasts Per Second
Total	Provides total statistics about network activity that originates from or that is sent to the computer (station) that is using Network Monitor and includes many statistics in each of the following categories: Network Statistics, Captured Statistics, Per Second Statistics, Network Card (MAC) Statistics, Network Card (MAC) Error Statistics
Session	Provides statistics about traffic from other computers on the network, which include the MAC (device) address of each computer's NIC, and data about the number of frames sent from and received by each computer
Station	Provides total statistics on all communicating network stations, which include: Network (device) Address of each communicating computer, Frames Sent, Frames Received, Bytes Sent, Bytes Received, Directed Frames Sent, Multicasts Sent, and Broadcasts Sent

The Graph pane presents a snapshot of the current network performance:

- *% Network Utilization:* Shows how much of the network bandwidth is in use.

- *Frames Per Second:* Shows total traffic in frames for broadcasts, unicasts, and multicasts. (A **frame** is a unit of data transmitted across the network. A **broadcast** sends one copy of each frame to all points on the network. A **unicast** sends one copy of each frame to each designated destination on a network, while a **multicast** sends one frame to multiple destinations.)

- *Bytes Per Second:* Shows total traffic in bytes for broadcasts, unicasts, and multicasts.

- *Broadcasts Per Second:* Shows how much network traffic is due to broadcasts from servers, workstations, and print servers.

- *Multicasts Per Second:* Shows how much network traffic is due to multimedia servers.

The Total pane shows statistics about the general activity on the network and is a valuable tool for assessing overall network performance since starting the session to monitor network statistics. Another valuable feature of this tool is that it provides information about network error conditions. There are five groupings of the total statistics: Network Statistics, Captured Statistics, Per Second Statistics, Network Card (MAC) Statistics, and Network Card (MAC) Error Statistics. Table 4-3 summarizes the statistics in the Total pane.

Media access control (MAC) is a level or layer of standardized network communications that examines physical address (address of a computer's network interface card, for example) information in frames, and controls the way devices share communications on a network.

Table 4-3   Network Monitor Total Pane Statistics

Grouping	Individual Statistics
Network Statistics: Total statistics that have been gathered since starting the current monitoring session	■ # Frames: Number of frames transmitted ■ # Broadcasts: Number of broadcasts transmitted to every point on the network ■ # Multicasts: Number of multicasts sent to specific points on the network since starting the current monitoring session ■ # Bytes: Number of bytes (characters) transmitted ■ # Frames Dropped: Number of frames that have been discarded due to problems ■ Network Status: Indicates if the network is running normally, and on an Ethernet network displays the word "Normal," while on a token ring network the status will show if the ring is intact or is beaconing
Captured Statistics: Total statistics that have been gathered since starting the current capture session	■ # Frames: Number of frames that have been examined for reporting ■ # Frames in Buffer: Number of frames in the file created for the capture to hold data for the capture session (so you can determine how fast the file is filling up) ■ Frames lost when buffer exceeded: Number of frames that could not be analyzed because the capture file is filled to the limit ■ # Bytes: Number of bytes that have been examined for reporting ■ Bytes in Buffer: Number of bytes in the file created to hold data for the capture ■ % Buffer Utilized: Amount of the total space allocated for the capture file that is already filled with data ■ # Frames Dropped: Number of frames not analyzed by Network Monitor because of problems with the frames, or because the capture file is full
Per Second Statistics: Data measured on a per second basis	■ % Network Utilization: Amount of the network that is active in a given second ■ # Frames/second: Frames transmitted from all sources within a second ■ # Bytes/second: Bytes transmitted from all sources within a second ■ # Broadcasts/second: Broadcasts transmitted from all sources within a second ■ # Multicasts/second: Multicasts transmitted from all sources within a second
Network Card (MAC) Statistics: Data gathered by the network card in a server or workstation that is currently running Network Monitor Driver	■ # Frames: Number of frames monitored from all sources ■ # Broadcasts: Number of broadcasts monitored from all sources ■ # Multicasts: Number of multicasts monitored from all sources ■ # Bytes: Number of bytes monitored from all sources

4

Table 4-3 Network Monitor Total Pane Statistics (continued)

Grouping	Individual Statistics
Network Card (MAC) Error Statistics: Error data that is detected at the network card on the MAC or frame level	■ CRC Errors: Cyclic redundancy check errors in which the size of the frame calculated at the time it was sent does not match the size when it was received ■ # Frames Dropped (No Buffers): Frames that could not be analyzed because the capture file is full ■ # Frames Dropped (Hardware): Frames that could not be analyzed because of hardware or physical network problems at the network interface card

The Session pane provides information about any two computers that are currently communicating, which includes the network addresses of those computers and the number of frames transmitted between them. The Session pane provides a good snapshot of the number of users who are currently communicating on the network, which is useful in determining the user base at any one point in time. One session represents full communication from start to finish, and consists of the following captured information:

- *Network Address 1:* The physical or device address of the network interface card that is installed in the computer that starts the communication. This information often includes the name of the card, such as Intel, and the address represented as a hexadecimal number.

- *1 → 2:* The number of frames sent from the computer that started the communication session to its companion computer in the session.

- *1 ← 2:* The number of frames sent from the companion computer to the computer that started the session.

- *Network Address 2:* The physical or device address of the network interface card that is installed in the companion computer in the two-way session.

The Station pane also provides a valuable snapshot of the user base, because it records information about the individual workstations and servers that are communicating, as well as total broadcasts and multicasts. If you scroll through this pane, you can determine the number of workstations that are contributing to the network utilization. Table 4-4 explains the information that is collected in the Station pane.

Table 4-4   Network Monitor Station Pane Statistics

Statistic	Description
Network Address	Physical or device address in hexadecimal that is assigned to the connected workstation's or server's network interface card
Frames Sent	Number of frames sent by the workstation or server
Frames Rcvd	Number of frames from other computers that have been received by the workstation or server
Bytes Sent	Number of bytes sent by the workstation or server
Bytes Rcvd	Number of bytes from other computers that have been received by the workstation or server
Directed Frames Sent	Number of frames that have been sent by the workstation or server that are not broadcast or multicast frames, such as unicasts
Multicasts Sent	Number of multicast frames that the workstation or server has sent, such as those for multimedia applications
Broadcasts Sent	Number of broadcast frames that the workstation or server has sent, such as frames advertising that the computer is connected and active

The information captured by Network Monitor also includes traffic generated by network devices such as print servers and routers.

When you analyze the user base of an organization, ask if the organization has established benchmarks by using network analysis tools such as Network Monitor. A **benchmark** is a measurement standard for hardware or software used to establish performance baselines under varying loads or circumstances. Some organizations establish benchmarks to have information about typical network performance situations so that they can plan for growth and use the information to help troubleshoot problems. Common benchmarks are:

- Slow, average, and peak network activity in relation to the work patterns at your organization

- Typical network utilization during slow, average, and peak periods

- Network activity that is related to specific protocols, such as TCP/IP

- Typical broadcast and multicast traffic

- Network activity that is related to specific servers and host computers

- Network activity that is related to specific workstations

- Network activity on individual subnets or portions of a larger network

- Network traffic related to WAN transmissions

- Network traffic created by particular software, such as client/server and multimedia applications

If benchmarks do not exist, you can use Network Monitor to gather benchmarks for your analysis. For example, you might observe %Network Utilization, Frames Per Second, Broadcasts Per Second, and Multicasts Per Second in the Graph or Total panes in relation to the number of users shown to be active in the Station pane. Acquire these statistics during slow, average, and peak periods.

Gathering benchmarks on broadcasts and multicasts can provide information about the traffic generated by workstations, and by servers that are broadcasting their presence on the network or that are running multimedia applications over the network. Information from the Session and Station panes can help you determine if there are specific workstations or servers that are particularly active in their transmissions. For example, a server at Jefferson Philately that is used to publish software may not be as active as a server that stores the database of customer service information. Try Hands-on Project 4-3 to practice using Network Monitor.

The Windows 2000 System Monitor is another tool that can be used to study network activity.

ANALYZING USER ACCESS AND PRODUCTIVITY

Part of analyzing the user base includes analyzing user access patterns and how existing resources enable users to be productive. One way to approach analyzing user access patterns is by using Network Monitor to study low, medium, and high use of resources. A common peak usage pattern, for example, occurs when all users first come to work and log on to the network. There may be other peak or slow periods throughout the day, depending on business patterns and other factors unique to an organization. For instance, the customer service representatives at Jefferson Philately are often at their busiest entering new orders during the noon hours for the four time zones in the U.S. and in the evenings. User access patterns are valuable to analyze for the following reasons:

- Determining the placement and number of DCs
- Determining the placement and number of global catalog servers
- Tuning access to Active Directory and network resources by implementing subnets and Active Directory site designations

Monitoring user access patterns can directly contribute to user productivity, because you can use this information to determine how to reduce delays in access for users. For example, your monitoring may determine that the users at a branch site of an organization sometimes have to wait while searching the global catalog on the main office's server over a slow WAN link, or all branch office users may have a long wait as each account's authorization is checked when users log on in the morning. Your research may show that users' productivity can be increased through faster access when a DC and global catalog server is placed in the branch office.

When you analyze user access patterns, be sure to consider the following checklist of questions:

- What types of user access are associated with low, medium, and high monitored network traffic?

- What user access patterns exist on local networks and across WANs?

- How is user access affected by branch offices, subsidiaries, and partner relationships?

- How is user access affected by outsourcing relationships?

- What productivity needs are associated with user access, such as improving the speed of access to make users more productive?

4

EVALUATING EXISTING SOFTWARE AND SOFTWARE SYSTEMS

Access to software is vital for all organizations. When you analyze the software currently in use at an organization, look for the following general types of software:

- Accounting software

- Office software

- E-mail software

- Specialized business software

- Development software

Most organizations have some combination of accounting and administrative software modules that include general ledger, accounts receivable, accounts payable, payroll, purchasing, and human resources. General ledger is a core software module that is used to track accounting activity in terms of income and expenses. Other modules that involve financial transactions feed into the general ledger module, such as accounts receivable, accounts payable, payroll, and purchasing. The accounts receivable module is used to track money owed to an organization, while accounts payable is a module for tracking money that the organization owes. Payroll modules enable an organization to pay its employees, and are sometimes combined with human resources modules that contain information about the employees.

Some organizations purchase accounting packages that can be adapted for their particular needs, and other organizations write their own accounting software. Typically, the payroll and human resources modules involve the most maintenance, because federal and state employment laws change yearly. When you analyze accounting software, Active Directory issues focus especially on creating security groups and group policies that establish reliable access and security.

Another factor in your analysis is determining how different modules communicate in an integrated accounting system, particularly if the modules are stored in different folders and their databases are stored in still different folders or on different servers. For example, because accounts receivable, accounts payable, payroll, and purchasing feed into the general ledger, it is necessary to make sure that users of these modules have the appropriate security access to the folders and databases that hold the general ledger module. A payroll clerk, for example, will need security access to that portion of the general ledger that is updated for the payroll checks that he runs—but not full access that would enable him to make other changes to the general ledger.

Large organizations, such as Interstate Security Bank and York Industries, often have "cafeteria" style payroll benefits with various health and retirement plans, each having different tax sheltering options. These payroll systems can be very complex to maintain, and yearly changes to state and federal tax laws can result in complex programming tasks. Large organizations often need secured test folders and test databases in which to make programming changes. Further, the specific testing and security requirements will be handled differently by each organization. As part of your analysis, find out how an organization handles program changes and testing. Also, research the requirements imposed by a company's financial auditors. Consider developing a checklist of the issues in these payroll systems such as:

- Anticipated programming changes to health, retirement, disability, and life insurance plans that may affect OU and security group designs

- Anticipated changes to programs because of payroll-based federal and state laws that will require special Active Directory structures for implementation and testing, such as OUs and security groups

- Anticipated requirements imposed by auditors for evaluating payroll-based program changes, such as creating a secure Active Directory OU for tracking and evaluating program changes

Another factor in analyzing accounting software is that upgrades are handled by the software vendor, or by a team of specialized applications programmers in the organization, which means that these programmers need special security access during upgrades, but their access security is changed after upgrades are completed.

Office software is usually composed of modules that include a word processor, spreadsheet, and database software. Other software may be implemented for office functions, such as Web design software, business reference software, a dictionary, an encyclopedia, and slide-making software. Often there is a need to create and publish shared data folders for users, and to offer Dfs. There may also be a need to set up security groups to limit access to shared folders. Office software is often installed and upgraded by individual users, which means that security and shared folders must be designed to enable users to perform these functions.

 Sometimes office software databases are accessed by multiple people on a network. Large databases and some database queries can be a source of extra network traffic and necessitate the creation of subnets to help control the traffic, which influences how sites are created in Active Directory.

E-mail software is important to most organizations. Some organizations use only one e-mail system and some use multiple e-mail systems, such as one system for internal e-mail that works with another SMTP-based (Simple Mail Transfer Protocol) mail system for Internet e-mail. Also, some organizations use calendar and scheduling software in combination with e-mail systems so that meetings can be scheduled electronically. E-mail systems may require firewalls for inbound and outbound security, and to reduce the likelihood that a virus can be sent or received.

Specialized business software can include all kinds of software for business functions such as inventory, manufacturing, marketing, fundraising, management, e-commerce, and others. Jefferson Philately, for example, has developed its own specialized software to handle subscription programs, mass mailings, and marketing promotions. Interstate Security Bank has developed software to enable it to act as a clearinghouse for automatic deposit payrolls. York Industries has specialized manufacturing software that controls the production of circuit boards that are used in appliances. Another York Industries software system performs a quality assurance check on specific circuits to make sure they are working before a board goes into an appliance. York Industries' engineers use computer-aided design (CAD) and computer-aided manufacturing (CAM) software to help design and manufacture appliances.

Many companies develop their own software or perform their own modifications to vendors' software packages to customize that software for specific business needs. The application development programmers in these companies may use compilers, such as COBOL, C++, Pascal, Fortran, and Basic. They also may use RAD (rapid application development) tools, such as Visual Basic. Developers may have software tools for developing reports and queries. These tools may influence Active Directory design in that a separate area, such as a development domain, may be created in which to develop and test programs before they are copied into a production domain for users to access.

Try Hands-on Project 4-4 to practice assessing the software used in an organization.

ANALYZING DATABASES AND DATA STRUCTURES

Many software systems store data in one or more databases. Many of the earliest databases are **flat file databases**, simple structures that consist of basic files, often in the same directory, in which data is sequentially stored on a first-in basis. The front of a file contains the data stored first, and the back of the file contains data stored most recently. Data that is stored in multiple files is linked by one or more programs. Security for a flat file database is set on files and folders. Access to data in flat file databases is typically slower than for other types of databases, particularly for complex or large data queries.

Network databases are a form of flat file database that use a basic table in which to store data or that use tables that are in a sequential relationship: one table is connected to the next table, which is connected to the next table. Security for network databases is established in a way that is similar to flat file databases, on files and folders, but access to a table can be faster than that for regular flat file databases (depending on the design).

The most efficient type of database (also depending on the design) is a relational database. **Relational databases** consist of multiple tables that have optimized relationships to one another for fastest data access. The process of optimizing the table relationships is called normalization. The security for a relational database has several levels, because it can be set on files and folders as well as internally in the database. Internally, the database administrator can specify what users or user group can access the database, specific tables in the database, specific rows or columns of data, and even specific cells. Access to data and data queries can be very fast in relational databases.

Besides the ability to normalize the database, there are other advantages to using relational databases. One advantage is that one or more views of specific data can be created, so that data can be accessed without having to search the entire database. Another is that statistics can be generated for a data query or report to document the fastest routes through which to obtain data. If the data changes over time, the statistics can be regenerated to establish the fastest search routes.

The access to databases and tables in many relational database systems is facilitated by Microsoft **Open Database Connectivity (ODBC)**, which is an application programming interface in Windows-based operating systems and a standard for accessing data inside a relational database. ODBC is designed to enable an application to use standard methods for accessing data inside a database. This is accomplished through three elements. First, the application must be written to use ODBC. Next, there must be an ODBC driver that is called by the application and that acts as an intermediary between the application and the database. Last, the database must be designed to be ODBC-compliant, which means that it offers a doorway through which ODBC can access data. ODBC is used by many database query and report-writing applications developed by Microsoft and by many third-party vendors.

Understanding the databases used by an organization and the types of access to databases is important for several reasons. One reason is that many organizations use ODBC to enable report-writing software, such as Crystal Reports, and office software, such as Microsoft Access and Excel, to access the contents of databases. These organizations typically make sure that the most current ODBC drivers are available to authorized users, such as those in specific security groups, so that they can download the drivers from a network server. New and upgraded versions of report-writing software and other office software require the most current versions of ODBC. Figure 4-7 illustrates ODBC drivers that are included with Windows 2000.

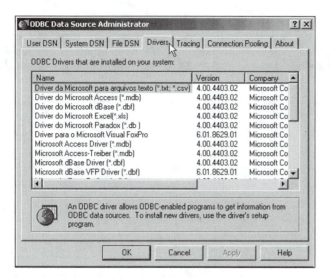

Figure 4-7   ODBC drivers

Another reason for understanding how databases are accessed is so that you can design Active Directory OUs and security groups to make sure that database access is restricted to authorized users. ODBC is a powerful access tool and in the wrong hands can be used to compromise an entire database, unless the access is well protected.

A last reason for analyzing the databases used by an organization is so that you know the user base associated with each database. You may need to design OUs and security groups to help manage the kinds of users and the number of users who access each database.

 ODBC drivers are available for most versions of Windows and are usually installed automatically with Microsoft Access. The latest ODBC drivers for any Microsoft operating system, such as Windows 2000, can be obtained from Microsoft. Some organizations regularly obtain the latest ODBC drivers for the operating systems they use and make these drivers available for authorized downloading through a server.

Develop a checklist or form for your analysis of an organization to help you look for typical software and databases, as illustrated in Table 4-5 for York Industries.

Table 4-5   Software and Database Analysis Form

Software	Vendor/ Version(s)	Number of Users	Country Locations	Server/Client Network Locations	Future Upgrade Plans
General ledger (GL)					
Accounts payable (AP)					
Accounts receivable (AR)					
Payroll					
Human resources (HR)					
Purchasing					
Word processing					
Spreadsheet					
Database					
Database access driver (ODBC)					
Report writing software					
E-mail software					
Specialized software					
Manufacturing software					
Inventory software					

ANALYZING THE EXISTING CORPORATE CULTURE AND SOFTWARE IMPLEMENTATION

In any corporation, business, or other organization, the "corporate culture" can affect how software is implemented. The corporate culture represents a set of conventions or what sociologists call *folkways* and *mores*, practices that everyone is expected to follow. Folkways are behaviors that are expected; however, people simply frown on you for not following them. Mores are behaviors that are expected and for which you will receive a punishment if they are not followed.

In some corporations, folkways dictate that relationships and dress are informal. Any employee can freely talk with a manager or the president about a suggestion or a concern.

In other corporations, there are mores about behavior, such as firing an employee who is too talkative, or who goes over a supervisor's head to lodge a concern directly with a manager.

A basic analysis of the corporate culture can provide you with insights about how software is implemented and maintained. For example, at one university the mores are that all programming changes to accounting software and all new reports are made by applications programmers only. In a different situation, an accounting firm, the company mores dictate that the accounting manager oversees all programming changes and makes most of the changes himself.

Many IT departments have a set of folkways and mores that employees follow. For example, the computer operators in one IT organization may be prohibited from creating accounts, tuning servers, or setting security because only system programmers perform these functions. In another IT organization, the computer operators may handle all of these functions, because the primary job of the system programmers is to implement new servers and then turn them over to the operators for day-to-day administration.

As the examples in this section show, many of the issues related to corporate culture affect Active Directory design in terms of the delegation of tasks and how security is established. The corporate culture also determines who installs and manages software—sometimes a sensitive issue. Plan to learn about the corporate culture as a way to understand how decisions are made, reflecting an organization's relationship to its software assets.

A checklist for analyzing corporate culture can include:

- Who decides to purchase software?

- Who funds software purchases?

- Who installs software?

- Who manages software after it is installed?

ANALYZING SOFTWARE SYSTEM PERFORMANCE ISSUES

Software system performance directly affects user productivity on a network. Slow or hard-to-access systems mean that users spend valuable time waiting for computer systems when they could be doing work. Find out what software performance is acceptable in an organization, and design Active Directory services to match the need. Consider the following examples:

- In an investment services company, software is accessed over a WAN link using Terminal Services, but the access is slow. The company perceives that it is saving money by using Terminal Services, which is why they have implemented this structure. Your analysis may be able to show the company how to lower their TCO by suggesting that they publish software instead of using Terminal Services, and thus have users perform only a one-time installation of software over the WAN link.

- At a remote manufacturing plant, users must wait for logon authentication after entering their account names and passwords because they have to access a remote DC. Logon authentication can be significantly speeded up by installing a combined DC and global catalog server on the same LAN that those users access, so they do not have to wait for the remote connection.

- In a nuclear research lab, performance is not an issue, but security is critical, because files must never leave a top-security area. One way to guarantee the security is to use Terminal Services, and set up access security so that the files can only be accessed from a server's hard drive in the security area. The security ensures that the files cannot be copied to another server or computer, and the hard drive in the server is permanently installed and guarded.

- At Jefferson Philately, the data files used by customer service representatives must always be available for use, even when a hard drive fails. They can ensure performance and fault tolerance in this situation by having more than one domain controller, and by using Dfs to spread the data files across multiple servers. In this way, performance is improved because the customer service representatives are not contending for the same server and hard drive. Also, if a server or hard drive fails, the data can be obtained from another Dfs server.

- York Industries maintains expensive banks of modems and multiple telephone lines so that users can access company networks, including software and user files, through RAS (Remote Access Services) servers. One recommendation for York Industries to set up **virtual private networks (VPNs)** at each company site so that users can access the company networks through the Internet. A VPN is similar to a tunnel through a larger network—such as the Internet, an enterprise network, or both—that is restricted to only designated member clients. This enables each company site to pay for one or two Internet telecommunications lines for multiple users to access, instead of paying for 40 to 100 regular telephone lines and maintaining the same number of modems at each company site. The TCO for remote access can be reduced by over 80 percent, and user access to resources is even faster through high-speed Internet access options, such as **Integrated Services Digital Network (ISDN)** and **digital subscriber line (DSL)**. ISDN delivers data services over specialized digital telephone lines using 64 Kbps channels. The channels are combined to offer different types of services; for example, an ISDN basic rate interface consists of three channels. Two are 64 Kbps channels for data, voice, and graphics transmissions. The third channel is a 16 Kbps channel used for communications signaling. The theoretical limit of ISDN is 622 Mbps. DSL technology uses regular copper telephone lines that enable upstream (sending from the client) communication at up to 2.3 Mbps, and downstream (receiving at the client) communication at up to 55 Mbps and higher. These and other high-speed telecommunications technologies can significantly improve remote access to software as compared to regular 56- Kbps asynchronous modem communications over dial-up lines.

Security for a VPN can be configured through Active Directory by limiting access via any of the following four means (try Hands-on Project 4-5 to set up remote access policies for a VPN server):

- IP address
- User account
- Network subnet address
- Remote access policies (including using authentication and encryption)

Figure 4-8 illustrates the dialog box used to configure authentication in the remote access policies of a VPN server.

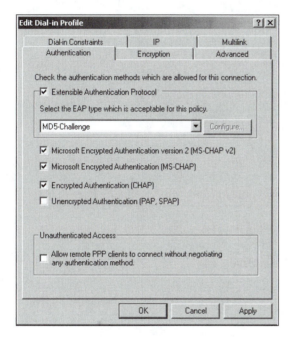

Figure 4-8   Configuring authentication

As a last example, consider Interstate Security Bank, which uses a client/server accounting system at their main and regional offices. Currently, they have set up this system so that the accounting software runs on a Windows 2000 server and so that the database software runs on a Windows 2000 Datacenter server. The performance is fine at the main office, but access for the branch offices over a WAN link is slow to each regional office's Datacenter server, particularly when the branch offices need to generate a report or to query data on a workstation screen. One way to improve performance is to place a database server in each branch office, using Dfs to replicate and update the databases at each site (with the master database at the respective regional office), as shown in Figure 4-9. Dfs and Active Directory replication can be set up so that it occurs at specific light-business intervals to keep the WAN link free for other work, such as at 7:30 in the morning before the branch offices open, and during the 2:00 business lull in the afternoon.

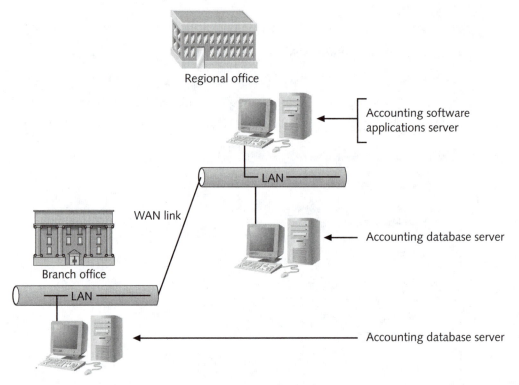

Regional office

Accounting software applications server

LAN

WAN link

Branch office

LAN

Accounting database server

Accounting database server

Figure 4-9   Using multiple database servers

Analyzing Software Security Issues

To analyze software security, you will need to link the software used by an organization with whomever accesses it, and also determine what security should be set up for individual software. One approach to linking the software, users, and the necessary security is to perform an inventory of the software, and to develop a table or spreadsheet that associates the users and security needs with the software, as shown in Table 4-6.

Table 4-6 Inventory of Software and Folder Security

Software	Users	Security
Accounting: general ledger, accounts receivable, and accounts payable	Accounting staff, vice president of finance, accounting manager	Folder permissions = Modify Share permissions = Change
Accounting: payroll	Payroll staff, vice president of finance, accounting manager	Folder permissions = Modify Share permissions = Change
Accounting: human resources	Human resources staff, vice president of finance, human resources manager	Folder permissions = Modify Share permissions = Change
Accounting: purchasing	Purchasing office staff, vice president of finance, purchasing officer	Folder permissions = Modify Share permissions = Change
Microsoft Office	All company users	Folder permissions = Read & Execute Share permissions = Read
User home folders	Home folder associated with each user account	Folder permissions = Full Control (each user has Full Control of her or his home folder)
Subscription, mass mailing, and marketing software	Marketing staff, vice president of marketing, product managers	Folder permissions = Modify Share permissions = Change
Manufacturing software	Manufacturing and warehouse staff, vice president of operations	Folder permissions = Modify Share permissions = Change
Distribution software	Warehouse and distribution staff, vice president of operations	Folder permissions = Modify Share permissions = Change
Inventory software	Warehouse and inventory staff, vice president of operations	Folder permissions = Modify Share permissions = Change
IT utility software	IT staff, vice president of finance, IT manager	Folder permissions = Modify Share permissions = Change

4

The security shown in Table 4-6 is one example of the security that can be set up to protect software, which is based on Windows 2000 Server shared folder and NTFS folder permissions. **NTFS permissions** are associated with folders and files, controlling the way accounts or groups access information. **Share permissions** are permissions that apply to a particular shared object, such as a shared folder or printer. Share permissions do not offer as many options as NTFS permissions, in part because they are matched to the characteristics of the shared object, such as the ability to manage print jobs on a shared printer. Table 4-7 illustrates the NTFS folder share permissions, and Table 4-8 shows the share permissions in Windows 2000 Server.

Table 4-7   NTFS Folder and File Permissions

Permission	Description	Applies to
Full Control	Can read, add, delete, execute, and modify files plus change permissions and attributes, and take ownership	Folders and files
List Folder Contents	Can list (traverse) files in the folder or switch to a subfolder, view folder attributes and permissions, and execute files, but cannot view file contents	Folders only
Modify	Can read, add, delete, execute, and modify files; but cannot delete subfolders and their file contents, change permissions, or take ownership	Folders and files
Read	Can view file contents and view folder attributes and permissions, but cannot traverse folders or execute files	Folders and files
Read & Execute	Implies the capabilities of both List Folder Contents and Read (traverse folders, view file contents, view attributes and permissions, and execute files)	Folders and files
Write	Can create files, write data to files, append data to files, create folders, delete files (but not subfolders and their files), and modify folder and file attributes	Folders and files

Table 4-8   Folder Share Permissions

Permission	Description	Applies to
Change	Enables users to read, add, modify, execute, and delete files.	Shared folders and the files in the folders
Full Control	Provides full access to the folder, including the ability to take control or change permissions.	Shared folders and the files in the folders
Read	Permits groups or users to read and execute files.	Shared folders and the files in the folders

Besides determining what security to apply to specific software, you will also need to analyze who is responsible for assigning the security. For example, security assignment may be done only by IT department server administrators, or it may need to be delegated to someone else. At Jefferson Philately, setting up security for general ledger, accounts receivable, accounts payable, payroll, and purchasing is delegated to the accounting manager. Security for the human resources accounting module is delegated to the human resources manager.

Windows 2000 Server offers the Security Configuration and Analysis tool, which is an MMC snap-in to help you monitor and analyze security. This tool works by creating a database from which to configure group policies on a server and perform a security check of specific group policies. For example, if you are setting up the first DC, you can use this tool to configure the server for the default domain security policy, such as requiring a minimum password length or enabling auditing. Later, you can use the tool to perform an analysis of the policy to determine if you need to make modifications on the basis of growth in server use or changes in an organization (see Figure 4-10). You can use the tool to import an existing template or to import a new security template that you have created. A **security template** is a file that contains preconfigured group policy settings that can be imported into a set of group policies linked to a domain or OU. Security templates are created by using the MMC Security Templates snap-in in Windows 2000 Server. The database may be built from an existing group policy, a security template, or you can construct a database the first time that you run the tool. After a database is in place, such as for the domain or for an OU, you should periodically analyze it to see if it meets the system's security recommendations. Also, use the Security Configuration and Analysis tool to analyze the security and group policies in an organization for which you are designing Active Directory Services. Try Hands-on Project 4-6 to practice analyzing security in Windows 2000 Server.

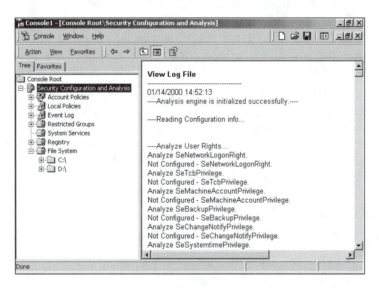

Figure 4-10   Analyzing security

ANALYZING BACKUP AND DISASTER RECOVERY METHODS

All organizations that value their software and data assets regularly back up their systems and have a disaster recovery plan. A **backup** involves making a copy of the data so that it can be restored in the event of a system failure or accidental data deletion.

A **disaster recovery plan** entails creating a plan to continue computer operations after a disaster such as a fire, flood, or earthquake.

Data backups are typically performed on tape systems, on CD-RW media, and on Zip media using one or more of several backup methods. Most popular is a **full backup** where all volumes, folders, and files are backed up. One form of the full backup creates an exact image of the disk files on tape. Image backups are performed in binary format, storing the information bit by bit. Image backups are fast, but have the disadvantage that if only a few files on the hard disk are accidentally deleted or corrupted, all files must be restored from tape. There is no option to restore selected files, selected folders, or directories. A more widely used full backup procedure is called file-by-file, which stores data as files on tape. In this format, the system administrator and backup operators can restore single files, selected folders, or directories as needed. The backup software that accompanies Windows 2000 Server has file-by-file backup options, but no image backup capabilities. Backup software from tape system vendors may come with image backup options.

Another method is the **incremental backup,** which backs up only those files that have changed since the previous backup. Many organizations combine full and incremental backups because there is not enough time to back up all files after each workday. One method is to perform full file-by-file backups on a Friday night or a weekend day, when there is less activity on servers. During the week, incremental backups are performed at the end of each workday. If a disk fails on Wednesday, the restore procedure is to first restore the volume from the weekend's full backup, then to restore from Monday's incremental backup, followed by Tuesday's incremental backup.

The Windows 2000 Server backup software recognizes five backup options, which are variations of full or incremental backups (see Figure 4-11). A full backup in Windows 2000 Server is called the *normal* backup, which is the same as a full file-by-file backup. A normal backup includes all files that you have selected, usually an entire partition or volume. The normal backup changes each file's archive bit to show that file has been backed up. The advantage of performing full backups each night is that all files are on one tape or tape set.

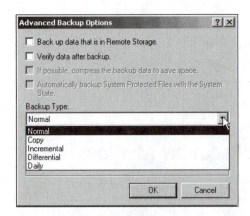

Figure 4-11   Windows 2000 Server backup options

- Are backup tape rotation plans and off-site vault storage used?

- Is Dfs implemented to provide fault tolerance and disaster recovery for important files and software applications?

- Is there more than one DC per domain, and are the DCs set up in a topology that enables Active Directory replication for fault tolerance and disaster recovery?

NG TECHNICAL SUPPORT, USER HELP, AND TRAINING

any organizations have groups that offer technical support, user help, and training for their ftware systems. *Technical support* is usually a higher support level for major software prob- ns. The kinds of problems that technical support professionals handle are assistance with stalling software, and troubleshooting major software problems. In an organization, the chnical support professionals are often in the IT department as part of the operations oup, the systems group, or the user support group. Software vendors also have technical pport professionals, who usually work directly with members of the IT department or who metimes assist users with special problems. For example, Jefferson Philately uses the tech- cal support professionals available from its accounting software vendor to help install grades to modules, such as to the payroll module at the end of the year for preparing W2s d 1099s. They also call the vendor's technical support team at times when they have dis- vered corrupt data and when they have made errors in the fiscal year-end closing steps. he vendor has a dial-up line into the computer that runs the software and can be given cess to work on software problems, when necessary. Jefferson Philately pays a yearly sup- rt fee for this technical support service.

fferson Philately also employs two technical support professionals in the operations group ho take turns being on call during the business day and after hours. They respond to any roblems that develop in operations, such as when a disk drive fails on a server and needs to e replaced and resynchronized with the other drives, or when a system backup experiences roblems and will not complete normally.

echnical support professionals usually need extensive access to systems, and often have ccounts that belong to the Administrators or Server Operators groups (both are preestab- shed groups in Windows 2000 Server, see Chapter 8). Because technical support profes- onals have extensive privileges, sometimes the external auditors of an organization require at there be a means to document the work that they perform. In Windows 2000 Server, is is accomplished by setting up group policies and folder security to audit the activities of e technical support professionals. In other systems, a more basic method is used, which is keep the password of the administrator account in a sealed envelope. When the technical pport person needs to use administrator privileges, he or she opens the envelope, does the ecessary work as administrator, and records a log of his or her activity in a word-processed udit report. Afterward, a security officer changes the administrator password and seals it ii nother envelope for the next time. When you analyze an organization, you will find th

An incremental backup includes only files that are new or that have been updated. Windows 2000 Server has an *incremental* option that backs up only files that have the archive attribute. When it backs up a file, the incremental backup removes the archive attribute to show that it has been backed up. A *differential* backup is the same as an incremental backup, but it does not remove the archive attribute. Incremental or differential backups are often mixed with full backups. The advantage of the differential backup is that only the most recent full backup and the most recent differential backup are required to restore data. This saves time over incremental restores, which require the full backup and all incremental backups since the last full backup.

Another Windows 2000 Server option is the *copy* backup, which backs up only the files or folders selected. The archive attribute, showing a file is new or updated, is left unchanged. For example, if the archive attribute is present on a file, the copy backup does not remove it. Copy backups are used in exceptional cases where a backup is performed on certain files, but the regular backup routines are unaffected because the copy backup does not alter the archive bit.

The *daily* backup option backs up only files that have been changed or updated on the day the backup is taken. It leaves the archive attribute unchanged, so regular backups are not affected. A daily backup is valuable, for example, when there is a failing hard disk and little time to save the day's work to that point. It enables the administrator to save only that day's work, instead of all changed files, which may span more than a day. The Windows 2000 Server backup options are summarized in Table 4-9.

Table 4-9   Windows 2000 Server Backup Options

Backup Option	Description
Normal	The same as a full file-by-file backup, backing up one or more volumes
Incremental	Only backs up files that have the archive attribute, and removes the archive bit after each file is backed up
Differential	Only backs up files that have the archive attribute, but does not remove the archive bit after a file is backed up
Copy	Backs up files and folders that have been selected, but does not remove the archive bit
Daily	Only backs up files that have been changed or added on the day of the backup, but does not remove the archive bit

For Windows NT servers, an organization should plan to regularly back up the Registry, which contains information about all software and hardware setups on the server. For Windows 2000 servers, the backup plan should include backing up the system state data (see Figure 4-12) and system protected files (try Hands-on Project 4-7). In Windows 2000 Server, the system state data includes:

- System and boot files

- Active Directory

- SYSVOL folder

- Registry

- COM+ Class Registration information

- DNS zones (when DNS is installed and integrated with Active Directory)

- Certificate information (when certificate services are installed)

- Server cluster data (when server clustering is used)

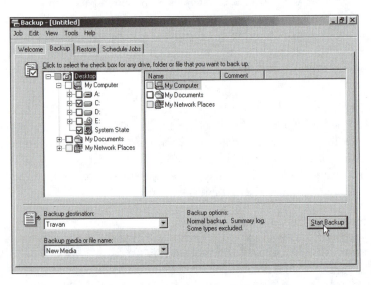

Figure 4-12   Backing up system state data

Backups of Windows 2000 Server should also include the system protected files, which are:

- *Ntldr:* A boot program that initiates the startup process, operating system selection, and hardware detection

- *Bootsect.dos:* A file that is used for dual-boot systems

- *Boot.ini:* An initialization file that is used by Ntldr to obtain startup information, such as which operating systems are available and their locations

- *Ntdetect.com:* A program that detects the computer's hardware

- *Ntbootdd.sys:* A driver for SCSI adapters

- *Ntoskrnl.exe:* The program that is the Windows 2000 kernel

- *Hal.dll:* The hardware abstraction layer (a driver for CPUs)

All organizations should have a disaster recovery plan to ability to continue business if a disaster strikes. The simp have a remote site for storing a copy of certain backups. F store the most recent full backup in a bank vault. The org incremental backups in the same vault during the week. A ter recovery method is to use backup media rotation. Ma media rotation method to ensure alternatives in case ther ple. One common tape rotation method is called the Tov there are two or more complete tape sets. This method r more frequently than others. If one of the frequently used tape is likely to be intact (although some recent data cann can be rotated on a weekly basis, so that one set is in the b for the current week's backups.

The use of Dfs and DCs enables a disaster recovery plan to extra tape sets. For example, Interstate Security Bank, with aster recovery plan in which Active Directory information regional, and branch sites. By placing DCs in each of the m bank can replicate Active Directory data to any combinat can also be used to create backups of data at any site. Thus, one or more other sites can be used to perform the busir formed at the site that has experienced the disaster. York I in that DCs and Dfs can be used to replicate data in case of

Because Jefferson Philately has only one site, they are alr approach. Besides using tape backups and bank vault storage a company that specializes in disaster recovery. This compa (Jefferson Philately is located in Cleveland), provides a WA dedicated to Jefferson Philately. The Active Directory is replic is used to regularly back up critical data from Jefferson Phila aster recovery plan includes the ability for members of Jeffe tion of the disaster recovery company and use workstations DC. If a disaster occurs, Jefferson Philately can still perform operations would be cut back in a disaster, but the company

When you analyze the backup and disaster recovery metho you consider the following questions:

- What type of backup methods are used, such as a c and incremental backups?

- What type of backup plans are in place for the Reg servers and the system state data for Windows 2000

- What type of backup plans are in place for system Windows 2000 servers?

An incremental backup includes only files that are new or that have been updated. Windows 2000 Server has an *incremental* option that backs up only files that have the archive attribute. When it backs up a file, the incremental backup removes the archive attribute to show that it has been backed up. A *differential* backup is the same as an incremental backup, but it does not remove the archive attribute. Incremental or differential backups are often mixed with full backups. The advantage of the differential backup is that only the most recent full backup and the most recent differential backup are required to restore data. This saves time over incremental restores, which require the full backup and all incremental backups since the last full backup.

Another Windows 2000 Server option is the *copy* backup, which backs up only the files or folders selected. The archive attribute, showing a file is new or updated, is left unchanged. For example, if the archive attribute is present on a file, the copy backup does not remove it. Copy backups are used in exceptional cases where a backup is performed on certain files, but the regular backup routines are unaffected because the copy backup does not alter the archive bit.

The *daily* backup option backs up only files that have been changed or updated on the day the backup is taken. It leaves the archive attribute unchanged, so regular backups are not affected. A daily backup is valuable, for example, when there is a failing hard disk and little time to save the day's work to that point. It enables the administrator to save only that day's work, instead of all changed files, which may span more than a day. The Windows 2000 Server backup options are summarized in Table 4-9.

Table 4-9   Windows 2000 Server Backup Options

Backup Option	Description
Normal	The same as a full file-by-file backup, backing up one or more volumes
Incremental	Only backs up files that have the archive attribute, and removes the archive bit after each file is backed up
Differential	Only backs up files that have the archive attribute, but does not remove the archive bit after a file is backed up
Copy	Backs up files and folders that have been selected, but does not remove the archive bit
Daily	Only backs up files that have been changed or added on the day of the backup, but does not remove the archive bit

For Windows NT servers, an organization should plan to regularly back up the Registry, which contains information about all software and hardware setups on the server. For Windows 2000 servers, the backup plan should include backing up the system state data (see Figure 4-12) and system protected files (try Hands-on Project 4-7). In Windows 2000 Server, the system state data includes:

- System and boot files

- Active Directory

- SYSVOL folder

- Registry

- COM+ Class Registration information

- DNS zones (when DNS is installed and integrated with Active Directory)

- Certificate information (when certificate services are installed)

- Server cluster data (when server clustering is used)

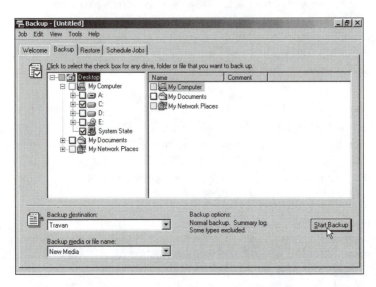

Figure 4-12   Backing up system state data

Backups of Windows 2000 Server should also include the system protected files, which are:

- *Ntldr:* A boot program that initiates the startup process, operating system selection, and hardware detection

- *Bootsect.dos:* A file that is used for dual-boot systems

- *Boot.ini:* An initialization file that is used by Ntldr to obtain startup information, such as which operating systems are available and their locations

- *Ntdetect.com:* A program that detects the computer's hardware

- *Ntbootdd.sys:* A driver for SCSI adapters

- *Ntoskrnl.exe:* The program that is the Windows 2000 kernel

- *Hal.dll:* The hardware abstraction layer (a driver for CPUs)

4

All organizations should have a disaster recovery plan to protect data and the organizations's ability to continue business if a disaster strikes. The simplest form of disaster recovery is to have a remote site for storing a copy of certain backups. For example, the organization might store the most recent full backup in a bank vault. The organization might also store specific incremental backups in the same vault during the week. Another example of a simple disaster recovery method is to use backup media rotation. Many server administrators develop a media rotation method to ensure alternatives in case there is a bad or worn tape, for example. One common tape rotation method is called the Tower of Hanoi procedure, in which there are two or more complete tape sets. This method rotates tapes so that some are used more frequently than others. If one of the frequently used tapes is bad, a less frequently used tape is likely to be intact (although some recent data cannot be restored). Different tape sets can be rotated on a weekly basis, so that one set is in the bank vault while the other is in use for the current week's backups.

The use of Dfs and DCs enables a disaster recovery plan to go beyond using bank vaults and extra tape sets. For example, Interstate Security Bank, with its many locations, can have a disaster recovery plan in which Active Directory information and data is duplicated at the main, regional, and branch sites. By placing DCs in each of the main, regional, and branch sites, the bank can replicate Active Directory data to any combination of sites or all of the sites. Dfs can also be used to create backups of data at any site. Thus, if one site experiences a disaster, one or more other sites can be used to perform the business that would normally be performed at the site that has experienced the disaster. York Industries has the same advantage in that DCs and Dfs can be used to replicate data in case of a disaster.

Because Jefferson Philately has only one site, they are already using a somewhat different approach. Besides using tape backups and bank vault storage of tapes, they pay a yearly fee to a company that specializes in disaster recovery. This company, which is in Cincinnati, Ohio (Jefferson Philately is located in Cleveland), provides a WAN link and a remote DC that is dedicated to Jefferson Philately. The Active Directory is replicated to the remote DC. Also, Dfs is used to regularly back up critical data from Jefferson Philately to the remote DC. The disaster recovery plan includes the ability for members of Jefferson Philately to go to the location of the disaster recovery company and use workstations there that are connected to the DC. If a disaster occurs, Jefferson Philately can still perform work at the recovery site, so that operations would be cut back in a disaster, but the company would continue functioning.

When you analyze the backup and disaster recovery methods of an organization, make sure you consider the following questions:

- What type of backup methods are used, such as a combination of full (or normal) and incremental backups?

- What type of backup plans are in place for the Registries of Windows NT servers and the system state data for Windows 2000 servers?

- What type of backup plans are in place for system protected files on Windows 2000 servers?

- Are backup tape rotation plans and off-site vault storage used?

- Is Dfs implemented to provide fault tolerance and disaster recovery for important files and software applications?

- Is there more than one DC per domain, and are the DCs set up in a topology that enables Active Directory replication for fault tolerance and disaster recovery?

ANALYZING TECHNICAL SUPPORT, USER HELP, AND TRAINING

Many organizations have groups that offer technical support, user help, and training for their software systems. *Technical support* is usually a higher support level for major software problems. The kinds of problems that technical support professionals handle are assistance with installing software, and troubleshooting major software problems. In an organization, the technical support professionals are often in the IT department as part of the operations group, the systems group, or the user support group. Software vendors also have technical support professionals, who usually work directly with members of the IT department or who sometimes assist users with special problems. For example, Jefferson Philately uses the technical support professionals available from its accounting software vendor to help install upgrades to modules, such as to the payroll module at the end of the year for preparing W2s and 1099s. They also call the vendor's technical support team at times when they have discovered corrupt data and when they have made errors in the fiscal year-end closing steps. The vendor has a dial-up line into the computer that runs the software and can be given access to work on software problems, when necessary. Jefferson Philately pays a yearly support fee for this technical support service.

Jefferson Philately also employs two technical support professionals in the operations group who take turns being on call during the business day and after hours. They respond to any problems that develop in operations, such as when a disk drive fails on a server and needs to be replaced and resynchronized with the other drives, or when a system backup experiences problems and will not complete normally.

Technical support professionals usually need extensive access to systems, and often have accounts that belong to the Administrators or Server Operators groups (both are preestablished groups in Windows 2000 Server, see Chapter 8). Because technical support professionals have extensive privileges, sometimes the external auditors of an organization require that there be a means to document the work that they perform. In Windows 2000 Server, this is accomplished by setting up group policies and folder security to audit the activities of the technical support professionals. In other systems, a more basic method is used, which is to keep the password of the administrator account in a sealed envelope. When the technical support person needs to use administrator privileges, he or she opens the envelope, does the necessary work as administrator, and records a log of his or her activity in a word-processed audit report. Afterward, a security officer changes the administrator password and seals it in another envelope for the next time. When you analyze an organization, you will find that these auditing procedures are most likely to be used on systems that involve handling money, such as accounting systems or systems in organizations such as Interstate Security Bank.

 The extensive auditing capabilities in Windows 2000 make this operating system particularly well suited for software applications that need to be checked regularly by financial auditors or computer security auditors. Besides systems that involve money transactions, the auditing capabilities are important for systems that contain confidential records, credit card transactions, or top-secret research.

Everyday user help activities are typically performed by an organization's *user support* professionals. Vendors also employ user support professionals to answer typical questions about their software. Jefferson Philately, Interstate Security Bank, and York Industries all have user support groups or departments. A user support professional works directly with users and is likely to respond to a full range of problems from simple to complex. In a single day, a user support person may:

- Show a user how to format a table in a word processor
- Help a user diagnose and replace a defective network interface card
- Show a user how to install a printer driver in Windows 2000 Professional
- Demonstrate how to use a CD-ROM
- Teach a user to back up his or her data
- Demonstrate how to perform a calculation in a spreadsheet
- Diagnose a simple printer problem by reminding a user how to press the online button

Most organizations set up special security privileges for user support professionals. When you analyze an organization, determine the population of users that are helped and how they are helped by user support professionals. For example, there are two user support professionals for each of the executive, finance, operations, and marketing areas at Jefferson Philately. When you analyze a company such as this, you might suggest that each user support professional has access to resources in each of her or his areas. For the two user support professionals assigned to the finance area, for instance, this means that they would have Account Operators privileges (a preestablished Windows 2000 security group, see Chapter 8) for those users. This gives the user support professionals access to assist in creating accounts and changing passwords for users who forget their passwords. The user support professionals in the finance area might also have read access to specific folders and limited permissions for the accounting system to help with problems. Another option is to make these user support professionals members of the security groups used in the finance area.

In organizations that use Terminal Services, the user support professionals can be given access to control a session manually. This enables them to watch the steps that a user performs without leaving their office. They can also enter keystrokes as if working from the user's workstation, to demonstrate a particular procedure. The ability to control a session manually in Terminal Services enables user support professionals to help more people, because they do not have to spend time traveling from department to department.

Many organizations offer training for their software systems, which is performed by their in-house trainers or by outsourced trainers. When there are in-house trainers, they often work in the IT user support group or under the Human Resources department. Some organizations have training labs in which to train individuals or groups of users. In other situations, the trainer works with individual users at each user's workstation. Some organizations maintain a training server that has copies of the software that employees must learn, and sample data for practice. Employees can practice in this environment, including entering, updating, and deleting data, without worrying about making a mistake on a live system.

There is a training lab at each of the York Industries locations, where trainers work under the user support manager in each of the seven IT departments. Because it is so large, York Industries has set up a special training domain that can be accessed from any of the locations. The training domain contains servers that have training versions of all of the software used by the companies that make up York Industries. Each location has a training lab that is connected to the training domain, and the trainers coordinate with one another on how they use the labs and training domain. The trainers all belong to the Server Operators and Account Operators groups for the servers in the domain. They have security privileges to install software, configure software, create training accounts, and restore data files.

York Industries sometimes also hires outsourced trainers for specialized training—for example, in situations where they introduce new software. For instance, the York Industries home site in Toronto hired trainers to teach server administrators when they changed from using UNIX servers to Windows NT 4.0 servers in 1997. For part of the training, the trainers used a WAN connection to access their own training domain. In this instance, the trainers and their students needed security access to use the WAN connection from the training lab. The trainers also brought training servers into the lab. For this portion of the training, they used a router to isolate the training lab from the rest of the company network and created a temporary training domain for the lab servers. Employees participating in the training were given Administrator privileges to enable them to train and experiment with the training servers.

When you analyze technical support, user help, and training, be sure to consider the following questions:

- Who provides technical support to the computer professionals in an organization, and what type of access do they require?

- Who provides user help functions in the organization, and what access do they need to perform their jobs?

- How is training provided, and what computer resources are needed for training?

- What access is needed to enable training?

- Is training software used, and what resources are needed to make it available to users?

CHAPTER SUMMARY

❐ Software resources and data are among a company's most important assets. Planning for Active Directory design involves analyzing the organization's software resources, such as the user base, which consists of user workstations that have operating systems that will connect to Windows 2000 Server. Among the client operating systems that you may encounter in an organization are MS-DOS, Windows 3.1, Windows 3.11, Windows 95, Windows 98, Windows NT, Windows 2000, Windows ME, Macintosh, and UNIX. As you analyze the user base, plan to use network traffic analysis tools, such as Network Monitor, to understand how the user base functions. Network Monitor can provide insights into user access patterns and how to improve network performance for user productivity.

❐ There are many kinds of software and software systems that organizations use. Plan to inventory the software systems and determine how Active Directory services, such as security and publishing software, can be set up to help an organization. Databases closely accompany software systems, and require analysis for their effect on security and software performance.

❐ Analyzing the software that is used in an organization can be linked to factors such as the corporate culture, software performance issues, and security. All of these affect Active Directory design. The corporate culture is related to security issues. Software performance is affected by factors such as the placement of DCs and using Dfs. Security needs affect how group policies and folder security are implemented.

❐ Most organizations use backups to protect data and software systems, including backing up Active Directory elements. Analyze the methods that an organization uses for backups to make sure that the organization has the protection that it needs. Also, analyze its disaster recovery plans. In some cases you may be surprised to find an organization that has millions of dollars invested in data and computer resources, but no disaster recovery plan.

❐ Technical support, user support, and training are factors that influence how Active Directory resources are set up, so that support personnel can access the resources they need to troubleshoot problems and so that users can train without fear of damaging live data.

In the next chapter you will learn how to analyze the hardware and network resources in an organization, such as LANs, WANs, and network management approaches.

KEY TERMS

backup — Making a copy of software and data so that they can be restored in the event of a system failure or accidental data deletion.

benchmark — A measurement standard for hardware or software used to establish performance baselines under varying loads or circumstances. Also called a baseline.

broadcast — A transmission that sends one copy of each frame to all points on a network, regardless of whether or not a recipient has requested to communicate with the sender.

digital subscriber line (DSL) — A technology that uses advanced modulation technologies on regular telephone lines for high-speed networking at speeds of up to 55 Mbps and higher between subscribers and a telecommunications company.

disaster recovery plan — Creating a plan to continue computer operations after a disaster such as a fire, flood, or earthquake.

file lock — Flagging a file so that it cannot be updated by more than one user at a time, giving only the first user to access it the ability to perform an update.

flat file database — A database in which data is stored sequentially in regular files in the same directory on a first-in basis.

frame — A unit of data that is transmitted on a network that contains control and address information (OSI Layer 2), but not routing information.

full backup — A backup of an entire system, including all system files, programs, and data files. In many Windows-based and other file systems, the archive bit (or equivalent) is removed on each file after the backup is complete.

incremental backup — A backup of new or changed files. In Windows NT and Windows 2000, an incremental backup removes the archive bit after backing up the files.

Integrated Services Digital Network (ISDN) — A telecommunications standard for delivering data services over digital telephone lines with a current practical limit of 1.536 Mbps, and a theoretical limit of 622 Mbps.

media access control (MAC) sublayer — A network communications function that examines physical address information in frames and controls the way devices share communications on a network.

multicast — A transmission method in which a server divides recipients of an application, such as a multimedia application, into groups. Each data stream is a one-time transmission that goes to one group of multiple addresses, instead of sending a separate transmission to each address for each data stream. The result is less network traffic.

named pipe — A communication link between two processes, which may be local to the server or remote, such as between the server and a workstation.

network database — A flat file database that uses a simple table structure.

Network File System (NFS) — A TCP/IP file transfer protocol that transfers information in record streams instead of in bulk file streams, and that is typically used by UNIX systems.

Network Monitor — A Windows NT and Windows 2000 network monitoring tool that can capture and display network performance data.

Network Monitor Driver — Enables a Microsoft-based server or workstation NIC to gather network performance data for assessment by Microsoft Network Monitor.

NTFS permissions — In Windows 2000, privileges set up via NTFS to access and manipulate resource objects, such as folders and printers; for example, privilege to read a file, or to create a new file.

Open Database Connectivity (ODBC) — A set of rules and an application programming interface developed by Microsoft for accessing databases and providing a standard doorway to database data. An ODBC driver is used between an application and a database to enable data to be queried and manipulated.

relational database — A database in which data is stored in tables that can be designed with optimized relationships to one another for fast data access.

security template — A file that contains preconfigured group policy settings for security, which can be imported into a group policy object linked to a domain or OU.

share permissions — Permissions that apply to a particular shared object, such as a shared folder or printer and that control access to that object over a network.

unicast — A transmission method in which one copy of each packet is sent to each targeted destination.

virtual private network (VPN) — A private network that is like a tunnel through a larger network—such as the Internet, an enterprise network, or both—that is restricted only to designated member clients.

4

REVIEW QUESTIONS

Answer questions 1–9 using this case information:

Vittali's Pizza is a company that prepares frozen pizza for convenience and grocery stores. The company headquarters is in Chicago and has 32 Windows 2000 servers. There are 752 people employed at the headquarters plant who use workstations on the network. The operating systems used on the workstations are UNIX, older Mac OS versions, and Windows 95. The Accounting department accesses its accounting software, which is a third-party software system, using Windows 95.

1. What accounting modules would you expect to find in the accounting software?

    a. payroll

    b. general ledger

    c. accounts payable

    d. accounts receivable

    e. all of the above

    f. only a and b

    g. only b and c

2. How would you expect the Macintosh clients to connect to the Windows 2000 domain?

    a. through NFS

    b. through Services for Macintosh

    c. by using a Windows 95 gateway

    d. all of the above

    e. none of the above

    f. only a and b

    g. only b and c

3. When Vittalli's Pizza has to restore data on a Windows 2000 server that has failed, they use a full backup and one other backup, at most. What is the other backup likely to be?

   a. differential

   b. incremental

   c. copy

   d. daily

   e. none of the above

4. Vittali's Pizza has a user support team that works out of the IT department. Which of the following types of users is user support most likely to help?

   a. Macintosh users

   b. server administrators in the IT department

   c. the managers of the company

   d. Windows 95 users

   e. all of the above

   f. only a and b

   g. only c and d

   h. only a, c, and d

5. The Vittali's Pizza accounting system uses a relational database. What type of security is most likely to be set for this database?

   a. folder and file

   b. access to rows and columns

   c. access to tables

   d. all of the above

   e. only a and b

   f. only a and c

6. Vittali's Pizza uses a report-generating tool to create reports from their database. Some of Vittali's users also use the Microsoft Access query capability to access the database to write reports. This means that the database is:

   a. in need of normalization

   b. ODBC-compliant

   c. in need of security analysis to make sure only authorized users can access it

   d. small

   e. all of the above

   f. none of the above

   g. only a and b

   h. only b and c

7. At Vittali's Pizza, the user support professionals manage user accounts. What Active Directory element might be useful in this situation to help with security?

   a. Give the user support professionals Modify access to each user's home folder.

   b. Give the user support professionals Full Control access to each user's home folder.

   c. Join the user support professionals' accounts to the Account Operators group.

   d. Join the user support professionals' accounts to the Administrator group.

   e. all of the above

   f. only a and d

   g. only b and d

8. The Vittali's Pizza auditors are concerned that the technical support professionals could pose a potential security threat because of their extensive access on certain Windows 2000 servers. What can you recommend to help satisfy the auditors?

   a. Limit the scope of the work done by the technical support professionals and give some of their responsibilities to the user support professionals.

   b. Use the Windows 2000 Server auditing capabilities.

   c. Outsource many of the technical support professionals' duties to a bonded company.

   d. Ignore the auditors' recommendations because there is no alternative.

   e. none of the above

9. Vittali's Pizza has two regional production plants, one in St. Louis, Missouri and one in Cedar Rapids, Iowa. At both sites, users are authenticated by the DCs in Chicago. What problems might this cause?

   a. There will be too many accounts for those DCs to handle.

   b. Logon access may be unacceptably slow for the St. Louis and Cedar Rapids users.

   c. Active Directory elements are not backed up to an offsite location.

   d. all of the above

   e. none of the above

   f. only a and c

   g. only b and c

Answer questions 10–19 using this case information:

Feather Soft manufactures mattresses in Vancouver, Philadelphia, and Mexico City. This company uses an accounting package from PeopleSoft in a Windows 2000 Server environment. The database for the accounting package is Oracle. Users at Feather Soft use Windows NT Workstation, Windows 98, Macintosh, and UNIX workstation operating systems. The company also uses Microsoft Office for the 250–300 employees at each site.

10. How would you expect the Windows 98 clients to access resources in Windows 2000 Active Directory?

    a. using DSClient

    b. using Active Directory gateway

    c. using My Network Places

    d. all of the above

    e. none of the above

    f. only a and b

    g. only a and c

11. When you begin analyzing security, what tool(s) can you use to determine how group policies are set up?

    a. Services icon in the Control Panel

    b. Network Monitor

    c. Security Configuration and Analysis Tool

    d. My Computer

    e. all of the above

    f. none of the above

    g. only a, c, and d

    h. only a and d

12. You want to verify that the Philadelphia location is backing up Active Directory data in their regular backups. What should they be backing up?

    a. system state data

    b. system protected files

    c. all user files

    d. the Hal.dll file

    e. all of the above

    f. none of the above

    g. both a and b

    h. both a and c

13. All three sites have many users who work one day a week from home. To support these users, the company maintains large modem banks and an array of telephone lines into each site's LAN. Is there an alternative that they can explore?

    a. a RAS network

    b. a VPN

    c. Terminal Services

    d. adding more technical support services

14. The managers of Feather Soft have several confidential shared folders that they access through the network using Windows 98. What security should you analyze for these shared folders?

    a. NTFS permissions

    b. share permissions

    c. the auditing of the folders

    d. the NFS permissions

    e. all of the above

    f. only a and b

    g. only a, b, and c

    h. only b, c, and d

15. When the company backs up the Ntldr file, this is an example of backing up:

    a. user data

    b. an Oracle database file

    c. system protected file

    d. an Oracle index file

    e. system permissions

    f. none of the above

16. Which of the following might be elements of a disaster recovery plan for Feather Soft?

    a. using Dfs

    b. eliminating tape rotation

    c. placing DCs at each site

    d. storing backup tapes in an offsite vault

    e. all of the above

    f. only a and d

    g. a combination of a, b, and d

    h. a combination of a, c, and d

17. What tool(s) can help in analyzing the user base and user traffic on the company networks?

    a. Services icon in the Control Panel

    b. Network Monitor

    c. Security Configuration and Analysis tool

    d. My Computer

    e. all of the above

    f. none of the above

    g. a combination of a, c, and d

    h. a combination of a and d

18. What programming tools might you analyze at Feather Soft, and what Active Directory elements might they affect in your analysis?

    a. office software and domains

    b. compilers and security access

    c. published software and OUs

    d. accounting software and trees

19. Which of the following may be affected through your analysis of the number of users and their location?

    a. the location of DCs

    b. performance optimization through creating sites

    c. the location of global catalog servers

    d. whether to use distribution groups in place of security groups

    e. all of the above

    f. only a and b

    g. only a, b, and c

Answer questions 20–25 using this case information:

Wick's Motobikes manufactures scooters and motorized bicycles and is located in London. This is a very traditionally run company that follows a centralized decision-making structure. The organization uses Windows 2000 servers and an IBM mainframe for computing resources. User workstations are UNIX, Windows 3.11, Windows 95, and Windows NT Workstation.

20. Wick's Motobikes uses Dfs. What would you expect to be installed in Windows 95 for this operating system to use Dfs?

a. DSClient

b. Active Directory driver

c. Bootsec.dos

d. Ntdect.com

e. all of the above

f. a combination of a and b

g. a combination of a, c, and d

21. The Windows 3.11 clients at Wick's Motobikes use Terminal Services. What Terminal Services feature are the user support professionals likely to use to help them be more productive?

a. Network Monitor Driver

b. user viewer

c. user computer search and redirector feature

d. ability to control a session manually

22. At a remote plant, 52 Windows NT clients use Terminal Services over a slow 1.544 Mbps WAN link. Which of the following would be possible solutions to help make these users more productive?

a. Increase the speed of their NICs from 10 Mbps to 100 Mbps.

b. Remove the router they must go through.

c. Publish the software that they use and enable users to install it remotely.

d. Use a firewall between the remote plant and the main site.

e. all of the above

f. a combination of a, b, and c

g. a combination of a, c, and d

23. Wick's Motobikes uses a client/server accounting system. The programs for the system are on one server, and the database is on another server. Many of the managers complain that the system is slow when several users run reports against it. The system designer responds by recommending that they upgrade the memory in the server that runs the programs. What is your response?

a. You agree that this is the best solution.

b. You recommend a faster network link in addition to added memory, so that the network can keep up with the machine.

c. You recommend implementing an additional server for reports and periodically copying the main database to that server.

d. You recommend placing the server with the programs in a different domain than the server with the database.

24. You want to analyze security, such as whether auditing is enabled for an OU, or whether all users in the domain must enter a password that is a minimum length. Where would you look?

    a. at folder permissions

    b. at individual user accounts

    c. at the security groups that have been created

    d. at the group policies

    e. none of the above

25. Which of the following in Network Monitor would give you the best idea about the individual workstations that are communicating on a network?

    a. Station pane

    b. Total pane

    c. Session pane

    d. Graph pane

    e. Network Monitor does not provide this information.

    f. a combination of a and c

    g. a combination of b and d

HANDS-ON PROJECTS

Project 4-1

In this activity, you view the number of users logged on to a Windows NT 4.0 server and then the users connected to a particular share. You will need access to a Windows NT 4.0 server and to log on to an account that has Administrator privileges.

To check the user connections:

1. Click **Start**, point to **Settings**, and click **Control Panel**.

2. Double-click the **Server** icon.

3. Click the **Users** button. How many users are connected? Record your observations in your lab journal or in a word-processed document. Click a user to see what resources that user is using. Record your observations. Click **Close**.

4. Click the **Shares** button. Click a shared resource under Sharename and look under Connected Users for those accounts using the resource. Click **Close**.

5. Click the **In Use** button. The Open Resources dialog box shows which resources are in use, the type of use, such as reading a folder, if any locks are set, and the path to the resource. Record your observations about which resources are in use. Click **Close**.

6. Click **OK** in the Server dialog box. Close the Control Panel.

Project 4-2

In this project, you practice viewing the users who are connected to a Windows 2000 server and determining which files are locked. You will need access to an account that has Administrator privileges.

To view the user connections:

1. Click **Start**, point to **Programs**, point to **Administrative Tools**, and click **Computer Management**.

2. Double-click **Shared Folders** under System Tools in the tree.

3. Click **Sessions** in the tree.

4. How many users are connected to the server? How many of those users have open files? Record your observations.

5. Click **Open Files** in the tree.

6. Are there locked files? If so, record some examples of files that are locked. How might this information provide clues about the software that is used?

7. How would you view the shares that are set up on a server and the number of clients connected to each share?

8. Close the **Computer Management** tool.

Project 4-3

This project enables you to use Network Monitor to analyze network activity and the user base. Network Monitor Driver and Network Monitor should already be installed on a computer running Windows 2000 Server before you start.

To use Network Monitor:

1. Click **Start**, point to **Programs**, point to **Administrative Tools**, and click **Network Monitor**. If a warning box is displayed that indicates a default network is not selected, click OK. Also, click OK if the Select Default Network dialog box is displayed (or select a network per your instructor's advice). (If you select a network, make sure that the NET Dial-up Connection Capture Window is not displayed in the Network Monitor title bar, for capturing through the modem connection. If it is, and after Network Monitor starts, click the Capture menu, click Networks, click Local Computer, and double-click a selection that has the device address of the server's NIC instead of the modem.)

2. Maximize one or both Network Monitor screens, if the display is not maximized.

3. Click the **Start Capture** button on the tool bar (it resembles a right arrow).

4. Scroll the Graph pane. What is the current network utilization? Are there any multi-casts, suggesting the use of multimedia software? Record your findings.

5. Scroll the Total pane to determine the network utilization.

4

6. Scroll through the Session pane. How many computers are communicating with other computers?

7. Scroll through the Station pane and determine the number of computers that are communicating. How many broadcasts have been sent? Is there any network traffic because of multicasts? Record your observations.

8. Compare the network utilization to the number of computers that are active. For example, if there are 20 computers that are active and the network utilization is under 30 percent, then the network is handling the load without problems. If there are 20 active computers, the network utilization is 80 percent, and there is a high number of multicasts, then the network is excessively busy, possibly because of multimedia applications. Record your observations.

9. Click the **Window** menu. Click to remove the check in front of **Total Stats**.

10. Click the **Window** menu again. Click to remove the check in front of **Session Stats**. How might the view of the two remaining panes be helpful in your analysis?

11. Click the **Stop and View Capture** button on the button bar (a black box with eyeglasses over it).

12. What kind of information is now available for your analysis?

13. Close Network Monitor.

14. Click **No** so that you do not save the captured information in a file—but note in your lab journal or in a word-processed document why it might be useful to save the data. Also, click **No** if you are asked to save any unsaved entries in the address database.

Project 4-4

In this project, you determine what administrative software is used at your school. For this project you will need to contact the business manager or a member of the business office. (An alternative is for your instructor to arrange for someone from the business office to field questions from the entire class.)

To analyze the software used at your school:

1. Arrange an interview (or attend the in-class presentation).

2. Develop a set of questions to ask during the interview (and record these in your lab journal or in a word-processed document). Some sample questions are:

   ❑ What administrative software is used?

   ❑ Are there administrative software modules that perform specific functions, such as general ledger and accounts receivable?

    ❐ What security measures are important for use of the administrative software?

    ❐ What office productivity software is used, such as word-processing software?

    ❐ What other software is used by the business office? Is any of this software developed here at the school?

3. Record your findings in your lab journal or in a word-processed document.

4. What Active Directory design issues would you anticipate with the use of this software?

Project 4-5

In this project, you set up remote access policies and edit the profile of a VPN server. You will need access to a VPN server (ask your instructor).

To set up the VPN access policies and edit the profile:

1. Click **Start**, point to **Programs**, point to **Administrative Tools**, and click **Routing and Remote Access**.

2. Double-click the VPN server in the tree (or single-click it, whichever is necessary to display the child objects under the server in the tree).

3. Click **Remote Access Policies** in the tree.

4. Double-click **Allow access if dial-in permission is enabled** in the right pane.

5. Double-click the **Day-And-Time Restrictions matches** parameter in the *Specify the conditions to match* box.

6. Drag the pointer to select all of the times of day boxes in the row for Sunday (the top row) and click **Denied**. What happens to the boxes?

7. Drag the pointer to select all of the times of day boxes in the row for Saturday (the bottom row) and click **Denied**.

8. Click **OK**.

9. Click the **Grant remote access permission** radio button, if it is not already selected.

10. Click the **Edit Profile** button.

11. Click the **Authentication** tab. What protocols are selected by default? Record your observations. Click the box to check the **Extensible Authentication Protocol**, if it is not checked. What box is activated after Extensible Authentication Protocol is checked?

12. Click the **Encryption** tab. What selections are already made? Record your observations. Also, make sure that **Strong** is checked. If it is not, check it.

13. Click the **Dial-in Constraints** tab. How would you disconnect users who have had no activity for over 15 minutes?

14. Click **OK**. Click **No** if an information box appears to display help information because you have changed authentication methods.

15. Click **OK**. Close the Routing and Remote Access tool.

Project 4-6

In this project, you practice analyzing security on a database (group policies) that your instructor has already provided. Ask your instructor for the name of the database to select once you are in the Security Configuration and Analysis tool.

To analyze security:

1. Click **Start**, click **Run**, and type **mmc** in the Open box. Click **OK**.

2. Maximize both console windows, if they are not already maximized.

3. Click the **Console** menu, and click **Add/Remove Snap-in**.

4. Click the **Add** button, and then double-click **Security Configuration and Analysis**.

5. Click **Close** and then **OK**.

6. Right-click **Security Configuration and Analysis** in the tree, and click **Open database**. What database options are available from which to select? Why might there be more than one database shown?

7. Click the database specified by your instructor and then click **Open**. What is now displayed in the right-hand pane? (Click **Security Configuration and Analysis** if no information is displayed.)

8. Right-click **Security Configuration and Analysis** again, and then click **Analyze Computer Now**.

9. Where is the error log file written? Can you change its location? Record your observations. Click **OK**.

10. What information is displayed next as the tool performs the analysis? Wait until the analysis is complete.

11. If the log file contents are not displayed in the right pane, right-click **Security Configuration and Analysis** and check **View Log File**. If View Log File is already checked, remove the check, right-click **Security Configuration and Analysis** again, and check **View Log File**. If the log file is still not displayed, double-click **Security Configuration and Analysis** in the right-hand pane.

12. Scroll through the log file in the right-hand pane. What kind of information is analyzed?

13. How can you view information about current security settings?

14. Close the MMC, and click **No** if you are asked if you want to save the console settings.

Project 4-7

In this project, you practice backing up system state data in Windows 2000 Server. You will need a tape drive installed in the server and a tape. (If you do not have a tape drive, you can specify a file in Step 6 and complete all steps through Step 14.)

4

To back up the system state data:

1. Insert the tape in the tape drive.

2. Click **Start**, point to **Programs**, point to **Accessories,** point to **System Tools**, and click **Backup**.

3. Click the **Backup** tab.

4. Click a drive to back up under My Computer, such as drive **C:**.

5. Click the **System State** box so that a check appears in it (refer to Figure 4-12).

6. In the Backup destination box, select the backup medium, which reflects the type of tape you are using, such as **Travan** or **4mm DAT**.

7. Click the **Start Backup** button.

8. Enter a description and label for the backup. If you are using a new tape or an old one that you can write over, click **Replace the data on the media with this backup**. If you want to retain data already on the tape, click **Append this backup to the media**.

9. Click the **Advanced** button.

10. Click **If possible, compress the backup data to save space**, if this option is available for the medium you selected in Step 6.

11. How would you back up the system protected files?

12. Click the **Backup Type** list box and view the options. Record the options in your lab journal or in a word-processed document, and note which dialog box enables you to access them. Select **Normal** as the option for this backup.

13. Click **OK**.

14. Click the **Start Backup** button (or you can click Cancel if you do not have a tape for practice).

15. Click **Close** when the backup is complete, and then close the Backup utility.

CASE PROJECT

Aspen Consulting Project: Analysis of a Company's Software Environment

The Printed Page is a bookstore chain that has large stores in every major city of the United States. The central office is located in Louisville, Kentucky, and all stores are connected to servers on the central office's LAN through telecommunications-based WAN links. Your main job today is to analyze the software used at the central corporate office building in Louisville. The building is completely networked, and the company has 22 Windows 2000 servers and 5 UNIX servers. They employ 455 users at this site and each employee has a workstation that is connected to the network.

1. What types of workstation operating systems would you look for at this company? How would you inventory the different workstation operating systems?

2. What Windows 2000 Server tools might you use to analyze the user base and user access patterns?

3. What type of software would you expect to find in use at the corporate offices? How would you inventory the software? How might the software affect Active Directory design?

4. As you are analyzing this company, you learn that it uses a book purchasing software system which all of the bookstores must access remotely when they order books for their own inventories and for customers. One of the complaints from most of the bookstores is that the access is often slow over the WAN links. What suggestions do you have that might help?

5. The corporate office has a backup plan that consists of using full and incremental backups. All backup tapes are kept onsite for easy access when they need them. Also, the company has grown so fast that it has no disaster recovery plan. What general recommendations would you make regarding the backup and disaster recovery practices of the corporate office?

6. When a new employee is hired, the employee is trained on a live system at his or her desk. The employee receives a training book and a training tape, and is left to learn as much as possible on his or her own. What would you suggest to improve the training practices?

OPTIONAL CASE PROJECTS FOR TEAMS

Team Case One

Mark Arnez is curious about accounting packages that can be purchased for companies that have over 1000 employees. He asks you to form a team to use the Internet to research accounting packages that companies of this size are likely to use. Create a report of your research findings to show the vendors that make accounting packages, the server or mainframe operating systems they use, and the databases that they use.

Team Case Two

To supplement your team's study of accounting software, Mark asks the team to research which databases are compatible with Windows 2000 Server. Make a list of the databases along with a brief description of each one, including the general security features.

5

ANALYZING HARDWARE AND NETWORK REQUIREMENTS

After reading this chapter and completing the exercises, you will be able to:

♦ Analyze hardware systems used in organizations

♦ Analyze local area networks and bandwidth

♦ Analyze wide area networks and bandwidth

♦ Analyze network management

♦ Analyze user access, productivity, and performance issues

♦ Analyze network and Internet security

In preparing for Active Directory design, determining the hardware and network resources used by an organization is as important as documenting the software and operating systems. The hardware includes workstations, servers, hosts, mainframes, and other systems. The network resources are network devices such as hubs, switches, routers, network server operating systems, LAN and WAN designs, telecommunication links, network protocols, DNS servers, and WINS servers.

In this chapter you will learn to analyze the existing hardware and network resources in an organization. You will learn about analyzing hardware systems such as workstations and host systems. You will also learn to inventory a wide range of network resources and how to prepare network diagrams of resources. Another critical part of analyzing network resources is evaluating security for general network and Web-based communications.

ANALYZING HARDWARE SYSTEMS

When you analyze hardware systems, consider dividing them into at least three categories:

- Workstations
- Host computers
- Network devices

Workstations

The workstations that you will find in an organization include all of the kinds of devices users employ to access network resources. These may be Pentium-based computers, Intel-based computers such as 386 and 486 computers, Alpha-based and Sun Microsystems computers (for UNIX), Macintosh computers, hand-held devices, thin-client computers, and other devices. In addition to using workstations, some organizations may still use terminals. A thin-client computer and a terminal are similar devices in that both access programs on a host computer or server on which the programs run. The difference is that a **thin-client** computer has a CPU and a minimal GUI-based operating system. A **terminal** is a device that consists of a monitor and keyboard to communicate with and run programs on host computers. The terminal does not have a processor to use for running programs locally.

When you assess the workstations on a network, include the speed of workstation network interface cards (NICs), which is likely to be 10 Mbps, 100 Mbps, or an autosensing 10/100 Mbps. Also, consider the speed of the expansion slot of the NIC. A PCI expansion slot is faster than an ESDI expansion slot, for example.

 At this writing, 1 Gbps NICs are becoming available, particularly for servers.

Another workstation element you should assess is the **basic input/output system (BIOS)** on the computers, particularly because this can affect operating system upgrades. BIOS is a program on a read-only or flash memory chip that establishes basic communication with components such as the monitor and disk drives. The advantage of a flash chip is that you can update the BIOS.

When you analyze the workstation hardware, compile the data into a spreadsheet or table that integrates the information with your list of operating systems, as in Table 5-1, a blank form that could be used for York Industries.

Table 5-1   Form for Determining the Workstation User Base and Hardware Base at York Industries

Operating System	Hardware, Including NIC Speed	Number of Users	Country Locations	Future Upgrade Plans
Windows 2000				
Windows NT				
Windows 98				
Windows 95				
UNIX				
Mac OS				

Host Computers

Host computers can include any computer to which others connect for information or to run programs. There are many types of host computers that can be present on a network:

- Computers running Windows 3.11, Windows 95, Windows 98, Windows ME, Windows NT Workstation, and Windows 2000 Professional that offer shared folders and printers

- Computers running Windows NT Server and Windows 2000 Server

- Computers running DNS and WINS

- Computers running DHCP

- Computers operating as RAS (Remote Access Services) servers

- Computers operating as VPN (virtual private network) servers

- Computers operating as Web servers

- Computers running NetWare

- Computers running UNIX that operate as servers

- Mainframe computers, such as an IBM mainframe running MVS or another mainframe operating system

For example, a company might have workstations that share files, Windows NT and Windows 2000 servers, UNIX servers, RAS servers, VPN servers, DNS servers, DHCP servers, and Web servers. At York Industries, information about such host systems could be compiled in a form such as Table 5-2.

Table 5-2   Form for Determining Host Computers at York Industries

Host System	Country Locations	Number and Network Locations	Purpose/Function	Future Upgrade Plans or Changes
Shared folders on workstations				
Windows NT servers				
Windows 2000 servers				
UNIX servers				
DNS servers				
DHCP servers				
RAS servers				
VPN servers				
Web servers				

Network Devices

When you inventory network devices, use the following checklist to determine the number and locations of these devices:

- **Print servers:** Printers, such as dot matrix, laser, and ink-jet printers, and plotters, that are directly connected to the network through a print server card or print server device

- **Repeaters:** Network transmission devices that amplify and retime a packet- or cell-carrying signal so that it can be sent along all outgoing cable segments attached to that repeater

- **Active hubs:** Network transmission devices that connect nodes in a star topology, regenerating, retiming, and amplifying the data signal each time it passes through the hub

- **Passive hubs:** Network transmission devices that connect nodes in a star topology, performing no signal enhancement as the data signal moves from one node to the next through the hub

- **Bridges:** A network transmission device that connects different LAN segments using the same access method, for example connecting one Ethernet LAN to another Ethernet LAN, or a token ring LAN to another token ring LAN

- **Routers:** Network devices that connect networks having the same or different access methods and media, such as Ethernet to token ring. Routers forward packets to networks by using a decision-making process based on routing table data, discovery of the most efficient routes, and preprogrammed information from the network administrator. Routers can also act as firewalls on a network.

- **Brouters:** Network devices that can act as bridges or routers, depending on how they are set up to forward specific protocols

- **Switches:** Network devices that link a network into a star topology and that forward data packets from one segment to another, amplifying the signal to each segment. An advantage of switches as compared to hubs is that they can filter packets.

- **Multiplexers:** Types of switches that divide a communication medium into multiple channels so several nodes can communicate at the same time. When a signal is multiplexed, it must be demultiplexed at the other end.

- **Channel service units (CSUs):** Devices that provide a physical interface between a network device, such as a router, and a telecommunications line. A CSU is used with a DSU.

- **Data service units (DSUs):** Devices used with CSUs for communication over a T-carrier line. DSUs convert data to be sent over the line and convert data received from the line into a format for the receiving network.

- **Access servers:** Devices that link networks to telecommunication lines—for example, by offering modem banks, T-carrier connectivity, and ISDN connectivity

- **Redundant array of inexpensive** (or **independent**) **disks (RAID)** or **RAID arrays:** Sets of disks in arrays that are used to store data and provide fault tolerance

- **CD-ROM arrays:** Arrays of CD-ROM drives that provide access through a network

- **Packet assembler/disassemblers (PADs):** Devices that encapsulate packets into X.25 format and that add X.25 address information. (**X.25** is among the oldest, most reliable transmission methods and uses packet-switching techniques that were developed in the 1960s and 1970s.) The PAD removes the X.25 format information when the packet reaches its destination LAN.

In some organizations, a culture can develop around hardware in which certain hardware is preferred, and specific employees work on specific hardware or hardware-related tasks. IBM mainframes, for example, have spawned hardware cultures of system programmers, COBOL programmers, schedulers, and computer operators who perform specific functions. Network devices also can spawn a particular culture associated with a vendor, because different network device vendors have different equipment to match different design plans. You may find that you are in a situation in which you are analyzing an organization that is growing into a new technology from an older one—for example, switching from a mainframe-based environment to a server-based environment. When you design Active Directory services, keep in mind that the culture will change along with the hardware and software—and avoid reflecting outmoded aspects of the old culture in your design. In the IBM mainframe example, some types of jobs may disappear, such as schedulers. The functions of other jobs will change, particularly for applications development programmers and computer operators.

One place to begin analyzing network devices is by developing an understanding of the types of network devices an organization uses and where those devices are located. Later you can obtain network diagrams, as discussed in the next section of this chapter, which show the role those devices play on specific networks. For instance, York Industries uses switches, brouters, network printers, CSU/DSU modules built into some brouters, access servers, and RAID and CD-ROM arrays. Table 5-3 illustrates how this information might be gathered for York Industries. Also, Figure 5-1 shows how network devices are shown in a network diagram that provides a partial view of how the York Industries network connects to a WAN using devices such as routers and switches.

Table 5-3   Form for Determining Network Devices at York Industries

Network Device	Country Location	Number of Devices and Network Locations	Function	Future Upgrade Plans or Changes
Switches				
Brouters without CSU/DSU				
Brouters with CSU/DSU				
Network printers				
Access servers				
RAID arrays				
CD-ROM arrays				

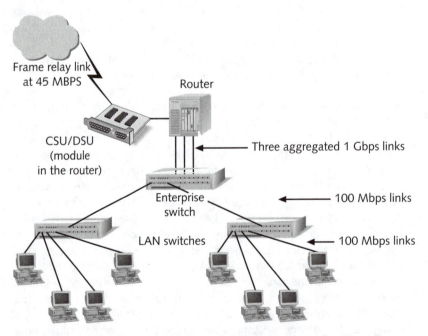

Figure 5-1   A small portion of the York Industries network in Toronto connecting to a WAN

LOCAL AREA NETWORK SYSTEMS AND BANDWIDTH

Many organizations maintain network diagrams, which can be an invaluable source of information for analyzing both LANs and WANs. If your organization does not have diagrams of its LANs and WANs, consider making your own. Software is available for diagramming networks that comes with clip art or stencils of typical network devices. Also, some network management software comes with the ability to inventory hardware and produce a diagram or report. Ideally a LAN diagram will contain the following information:

- Network backbone (communications cable or wireless infrastructure that joins different LANs)

- Servers, including their locations and IP addresses

- Host computers, including their locations and IP addresses

- Workstations, including their locations and IP addresses, subnet masks, and subnet address information

- Network devices, including their locations and IP addresses

- Telecommunications links, including copper, fiber-optic, and wireless

- Internet connectivity

- Intranets

- Remote links

- Building locations

- Cable types

- Wireless communications links and frequencies (as measured in hertz, such as 902 megahertz)

If you create your own diagrams for a medium-to-large organization, consider first creating a general diagram of the entire network, including LANs and WANs, without showing all of the devices or workstations. Figure 5-2 illustrates a general network diagram for a company that does business in four cities around the world. Also, create diagrams of local interconnected LANs for a closeup view of a particular site in a larger WAN. If your organization has network management software, then you may be able to use this software to provide an understanding of a local site. Figure 5-3 illustrates how to display this information for a university campus, using SunNet Manager network management software (network management software is discussed more extensively later in this chapter). Try Hands-on Projects 5-1 and 5-2 to practice interpreting a network diagram and creating one of your own.

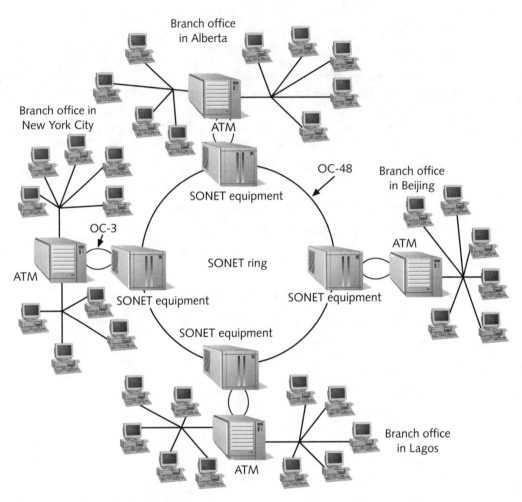

Figure 5-2   Large network diagram

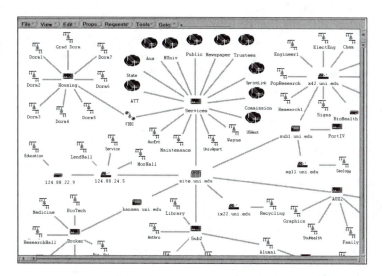

Figure 5-3   Resource inventory created with SunNet Manager

 Tip Some examples of software that enables you to create diagrams to model a network are Autodesk's AutoCAD, LANflow by Pacestart Software, Altima's NetZoom, netViz by netViz, RFF Electronic's RFFlow, Smartdraw by SmartDraw, and Microsoft Visio.

Analyzing LAN Transmission Methods

The most common LAN transmission methods are Ethernet and token ring. Fiber Distributed Data Interface (FDDI) is another LAN transmission technology that you will find on some network backbones.

Ethernet uses a control method known as Carrier Sense Multiple Access with Collision Detection (CSMA/CD). CSMA/CD is an algorithm (computer logic) that transmits and decodes formatted data packets. Using CSMA/CD, the Ethernet sending node encapsulates the frame to prepare it for transmission. All nodes that wish to transmit a frame on the cable are in contention with one another. No single node has priority over another node. The nodes listen for any packet traffic on the cable. If a packet is detected, the nonsending nodes go into a "defer" mode. The Ethernet protocol permits only one node to transmit at a time. Transmission is accomplished by sending a carrier signal. Carrier sense is the process of checking the communication cable for a specific voltage level indicating the presence of a data-carrying signal. When no signal traffic is detected on the communication media for a given amount of time, any node is eligible to transmit. An Ethernet network can use a bus (straight line) or physical star layout (topology), with the physical star layout via a hub or switch being the most popular.

Occasionally in Ethernet transmissions more than one node will transmit at the same time, which results in a collision. The transmitting node detects a collision by measuring the signal strength. A collision has occurred if the signal is at least twice the normal strength.

A transmitting node uses the collision detection software algorithm to recover from packet collisions. This algorithm causes the stations that have transmitted to continue their transmission for a designated time. The continued transmission is a jam signal of all binary 1s, which enables all listening nodes to determine that a collision has occurred. The software at each node then generates a random number, which is used as the amount of time to wait before transmitting again. This ensures that no two nodes will attempt to transmit again at the same time.

The **token ring** access method was developed by IBM in the 1970s and remains a primary LAN technology. The token ring transport method uses a physical star topology along with the logic of a ring topology. Although each node is connected to a central hub, the packet travels from node to node as though there were no starting or ending point. Each node is joined through a **multistation access unit (MAU)**. The MAU is a specialized hub that ensures the packet is transmitted around the ring of computers.

 MAU technology has evolved into new hub devices, such as the controlled access unit (CAU), which allows several units to be connected (stacked) together and count as one MAU. CAUs also can have options to gather information that is used in network performance management.

A specialized frame, called the token, is continuously transmitted on the ring to determine when a node can send a packet. In most implementations, there is only one token available on the ring, although the official token ring specifications permit two tokens for networks operating at 16 Mbps or faster. When a node wishes to transmit, it must capture the token. No other node can capture the token and transmit until the active node is finished. The station that captures the token builds a frame that consists of data along with the token. The data-carrying frame is sent around the ring until it is received by the target node. The target node changes two bits to show that the frame reached its destination and that the data was read. Next, the target node places the frame back on the network and it continues around the ring until the transmitting station picks it up, checking the token to determine if it was received. The transmitting station then encapsulates the next frame of data with the token, or it builds a token without data to return to the ring so a different station can capture it.

The **Fiber Distributed Data Interface (FDDI)** standard was developed in the mid-1980s to provide higher-speed data communication than was originally offered by Ethernet or token ring. FDDI uses fiber-optic cable as the communications medium; a common application of FDDI is to provide fast access to network servers. FDDI is similar to the token ring access method because it uses token passing for network communication. It differs from standard token ring in that it uses a timed token access method. An FDDI token travels along the network ring from station to station. If a station does not need to transmit data, it picks up the token and sends it to the next station. If the station possessing the token does need to transmit, it can send as many frames as desired for a fixed amount of time, called the target token rotation time (TTRT). Because FDDI uses a timed token method, it is possible for several frames from several stations to be on the network at a given time, providing high-capacity communication. FDDI employs two routes or rings, so that if one ring malfunctions, data can reach its destination on the other ring.

Analyzing Protocols

It is important to inventory the protocols that are used on a network because Active Directory offers more services for some protocols than for others. The protocol of the Internet, TCP/IP, has the most Active Directory options, including security and site creation capabilities. Typical protocols to include in your inventory can be any combination of the following:

- TCP/IP
- NetBEUI
- IPX/SPX
- AppleTalk
- SNA and DLC

Transmission Control Protocol/Internet Protocol (TCP/IP) is a protocol combination that was developed early in the evolution of the Internet for robust communications. TCP is a transport protocol that establishes communication sessions between software application processes initiated by users on a network. TCP provides for reliable end-to-end delivery of data by controlling data flow. Nodes agree upon a "window" for data transmission that includes the number of bytes that will be sent. The transmission window is constantly adjusted to account for existing network traffic. The essential TCP functions are to monitor for session requests, to establish sessions with other TCP nodes, to transmit and receive data, and to close transmission sessions.

IP is designed to provide for data transfer, packet addressing, packet routing, packet fragmentation, and simple detection of packet errors. Successful data transfer and routing to the correct network or subnetwork are made possible by IP addressing conventions. Each network station has a 32-bit IP address, which also correlates with its 48-bit MAC (device) address for network communication. The address identifies a given network as well as a specific station on the network.

NetBIOS Extended User Interface (NetBEUI) was developed as the native protocol for LAN Manager and LAN Server, which are early server network operating systems that were developed as a joint IBM and Microsoft venture. NetBEUI later became the native protocol for Windows NT. NetBEUI was developed by IBM in 1985, as an enhancement of **Network Basic Input/Output System (NetBIOS)**. NetBIOS is a method for interfacing software with network services, and it provides naming services that are used on many Microsoft networks. It is not a protocol. NetBIOS names are used to name objects on a network, such as a workstation, server, or printer. NetBEUI was developed when computer networking primarily meant local area networking for a relatively small number of computers, from just a few to as many as 200. It was not developed to take into account enterprise networks on which packets are routed from LAN to LAN, and it does not have routing capabilities.

5

If you encounter NetBEUI in your analysis of a Microsoft-based network, recommend converting to TCP/IP, if possible.

The **Internet Packet Exchange (IPX)** protocol was developed for Novell NetWare as an adaptation of the earlier Xerox Network System protocol. Although it's an early network protocol, one advantage of IPX over some other early protocols is that it can be routed, meaning that it can transport data over multiple networks in an enterprise. A disadvantage is that IPX is a "chatty" protocol because live stations using IPX frequently broadcast their presence across the network. When there are multiple IPX-configured NetWare servers and several hundred clients, the IPX broadcasts can amount to significant network traffic. Along with IPX, Novell implemented a companion protocol called **Sequence Packet Exchange (SPX)**. SPX enables the exchange of application-specific data with greater reliability than IPX.

The presence of IPX/SPX usually means that there are older NetWare servers (pre-NetWare version 5) on the network. As is true for Windows 2000 Server, newer versions of NetWare use TCP/IP as the protocol of preference.

Apple developed the **AppleTalk** protocol suite to network Macintosh systems. AppleTalk is a peer-to-peer network protocol, which means it is designed to enable Macintosh workstations to communicate regardless of the presence of a server, and it provides options to connect to Novell NetWare, MS-DOS, Microsoft Windows 3.x, Windows 95, Windows 98, Windows ME, Windows NT, and Windows 2000. AppleTalk Phase II handles an increased number of networked computers and is interoperable with large heterogeneous networks that host multiple protocols.

Older IBM mainframe computer installations may use **Systems Network Architecture (SNA)** instead of TCP/IP. When workstations running Microsoft Windows 95, Windows 98, Windows ME, Windows NT, or Windows 2000 are used to access an SNA-based mainframe, an alternative to using an SNA gateway is to install the **Data Link Control (DLC)** protocol at the workstation. DLC emulates SNA, and is also used to communicate with some types of network printers, such as older Hewlett-Packard printers.

The simplest way to determine which protocols are in use is by means of the Network and Dial-up Connections tool from the Control Panel in Windows 2000 or, in Windows NT 4.0, by using the Network tool in the Control Panel. Try Hands-on Project 5-3 to check the protocols used by a Windows 2000 server on a network.

One way to document how different protocols are used on a network is to include them in a network diagram. For example, Jefferson Philately uses TCP/IP for its Windows 2000 servers and IPX/SPX for its NetWare 4.1 servers. Figure 5-4 shows how a network diagram might be prepared for analysis, showing part of Jefferson Philately's network and the protocols that are in use.

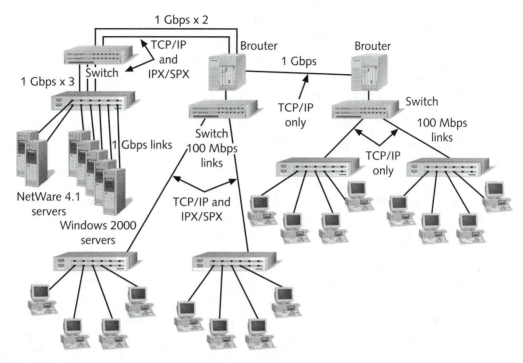

Figure 5-4 Protocols used on the Jefferson Philately network

Analyzing IP Addresses, Subnets, and Subnet Masks

Determine the IP addresses of servers, workstations, and host computers as part of your analysis. Also, determine what subnets are used on a network. This information is vital for planning the locations of DCs, global catalog servers, and DNS servers, and how to set up sites in Active Directory.

Most current networks use IP version 4 (IPv4) addresses that are assigned either statically or dynamically. Static addressing means that a network administrator assigns addresses, often keeping track of who has what address in a database of IP addresses. Dynamic addressing means that there is a **Dynamic Host Configuration Protocol (DHCP)** server. DHCP is a protocol in the TCP/IP suite that is used along with DHCP services to detect the presence of a new network client and assign an IP address to that client. For example, if your analysis shows that Windows 95, 98, NT, or 2000 clients are set up to automatically obtain IP addresses, this means that each client contacts a DHCP server to obtain an address. The DHCP server has a preassigned range of IP addresses that it can give to new clients. Each address is assigned for a specific period of time, such as eight hours, two weeks, a month, or a year. A range of contiguous addresses is called the scope.

The IP address format is called the dotted decimal notation address. It is 32 bits long and contains four fields, decimal values representing 8-bit binary octets. An IP address in binary octet format looks like this: 10000001.00000101.00001010.1100100, which converts to 129.5.10.100 in decimal format.

A special-purpose form of addressing is the **subnet mask**. A subnet mask is used for two purposes: to show the class of addressing used, and to divide a network into subnetworks to control network traffic. For class addressing, the subnet mask enables an application to determine which part of the address is for the network ID and which is for the host ID. The *network ID* is the first part of the address and is used to differentiate one network from another, while the *host ID* is the second part of the address and is used to identify a specific computer or device on the network.

To accomplish the second purpose, dividing the network into subnetworks, the subnet mask consists of a subnet ID within the network and host IDs, which is determined by the network administrator. For example, the subnet mask 255.255.255.0 (11111111.11111111.11111111.00000000 in octets) designates the first three octets as the network ID and subnet, and the last octet as the host ID. Thus in the address 129.70.10.22, the network ID is 129.70, the subnet is .10, and the host ID is .22. Using the subnet mask to divide a network into a series of smaller networks enables IP-aware network devices such as routers to effectively ignore traditional address class designations, enabling more options for segmenting networks through multiple subnets and to provide additional network addresses to overcome the four-octet length limitation. A new way to ignore address class designation is by using **Classless Interdomain Routing (CIDR)** addressing, which puts a slash (/) after the dotted decimal notation. CIDR provides more IP address options for medium-sized networks, for which there is a particular shortage of addresses. The shortage is due to the proliferation of networks combined with the finite number of addresses numerically possible in the basic four-octet address scheme. For example, a CIDR network addressing scheme for a network that needs up to 16,384 (2^{14}) stations might be 165.100.0.0/14.

Microsoft and other vendors have made a commitment to implement IP version 6 (IPv6) capability on networks, which will help overcome IP address shortages and provide new services. The purpose of IPv6 is to provide a logical growth path from IPv4 so that applications and network devices can handle new demands as they arise. Currently, IPv4 is used on most networks throughout the world, but the transition to IPv6 is beginning. Among the new features of IPv6 are:

- 128-bit address capability
- A single address can be associated with multiple network interfaces
- Address autoconfiguration and CIDR addressing
- A 40-byte header instead of IPv4's 20-byte header (for more services)
- New IP extension headers that can be implemented for special needs, including more routing and security options

In your analysis of a network, determine IP-related information such as:

- What version of IP is used, IPv4 or IPv6
- Whether IP addresses are assigned dynamically or statically
- What IP address ranges are used (or scopes when DHCP is in use)
- The subnets that are used and their locations
- The reasons why subnets are used

Try Hands-on Project 5-4 to examine scopes on a Microsoft DHCP server.

When you analyze scopes, keep in mind that a Microsoft DHCP server can have up to 1000 different scopes and up to 10,000 DHCP clients.

Analyzing DNS and WINS Servers

The **Domain Name System (DNS)** servers on a network can be Windows 2000 servers, UNIX servers, or another host computer that provides DNS services. DNS resolves IP addresses to computer names—for example, resolving 124.92.1.145 to the computer name Wilson; it also resolves computer names to IP addresses. **Windows Internet Naming Service (WINS)** is used with DNS Server to resolve IP addresses and computer names on networks in which NetBIOS applications are still in use, including NetBIOS computer names for pre-Windows 2000 clients, such as Windows 95, Windows 98, and Windows NT.

Typically, two zones of data are created on a DNS server. One zone, called the **forward lookup zone**, holds host name records, called address records, to map a computer name to the IP address. Each IP-based server and client should have a host record so that it can be found through DNS. For example, if the DNS server name is Research, with the IP address 145.85.22.5, then the forward lookup zone maps Research to 145.85.22.5. In IP version 4, a host record is called a *host address (A) resource record*. An IPv6 host record is called an *IPv6 host address (AAAA) resource record*. Figure 5-5 shows the forward lookup zone host records as displayed in the Microsoft DNS management tool. When Microsoft DNS is installed on a DC in a domain, a forward lookup zone is automatically created for the domain with the DNS server record already entered. The network administrator must enter the records of other hosts or configure DHCP to automatically update the DNS forward lookup zone each time it assigns an IP address. Depending on the domain structure and Internet connectivity, a DNS server can have several forward lookup zones, but there should be at least one for the parent domain.

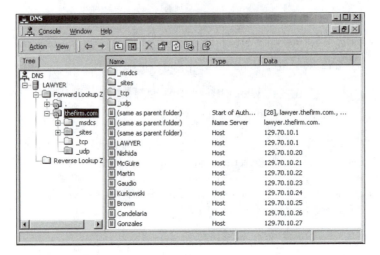

Figure 5-5 DNS forward lookup zone

A second type of zone, called the **reverse lookup zone**, holds the *pointer (PTR) resource record*, which contains the IP address resolved to the host name. The reverse lookup zone is not as commonly used as the forward lookup zone, but can be important to create for those instances when a network communication requires associating an IP address to a computer name—for example, for monitoring a network using IP address information. Because it is used less commonly, the reverse lookup zone is not automatically created when Microsoft DNS is installed. Try Hands-on Project 5-5 to practice examining forward and reverse lookup zones.

When you analyze DNS on a network, look at the following:

- The operating system of the DNS server, such as Windows 2000 Server or UNIX
- Where DNS servers are located on the network
- The placement of primary and secondary (backup) DNS servers
- Information in the forward and reverse lookup zones
- Whether or not DNS zones are automatically updated when a new device is connected

When you analyze the use of WINS servers, determine the:

- Reason why WINS is used, such as for pre-Windows 2000 object naming
- NetBIOS naming conventions used on a network
- Locations of WINS servers

Analyzing Bandwidth

Bandwidth is the transmission capacity of a communication medium, which is typically measured in bits per second (bps, for data transmissions) or hertz (Hz, for combined data, voice, and video transmissions in wireless communications). Technically, bandwidth is determined by the maximum minus the minimum transmission capacity of a communication medium.

Bandwidth is related to the capacity of the communication medium and to the transmission method. The following are some typical bandwidth capacities that you will find in your analysis of a network:

- 10 Mbps Ethernet

- 100 Mbps Ethernet (Fast Ethernet)

- 1 Gbps Ethernet (Gigabit Ethernet)

- 10 Gbps Ethernet

- 4 Mbps token ring (on older networks)

- 16 Mbps token ring

- 100 Mbps token ring

- 100 Mbps FDDI

- Wireless spread spectrum at 902–928 MHz (megahertz), 2.4 GHz (gigahertz), and 5.72–5.85 GHz yielding an equivalent of 1–10 Mbps, depending on the transmission equipment

- Wireless infrared at 100 GHz–1000 THz (terahertz) yielding up to 16 Mbps for directional communications and under 1 Mbps for omnidirectional communications

- Wireless microwave at 4–6 GHz and 21–23 GHz currently yielding 1–10 Mbps, depending on the transmission devices used

- Wireless satellite at 11–14 GHz, currently yielding 1–10 Mbps, depending on the transmission devices used

- Wireless low orbiting satellite (LEO) at 11–14 GHz, which is currently under development, yielding 2 Mbps for uplink transmissions and 64 Mbps for downlink transmissions (and with the potential to reach 155 Mbps)

When you study a network diagram, look for information about bandwidth, or if you make your own diagram, include bandwidth information as in Figure 5-6.

Try Hands-on Project 5-6 to analyze bandwidth and the LAN transmission method on a Windows 2000 server.

5

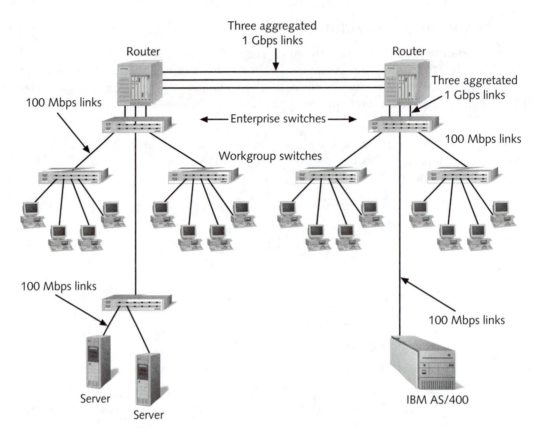

Figure 5-6   Bandwidth information

Create a checklist of the information that you should analyze in relation to LAN resources, such as the following:

- Obtain or create network diagrams showing information about the network layout (topology)

- Determine the LAN transmission methods, including Ethernet, token ring, and FDDI

- Determine the LAN protocols, such as TCP/IP, IPX/SPX, NetBEUI, AppleTalk, SNA, and DLC

- Determine IP addressing conventions, including subnet masks

- Determine how IP subnets are used

- Assess the deployment of DNS, WINS, and DHCP servers

- Determine the Ethernet, token ring, FDDI, and wireless bandwidths of specific links

For an organization such as Jefferson Philately, Interstate Security Bank, or York Industries, create or obtain a network diagram that shows everything on this checklist, such as protocols, bandwidth, transmission methods, locations of IP subnets, and current placement of DNS, DHCP, and WINS servers. Also, contact the DNS server manager and ask him or her to print out the contents of all information that is contained in DNS tables, such as all forward and reverse lookup zones, plus subnet information.

 Identifying subnets and their locations via a network diagram provides help in deciding how to design Active Directory sites.

5

WIDE AREA NETWORK SYSTEMS AND BANDWIDTH

Analyzing WAN links on a network is just as important as analyzing LANs, particularly for companies like Interstate Security Bank and York Industries. There are many WAN options available to organizations, depending on local, regional, and long-distance telecommunications companies and the part of the world in which the organization is located. When local, regional, or long-distance telecommunications companies do not offer appropriate WAN communications options, some organizations build their own. Factors that are important for analyzing WAN communications are:

- WAN transmission methods

- WAN technologies transmitted over other WANs

- WAN bandwidth

Analyzing WAN Transmission Methods

WAN transmission methods have evolved from early and tested technologies to new and complex technologies. Simple modem communications and X.25 communications are two examples of early technologies that are still widely used. DSL and SONET are examples of new technologies offered by some telecommunications companies.

The WAN technologies that you should look for in your network analysis are:

- *Modem communications over regular telephone lines:* Modem communications involve modulating and demodulating data signals over telephone lines, often called plain old telephone service (POTS), or more recently called public switched telephone network (PSTN).

- *X.25:* X.25 defines how data is sent from data terminal equipment (DTE), such as computers, to data circuit equipment (DCE), such as a packet switch or access device into a public data network. X.25 is a point-to-point connection-oriented WAN protocol rather than a point-to-multipoint connectionless protocol, which is used in some other WAN approaches. Because it is connection-oriented, X.25

includes techniques to verify the continuity of the WAN connection and to ensure that each packet reaches its intended destination. Each DTE is connected to a DCE through a PAD. A PAD has multiple ports, which enable it to set up a different virtual circuit for each computer system that attaches to it. The DCE connects to a vendor's *packet switching exchange (PSE),* which is a switch in the X.25 WAN network located at the vendor's site. X.25 is primarily intended for data communications (see Figure 5-7).

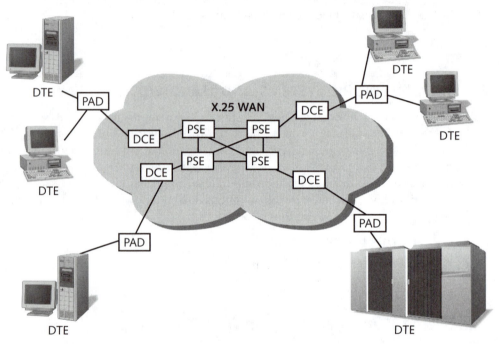

Figure 5-7   X.25 WAN architecture

 Packet switching is a data transmission technique that establishes a logical (virtual) channel between two transmitting nodes, but uses several different paths of transmission to continually find the best routes to the destination.

- *Frame relay:* **Frame relay** was first proposed in 1984 as a WAN transport method. Frame relay has several elements in common with X.25—for example, both use packet switching over telecommunication lines. In frame relay, a DTE might be a router, bridge, or computer that is connected to a DCE, which in frame relay is a network device that connects to the frame relay WAN. Instead of using a PAD to convert packets as in X.25, frame relay uses a frame relay access device (FRAD), which is often a module in a router, switch, or chassis hub (see Figure 5-8). Unlike X.25, frame relay is designed to interface with modern networks that do their own error checking. It achieves high-speed data transmission by recognizing that newer network technologies have error checking on intermediate stations, and therefore it does not incorporate extensive error checking, which means it is a connection-less service. Frame relay is often used as a WAN link between TCP/IP- and IPX-based networks. Besides data communications, frame relay can also be adapted for voice communications by using *voice over frame relay* techniques.

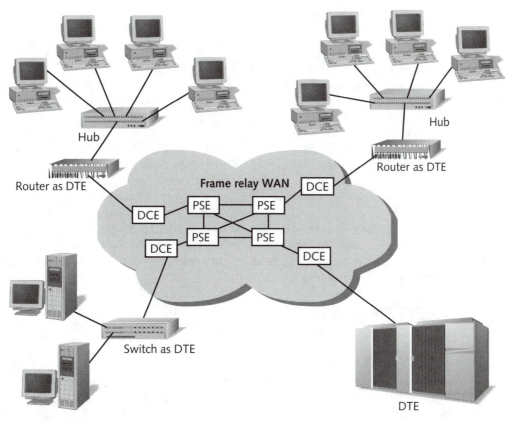

Figure 5-8   Frame relay WAN architecture

- *ISDN:* **Integrated Services Digital Network (ISDN)** was first proposed in the 1970s to provide voice, data, graphics, and video digital transmission services, and was standardized in 1984 and 1988. Many telecommunications companies offer ISDN over digital telecommunications lines. "Single line service" digital ISDN for individual residences is available from local telephone companies. Single line service enables the end user to connect several devices to the line, such as a fax, computer, and digital telephone. Organizations that connect one LAN to another over an ISDN WAN generally do so through a T-carrier type of line. One advantage of ISDN communications is that multiple ISDN lines can be aggregated for a total communication speed that is equal to the speed of all lines added together.

- *SMDS:* **Switched megabit data service (SMDS)** was developed by Bell Communications and was first demonstrated in 1990 as a telecommunications-based system. SMDS is a cell-based data transmission technology instead of a packet-based one. Cells offer an advantage over packets in that they can contain a higher payload of data (more data per cell). As SMDS has developed, it has been designed to be compatible with high-speed broadband ISDN to provide extremely fast transport of SMDS over long distances. SMDS cells are handled through SMDS switches that are joined by high-speed digital lines. SMDS is a connectionless transport system intended to reduce overhead by leaving error checking to intelligent end devices such as switches and routers.

- *DSL:* **Digital subscriber line (DSL)** uses advanced modulation technologies on existing copper telephone line networks for high-speed networking between a subscriber and a telecommunications company. DSL supports transmission of data, voice, and video communications, including multimedia applications. Originally intended for telecommuters and small businesses, DSL is increasingly used by medium and large businesses and corporations as a "last mile" connectivity option to a telecommunications company. Last mile connectivity involves providing access between a company, business, or home and the local telecommunications company or network services provider. When used in a home office, a workstation is connected to DSL using a DSL modem in a computer. When DSL is made available to multiple workstations on a LAN, a DSL adapter is used to connect the telecommunications line to a router, which in turn is connected to a WAN (see Figure 5-9).

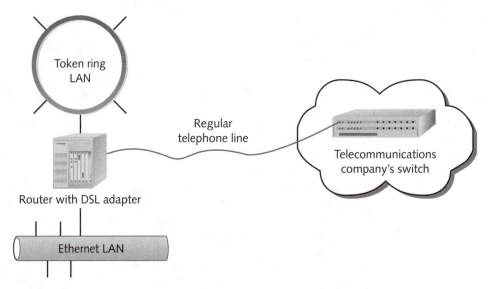

Figure 5-9   DSL WAN architecture

- *ATM:* **Asynchronous transfer mode (ATM)** is a high-speed cell-based technology in which different classes of service can be allocated to different types of transmissions—for example, simple data transmissions as compared to complex multimedia transmissions. Telecommunications companies offer ATM for WAN communications and often complement these services with SONET and frame relay. The advantages of ATM are numerous. It is scalable, so speeds can be increased as a LAN or WAN grows, or as a LAN grows into a WAN. It is used to solve congestion problems and help segment networks. Originally intended only for WAN applications, ATM is also used to provide high-speed backbone connectivity for LANs. Large banks and universities use ATM for WAN communications between distant sites, and the film industry uses it to transport motion pictures. ATM supports transmission of voice, video, and multimedia applications.

- *SONET:* **Synchronous optical network (SONET)** is a fiber-optic technology that can transmit data over a WAN at extremely high speeds. SONET has grown rapidly, and more and more telephone companies have added it to their service options. In Europe, synchronous digital hierarchy (SDH) is a telecommunications technology that is very similar to SONET. Both technologies use cell-based transmissions instead of packets. SONET and SDH are fiber-optic communications technologies that provide multiple levels of data recovery capabilities, which are selected as different services by users.

Analyzing Protocol Support over WANs

Many WAN technologies enable other LAN and WAN technologies to operate through them. For example, FDDI can operate over SONET. This provides compatibility for situations in which one technology must be used for part of the distance and another technology for the remaining distance. It also provides compatibility with technologies already used on LANs. For example, SMDS and ATM can be transmitted over broadband ISDN, and FDDI, SMDS, and ATM can be transmitted over SONET. When you analyze network connectivity, determine if a WAN technology is being used over another WAN technology.

York Industries, for example, employs a WAN technology between Toronto and Palisades in which SMDS is transported over SONET, which is documented in a network diagram.

Analyzing WAN Bandwidth

The transmission speeds for different WAN technologies can vary, depending on how that technology is implemented. The following are typical bandwidths for the WAN technologies discussed in this chapter:

- *Modem communications over regular telephone lines:* Transmission rates can vary from 300 bps to 56 Kbps and higher.

- *X.25:* Transmission rates are usually from 64 Kbps to 2.048 Mbps, but some European networks support only 9.6 Kbps.

- *Frame relay:* Initially, the most common implementations of frame relay were at 56 Kbps and 2 Mbps, but modern frame relay implementations can reach speeds up to 45 Mbps.

- *ISDN:* There are typically two ISDN service interfaces available in most areas. The *basic rate interface (BRI)* has an aggregate data rate of 144 Kbps. The BRI consists of three channels: two are 64 Kbps B channels for data, voice, and graphics transmissions, and the third is a 16 Kbps D channel used for communications signaling, packet switching, and credit card verification. ISDN BRI is not suitable for some network applications, such as large file transfers and graphics applications, without aggregating or "bonding" channels together. For example, one BRI line with two 64 Kbps channels can be bonded to achieve a 128 Kbps connection, and with channel D added the total rate is 144 Kbps. Another example is the bonding of three BRI lines consisting of six 64 Kbps channels for an aggregate speed of 384 Kbps. The primary rate interface (PRI) supports faster data rates, with an aggregate of switched bandwidth equal to 1.536 Mbps. In the United States and Japan, PRI consists of twenty-three 64 Kbps channels and one 64 Kbps channel for signaling communications and for packet switching. European PRI ISDN is thirty 64 Kbps channels and one 64 Kbps signaling or packet switching channel. Figure 5-10 is a simple network diagram showing PRI ISDN architecture. Broadband ISDN is under development and has a theoretical limit of 622 Mbps.

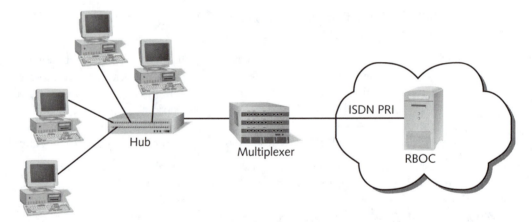

Figure 5-10   ISDN PRI architecture

- *SMDS:* Transmission is typically over a T-carrier telecommunications line. The normal T-1 speed is 1.544 Mbps, but SMDS over a T-1 line transports data at 1.17 Mbps. When a T-3 line is used with DS-3 access rates, SMDS divides the line into different service classes that transmit at a combination of speeds, which are 4, 10, 16, 25, and 34 Mbps.

- *DSL:* The speed of DSL depends on what type of DSL technology is used. Table 5-4 shows the DSL technologies and their associated transmission rates.

Table 5-4 DSL Bandwidth

DSL Technology	Bandwidth
Asymmetrical digital subscriber line (ADSL)	Transmits at 576–640 Kbps for upstream (to the telecommunications company), and up to 6 Mbps for downstream (to the customer)
Rate adaptive asymmetric digital subscriber line (RADSL)	Transmits at 1 Mbps upstream and 7 Mbps downstream
High bit-rate digital subscriber line (HDSL)	Uses full-duplex (both ways at the same time) transmissions at 768 Kbps
Very high bit-rate digital subscriber line (VDSL)	Transmits upstream at 1.6–2.3 Mbps and downstream at 51–55 Mbps
Symmetric digital subscriber line (SDSL)	Transmits upstream and downstream at 384 Kbps

5

- *ATM:* The possible ATM transmission speeds are 25 Mbps, 51 Mbps, 155 Mbps, 622 Mbps, 1.2 Gbps, and 2.4 Gbps. The lower speeds, 622 Mbps and below, are used for LAN implementations, and speeds above 622 Mbps are used for WANs.

U.S. and international vendors have worked to ensure uniform operability no matter who manufactures ATM devices, which makes ATM very suitable for global WAN implementations.

- *SONET:* SONET operates at a base level of 51.84 Mbps, or optical carrier level 1 (OC–1), and the electrical equivalent is called Synchronous Transport Signal Level 1 (STS–1). The signal can be incrementally switched to higher speeds as needed for a particular type of service. The currently available range of speeds is shown in Table 5-5. Future SONET transmission speeds are expected to reach STS level 256 at 13.271 Gbps.

Table 5-5 SONET Bandwidth

Optical Carrier Level	STS Level	Transmission Rate in Mbps
OC–1	STS–1	51.84
OC–3	STS–3	155.52
OC–9	STS–9	466.56
OC–12	STS–12	622.08
OC–18	STS–18	933.12
OC–24	STS–24	1244
OC–36	STS–36	1866
OC–48	STS–48	2488

Use the following checklist when you analyze WAN communications:

- Determine which WAN technologies are in use, such as modem communications, X.25, frame relay, ISDN, SMDS, DSL, ATM, and SONET.

- Determine if one WAN technology is also transporting another WAN technology, such as SONET transporting ATM.

- Determine the bandwidth of all WAN links.

For an organization such as Jefferson Philately, Interstate Security Bank, or York Industries, use a network diagram to help in your analysis of the WAN links. A network diagram that shows the WAN links between each networked location, WAN technologies, and bandwidths is a significant aid for designing Active Directory sites (see Chapter 7).

ANALYZING NETWORK MANAGEMENT

Network management involves using specialized tools, software, and protocols to assess network performance and troubleshoot problems. As an Active Directory designer, network management affects you in a couple of ways. One is when a network employs network management protocols that are compatible with Active Directory. A second way that network management affects Active Directory design is when management software that complements Active Directory functions is deployed.

One important example of a network management protocol is **Simple Network Management Protocol (SNMP)**. SNMP enables network managers to continuously monitor network activity and is compatible with Windows NT and Windows 2000, including Active Directory. A more recent version of SNMP called SNMPv2 has been developed to provide better security.

Another network management protocol that might be in use instead of SNMP is the **Common Management Interface Protocol (CMIP)**. Most hardware and network management software vendors have chosen to implement SNMP instead of CMIP because TCP/IP is widely used, and because SNMP is easier to use. Several hundred types of networking devices support SNMP, including file servers, network interface cards, routers, repeaters, bridges, switches, and hubs. In contrast, CMIP is used by IBM in some token ring applications, but is not used on many other networks.

SNMP functions through two types of nodes, the *network management station (NMS)* and *network agents*. The NMS monitors networked devices that are equipped to communicate via SNMP. The managed devices run agent software that is in contact with the network management station. Most devices connected to modern networks are agents. These include routers, repeaters, hubs, switches, bridges, PCs (via the NIC), print servers, access servers, and UPSs.

You can use the console at the NMS to send commands to network devices and obtain statistics on performance. The NMS can build a map of the entire network. If a new device is added, the NMS can discover it immediately. Software on the NMS has the ability to detect when an agent is down or malfunctioning. That agent may be highlighted in red, an alarm may sound, or both. All NMS software is now written in GUI format so it is easy to interpret.

Many NMS software packages have a graphical display to show network utilization, flow of packets, and other network performance information. The graphical representations are important in identifying what type of agent the metering represents and the severity of the problem. Some also have application programming interfaces (APIs) that act as doors into the NMS software to enable you to customize programming features through Visual Basic, for example.

Each agent keeps a database of information, including the number of packets sent, the number of packets received, packet errors, the number of connections, and more. An agent's database is called the Management Information Base (MIB). The NMS uses a range of commands to obtain or alter MIB data. SNMP communications contain a community name or "string," which is a password shared by the NMS and the agent. The MIB on each network agent stores data on the network object on which it is activated, such as workstations, servers, bridges, routers, switches, hubs, and repeaters.

 A newer MIB standard, MIB II, provides improved security, support for token ring, support for high-speed interfaces, and support for telecommunications interfaces.

Remote Network Monitoring (RMON) is an SNMP-based tool used to monitor LANs connected through WANs. RMON not only employs SNMP, but also incorporates a special database, called RMON MIB-II, for remote monitoring. This database enables remote network stations to gather network analysis data at virtually any point on a LAN or WAN (see Figure 5-11). The remote nodes are agents or probes. Information gathered by the probes can be sent to a management station that compiles it into a database. RMON MIB-II standards are currently in place for FDDI, Ethernet, and token ring networks. Both Interstate Security Bank and York Industries use SNMPv2 and RMON for network monitoring throughout their WANs.

To determine how network management is deployed, use a checklist of what to assess, such as:

- Determining if network management protocols are used, such as SNMP or CMIP.

- Determining which stations act as network agents and NMSs.

- Using the NMS and network management software to your advantage for gathering information about how a network is set up.

- Finding out what network management software is used, such as software created by Sun Microsystems, IBM, and Hewlett-Packard, and determine how it is used to manage a network.

- Assessing the security in place for SNMP or CMIP.

- Determining if RMON is used.

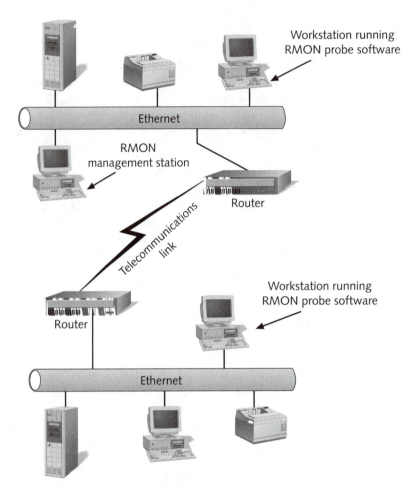

Figure 5-11 RMON architecture

 Full-system network management software includes CiscoWorks 2000 from Cisco, Tivali's NetView, IBM's Nways Manager, Hewlett-Packard's Openview, and Sun Microsystems' Solstice (which includes SunNet Manager).

York Industries, for example, uses SNMPv2, Windows 2000 Network Monitor, CiscoWorks 2000, and Hewlett-Packard's Openview software, all of which enable them to manage network devices, inventory computers connected to the network, monitor network performance, and monitor for devices that are down. They also use an Openview software module that has RMON capabilities. All of these simplify the process of obtaining network information for Active Directory design analysis. Also, through Active Directory compatibility with SNMPv2, they are able to set community names for security and to set traps for recording network performance information and for troubleshooting through Windows 2000

System Monitor, CiscoWorks, and Openview. A *trap* is a specific situation or event that SNMP can track and report to a network management station, provide a warning to a network administrator, or both.

ANALYZING USER ACCESS, PRODUCTIVITY, AND PERFORMANCE ISSUES

Determining what hardware and network resources are used by an organization is valuable for analyzing access and productivity issues. Your analysis may show that users are not as productive as they might be because they are using workstations that do not take full advantage of the network resources, or some older workstations may not be able to keep up with the network speed. Another possibility is that you will find that there is not enough bandwidth to servers—for example, 10 Mbps when there should be 100 Mbps, or even 1 Gbps, for maximum user productivity.

Studying network bandwidth also is valuable because it can help determine how to set up Active Directory services for DC and global catalog replication. Replication may need to be set to occur less often over WAN links that have less bandwidth than over other WAN links. The bandwidth will also determine the best placement of DCs and global catalog servers, as well as RAS, Web, and VPN servers.

Protocols can be another factor that influences user productivity. NetBEUI is designed for small networks and can cause problems on medium- and large-sized networks, because brouters have to be set in a slower bridge mode rather than the faster router mode. IPX/SPX is a chatty protocol that can cause extra network traffic, reducing the productivity of users. TCP/IP offers advantages over other protocols because there is a huge suite of TCP/IP-related protocols that can be used to troubleshoot network problems, adapt a network for multimedia communications, handle Internet mail, and more.

The LAN transmission method is important for user access, particularly from the standpoint of network growth. There are more options to expand an Ethernet network than to expand either token ring or FDDI networks. This is an important consideration when there is rapid network growth, and the network backbone, for example, needs to be expanded easily from 100 Mbps Ethernet to 1 Gbps.

The following checklist provides some guidelines for analyzing user access, productivity, and performance issues.

- Determine if users can be more productive and have better access by upgrading their computers or workstation operating systems.

- Assess if the most effective protocols are in use and if some protocols can be retired, such as IPX/SPX or NetBEUI.

- Assess whether the network bandwidth is adequate for the type of work and traffic on specific network segments.

- Determine if the network access order can be tuned on some workstations, such as those running Windows NT 4.0 or Windows 2000, when multiple protocols are in use.

- Assess whether the network access method is appropriate for anticipated growth in user access.

For example, all of the Interstate Security Bank branch offices located in Oregon have the cabling and network interface cards to support 100 Mbps Ethernet access, but the switches used to connect the computers operate only at 10 Mbps. The branch office employees report that network access is often slow when business is heavy, causing delays in helping customers. The branch offices can enjoy faster network access by replacing the 10 Mbps switches with ones that operate at 100 Mbps. This simple upgrade can affect Active Directory design, because the faster access may mean that a single domain controller at each branch office is not enough to keep up with the faster access, requiring the addition of another DC at each branch. Although some expense is involved in making the upgrades, the branch office employees benefit because their access is much faster and so their productivity is greater. The result is that customers are happier, and business is better at each branch office.

ANALYZING NETWORK AND INTERNET SECURITY

The network and Internet security can be analyzed in terms of many factors. Some of these are:

- Windows 2000 server user account security policies

- Use of Kerberos security and certificates

- Use of encryption and authentication in Windows 2000 RAS and VPN security policies

- Protecting Web sites through encryption and authentication security

- Protecting Web and intranet sites through subnet, IP address, and account access restrictions

- Using proxy servers and firewalls for network security

- Configuring routers to provide network security and traffic management

For example, account policies will likely include account restrictions, such as those requiring a minimum password length or restricting a password from being repeated immediately. Account lockout prevents someone from accessing an account by repeatedly trying multiple account names or passwords. In Windows 2000 Server, you can determine this information by examining the local computer and default domain policies that are set up in Windows 2000 servers and in Active Directory. UNIX and Windows 2000 systems also may be set up to use Kerberos security across the network.

Windows 2000 RAS and VPN servers will have remote access security policies and profiles for encryption and authentication. The following are examples of authentication policies that may be used in Windows 2000 server:

- *Extensible Authentication Protocol (EAP):* Used for clients who access a RAS or VPN server through special devices such as smart cards, token cards, and others that use certificate authentication

- *Challenge Handshake Authentication Protocol (CHAP):* Used to require encrypted authentication between the server and the client, but uses a generic form of password encryption, which enables UNIX computers and other non-Microsoft operating systems to connect to a RAS or VPN server

- *CHAP with Microsoft extensions (MS-CHAP):* Designed as a version of CHAP that uses a challenge and response form of authentication along with encryption

- *CHAP with Microsoft extensions version 2 (MS-CHAP v2):* Developed especially for VPNs, it provides better authentication than MS-CHAP, because it requires the server and the client to mutually authenticate one another. It also provides more sophisticated encryption by using a different encryption key for receiving than for sending.

- *Password Authentication Protocol (PAP):* Can be used to perform authentication, but does not require it, which means that operating systems without password encryption capabilities, such as MS-DOS, are able to connect to a RAS or VPN server

- *Shiva's Password Authentication Protocol (SPAP):* Provides PAP services for remote access clients, network equipment, and network management software manufactured by the Shiva Corporation, which is owned by Intel Network Systems, Inc.

The encryption policies that can be established for a Microsoft RAS or VPN server use *IP Security (IPSec)* and *Microsoft Point-to-Point Encryption (MPPE)*. IPSec is a set of IP-based secure communications and encryption standards created through the Internet Engineering Task Force (IETF). MPPE is a starting-to-ending-point encryption technique that uses special encryption keys, varying in length from 40 to 128 bits. Try Hands-on Project 5-7 to analyze encryption and authentication on a RAS server.

When you analyze a Web site, determine if there are specific IP addresses, accounts, or subnets that are not authorized to access that site. Figure 5-12 shows a site in which specific IP addresses are restricted.

As you examine the security that a router enforces on a network, determine the placement of the router. For example, if the router is placed between the network backbone and specific servers, it has the function of protecting those servers. Obtain information from the router's table to determine which IP addresses or subnets have access to those servers and which do not have access. Figure 5-13 illustrates how a router might be positioned to control access to five servers.

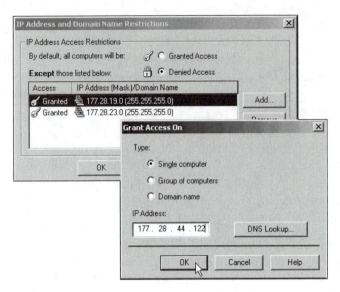

Figure 5-12   Restricting access to a Web site

Use the following checklist to help you examine network and Internet security:

- Determine what account security policies are implemented on existing servers.
- Determine if Kerberos and certificate security is used or if there are plans to use it.
- Assess the remote access policies for RAS and VPN servers.
- Assess the use of encryption and authentication on all servers and hosts.
- Determine how routers, proxy servers, and firewalls are used for network security, including the location of those devices.
- Assess what IP- and account-based restrictions are used for security on Web, RAS, VPN, and other servers.

For example, Jefferson Philately, Interstate Security Bank, and York Industries all use password security measures that require users to set passwords over a minimum length. Also, they all plan to set up encryption and authentication on their RAS and VPN servers. Interstate Security Bank plans to use IPSec, and its regional offices currently connect to branch offices through routers that also function as firewalls. All of this information is important for planning Active Directory because: (1) the password security measures and IPSec are set up in group policies, (2) the RAS and VPN encryption and authentication are set up in remote access policies, and (3) router information can be used for setting up links between sites.

5

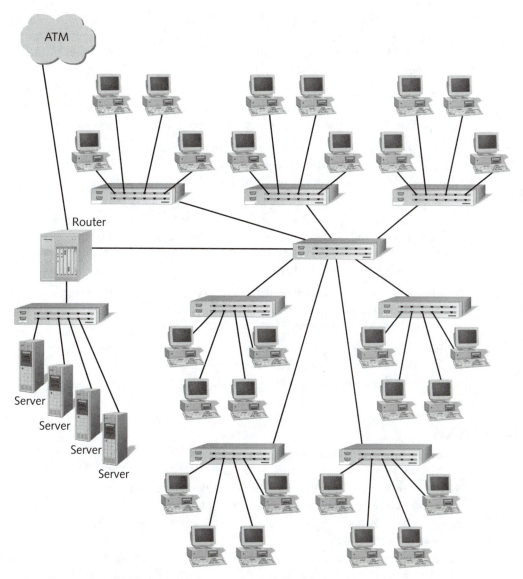

Figure 5-13   Router used to secure access to servers

CHAPTER SUMMARY

- ❒ Analyzing computer and network hardware involves inventorying workstations, servers, host computers, and a wide range of network equipment, such as switches and routers.

- ❒ The process of analyzing LANs entails determining factors such as the LAN transmission methods and the protocols in use. Many LANs use TCP/IP as the main protocol, particularly if there is Internet or intranet connectivity. When TCP/IP is used, plan to determine the IP characteristics of the LAN, such as IP address ranges, subnets, and DNS and DHCP implementations. Another important factor to assess is the bandwidths of different portions of LANs.

❑ The analysis of WANs includes determining the transmission methods, such as when a WAN uses both ATM and SONET. Determining the bandwidths of WAN links is important for assessing Active Directory services, such as replication.

❑ Many networks employ network management techniques that are made possible through the use of SNMP. SNMP and network management software can be valuable tools for your analysis of a network as well as aids for studying network performance issues.

❑ User access, productivity, and performance can be analyzed by determining what types of computers are deployed as workstations, what operating systems are in use, the bandwidth that is available to users, the protocols in use, and other factors. Changes to any one of these factors can make a difference, such as upgrading to faster workstations in a high-bandwidth network or using a more efficient access protocol.

❑ Security has become a vital element in networking. Analyze how network security is handled, such as the use of account policies, Kerberos, encryption, authentication, and strategically deployed routers.

In the next chapter, you will apply the organizational, software, hardware, and network analyses that you learned to the actual large-scale design of Active Directory—for example, designing forest, tree, and domain structures. You also learn about schema design and modification.

KEY TERMS

access server — A network device that links a network to telecommunications lines, for example by offering modem banks, T-carrier connectivity, and ISDN connectivity.

active hub — A network transmission device that connects nodes in a star topology, regenerating, retiming, and amplifying the data signal each time it passes through the hub.

AppleTalk — A peer-to-peer protocol used on networks for communication between Macintosh computers.

asynchronous transfer mode (ATM) — A transport method that uses cells, multiple channels, and switching to send voice, video, and data transmissions on the same network.

bandwidth — The transmission capacity of a communications medium, which is typically measured in bits per second (for data transmissions) or hertz (for data, voice, and video transmissions), and which is determined by the maximum minus the minimum transmission capacity.

basic input/output system (BIOS) — A program on a computer's read-only or flash memory chip that establishes basic communications with components such as the monitor and disk drives. The advantage of a flash chip is that you can update the BIOS.

bridge — A network transmission device that connects different LAN segments using the same access method, for example connecting one Ethernet LAN to another Ethernet LAN, or a token ring LAN to another token ring LAN.

brouter — A network device that acts as a bridge or a router, depending on how it is set up to forward a given protocol.

CD-ROM array — Multiple CD-ROM drives connected into a single unit or device for access through a network or through a network server.

channel service unit (CSU) — A device that is a physical interface between a network device, such as a router, and a telecommunications line.

Classless Interdomain Routing (CIDR) — A new IP addressing method that ignores address class designations and that uses a slash at the end of the dotted decimal address to show the total number of available addresses.

Common Management Interface Protocol (CMIP) — A protocol that is a standard for network management, that gathers network performance data, and that is primarily used on networks that deploy IBM devices.

Data Link Control (DLC) protocol — A protocol that is designed for communication with an IBM mainframe or minicomputer, and that is set up to use SNA communications.

data service unit (DSU) — A device used with a channel service unit (CSU) for communications over a telecommunications line. The DSU converts data to be sent over the line and converts data received from the line into a format for the receiving network.

digital subscriber line (DSL) — A technology that uses advanced modulation technologies on existing telecommunications networks for high-speed networking between a subscriber and a telecommunications company, and that has communication speeds up to 60 Mbps.

Domain Name System (DNS) — A TCP/IP application service that resolves domain and computer names to IP addresses; or IP addresses to domain and computer names. In Active Directory implementations, DNS is also used to enable clients to find domain controllers.

Dynamic Host Configuration Protocol (DHCP) — A TCP/IP-based network protocol that provides a way for a server running DHCP services to automatically assign, through a lease, an IP address to a workstation or client computer on its network.

Ethernet — A transport system that uses the CSMA/CD access method for data transmission on a network. Ethernet typically is implemented in a bus or bus–star topology.

Fiber Distributed Data Interface (FDDI) — A fiber-optic data transport method capable of a 100 Mbps transfer rate using a dual-ring topology.

forward lookup zone — A DNS zone or table that maps computer or domain names to IP addresses.

frame relay — A communications protocol that relies on packet switching and virtual connection technology to transmit data packets, and that achieves higher transmission rates by leaving extensive error checking functions to intermediate nodes.

Integrated Services Digital Network (ISDN) — A standard for delivering data services over telephone lines, with a current practical limit of 1.536 Mbps and a theoretical limit of 622 Mbps.

Internet Packet Exchange (IPX) — A protocol developed by Novell for use with its NetWare file server operating system.

multiplexer — A switch that divides a communication medium into multiple channels so several nodes can communicate at the same time. When a signal is multiplexed, it must be demultiplexed at the other end.

multistation access unit (MAU) — A central hub that links token ring nodes into a topology that physically resembles a star, but in which packets are transmitted in a logical ring pattern.

NetBIOS Extended User Interface (NetBEUI) — Developed by IBM in the mid-1980s, this protocol incorporates NetBIOS for communications across a network and is used on early, small Microsoft-based networks.

Network Basic Input/Output System (NetBIOS) — Used on many Microsoft networks, a method for interfacing software with network services; it provides network object naming services.

packet assembler/disassembler (PAD) — A device that encapsulates a packet into X.25 format and adds X.25 address information. The PAD removes the X.25 format information when the packet reaches its destination LAN.

passive hub — A network transmission device that connects nodes in a star topology, performing no signal enhancement as the data signal moves from one node to the next through the hub.

print server — A network computer or server device that connects printers to the network for sharing and that receives and processes print requests from print clients.

redundant array of inexpensive (or **independent**) **disks (RAID)** — A set of disks in arrays that are used to store data and provide fault tolerance.

repeater — A network transmission device that amplifies and retimes a packet- or cell-carrying signal so that it can be sent along all outgoing cable segments attached to that repeater.

reverse lookup zone — A DNS server zone or table that maps IP addresses to computer or domain names.

router — A network device that connects networks having the same or different access methods and media, such as Ethernet to token ring. It forwards packets to networks by using a decision-making process based on routing table data, discovery of the most efficient routes, and preprogrammed information from the network administrator.

Sequence Packet Exchange (SPX) — A Novell protocol that is used for network transport for application software where there is a particular need for data reliability.

Simple Network Management Protocol (SNMP) — A TCP/IP-based protocol that enables servers, workstations, and network devices to gather standardized data about network performance and identify problems. SNMP also provides a means to manage specific network services and devices.

subnet mask — A subnet mask is a designated portion of an IP address that is used to indicate the class of addressing on a network and to divide a network into subnetworks as a way to manage traffic patterns.

switch — A network device that has incoming and outgoing circuits and that can direct network traffic along a specific path using a process of filtering and forwarding data frames. On Ethernet networks, modern switches have replaced hubs in popularity because they support the use of the star topology and can direct frames and packets to a specific device or IP addresses, enabling fast communication.

switched megabit data service (SMDS) — Also called switched multimegabit data service, this is a transport method developed by regional telephone companies to provide cell-based, high-speed communication over WANs.

synchronous optical network (SONET) — A fiber-optic communications technology that is capable of high-speed (over one gigabit per second) data transmission. Networks based on SONET can deliver voice, data, and video communications.

Systems Network Architecture (SNA) — A layered communications protocol used by IBM for communication between IBM mainframe computers and terminals.

terminal — A device that consists of a monitor and keyboard, and is used to communicate with host computers that run the programs. The terminal does not have a processor to use for running programs locally.

thin client — A specialized personal computer or terminal device that has a minimal Windows-based or GUI-based operating system. A thin client is designed to connect to a host computer that does most or all of the processing. The thin client is mainly responsible for providing a graphical user interface and network connectivity.

token ring — An access method developed by IBM in the 1970s and which remains a primary LAN technology. This transport method uses a physical star topology along with the logic of a ring topology. Although each node is connected to a central hub, the packet travels from node to node as though there were no starting or ending point.

Transmission Control Protocol (TCP)/Internet Protocol (IP) — The key protocols, used for network and Internet communications, combined into a suite. TCP is a transport protocol that establishes communication sessions between networked software application processes and that provides for reliable end-to-end delivery of data by controlling data flow. IP is a protocol that is used in combination with TCP or UDP to enable packets to reach a destination on a local or remote network by using dotted decimal addressing.

Windows Internet Naming Service (WINS) — A Windows 2000 Server service that enables the server to convert IP addresses to NetBIOS computer names for network and Internet communications. WINS is needed to provide naming services for Windows NT, Windows 98, and earlier Windows operating systems.

X.25 — An older, very reliable packet-switching protocol for connecting remote networks at speeds up to 2.048 Mbps.

REVIEW QUESTIONS

Answer questions 1–9 using this case information:

Whole Earth Juices produces healthy juice drinks that are sold throughout Canada and the United States. The corporate offices of Whole Earth Juices are in Austin, Texas, and there are production plants in Toronto, Montreal, Austin, San Francisco, Chicago, Denver, New Orleans, and Newark. All of the production plants are linked to the corporate offices through WAN links. There are Windows 2000 and NetWare version 4 servers at the corporate offices. The corporate offices also have an older IBM mainframe.

1. The IBM mainframe uses SNA. What protocols would you anticipate that would be in use on the Windows 2000 Professional and Windows 98 workstations used in the corporate offices?

    a. IPX/SPX

    b. DLC

    c. TCP/IP

    d. NetBEUI

    e. all of the above

    f. only a and b

    g. only a, b, and c

2. The backbone at the corporate offices site is Ethernet. What bandwidths might you expect to find?

    a. 16 Mbps

    b. 100 Mbps

    c. 1 Gbps

    d. all of the above

    e. none of the above

    f. only a and b

    g. only b and c

3. The production site in Montreal uses token ring on its LAN. What bandwidths might you find at this site?

    a. 16 Mbps

    b. 100 Mbps

    c. 1 Gbps

    d. 10 Gbps

    e. all of the above

    f. only a and b

    g. only b and c

    h. only b, c, and d

4. You want to get an overall view of how the LANs and WANs are interconnected for Whole Earth Juices. Which of the following might you do first?

    a. Call the WAN providers for information about the bandwidths.

    b. Determine how many computers are Pentiums.

    c. Obtain a network diagram.

    d. Install network management software to survey all connections.

5. The new IT manager at the San Francisco production site reports that this site uses the same technology for its LAN backbone and for its WAN connection. However, he is not sure what that technology is. Which of the following is most likely to be that technology?

a. ATM

b. ISDN

c. DSL

d. frame relay

e. none of the above

6. The Chicago production plant has only Windows 2000 servers, and most of the employees run programs on the servers via Terminal Services, because the managers determined that this would reduce the cost of devices used on the employee's desktops. What type of desktop devices would you most expect to inventory?

a. Pentium III computers

b. thin-client computers

c. UNIX computers

d. Apple computers

e. none of the above

7. The corporate headquarters uses several VPN servers. Where would you look to analyze the encryption security used on those servers?

a. in the account lockout policies

b. in the Control Panel System applet

c. in the Control Panel Server applet

d. in the remote access policies

8. The Newark production plant has experienced a network problem, and the senior level network administrator at the corporate headquarters has discovered the problem before anyone in Newark. What would you expect to find that would make this possible?

a. clustered Windows 2000 servers

b. RMON

c. SNMP

d. TCP/IP

e. only a and d

f. only a, b, and c

g. only b, c, and d

9. The New Orleans plant uses a router to separate its servers from the rest of the network. Why might they do this?

    a. because they have an older network

    b. because they use token ring

    c. because they want to create "firewall" security for access to the servers

    d. because they use NetBEUI

    e. none of the above

    f. only b and d

    g. only a, b, and c

Answer questions 10–19 using this case information:

Pegasus Products manufactures accessories for trucks, such as tool boxes, mud flaps, and specialty cab lights. The company employs 820 people who work on an industrial campus in Detroit. They use a switched-based Ethernet network, but the backbone is FDDI. Data transmissions are routed on the network, which is divided into subnets. The workstations are Pentium and Apple computers. Their WAN communication is through frame relay. The company has two Web servers that are used to advertise products and take orders from distributors. They also have a specialized server that contains modem banks.

10. What is the bandwidth of the FDDI backbone?

    a. 10 Mbps

    b. 16 Mbps

    c. 100 Mbps

    d. 2.5 Gbps

    e. none of the above

11. Pegasus Products uses SNMP for network management. Knowing this, what other components should you research in your analysis?

    a. network management station

    b. network configuration coordinators

    c. network agents

    d. network bugs

    e. all of the above

    f. only a and b

    g. only a and c

    h. only b, c, and d

12. Your analysis of the workstations at Pegasus Products shows that there are over 300 486 workstations that cannot keep up with the 100 Mbps network segments to which they are connected. What is your recommendation along with implementing Active Directory?

   a. Put these workstations in a separate domain.

   b. This is a good time to begin replacing these workstations to help increase user productivity and network performance.

   c. Change the network access order to emphasize using NetBEUI.

   d. Add more routers to increase network performance.

13. As part of your analysis, you are performing an inventory of network devices used by Pegasus Products. Which of the following would you expect to include in the inventory?

   a. FRAD

   b. switches

   c. routers

   d. access server

   e. all of the above

   f. only b and c

   g. only b, c, and d

14. The employees of Pegasus Products are able to remotely access information in several different ways. Which of the following are remote access methods that you might expect to inventory?

   a. Web servers

   b. RAS servers

   c. VPN servers

   d. all of the above

   e. only a and b

   f. only a and c

15. Which of the following is the bandwidth of the frame relay WAN link?

   a. 45 Mbps

   b. 144 Mbps

   c. 155 Mbps

   d. 1 Gbps

   e. all of the above are possible

   f. only a and b are possible

   g. only b, c, or d are possible

5

16. Which of the following might you find as encryption techniques used for the Windows 2000 servers that are accessed remotely?

    a. IPSec

    b. MPPE

    c. RSVP

    d. ARP

    e. all of the above

    f. only a and b

    g. a combination of a, b, and d

    h. a combination of a, c, and d

17. Pegasus Products uses a DNS server. What information should you inventory on this server?

    a. forward lookup zones

    b. router zones

    c. reverse lookup zones

    d. DNS delay setting

    e. all of the above

    f. none of the above

    g. only a and c

    h. only b, c, and d

18. Pegasus Products has implemented some wireless data communications. Which of the following technologies should you look for in your analysis of network links?

    a. spread spectrum

    b. microwave

    c. AM radio wave

    d. FM radio wave

    e. all of the above

    f. only a and b

    g. only b and d

    h. only a, c, and d

19. Pegasus Products uses a Windows 2000 DHCP server. What information should you investigate on this server in your analysis of the company?

   a. the reverse lookup zone

   b. the scopes

   c. the server zones

   d. the server ranges

   e. all of the above

   f. only a and c

   g. only a, b and d

Answer questions 20–25 using this case information:

Outdoor Comfort makes patio furniture that sells in retail furniture stores. They have a location in Phoenix, Arizona and another location in Beijing, China. The two sites are linked by satellite communications. There are 2710 total employees in the company. Besides using UNIX servers and an older IBM mainframe computer, they use Windows 2000 servers for DNS, DHCP, Web, and multimedia services. Routers are used to help segment network traffic. They also use Windows 2000 servers as data warehouse (fast database lookup) servers for the IBM mainframe.

20. In your investigation of IP addressing, what type of addressing would you expect to find?

   a. subnet masks and subnets

   b. IPv4 or IPv6 addresses

   c. device addresses that double as IP addresses

   d. IP addresses that all begin with 255.255

   e. all of the above

   f. only a and b

   g. only b and d

21. The WAN communications between Phoenix and Beijing are via regular satellite. What is the likely bandwidth of these communications?

   a. 1 Gbps

   b. 70–80 Mbps

   c. 56–64 Kbps

   d. 1–10 Mbps

22. The IT director says that users are locked out from their accounts after seven failed attempts to access that account. However, when you test this during your analysis, you are never locked out. Where would you look to analyze and verify the information provided by the IT director?

    a. Examine the account policies.

    b. Examine the remote access policies.

    c. Ask the users about their experiences.

    d. Determine if IPSec is used.

23. What information would you investigate regarding the DNS server(s)?

    a. the location of the primary DNS server

    b. whether DNS zones are automatically updated when a new device is connected

    c. information about host address (A) resource records

    d. whether there are secondary DNS servers

    e. all of the above

    f. only b and c

    g. only a, c, and d

    h. only b, c, and d

24. Which of the following protocols might you expect to find in your analysis of protocols?

    a. IPX/SPX

    b. AppleTalk

    c. SNA

    d. TCP/IP

    e. all of the above

    f. only a and c

    g. only c and d

    h. only a, c, and d

25. Outdoor Comfort uses SNMP. What types of devices should you investigate that might support SNMP?

    a. routers

    b. hubs

    c. servers

    d. workstations

    e. all of the above

    f. a combination of a and b

    g. a combination of c and d

    h. a combination of b, c, and d

HANDS-ON PROJECTS

Project 5-1

In this project you practice reading a network diagram. To complete this project you will first need to obtain a network diagram from your instructor or from the IT director at your school.

To read the network diagram:

1. Obtain the network diagram from your instructor or from the IT director.
2. Are routers shown on the diagram, and if so, are their locations and IP addresses shown?
3. Are switches shown on the diagram, and if so, are their locations and IP addresses shown?
4. Are subnets shown on the diagram, and if so, are their locations and IP addresses shown?
5. Are servers and host computers shown on the diagram, and if so, are their IP addresses shown?
6. Are workstations shown on the diagram, and if so, are their IP addresses shown?
7. Are network links shown on the diagram?
8. Are there any ways in which you would change the diagram to make it even more useful for Active Directory design analysis?
9. Record your observations in your lab journal or in a word-processed document.

Project 5-2

This project enables you to practice creating a simple network diagram. You will need access to diagramming software, such as AutoCAD, Visio, or Microsoft Paint.

To create the network diagram:

1. Start the diagramming software available at your school, such as AutoCad, Visio, or Microsoft Paint.
2. Open to a clear drawing area.
3. Select a simple hub or switch from a stencil or from clip art that accompanies the drawing package. If there is no hub or switch included, use the switch.bmp figure file that is available from your instructor.
4. Place the switch at, or drag it to, the center of the drawing.
5. Select a router from a stencil or from clip art that accompanies the drawing package. If a router is not included, use the router.bmp clip art file available from your instructor.
6. Place or drag the router so that it is centered above the switch.
7. Activate the line draw capability in the drawing package or click the line button, if you are using Microsoft Paint. Create a thick dark line between the router and the switch, and label it **Backbone**.

8. Select a PC from a stencil or from clip art that accompanies the drawing package. If none is included, use the pc.bmp clip art file available from your instructor.

9. Place the PC at, or drag it to, the upper-left corner above the hub or switch.

10. Copy the PC or repeat Step 8, and place another PC in the upper-right corner above the hub or switch.

11. Add two more PCs, one in the lower-left corner and one in the lower-right corner below the hub or switch.

12. Activate the line draw capability in the drawing package or click the line button, if you are using Microsoft Paint. Create a line between each PC and the hub or switch.

13. The final product should look similar to Figure 5-14.

14. Save your work as a file called **network**.

15. Print the network drawing.

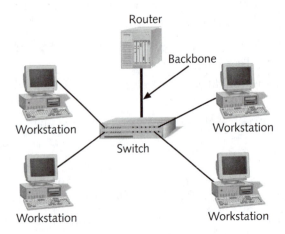

Figure 5-14   Network diagram

Project 5-3

In this project, you practice determining the protocols used by a Windows 2000 server. You will need access to an account with Administrator or Server Operator privileges.

To determine the protocols used by a Windows 2000 server:

1. Click **Start**, point to **Settings**, and click **Network and Dial-up Connections**.

2. Right-click **Local Area Connection** and click **Properties**.

3. Which protocols listed in the box entitled *Components checked are used by this connection?* Record your observations in your lab journal or in a word-processed document.

4. If Internet Protocol (TCP/IP) is used, select it and click **Properties**.

5. What IP addressing information is available from this dialog box? Record your observations.

6. Click **Cancel** and click **Cancel** again.

7. Close the Network and Dial-up Connections window.

Project 5-4

In this project you practice analyzing a scope on a DHCP server. In addition to a DHCP server, you will need an account with Administrator privileges, or one that is a member of the DHCP Administrators security group.

To analyze a DHCP scope:

1. Log on to the DHCP server.

2. Click **Start**, point to **Programs**, point to **Administrative Tools**, and click **DHCP**.

3. Double-click **DHCP** in the tree, if the DHCP server name is not already displayed.

4. Double-click a DHCP server in the tree, if its child objects are not listed.

5. Double-click a scope in the tree. What information is displayed in the right-hand pane?

6. Right-click the scope in the tree and click **Properties**. Make sure that the General tab is displayed. What is the IP address range for the scope? What is the subnet mask? Record your observations.

7. Click **Cancel**.

8. Right-click another scope, if there is one, and click **Properties**. Record the IP address range and subnet mask for that scope.

9. Click **Cancel**.

10. Close the DHCP server tool.

Project 5-5

In this project you practice viewing the contents of Microsoft DNS forward and reverse lookup zones. A Microsoft Windows 2000 DNS server should be installed on the network. You will need access to an account with Administrator privileges or one that is a member of the DnsAdmins security group.

To view the contents of the forward and reverse lookup zones:

1. Click **Start**, point to **Programs**, point to **Administrative Tools**, and click **DNS**.

2. In the tree, double-click **DNS**, if necessary, to display the DNS server.

3. Double-click the computer name of the DNS server, if necessary, to display the child objects under it.

4. Double-click **Forward Lookup Zones** in the tree, and double-click a domain, if there are more than one.

5. In your lab journal or in a word-processed document, note the entries that you see in the right pane for hosts. What is the entry for the DNS server?

To view the reverse lookup zone:

1. Double-click **Reverse Lookup Zones** in the tree to display its child objects.

2. What reverse lookup zones exist for the DNS server?

3. Double-click a zone to display the folders under it for subnets. What folders exist for subnets?

4. Double-click one of the folders. What entries exist in the folder? Record the entries in your lab journal or in a word-processed document.

5. Close the DNS management tool.

Project 5-6

In this project, you first practice analyzing the bandwidth of a Windows 2000 Server connection. Next, you determine the LAN transmission method. You will need access to an account that has Administrator privileges.

To analyze the bandwidth:

1. Click **Start**, point to **Settings**, and click **Network and Dial-up Connections**.

2. Double-click **Local Area Connection**.

3. What information is provided in the Local Area Connection Status dialog box?

4. At what speed is this server connected to the network? Record your observations.

5. Click **Close**.

6. Close the Network and Dial-up Connections window.

To analyze the LAN transmission method:

1. Right-click **My Computer** on the desktop and click **Manage**.

2. Double-click **System Information** in the tree.

3. Double-click **Components** in the tree.

4. Double-click **Network** in the tree. Is there an option that would provide information about the protocol in use on the server? Record your observations.

5. Click **Adapter**.

6. What is the LAN transmission type indicated for the Adapter Type parameter?

7. What other information in this window might be useful for your network analysis?

8. Record your observations in your lab journal or in a word-processed document.

9. Close the Computer Management window when you are finished.

Project 5-7

In this exercise, you analyze the encryption and authentication used on a RAS server. You will need access to a RAS server, and be able to log on using an account that has Administrator privileges.

To analyze the encryption and authentication:

1. Click **Start**, point to **Programs**, point to **Administrative Tools**, and click **Routing and Remote Access**.

2. Double-click the RAS server in the tree, if necessary to display the child objects under the server.

3. Click **Remote Access Policies** in the tree.

4. Right-click **Allow access if dial-in permission is enabled** in the right-hand pane. Click **Properties**.

5. Click the **Edit Profile** button.

6. Click the **Authentication** tab. What protocols are selected by default? Record your observations. What protocol would you check to enable the use of smart cards?

7. Click the **Encryption** tab. What selections are already made? Record your observations.

8. What other tabs might be useful to check for information as part of your analysis?

9. Click **Cancel**.

10. Click **Cancel**. Close the Routing and Remote Access tool.

CASE PROJECT

Aspen Consulting Project: Analysis of a Company's Hardware and Network Environment

The Richardson News Service owns 174 TV and radio stations in cities across the United States. The networks between these TV and radio stations are linked by satellite, ATM, and SONET WAN communications. The number of users on all of the combined networks is 8452. The company is working to retire an IBM mainframe and implement more Windows 2000 and UNIX servers. Also, it uses NetWare servers in several sites. You are asked to perform an analysis of the hardware and network resources in preparation for implementing Active Directory.

1. About what types of hardware would you gather information?

2. How might you get an overall understanding (overview) of the layout of all of the LANs and WANs in this organization?

3. What protocols would you research in your analysis of Richardson News Service? How might research about protocols help in your Active Directory design?

4. What types of servers would you research and how would you research them?

5. Explain how you would analyze the following in regard to network security:

   ❑ Account security

   ❑ Remote access security

   ❑ Authentication

   ❑ Encryption

   ❑ Router and firewall security

6. How would you investigate the IP addressing methods that are used by this company?

7. What aspects of the WAN links would you research? Why?

8. What network management elements would you look for in your analysis?

OPTIONAL CASE PROJECTS FOR TEAMS

Team Case One

Mark Arnez is curious about all of the kinds of devices that support network management. He asks you to form a team to develop a comprehensive list of devices that can support network management in some way.

Team Case Two

Using the same team as in Team Case 1, Mark asks you to develop a list of the tools in Windows 2000 that can help you analyze hardware and network resources in an organization. In developing the list, he also asks your team to prioritize the tools in terms of the level of importance of information that they can yield.

6

DESIGNING FORESTS, TREES, AND DOMAINS

After reading this chapter and completing the exercises, you will be able to:

♦ Understand Active Directory design issues

♦ Develop a forest design, including a forest modification policy

♦ Develop a tree and domain design, including a tree and domain modification policy

♦ Develop a schema design, including a schema modification policy

♦ Design Active Directory services in relation to organizational and business management models

♦ Design Active Directory services in relation to network models

Thorough analysis of the business, IT organizational model, software, hardware, and network requirements of an organization provides the background research that you need to carefully plan Active Directory services. With your analysis in hand, you are ready to address large-scale design issues that affect how you set up forests, trees, and domains. Once you have a design for these elements, then you will be ready to address smaller-scale design elements that include OUs, groups, group policies, and security.

In this chapter you will learn how to develop designs for forests, trees, domains, and schemas. You will learn to link your design plans to factors that you have analyzed, such as the business model, the IT management model, and network resources. You will learn about tailoring your design approach to considerations such as design techniques and namespaces. You also will learn about schema design and modification techniques.

GENERAL DESIGN ISSUES

When you begin designing Active Directory, keep several design strategies in mind:

- Complete your analysis of the business organization, IT organization, and software, hardware, and network resources.

- Allow adequate time to prepare a thorough design.

- Create a main design and one or more alternate designs to give you and your organization flexibility in choosing among options.

- Keep your design as simple as possible, because as your design becomes more complex, so does eventual Active Directory maintenance.

- Create a design that is easy to build on as your organization grows.

- Use a design that enables modifications when organizational restructuring occurs.

- Review your design with other people who are knowledgeable about the organization and consider design modifications on the basis of their input.

Designing Active Directory services is a top-down, modular process. It is a top-down process because the design begins with the forest structure and continues down through developing a site structure. The design is also modular because you develop a plan for each design phase, including a forest plan, a tree and domain plan, an OU plan, and a site plan. If you have developed computer programs, you will find that the process of designing Active Directory is somewhat similar. When you write a program, you begin by gathering information about the needs of the organization and the purpose of the program in relation to those needs. Next, you create an overall plan using a top-down flow diagram. Then you divide the programming into several smaller modules (such as subroutines) that make the programming tasks easier to accomplish than if you try to tackle the whole program at once. Finally, you write the program code from your planning documents, creating modules that will be joined into one large application.

In designing Active Directory, you make the process less formidable by dividing the process into plans for each Active Directory entity: forests, trees and domains, OUs, and sites. Besides developing forest, tree and domain, OU, and site plans, you may also decide to develop other plans for group structures, group policies, and additional Active Directory services.

CREATING A FOREST PLAN

When you develop a forest plan, keep in mind the basics of a forest from earlier chapters (particularly see Chapters 1, 2, and 3):

- *Forests are the largest containers in Active Directory:* Forests contain trees, domains, OUs, a schema, and other smaller containers.

- *Trees under a forest reflect disjointed namespaces:* There can be multiple trees in one forest with disjointed namespaces, such as tools.com and gardens.com.

- *Trees and domains within a forest use the same schema:* All trees and domains in a forest use the same schema, which defines the object classes, such as user accounts, computers, and groups along with the specific attributes associated with each object class.

- *There is one global catalog for a forest:* A forest contains just one global catalog, which makes finding objects, such as printers, faster than if there were multiple global catalogs to search (as in when there are multiple forests). When users search for a person, computer, shared folder, or shared printer in Windows 2000, they simply access the Entire Network just after opening My Network Places, as in Figure 6-1. Alternately, they can search the global catalog by opening My Network Places, double-clicking Entire Network, clicking the entire contents link, and then double-clicking Directory (see Figure 6-2). Try Hands-on Project 6-1 to search the global catalog using a different method than opening My Network Places.

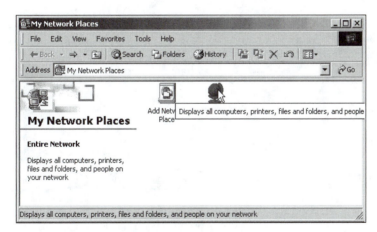

Figure 6-1   Searching the entire network

6

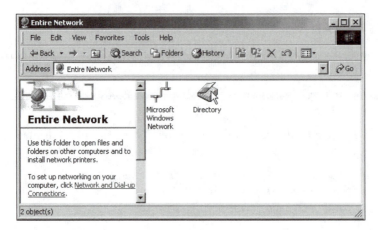

Figure 6-2   Using the Directory option to search the global catalog

■ *Transitive trusts exist between all domains in a forest:* All domains in a forest have two-way security access to resources in all other domains. For example, consider a technical university setting in which there are two trees in a forest and three domains in each tree, as shown in Figure 6-3. By the rules of two-way transitive trusts, the westbranch.admintech.edu domain has access to resources in the parttime.students.academictech.edu domain. Similarly, the development.admintech.edu domain can access resources in faculty.academictech.edu.

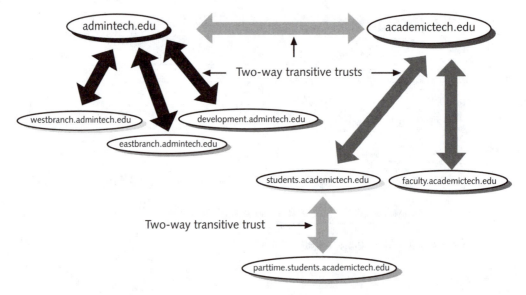

Figure 6-3   Two-way transitive trusts in the same forest

- *User logon security is performed using the UPN (user principal name):* When a user logs on to access resources in a forest, that user employs his or her user principal name, such as tmelizo@academictech.edu. The UPN enables Active Directory services to combine Internet, e-mail, and forest access by using the same name. As you learned earlier in this book, the UPN is a common naming convention specified in RFC 822.

- *There is only one configuration container per forest:* The **configuration container** holds information that some applications use or store in Active Directory. For example, the configuration container holds information about the site configuration that is used by distributed applications and for ensuring that replication of DCs is correctly performed across the network. The configuration container also holds information about certain Windows display specifications, extended rights setups, and security principal objects, such as the Everyone security group. A **security principal object** is an object, such as a user account, group, or computer, that can be assigned a security ID that is used to give that object access to a resource. For example, the user account tmelizo is assigned a unique security ID that can be placed on the ACL of a domain or shared folder to show that tmelizo has access to that domain or folder (see Chapter 10 for more information about security IDs). You can see partial views of the contents of the configuration container by using the Windows 2000 Administrative Tools (click Start, point to Programs, and point to Administrative Tools): Active Directory Sites and Services (for managing objects, see Figure 6-4), and Active Directory Domains and Trusts (for managing trusts between domains). Also, you can manage the schema objects in the configuration container by using the Active Directory Schema Microsoft Management Console (MMC) snap-in tool. The full contents of the configuration container are viewed by using the ADSI Edit tool, which is available when you install the Microsoft Active Directory Support Tools on the Windows 2000 Server CD-ROM.

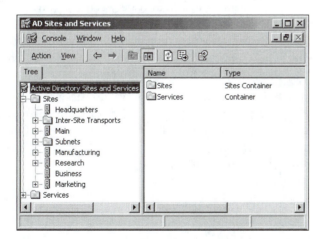

Figure 6-4   Using the Active Directory Sites and Services tool to view site objects in the configuration container

When you create the forest plan, first consider two general elements: (1) the effort you will have to spend in managing forests, and (2) how your forest design affects users. For example, in terms of management, it is easier to manage only one forest than to manage two or more. This is true because when there are multiple forests, you have to maintain a schema, configuration container, and Active Directory objects for each forest, which can double the work when there are two forests or triple the work when there are three. Having multiple forests also makes setting up and troubleshooting security more complex. For instance, the domains in one forest do not initially have trust relationships with domains in another forest. The trusts between domains in separate forests must be created manually, and are one-way trusts instead of two-way transitive trusts. If there is a security problem between domains in separate forests, then you have to troubleshoot the trust relationships along with other security factors, such as permissions and account authorizations.

 There are times when it is advantageous to create multiple forests. For example, your analysis of the IT organization may show that there are separate IT groups, or that some IT functions are outsourced, and thus you require two or more forests for two or more IT management groups.

The forest design affects users because the users in one forest cannot readily access the global catalog of another forest. Instead, there first must be a trust relationship defined between a domain of users in one forest and a domain in another forest. Once the trust relationship is defined, then users in one domain can use My Network Places in Windows 2000 Professional, for example, to find the domain in the other forest and then search that domain for the resources that they can access. The bottom line is that when there are two or more forests, it is more difficult and confusing for users in one forest to access the resources in another forest. If only one forest is created, the search for resources is much more transparent to users, because users simply search Entire Network in My Network Places without the need to distinguish between domains. Logging on is also easier for users when there is only one forest. If there are multiple forests, users need to log on using their UPN names to access resources in other forests. For example, the user Tom Melizo, whose home domain is academictech.edu, would need to log on as tmelizo@academictech.edu instead of using the simpler tmelizo.

Another factor to consider when there are two or more forests is that replication becomes more complex, because if you need to replicate information between forests, you will have to do this manually—replication is not automatic between forests. Also, whereas accounts and other objects can easily be moved between domains in the same forest, they are not easily moved between domains in separate forests.

DEVELOPING A FOREST MODIFICATION POLICY

A forest change control or change management policy should be developed as part of the forest plan. As you learned earlier in the text, change management is the creation of processes and capabilities that enable organizations to control how changes are made and whom they affect. Change management is vital because it directly affects user productivity and system management. A forest change management plan is typically developed by a team of individuals in an organization, such as representatives from the IT, management, and user groups. The forest change management plan also includes change management for the configuration container. The forest change management plan should include:

- How people are selected to manage and change objects in a forest and in the configuration container

- A list of the team members who are authorized to make changes in a forest and in the configuration container

- How security will be assigned to those who manage forest and configuration container objects

- The general circumstances under which changes are to be made, such as the addition of a new domain, moving a domain from one forest to another, creating a new site, or creating a new forest

- How changes are planned and how the changes will affect the organization and its users

- How changes are evaluated in the planning stage before they are implemented

- How changes are implemented, such as by developing an implementation scenario or script of the implementation steps

Typically, a change to a forest is made because there is a corresponding change in an organization, such as a dramatic increase in the organization's size, a merger, or a shift in how the organization manages its computer resources. Successful change management can ensure that forest changes are made carefully and with the least amount of confusion to users so that productivity is not impaired.

The Windows 2000 Server Resource Kit includes tools that enable you to move objects between forests. Security principal objects, such as accounts, can be cloned by using the ClonePrincipal tool. Active Directory objects can be moved on a large scale by using the LDAP Data Interchange Format tool (Ldifde.exe).

CREATING A DOMAIN AND TREE PLAN

After you develop the forest plan and a plan for forest change management, create a plan for the domain and tree structure. Domains, trees, and the namespace are all interlinked, because the namespace plan affects domain naming and the number of domains that are needed. Also, the namespace plan and the number of domains needed affects how many trees are created. Reciprocally, the number of domains needed affects the namespace plan. The best place to start is to create a domain and tree plan and then determine the namespace plan, because the need for domains is related to more factors than simply the namespace plan.

Before you begin creating a domain and tree plan, consider the basic characteristics of domains and trees. The characteristics of domains are:

- *Only one domain is housed per domain controller:* Each domain is associated with one or more domain controllers that exist in a multimaster relationship in which the domain information is replicated among those controllers. However, any single domain controller houses only one domain. For example, if there are two domains, then there must be at least two domain controllers, and preferably more to replicate each domain (see Figure 6-5).

- *Domains are partitions of forests:* Forests are partitioned into domains. When you consider the entire Active Directory database, recognize that it can grow to be very large, because a portion of it is distributed in each domain. If there are three domains, then there are three partitions in a forest, each containing a designated portion of the Active Directory database. This is why one domain controller can hold only one domain, because that domain controller houses the portion of the Active Directory database that contains information for that domain. This design has the advantage that the Active Directory database can be distributed across a network so that network performance and network access are optimal for any user in any location.

- *Domains enable you to draw security and administrative boundaries:* Each domain can act as a boundary that protects access via security principal objects that include user accounts and computers. A domain verifies the access of security principal objects to its resources, such as access to a shared folder. Another advantage of a domain is that it enables delegation of Active Directory administration. For example, members of the Enterprise Admins (enterprise administrators) security group can administer any resource or domain in a forest. However, forests can be large and require that there be several kinds of administrators. In contrast to the Enterprise Admins group, the Domain Admins security group has administrative powers only in a specific domain. This means that enterprise administrators can delegate administrative authority over a domain to Domain Admins to make their workload more manageable.

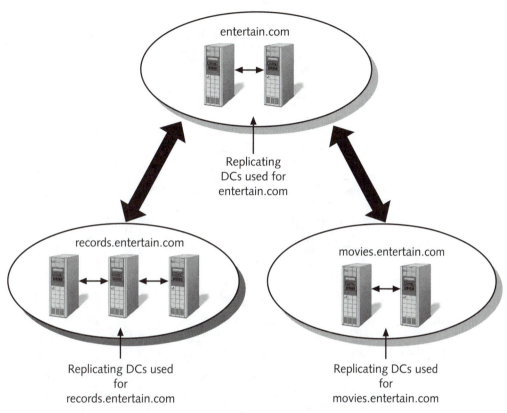

entertain.com

Replicating
DCs used for
entertain.com

records.entertain.com

movies.entertain.com

Replicating DCs used
for
records.entertain.com

Replicating DCs used
for
movies.entertain.com

6

Figure 6-5 Domains in the same tree using individual DCs

■ *Domains act as natural boundaries for group policies:* When a domain is created, so is a default domain group policy. The default domain group policy can be tailored to match the unique requirements of each domain, particularly security requirements. Through the default domain group policies, one domain can have very strict password requirements for accounts while another domain uses less strict requirements. One domain can use a specific desktop setup for all of its clients while another domain enables clients to customize their own desktop setups.

■ *Domains can be hierarchical:* Domains can be arranged in parent and child relationships, which are hierarchical relationships in which the child is created under the parent. When parent and child relationships are created, the parent and child domains are in a contiguous namespace, in which every child object contains the name of the parent object. Figure 6-6 illustrates the parent and child relationships between domains in which the domain wireless.telecom.com is the parent of voice.wireless.telecom.com, for example. Also in Figure 6-6, voice.wireless.telecom.com and data.wireless.telecom.com are **grandchild domains** of telecom.com.

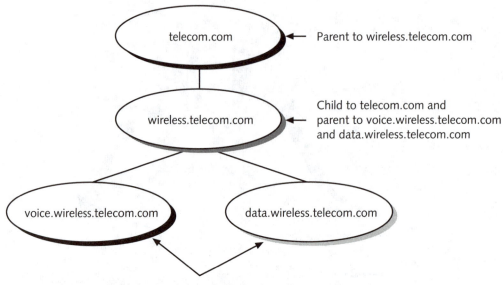

Figure 6-6   Domain parent and child relationships

The characteristics of trees are:

- *Trees contain domains that are in a contiguous namespace:* When there are domains that exist in a contiguous namespace, they can exist in the same tree within a forest.

- *There can be multiple trees in a forest:* When there are multiple trees in a forest, each tree has a disjointed namespace in relation to other trees in the same forest.

- *There is a root domain in each tree of a forest:* The **tree root domain** is the highest-level parent domain (a domain that has no higher level parent domain). For example, the root domain for the tree in Figure 6-6 is telecom.com.

- *Two-way security trust relationships exist between domains in trees:* The two-way transitive trust relationships among domains in the same tree flow from parent to child. The two-way transitive trust relationship among domains in two or more trees in the same forest flow from tree root domain to tree root domain, as shown in Figure 6-7. These trust relationships enable a domain in one tree to access the resources in a domain in a different tree. In Figure 6-7, the two-way transitive trust is automatically established between the telecom.com and satellite.com tree root domains.

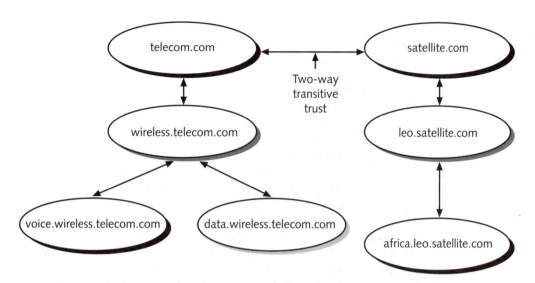

Figure 6-7   Two-way transitive trusts between trees and domains

Even though one domain is parent to another, the domain boundary concept still holds. The default domain policy of the parent can be applied to the child or the child can have a completely different default domain policy. Also, the Domain Admins (domain administrators) group in the parent domain does not automatically have administrative privileges over a child domain, unless privileges are granted to them by the Domain Admins in the child domain. Only the Enterprise Admins group has administrative privileges for all domains under the root domain.

When you begin the domain and tree plan, start by planning domains, and let the tree plan fall into place on the basis of the number and types of domains that are to be created. Planning domains involves several steps:

- *Complete your analysis of the business, IT organizational, software, hardware, and network requirements of the organization.*

- *Form a planning team* or consult with server, network, domain, and DNS server administrators. Also, consult with other key IT personnel, such as security analysts and systems and applications programmers. Further, include the organization's managers and users in your consultations.

- *Consider the number of domains that are required* on the basis of the geographic, administrative, and network requirements of the organization.

- *Determine the root domains for the forest.*

- *Determine the namespace for DNS naming of domains.*

- *Establish the best methods for fast user authentication.*

- *Determine the operations master roles.* When you create a forest, there must be DCs that are designated as the **operations masters** in one or more domains. There are five operations master roles: relative identifier master, primary domain controller emulator master, infrastructure master, schema master, and domain naming master. The **relative identifier master** is a DC that assigns a group of special (relative) ID numbers to every other DC. These relative IDs are used for security when creating a user principal object, such as an account. This helps ensure that only DCs registered in Active Directory can create certain objects. The **primary domain controller (PDC) emulator master** is used to emulate a Windows NT 4.0 PDC when there are still Windows NT 4.0 backup domain controllers (BDCs) operating. It is also needed when there are network computers operating without Windows 2000 client software. The **infrastructure master** is used to update the contents of a security group when a user or computer account is added, deleted, or renamed. It is also needed to ensure that the group membership is not changed when a group is renamed. The schema master and domain naming master are both discussed later in this chapter. When there is only one domain, that domain handles all five roles. In a tree structure within a forest, the first tree root domain created typically handles the schema and domain naming master roles. Each domain in the tree is also assigned the roles of relative identifier master, primary domain controller emulator, and infrastructure master for that domain. See Chapter 10 for a full description of the operations masters and for sample designs that show how to implement them. Try Hands-on Project 6-2 to determine the operations masters in a domain.

Beginning Domain and Tree Design

When you begin work on the domain and tree plan, start by examining the information you have gathered from your analysis of the organization. As part of your analysis, make sure that you obtain a network diagram or create one of your own. As discussed earlier in the text, the network diagram should provide information about LANs and WANs. LANs are typically considered fast links with fast backbones, such as 10 Mbps to the desktop (to ordinary computers), and 100 Mbps on network backbones. Backbones provide major connections between areas encompassed in the LANs and to servers. LAN links are usually considered reliable, because they are typically less susceptible to outages or network saturation when compared to WANs.

WAN links are typically slower than LAN links and less reliable, although this depends on the WAN technology. SONET, for example, is fast and can have up to a 99 percent assurance of reliable access. X.25, though, is a slow WAN link and less reliable. The actual reliability of a WAN link may also be related to the reliability of the WAN provider and not to the technology. Sometimes the WAN provider does not have sufficient equipment or resources to ensure reliability.

In the context of planning domains, recall from Chapter 1 that a **site** is one or more TCP/IP-based subnets that are aggregated into a logical Active Directory container object (a site). The links between subnets in a single site are relatively fast (512 Kbps or faster) and reliable. Consider a group of sites to be a group of interconnected LANs, some or all of which may be joined by WANs. For example, the Interstate Security Bank headquarters, regional offices, and branch offices are all individual sites. Also, for planning domains, Microsoft uses the term **site link** to refer to WANs that are slower and less dependable than the LANs they join together. The WAN link between a branch office and a regional office at Interstate Security Bank is an example of a site link.

The network diagram should enable you to distinguish between LANs (sites) and WANs (site links). The connection speeds on each LAN (to the desktop, to servers and hosts, and on the backbone) should be labeled on the diagram for easy reference. Also, the connection speed of each WAN should be shown along with information about each WAN, such as estimated level of use, type of use (data, voice, video, multimedia), dependability, times when the link is activated for use (such as only during the day), and the cost of the link. For example, a company may use frame relay for data and for voice communication, which means that the bandwidth is not fully allocated to data. Another company may use voice over IP on an ATM WAN. Also, make sure that there is information about whether a link is used only for Internet access or only for e-mail services.

Your analysis may show that a WAN link has an undependable track record. For example, consider one university that initially established its Internet access as a microwave link to another university. The microwave link became unreliable because of an intermittent equipment problem, and was sometimes down for hours or even several days at a time. The link remained unreliable for nearly six months because neither university could agree about which location was the source of the problem.

The analysis of a site link may show that it is already saturated with traffic and that it will not bear much additional traffic, such as that from DC or global catalog replication. Another possibility is that a particular site link is expensive to operate and that the goals of the organization are to use it primarily for certain kinds of business traffic, such as for multimedia presentations and conferencing.

Also, some site links may be indirect connections, such as sending e-mail through the Internet. Note these types of connections on the network diagram so that you do not assume a physical connection where one does not exist.

In addition to completing your analysis before starting the domain and tree plan, determine how others will provide input into the plan. Some organizations prefer to form a committee to either work on the plan or to provide input. Other organizations prefer to have one person working on the plan, but expect that person to consult with key individuals, such as current domain administrators, network and server administrators, and security analysts.

Begin your domain and tree plan with several considerations in mind:

- *Use the minimum number of domains and trees*, if possible, to reduce the TCO of maintaining domains.

- Because Windows 2000 Server domains can be administered differently from Windows NT Server domains, it may be possible to *consolidate multiple existing Windows NT Server domains into fewer Windows 2000 Server Active Directory domains.*

- *Avoid using domains to reflect the structure of an organization*, because the organizational structure may change. Instead focus on designing the domain structure on the basis of geography, which is related to site and site link requirements.

- *Create a domain and tree plan that can easily accommodate growth.*

- *Review and revise your plan with the goal to make it as optimal as possible.*

- *Create a plan that enables you to keep domain controllers in secure locations*, because they contain sensitive account and domain access information.

One example of how converting from Windows NT to Windows 2000 Server can result in fewer domains is the use of OUs in Windows 2000 Server Active Directory. Historically, some organizations have created two domains in Windows NT Server environments, one from which to manage user accounts and a second from which to manage access to resources, such as servers, shared folders, and shared printers. When these organizations convert to Windows 2000 Server, they can use one domain instead of two. OUs within a single domain (instead of using two or more domains) can be used to manage or delegate management of accounts and resources. OUs offer another significant advantage because it is much easier to transfer accounts and resources from one OU to another than it is to transfer them between domains.

Determining How Many Domains and Trees to Create

There are three general models for creating domains and trees in Active Directory. The simplest model is to create one domain and administer that domain by delegating authority through OUs. A second model is to create two or more domains in a single tree and to use the domains to manage LAN locations or sites. The third model is to create multiple domains in two or more trees that are members of the same forest, using the trees to manage disjointed namespaces, and the multiple domains to manage resources at different sites. Figure 6-8 illustrates the three models that can be used.

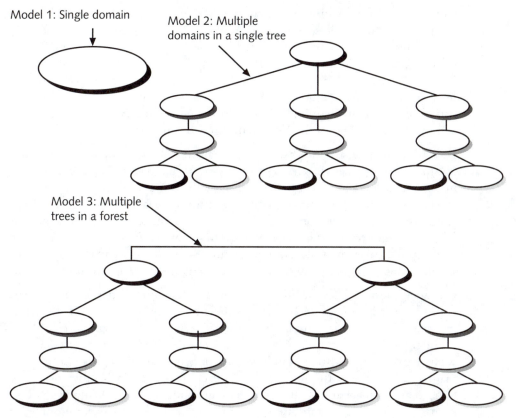

Figure 6-8   General domain and tree designs

 Because Active Directory can easily be scaled, one approach is to start off simply with only one or two domains, and then to scale Active Directory domains and trees as you become more comfortable in handling design issues or as your organization grows.

The particular model that you use in your domain and tree design is affected by the information that you will have from your analysis of an organization. First, it is affected by your determination of the organizational and business management models. For example, if the organizational model is best analyzed by geography and you have performed a thorough analysis of the network structure, then the number of domains and trees that you establish will be related to the physical requirements of geography. Consider a community college that has one main location and two large branch locations in different parts of the same state, and that has slow 56 Kbps WAN links between each site. One design idea for this college is to have a domain at each site (under one tree) so that users are authenticated quickly without having to access a server at a remote location, and so that each location has its own security boundary. Also, having three domains reduces the replication traffic over the slow WAN links.

Consider another situation in which there is a private liberal arts college that has a main campus, two branch sites, and fast ATM WAN links between all three sites. The college has a centralized business management model that is particularly applicable to the IT organization. In this instance, the determining factor in terms of the number of domains is that the school's management and IT organization want to have tight control over management of the branch sites. This example is an instance in which the political situation dictates that there will be one domain (overruling geography), and the domain administrators will be in the IT organization on the main campus.

In a third example, assume that you are analyzing a large food company that consists of 20 smaller companies that have gradually been purchased by the parent company. The management model is decentralized, and the various companies use many project teams. WAN communications between the companies are a mix of ISDN, DSL, and frame relay. Also, many of the companies have domain names and Web sites that existed prior to their merger with the larger company. In general, this is a scenario that is most likely to be suited for a multiple-domain, multiple-tree design, particularly because there is decentralization of authority and because the companies use disjointed namespaces.

Consider a fourth example, in which you are designing Active Directory services for a company in which your analysis shows there are eight Windows NT 4.0 servers, including two that are in a remote location for a research unit, which has a T-1 WAN link. All of the servers are older models of Pentium and Pentium II computers, and the company wants to keep the existing Windows NT domain design of three domains, two at the main site, and one at the remote site. This company uses a combination of the decentralized and path-goal business management models. On the Windows NT servers, one domain is set up to contain user accounts, one is used to manage resources at the main site, and one is used to manage resources at the remote site. In this context, you can simply use the same domain structure when you convert to Windows 2000 Server. An alternative (if you choose to confront the politics) is to recommend consolidating into one or two domains (depending on the traffic over the WAN link) and using OUs to delegate administration—depending on the company's willingness to consider lowering its TCO for managing the domains.

In a last example, security is of primary importance to a large financial services company that offers different products, such as investment funds, online trading, annuities, insurance, and credit card services. A multiple-domain design using one forest can be used so that each product or service is handled within its own domain, such as a domain for online investors and another domain for credit card services. Because each domain acts as a security boundary, each product or service is individually protected by customized management and group policies.

To summarize, the main factors that affect the number of domains and trees in relation to the general organizational, business management, IT organizational, and network factors include:

- The combination of geography, sites, and site links—which represent *physical topology* factors that influence replication traffic and how fast users are authenticated when they log on

- *How domains and resources will be administered*, as determined by general organizational, business management, and IT organizational factors

- How closely *legacy Windows NT domains* must be duplicated

- The particular *security needs of an organization*, such as a need to protect financial services or a top-secret research group

In situations where you decide to use multiple domains or multiple trees, as in models 2 and 3 in Figure 6-8, bear in mind that there are several consequences that can increase the TCO:

- There will be more domain administrators and more default domain policies to set up and maintain.

- Security should be reviewed constantly for holes, because there are more default domain and group policy objects, resulting in more possible points for intrusion.

- The probability of having to move accounts, groups, and other objects among domains is increased, thus increasing maintenance.

- It is necessary to purchase more domain controllers (plan to purchase at least two per each domain for replication of Active Directory elements).

- Redundancy should be built in for site links, to ensure uninterrupted access to all resources in the forest.

- There will be more two-way transitive trust relationships, resulting in more possible failure points should there be a LAN, site link, or domain controller failure. For example, in Figure 6-7 shown earlier in this chapter, there are six possible failure points, because there are six two-way transitive trusts. If the site link is broken between the data.wireless.telecom.com domain and the wireless.telecom.com domain, then only one domain (data.wireless.telecom.com) is unable to access the resources in the rest of the forest. Also, none of the other domains can access the resources of the data.wireless.telecom.com domain. If the site link between the tree root domains telecom.com and satellite.com fails, then none of the domains under one tree can access resources in any of the domains of the other tree. Wireless.telecom.com cannot access resources in africa.leo.satellite.com, for instance.

6

Determining a Root Domain in a Forest

When you determine which domain should be a root domain, consider several factors. Often the root domain is *located at a central site,* such as at the company headquarters, and child domains radiate outward toward the boundaries. Typically, root domains are smaller than child domains and are used for enterprise administration. Root domains generally do not host a large number of user accounts or computers, other than those needed by administrators. The root domain is *dedicated for tree-wide administration,* such as controlling the membership of the Enterprise Admins, Schema Admins, and Cert Publishers groups. Child domains are on the boundaries, such as in regional or branch offices. Typically larger than root domains, child domains are used to host user accounts and computer accounts, as well as resources.

Make sure that the root domain name is one that reflects an important aspect of a company or division, such as reflecting the company function or the products made by the company. Also, *make sure that each child domain is only one name different from its parent,* such as the child, wireless.telecom.com, of the parent, telecom.com.

Usually, a root domain is one that is already registered as a unique domain on the Internet.

Determining the Namespace for DNS Naming of Domains

Active Directory uses DNS names for domain naming, but it also recognizes NetBIOS Name System names. **DNS naming** is used because it has wide recognition and because it is employed all over the world for Internet and intranet naming. DNS names have another advantage in that they can be registered and protected from being used by someone else. A DNS name is hierarchical and is in the dotted format, such as 207.46 for Microsoft. A root domain name is usually composed of two parts, a top-level domain (TLD) name, such as the country or organization type, and a subdomain name, such as a university or business name, as in microsoft.com. Table 6-1 shows Internet TLD naming conventions for many types of organizations, and Table 6-2 shows TLD conventions for a representative set of countries. Also, at this writing, the International Corporation for Assigned Names and Numbers (ICANN) is considering additional global TLDs, as shown in Table 6-3.

Table 6-1   TLDs for Organizations

Type of Organization	Domain Naming Convention
Air transportation	aero
Small-to-large businesses, including partnerships, proprietorships, and corporations	biz
General commercial	com
Business cooperatives (owned by the people who use them)	coop
Educational	edu
Government	gov
Domain name registration organizations	info
International treaty organizations	int
Museums	museum
Domains for individual or personal use	name
Network provider	net
Nonprofit organization	org
Professionals such as physicians, accountants, and lawyers	pro

6

Table 6-2   Country Names for Domains

Country	Domain Naming Convention	Country	Domain Naming Convention
Australia	au	Mozambique	mz
Canada	ca	Nigeria	ng
Chile	cl	Poland	po
Finland	fi	Qatar	qa
France	fr	Samoa	ws
Hungary	hu	Sweden	se
Italy	it	United Arab Emirates	ae
Japan	jp	United Kingdom	uk
Jordan	jo	United States	us

Table 6-3   Proposed Global TLD Names

Type of Organization	Proposed Global TLD Names
Arts-related organizations	arts
Businesses that sell products	shop or mall
Entertainment and recreational organizations	rec
General businesses and firms	firm
Individual naming options for unique organizations	nom
General identification by telephone number	tel
Trade unions	union
Health organizations	health

Domain names in the **NetBIOS Name System (NBNS)** can be any name recognized by NetBIOS and designated as a domain name, such as "thefirm" or "gordoncollege." NBNS uses single names that cannot be set up hierarchically, and thus cannot be scaled in the same way as DNS names. When you operate in a **mixed mode** of Windows 2000 servers and Windows NT servers (4.0 or below), Windows 2000 Server domains are given both DNS and NBNS names, such as telecom.com and telecom. Windows NT 4.0 (and below) domains have NBNS names only. Active Directory can register and look up both types of names, but DNS naming is native to Active Directory.

A DNS server is used to resolve DNS names, and a WINS server is used to resolve NBNS names. Also, even though Microsoft DNS Server is not required for managing the namespace, using it offers the ability to more fully take advantage of Active Directory features, such as protection for DNS information through multimaster replication.

When you create domain names, plan to follow some basic naming guidelines:

- If you are running in mixed mode with Windows NT and Windows 2000 Server domains, *set up Windows 2000 domains to have consistent DNS and NBNS names*. For example, if the DNS name is freshfoods.com, then make the NBNS name freshfoods. There are some exceptions to this guideline, such as when you need to use a different NBNS name because an existing Windows NT domain uses characters that are not recognized by DNS naming standards. For example, "The Bank," which has white space between The and Bank, is not a valid DNS name because DNS naming does not recognize the white space. Another similar exception occurs when you are completely revamping old domain naming for your organization and have to keep old domain names for a while during a conversion to Windows 2000 Server.

- If your domains are recognized internationally, consult with a language expert to *make sure that you are not using a name that has an inappropriate or offensive meaning when it is translated into other languages*. This can be true even for a United States English name that is used by Canadian or United Kingdom clients.

- *Use names that uniquely apply to your organization* and that help distinguish it from all others—particularly from organizations that make similar products or offer similar services. Also, *use unique names to separate Internet-based domains from intranet-based domains.* For example, if your company has an Internet-based domain called handtools.com, use a name such as handtoolscorp.com for your intranet.

- *Use names that you have already registered via the Internet, or plan to register your names* (check first to make sure that a name is not already registered). This practice provides better Internet interaction and protects the names that you select so that they are always unique as far as the Internet is concerned. The cost of registering names is minor compared to the business advantage that registering can provide.

- *Make sure all characters in the domain name conform to DNS naming standards.* You can use uppercase and lowercase letters of the alphabet, the hyphen character, and whole numbers between 0 and 9. For example, the name FineFoods.com is acceptable, but Fine/Foods.com is not acceptable.

- *Use names that can be related to a meaningful phrase and that are not too long to remember.* The name FineFoods.com is much easier to remember and to decipher than the name FnFoods.com or the name JjsvryFineFoods.com.

- *Never use identical names for two domains that are on different networks.* In some instances, you might be tempted to use identical names for two domains that are on different networks. For example, because York Industries has a main location in Toronto and another location in Buenos Aires, they might be tempted to use the domain root name york.com on both networks. To avoid confusion and administrative problems, the better approach is to have a york.com root domain in Toronto and a pampas.york.com (or pampas.com) domain, which reflects the name of the Buenos Aires company owned by York Industries.

 The incompatibility between some NetBIOS names and DNS naming standards offers a strong reason for using Microsoft DNS services when you convert from Windows NT servers to Windows 2000 servers. Microsoft DNS supports non-standard characters that might be used in NetBIOS names, such as extended ASCII characters and unicode characters, such as $, %, and {.

Establishing the Best Methods for Fast User Authentication

Part of the planning for domains should include examining ways to make the user authentication process as fast as possible, so users can be more productive. One way to streamline authentication that has been discussed already in this book is to place domain controllers and global catalog servers so that users do not have to access them over a site link. Another way is to determine places in the domain structure that can benefit from cross-link trusts. A **cross-link trust** is a manually created trust that provides a one- or two-way trust (two-way when you create two cross-link trusts) between two specific domains, which provides a shortcut through the normal transitive trust verification process.

Refer to Figure 6-7 and assume that users in the africa.leo.satellite.com domain frequently need access to resources in the data.wireless.telecom.com domain (but not vice versa). Because transitive trusts are already established, the current way for a user in africa.leo.satellite.com to access a shared database folder in data.wireless.telecom.com is to go through all of the transitive trust links, as shown in Figure 6-9.

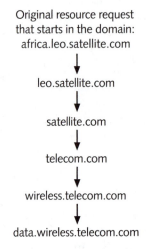

Original resource request
that starts in the domain:
africa.leo.satellite.com

leo.satellite.com

satellite.com

telecom.com

wireless.telecom.com

data.wireless.telecom.com

Figure 6-9 Resource access verification through multiple transitive trusts in a forest

As Figure 6-9 illustrates, going from the lowest end of the satellite.com tree to the lowest end of telecom.com tree takes time and resources, because each domain has to be queried, and the query then has to be sent to the next domain. The users' access to a resource is slowed by each search, plus the search takes valuable server CPU time. Time and resources can be saved by creating a cross-link trust between the africa.leo.satellite.com domain and the data.wireless.telecom.com domain, as shown in Figure 6-10. Instead of verifying user access by traversing the transitive trust relationships between six domains, the cross-link trust enables the user to quickly go through the cross-link trust relationship between two domains (see Figure 6-10). Try Hands-on Project 6-3 to practice setting up a cross-link trust.

A cross-link trust between two trees is really an **explicit one-way nontransitive trust**. This type of trust is different from a two-way transitive trust because (1) the trust relationship does not go beyond the two domains, and (2) the trust relationship is one-way. In Figure 6-10, if users in the data.wireless.telecom.com domain also need access to resources in africa.leo.satellite.com, then a second explicit one-way nontransitive trust can be created going in the opposite direction.

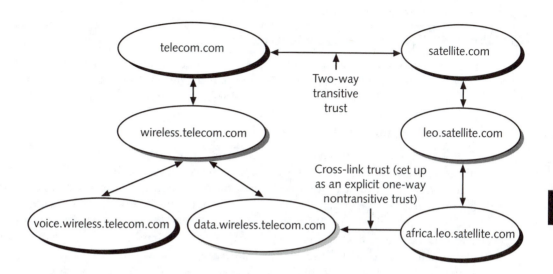

Figure 6-10   Using a cross-link trust

Developing a Tree and Domain Modification Policy

Part of the tree and domain plan should include a policy for change control, which is often integrated with the forest change control policy. Such a policy helps to ensure that there is an organized and known approach to making any changes, such as adding a new tree or domain. The elements that should go into this policy are:

- *Determine the location of the domain naming master.* Each forest must have one DC that is designated as the domain naming master. The **domain naming master** is the only DC that can add a new domain or delete a domain. See Chapter 10 for more information about how to locate the domain naming master.

- *Determine the composition of the team that is authorized to make changes to the tree and domain structure.*

- *Determine how security will be assigned to those who manage trees and domains.*

- *Specify the circumstances under which changes are to be made,* and relate these to the forest change control policy.

- *Specify how changes are planned* and how the changes will affect the organization and its users.

- *Determine how changes are evaluated* in the planning stage before they are implemented.

- *Prepare guidelines for how changes are implemented,* such as developing an implementation scenario or script of the implementation steps.

SCHEMA DESIGN AND MODIFICATION

Earlier in this book you learned that Active Directory objects are defined through a schema. Also called the **directory information tree (DIT)**, the schema is a database that consists of object classes, such as computers and user accounts, and the attributes associated with each object class. A schema is also one of four namespaces that are used in Active Directory and DNS.

The namespace with which you are most familiar is the one that is associated with domains and trees in a forest. This is the namespace that is resolved by a DNS server and that is used to locate a particular domain or a resource in a domain. Active Directory has three additional namespaces that are stored and replicated on every domain controller within a single domain. The first namespace is the **domain partition namespace**, which is a database of the objects, such as user accounts and printers, contained in a single domain. Figure 6-11 illustrates this namespace as shown through the ADSI Edit tool, which is one of the Active Directory Support Tools. The domain partition namespace information is displayed in the right-hand pane in Figure 6-11.

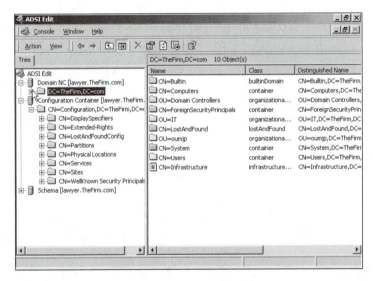

Figure 6-11   Domain partition namespace viewed using the ADSI Edit tool

The **schema namespace** is the second namespace in Active Directory and contains object classes and the attributes associated with those classes. Figure 6-12 shows the object classes in this namespace as viewed through the Active Directory Schema MMC snap-in (you can also view it using the ADSI Edit tool). The schema namespace is identical on all DCs for all domains in a forest. Third is the **configuration namespace**, which is the same as the configuration container and holds information about the layout of sites in a forest. You can view the configuration namespace contents by using the Active Directory Sites and Services tool (refer to Figure 6-4), or through the ADSI Edit tool (see the objects under Configuration Container in the tree in Figure 6-11). Try Hands-on Project 6-4 to install the Active Directory Support tools, which include the ADSI Edit tool. Also, try Hands-on Project 6-5 to use the ADSI Edit tool to examine the domain, configuration container, and schema namespaces.

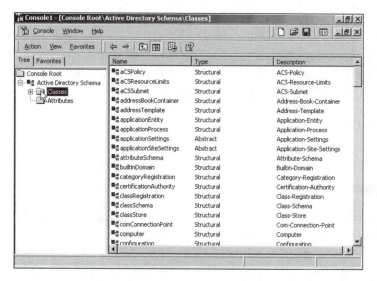

Figure 6-12　　Schema namespace shown via the Active Directory Schema MMC snap-in

The object classes in a schema are technically called *classSchema* objects, and attributes are *attributeSchema* objects. When broken down further, there are two kinds of attributeSchema objects, those that must be defined, described as *mandatory attributes* and technically called *mustContain* attributes, and those that are optionally defined, described as *optional attributes* and called *mayContain* attributes. For example, when the classSchema object *user* is configured, the attribute *homeDirectory* is a mayContain attribute, because assigning a home directory to an account is optional. However, for the classSchema object *group*, there is a mustContain attribute, called *groupType*, which is mandatory because the type of group, security, or distribution must be designated (see Figure 6-13).

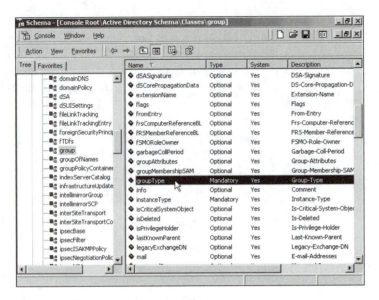

Figure 6-13   A mandatory attribute

When you install Windows 2000 Active Directory, it is automatically set up to have a fully functioning schema of nearly 200 classSchema objects and over 900 attributeSchema objects. The original set of classSchema objects is called the **base DIT class listing**, and the original set of attributeSchema objects is the **base DIT attribute listing**. Some examples of self-explanatory object classes are:

- addressBookContainer
- computer
- container
- device
- group
- groupPolicyContainer
- printQueue

- securityPrincipal
- server
- site
- subnet
- user
- volume

Use the Active Directory Schema MMC snap-in to view object classes and the attributes for a specific class (refer to Figure 6-13). If the Active Directory Schema snap-in is not available in the MMC, install the Windows 2000 Administration Tools. Try Hands-on Project 6-6 to install the Windows 2000 Administration Tools, and then try Hands-on Project 6-7 to practice viewing the schema contents by using the Active Directory Schema snap-in.

After the Windows 2000 Administration Tools are installed, you can view the schema by using either the Active Directory Schema snap-in or the Schema option in the Administrative Tools menu (click Start, point to Programs, point to Administrative Tools, and click Schema).

The object classes are arranged in a hierarchy within the schema. Objects that are below other objects inherit the attributes of the objects above them. At the top of the hierarchy is an object class called Top. All object classes below this object inherit its attributes, such as the attribute objectClass, which is used to show that this is an object class.

There are class 1 and class 2 schema objects. Class 1 schema objects are those provided in the base DIT class and base DIT attribute listings. Class 2 schema objects are those that represent additions to the schema that are made by a schema administrator. One copy of the existing class 1 and class 2 objects is always resident on the hard disk of a DC, and one copy is also resident in RAM. When you add a new schema object, it does not become available immediately because it takes about five minutes for the RAM copy to be updated from disk. Also, when you update the schema, the update is replicated to all DCs in the forest.

Designing a Schema Structure

The Windows 2000 schema is designed so that you can add schema object classes and attributes to supplement those included in the base DIT class and base DIT attribute listings. For many organizations, it is possible to use only the default Windows 2000 Server schema. Use the Active Directory Schema MMC snap-in to examine the existing schema structure to determine if the structure you want already exists. If not, there are two ways to extend the schema:

- By creating a new object class from an existing object class, such as creating a new object under the *user* object
- By creating additional attributes for an existing object class

Generally, creating a new object under an existing object class is preferable to simply adding an attribute to an existing class. This practice helps to ensure that the intent of the base DIT class listing is not altered in an unexpected way, which can lead to some applications no longer working. For example, if you want to add a new attribute under the user object, you would create a subclass under user, such as customUser, which would inherit all of the properties and attributes of the original user object class. Next, you would add one or more attributes to customUser (see Figure 6-14).

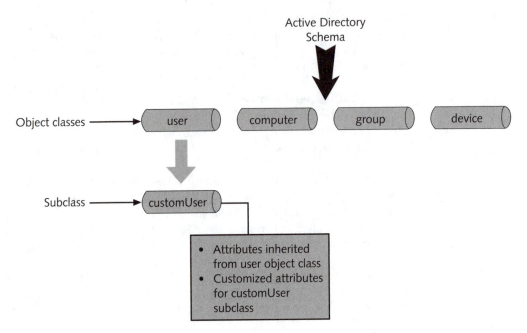

Figure 6-14   Creating a new subclass under an existing object class

When you determine that it is necessary to extend the schema, develop a schema plan. For this plan:

- Determine which user accounts will belong to the Schema Admins group and have the authority to modify the schema.

- Determine how modifications will affect existing schema objects, programs, and users.

- Determine the specific procedures that will be used for modifying the schema, such as when schema modifications will be made and how modifications will be handled in case there are errors.

- Determine how to handle invalid objects that are the result of a schema modification (an invalid object can occur when a schema change deletes an object causing the linkage to other objects to be broken, or when a modification changes the mayContain or mustContain properties of an object).

- Determine if existing Windows 2000 schema modification tools can correctly add and manage the schema changes, because some modifications may not be handled by the existing tools. You may need to program extensions into the tools, or purchase additional schema management tools from a third–party vendor.

- Determine how schema modifications will affect the schema replication to outer-lying DCs, because in some cases a DC may attempt to access a schema modification before it has been replicated to that DC (however the schema master DC will perform a full schema replication if it detects an error condition at another DC).

- Determine the names for new object classes and new attributes. Names added to the Active Directory schema must conform to two standards, LDAP (Lightweight Directory Access Protocol) and common name. A schema object will have an LDAP name that is typically two or more words combined, with the first word in lowercase and the second and subsequent words each capitalized, such as siteLink or siteLinkBridge. The common name usually consists of the same combined words as the LDAP name, but is hyphenated or shortened to fewer words for easier reading, as in Site-Link (for LDAP name siteLink) or Reports (for LDAP name directReports). LDAP and common names must be unique in the schema.

- Obtain an **object identifier (OID)** for each new object class and attribute. An OID is a unique, dotted number that is associated with each object class and attribute; the format is defined by the X.500 standard. For example, the OIDs for the object classes siteLink and siteLinkBridge are 1.2.840.113556.1.5.147 and 1.2.840.113556.1.5.148. New OIDs are obtained by contacting either the American National Standards Institute (ANSI, found at www.ansi.org) or the International Organization for Standardization (ISO, found at www.iso.ch). Try Hands-on Project 6-8 to practice viewing the OID of an object class.

It is possible to generate your own OID by using the OIDGEN utility that is part of the Windows 2000 Server Resource Kit. The disadvantage of using this method is that it is possible to create an OID that is in conflict with one that is added later by Microsoft or by a software vendor. Consequently, you should avoid using this tool and plan to obtain OIDs from ANSI or the ISO.

- Determine which domain controller will be the schema master, and then authorize that DC to modify the schema. Try Hands-on Project 6-9 to practice authorizing a DC.

Each forest can have only one DC that is designated as the **schema master**, from which all schema modifications are made and replicated. See Chapter 10 for information about how to locate the schema master in a network.

- Determine which class type to designate for a new object class. There are three possibilities: auxiliary, abstract, and structural. The *auxiliary class type* is used to designate a group of existing attributes to apply later to another class that is designated as structural. The *abstract class type* is like a template of

6

attributes that can be applied later to a structural object class. Both the auxiliary and abstract class types can be thought of as preparatory steps to creating an object class that will have a specific application. The *structural class type* is used for a specifically applied object class, such as one used by a third-party software application that enhances network printing operations. The structural class type can be created as a product of an auxiliary or abstract class type.

Whenever you extend the schema, Windows 2000 Server automatically checks your work for possible problems. One set of checks makes sure that any modifications to object classes or attributes are consistent. For example, the system will report an error if you specify an attribute to mayContain or mustContain, but you do not link it to an existing object class. It will also report an error if the OID is not unique.

A second set of checks are safety checks. These help to make sure that you have not damaged the schema or created problems for an existing application. For example, it will find instances in which you have deleted the mandatory or optional designation for an attribute. Also, it will report an error when you have deactivated an object from the base DIT objects list.

Designing a Schema Modification Policy

Change management must be used for schema modifications to protect the integrity of the schema. Your organization may develop a schema change management policy that is incorporated into the forest change management policy, or the schema change management policy may exist as a separate policy. Having a schema change management policy is as important as having a forest change management policy, because changes in either policy affect all users and resources in the forest.

A schema change management policy is often developed by a combination of IT, management, and user representatives in an organization, and it should address the following topics:

- How people are selected to manage and change object classes and attributes in a schema

- A list of the team members who are authorized to make changes in the forest-wide schema

- How security will be assigned to those who manage the schema

- How to keep the schema master DC secure

- The circumstances under which changes are to be made, such as changes required by new software or special security conditions

- How changes are planned and how the changes will affect the organization and its users

- How the changes are implemented, including developing an implementation scenario or script

Another consideration that is sometimes overlooked is providing a location from which to easily access the forest and schema change management policies, along with the forest and domain and tree plans. For example, these documents can be made available in a shared folder, or on an intranet so that they are easily accessed by schema, forest, and domain administrators.

ACTIVE DIRECTORY DESIGN EXAMPLES: ORGANIZATIONAL AND BUSINESS MANAGEMENT MODELS

Once you have learned the design concepts and how to create a forest, domain and tree, and schema plan, you are ready to put these concepts to work in an actual design. In this and the next section, design examples are discussed for the three companies, Jefferson Philately, Interstate Security Bank, and York Industries.

Consider Jefferson Philately, a company that is entirely situated in one geographic location, which reflects its organizational model. Also, the analysis of the company shows that it has a centralized business management model that applies to the organization as a whole and particularly to the IT department (see Chapter 2). The company can be analyzed in terms of management units, with the IT department as a unit under the vice president of finance. Also, it can be analyzed in terms of functional units, with information technology playing an important role. Given these findings, one way to design the Active Directory structure is to have only one domain for the entire company. This conforms to the design issues already discussed in several ways:

- The design is kept simple.

- Because the network is in one geographic location, and there are no site links other than Internet connectivity, there is a need for only one domain.

- Having one domain helps to lower the TCO for this company, which is relatively small at 295 employees.

- Because the company and the IT department use the centralized model, having one domain enables management of the computer resources to be centralized in the IT department—which is consistent with their defined role in the company.

In the single-domain model, the company might register a domain, such as jefferson.com or stamps.com, depending on what is available. If they later develop an intranet or VPN, they might add a child domain in the same tree called jeffersoncorp.com or stampscorp.com.

6

An alternate way to design Active Directory services for Jefferson Philately is to start with two domains, one for company resources and the other for Web access by customers. The Web domain might also be configured to provide purchasing information for the outside vendors who sell materials to Jefferson Philately, such as the vinyl, plastics, and cardboard that the company uses for manufacturing notebooks. This enables the company to have a tight security boundary around the accounts and resources used internally, and to customize another security boundary for those who access its network resources through the Web site and Internet. The Web domain would be registered and might be called stamps.com, and the company domain might be a registered child domain (with a different domain security policy) called corp.stamps.com, as shown in Figure 6-15.

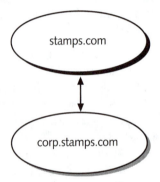

Figure 6-15   Two-domain model for Jefferson Philately

In the plan shown in Figure 6-15, stamps.com is the root domain in the tree. The root has few accounts, other than those for administrators, for outside vendors, and for Internet access (usually one account).

The organizational model of Interstate Security Bank, in contrast, involves national geographic separation among sites, with offices spread throughout Idaho, Montana, Oregon, Washington, and Wyoming. Also, the organization of Interstate Security Bank can be analyzed in terms of business units consisting of the main headquarters, regional offices, and branch offices. It can also be analyzed in terms of departments, such as the Loans department, Business department, and Information Technology department. The management model in many of the departments, including in the IT department, is more decentralized than centralized (see Chapter 2 for the analysis of Interstate Security Bank).

The tree and domain structure for Interstate Security Bank can focus on the business units, which also reflect the geographic organization. A root domain can be created, such as isb.com, from which to manage all other domains. The root domain would be located in the headquarters office and would also act as the schema master and the domain naming master. Under the root domain there would be five child domains, one for each regional office and all in a single tree: idaho.isb.com, montana.isb.com, oregon.isb.com, washington.isb.com, and wyoming.isb.com (see Figure 6-16).

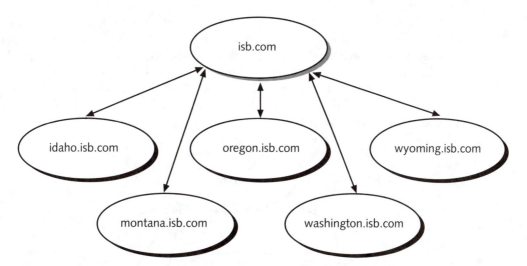

Figure 6-16 Sample domain structure for Interstate Security Bank

This tree and domain proposal satisfies several needs of Interstate Security Bank:

- The domain structure mirrors the geographical and business unit structure, which is likely to be more permanent than the department structure (the business unit and geographic structure has existed for years, but the department structure is sometimes reorganized).

- Each major location (headquarters and regional office location) has a domain as a security boundary, which satisfies the external and federal auditors' recommendations for security.

- This domain structure meets the regulations of several states that require records of bank transactions to remain secure and to stay within the state (instead of processing transactions at the headquarters office).

- Having multiple domains enables the administrative responsibility for each domain to be decentralized to each location, which is consistent with the organization of the IT department.

- Because some departments maintain their own servers, it would be possible in the future for a department to have its own child domain that it administers.

- Because the bank enables customers to transact business via the Web, it should register all of its domains. The isb.com domain might act as the central Web site from which to direct customers in each state to their appropriate state Web site for account transactions.

An alternative for the Interstate Security Bank design is to add another domain for the payroll clearinghouse service that the bank offers. As discussed in Chapter 2, the clearinghouse enables organizations to send direct payroll deposits to the Interstate Security Bank headquarters, which then transfers the deposits to other banks used by the employees of those organizations. Because the payroll clearinghouse operates out of the headquarters office, this domain would be another child domain under isb.com, such as clearinghouse.isb.com as in Figure 6-17.

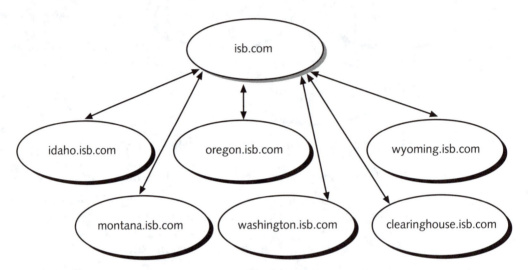

Figure 6-17   Alternate tree and domain design for Interstate Security Bank

ACTIVE DIRECTORY DESIGN EXAMPLES: NETWORK MODEL

The network and international geographical organization for York Industries provides a good place to start for its forest, domain, and tree plan. As a first step, create a very basic network diagram to show the network technologies and speeds of the site links as in Figure 6-18. Additional information that you might add that is not in the figure includes the reliability and cost of each connection.

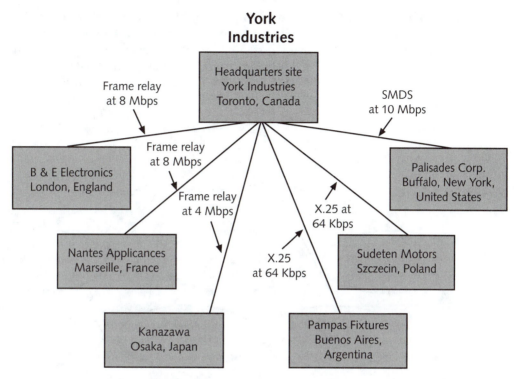

Figure 6-18   Network site links for York Industries

Some of the site links are slow, particularly the X.25 links. The fastest link is the SMDS 10 Mbps link between Toronto and Buffalo. None of the site links are as fast at the back-bone connections on each site, which are 100 Mbps or 1 Gbps, depending on the site. Some of the site links also have a history of unreliability, such as the site link to B & E Electronics in London, and the one to Sudeten Motors in Szczecin, Poland. Overall, the tree and domain plan should note that all of the site links are relatively slow, all are expensive, and some are unreliable.

Next, as you consider the tree and domain structure, recognize that the analysis of the organizational structure shows that York Industries implements the project-based structure and that it uses a primarily decentralized management model (see Chapter 2). Further, the analysis shows that each business organization has its own goals and strategies, including individual mission statements, business objectives, and strategic, operating, and project plans. The IT area reflects the decentralization because each business location has its own IT department.

Begin forest, tree, and domain planning for this organization by creating one forest with one tree that has seven domains representing a contiguous namespace. Additional child domains can be added at each location in the future, but the plan for now is to start relatively simply for this large organization of 21,400 employees. The initial domains are york.com for the tree root domain and be.york.com, nantes.york.com, kanazawa.york.com, pampas.york.com, sudeten.york.com, and palisades.york.com (see Figure 6-19).

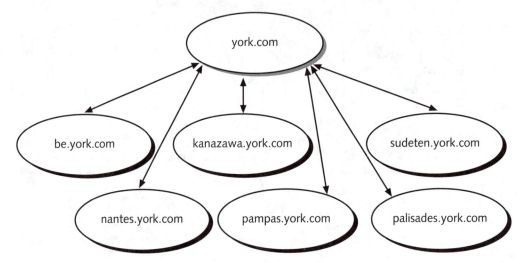

Figure 6-19   Sample domain structure for York Industries

This plan addresses several network, organizational, and business process factors for York Industries:

- It reduces replication over the site links to primarily global catalog and schema replication, which can be set up as less frequent than full-scale domain replication among DCs in the same domain. This reduces the administrative traffic across these expensive site links, so more bandwidth can be allocated for business communications.

- It enables users at each site to have fast logon authorization, and the logon authorization is not affected by slow or unreliable site links.

- It creates a security boundary around each company.

- It honors the decentralized mode of operation for each company, including having different business goals, strategic plans, operating plans, and business cycles.

- It enables each IT department to be autonomous in managing its own domain and to manage future child domains that might be created at a particular site.

An alternate plan is to have one forest, but seven trees. The advantage of this approach is that each company can have its own tree and root domain, giving each company even more independence in creating domains under its tree. In this design, the tree root domains are york.com, be.com, nantes.com, kanazawa.com, pampas.com, sudeten.com, and palisades.com (see Figure 6-20). Each tree root is used for parent and child domain administration and for Web access. The domain and tree plan is easily modified later to add child domains under each tree root as needed. The disadvantage of this plan is that there is more forest, tree, domain, and schema administration required, thus creating a higher TCO. Another consideration is that cross-link trusts will likely be needed for fast access to resources between certain trees.

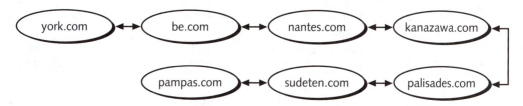

Figure 6-20   Alternate tree and domain plan for York Industries

CHAPTER SUMMARY

❑ Active Directory design begins with the analysis phase that you have learned about in Chapters 2 through 5, and next focuses on applying your analysis, beginning with designing the forest, tree, domain, and schema structure.

❑ Start your actual design by creating a forest plan that can grow as your organization grows. Make sure that you understand the function of a forest and the issues associated with creating more than one forest. Also, develop a forest change control policy to ensure that changes are considered and implemented with the minimum disruption to your company or organization.

❑ After creating the forest plan, develop a tree and domain plan. Two important considerations for the plan are how many domains and trees are needed. A simpler design is less expensive and less confusing to manage, but a more complex design may be required to match the way your organization does business. Another important element of the design is the namespace that is used by your organization.

❑ The schema design affects the entire forest and should be carefully planned. For many organizations, it is possible to use the schema that comes with Windows 2000 Server. In other situations, your organization will have special needs or applications that require schema modifications. Approach schema modifications by preceding them with careful planning and by having a change control policy in place, because a mistake in a schema change can cause an application or process to malfunction.

In the next chapter, you will continue learning about Active Directory design by focusing on site design, OUs, delegation, and DNS implementation.

KEY TERMS

base DIT attribute listing — The original set of schema attributes (attributeSchema objects) that are set up when Active Directory is installed.

base DIT class listing — The original set of schema object classes (classSchema objects) that are set up when Active Directory is installed.

configuration container — A master container in a forest that holds information used or stored by some applications, such as the site topology that is used by the DC replication process.

configuration namespace — See configuration container.

cross-link trust — A manually created trust that provides a one- or two-way trust between two specific domains, and that provides a short-cut through the normal transitive trust verification process.

directory information tree (DIT) — Another name for the schema, which contains object classes and their associated attributes for defining all objects in Active Directory.

domain naming master — The single domain controller in a forest that has the authority to create new domains or delete existing domains.

DNS naming — A naming system that is based on a dotted notation and that can reflect a hierarchy of domains.

domain partition namespace — A database of the objects, such as user accounts, computers, and printers, contained in a single domain.

explicit one-way nontransitive trust — One of two types of trust relationships used in Windows 2000. This type of trust is different from a two-way transitive trust because (1) the trust relationship does not go beyond the two domains specified in the trust, and (2) the trust relationship is one-way. An explicit one-way nontransitive trust is typically used between two domains in two different trees in the same forest.

grandchild domain — A domain that is more than one level removed from an upper-level domain. For example, voice.wireless.telecom.com is a grandchild of the telecom.com domain.

infrastructure master — A domain controller that replicates to other domains changes to the user accounts in a group, such as when an account is added to the group or an account already in a group is renamed. It is also needed to ensure that the group membership remains intact when a group is renamed.

mixed mode — When Active Directory has both Windows NT 4.0 domain controllers (BDCs) and Windows 2000 Server domain controllers (DCs) that coexist in the same domain.

NetBIOS name system (NBNS) — A domain name that is recognized by NetBIOS and that consists of a single name. NBNS names cannot be scaled in the same way as DNS names.

object identifier (OID) — Assigned to each object class and attribute in a schema, an OID is a unique dotted number as defined by the X.500 standard.

operations masters — A domain controller that plays one or more critical "roles" for Active Directory, such as generating a unique pool of numbers from which to create unique security identifiers (SIDs) for new objects or creating new domains. The operations master roles are: relative ID master, infrastructure master, primary domain controller emulator master, domain naming master, and schema master.

primary domain controller (PDC) emulator master — A domain controller that duplicates the role of a Windows NT 4.0 primary domain controller (PDC) when Active Directory is operating in mixed mode, because there are Windows NT 4.0 or earlier backup domain controllers in a domain. Two important roles of the PDC emulator are to enable password changes for computers running non-Windows 2000 operating systems and to replicate specific Active Directory information to Windows NT 4.0 or earlier backup domain controllers.

6

relative identifier master — A domain controller that assigns a pool of relative ID numbers to every DC in the same domain. Creating pools of relative ID numbers enables the other DCs to assign security identifier numbers to newly created security principal objects, such as accounts, computers, and groups. There is only one relative identifier master per domain.

schema master — A single DC in a forest from which all schema modifications and management is handled and that replicates the schema to all other DCs in the same forest.

schema namespace — An Active Directory namespace that holds object classes and the attributes associated with each object class.

security principal object — A main security object in a domain, such as a group, user account, or computer name, that enables users to access the domain and that enables verification of access to domain resources. The Everyone security group is an example of a security principal object.

site — Set up to enable efficient Active Directory operations on a network, one or more TCP/IP-based subnets that are aggregated into a logical Active Directory container object (a site). The links between subnets within a site are relatively fast (512 Kbps or faster) and reliable.

site link — A WAN link that is often slower and less dependable relative to the LANs or sites that it connects. Active Directory replication can be enabled and scheduled over site links.

tree root domain — The highest-level parent domain in a tree. The tree root domain has no higher-level parent domain.

REVIEW QUESTIONS

Answer questions 1–9 using this case information:

Music Master Recordings is a music production company that signs recording artists and produces digital recordings, CDs, and tapes that are sold in Canada, Europe, and the United States. The company has recording studios in Los Angeles (under the label Music Master Recordings, or MMR), Toronto (under the label World Music, or WM), and London (under the label HMS Music, or HMS). Each site has a LAN with a 100 Mbps backbone, and an IT department that manages the Windows 2000 Servers, Windows NT 4.0 Servers, and network resources. The management style of the company is decentralized.

1. What type of domain naming would you expect to find used by this company?

   a. DNS naming

   b. RAS naming

   c. NetBIOS name system

   d. AppleTalk naming

   e. all of the above

   f. only a and b

   g. only a and c

   h. only a, c, and d

2. Music Master Recordings is using three domains, mmr.com, wm.mmr.com, and hms.mmr.com. How many trees are in this Active Directory design?

   a. 1

   b. 2

   c. 3

   d. 4, counting the Web server

   e. There are no trees, only one forest.

3. Using Question 2 as a reference, which domain most likely contains the schema master?

   a. mmr.com

   b. wm.mmr.com

   c. hms.mmr.com

   d. The schema master is the DNS server, which is offsite.

   e. none of the above

4. Referring to the information in Question 2, the Active Directory design focuses primarily on:

   a. departments

   b. a centralized IT department approach

   c. geography, or the physical characteristics of the network

   d. the assumption that the WAN links are fast and reliable

   e. none of the above

5. The WAN connection between the Los Angeles and London locations is called a:

   a. site

   b. site link

   c. cross-link

   d. relay link

   e. all of the above

   f. only a and d

   g. only a, b, and c

6. Instead of dividing Active Directory into three domain partitions, an alternate way to set up this Active Directory design for even less Active Directory maintenance is to:

   a. have three trees

   b. have three separate forests

   c. have one domain only

   d. have no domains, only sites

   e. none of the above

   f. only a and b

7. The networks of this company are TCP/IP-based, and they are divided into IP subnets. Where in Active Directory would you expect to find information about how the IP subnets are divided into sites?

   a. in the schema master

   b. in the backup domain controller

   c. in the directory information tree

   d. in the configuration container

   e. site information is not stored in Active Directory, but in the SAM in the Registry

8. You are in a meeting with the chief technology officer for Music Master Recordings and he expresses the concern that security is lax, because having the parent-child domain structure used by the company means that the two child domains must have identical domain group policies to the parent domain. What is your response?

   a. You observe that this is a limitation of Windows 2000.

   b. You comment that the rules of group policy inheritance mean that only the account and security policies must be the same between parent and child domains.

   c. You note that all three domains can have completely different domain group policies.

   d. You recommend overcoming this limitation by creating one large OU for each domain and assigning special group policies for each OU.

9. What type(s) of trusts are automatically created between the three domains used by Music Master Recordings?

   a. explicit one-way nontransitive trusts

   b. cross-link trusts

   c. multilink aggregate connections

   d. two-way transitive trusts

   e. all of the above

   f. only a and b

   g. only b and d

   h. only a, b, and d

Answer questions 10–19 using this case information:

Advanced Scanners manufactures a full product line of computer-based scanners. This company employs 492 people at one site in Vancouver and has an Internet connection to an ISP via ISDN. The company owns five buildings, one for business operations, one for marketing and research, two for manufacturing, and one for shipping. The occupancy of the buildings also reflects the actual business departments: Business Operations, Marketing, Research, Manufacturing, Inventory, and Shipping.

10. You have formed a team to help you in planning Active Directory services for Advanced Scanners. One of the system programmers on your team has just attempted to make a case for creating one domain for each of the five business departments. His main reasoning is that this is necessary for proper administration of departmental resources. What is your response?

    a. You agree that five domains are the best design solution.

    b. You agree with the idea of five domains, but you decide to add a sixth domain for Web services.

    c. You point out that the company has reorganized twice in the past, and that it is wiser for the sake of administration to have only one domain initially.

    d. You point out that the company has reorganized twice in the past, and thus it is wise to create at least two extra domains, five for the existing departments and two in reserve, in case there are more reorganizations.

    e. none of the above

11. Which of the following is wise to cover in a schema modification policy for Advanced Scanners?

    a. providing information about how security will be assigned to those who manage the schema

    b. developing a way to keep the schema master secure

    c. developing a methodology for how schema changes are implemented

    d. creating of list of those who are authorized to make schema changes

e. all of the above

f. only a and b

g. only a and d

h. only b, c, and d

12. Which of the following should you have in planning Active Directory design for Advanced Scanners?

a. a forest plan

b. a tree and domain plan

c. a schema plan

d. change control plans

e. all of the above

f. only c and d

g. only a, c, and d

13. Each of the 492 employees will have user accounts. This is an example of:

a. security principal objects

b. group objects

c. group attributes

d. ACLs

e. none of the above

14. Which of the following should Advanced Scanners have defined in Active Directory?

a. operations master

b. infrastructure master

c. IP subnet master

d. application verification container

e. all of the above

f. only a and b

g. only a, b, and d

15. When considering how many domains to create, which of the following factors should Advanced Scanners take into account?

a. the geographical locations of company sites

b. the number of users

c. the number of IP subnets

d. none of the above

e. all of the above

f. only a and b

g. only b and c

16. After the company determines a namespace, what should they do?

    a. train users how to log on with user principal names

    b. register domain names

    c. create a Web site as their first domain

    d. create a child domain as a backup to a parent domain

    e. all of the above

    f. only a and d

    g. only a, b, and d

17. Advanced Scanners is considering using the name 123-Scan.com. Which characters, if any, are not compatible with DNS naming standards?

    a. the numbers 2 and 3

    b. the number 1

    c. the capital S

    d. the hyphen (-)

    e. all of the above are compatible with DNS naming standards.

    f. all of the above are incompatible with DNS naming standards.

    g. only a and d are incompatible with DNS naming standards

    h. only a, b, and d are incompatible with DNS naming standards

18. You have just installed Active Directory and are reviewing the schema contents. Which of the following would you expect to find?

    a. a base DIT attribute listing

    b. a base DIT class listing

    c. class 1 schema objects

    d. class 2 schema objects

    e. all of the above

    f. only a and c

    g. only a, b, and c

19. Advanced Scanners has several users who do not have Directory Services Client software and are using very old versions of MS-DOS. What should be in use via Active Directory to help handle these clients?

    a. Windows NT BDC

    b. the schema object class intellimirrorGroup

    c. primary domain controller (PDC) emulator master

    d. the schema attribute flatName

    e. all of the above

    f. only a and b

    g. only b, c, and d

Answer questions 20–25 using this case information:

Wholesale Distribution is a company that provides walnuts, almonds, peanuts, cashews, and pistachio nuts to grocery store chains throughout the United States. This company has 10 large regional distribution centers that each employ 171 to 452 people. There is also a national office located in New York. The company is already considering an Active Directory structure that has two parent domains. One is called nuts.com, which would be housed in New York and would have a child domain under it for each regional office. Nuts.com would be the first domain created. The second parent domain called vendors.com, is also housed in New York. Vendors.com would have two child domains, one for U.S. suppliers (called us.vendors.com) from which the company purchases products for distribution, and another for foreign suppliers called foreigners.vendors.com.

20. Which of the following is a problem with the domain namespace thus far?

    a. There should be more child domains under vendors.com, such as one for each state in the U.S.

    b. The domain foreigners.vendors.com is likely to be offensive to some non-U.S. suppliers.

    c. The name foreigners.vendors.com has too many letters for a domain name.

    d. A child domain name should have a hyphen, such as us-vendors.com instead of us.vendors.com.

21. How many trees are in this proposed domain structure?

    a. 1

    b. 2

    c. 3

    d. 4

    e. none

22. Which of the following will be housed in the nuts.com domain after all of the domains are created, and is (are) an example(s) in which there is only one per forest?

    a. infrastructure master

    b. operations master

    c. schema master

    d. domain naming master

    e. all of the above

    f. none of the above

    g. only a and b

    h. only c and d

    i. only a, b, and c

23. How many schemas should Wholesale Distribution plan to implement?

    a. one schema for the entire forest

    b. one schema for each parent domain

    c. one schema for each domain

    d. one schema for the parent domains and one schema for the child domains

24. One of the planners of Active Directory services is worried about slow access to resources because a user might have to go through several domains to reach the resources she or he needs. Do you have a solution to suggest?

    a. add more domain administrators

    b. purchase faster CPUs for the servers and more replication servers

    c. use IPSec, which provides faster security

    d. create cross-link trusts

    e. all of the above

    f. only a and b

    g. only a, b, and c

25. Wholesale Distribution is planning to add some object classes and attributes to the schema. What should go into their design plan?

    a. obtain unique OIDs

    b. determine what LDAP and common names to use

    c. duplicate existing object class and attribute names wherever this is appropriate

    d. delete the object classes that initially came with the Windows 2000 schema, but that are not in use

    e. all of the above

    f. only a and b

g. only b and c

h. only a, c, and d

HANDS-ON PROJECTS

Project 6-1

In this project, you search the global catalog via the Start button using Windows 2000 Server.

To search the global catalog:

1. Click **Start** and point to **Search**.
2. What options are available? Record your observations in your lab journal or in a word-processed document.
3. How would you find a folder shared from a server?
4. Click **For Printers**.
5. How would you search for a specific printer?
6. Leave the Name, Location, and Model boxes empty. Click the **Find Now** button.
7. How many printers are found? Record the names of one or two printers.
8. Close the Find Printers window.

Project 6-2

In this project, you view the relative identifier, PDC emulator, and infrastructure masters. You also learn where to transfer an operations master role from one domain controller to another. Ask your instructor what DC to access for this assignment, or if there is only one DC on your network, log on to it using an account that is a member of the Enterprise Admins or Domain Admins security groups.

To determine the operations masters:

1. Click **Start**, point to **Programs**, point to **Administrative Tools**, and click **Active Directory Users and Computers**.
2. Make sure that **Active Directory Users and Computers** is selected in the tree.
3. Click **Action** and click **Operations Masters**.
4. Make sure that the RID tab is displayed.
5. What computer is the relative ID master? Record your observations in your lab journal or in a word-processed document.
6. What button is available to change the relative ID master role to another computer? Record your observations.
7. Click the **PDC** tab and record which computer is the PDC emulator master. Is there a button available to change the PDC emulator master?

6

8. Click the **Infrastructure** tab and record which computer is the infrastructure master. What button is used to change the infrastructure master?

9. Click **Cancel**.

10. Close the Active Directory Users and Computers tool.

Project 6-3

This project gives you an opportunity to practice setting up a cross-link trust. Obtain information from your instructor about which domains to access for this assignment (or you can practice on a single domain without actually setting up the trust). You will need an account that is in the Enterprise Admins or Domain Admins security groups.

To create a cross-link trust:

1. Click **Start**, point to **Programs**, point to **Administrative Tools**, and click **Active Directory Domains and Trusts**.

2. Right-click a domain in the tree.

3. Click **Properties**.

4. What is the pre-Windows 2000 domain name? What type of domain name is this?

5. What domain operation mode is in effect?

6. Click the **Trusts** tab.

7. Are any trusts already set up? If so what are they?

8. Click the bottom **Add** button in the dialog box, which is next to the box, *Domains that trust this domain*.

9. What information do you need to complete to create a one-way trust between the current domain and another domain in the forest?

10. Complete the information, if it has been provided by your instructor, click **OK**, and then click **Yes** if asked to verify the trust. If the information has not been provided by your instructor, click **Cancel**.

11. Click **OK**.

12. Close the Active Directory Domains and Trusts tool.

Project 6-4

In this project, you find out how to install the Active Directory Support Tools as a group. You will need access to the Windows 2000 Server (or higher) CD-ROM and to log on using an account with Administrator privileges.

To install the Active Directory Support Tools:

1. Insert the Windows 2000 Server CD-ROM.

2. Click **Browse This CD**.

3. Double-click the **SUPPORT** folder.

4. Double-click the **TOOLS** folder.

5. Double-click **SETUP** to start the Windows 2000 Support Tools Wizard.

6. Click **Next**.

7. Click **Next** in the User Information window.

8. Make sure that **Typical** is selected and click **Next**.

9. Click **Next** to begin the installation.

10. Click **Finish**.

11. Close the TOOLS window and then click **Exit** to leave the Microsoft Windows 2000 CD window.

6

Project 6-5

In this project, you use the ADSI tool to examine the domain, configuration container, and schema namespaces. The Active Directory Support Tools should already be installed for this project through Hands-on Project 6-4. You will need to log on using an account that is a member of the Enterprise Admins security group.

To examine the namespaces:

1. Click **Start**, point to **Programs**, point to **Windows 2000 Support Tools**, and point to **Tools**.

2. What support tools are available? Record your observations in your lab journal or in a word-processed document.

3. Click **ADSI Edit**.

4. What namespaces do you see under the tree? Record your observations.

5. Double-click **Domain NC** in the tree to view the domains under it, if they are not already displayed. In what format are the domain names provided?

6. Click a domain under Domain NC in the tree. What information is displayed in the right-hand pane?

7. Double-click **Configuration Container** in the tree to view the information under it, if the information is not already displayed. What information is displayed? What naming format is used for the information?

8. Click a folder under Configuration Container in the tree. What information is displayed in the right-hand pane?

9. Double-click **Schema** under the tree to view the information under it, if the information is not already displayed.

10. Click the folder under Schema in the tree. What information is shown in the right-hand pane?

11. Close the ADSI Edit tool.

Project 6-6

In this project, you learn how to install the Windows 2000 Administration Tools. If you find that an administrative tool or MMC snap-in such as the Active Directory Schema snap-in is not available, install the Windows 2000 Administration Tools.

To install the Windows 2000 Administration Tools:

1. Insert the Windows 2000 Server CD-ROM.

2. Click **Browse This CD**.

3. Double-click the **I386** folder.

4. Double-click **ADMINPAK**, which is a Windows installer package.

5. Click **Next**.

6. Click **Finish**.

7. Close the I386 window.

8. Click **Exit** to leave the Microsoft Windows 2000 CD window.

One way to remotely manage a Windows 2000 server is to install the Windows 2000 Administration Tools, and then to assign or publish the tools by (see Chapter 8): (1) creating an OU for the server administrators, (2) creating a group policy object for the OU, (3) use the software installation option in the group policy object to assign or publish the file, \%SystemRoot%\System32\Adminpak.msi.

Project 6-7

This project enables you to practice viewing the schema contents in a tree by using the Active Directory Schema MMC snap-in. The Windows 2000 Administration Tools should already be installed (see Hands-on Project 6-6). You will need to log on using an account that is a member of Enterprise Admins or Schema Admins.

To view the schema contents:

1. Click **Start**, click **Run**, and enter **mmc** in the Open box. Click **OK**.

2. Maximize the console windows, if necessary.

3. Click **Console** on the menu, and then click **Add/Remove Snap-in**.

4. Click **Add**.

5. Double-click **Active Directory Schema** in the *Available Standalone Snap-ins* dialog box, and click **Close**.

6. Click **OK**.

7. Double-click **Active Directory Schema** in the tree.

8. What child objects (folders) do you see under Active Directory Schema in the tree and in the right-hand pane? Record your observations.

9. Click **Classes** in the tree. Scroll to view the object classes. What information is shown in the right-hand pane?

10. Record four or five examples of object classes.

11. What type of object is addressTemplate? What type of object is leaf? What type of object is samDomain? Record your observations.

12. Click **Attributes** in the tree.

13. What information is now shown in the right-hand pane for the attributes?

14. Double-click **Classes** in the tree and click the aCSPolicy class in the tree. How does the right-hand pane display change?

15. Leave the Active Directory Schema tool open for the next hands-on project.

Project 6-8

This hands-on project enables you to determine the OID of an object class and of an attribute.

To view the OID:

1. Make sure that the Active Directory Schema tool is open, or if it is not, open it.

2. Click **Classes** under the tree (if the classes information is not currently shown in the right-hand pane).

3. Right-click **computer** in the right-hand pane, and then click **Properties**.

4. What is the OID of this object class? Record the OID in your lab journal or in a word-processed document.

5. While you are in the computer Properties dialog box, record how you would determine the attributes associated with the computer object class. How many attributes are associated with the object class? Record two or three of the attributes.

6. In terms of the hierarchical structure of the schema, how would you determine the relationship of the computer object class to another object class, such as the parent object just above it?

7. Click **Cancel** in the computer Properties dialog box.

8. Click **Attributes** under the tree.

9. Right-click an attribute, such as **accountExpires**.

10. Click **Properties**.

11. What is the OID for this attribute? Record your observation.

12. Click **Cancel**.

13. Find the OID of one other attribute and record your observation.

14. Leave the Active Directory Schema tool open for the next hands-on project.

Project 6-9

In this project, you practice authorizing a DC for making schema modifications.

To authorize a DC for schema modifications:

1. Open the Active Directory Schema tool, if it is not already open.

2. Right-click **Active Directory Schema** in the tree under Console Root.

3. Click **Operations Master** on the shortcut menu.

4. Check the box for **The Schema may be modified on this Domain Controller**, if it is not already checked.

5. Click **OK** if you had to check the box, or click **Cancel** if the box is already checked.

6. Close the Active Directory Schema tool.

7. Click **No** if you are asked about saving the console settings.

CASE PROJECT

Aspen Consulting Project: Designing a Forest, Tree, Domain, and Schema Structure for a Company

World Wide Communications Cable is a company that installs fiber-optic cable in countries all over the world. The headquarters office is in Cambridge, Massachusetts and there are regional offices in Bonn, Germany; Barcelona, Spain; Amsterdam, Netherlands; Gaborone, Botswana; New Delhi, India; and Brasilia, Brazil. The WAN links are as follows from the main office:

- 8 Mbps frame relay to Bonn

- 8 Mbps frame relay to Barcelona

- 4 Mbps frame relay to Amsterdam

- 2 Mbps satellite to Gaborone

- 1 Mbps satellite to New Delhi

- 2 Mbps satellite to Brasilia

Your prior analysis of the company shows that the management is very centralized in the Cambridge office. The IT department also is very centralized, although they do use some teams for specific projects, with each team reporting daily to the IT management. Further, each regional office is required to prepare a mission statement, a set of business objectives, and an operating budget—all of which are edited and rewritten as necessary in the central office.

1. What factors would you consider in developing the forest plan for this company? What factors would go into a forest change control policy?

2. Prepare a basic diagram of the site and site link structure of this organization.

3. What factors would you consider in developing the tree and domain plan? How many domains do you recommend for World Wide Communications Cable?

4. What factors would you consider in developing the schema plan for this company? What recommendations would you make in terms of whether or not to modify the DIT?

5. The IT director of the company is concerned about having fast access to resources in domains. What techniques can you recommend in general to help achieve fast access?

OPTIONAL CASE PROJECTS FOR TEAMS

Team Case One

Mark Arnez has hired several new consultants. He wants you to form a team and prepare a document that discusses the information that is available by using the Active Directory Schema tool, compared to the ADSI Edit tool.

Team Case Two

Mark is impressed with the document that your team developed in Team Case One. Now he wants you to research the schema hierarchy, and to develop a chart that documents it.

7

DESIGNING ORGANIZATIONAL UNITS, SITES, AND DNS IMPLEMENTATION

After reading this chapter and completing the exercises, you will be able to:

♦ Create and implement an OU plan that includes delegating authority and managing group policies

♦ Create and implement a site plan

♦ Create and implement a DNS server plan

♦ Plan for coexisting with other directory services

The large-scale design elements—forests, trees, domains, and schemas—provide the starting point for Active Directory design. After you have developed plans for these large-scale elements, it is time to refine your design by working on the smaller elements, such as OU planning, site planning, and DNS planning. These elements enable you to fine-tune administration of resources, enhance Active Directory performance, and provide better security.

In this chapter, you learn how to create an OU plan that enables you to delegate administration and link group policies to OUs. After creating the OU plan, you learn how to plan and set up sites as a way to improve response for users and to better control Active Directory replication. Also, DNS implementation strategies are discussed, such as how to implement zones and where to place DNS servers. Last, you learn about how Active Directory can interoperate with other directory services and DNS systems.

CREATING AN OU PLAN

Following your work on the forest, domain and tree, and schema plans (see Chapter 6), your next step is to develop an OU plan. Before starting on the OU plan, consider the following aspects of OUs:

- *OUs are containers for user accounts, computers, contacts, groups, printers, shared folders, and child OUs.* An OU is an Active Directory container that is used to house any combination of user accounts, computers, groups, contacts, printers, shared folders, and child OUs. The typical purpose of an OU is to provide flexibility in administering any of these Active Directory resources (see Figure 7-1).

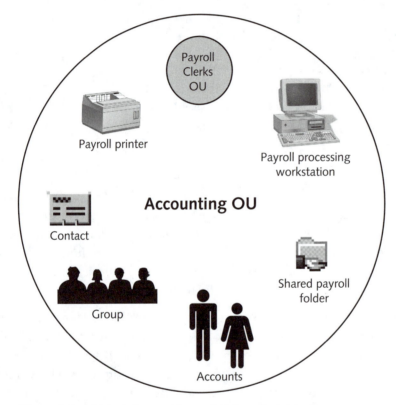

Figure 7-1   Objects housed in an OU for administration

A contact is like an electronic rolodex card that contains information about a person who may or may not have a user account. Contacts are particularly useful for sending e-mail, and as members of distribution groups for e-mail.

- *There is one default OU created when you create a domain.* The default *Domain Controllers* OU contains the computers that function as DCs for the domain. Besides the Domain Controllers OU, Active Directory creates six default folders under a domain: Builtin, Computers, ForeignSecurityPrincipals, LostAndFound, System, and Users. The *Builtin* folder houses groups that are used to help manage a server, such as the Account Operators, Administrators, and Server Operators groups. Many of these groups are groups that were introduced in Windows NT Server. The *Computers* folder contains computer accounts for computers running Windows 2000 and Windows NT that need access to resources in the domain. The *ForeignSecurityPrincipals* folder houses security principal objects, such as groups and printers, from a trusted domain. A trusted domain is another domain that has given the current domain access to its resources, such as domains in two-way transitive trust relationships (see Chapter 1). *LostAndFound* is used for objects in the domain that have been orphaned—as happens, for example, when you want to delete an OU, but temporarily to save certain accounts in that OU. *System* contains system-related Active Directory containers, such as group policy object containers and IP Security (IPSec) settings. *Users* is home to user accounts and groups used to manage the server, domain, and enterprise. Two examples of groups that are created by default in this folder are Domain Admins and Enterprise Admins. *The default folders are different from regular OUs because you cannot link a group policy object to them.* You can view the default OU and folders in a domain by opening the Active Directory Users and Computers tool, and viewing them under the domain in the tree, as in Figure 7-2. Try Hands-on Project 7-1 to practice viewing the OUs and folders in a domain. Also, try Hands-on Project 7-2 to create an OU.

The icon for an OU is an open book inside a folder, whereas the icon for a folder is a folder with no figure inside it. Also, to display the LostAndFound and System folders in the Active Directory Users and Computers tool, you must click the View menu and check Advanced Features.

- *OUs can be used to delegate authority.* One advantage of OUs is that you can use them to delegate authority; for example, for managing accounts. This is particularly important in organizations that have decentralized or project-based decision structures. It is also useful to reflect different administrative groups within an IT department or administrative groups that are spread among different departments. For example, your analysis of an organization may show that the operations group is responsible for creating accounts, and the user support group within the IT department is responsible for resetting passwords when users forget them. You can create an Accounts OU, put all user accounts into that OU, and then delegate authority to create accounts to the operations group and authority to change passwords to the user support group. Try Hands-on Project 7-3 to delegate authority over OUs.

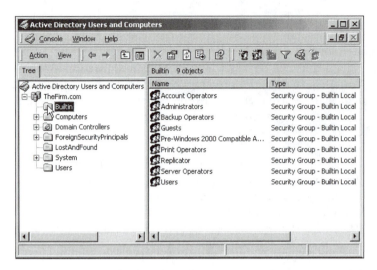

Figure 7-2   OUs displayed in the Active Directory Users and Computers tool

- *OUs can be used to reflect the organizational structure of a company.* OUs can be designed to reflect the division, department, and unit organization of a company. Although it is not necessary to use OUs in this way, the option is there for companies that need or desire this capability. The capability may be particularly effective in organizations that are more decentralized than centralized.

- *OUs can be useful to reflect different strategies or policies in organizations.* One example in which OUs might reflect different strategies is York Industries. Each York company might have an OU that contains shared folders for different strategies, business objectives, strategic plans, operating plans, and team plans. Also, each OU can be administered by each company within York Industries.

- *OUs can be assigned specific group policies.* One or more OUs can have a particular GPO (group policy object) assigned to them. Consider a situation at Jefferson Philately, for example, in which server disk quotas are enforced on marketing personnel for large files that they store on two servers. The disk quotas are necessary to ensure that the servers do not run out of disk space. Also, the Jefferson Philately human resources personnel need to have a special desktop folder on each client workstation that redirects access to employee documents to one highly secured centralized folder on a particular server. You can create one OU for the marketing personnel and assign one GPO that enables disk quotas for objects in that OU, and create another OU for the human resources staff with a different GPO that includes folder redirection.

Keep track of the group policies that you assign to OUs, so that you have a strong understanding of the security and other differences between OUs. One way to keep track of the differences and to periodically review group policies is to use the Security Configuration and Analysis tool, which is an MMC snap-in (see Chapter 4, including Hands-on Project 4-6).

- *OUs can contain security principal objects, but they are not themselves security principal objects.* Unlike user accounts or groups, OUs cannot be placed on a DACL (discretionary access control list), such as the DACL of a shared folder. However, they can contain objects, such as user accounts or groups, that can be placed on the DACL of an object. In this sense, OUs are not used to help control security, but simply act as containers for delegating authority. However, in another sense, security can be associated with OUs through assigning group policies to OUs. For example, you can create a group policy object that enables auditing of accounts and that requires accounts to have passwords over 10 characters. Next, you can assign that group policy object to an OU that contains user accounts, thus enforcing specialized account security for those accounts.

- *OUs can be set up hierarchically.* OUs can be nested within OUs, similar to nesting subfolders inside of folders. For example, Jefferson Philately might consider nesting OUs to reflect different levels of the accounting department, with the top level called Accounting, a level under that called AR (for accounts receivable), and a level under that called Cash (for cashiers)—thus creating three layers of nested OUs (see Figure 7-3).

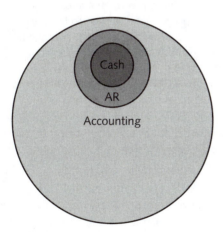

Figure 7-3 OUs nested three levels deep

- *The CPU must trace the OU hierarchy, but users do not have to.* When you nest OUs, the CPU must go through each level to find a specific resource. For example, if you nest OUs 20 layers deep and put user accounts in the bottom layer, then the CPU must trace down through 20 layers to find that account when the user logs on. In another example, you might keep a group of published shared network printers in an OU that is nested in the 10th layer of a set of OUs. Each time a user accesses a printer, the CPU goes through each of the 10 layers to find it. In both examples, though, the users do not have to traverse the OU hierarchy. For example, the user does not have to visually search through 20 OU layers to find her or his account to log on; she or he simply provides the account name, domain, and password. Also, in the printer example, it is not necessary for a user to personally look through 10 OU layers to find a published shared printer. For example, in Windows 2000 Professional, the user simply clicks Start, points to Search, clicks For Printers, enters the name of the printer, and clicks Find Now. If the user clicks Find Now without entering the name of the printer, then all published printers are displayed. The CPU does the looking through multiple layers of OUs. The bottom line is that the OU structure makes no difference to users when they access resources; it is set up primarily to satisfy the needs of administrators, such as the need to delegate authority over the printers in the 10th OU layer to a particular employee in an office. *The OU structure does make a difference in terms of the load placed on the CPU when Active Directory must go through a hierarchy of OUs in order to find a certain resource.*

In the example of the nested printers, one way to centralize control of printers that are directly connected to the network, printers connected to a server, and printers that are shared by individual workstations, is to set each one up as a network printer via the Printers folder on a Windows 2000 server. Next, publish the printers in the desired OU. Use OU delegation and the Security tab on each printer's Properties dialog box to set up who can manage and who can use the printers.

Avoid making OUs more than 10 layers deep, because this is the point at which the demand on the CPU begins to be noticeable.

When you develop the OU plan, start by using the same general rule that applies to the domain plan: *Keep the OU design as simple as possible.* Although OUs are easier to restructure than domains and it is easier to reorganize objects in OUs, each OU still requires someone to administer it. Also, every level of OUs is another level of administration. Another general rule is to gear your OU design to *first reflect the business management model* of your organization, and second, if necessary, to reflect the organizational model.

For example, the following is one way to implement a simple OU plan and to design around the business management model for Interstate Security Bank (see Figure 7-4):

1. Create a tree root domain for the headquarters office and a child domain for each regional office.

2. Use the existing default OUs/folders in each domain, such as Users to contain groups and user accounts, and Computers to contain computers.

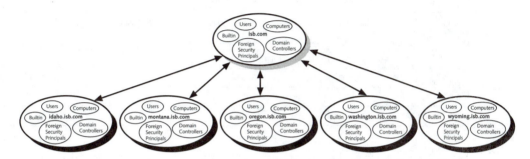

Figure 7-4   Sample OU structure for Interstate Security Bank

This design is relatively simple because it focuses on using the existing OUs and folders, which would be managed by server administrators at each location. Also, it reflects the decentralized business model by delegating administration of the OUs and folders to the server administrators at each location (who may or may not be in the IT department)—instead of centralizing all OU and folder administration with the IT department at the headquarters location.

> You can delegate control of a folder object, such as the Users folder, in a way that is similar to delegating control over an OU.

A modification of the OU design is to create additional OUs in the headquarters root domain and in each regional child domain to reflect the organizational model. This modification would incorporate the following departments and business units, including the outside relationships with the federal and the external auditors, as shown in Table 7-1. Also, Figure 7-5 illustrates how this modification would look in the isb.com domain, as viewed in the Active Directory Users and Computers tool.

Table 7-1 Additional OUs for the Headquarters and Regional Offices to Reflect the Organizational Model

OU	Department, Business Office, or Outside Relationship
Board	Board of directors
Exec	Executive officers of the company
Loans	Loans department
Marketing	Marketing department
Business	Business department (which includes the tellers at each branch office)
IT	Information Technology department
Invest	Investments department
CS	Customer Service department
Fed	U.S. government auditors
Hutton	External auditors, R.D. Hutton

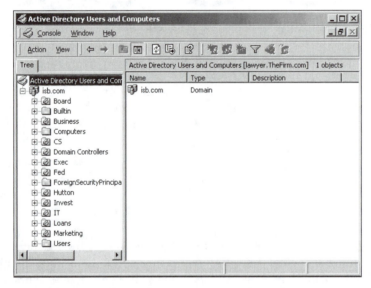

Figure 7-5 Additional OUs for Interstate Security Bank

The advantage of the modified structure, which includes the organizational model, is that it enables the company to delegate administration of OUs and to reflect the decentralized decision structure of the company. The disadvantage is that the additional OUs create more administrative work. For example, in the first design that uses only the default OUs and folders, when an employee transfers from one department to another, there is no Active Directory maintenance because all employee user accounts are in the Users folder. There is no need to move the employee's account. In the modified alternative that reflects the organizational model of the company, if an employee is transferred from the

Loans department to the Investments department, one or more administrators must move that employee's user account from the Loans OU to the Invest OU. This can become significant extra work in an organization in which employees often transfer or when there are frequent reorganizations. The extra work includes:

- Developing a paper or electronic notification system to indicate that an employee has moved

- Coordinating among OU administrators the move of the user account and the necessary security changes

- The time required for each OU administrator to move employees between OUs (the time is not much for one transferred employee, but it can add up if there are lots of employees who transfer, or if there is a company reorganization or merger)

Reasons to Create OUs

There are three broad reasons for creating OUs:

- *To delegate Active Directory management tasks.* This is the most common reason to create OUs, because OUs enable you to design Active Directory resource management to reflect the full spectrum of centralized to decentralized business models. Generally, you will create fewer OUs for centralized management and many more OUs when management is decentralized. In a decentralized management situation, delegating control empowers managers, supervisors, and team leaders so that they can accomplish certain tasks instantly, such as creating an account for a new employee on that employee's first day. This saves time for the server administrator, because she or he can delegate the account creation and password-changing tasks to others who are closer to managing the employees or resources (such as shared folders and printers). It can also save the OU administrator time—for example, by being able to immediately create a new user account, rather than having to complete an electronic form or paper request to have the IT group create the account. In some organizations, the electronic forms and paperwork can be more time-consuming and expensive than the time and expense to create an account. Another advantage of delegating control is that it limits the scope of potential mistakes. In the Interstate Security Bank example, consider the scope when the first proposal is deployed and all user accounts are kept in the Users folder, which is managed by a server administrator. A mistake by the administrator can have a very broad scope, such as inadvertently deleting all accounts and groups in the Users folder for the entire idaho.isb.com domain. In contrast, consider the implications of a mistake when the modified proposal is deployed that creates OUs to reflect the organizational structure. In this design, if the business manager at the Interstate Security Bank regional office in Idaho inadvertently deletes the contents of the Business OU in the idaho.isb.com domain, the scope of the damage is limited to only

7

those in his or her department. Try Hands-on Project 7-3 to see the options for delegating authority over an OU, including how to control the scope of authority within an OU.

■ *To associate a particular group policy object with an OU.* Besides delegating administration, another important reason for creating an OU is to associate a customized group policy object with that OU. In the example of Interstate Security Bank, there is a need for each of the computers used by the tellers to have identical desktops that access the programs they need for monetary transactions. The tellers' computers are set up to have a cash drawer that operates in conjunction with their workstations. Also, any teller may need to work at any customer station, which makes it vital that all of the workstations have the same desktop. To accomplish this, the bank can create a Tellers OU that is a first-level OU, or they can nest the Tellers OU inside the Business OU in each domain. The general steps for associating a group policy object with an OU are to: (1) open the Active Directory Users and Computers tool, (2) open the Properties dialog box for the OU, (3) click the Group Policy tab, and (4) click the New button to create a new group policy to associate with the OU. Try Hands-on Project 7-4 to practice creating a group policy object for an OU.

■ *To remove specific objects from view or access.* Objects can be hidden through creating an OU, specifying only certain accounts on the OU's DACL, and then placing the objects to be hidden in that OU.

Managing OUs

Besides creating an OU, delegating authority, and setting up a group policy object, there are several other OU management functions that you can perform. For example, one function is to move an OU, which is a vital feature that you will use if you have to modify the OU structure or when there is a company reorganization. Assume, for instance, that Interstate Security Bank at first creates a Tellers OU at the same level as the Business OU, but later decides to nest the Tellers OU under the Business OU. The administrator could easily move the OU by using the following steps:

1. Click Start, point to Programs, point to Administrative Tools, and click Active Directory Users and Computers.

2. Right-click the Tellers OU and click Move.

3. Click Business in the Move dialog box (see Figure 7-6).

4. Click OK.

5. Close the Active Directory Users and Computers tool.

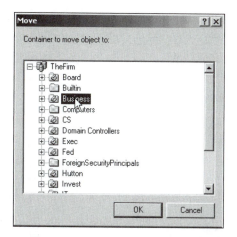

Figure 7-6   Moving an OU to nest it in another OU

 As you can determine from these steps, the process of moving an OU is far easier than the process of changing domains from parent to child or from child to parent. Domains are much more complicated to restructure because you have to delete and recreate them.

Another OU management task that can be useful is the ability to rename an OU. The general steps for this process are to right-click the OU in the Active Directory Users and Computers tool and to click Rename. The OU contents remain the same, as does any group policy object that is associated with the OU.

If you need to delete an OU, right-click it in the Active Directory Users and Computers tool and click Delete. Make sure that you move the OU contents or that the contents are not needed before you delete the OU. Try Hands-on Project 7-5 to move, rename, and delete an OU.

Creating an OU Change Management Plan

As you have done for other Active Directory planning (see Chapter 6), create an OU change management plan so that changes are conceived in a way that benefits the organization and are consistent with the OU planning process. Consider the following recommendations for your OU change management plan:

- Specify who has the authority to add, remove, and manage OUs in each domain.

- Determine how security will be assigned to those who manage OUs.

- Set up a policy to describe how changes are to be planned in the OU structure for each domain and how they will benefit the organization.

- Document how changes will affect domain security, including providing documentation for the financial auditors.

- Determine how changes are evaluated in the planning stage before they are implemented.

- Determine how changes are implemented—for example, by developing an implementation document.

CREATING A SITE PLAN

Planning sites is different from planning forests, trees, domains, and OUs, because sites are anchored in the physical topology of the network. Forests, trees, domains, and OUs are related to the logical aspects of an organization and its network. When you begin planning sites, consider the following characteristics:

- *Sites are planned on the basis of sites and site links.* The starting point for planning sites is to determine the site locations and site links. This is another reason for obtaining or creating a network diagram that clearly illustrates the sites and site links. For the purpose of planning a site container in Active Directory, consider a site to be a LAN that has a relatively fast transmission speed and on which connections are reliable. Consider a site link to be a WAN connection, such as frame relay or DSL, that connects one site to another. Sometimes you may be in doubt about whether a location is one site or two sites joined by a site link. For example, consider Jefferson Philately, which has plans to build a new manufacturing facility to house the Manufacturing department. In one plan for the facility, the new building would be close to its original building. In this plan, the LANs in both buildings would be connected by a 155 Mbps ATM backbone link. When you create a site plan for this model, you can consider the two LANs as one site, because they are linked by a reliable, high-speed backbone. A second plan for the new manufacturing facility proposes to build it in Cambridge, Ohio, which is over 180 miles away from the main location in Cincinnati. In this proposal, the LANs at each location would be connected by a 256 Kbps frame relay link. The second plan entails two sites joined by a site link, because the 256 Kbps link is a slow connection and is less reliable than the ATM backbone link in the first plan.

■ *Access to sites can be optimized further by using subnets.* One physical LAN site can have several subnets. You can optimize logon and network access by using existing subnets or by creating additional subnets on a medium- or large-sized LAN. A group of subnets can be associated with one Active Directory site designation, and DCs can be placed at each site within a LAN. For example, assume that Jefferson Philately decides to build its new manufacturing facility near the original building in Cincinnati. After the new facility has been in operation, network administrators discover that manufacturing applications create a large amount of traffic on the manufacturing facility's network and on the ATM backbone. One option for Jefferson Philately is to create two subnets, one for the main building and one for the manufacturing building, using one or more routers to control traffic. In this situation they have more options for creating Active Directory sites. They can associate both subnets with one site and locate all domain controllers on one subnet, which matches the centralized IT organization used by Jefferson Philately. Another option is to locate one or more domain controllers on each subnet, which will help control the traffic associated with each subnet. The disadvantage of locating domain controllers on each subnet is that this creates domain controller replication traffic over the link between buildings. If they need to have domain controllers in both the main and manufacturing buildings, a better alternative is to create two sites in the same domain, one for each subnet. The advantage of the latter alternative is that they can place DCs on both sites, while enabling Active Directory to use the site information to determine which DC is closest to a user who is accessing the network (see Figures 7-7 and 7-8). Another advantage is that the replication traffic between the two sites can be controlled, so that the link between the buildings is less congested. The users' access is faster, which makes users more productive, and the network traffic to DCs is more efficient, which also makes users more productive.

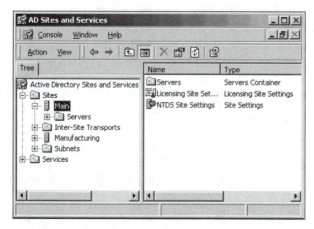

Figure 7-7   Using two sites in Active Directory

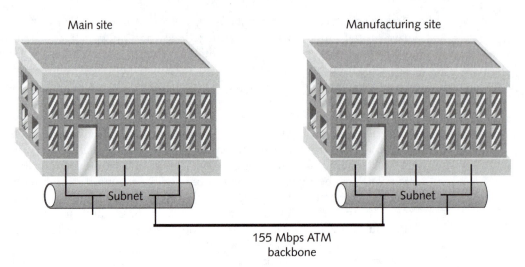

Figure 7-8   Associating subnets with different sites

Sites, site links, and subnets are created and managed by using the Active Directory Sites and Services tool. You can access this tool as an MMC snap-in or by clicking Start, pointing to Programs, pointing to Administrative Tools, and clicking Active Directory Sites and Services.

Aggregating subnets into multiple sites can be a particularly powerful tool on a large network that is subject to congestion, such as one on a large business or university campus that has multiple buildings.

- *Site designations enable computers to seek the DCs and global catalog servers at the closest site.* When a computer first logs on to the network, it works with Active Directory services and a DNS server to find the DC that is closest and on the same site. Once the client is logged on, the client caches this information so that for the duration of the logon session, it can quickly access the resources nearest to it without continually querying Active Directory and creating unnecessary network traffic. This characteristic helps to reduce network traffic between subnets and over site links.

- *Site, site-link, and subnet information is stored in the Active Directory configuration container.* As you learned in Chapter 6, each DC in a forest has a copy of the configuration container and therefore has site information. That enables any DC to work with a DNS server to quickly inform a client about the closest DC and site.

- *Replication between DCs uses site and site-link information.* Site and site-link information is used by the **Knowledge Consistency Checker (KCC)** to ensure Active Directory replication for operations masters, DCs, and global catalog servers. The KCC is a process run by Active Directory to establish network connections between DCs and to ensure that replication services take place. It obtains site and site-link information from the configuration container and assesses the locations of DCs, site-link costs, and the replication strategy of server administrators. Unless it is changed by server administrators, the KCC runs at 15-minute intervals. Besides ensuring replication, it continuously determines the status of sites, site links, and DCs so that it can carry out the replication process.

Considering Active Directory Replication

As you design the site plan, consider how Active Directory replication works along with the physical layout of the network. For example, within a site, the default setup for replication assumes that there are fast links. Data is not compressed to save on network traffic. When an Active Directory change is made on one DC, it notifies other DCs of the change. Also, DCs on the same site frequently poll one another to determine if there are any changes. The protocol that is employed for replication on the same site is the **remote procedure call (RPC) protocol**. RPC protocol is used by one computer to run a program process on another computer.

 If you experience problems with DC replication, make sure that the Remote Procedure Call (RPC) and Remote Procedure Call (RPC) Locator services are running on all DCs in a forest. To check, right-click My Computer, click Manage, double-click System Information in the tree under System Tools, double-click Software Environment in the tree, and click Services. Scroll the right pane to view these services and make sure that they are running and set to start automatically.

When replication occurs across site links, it is designed by default to use fewer network resources and to have a smaller footprint. Replication across a site link is compressed so that valuable bandwidth can be allocated for other traffic. DCs in sites at different ends of the site links do not automatically contact one another when an Active Directory change has been made. Performed every three hours by default, polling between DCs across site links is less frequent than polling between DCs on the same site. Replication across a site link is accomplished using TCP/IP for regular links, or SMTP for SMTP (mail-based) links.

When you replicate over a site link, the replication occurs only between two bridgehead servers. A **bridgehead server** is a DC at each site, as designated by the KCC, that exchanges replication information. There is only one bridgehead server per site so that site-link traffic is kept to a minimum. Otherwise, having multiple DCs replicating with partners across a site-link could take up considerable bandwidth. Each bridgehead server replicates Active Directory information to the other DCs on the same site (see Figure 7-9). When there are multiple site links between sites, bridgehead servers usually replicate over the site link that is designated by the server administrator as the link with the lowest cost, unless the bridgehead servers cannot be reached over those site links. A site link can be configured to have a cost, which represents the value of the link in terms of factors such as expense and use for critical communications. A less expensive or less critical link can be given a lower cost than other site links so that replication traffic is performed over that link.

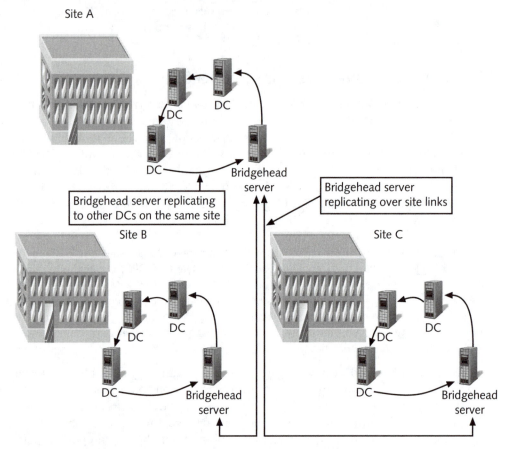

Figure 7-9   Bridgehead servers

 The KCC automatically sets up connections for replication between DCs that are in the same site. It does not automatically set up connections between DCs on two different sites connected by a WAN unless two conditions are satisfied. One condition is that there must be at least one DC at both sites, and the second is that each site must be set up with a site link.

When you configure a site link, you must take into account several factors: the site name, cost, replication schedule, replication interval, and protocol. Create a name for the site link that reflects information about that link—for example, by combining the names of the sites it joins. By specifying the cost of a site link, you enable the replication process to go over the lowest-cost link when there are two or more links. For example, if there are two site links, one which is a 1.536 Mbps PRI ISDN link used for critical data and media communications, and the other a 256 Kbps frame relay link that is used for less critical communications, you would give the frame relay link the lowest cost. The replication schedule is the schedule according to which information is replicated for the site link. For example, you might specify that replication only occurs after business hours. Another possibility is to schedule replication to occur every hour when you are making lots of Active Directory changes that you want to go into effect as soon as possible. The replication interval determines how frequently bridgehead servers poll one another for changes, and you can make the interval greater or less than the three-hour default. Also, when you create a site link, you can specify whether the replication protocol over the link is TCP/IP or SMTP. Try Hands-on Project 7-6 to set up a site and then try Hands-on Project 7-7 to set up a site link. Also, try Hands-on Project 7-8 to designate a subnet to Active Directory and then associate that subnet with a site.

Starting the Planning Process

When you create the site plan, start by performing the following steps:

1. Create a team that can help you plan sites, such as one consisting of network administrators, server administrators, and domain and enterprise administrators.

2. Use your physical network diagram to determine the locations of sites, subnets, and site links.

3. Plan to set up an Active Directory site for each LAN.

4. Create additional Active Directory sites within LANs on the basis of IP subnets, taking into account network traffic patterns.

5. Set up an Active Directory site for each remote e-mail based connection via SMTP.

6. Determine which linked sites will have DCs, taking into account the bandwidth and reliability of the site links in relation to user productivity, and the need for Active Directory redundancy.

7. Set up the Active Directory site links.

8. Determine the replication characteristics between site links, including the replication schedule and polling interval.

9. Determine the protocol to use for a site link: TCP/IP or SMTP.

Creating a Site Change Management Plan

As part of the site planning process, develop a site change management plan that emphasizes periodically evaluating the site plan to improve network performance and user access. Some recommendations for the site change management plan are to:

- Specify who has the authority to add, remove, and manage sites, including the management of the replication setup.

- Determine how security will be assigned to those who manage sites.

- Set up a policy to describe how changes are to be planned in the site structure for a forest. Require documentation to show how changes will improve the network performance or response time for users. Also, show how the DC replication setup will be affected or changed.

- Document how changes will affect domain security, such as how Active Directory information will be guarded as it is sent over site links.

- Determine how changes are evaluated in the planning stage before they are implemented.

- Determine how changes are implemented—for example, by developing an implementation planning document.

- Determine a schedule for periodically reviewing the site plan to make improvements in server and network performance.

Sample Site Designs

One example of a basic site plan is for the headquarters isb.com domain at the Interstate Security Bank in Seattle. The bank's headquarters is located in a 10-floor building in which the departments are on different floors. The executive offices are on the top floor, and these are on one subnet. The Marketing department is on floors eight and nine, and there is one subnet for both of these floors. The Business department is on floors five, six, and seven, and has two subnets associated with it. The IT, Loans, and Investments departments are on the second, third, and fourth floors, and each is segmented by a subnet. The first floor consists of the Customer Service department and the payroll clearinghouse unit, each on its own subnet. The backbone for the network is 1 GB Ethernet, with a router located in the IT department, and 1 GB switches on each floor. The Internet connection for the bank's Web site also comes into the router, as shown in Figure 7-10.

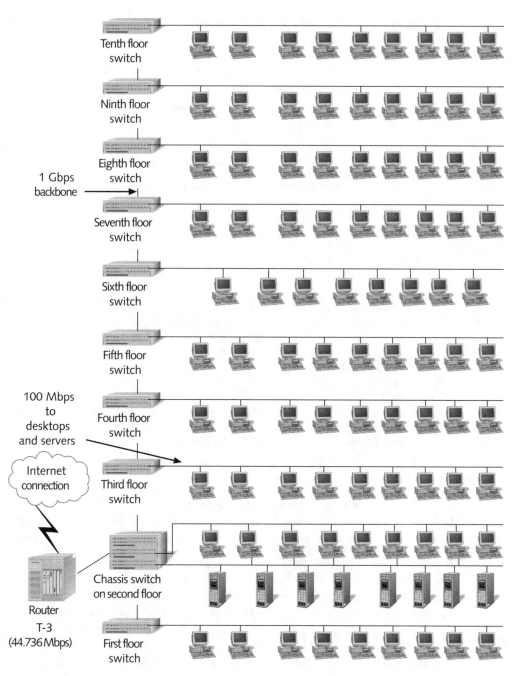

Figure 7-10   Headquarters network

The simplest way to set up the site plan is to have only one site in the isb.com domain and to have all subnets associated with that site. A better approach is to analyze the network traffic to determine which areas are most congested, if any. For example, consider that your analysis of the network traffic shows that there is significant traffic on the Marketing, Customer Service, Business, and IT subnets. In this case, you can provide better service to the users relocating specific domain controllers and by creating five sites, one for each of the following areas:

- Executive offices, Loans department, Investments department, and payroll clearinghouse (with four associated subnets)

- Marketing department (with two associated subnets)

- Customer Service department (with one subnet)

- Business department (with two subnets)

- IT department (with one subnet)

Creating five sites has several advantages in terms of using the Active Directory capabilities:

- Creating sites enables the bank to locate particular domain controllers on the sites containing the users of those DCs, such as locating the domain controller that contains the Marketing department user files on the Marketing department's site. This will enable users to log on to the nearest domain controller, which gives users faster response and also helps to reduce unnecessary network traffic.

- Active Directory replication traffic between sites can be controlled—for example, replicating over site links at eight-hour intervals. This will help reduce some of the network congestion.

- Each site link can be assigned a cost, so that replication traffic goes over relatively less critical network paths.

As part of the site plan, you can advocate locating one DC at each site, either immediately or over a period of months. In a situation like this, you can very likely justify the cost of the plan by relating the TCO to the cost savings in user productivity.

Another modification for the headquarters site plan is to implement the clearinghouse.isb.com domain for the payroll clearinghouse, as discussed in Chapter 6, and then to create a separate site for that domain. Adding the child domain and the separate site, which implies setting up DCs for that domain, will enhance the security, the management, and the network response for the sensitive payroll clearinghouse business. This modification will also be likely to have extra appeal to the financial auditors who typically like to have strong security boundaries around different types of business functions.

Consider another company situation, which is Pampas Fixtures, one of the companies belonging to York Industries. Pampas Fixtures has manufacturing business units in five different buildings that are spread throughout Buenos Aires. These manufacturing units all have 10 Mbps LANs that are connected to one another using 128 Kbps X.25 connections through a local telecommunications company. Three of the X.25 connections are very reliable, but the other two connections are often down or under repair. One approach to creating the site plan is to combine the three LANs with reliable X.25 links into one site in the Pampas Fixtures domain, and to separately designate one site at each of the two LANs that are connected through the unreliable links. One DC would be placed at each site, which means that two of the LANs in the site that contains three locations would not have DCs (see Figure 7-11). By using three sites, the company targets the sites to match the locations of the most unreliable site links, while saving money by not having DCs on each LAN. The disadvantage of this plan is that users where there are no DCs may have a long wait to access network resources.

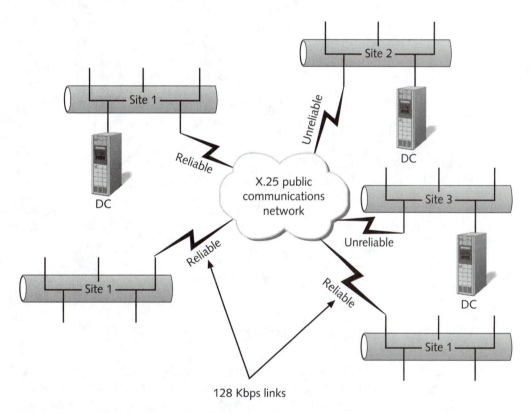

Figure 7-11   Planning three sites for Pampas Fixtures

An alternate approach is to create five sites, one for each LAN location (see Figure 7-12), with a DC at each site. This is most likely to be the best approach, because there are no locations in which users are frequently waiting to access resources and are therefore less productive. Also, no matter where a site link is down, users can continue to access server resources.

In either model, replication can be set up so that it occurs after working hours. In this way, important daytime WAN traffic is devoted exclusively to business functions, while the evening hours are used for replication and other network maintenance tasks.

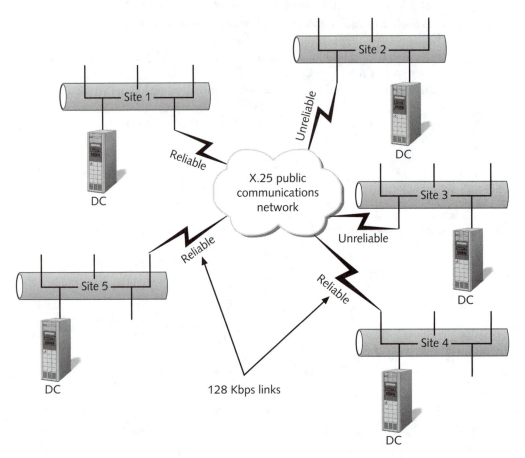

Figure 7-12 Planning five sites for Pampas Fixtures

  As you plan sites, keep in mind that global catalog servers are important to user access as well as DCs. Just as you would locate one or more DCs on LANs joined by unreliable site links, consider locating global catalog servers, too. For example, in Figure 7-11, consider having each DC double as a global catalog server so that there is one global catalog server for the reliable site links, and one for each of the two unreliable site links. In Figure 7-12, also consider designating each DC as a global catalog server (see Chapter 10 for more information about placing global catalog servers) to provide even faster access to network resources.

PLANNING DNS IMPLEMENTATION

When you implement Active Directory, there must one or more DNS servers available on the network. If there are no DNS servers that have been implemented prior to using Windows 2000, plan to implement Windows 2000 DNS because it is most compatible with Active Directory. If non–Microsoft DNS servers are already in use, make sure that the servers are compatible with Active Directory.

 Although Active Directory will work with other standardized versions of DNS, Windows 2000 DNS is specifically tailored for compatibility with Active Directory, particularly in terms of using DC replication and security features.

DNS servers maintain the namespace for an enterprise and provide a way to resolve computer names to IP addresses and IP addresses to computer names. They do this by maintaining tables of information that link computer names and IP addresses. The tables are associated with partitions in a DNS server that are called **zones** and that contain **resource records (RR)**. Each zone houses tables, called the zone file or zone database, of different types of resource records, such as records that link domain servers to the services they provide, SMTP (e-mail) or DHCP (IP address leasing), for example. Other types of resource records link a computer name to an IP address.

The zone that links computer names to IP addresses is called the **forward lookup zone**, which holds host name records, also called address records. Each IP-based server and client should have a host record so that it can be found through DNS. For example, if the DNS server name is Lawyer, with the IP address 129.70.10.1, then the forward lookup zone maps Lawyer to 129.70.10.1. In IP version 4, a host record is called a **host address (A) resource record**. IP version 6 (IPv6) is a newer version of IP that is still under development and consists of a 128-bit address. An IPv6 record is called an **IPv6 host address (AAAA) resource record**. Microsoft, along with other major network software and hardware vendors, has made a commitment to implement IPv6. Figure 7-13 shows the forward lookup zone host records as displayed in the DNS management tool. When you install DNS on a DC in a domain, a forward lookup zone is automatically created for the domain with the DNS server record already entered. You must enter the records of other hosts, or configure DHCP to automatically update the DNS forward lookup zone each time it assigns an IP address.

Another zone, called the **reverse lookup zone**, holds the **pointer (PTR) resource record**, which contains the IP-address-to-host name. The reverse lookup zone is not used as commonly as the forward lookup zone, but can be important to create for those instances when a network communication requires associating an IP address to a computer name, such as for monitoring a network using IP address information. Because it is used less commonly, the reverse lookup zone is not automatically created when DNS is installed. If you anticipate that there will be users who access your network offsite, such as over the Internet, however, plan to implement a reverse lookup zone. Table 7-2 summarizes the commonly used resource records in DNS.

7

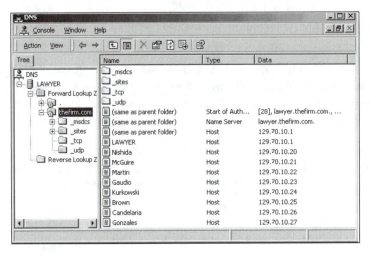

Figure 7-13   Forward lookup zone

Table 7-2   DNS Resource Records

Resource Record	Description
Address (A)	Links a computer or network host name to its IP address
Canonical name (CNAME)	Links an alias to a computer name, so that the actual computer naming scheme of a network is difficult to determine
Load sharing	Used to spread the load of DNS lookup requests among multiple DNS servers as a way to provide faster resolution for clients and better network response
Mail exchange (MX)	Provides the link to which e-mail is sent for users in a domain
Name server (NS)	Provides the links to secondary DNS servers for an authoritative server (described later in this section) and the links to off-site primary servers that are not authoritative for the domain
Pointer record (PTR)	Links an IP address to a computer or network host name
Service (SRV)	Links a particular TCP/IP service to a server along with the domain of the server and its protocol
Start of authority (SOA)	Is the first record in a zone and also indicates if this server is authoritative for the current zone
Windows Internet Naming Service (WINS)	Used to forward a lookup request for a NetBIOS name to a WINS server when the host name cannot be found in DNS
Windows Internet Naming Service Reverse (WINS-R)	Used to forward a reverse lookup (IP address to computer name) request to a WINS server

DNS servers on a network fall into two broad categories: primary and secondary. A **primary DNS server** is the DNS server that is the main administrative server for a zone and thus is also the *authoritative* server for that zone. For example, when you first create a forward lookup zone on a DNS server for the york.com domain, you create an SOA resource record that identifies that DNS server as authoritative for york.com. This means that all changes to the zone, the creation of address (A) resource records, new SRV resource records, and so on must be made on that DNS server.

You have the option to create one or more backup DNS servers, called **secondary DNS servers**, for a primary DNS server. A secondary DNS server contains a copy of the primary DNS server's zone database, but is not used for administration. It obtains that copy through a zone transfer over the network. There are three vital services performed by secondary DNS servers. One is to make sure that there is a copy of the primary DNS server's data, in case the primary server fails. Another function is to enable DNS load balancing (via the load sharing resource records) among a primary DNS server and its secondary servers. Load balancing means that if the DNS primary server is busy performing a name resolution, a different request for a name resolution that is received at the same time can be fielded by a secondary DNS server for faster response to users. A third advantage to using secondary DNS servers is that they can be spread to different parts of a network, such as to different sites, so that you can reduce the congestion in one part of the network.

 One DNS server can be authoritative for multiple domains because it can have multiple zones. Also, because one server can have multiple zones, a single DNS server can be a secondary server for more than one primary server. Plus, one DNS server can be a primary server for one zone, and a secondary server for another zone.

Non-Microsoft DNS servers that are authoritative on the network must support two DNS standards: service resource records and the DNS dynamic update protocol. Outlined in RFC 2052, a **service resource record (SRV RR)** is a type of DNS record that enables DNS to recognize multiple servers in a single domain, and to locate commonly used TCP/IP services that are associated with specific servers. SRV RRs allow a DNS server to generate a list of network servers that provide TCP/IP services and the protocols supported by those servers, and to determine a preferred server for a specific service. The SRV record is formatted to include information about the service that is provided by a server, the domain that is serviced by a server, and the protocol used by the server. The **DNS Dynamic Update Protocol** is outlined in RFC 2136 and enables information in a DNS server to be automatically updated; for example, enabling a Windows 2000 Professional workstation to update its DHCP-leased IP address. The DNS Dynamic Update Protocol can save network administrators a great deal of time, because they no longer have to manually register each new workstation or to register a workstation each time its IP lease is up and a new IP address is issued.

To use the DNS Dynamic Update Protocol, make sure that you complete two steps in the Windows 2000 Server environment. First, configure Windows 2000 DNS zones in a domain particularly the forward and reverse lookup zones, to accept dynamic updates by opening the DNS tool in Administrative Tools, displaying the zone and its child objects in the tree, displaying the child objects under the domain, right-clicking the domain under the zone, and clicking Properties (see Figure 7-14). Second, if you are using DHCP, configure it to dynamically update DNS or to have clients perform the dynamic update. To configure DHCP, open the DHCP tool in the Administrative Tools, right-click the DHCP server in the tree, click Properties, and click the DNS tab (see Figure 7-15).

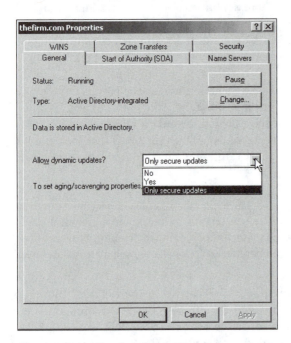

Figure 7-14   Configuring DNS for dynamic updates

These two requirements apply only to DNS servers that are authoritative. If you are not using Microsoft DNS for authoritative servers on a network, consult the documentation for the currently used DNS versions to determine if they support SRV records and the DNS Dynamic Update Protocol. If they do not, find out if you can obtain an update, or convert DNS authoritative servers to Microsoft DNS. *DNS servers that do not function in an authoritative role do not have to support these standards.*

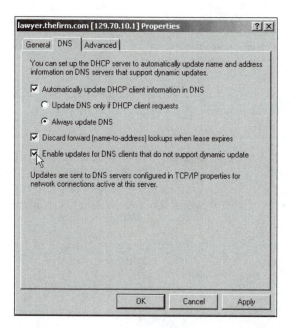

Figure 7-15   Configuring DHCP for dynamically updating DNS

There are several advantages to using Microsoft Windows 2000 DNS integrated with Active Directory. A significant advantage is that the zone databases are stored in Active Directory. When there are multiple DCs, this means that there are multiple copies of the zone databases stored on the network for extra fault tolerance. Another advantage to this design is that the multimaster DC model enables *all DNS servers to act as authoritative DNS servers*, processing new records and record modifications—in the same way that any DC in a domain can process the addition of a new account. Once it is added, a new DNS record or modification is automatically replicated to other DNS servers through the normal DC replication process. The result is a reduction in network traffic, and even more fault tolerance than is provided by non-Microsoft DNS servers.

The option to integrate DNS with Active Directory services is selected when you create a new zone in DNS. To create a new zone and select the option:

1. Open the DNS tool in the Administrative Tools (or open the MMC snap-in).

2. Right-click the DNS server in the tree.

3. Click New Zone.

4. Click Next after the New Zone Wizard starts.

5. Select the type of zone that you want to create (see Figure 7-16). The selections are to create a zone that is integrated with Active Directory, to create a standard primary zone that is not integrated with Active Directory, or to create a standard secondary zone that is not integrated.

6. Click Next.

7. Specify whether you want to create a forward or reverse lookup zone.

8. Click Next.

9. Enter the name for the zone (or for a reverse lookup zone you can enter the network ID or name for the zone).

10. Click Next.

11. If you are creating a zone that is integrated with Active Directory, go to Step 14. If you are creating a standard primary zone, proceed with Step 12. Or, if you are creating a standard secondary zone, enter the IP address of the primary DNS server from which to copy the zone data, click Add, and go to Step 13.

12. Specify the zone filename, or use the default name, which is derived from the name you entered in Step 9 plus the ".dns" extension.

13. Click Next.

14. Click Finish.

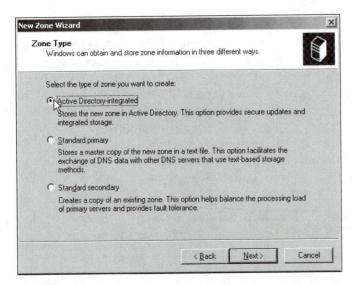

Figure 7-16 Selecting the zone type

When you choose to create a standard primary zone or a standard secondary zone, the zone file is not stored in Active Directory and is not automatically replicated as part of the DC replication, and there is only one authoritative (primary) server, instead of many for that zone.

Another advantage of Windows 2000 DNS is a feature called *secure dynamic update*. By using this feature, you can specify which computers can access DNS information for dynamic updating. For example, if you suspect that your network is subject to intrusions from a computer over the Internet, you can prevent that computer from obtaining DNS resolution information. Similarly, you can specify that some computers cannot automatically update the DNS resource records, so that these computers are known to DNS servers only if you manually enter resource records for them. This is another important security feature so that you can limit the harm done by a network intruder, or prevent an unauthorized user from registering his or her computer name and IP address.

Yet another advantage of using Windows 2000 DNS is that DCs can automatically create a set of *locator records*. These are SRV records that identify the specific services that each DC can offer. Any client computer can query a DNS server about the available services on DCs and then receive information about which DCs provide that service, such as e-mail or IP address leasing.

Additional DNS Server Roles

DNS servers can play several specialized roles in addition to or other than those of authoritative/primary or secondary DNS server. For instance, when there are multiple sites or when there is Internet connectivity, it is common to designate one DNS server to *forward name resolution requests* to a specific remote DNS server. One example of how forwarding works is a set of state community colleges that operate under a community college commission. Each college maintains DNS servers for resolution of addresses within its own namespace. Each college also has designated one onsite DNS server to automatically forward name resolution requests involving another college or the commission. If there is a name resolution request that involves finding a server at the community college commission, the DNS forwarder server on the college network forwards the resolution request to a DNS server on the commission's network (see Figure 7-17). Or, if a professor at one college needs to access a shared folder offered by a professor at another college, the DNS forwarder server at the first college transfers the resolution request to a DNS server at the other college.

When one DNS server is set up as the forwarder, then all other DNS servers that have queries to send to an offsite DNS server send those queries to the single DNS forwarder server. By designating only one DNS forwarder server, you ensure that only one server is sending queries over a site link, instead of having multiple servers sending queries and creating extra traffic over the site link.

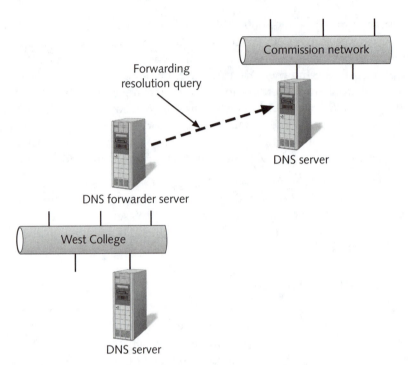

Figure 7-17   DNS forwarder server

DNS forwarding can be set up so that if the DNS server that receives the forwarded request cannot resolve the name, then the server that originally forwarded the request attempts to resolve it. This is called *nonexclusive forwarding*. When DNS forwarding is set so that only the DNS server receiving the request attempts resolution (and not the server that forwarded the request), this is called *exclusive forwarding*. In exclusive forwarding, the DNS server that initially forwards the request is called a *slave DNS server*.

Another role that a DNS server can perform is that of a *caching server*. A caching server is used to provide fast queries, because the results of each query are stored in RAM. As more resolution queries are performed, a large base of information is stored in RAM for fast response to users. Usually a caching server does not contain zone databases, but queries a primary or secondary DNS server and caches the results to provide a fast response for the next identical query. Caching servers are used as a way to reduce the number of secondary DNS servers required, and therefore reduce the extra network traffic that results because of replicating zones from the primary to the secondary servers. One limitation of using caching servers is that it takes time for each one to build up a comprehensive set of resolved names to IP addresses, and every time a caching server goes down, it must rebuild its information from scratch.

Try Hands-on Project 7-9 to gain first-hand experience with zones, resource records, security, and forwarding in a DNS server.

Creating a DNS Implementation Plan

When you plan a DNS implementation, consider the following recommendations:

- If possible, implement Windows 2000 DNS server, using the option to integrate DNS zones with Active Directory. This makes every DC that is also a DNS server an authoritative server (in effect a primary server). The advantage is that the DNS servers, like the DCs, exist in a multimaster relationship. The multimaster relationship reduces the need to use caching servers, because DNS zone transfers from DNS server to DNS server occur as a built-in process along with normal DC replication. Also, when you use Windows 2000 DNS server, you can take advantage of Dynamic DNS updating, which will save you time as an administrator and make your A and PTR resource records more accurate.

- Plan to locate a DNS server across most site links, just as you would locate DCs. The exceptions may be when there are not enough users across certain site links, or when the site links are very reliable and high-speed, such as SONET (see Chapter 5).

- Just as you should create two or more DCs per domain, also create two or more DNS servers to take advantage of load balancing, multimaster relationships, and fault tolerance.

- When you have off-site links between different domains, designate one DNS server as a forwarder to reduce traffic over those links.

- The number of DNS servers that you set up can be related to your analysis of an organization. For example, an organization that is centralized will typically have fewer domains and therefore fewer DNS servers and DNS server administrators. An organization that is decentralized will likely have more domains, more DNS servers, and more DNS server administrators.

Creating a DNS Change Management Plan

After you have created a DNS implementation plan, make sure that you also have a policy to guarantee planned changes in the future. Here are some recommendations:

- Delineate who has the authority to add, remove, and manage DNS servers and DNS zones.

- Determine how security will be assigned to those who manage DNS servers, such as through the Domain Admins and DnsAdmins security groups.

- Create a policy to describe how changes are to be planned in the DNS structure for a forest.

- Determine how changes are evaluated in the planning stage before they are implemented.

- Determine how changes to the DNS server implementation will affect users and network performance.

DNS Implementation Examples

A DNS implementation plan for Jefferson Philately would include two DNS servers that are also configured as DCs. By using Windows 2000 DNS, the servers would be configured to integrate with Active Directory services so that zone information is stored in Active Directory. Zone transfers would be made automatically between the two servers, which means that both servers would function as primary DNS servers, because zone updates can be made from either server. At least a forward lookup zone should be configured with host address (A) resource records for all of the computers on the network. Also, the analysis of software and hardware systems shows that Jefferson Philately is upgrading its workstations over the next year to use Windows 2000 Professional. This means that they can set up DNS to implement dynamic updates from the Windows 2000 Professional workstations. The advantages of this plan are:

- Both DNS servers are configured to take advantage of automated Active Directory zone transfers.

- Both DNS servers are in a multimaster-type DNS primary server relationship.

- There are two DNS servers that can balance the load of DNS queries to reduce response time and network traffic.

- The zone databases are replicated between the two servers, which provides fault tolerance.

- Dynamic updating ensures that forward lookup zone resource records are kept up to date.

 If there is much offsite traffic from the vendors with which Jefferson Philately transacts business, such as those used for vinyl, plastic, and cardboard purchases, then the company should consider creating a reverse lookup zone for visitors who are first known to the network by IP addresses. Also, if Jefferson Philately engages in electronic transfers with these companies, then Jefferson should consider designating one of its DNS servers as a forwarder, with pointers to the DNS servers of the vendors from which it purchases manufacturing supplies.

Figure 7-18 illustrates this DNS implementation model for Jefferson Philately.

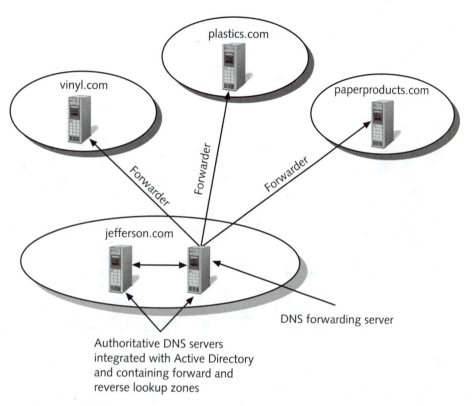

Figure 7-18   Implementing DNS servers for Jefferson Philately

When Jefferson Philately opens its new manufacturing facility, the DNS implementation will change, depending on where they locate the facility. If the facility is in the same city and joined by a reliable high-speed ATM link, then having only two DNS servers on the network at the main location will likely be sufficient. If the facility is built in Cambridge, Ohio, using a 256 Kbps frame relay site link, then they should consider adding a third DNS server that would be integrated with Active Directory and located in the network in Cambridge. This would provide faster access for users at the Cambridge location and fault tolerance.

The DNS implementation model for Interstate Security Bank involves more domains than for Jefferson Philately. One way to approach this implementation is to set up two Active Directory integrated DNS servers in each domain. Also, for the payroll clearing-house business, the company should consider creating a reverse lookup zone to provide a way to identify offsite resolution requests that start with IP addresses instead of computer names. Figure 7-19 shows an example of this implementation for the Interstate Security Bank domain plan that does not have a separate domain for the payroll clearinghouse business.

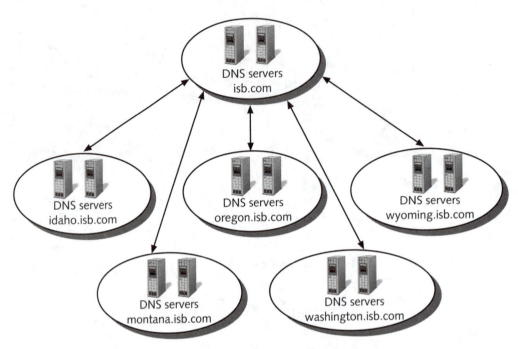

Figure 7-19   Implementing DNS servers for Interstate Security Bank

The advantages of the plan shown in Figure 7-19 are:

- There is load-balancing and fault tolerance among DNS servers within the domains.

- There are DNS servers at each site, so that no site is dependent on the DNS server to another site.

- The reverse lookup zone enables resolution of offsite IP addresses.

- One DNS server per site can be designated as a forwarder to all other sites as a way to reduce site-link traffic.

- Administration of DNS servers at each site is independent, which reflects the decentralized management structure.

In this DNS implementation plan, the two DNS servers in the isb.com domain are authoritative only for that domain. The two DNS servers in the idaho.isb.com domain are authoritative only in that domain, and so on for the DNS servers in each child domain. Also, for a DNS server in any domain, you have the option to add a forward lookup zone from a DNS server in another domain, and to make that zone integrated with Active Directory—which makes it authoritative—or to make it a secondary zone. One way to use this capability is to make one DNS server in the isb.com domain authoritative for the forward lookup zones of DNS servers in each of the other domains: idaho.isb.com, montana.isb.com, oregon.isb.com, washington.isb.com, and wyoming.isb.com. This provides a disaster recovery plan, so that if both DNS servers in a domain other than isb.com go down, the users in that domain still have DNS services, and those DNS servers can be rebuilt quickly via the DNS server in the isb.com domain. It also means that a DNS administrator in the isb.com domain can modify the DNS server forward lookup zones in any other domain, if necessary. If the bank does not want a DNS server in the isb.com domain to be authoritative for the forward lookup zones in the child domains, another option is to set up the redundant zones on the isb.com DNS server as standard secondary zones, instead of being integrated with Active Directory (refer to Figure 7-16). This would make the DNS server in the isb.com domain a secondary DNS server to the DNS servers in each of the other domains. Last, this capability also means that you could modify the original plan to have only one DNS server in each of the child domains. One DNS server in the isb.com domain would be a secondary server for each of the forward lookup zones on the single DNS servers in the child domains (see Figure 7-20). This option may be attractive, if the bank needs to take cost saving measures.

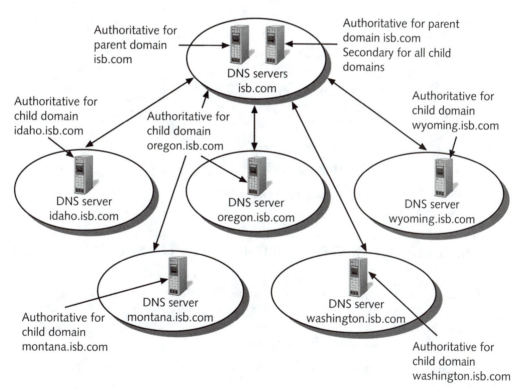

Figure 7-20   Alternate DNS implementation model for Interstate Security Bank

Yet another alternative that can make DNS server maintenance simpler is to create a separate child domain for the payroll clearinghouse business, implement one or two DNS servers in that domain, and primarily maintain the reverse lookup zone for the DNS servers in that domain.

A DNS implementation plan for York Industries has at least two DNS servers in each domain, and more for those domains that span two or more sites. Because the distances are so great over the site links, zone transfers will stay within each domain (except for the possibility of using secondary servers in other domains for disaster recovery). Active Directory integration would be used among the two or more DNS servers within each domain. Most of the York Industries domains would use both forward and reverse lookup zones, because the international network traffic and Internet access makes a need for both very likely. Also, there would be extensive use of forwarders between sites as a way to save on traffic across the site links. Figure 7-21 illustrates how a forwarder might be set up between the Nantes company site and the other sites.

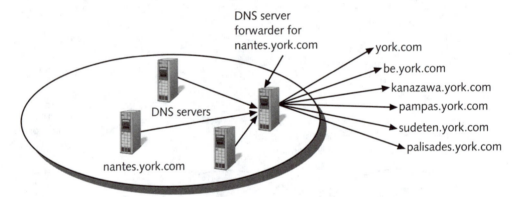

Figure 7-21   Using forwarding between York Industries domains

PLANNING FOR COEXISTENCE WITH OTHER DIRECTORY SERVICES

Often there are other directory services and other versions of DNS on a network. Your best approach in planning for coexistence with these other services is to recognize that Active Directory and Windows 2000 DNS are based on modern standards. Check on the standards used by other directory services and other versions of DNS to make sure that they also use industry standards.

Active Directory uses the following important standards for directory services (see Chapter 1):

- LDAP (Lightweight Directory Access Protocol) version 3, which is a standard directory services protocols (used by IBM, Novell, Netscape, and Lotus, and developed to be consistent with X.500 standards but easier to implement)

- NSPI (Name Service Provider Interface), which is the protocol used by Microsoft Exchange for e-mail services

- TCP/IP (Transmission Control Protocol/Internet Protocol), which is the protocol of choice for most networks, the Internet, intranets, extranets, and virtual private networks

- DNS (Domain Name System), which is the TCP/IP-based name resolution service

For optimum communication between Active Directory and other directory services, make sure that the other directory services also support these standards. If you are using directory services that are not compatible, but that can be upgraded to be compatible, perform the upgrade. For example, Novell Directory Services (NDS) used in NetWare version 5 and higher is compatible with these standards and can interoperate with Microsoft Active Directory. Earlier versions of NetWare, such as versions 2, 3, and 4, are not fully compatible and should be upgraded to version 5 or higher.

Also, make sure that non-Windows 2000 DNS services on your network are compatible. As you learned earlier in this chapter, if there are non-Windows 2000 DNS authoritative servers, they must support SRV resource records and DNS Dynamic Update Protocol. In addition to these requirements, they should be compatible with **Berkeley Internet Name Domain (BIND)** version 8.1.2 or above. BIND is a standardized version of DNS that is specified by the Internet Software Consortium (ISC) and that was first developed for UNIX operating systems. Although you can configure Active Directory to work with lower BIND versions, you will be able to take advantage of more functionality if the other DNS servers are using BIND 8.1.2 or above—or if you migrate to Windows 2000 DNS.

 If you are using Windows NT 4.0 DNS services, these can be upgraded for compatibility with Windows 2000 DNS by installing Windows NT 4.0 service pack 4 or higher, which implements SRV RRs and DNS Dynamic Update Protocol.

Active Directory information can be exported to and imported from other directory services by using either of two utilities available from Microsoft:

- *LDIFDE:* This is a command prompt utility that works in a batch mode to import information from other directory services or to export information from Active Directory into other directory services. Before using this command, enter *LDIFDE* at the command prompt to view the switches that can be used with it. You might use this utility to import information from Novell Directory Services into Active Directory when your network uses both Windows 2000 and NetWare servers, for example (see Chapter 9 for additional ways to import and export directory service data).

- *CSVDE:* This is a command prompt utility that enables you to export or import directory services information in a comma-delimited format (with a comma after each record or information field). The comma-delimited format is compatible with a range of directory services applications as well as with most spreadsheet software, such as Microsoft Excel. Enter the command *CSVDE* to view the switches that are available with this command.

 Other third-party utilities are available that enable Active Directory to inter-operate with different directory services.

Chapter Summary

❑ Organizational units (OUs) enable you to manage server resources more flexibly than through a domain. By creating OUs, you can delegate authority over objects such as user accounts, groups, shared folders, and printers. Also, you can implement OUs to set specific group policies, such as those for particular groups and users in a domain. OUs also come with tools that enable you to manage and restructure their contents.

❑ Sites reflect the physical layout of a network and are therefore a different concept than forests, trees, domains, and OUs, which are logically based. Use sites to enhance network and Active Directory performance, such as by reflecting the traffic control techniques used in IP subnets.

❑ DNS servers are implemented to perform name resolution. Carefully plan the placement and use of DNS servers to accomplish load balancing, fast name lookup, and fault tolerance.

In the next chapter, you will learn about Windows 2000 groups and about managing group policies from large-scale levels, such as the domain level, to smaller levels, such as OUs.

Key Terms

Berkeley Internet Name Domain (BIND) — A standardized version of Domain Name System that is specified by the Internet Software Consortium (ISC).

bridgehead server — A DC at each site across a site link which is designated by the KCC to exchange replication information. There is only one bridgehead server per site.

DNS Dynamic Update protocol — A TCP/IP-based protocol that enables information in a DNS server to be automatically updated; for example, when a Windows 2000 Professional workstation updates its leased DHCP IP address.

forward lookup zone — A DNS zone or table that maps computer names to IP addresses.

host address (A) resource record — A record in a DNS forward lookup zone that consists of a computer or domain name correlated to an IP version 4 (or 32-bit) address.

IPv6 host address (AAAA) resource record — A record in a DNS forward lookup zone that consists of a computer or domain name mapped to an IP version 6 (or 128-bit) address.

Knowledge Consistency Checker (KCC) — A process run by Active Directory to establish network connections between DCs and to ensure that replication services take place. It obtains site and site-link information from the configuration container and assesses the locations of DCs, site-link costs, and the replication strategy of server administrators.

pointer (PTR) resource record — A record in a DNS reverse lookup zone that consists of an IP (version 4 or 6) address correlated to a computer or domain name.

primary DNS server — A DNS server that is used as the main server from which to administer a zone, such as for updating records in a forward lookup zone for a domain. A primary DNS server is also called the authoritative server for that zone.

remote procedure call (RPC) protocol — A protocol that is used by an initiating computer to run a program process on another computer.

resource record (RR) — A record that is used to provide data in a DNS zone or lookup table. The information in a DNS server is built from resource records.

reverse lookup zone — A DNS server zone or table that maps IP addresses to computer or domain names.

secondary DNS server — A DNS server that is a backup to a primary DNS server and therefore is not authoritative.

service resource record (SRV RR) — A record in a DNS zone that is created to locate commonly used TCP/IP services. The SRV record is formatted to include information about the service that is provided by a server, the domain that is serviced by a server, and the protocol used by the server.

zone — A partition or subtree in a DNS server that contains specific kinds of records in a lookup table, such as a forward lookup zone that contains records in a table for looking up computer and domain names in order to find their associated IP addresses.

REVIEW QUESTIONS

Answer questions 1–9 using this case information:

College of the Pines is a community college of 7,452 students that has a main campus of 4,930 students and four branch campuses consisting of 270, 1,200, 322, and 730 students. The main and branch campuses each have administrative offices, instructor offices, classrooms, and labs, all of which are networked at each site. The WANs that join the branch campuses to the main campus are all connected by 128/144 Kbps ISDN links.

1. When planning how to set up sites for this college, which of the following should you do?

   a. Create a network diagram.

   b. Determine who will manage sites.

   c. Create no more than two subnets per each site.

   d. Create no more that two OUs per each site.

   e. all of the above

   f. only a and b

   g. only b and c

   h. only b, c, and d

2. Your analysis shows that there are four WANs. How many site links are there?

   a. 1

   b. 2

   c. 3

   d. 4

   e. 8

3. The college has a User Consulting department on the main campus and at each of the branch campuses. The academic vice president would like the user consultants in this department, but not faculty or staff, to be able to reset passwords for students. Which of the following is the best solution?

   a. Create an OU called Students in the college's domain, move the student user accounts to that OU, and delegate authority to the user consultants to reset passwords.

   b. Create a child domain called students.pines.edu and delegate authority for that domain to the user consultants.

   c. Create an OU called Students, move the student user accounts to that OU, and delegate authority to create user accounts to the user consultants.

   d. Make the user consultants members of the default OU Administrators group.

   e. Inform the vice president that there is no way to grant authority to reset passwords without making the user consultants enterprise administrators.

   f. only b and c

   g. only c and d

4. You want to put two DNS servers on the branch campus that has 1200 students, making one an authoritative DNS server and one a backup DNS server that is not authoritative. What type of DNS server is the backup server?

   a. Active Directory integrated

   b. standard primary

   c. standard secondary

   d. caching

   e. none of the above

   f. all of the above

   g. only a and b

   h. only a, b, and d

5. Your analysis shows that all of the site links have had periods when they were down. Which of the following would you include in your Active Directory design?

   a. Make each branch a separate forest.

   b. Make each branch a site (or more than one site, depending on the subnet structure).

   c. Create only reverse lookup zones for the branches, and one forward lookup zone for the main campus in DNS servers.

   d. Make the main campus a site (or more than one site, depending on the subnet structure).

   e. all of the above

   f. only a and c

   g. only b and d

6. When you integrate a DNS zone with Active Directory:

   a. The zone must be a forward lookup zone.

   b. The zone information is stored in Active Directory.

   c. The DNS server must also be set up as a caching server.

   d. There can only be one computer designated as a DNS server.

   e. none of the above

   f. only a and c

   g. only a, b and c

7. College of the Pines has a limited budget until the new fiscal year starts in July, which is five months away. One of their DNS servers is running Windows NT Server 4.0, and the college does not have the funds budgeted to upgrade it. How can they continue to use this NT 4.0 DNS server when all of the other DNS servers are running Windows 2000 Server?

   a. Install DHCP on the Windows NT 4.0 server.

   b. Create a special Windows 2000 DNS partition in the Windows NT 4.0 version of DNS.

   c. Install service pack 4 or higher on the Windows NT 4.0 server.

   d. They are out of luck, unless they can convince an alumnus to donate the money to upgrade the server to Windows 2000.

8. The college's five lab servers are running NetWare version 5 and NDS. What can they do to interoperate with Active Directory?

   a. Install Active Directory NDS client in NetWare, and configure NetWare to use NetBEUI.

   b. NDS and Active Directory are capable of interoperating because they both use the same directory services standards.

   c. Run Active Directory in mixed mode.

   d. all of the above

   e. none of the above

   f. only a and c

   g. only a and b

9. College of the Pines uses DHCP and has many Windows 2000 Professional workstations. Which of the following should they consider?

   a. Configure DNS to enable dynamic updating.

   b. Configure the Windows 2000 Professional workstations to use DHCP.

   c. Configure DHCP to enable DNS dynamic updating.

   d. Disable DNS, because all that they need is DHCP.

   e. all of the above

   f. only a and c

   g. only a, b, and c

   h. only b, c, and d

Answer questions 10–19 using this case information:

Phone Accessories is a company that manufactures answering machines, pagers, cell phone antennas, caller ID devices, and other accessories that are used with telephones. They have one large facility that consists of three buildings, one for business and research, one for manufacturing, and one for warehousing and shipping. The company employs 418 people.

10. Each of the company's buildings is joined by a 1 GB fiber-optic Ethernet link. Would it be possible to consider the LANs in all three buildings as one site?

    a. No, because 1 GB Ethernet is not a fast link between the LANs.

    b. No, because one site cannot go beyond the range of a single building.

    c. No, because each building has a subnet.

    d. Yes, because 1 GB Ethernet can be considered a fast and reliable link between the buildings.

11. Phone Accessories has an existing UNIX-based DNS server, and they want to make it authoritative on their network that consists of UNIX and Windows 2000 servers. What requirements should this DNS server meet so that it can work alongside Windows 2000 DNS?

a. It should support SRV resource records.

b. It must be configured as a forwarding server.

c. It should be compatible with DNS dynamic updating.

d. All UNIX-based DNS servers are compatible with Windows 2000 DNS, thus there is no problem.

e. only a and b

f. only a and c

g. only a, b, and c

12. The research unit of the company is considered to be a top-secret group, because the company is worried about the possibility of employees in the group sharing technical secrets with the competition. As a result, the company would like to enforce special security measures on those who are in the research unit. Which of the following can help?

a. Create multiple sites and associate a secure site group policy with each site.

b. Create an OU containing the accounts and resources used by members of the research unit and delegate full control to a special security official for the group.

c. Associate a special group policy object with an OU that contains the accounts and resources used by members of this unit.

d. Create multiple roving OUs and change their contents so that only those who need access will know the contents.

e. none of the above

f. only a and b

g. only b and c

h. only a, b, and d

13. Because of the centralized authority structure in the IT department, the company wants to place the UNIX-based DNS server in the business and research building and use it to manage DNS services. The company also wants to place a Windows 2000 DNS server in each of the other two buildings, but not use these servers for DNS management. What DNS implementation plan should the company use?

a. Make the UNIX-based DNS server an integrated server with Active Directory.

b. Make the UNIX-based DNS server a primary server.

c. Make one of the Windows 2000 DNS servers a primary server and one a secondary server.

d. Make both of the Windows 2000 DNS servers secondary servers.

e. only a and c

f. only b and c

g. only b and d

14. Which of the following is true about the design proposed in Question 13?

    a. All three DNS servers will participate in Active Directory-based DNS zone replication.

    b. Only the Windows 2000 DNS servers will participate in Active Directory-based DNS zone replication.

    c. None of the Windows 2000 DNS servers will participate in Active Directory based DNS zone replication.

    d. The UNIX-based DNS server is a bridgehead server.

    e. none of the above

    f. only a and d

    g. only b and d

15. The company auditors want all user accounts in the Business department to be created by a single manager in that department and for that manager to have one backup person, who is his administrative assistant. How can you address this strong recommendation from the auditors?

    a. Create an OU containing the Business department's user accounts, and delegate account management to the manager and his administrative assistant.

    b. Create a separate domain for the Business department, and delegate domain user account management to the manager and his administrative assistant.

    c. Create a subnet of only the Business department computers, and delegate subnet management to the manager and his administrative assistant.

    d. There is no way to address this request without giving the manager and his assistant Server Operators privileges.

16. Phone Accessories purchases electronic parts from two different companies that each have LANs, which they allow the engineers and parts inventory personnel at Phone Accessories to access. Phone accessories wants to designate only one of its Windows 2000 DNS servers to contact the DNS servers at the companies with which they transact business, and to not have Phone Accessories' DNS server resolve the off-site addresses of the remote companies. What can Phone Accessories do?

    a. Ask the other companies to make one of their DNS servers forwarders.

    b. Make a designated Phone Accessories DNS server an exclusive forwarder.

    c. Make a designated Phone Accessories DNS server a nonexclusive forwarder.

    d. Place a Phone Accessories DC on each of the other companies' sites for Active Directory replication.

    e. Make each of the other companies a subnet that is recognized by Phone Accessories' Active Directory.

7

17. The IT manager of Phone Accessories has asked you what protocol(s) is (are) used to replicate DCs on the same site. Which of the following is your answer?

    a. Microsoft NetBEUI

    b. remote procedure call (RPC) protocol

    c. BIND protocol

    d. LATA protocol

    e. only a and b

    f. only c and d

    g. only a, c, and d

    h. only a, b, and d

18. The board of directors at Phone Accessories wants to reorganize the company. Which of the following offer(s) the most flexibility and usefulness in planning for the reorganization so that the new administrative authority structures are reflected in Active Directory?

    a. DNS server placement

    b. sites and subnets

    c. domains

    d. OUs

    e. All of the above are equally flexible and useful.

    f. None of the above are particularly flexible nor useful.

19. Phone Accessories' auditors are sticklers for security, and they want to make it difficult for offsite users to determine the naming scheme on the Phones Accessories network. Which of the following resource records can be used to help accomplish this?

    a. SRV

    b. WINS-R

    c. MX

    d. PTR

    e. CNAME

    f. only a and b

    g. only b, c, and d

Answer questions 20–25 using this case information:

Iron Hearth manufactures wood and wood pellet stoves. Its headquarters office and manufacturing plant are within close proximity in Portland, Oregon. The company also owns another company, called Stove Fixtures, which is located in Crescent City, California. Iron Hearth uses the registered domain name ironhearth.com, and Stove fixtures has no registered domain name because it is in the same domain as Iron Hearth. Iron Hearth's

Portland location consists of five subnets, three in the large building that is their head-quarters office and two that are in the manufacturing plant. Your analysis shows that there is a 128 Kbps frame relay link between Iron Hearth and Stove Fixtures.

20. The network in the manufacturing plant is particularly busy, and the company is considering adding a third subnet in the plant. There is an old and very busy 10 Mbps copper link between the headquarters and the plant that they do not plan to upgrade for another year and a half. How many sites would you recommend creating, just at the Portland location?

　　a. No sites are needed, but they should create more subnets.

　　b. Create only one site for faster access.

　　c. Create at least two sites, one consisting of the headquarters subnets, and one consisting of the plant subnets.

　　d. No sites are needed, but they can better segment Active Directory traffic by creating nested OUs for the headquarters users and for the plant users.

21. The Iron Hearth IT department wants to make the LAN at Stove Fixtures a separate site and place at least two DCs at that location. Why is this a good idea?

　　a. It will provide fault tolerance.

　　b. It will give the Stove Fixtures users faster network access to resources.

　　c. It will enable the IT department to control the frequency of replication over the site link.

　　d. It will provide a form of disaster recovery for both the Iron Hearth and Stove Fixtures operations.

　　e. all of the above

　　f. only a and b

　　g. only a and c

　　h. only b, c, and d

22. What is the first DC that is set up at the Stove Fixtures location called?

　　a. a bridgehead server

　　b. a DNS server

　　c. a slave server

　　d. a forwarder

　　e. a site server

23. The IT vice president wants to simplify the management of user accounts so that accounts are managed by the server administrator and her assistant. What do you recommend?

   a. Create OUs for each department, and delegate authority for the OUs to the server manager and her assistant.

   b. Create two different OUs containing identical user accounts, one delegated to the server manager and one delegated to her assistant.

   c. Create one OU for the server manager that contains the user accounts, and nest an OU under the server manager's OU that is delegated to her assistant.

   d. Create all user accounts in the Users folder, and make sure that the server manager and her assistant have privileges to manage accounts in that folder.

   e. Change the IT vice president's mind, because most companies have department heads manage user accounts.

24. You are planning to set up one Windows 2000 DNS server at the headquarters LAN, one on the manufacturing LAN, and one on the LAN at Stove Fixtures. The IT vice president wants the DNS administrator to be able to modify zone information at any of the three servers. Which of the following is true?

   a. The zones in all three servers should be integrated with Active Directory.

   b. Zone transfers should occur between all three DNS servers.

   c. The zones in all three servers should be made standard primary zones to ensure that they are authoritative and that full replication occurs.

   d. The DNS server at the headquarters and the manufacturing plant should have standard primary zones, and the DNS server at the Crescent City location should be made a standard slave server.

   e. none of the above

   f. only a and b

   g. only a and c

   h. only a and d

25. When you set up the DNS servers, the members of the board of directors, who access the network from different locations in Washington, Oregon, and California, are having trouble accessing information and sending e-mail to Iron Hearth. What are you likely to have omitted from your planning and implementation?

   a. creating SRV RRs

   b. creating a forward lookup zone

   c. creating a reverse lookup zone

   d. creating a WINS RR pointer to Active Directory

   e. creating NS RRs

Hands-on Projects

Project 7-1

This project enables you to view the OUs in a domain.

To view the OUs:

1. Click **Start**, point to **Programs**, point to **Administrative Tools**, and click **Active Directory Users and Computers**.

2. Double-click a domain in the tree, such as TheFirm.com, if the child objects are not already displayed under the domain.

3. What OUs and folders are displayed in the tree under the domain? Record your observations in your lab journal or in a word-processed document.

4. Click **Builtin**. What groups are displayed in the right-hand pane for this container?

5. Click **Computers**. What computers are listed in the right-hand pane titled Computers?

6. Click **Domain Controllers**. How many domain controllers are displayed, and what are their names?

7. Click **ForeignSecurityPrincipals**. Are there any objects displayed in the right-hand pane, and if so what are they? What is the purpose of this container?

8. Click **Users** and notice the accounts and groups in this container.

9. Examine the contents of the tree and determine which OUs/folders are there by default, and which ones have been created in addition to the default OUs.

10. Record your observations.

11. Leave the Active Directory Users and Computers tool open for the next hands-on project.

Project 7-2

In this project, you create an OU and determine what elements can be put in the OU. Before starting, consult with your instructor about which domain should contain the OU that you create.

To create the OU:

1. Make sure that the Active Directory Users and Computers tool is open, and if not, open it.

2. Right-click the domain for which you have permission to create a new OU, point to **New**, and click **Organizational Unit**.

3. In the Name box, enter your initials plus TestOU, as in MJPTestOU.

4. Click **OK**.

5. Scroll to find the OU that you created in the tree and right-click the new OU.

6. What are the options shown on the shortcut menu? Record these in your lab journal or in a word-processed document.

7. Point to **New** on the shortcut menu. What are the elements that can be placed in an OU? How would you create another OU within the current OU?

8. Move the pointer down to **All Tasks** on the shortcut menu for the OU. What are the options associated with All Tasks?

9. Record your observations.

10. Move the pointer away from the shortcut menus and into a blank area of the Active Directory Users and Computers tool. Click the blank area to close the menus.

11. Leave the Active Directory Users and Computers tool open for the next project.

Project 7-3

7

In this project, you practice delegating authority to an OU. This project gives you a more thorough look at the delegation options than you got from the OU delegation hands-on project in Chapter 1.

To delegate authority over an OU:

1. Ensure that the Active Directory Users and Computers tool is open, and if not, open it.

2. Right-click the OU that you created in Hands-on Project 7-2, such as MJPTestOU, and click **Delegate Control**.

3. Click **Next**.

4. Click the **Add** button.

5. Double-click **Server Operators**, and then click **OK**.

6. How would you add another group or user account to the list of selected users and groups? Record your answer in your lab journal or in a word-processed document.

7. Click **Next**. What are the options in the Tasks to Delegate dialog box? Record your observations.

8. Leave **Delegate the following common tasks** selected.

9. Check the box for **Reset passwords on user accounts** and click **Next**.

10. What dialog box do you see now? Record your observations.

11. Click **Back** so that you can view other delegation options.

12. Click **Create a custom task to delegate**, and then click **Next**.

13. What options do you see now? Record your observations.

14. Select **Only the following objects in the folder**.

15. How would you specify delegation of administration so that it only applies to shared folders in the OU? How would you delegate control only over groups? Record your observations.

16. Check **Printer objects** in the scroll box. Also, check **User objects**.

17. Click **Next**.

18. What options do you see in the Permissions dialog box? How would you grant only Read permission?

19. Check **Full Control**. What happens when you check this permission?

20. Click **Next**.

21. What information is provided in the dialog box? Record your observations.

22. Click **Finish**.

23. Leave the Active Directory Users and Computers tool open for the next project.

Project 7-4

This project enables you to create a group policy object to associate with an OU.

To create the group policy object for an OU:

1. Open the Active Directory Users and Computers tool, if it is not already open.

2. Right-click the OU that you created in Hands-on Project 7-2, such as MJPTestOU, and click **Properties**.

3. What tabs are available? Record your observations.

4. Click the **Group Policy** tab.

5. Click the **New** button. Type in a name for the group policy that links it to the OU that you created, such as MJPTestOU Group Policy Object. Press **Enter**.

6. Make sure that the group policy name that you entered is highlighted and then click **Edit**.

7. In the tree and under User Configuration, double-click **Administrative Templates**.

8. What new options are displayed in the tree? Record your observations.

9. Click **Desktop** in the tree. What options are now displayed in the right-hand pane under Policy? Record your observations.

10. Double-click **Hide all icons on Desktop**.

11. Click the **Explain** tab to see what this policy accomplishes, and summarize this information in your lab journal or in a word-processed document.

12. Click the **Policy** tab, click **Enabled**, and click **OK**.

13. What is now displayed for Hide all icons on Desktop when you look under the Setting column?

14. How would you hide the Active Directory folder in My Network Places on the desktops of user accounts using this group policy object?

15. Close the Group Policy tool.

16. Click **Close** in the OU properties dialog box.

17. Leave the Active Directory Users and Computers tool open for the next project.

Project 7-5

In this project, you move, rename, and delete an OU. Before you begin, ask your instructor for the name of an OU under which to move the OU that you created in Hands-on Project 7-2, or you can use a default OU.

To move an OU:

1. Make sure that the Active Directory Users and Computers tool is open, and if not, open it.

2. Right-click the OU that you created in Hands-on Project 7-2, such as MJPTestOU, and click **Move**.

3. To what locations can you move the OU, such as other OUs?

4. Click the OU that your instructor has provided or click **Domain Controllers**, and then click **OK**.

To rename an OU:

1. In the tree, find the OU that you moved and then right-click it.

2. Click **Rename**.

3. Rename the OU by using your initials plus the word Rename, such as MJPRename.

4. Press **Enter**.

To delete an OU:

1. In the tree, find the OU that you renamed and right-click it.

2. Click **Delete**.

3. Click **Yes** to confirm the deletion.

4. Click **Yes**, if necessary, to the warning that the container's contents will be deleted.

5. Close the Active Directory Users and Computers tool.

Project 7-6

In this project, you create an Active Directory site.

To create a site:

1. Click **Start**, point to **Programs**, point to **Administrative Tools**, and click **Active Directory Sites and Services**.

2. Right-click **Sites** in the tree and click **New Site**.

3. Enter the name of the new site. Use your initials appended to Site, such as MJPSite.

7

4. Select a link for the site, such as the default link **DEFAULTIPSITELINK**, or use a link specified by your instructor.

5. Click **OK**.

6. What steps should you perform next to configure the site? Record your observations.

7. Click **OK** in the information box.

8. Where does your new site appear in the tree?

9. Right-click the new site and click **Properties**. What properties are associated with the site? How would you set a group policy for a site?

10. Click **Cancel**.

11. Click the new site in the tree. What is displayed in the right-hand pane?

12. Right-click **Servers** in the right-hand pane and point to **New**.

13. How would you associate a server with this new site?

14. Leave the Active Directory Sites and Services tool open for the next project.

Project 7-7

This project enables you to create a site link. There should be at least three sites already created before you start.

To create a site link:

1. Ensure that the Active Directory Sites and Services tool is open, or if it is not, open it.

2. Click **Inter-Site Transports** in the tree. What is now displayed in the right-hand pane?

3. Right-click the **IP** folder.

4. What options are displayed in the shortcut menu? Record your observations.

5. Click **New Site Link**.

6. Enter a name for the new site link that is a combination of your initials and SiteLink, such as MJPSiteLink.

7. In the *Sites not in this site link* box, click **Default-First-Site-Name** or another site specified by your instructor, and then click **Add**.

8. Click the site that you created, such as MJPSite, and click **Add**.

9. Click **OK**.

10. How can you check to make sure that the site link is created?

11. Leave the Active Directory Sites and Services tool open for the next project.

Project 7-8

In this project, you learn how to create a subnet in Active Directory. Obtain a subnet and subnet mask from your instructor before starting or use the examples in this project.

To create a subnet:

1. Make sure that the Active Directory Sites and Services tool is open, or if it is not, open it.

2. Double-click **Sites** in the tree. What information appears in the right-hand pane? Record your observations.

3. Right-click **Subnets** in the right-hand pane. What options are displayed in the menu? Record your observations.

4. Click **New Subnet**.

5. Enter the subnet address, such as 129.70.10.0 (press the period key to advance to the next field, if necessary).

6. Enter a subnet mask, such as 255.255.255.0.

7. In the Site Name box, click the site that you created in Hands-on Project 7-6, such as MJPSite. What are you accomplishing by clicking the site? Record your observations in your lab journal or in a word-processed document.

8. Click **OK**. (If you see a message that the name is already in use, click OK again and use a different subnet address.)

9. How can you verify that the subnet was created?

10. Close the Active Directory Sites and Services tool.

Project 7-9

This project enables you to view DNS zones, the DNS SOA resource record to determine the primary server, and other information about a DNS server. You will need access to a computer running Windows 2000 DNS. Also, address and pointer resource records should already be created.

To view the DNS zones and other DNS server information:

1. Click **Start**, point to **Programs**, point to **Administrative Tools**, and click **DNS**.

2. What computer (or computers) is (are) associated with DNS? What zones already exist, and what is their purpose? Record your observations.

3. Double-click the first computer in the tree.

4. Double-click **Forward Lookup Zones** in the tree.

5. Double-click a domain in the tree under Forward Lookup Zones, such as theFirm.com.

6. What information is displayed in the right-hand pane? Record your answers.

7. Right-click a domain in the tree under Forward Lookup Zones, and click **Properties**.

8. Make sure that the General tab is displayed. How can you set DNS to allow dynamic updates, such as those from a Windows 2000 Professional workstation?

9. Click the **Start of Authority (SOA)** tab. What computer is the primary server?

10. Click the **Name Servers** tab. What name servers are listed?

11. Click the **WINS** tab. How would you enable WINS forward lookup?

12. Click the **Zone Transfers** tab. What can you do using this tab?

13. Click the **Security** tab. Make sure that Administrators is selected in the Name box. What permissions are given to Administrators?

14. Is there a security group for DNS administrators? If so, what is it, and what permissions are granted?

15. Click **Cancel**.

16. Click **Reverse Lookup Zones** in the tree. What records are displayed?

17. Right-click the computer in the tree. How would you create a new zone?

18. Click **Properties**. How would you set up a forwarder? (If you see a message that forwarders are not available, determine why from the message, and record your observations.)

19. Click **Cancel**.

20. Close the DNS tool.

CASE PROJECT

Aspen Consulting Project: Designing OUs, Sites, and DNS Services

Harrisons Cards is a greeting card company that manufactures greeting cards, calendars, specialty mugs, and candles. The headquarters for Harrisons is located in London, England. There are four manufacturing plants; each has its own LAN and a WAN link to the headquarters office in London:

❏ Taos, New Mexico, which manufactures greeting cards and stationary, and is connected to London by a satellite at 2 Mbps

❏ Mexico City, Mexico, which manufactures specialty mugs and porcelain figurines, and is connected to London by 128 Kbps X.25 link

❏ Quebec, Canada, which manufactures candles and other wax products, and is connected to London by a 256 Kbps frame relay link

❏ New Orleans, Louisiana, which manufactures greeting cards and calendars, and is connected to London by a 256 Kbps frame relay link

Your analysis of the Harrisons Cards division in New Orleans shows that it has the following departments, each of which has a wide range of autonomy in a decentralized decision model and uses project-based organizational structures:

❐ Executive officers consisting of a vice president and her team of department managers

❐ Business department, which includes accounting, payroll, accounts receivable, and accounts payable

❐ Marketing department, which consists of all marketing personnel, copywriters, and advertising artists

❐ Art department, which consists of artists, photographers, and writers

❐ Manufacturing department, which consists of the manufacturing and inventory personnel

❐ Shipping department, which inspects products and sends them to their destinations

❐ IT department, which maintains the LAN, WAN link, Windows 2000 servers, and desktop computers

7

1. What questions would you ask when helping the company to formulate an OU plan for the New Orleans division? Based on what you know now, create a preliminary OU plan, including a change control plan.

2. Develop a basic network diagram of the LANs and WANs in the Harrisons Cards network. With your network diagram in front of you, create a site plan, including a site change control plan.

3. After creating your site plan, provide a basic explanation about how to create sites, site links, and subnets in Active Directory.

4. Create a DNS server implementation plan for Harrisons Cards. Include an explanation of how you would implement Active Directory integrated DNS zones, primary servers, and secondary servers. Also, explain how the DNS server implementation plan addresses load balancing and fault tolerance. Include a change control plan as part of your DNS server implementation plan.

5. Your analysis of software and hardware systems shows that the main location in London has four NetWare 4.1 servers running NDS, two Windows NT 4.0 servers (both configured as DNS servers), and nine Windows 2000 servers configured using Active Directory. What planning issues should you examine in relation to the Active Directory and DNS implementation?

OPTIONAL CASE PROJECTS FOR TEAMS

Team Case One

Mark Arnez is curious about the containers used by NDS in NetWare version 5 or higher. He asks you to form a team to research NDS and compare the containers to those used by Active Directory.

Team Case Two

Mark is aware that you are going to school, and he reports that your school has requested help in designing Active Directory. He asks you to form a team and create a site design and DNS implementation design proposal for your school.

CHAPTER 8

SECURITY GROUP AND GROUP POLICY DESIGN

After reading this chapter and completing the exercises, you will be able to:

♦ Plan and use Windows 2000 groups, including domain local, global, and universal groups

♦ Plan group policy and create new group policies

♦ Configure group policy objects

♦ Plan and configure group policy management of security and client workstation desktops

---

Two of the most powerful Active Directory management concepts are groups and group policies. Groups can be used to significantly reduce the time it takes to manage a large number of user accounts and Active Directory resources. When used with OUs and group management, group policies enable you to manage security, desktop settings, remote software installation, and many other Active Directory features on a large scale or on a very small scale. The introduction of group policies in Windows 2000 Server enables you to fine-tune how you manage resources while simplifying your domain structure, so that you can nimbly modify Active Directory to match unique corporate needs and corporate reorganizations.

In this chapter, you will learn about the Windows 2000 security groups, including groups that carry over from Windows NT Server and new groups that are tailored for Active Directory. You also will learn about the hundreds of ways that group policy objects can be configured to precisely customize the Windows 2000 Server environment, including network security and client computer desktops.

WINDOWS 2000 GROUPS

Groups provide a way for server and network administrators to save time in managing user accounts and resources. For example, if there are 800 user accounts in a domain, it is much simpler to put accounts into groups of users who access the same resources and have the same security needs than it is to manage each account separately. In this way, the management tasks simply involve changing properties associated with each group. This is much easier than managing 800 individual accounts and trying to remember the characteristics of each account, such as which shared folders each account can access.

The use of groups was introduced in Windows NT Server, in which there are two types of groups: local groups that are used to manage resources on a single server or on servers in one domain, and global groups that are used to manage resources across multiple domains. With the introduction of Active Directory, Windows 2000 Server expands on the use of groups through the concept of **scope of influence** (or scope), which is the reach of a group for gaining access to resources in Active Directory. When Active Directory is not implemented in Windows 2000 Server, the scope of influence is limited to the *standalone* server, and only local groups are created. In contrast, the implementation of Active Directory increases the scope from a local server to either a domain or an entire forest. The types of groups and their associated scopes are as follows:

- *Local group*: Used on standalone servers that are not part of a domain. The scope of this type of group does not go beyond the local server on which it is defined.

- *Domain local group*: Used when there is a single domain, or to manage resources in a particular domain so that global and universal groups can access those resources.

- *Global group*: Used to house accounts from the same domain so that those accounts can access resources in the same and in other domains.

- *Universal group*: Used to provide access to resources in any domain within a forest.

 A Windows 2000 server that is in a **standalone server** role is a networked server that is not a member of a domain, but that is a member of an existing workgroup or that establishes its own workgroup, as in peer-to-peer networking.

All of these groups can be used for security groups or for distribution groups. Security groups are used to enable access to resources on a standalone server or in Active Directory. Distribution groups are used for e-mail or telephone lists to provide quick mass distribution of information. In this chapter, the focus is on security groups.

Using Local Groups

A **local security group** is used to manage resources on a standalone server that is not part of a domain. For example, you might use a local group in a small office situation in which there are only a few users, such as 5, 15, or 30. Consider an office of travel agents in which there are 28 user accounts that are part of a workgroup established by the standalone server. Two of the accounts are used by the owners who oversee the business. Two other accounts are used by the office manager and the assistant office manager, who handle the details of employee hiring, payroll, employee schedules, and general accounting. Twenty-four accounts are for the individual travel agents. In this situation, the company may decide not to install Active Directory, and instead, divide these accounts into three local groups. One group would be called Owners and contain the two owners' user accounts. Another group would be called Managers and would hold the accounts of the office manager and his assistant. The third group, Agents, would consist of the travel agents' user accounts. Each group would be given different security access (added to ACLs) based on the resources at the server, which would include access to folders and to printers.

Using Domain Local Groups

A **domain local security group** is used when Active Directory is deployed. This type of group is typically used to manage resources in a domain and to give global groups from the same and other domains access to those resources. As shown in Table 8-1, a domain local group can contain members such as global groups, and it can be a member of access control lists and other domain local groups.

Table 8-1 Membership Characteristics of Domain Local Groups

Active Directory Objects That Can Be Members of a Domain Local Group	Active Directory Objects That a Domain Local Group Can Join as a Member
User and computer accounts in any domain in the forest	Access control lists for objects in the same domain, such as permissions to access a folder, shared folder, or printer
Domain local groups in the same domain	Domain local groups in the same domain
Global groups in any domain in a tree or forest (as long as there are transitive or two-way trust relationships maintained)	
Universal groups in any domain in a tree or forest (as long as there are transitive or two-way trust relationships maintained)	

8

The scope of a domain local group is the domain in which the group exists, but you can convert a domain local group to a universal group as long as the domain local group does not contain any other domain local groups. Also, to convert any group, the domain must be in native mode (all Windows 2000 servers) and not mixed mode (a combination of Windows 2000 and Windows NT servers).

Although domain local groups can contain accounts, *use domain local groups primarily (or exclusively) to provide access to resources.*

Even though a domain local group can contain any combination of accounts plus domain local, global, and universal groups, the typical purpose of a domain local group is to provide access to resources, which means that you grant access to servers, folders, shared folders, and printers to a domain local group. Access is granted to a shared folder, for example, by placing the domain local group on that shared folder's ACL. Under most circumstances you should plan to put domain local groups on access control lists only, and the members of domain local groups should be mainly global groups. For example, consider B & E Electronics, which makes timers, relay switches, and motors for appliances manufactured by York Industries. B & E Electronics has a shared folder, called Parts Inventory, that holds a database of the parts inventory such as wire, resistors, capacitors, LEDs, and other parts. The Parts Inventory shared folder is made available to members of the Inventory department and to the Manufacturing unit by creating two domain local groups, Inventory and Manufacturing. Each domain local group is placed on the Parts Inventory ACL to give it access to the database in the folder. Also, each domain local group consists of two global groups that contain user accounts. The Inventory domain local group holds the member global groups, GlobalInventory and GlobalWarehouse. The Manufacturing domain local group consists of the GlobalManufact global group and the GlobalMachinists global group, with both global groups containing user accounts (see Figure 8-1).

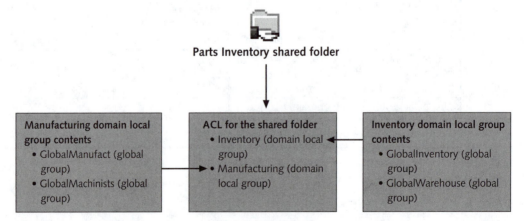

Figure 8-1   Accessing a shared folder via a domain local group

Generally, a domain local group does not contain accounts, because account management is more efficient when you handle it through global groups. More examples of using domain local groups with global groups are presented in the next section. Try Hands-on Project 8-1 to practice creating a domain local group.

Using Global Groups

A **global security group** contains accounts and other global groups from a single domain. A global group can also be set up as a member of a domain local group in the same or another domain (as long as the domain in which the global group is set up is trusted by the domain of the domain local group of which it becomes a member). This capability gives a global group a broader scope than a domain local group, because its members can access resources in other domains. The primary implementation of a global group is to:

1. Contain user and computer accounts as members

2. Become a member of a domain local or universal group that has access to resources, thus giving its members access to those resources

Table 8-2 shows which Active Directory objects can be members of global groups and which objects global groups can join.

Table 8-2   Membership Characteristics of Global Groups

Active Directory Objects That Can Be Members of a Global Group	Active Directory Objects That a Global Group Can Join as a Member
User and computer accounts from the domain in which the global group was created	Access control lists for objects in any domain in a forest (as long as a transitive trust relationship is maintained between domains)
Other global groups that have been created in the same domain	Domain local groups in any domain in a forest
Levels of global groups, so that global groups can be nested to reflect the structure of organizational units (OUs) in a domain	Global groups in the same domain
	Universal groups in a forest

Although it is possible to add a global group to an access control list, it is not recommended, because global groups normally gain access to resources through their membership in a domain local or universal group.

In native mode domains, nesting global groups to reflect the structure of OUs means that global groups can be layered. For example, in the IT operations for the Applications Development unit in Nantes Appliances, there might be an OU for applications development, an OU under applications development for database development, and an OU under database development for documentation—resulting in three levels of OUs. Also, there might be a global group composed of the accounts for software developers in the applications development OU, a global group of accounts for database administrators in the database development OU, and a global group of technical writers in the documentation OU. The global group membership (for AppDevelopers, DatabaseAdmins, and TechWrite) can be set up to reflect the structure of OUs (AppDev, DB, and Document) as shown Figure 8-2. Try Hands-on Project 8-2 to create and nest global groups.

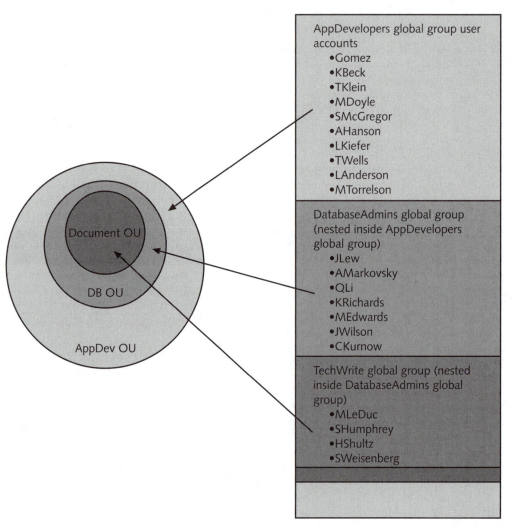

Figure 8-2 Nested global groups

When you nest groups, think through what resources that a group can access because it is nested in another group. In Figure 8-2, the members of TechWrite have access to all of the resources (provided through domain local and universal group memberships) that are accessible to both the DatabaseAdmins and AppDevelopers global groups. Also, the DatabaseAdmins global group has access to the same resources that the AppDevelopers global group can access. However, the access does not work in the reverse direction; for example, AppDevelopers does not automatically have access to the same resources as TechWrite.

Nested global groups can not be used in mixed mode domains, because Windows NT Server does not support them.

In a native mode domain, a global group can be converted to a universal group, as long as it is not nested in another global group or in a universal group. In the example shown in Figure 8-2, the TechWrite and DatabaseAdmins global groups cannot be converted to universal groups because they already are members of the DatabaseAdmins and AppDevelopers groups, respectively.

8

Although global groups can be on the ACLs of resources, such as shared folders, *use global groups primarily to hold user accounts in a domain*.

A typical use for a global group is to:

1. Build the global group so that it contains accounts from the same domain that need access to resources in the same or in another domain.

2. Make the global group in one domain a member of a domain local group in the same or another domain.

This model enables you to manage user accounts and their access to resources through one or more global groups, while reducing the complexity of managing accounts. For example, consider Interstate Security Bank in which there is a special executive group, consisting of the company president and the vice presidents from each of the regional offices, who need access to the isb.com, idaho.isb.com, montana.isb.com, oregon.isb.com, washington.isb.com, and wyoming.isb.com domains. One way to enable the executive group to have access is to create a domain local group called LocalExec in each domain that provides the appropriate access to folders, files, and other resources. Next, make sure that the president and all of the vice presidents have accounts in the same domain, such as the isb.com domain, and create a GlobalExec global group in that domain from which to manage the access. Add the GlobalExec global group as a member of the LocalExec domain local groups in each domain, as shown in Figure 8-3. These steps enable the GlobalExec group to manage security for all of the accounts. If the president or a vice president leaves to take another job, you simply delete (or disable) that person's account from the global group and later add an account (or rename and enable the old account) for her or his replacement. You also can manage access to resources in each domain at one time through each domain local group, resulting in much less management work. If a new printer is added to a domain, for example, you can give the domain local group full privileges to the printer, which automatically gives access to any global group that is a member of the domain local group.

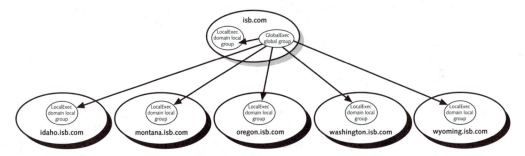

Figure 8-3   Using a global group to manage account access to multiple domains

When Active Directory structure becomes complex enough in a large organization so that many domains and trees are in use, global groups are used as members of universal groups to manage accounts, as described in the next section.

Using Universal Groups

In an Active Directory context in which there are multiple hierarchies of domains and trees, **universal security groups** provide a means to span multiple domains and trees. These groups can have members and can join the Active Directory objects, as shown in Table 8-3.

Table 8-3   Membership Characteristics of Universal Groups

Active Directory Objects That Can Be Members of a Universal Group	Active Directory Objects That a Universal Group Can Join as a Member
User and computer accounts from any domain in a forest	Access control lists for objects in any domain in a forest
Global groups from any domain in a forest	Any domain local group in a forest
Universal groups from any domain in a forest	Any universal group in a forest

You can create a universal group only if your domain structure has been converted from mixed mode (Windows 2000 and Windows NT servers), which is the default mode, to native mode (only Windows 2000 servers). If you attempt to create a new universal group, but find that the radio button in the New Object – (Group) dialog box is deactivated, this means that the domain is set up in mixed mode, and you must convert the domain to native mode before you can create the group. Once you convert a domain from mixed to native mode, it cannot be converted back. Try Hands-on Project 8-3 to find out how to convert a domain from mixed to native mode.

 A universal group cannot be converted to a smaller scope, such as to a global or domain local group.

 Although universal groups can hold accounts, *deploy universal groups primarily to provide access to resources in the forest.*

8

Universal groups are offered to provide an easy means to access any resource in a tree or among trees in a forest. If you carefully plan the use of universal groups, then you can manage security for multiple accounts with a minimum of effort. That planning is done in relation to understanding the scope of access that is needed for a group of accounts. Here are some guidelines to help simplify how you plan to use groups:

- Use global groups to hold accounts as members—and keep the nesting of global groups to a minimum (or do not use nesting) to avoid confusion. Give accounts access to resources by making the global groups to which they belong members of domain local groups or universal groups or both.

- Use domain local groups to provide access to resources in a specific domain. Avoid placing accounts in domain local groups. Make domain local groups members of ACLs for specific resources in the domain, such as shared folders and printers.

- Use universal groups to provide extensive access to resources when there are multiple domains and trees. *Make universal groups members of ACLs for objects, such as shared folders, in any domain within a forest.* Manage user account access by placing accounts in global groups and joining global groups to domain local or universal groups, depending on which is most appropriate to the scope required for access.

In the example of setting up access for the president and vice presidents of Interstate Security Bank, an alternative is to create one universal group, UniExec, that has access to all resources in the six domains. Also, create one global group, GlobalExec, that contains the president and vice presidents, and make that global group a member of UniExec, as shown in Figure 8-4. In this model there are only two groups to manage, compared to the model shown in Figure 8-3, in which there are seven groups to manage.

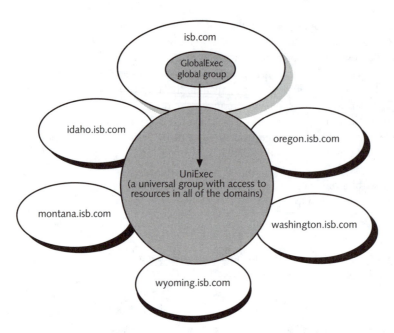

Figure 8-4   Implementing a universal group for enterprise-wide access

Creating and Managing Groups

Groups are created by using the Active Directory Users and Computers tool when Active Directory is installed, as shown in Figure 8-5. Each group has an associated set of properties that can be modified after the group is created—for example, to add user accounts to the group or to make a group a member of another group. You can access the properties by double-clicking the group after you create it, such as in the Active Directory Users and Computers tool, where you will find the group under the container in which you created it.

When you double-click a group (or right-click a group and click Properties), you will find four tabs in the Properties dialog box:

- *General*: Used to enter a description of the group, change the scope and type of group, and provide an e-mail address for a distribution group

- *Members*: Used to add members to a group, such as adding a global group to a universal group (click the Add button to add members; see Figure 8-6)

- *Member Of*: Used to make the group a member of another group (click the Add button to add the group to another group)

- *Managed By*: Used to establish an account or group that will manage the group, if the manager is other than the server administrator; also the location, telephone number, and fax number of the manager can be provided

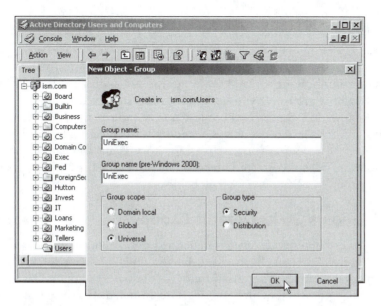

Figure 8-5   Creating a universal group

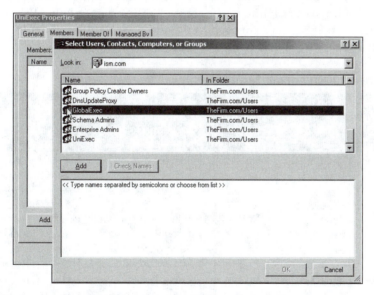

Figure 8-6   Adding members to a group

The General tab enables you to change group scope, but only in the permitted direction. For example, you can change a global group into a universal group, but not into a domain local group. In this example, the domain local group will be deactivated so that you cannot select it. Try Hands-on Project 8-4 to practice changing group scope.

Upgrading Windows NT Server Groups

When you upgrade Windows NT Server to Windows 2000 Server, the existing Windows NT local groups on a primary domain controller are automatically converted to Windows 2000 domain local groups, and the Windows NT global groups are converted to Windows 2000 global groups. If you continue to run in mixed mode because there are remaining Windows NT Server backup domain controllers, then the Windows NT servers recognize the converted groups as Windows NT local and global groups. A Windows NT server that does not use Active Directory client software cannot recognize a universal group. With the Active Directory client installed, a Windows NT server treats a universal group as a Windows NT global group.

Planning for Windows 2000 Default Groups

Windows 2000 Server comes with several predefined domain local, global, and universal groups when Active Directory is installed. For example, Domain Admins is one of the default groups and includes the Administrator account as a member. The predefined groups can vary, depending on which services are installed. For instance, there is a domain local DHCP Administrators group set up when you set up a DHCP server, and you will likely want to add the Domain Admins global group as a member. Table 8-4 shows many examples of predefined Windows 2000 Server groups. When Active Directory is installed, these groups are found in one of two default folders in a domain tree, Builtin and Users.

Table 8-4   Windows 2000 Default Security Groups

Security Group	Scope	Changes to Group Scope Permitted	Active Directory Container Location/Default Members	Description
Account Operators	Built-in local	No	Builtin	Used for administration of user accounts and groups
Administrators	Built-in local	No	Builtin/Administrator account; Domain Admins and Enterprise Admins groups	Provides complete access to all local computer and/or domain resources
Backup Operators	Built-in local	No	Builtin	Enables members to back up any folders and files on the computer
Cert Publishers	Global	No	Users	Used to manage enterprise certification services for security

Table 8-4   Windows 2000 Default Security Groups (continued)

Security Group	Scope	Changes to Group Scope Permitted	Active Directory Container Location/Default Members	Description
DHCP Administrators	Domain local	Yes	Users	Used to manage the DHCP server services (when DHCP server services are installed)
DHCP Users	Domain local	Yes	Users	Enables users to access DHCP services when DHCP is enabled at the client (when DHCP server services are installed)
DnsAdmins	Domain local	Yes	Users	Used to manage the DNS server services (when DNS server services are installed)
DnsUpdateProxy	Global	Yes	Users	Enables each user access as an update proxy, so that a DHCP client can automatically update the DNS server information with its IP address
Domain Admins	Global	No	Users/Administrator account	Used to manage resources in a domain
Domain Computers	Global	No	Users	Used to manage all workstations and servers that join the domain
Domain Controllers	Global	No	Users/all DC computers	Used to manage all domain controllers in a domain
Domain Guests	Global	No	Users/Guest account	Used to manage all domain guest-type accounts, such as those for temporary employees

8

Table 8-4   Windows 2000 Default Security Groups (continued)

Security Group	Scope	Changes to Group Scope Permitted	Active Directory Container Location/Default Members	Description
Domain Users	Global	No	Users/all user accounts	Used to manage all domain user accounts
Enterprise Admins	Global (mixed mode) Universal (native mode)	No	Users/Administrator account	Used to manage all resources in an enterprise
Everyone	Built-in local	No	Does not appear in a container and cannot be deleted	Used to manage default access to local or domain resources, and all user accounts are automatically members
Group Policy Creator Owners	Global	No	Users/Administrator account	Enables members to manage group policy objects
Guests	Built-in local	No	Builtin/Guest and IIS accounts, Domain Guests group	Used to manage guest accounts and to prevent access to install software or change system settings
NetShow Administrators	Domain local	Yes	Users/ NetShowServices	Created when Windows media servers are installed to manage the media services
Pre-Windows 2000 Compatible Access	Built-in local	No	Builtin/ pre-Windows 2000 Everyone group	Used for backward compatibility to the Everyone group on Windows NT servers and limits access to read
Print Operators	Built-in local	No	Builtin	Members can manage printers on the local computer

Table 8-4 Windows 2000 Default Security Groups (continued)

Security Group	Scope	Changes to Group Scope Permitted	Active Directory Container Location/Default Members	Description
RAS and IAS Servers	Domain local	No	Users	Enables member servers to have access to remote access properties that are associated with user accounts, such as security properties
Replicator	Built-in local	No	Builtin	Used with the Windows File Replication service to replicate designated folders and files
Schema Admins	Global (mixed mode) Universal (native mode)	No	Users/Administrator account	Members have access to modify the schema in Active Directory
Server Operators	Built-in local	No	Builtin	Used for common day-to-day server management tasks, including managing the contents, such as accounts, of OUs and groups in a domain
Users	Built-in local	No	Builtin/Domain Users group	Used to manage general user access, including the ability to be authenticated as a user and to communicate interactively
WINS Users	Domain local	Yes	Users	Used to grant access to view the WINS server contents

8

Developing a Group Plan

Developing an initial group plan, as well as a way to frequently revise the plan, can save you lots of time and confusion as you use more and more groups. If you create groups "on the fly" and fail to have a plan, months and years later you will have a confused mass of groups and security problems. Consider, for example, a medium-sized business that has 40 groups, some that are domain local and universal groups containing both accounts and global groups. Others are global groups created for reasons that no one currently remembers. Several groups have been created to enable someone to manage a specific server function, such as Web files and the company's accounting files. Also, consider that the company has hired two new server administrators, who are charged with tightening security, because the old server administrators have taken positions in a competing company. The new administrators come into the job with a confusing security maze that will take lots of time to sort out and then fix. Each time an administrator changes the composition of a group or deletes a group, there is always the worry that someone will unexpectedly lose vital access, including the server administrator. If the original server administrators had created a group plan from the start, the job of the new server administrators would have been simpler and safer.

When you develop a group plan, include and document the following:

- Who has access to create, modify, and delete groups

- Guidelines for how domain local, global, and universal groups are to be used

- What groups will be deployed, including why they are needed. Only create as many groups as are truly needed.

- Change control mechanisms, to make sure that changes will not interfere with the normal work performed by users

- The purpose of each group—for example, in a database or spreadsheet. Also, provide a description of each group in that group's properties.

- The security granted to each group, including the objects to which it has access

- All uses of nesting and how security is affected

- Guidelines for creating new groups and deleting old groups

- Plans for deleting old groups within a specific time period from when they are no longer needed, such as within a month or sooner

- Periodical review of groups, group memberships, and ACLs to make sure that you have the appropriate security set up for your organization, and that there are no security holes or surprises

AN EXAMPLE OF GROUP IMPLEMENTATION

Assume that you have already designed the OU structure for Jefferson Philately, and it involves starting with the default folders and OUs: Builtin, Computers, Domain Controllers, ForeignSecurityPrincipals, and Users. Now you want to create a plan in which all groups are housed in the Users folder for the domain. Also, after meeting with management, the decision is to have the group structure reflect the functional structure of the organization. The analysis of the functional structure (see Chapter 2) reveals the following functional areas (see Figure 8-7):

- Board of directors
- Management
- Accounting and payroll
- Cashiers
- Human resources
- Marketing and subscriptions

- Manufacturing
- Journeyman printer operators
- Customer service
- Information technology
- Inventory, warehouse, and distribution
- Physical plant

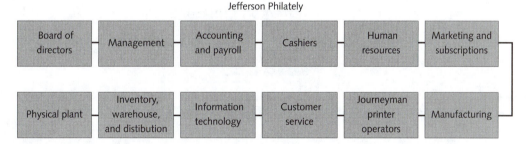

Figure 8-7   Organizational structure by function

Following your analysis of the functions, the next step is to determine what resources must be accessed in order to accomplish these functions. For example, the board of directors needs to access two shared folders, one that contains budget, sales, and financial reports created for the board, and one that contains company policy and general human resources information. To satisfy this requirement, you might create a domain local group called Board and place this group on the ACLs of both shared folders. Next, create a GlobalBoard global group that contains all members of the board and the company president. Access to the resources is created on the basis of company function, which in this case is participation on the board of directors. The access is set up by:

1. Creating the domain local group Board to access the resources

2. Creating the global group GlobalBoard

3. Making each of the board members' accounts a member of the GlobalBoard group

4. Making GlobalBoard a member of Board

Because 12 different functions are identified in the organizational analysis, create one domain local group for each function. Next, use the analysis of the Jefferson Philately department structure for the initial design of the global groups (see Figure 8-8):

- Board
- Human resources
- Information technology
- Accounting and payroll
- Customer service

- Marketing
- Print operations
- Warehouse operations
- Physical plant
- Manufacturing

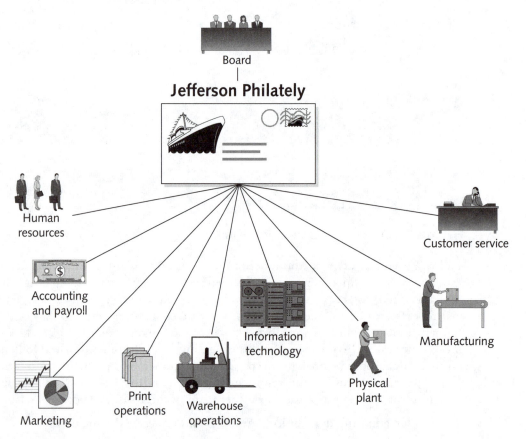

Figure 8-8   Jefferson Philately department structure

This example uses two types of organizational analysis of Jefferson Philately, analysis by function and analysis by department. The analyses are similar, but the analysis by function enables you to determine the resources that users need to access. The analysis by department enables you to identify who belongs to each department. Thus, you base the domain local group structure on your analysis of the organization by *function* (resources), and you base the global group structure on your analysis of organization by *department* (individual users).

Create one global group for each department, such as GlobalBoard, GlobalHR, and so on. Because each department has a manager, also create a Managers global group. Populate each global group with the appropriate accounts. Make the global groups members of the appropriate domain local groups, such as (see Figure 8-9):

- GlobalBoard (Board of directors) is a member of the Board domain local group.

- GlobalAccting (Accounting and payroll department) is a member of the Accting domain local group.

- GlobalManage (for the managers), is a member of the Manage, Accting, Cashiers, and HR domain local groups.

- GlobalHR (Human resources department) is a member of the HR domain local group.

- GlobalMarket (Marketing department) is a member of the Market and CS (Customer Service) domain local groups.

- GlobalManufact (Manufacturing department) is a member of the Manufact domain local group.

- GlobalPrintersOps (Print operations) is a member of the PrinterOps domain local group.

- GlobalCS (Customer service department) is a member of the Cashiers and CS domain local groups.

- GlobalIT (Information technology) is a member of the IT domain local group.

- GlobalWarehse (Warehouse operations department) is a member of the Warehse domain local group.

- GlobalPlant (Physical plant) is a member of the Plant domain local group.

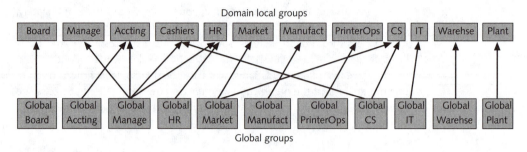

Figure 8-9   Sample group structure for Jefferson Philately

Finally, for future reference, document how each group is set up.

> Another way to use your analysis of an organization and to relate that analysis to groups is through examining the business processes. Most organizations, including Jefferson Philately, have business processes such as hiring and employee records, accounting, payroll, marketing, product research and design, production, inventory, and distribution. Instead of using the analysis by function, you may find that it is more effective to create domain local groups on the basis of specific business processes (which often are similar, but not identical to, analysis by function).

Another approach is to combine your analysis by function with your analysis of business processes. For example, the group structure for Jefferson Philately might be modified to reflect mail-order subscription programs, which are a business process. Some examples of programs to which customers can subscribe are Stamps of American Presidents and Duck Stamps of the 50 States. Domain local and global groups might be created for each subscription program, with the global group membership reflecting employee teams containing members from multiple departments. As soon as a subscription program ends, such as Stamps of American Presidents in the 1900s, Jefferson Philately would delete the corresponding domain local and global groups for that program.

USING GROUP POLICIES AND GROUP POLICY OBJECTS

Group policy is a Windows 2000 Server concept that enables you to standardize the working environment of clients and servers by setting policies in Active Directory. Through group policy, you can manage desktop configurations, logon security, resource auditing, software availability, remote access, remote installation of Windows 2000 Professional, scripts, and folder redirection. There are literally hundreds of policies that can be configured. Also, by using customized MMC Group Policy snap-in extensions, it is possible for organizations to develop their own specialized group policies.

Resource auditing is used to track who accesses a resource, such as a folder. Remote access entails using offsite resources, such as dial-up telephone lines to access a network. Scripts are files of commands that are run when the script is run, such as commands that are run when a user logs on to an account. Folder redirection enables access to folders, including My Documents, to be directed to a particular network location or shared folder.

Group policy has evolved from the Windows NT 4.0 concept of system policy. **System policy** is a set of basic user account and computer parameters that can be configured using the **system policy editor**, Poledit.exe. Parameters that are established in the system policy editor can apply domain-wide or just to specific groups of users. There are important differences between using system policy and group policy. For example, the largest scope for system policy is the domain, whereas group policy can extend to cover multiple domains in one site. There are fewer objects to configure in a system policy than in a group policy. Also, the system policy parameters focus mainly on the clients' desktop environment as controlled by Registry settings. Group policy is set for more environments, ranging from client desktops to account policies to remote installation of Windows 2000 on clients. System policy is less secure because it is possible for users to change system policy parameters that apply to them by accessing the Registry editors in their client operating systems (such as in Windows 98). Group policies are secured so that they cannot be changed by individual users. Another problem with system policies is that, because they are applied to the clients' Registries, the system policies can live on after they are no longer needed. This is not a problem with group policy because a group policy is dynamically updated and configured to represent the most current needs.

The general characteristics of group policy are:

- *Group policy can be set for a site, domain, or OU*: Group policy can be linked to any site, domain, or OU. An OU is the smallest container with which a group policy is linked. Group policy is not linked to security groups directly, but it can be filtered through these groups (see Chapter 9). Also, when the first domain is created, a default domain policy is automatically associated with that domain. The default domain policy is, by default, inherited by child domains, but can be changed so that a child domain has different group policy settings than its parent domain.

- *Group policy cannot be set for non-OU folder containers*: Default containers that are folders instead of OUs, such as the Builtin, Computers, ForeignSecurityPrincipals, and Users folders, are not truly OUs, and therefore you cannot link group policy with these containers. You can verify this by opening the Active Directory Users and Computers tool, right-clicking Users, and clicking Properties. There is no Group Policy tab in the Users Properties dialog box. Compare this to right-clicking the Domain Controllers OU and clicking Properties. The Domain Controllers OU does have a Group Policy tab.

8

- *Group policy settings are stored in group policy objects*: A **group policy object (GPO)** is an Active Directory object that contains group policy settings (a set of group policies) for a site, domain, OU, or local computer. Each GPO has a unique name and globally unique identifier (GUID, see Chapter 1). When Active Directory is installed, there is one local GPO for every Windows 2000 server, and a server is also governed by Active Directory GPOs for sites, domains, and OUs.

- *There are local and nonlocal GPOs*: The local GPO applies to the local computer. Nonlocal GPOs apply to sites, domains, and OUs. When there are multiple GPOs, their effect is incremental (local GPO first, default domain GPO next, site GPO next, and the GPOs for OUs next).

- *When there is a mixed mode domain that contains system policies and a group policy, the group policy prevails*: If a group policy specifies one desktop setting and a system policy specifies another, then the group policy setting prevails.

- *Group policy can be set up to affect user accounts and computers*: Group policy is set up to affect user accounts, computers, or both. If a policy is set up for one but is not the same as a policy set up for the other, then the policy set up for computers prevails over the policy for user accounts.

- *When group policy is updated, old policies are removed or updated for all clients*: Each time you update group policy, the new information is updated for clients, and the old information that no longer applies is removed.

- *Each group policy object has a discretionary access control list*: A **discretionary access control list (DACL)** is an access control list of users, groups, and computers that are granted some form of permission to an object, such as a group policy. Each DACL entry is called an access control entry (ACE). Users that are affected by a group policy are granted Apply Group Policy and Read permissions. Those who can create or change a group policy have Write or Full Control ACE entries on the DACL.

 You can optimize group policy execution performance by removing groups from the DACL that do not need to access a group policy object—or by removing Apply Group Policy and Read permissions from groups to which the group policy object does not apply (administrators will still need Read permission, but should not have Apply Group Policy permission). Also, you can improve performance by disabling the Computer Configuration or User Configuration settings (discussed later in this chapter), when one of these does not apply to a particular group of users. Try Hands-on Project 8-7 to practice optimizing the execution of a group policy.

- *Group policy objects can be delegated*: You can delegate authority over a group policy object, such as a group policy object associated with an OU, by customizing MMC Group Policy snap-in consoles and configuring the group policy permissions.

■ *Specific group policy parameters (extensions) can be set up to accommodate slow networks links, such as site links*: You can customize a group policy for clients who communicate to the main network over slow links. For example, you can turn off scripts or software installation over slow links.

Planning Group Policy Objects

Plan the group policy in conjunction with your designs for sites, domains, and OUs. A typical starting point is to plan the **default domain policy**, which is the group policy object that is automatically set up for a domain and can be modified by the domain administrator. This policy initially focuses on basic security policy issues that include account policies, account lockout policies, use of Kerberos, auditing policies, and other security measures. For example, account policies include:

■ *Enforce password history*: Enables you to require users to choose new passwords when they make a password change, because the system can remember the previously used passwords

■ *Maximum password age*: Permits you to set the maximum time allowed until a password expires

■ *Minimum password age*: Permits you to specify that a password must be used a minimum amount of time before it can be changed

■ *Minimum password length*: Enables you to require that passwords are a minimum length

■ *Passwords must meet complexity requirements*: Enables you to create a filter of customized password requirements that each account password must follow

■ *Store password using reversible encryption for all users in the domain*: Enables passwords to be stored in reversible encrypted format

After you plan the default domain policy, develop separate plans for site or OU group policies. Consider for example, Interstate Security Bank, which decides to create a Tellers OU for each regional office. They want to create this OU so that they can standardize the desktop and software available on each of the teller's computers, which function with an attached cash drawer. After the OU is created for each regional office, the next step is to create a group policy object to link to it.

A key element in planning a group policy object is to make sure that it reflects the business processes of an organization. Use your analysis of the organization to understand the business processes. For example, your analysis may show that most users need only basic logon security consisting of a minimum length password, but that you need to create a special OU and group policy object that enforces more complex account logon security for a top-secret research unit.

Another element in planning group policy is to include key users in your planning. Some organizations use a committee consisting of the server or Active Directory administrator and several managers and users. The server administrator presents the committee with

8

information about what group policies can be set, and the committee decides how to implement the group policies.

The following is a checklist for planning group policies:

- Determine who will create and manage site and default domain group policies.

- Determine who will participate in the planning for site, domain, and OU group policies—for example, by establishing a group policy planning committee.

- Determine who will create and manage OU group policies, including the specifics of how authority will be delegated.

- Create and track group policies by using the Security Templates tool (accessing this tool is discussed later in this chapter). Develop a group policy object naming scheme to help identify specific group policy objects.

- Configure local and default domain policies first. Set up account policies, account lockout policies, Kerberos security, and auditing from the beginning so that security is solid.

- Configure OU group policies to match the goals of your OU plans that call for creating OUs to have customized group policies. These will include needs for desktop configurations, remote installation services for Windows 2000 Professional, and software publication (any or all of these can also be configured in default domain policies).

- Create an implementation scenario for each group policy object that is created or modified.

As part of the group policy planning, develop a change control plan that includes:

- Who has the authority to make changes to each group policy object

- How permissions will be assigned to each group policy object

- Under what circumstances changes will be made to group policies

- How changes will affect server and network security

- How changes are to be evaluated before they are implemented

- How to implement changes with the least impact on users, including how to provide advance notification to users

Planning and Using Individual Group Policies

Group policies are typically organized under two categories: Computer Configuration and User Configuration. The Computer Configuration settings apply to computer accounts in Active Directory, and the User Configuration settings are policies for user accounts. Under Computer Configuration and User Configuration, there are three child categories: Software Settings, Windows Settings, and Administrative Templates (see

Figure 8-10). All of these are "typical" settings because group policy extensions can be added or removed, which means one group policy object can be customized to have somewhat different options than another.

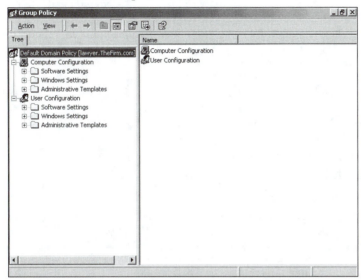

Figure 8-10   Group policy parameters

The typical options for Computer Configuration are similar, but not identical, to the options for User Configuration. For example, in the User Configuration subcategory, Administrative Templates, you can configure desktop settings. However, there are no desktop settings under the same subcategory for Computer Configuration. Table 8-5 summarizes the general subcategories of settings for Computer Configuration and User Configuration.

Table 8-5   Computer and User Configuration Settings

Software Settings	Description	Computer/User Configuration
Software installation	Used to manage how users access software (assigned or published)	Computer and User Configuration
Windows Settings	**Description**	**Computer/User Configuration**
Internet Explorer Maintenance	Used to manage Internet Explorer settings for clients, such as creating a set of favorite Internet links	User Configuration only
Scripts (Startup/Shutdown; Logon/Logoff)	Used to implement script command files when clients start up or shut down (such as powering off a computer at shutdown) their computers, and when clients log on or log off the network (such as mapping specific drives during logon)	Computer and User Configuration

Table 8-5   Computer and User Configuration Settings (continued)

Windows Settings	Description	Computer/User Configuration
Security Settings	Used to configure security settings Under Computer Configuration you can manage account policies, auditing policies, user rights, IP security policies (see Chapters 1 and 5), public key policies, and many other security settings; under User Configuration you manage public key policies.	Computer and User Configuration
Remote Installation Services	Used to manage options that are made available to users who install Windows 2000 Professional over a network	User Configuration only
Folder Redirection	Used to redirect specific folders so that they are housed on a network (such as redirecting the My Documents folder to obtain documents from a server—this means that documents can be accessed no matter what computer a user employs to access her or his account)	User Configuration only
Administrative Templates	**Description**	**Computer/User Configuration**
Windows Components	Used to manage NetMeeting, Internet Explorer, Task Scheduler, Windows Installer—in addition, Windows Explorer and MMC are included for User Configuration	Computer and User Configuration
System	Used to manage system-wide services, such as how to run logon scripts, enabling disk quotas, how to apply group policy, and managing Windows file protection—but options for User Configuration are limited to logon/logoff scripts and group policy management	Computer and User Configuration
Network	Used to manage network settings for offline files and network and dial-up connections (currently there are more options for User Configuration)	Computer and User Configuration
Printers	Used to manage access to printers, such as publishing printers and enabling Web-based printing	Computer Configuration only

Table 8-5   Computer and User Configuration Settings (continued)

Administrative Templates	Description	Computer/User Configuration
Start Menu & Taskbar	Used to customize Start Menu and Taskbar options for clients, such as removing the Run option on the Start Menu	User Configuration only
Desktop	Used to customize the desktop for clients, such as enabling or disabling Active Desktop or hiding the Internet Explorer icon	User Configuration only
Control Panel	Used to customize the Control Panel options that are available to users, such as disabling Add/Remove Programs or hiding specific Control Panel applets	User Configuration only

Configuring Default Domain Policy

Two of the most common ways to access the default domain policy are by using the Active Directory Users and Computers tool or the MMC Group Policy snap-in. To access the default domain policy from the Active Directory Users and Computers tool:

1. Click Start, point to Programs, point to Administrative Tools, and click Active Directory Users and Computers.

2. Right-click the domain for which you want to set up the default domain policy, and then click Properties.

3. Click the Group Policy tab.

4. Make sure that Default Domain Policy is selected, and click Edit (see Figure 8-11).

To access the default domain policy by using the Group Policy MMC snap-in:

1. Start MMC by clicking the Start button, clicking the Run option and entering mmc in the *Open* box. Click OK.

2. Click MMC's Console menu, and click Add/Remove Snap-in.

3. On the Add/Remove Snap-in dialog box, click Add, scroll to Group Policy and double-click it.

4. When the Select Group Policy Object Wizard starts, click the Browse button, double-click Default Domain Policy, and click Finish (see Figure 8-12).

5. Click Close, and click OK.

6. Maximize the console windows, if necessary.

7. Click Default Domain Policy in the tree, if the child objects are not displayed.

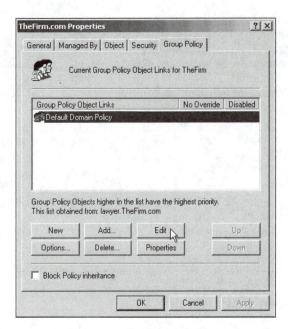

Figure 8-11   Accessing the default domain policy from the Active Directory Users and Computers tool

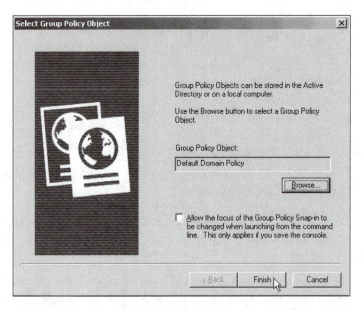

Figure 8-12   Accessing the default domain policy from the Group Policy snap-in

Configure the default domain policy to have policies that apply to everyone in the domain. These will typically be policies such as:

- Account policies for passwords, account lockout, and Kerberos
- Logon/logoff scripts
- Event log recording parameters
- Security for system services, such as for setting the default startup mode (automatic, manual, or disabled)
- IP security
- Public key security
- Disk quotas
- File protection scanning
- Publishing printers
- Offline file management
- Remote Installation Services (RIS) for Windows 2000 Professional

For example, all organizations should set up password, account lockout, and Kerberos policies (see Figure 8-13), as well as other forms of security, such as security for system services, IP security, and public key security (try Hands-on Project 8-5 to set up account policies for a domain). Also, most medium- and large-sized organizations like Jefferson Philately, Interstate Security Bank, and York Industries are concerned about managing disk capacity through setting disk quotas that limit how much disk space users can occupy. It is common for these organizations to enable disk quotas, and to set the default disk quota parameters in the default domain policy so that they apply to everyone. There are parameters, such as setting default quota limits for all users, setting the type of enforcement when users reach their quotas, and creating event log entries to report disk quota events (see Figure 8-14).

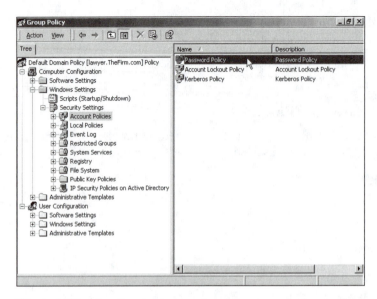

Figure 8-13   Configuring account policies

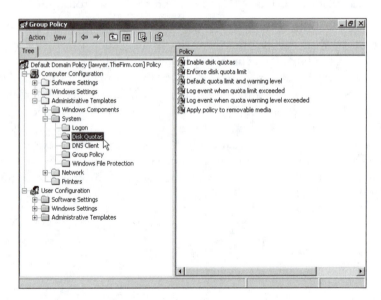

Figure 8-14   Configuring disk quotas

Managing disk capacity through disk quotas offers an important way for organizations to save money by encouraging users to clean up old files, rather than buying new disks while existing disks contain unused files. Disk quotas also are important as a way to ensure that an organization can conduct business normally. Organizations that do not enforce disk quotas can run out of disk space during important business cycles, such as during the end-of-year accounting closing or when launching a new product campaign.

Creating and Planning a New Group Policy Object for a Site

There are several reasons to set group policies for a site. One is when a site spans two or more domains and you want to apply a particular group policy object to all users in the domains, such as requiring IP security or publishing software. Another possibility is that one site has only Windows 2000 Professional clients, while another site has only Windows NT clients. Using different group policy objects for each site enables you to set up different desktop configurations for each site. Yet a third reason for linking a group policy object with a site is so that you can associate different account policies with the different sites.

The steps for creating and linking a group policy object with a site are:

1. Click Start, point to Programs, point to Administrative Tools, and click Active Directory Sites and Services.

2. Find the site to which you want to link a group policy object and right-click it in the tree.

3. Click Properties.

4. Click the Group Policy tab.

5. Click the New button.

6. Enter the name of the new group policy object and press Enter.

7. Make sure that the group policy object is highlighted and click the Edit button.

8. Configure the group policy settings.

9. Close the Group Policy tool.

10. Close the site Properties dialog box.

11. Close the Active Directory Sites and Services tool.

8

Creating and Planning a New Group Policy Object for an OU

You can create a new group policy object for an OU by using the Active Directory Users and Computers tool. The steps for creating a new group policy object are:

1. Open the Active Directory Users and Computers tool.
2. In the tree, right-click the OU for which you want to create the group policy and click Properties.
3. Click the Group Policy tab.
4. Click the New button.
5. Enter a name for the new group policy and press Enter.
6. Click the Edit button.
7. Configure the desired Computer Configuration and User Configuration settings.
8. Close the Group Policy tool when you are finished.
9. Click Close to exit the OU Properties dialog box.
10. Close the Active Directory Users and Computers tool.

Several common reasons why you would create a group policy object to associate with an OU are to:

- Create a common desktop for the members of the OU
- Publish or assign specific software for the OU members
- Create specialized security policies
- Set up customized Internet Explorer parameters
- Redirect files

The Tellers OUs at Interstate Security Bank represent one example of why you would customize the desktop in a bank, so that all of the computer/cash drawers have identical setups. In an organization such as Jefferson Philately, the customer service representatives might have their own OU so that a group policy object could be set up to *assign* specialized customer service software to appear on every customer service representative's desktop (see Figure 8-15). As mentioned in Chapter 3, assigning software means that the software is automatically started through a desktop shortcut or menu selection, while publishing software enables users to install that software themselves from a central network location. Another advantage of creating group policies to assign or publish software, as discussed in Chapter 3, is to provide change management so that all users are deploying the same software and software versions—which is particularly important for some business processes in an organization. For example, it is easier for multiple users to edit the same document when they are using the same version of the software used to create that document.

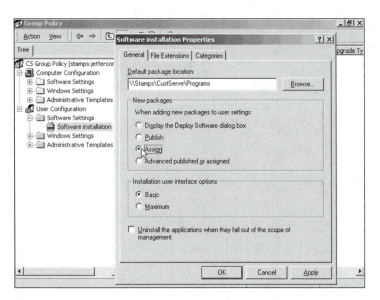

Figure 8-15   Assigning software through group policy

Redirecting files is another important group policy for some organizations. For example, assume that your analysis of business processes and communication flow for Interstate Security Bank reveals that each regional office sends out CD and IRA dividend statements each quarter. Each regional office collects the dividend statements from its branch offices and then prints those statements. Also, your analysis shows that customers call their branch offices when they have questions about a statement, and the branch offices write a personalized follow-up letter to customers after the call. So that the regional office and its branch offices can quickly find copies of the original statements and copies of the follow-up letters in the same place, the bank can create a group policy that includes folder redirection. The customer service representatives, tellers, and Business department would all have a desktop folder that is redirected to a centrally located folder at the regional office. The central folder would contain the original dividend statements and copies of letters to customers.

Last, consider your organizational analysis of York Industries, which shows the company has a top-secret research and development department for creating new advances in appliances. An OU can be created for this department that has a group policy focusing on specialized security. Supplementing the default domain policy that enforces password and account lockout restrictions, the OU's group policy would focus on enforcing secure server IP security and security through creating a specialized client desktop, including redirecting research folders to a secure server location (see Figure 8-16).

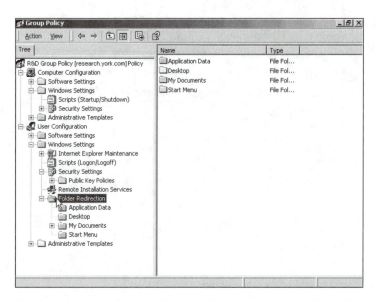

Figure 8-16   Configuring folder redirection in the Group Policy window

Try Hands-on Project 8-6 to set up a group policy for an OU that sets up IP security, and that disables the Control Panel so that it is more difficult for a user to reconfigure his or her workstation to be less secure.

Planning Group Policy Management for Client Computers

When you customize the desktop settings for client computers by using the Administrative Templates child object under User Configuration in a group policy object, make sure that you review the default Administrative Templates that are available in Windows 2000 Server. These are shown in Table 8-6.

Table 8-6   Administrative Templates Included with Windows 2000

Template	Purpose	Tool Used to Configure
Common.adm	Managing desktop settings that are common to Windows 95, 98, and NT	Poledit.exe
Ientres.adm	Default for managing Internet Explorer in Windows 2000 Professional clients	Group Policy snap-in or edit group policy by using the Active Directory Users and Computers tool
System.adm	Default for managing Windows 2000 Professional clients	Group Policy snap-in or edit group policy by using the Active Directory Users and Computers tool
Windows.adm	Managing Windows 95 and 98 clients	Poledit.exe
Winnt.adm	Managing Windows NT 4.0 clients	Poledit.exe

If there is a combination of Windows 95, Windows 98, Windows NT, and Windows 2000 clients, then you will likely want to use a combination of administrative templates, such as Common.adm and System.adm. Common.adm provides desktop configuration for Windows 95, 98, and NT clients, and System.adm provides desktop configuration for Windows 2000 clients. You can do this because the Administrative Templates setting under User Configuration enables you to add or remove multiple templates in one group policy object (see Figure 8-17). Try Hands-on Project 8-8 to add an administrative template to a group policy object.

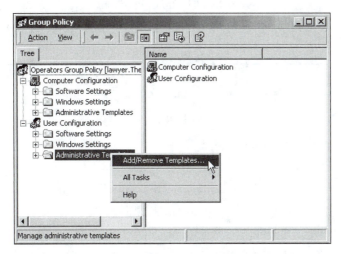

Figure 8-17   Adding an administrative template

Table 8-7 shows an expanded list of the Administrative Templates options under User Configuration.

Table 8-7   Options for Configuring Administrative Templates Settings Under User Configuration

Component	Description
Windows Components	Controls access to installed software such as NetMeeting, Internet Explorer, Windows Explorer, MMC, Task Scheduler, and Windows Installer
Start Menu & Taskbar	Controls the ability to configure the Start menu and Taskbar, the ability to access program groups from the Start menu, and the ability to use Start menu options including Run, Search, Settings, and Documents
Desktop	Controls access to desktop functions, including the icons for My Network Places and Internet Explorer, the ability to configure the Active Desktop, and the ability to configure Active Directory searches

Table 8-7 Options for Configuring Administrative Templates Settings Under User Configuration (continued)

Component	Description
Control Panel	Controls access to Control Panel functions such as Add/Remove programs, Display, Printers, and Regional Options—plus the ability to disable the Control Panel altogether and to hide or display only specific Control Panel icons
Network	Controls access to offline files and the ability to configure network access via Network and Dial-up Connections
System	Controls access to Logon/Logoff capabilities, scripts, Task Manager functions, Change Password, group policy refresh rate, slow link detection, and other system functions

To configure client desktops in the default domain policy, for example:

1. Open the Active Directory Users and Computers tool.

2. Right-click the domain you want to configure and click Properties.

3. Click the Group Policy tab.

4. Ensure that Default Domain Policy is selected and click Edit.

5. In the tree, double-click User Configuration, if its child objects are not displayed, and double-click Administrative Templates.

6. In the tree, click any of the component folders that you want to configure, as described in Table 8-7, such as Start Menu & Taskbar.

7. In the right-hand pane, double-click each of the entities that you want to configure, such as *Remove common program groups from Start Menu*.

8. Close the Group Policy tool when you are finished, and then close the domain Properties dialog box and the Active Directory Users and Computers tool.

Creating Group Policies Using the Security Templates Tool

There is a way to create a policy that focuses mainly on security. You can then associate this policy with a site, a domain, or an OU. This is accomplished by using the Security Templates tool, which contains a subset of the settings that you would find in a group policy object under Computer Configuration, Windows Settings, and Security Settings. The security settings include account policies, local computer policies, event log policies, restricted groups, system services, Registry, and file system (see Figure 8-18).

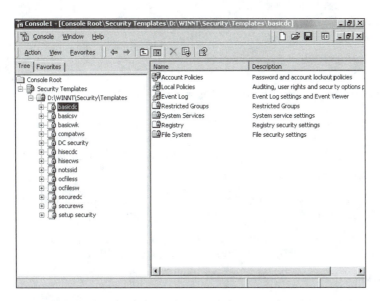

Figure 8-18   Using the Security Templates tool

This tool is particularly useful when you have multiple group policies to maintain or when you have multiple OUs, but many of those OUs share the same group policy. For example, if you have 20 OUs set up in a domain and use one security policy for eight OUs, a different one for eight OUs, and still another one for four OUs, then you would create three security templates. This approach is effective when your main concern is with security and not with other group policy settings, such as customizing the desktop.

When you are ready to create a new security template, use these general steps:

1. Make sure there is no default security template that already matches what you want to do (if there is, use the default security template).

2. Make sure that the Group Policy and Security Templates snap-ins are installed in the MMC.

3. Create a security template by clicking the main folder under Security Templates in the MMC (such as \WINNT\Security\Templates), clicking the Action menu, and clicking New Template. Enter a name for the new template and click OK. Double-click the template and configure the settings you want.

4. Import your newly created template into an existing group policy by installing the Security Configuration and Analysis snap-in, right-click that snap-in, open a database (previously created for the group policy; see Chapter 4) or create a new one, right-click Security Configuration and Analysis in the tree, click Import Template, click the template configuration file you created, and click Open. Right-click the Security Configuration and Analysis snap-in again, click Configure Computer Now, and click OK.

8

> **Note** When you apply a security template, it incrementally updates the group policy object to which it is applied.

There are several default security templates that come with Windows 2000 Server, which you can import to an existing group policy, instead of creating a new security template:

- *basicdc*: Provides basic security intended for domain controllers

- *basicsv*: Provides basic security settings for servers, but does not include default settings for user rights or restricted groups

- *basicwk*: Provides basic security settings for workstations, but does not include default settings for user rights or restricted groups

- *compatws*: Provides compatible workstation or server security settings for computers running Windows 2000 and Windows NT

- *DC security*: Default security for DCs that is updated beyond basicdc security

- *hisecdc*: Sets maximum (high-security) protection for domain controllers running Windows 2000

- *hisecws*: Sets maximum (high-security) protection for workstations running Windows 2000

- *notssid*: Used for user security in terminal server applications

- *ocfiless*: Used for optional component file security for servers

- *ocfilews*: Used for optional component file security for workstations

- *securedc*: Provides the recommended security on DCs, excluding files, folder, and Registry key security

- *securews*: Provides the recommended security on client workstations, excluding files, folder, and Registry key security

- *setup security*: Provides "out of the box" security, which leaves most security settings "not defined"

CHAPTER SUMMARY

- Windows 2000 security groups include domain local, global, and universal groups for Active Directory implementations. Groups enable you to manage access to Active Directory resources such as servers, shared folders, and shared printers. As a general rule, use domain local and universal groups to provide access to resources, and use global groups to contain user accounts.

❐ Group policy objects are configured to manage the default domain policy and group policies. The main categories of group policies in a group policy object are Computer Configuration, which is used to manage computer accounts, and User Configuration for user accounts. These objects provide ways to make software available to users over the network, implement domain and group security, and manage client computers from Active Directory.

In the next chapter, you will learn how to plan Active Directory object security and how to enable Active Directory to coexist with other directory services, such as Novell Directory Services.

KEY TERMS

default domain policy — Automatically set up when a domain is created, this is the group policy object that is used for a domain, that is inherited by child domains, and that can be modified to match the particular needs of an organization.

discretionary access control list (DACL) — A portion of an access control list (ACL) of users, groups, and computers that are granted or denied some form of permission for an object, such as to a group policy or a shared folder.

domain local security group — A security group that typically is placed on the access control lists of resources in a domain and that has global security groups as members.

global security group — A security group that typically contains user accounts and other global groups from its home domain—and that is a member of domain local groups in the same or other domains as a way to give that global group's member accounts access to the resources defined to the domain local groups.

group policy — A Windows 2000 Server concept that enables a server administrator to standardize the working environment of clients and servers by setting policies in Active Directory.

group policy object (GPO) — An Active Directory object that contains group policy settings for a site, domain, OU, or local computer. Each GPO has a unique name and a globally unique identifier.

local security group — A group of user accounts that is used to manage resources on a standalone Windows 2000 server that is not part of a domain.

scope of influence — The reach of a type of group, such as access to resources in a single domain or access to all resources in all domains in a forest (see domain local, global, and universal groups).

standalone server — A server that is not a member of a domain, but that is a member of an existing workgroup or that establishes its own workgroup, as in peer-to-peer networking.

system policy — A set of basic user account and computer parameters that can be configured in Windows NT 4.0 (and is contained in Windows 2000 for backward compatibility) to control the desktop environment and specific client configuration settings.

system policy editor — An editor, Poledit.exe, that is used to configure system policy parameters in Windows NT 4.0 and that is also available in Windows 2000 Server.

universal security group — A group that is used to provide access to resources in any domain within a forest. A common implementation is to make global groups that contain accounts members of a universal group that has access to resources. The universal security group is only available in native mode domains.

REVIEW QUESTIONS

Answer questions 1–9 using this case information:

Yablonsky's Siding manufactures aluminum and steel house siding. The main plant, which is in Richmond, Virginia, has the following organizational functions: management, sales, customer service, business, information systems (IS), manufacturing, shipping, and installation support. Windows Active Directory consists of three domains: siding.com, sales.siding.com, and manufact.siding.com.

1. The IS department wants to create a group called Managers that will contain the user accounts of the top-level company managers. They want this group to have access to shared folders in all three domains. What type of group should contain these users' accounts?

    a. domain local

    b. global

    c. local

    d. universal

    e. none of the above

2. Which of the following types of groups should be used to give the group of user accounts discussed in Question 1 access to resources in all three domains?

    a. domain local

    b. global

    c. local

    d. universal

    e. none of the above

3. The managers for Yablonsky's Siding want to make sure that all users must enter passwords that are at least seven characters in length and that must be changed every 30 days. How can this be set up?

    a. Set these object parameters in the default domain policies for all three domains.

    b. Create multiple OUs for each department in the company and set the password security in each OU.

    c. Create a universal group for all domain resources and configure the Computer Settings in the Software option in that group policy.

    d. Set one domain policy and make sure that you do not use any other group policies in Active Directory.

    e. only a and d

    f. only b and c

    g. only c and d

4. Yablonsky's Siding wants to make Microsoft Office software available for any employee to install, but they want to encourage all users to use the same version of this software. What do you recommend?

    a. Purchase multiple copies of Microsoft Office and develop a software checkout system so that users can access it on a temporary basis as needed (to save on license costs).

    b. Have users purchase their own copies individually and install their own copies.

    c. Publish the most recent version of Microsoft Office for users to install.

    d. Create one OU for users to access Microsoft Office on a restricted lease of 4 hours per session.

    e. There is no good solution to this need, without purchasing a specialized Microsoft Office server.

    f. none of the above

5. The company has recently upgraded all client workstations to Windows 2000 Professional. Now they want to manage the desktop setups via Active Directory, and they want to configure Internet Explorer on each desktop to have the same main links. Which of the following templates should they use?

    a. Common.adm

    b. System.adm

    c. Ientres.adm

    d. Windows.adm

    e. all of the above

    f. only a and d

    g. only b and c

    h. only a, b, and d

8

6. The Yablonsky's Siding IS department is not sure about how to create an OU and a group policy for an OU. Which of the following tools enables them to do both by starting one tool?

   a. Group Policy snap-in

   b. Security Templates MMC snap-in

   c. Active Directory Domains and Trusts tool

   d. Active Directory Users and Computers tool

   e. No one tool enables them to do both; they must use a and b.

   f. No one tool enables them to do both; they must use b and c.

7. Yablonsky's Siding considers their sales information to be confidential. Which of the following security measures would you recommend?

   a. Create an OU for sales personnel user accounts and create groups in the OU to manage the access to sales data.

   b. Create a group policy for the sales personnel that establishes special security measures, such as using IP security.

   c. Redirect sales data to a secured folder via a group policy.

   d. Hide the sales users in the domain so that no one can find out their user account or computer names, not even for e-mail contact.

   e. all of the above

   f. only a and b

   g. only a, b, and c

8. Users are not deleting old files on the server, and the IS department has noticed that IS often has to purchase new disks with greater frequency. What might the IS department do?

   a. Enable disk quotas via a group policy.

   b. Set default disk quotas via a group policy.

   c. Hide My Computer via a group policy so that clients cannot view server drives, making them harder to access and store data on.

   d. Periodically deactivate disks so that users cannot access them as frequently.

   e. all of the above

   f. only a and b

   g. only b and d

   h. only a, c, and d

9. The IS department wants to implement startup script files. From where would they do this?

   a. General properties tab associated with a group

   b. Group Policy

   c. General properties tab associated with an OU

   d. General properties tab associated with a site

   e. all of the above

   f. only a and b

   g. only c and d

   h. only a, c, and d

Answer questions 10–19 using this case information:

The Office of State Income Tax for a state in the U.S. is implementing Active Directory. This office has the following departments: Executive, Accounting Control, Forms and Printing, Legislative Liaison, and Collections. The Office of State Income Tax has 18 servers that are all in one child domain that is under the state's parent domain.

10. The state's IT department wants to convert a domain local group called Exec to a universal group, but the universal group option is deactivated. What might be the problem?

   a. The domain local group contains only one user account, but must contain two or more.

   b. The domain is set in mixed mode.

   c. The domain local group must first be converted to a global group, and then to a universal group.

   d. A universal group is not recognized in a child domain.

   e. all of the above

   f. only a and c

   g. only b and c

   h. only a, c, and d

11. The state's IT department is not sure what tool to use to edit System.adm. Which tool should it use?

   a. Poledit.exe

   b. Group Policy MMC snap-in

   c. Active Directory Users and Computers

   d. Regedit.exe

   e. Any of the above can be used.

   f. either a or d

   g. either b or c

   h. any of a, c, or d

12. The Office of State Income Tax wants to establish high security on its DCs. Which of the following security templates should they use?

    a. hisecdc

    b. basicdc

    c. compatws

    d. setup security

    e. none of the above

13. In a conversation with the director of collections, he asks why you would use group policy. Which of the following are reasons to use group policy?

    a. To reduce the need for more than two DCs in a domain

    b. To create a common desktop for the members of an OU

    c. To enable wider use of universal groups instead of global groups

    d. To redirect files for members of an OU

    e. all of the above

    f. only a and c

    g. only b and c

    h. only b and d

14. The director general of the Office of State Income Tax is mostly concerned about security for all of the group policies that the agency creates. Which of the following should your planning focus on in particular?

    a. software settings

    b. Internet Explorer settings

    c. security templates

    d. file templates

    e. none of the above

15. You have created a global group for each of the following departments: Executive, Accounting Control, Forms and Printing, Legislative Liaison, and Collections. Which of these groups should be on the ACLs of resources, such as shared folders?

    a. Only the global group for the Executive department

    b. Only the global groups for the Executive and Accounting Control departments, because they access highly sensitive information

    c. Only the global group for the Legislative Liaison department, because it accesses information in the parent domain

    d. Ideally, all of the global groups should be on the ACLs of shared resources.

    e. Ideally, none of the global groups should be on the ACLs of shared resources.

16. The State Auditor has mandated that all servers in the state system will use Kerberos. Where would you configure Kerberos for the Office of State Income Tax?

    a. On each user account when it is created

    b. As the audit policy for Computer Configuration

    c. As each OU's independent group policy

    d. As a security setting in the default domain policy

    e. only a and b

    f. only b and c

    g. only a, b, and c

17. Because the members of the Collections department use one another's computers, you need to make sure that each collection agent's desktop has an icon for this year's tax collection program and last year's tax collection program. Which of the following steps should you use to make sure?

    a. Create a Collect OU.

    b. Move all of the collection agents' accounts into the Collect OU, and create a two Collect groups, one for software resources and one for collection agent's accounts.

    c. Create a group policy that is linked to the Collect OU, and assign the two collection programs.

    d. Create a default domain policy for the Collect OU, and publish the two collection programs.

    e. Only a and b are the best choices.

    f. Only a, b and c are the best choices.

    g. Only a, b, and d are the best choices.

18. All of the Office of State Income Tax users in the Executive department have workstations running Windows 95 or Windows 98. What administrative template(s) should be set up in a group policy that applies to an OU containing their accounts?

    a. Common.adm

    b. System.adm

    c. Ientres.adm

    d. Windows.adm

    e. all of the above

    f. only a and b

    g. only a and c

    h. only a, c, and d

19. The state's IT director is new to Active Directory and is not familiar with the basic categories in a group policy. They are:

    a. User configuration

    b. Domain configuration

    c. Computer configuration

    d. Site configuration

    e. all of the above

    f. only a and c

    g. only b and c

    h. only a, b, and d

Answer questions 20–25 using this case information:

Montoya Containers manufactures cardboard boxes and packaging. The company has two manufacturing plants on the west coast, two in the midwest, and one on the east coast of the U.S. Each manufacturing plant has a network. There is one parent domain on the east coast and four child domains under the parent. The company employs 1722 people in all of its locations. Each of the five locations has units that perform human resources, business, marketing, computer support, materials purchasing, cardboard fabrication, and product distribution. The management model is centralized throughout all of the companies, and the computer support units at each location work to keep the tree, domain, and OU structures as simple as possible, and under the control of the computer support personnel. All of the company's users are running Windows 2000 Professional.

20. Given the centralized decision structure of this company, what model for organizing user accounts and groups would you expect to find?

    a. Distribution of user accounts into multiple OUs and with the authority over OUs delegated to department heads or team leaders

    b. User accounts mostly placed under the Users container in each domain

    c. Multiple group policies to correspond with multiple OUs that match the functional areas

    d. Groups mostly placed under the Builtin and Users containers

    e. all of the above

    f. only a and c

    g. only b and d

    h. only a, c, and d

21. Montoya Containers wants to enable Active Desktop for all users in the organization. What would you recommend to accomplish this?

    a. Enable Active Desktop under User Configuration and Administrative Templates in the default domain policy.

    b. Enable Active Desktop under all instances of Windows Settings in a group policy for all OUs that contain shared folders.

    c. Create a multimedia training program on a server in each domain that shows all of the users how to enable Active Desktop themselves.

    d. Enable Active Desktop as part of the Security Settings under all instances of Windows Settings in all group policies.

    e. Disable logon scripts under all instances of Windows settings.

22. The computer support group at the headquarters site for the company has created a universal group called InventoryManage and now wants to convert this group to a domain local group. The problem is that the domain local group selection is deactivated. What is the problem?

    a. The InventoryManage group has user accounts as members and therefore cannot be converted to any other type of group.

    b. The InventoryManage group has at least one other universal group as a member and therefore cannot be converted until its member group is removed.

    c. A universal group cannot be converted to another type of group.

    d. The InventoryManage group was created in the Users folder, which is not truly an OU.

    e. none of the above

23. The Human Resources department has gotten many complaints about employees who are playing games over the Internet. Since only 10 users at each site need to access the Internet, what do you recommend?

    a. Impose stiff penalties for using the Internet, such as docking a day's pay for each day a user is caught.

    b. Hide the Internet Explorer icon for all users via the default domain policy in each domain and assign a special Internet Explorer program access for users who need it.

    c. Configure the Builtin container's group policy to delete Internet Explorer for all groups other than a special group of the users who need to use the program.

    d. Configure all servers that users access to be Terminal Servers and then periodically monitor selected users for Internet Explorer violations.

    e. only b and c

    f. only a and d

24. The computer support personnel at Montoya Containers are not certain about what Active Directory containers other than OUs can have a group policy linked to them. Which of the following can have a group policy?

    a. a folder

    b. a site

    c. a group

    d. a domain

    e. all of the above

    f. only a and b

    g. only b and d

    h. only b, c, and d

25. Montoya Containers wants to establish a group policy that creates a common set of icons that are displayed on each domain controller. How can they do this?

    a. Create a common desktop for domain controllers in the default domain policy.

    b. Create a specialized group policy for the domain controllers and link it to the Domain Controllers container under each domain.

    c. Create a specialized group policy for the domain controllers and link it to the domain.

    d. Create a hardware profile for domain controllers and copy it to each domain controller.

    e. none of the above

HANDS-ON PROJECTS

Project 8-1

In this project, you create a new domain local group and place it on a folder's ACL.

To create a domain local group:

1. Click **Start**, point to **Programs**, point to **Administrative Tools**, and click **Active Directory Users and Computers**.

2. Click **Users** under a domain in the tree.

3. Click the **Action** menu, point to **New**, and click **Group**. (An alternate way to create a new group is to click the *Create a new group in the current container* icon.)

4. In the *Group name* box, enter a group name consisting of your initials and DomainGroup, such as MJPDomainGroup. What happens in the *Group name (pre-Windows 2000)* box when you enter the group name?

5. What options are available for the group scope? Are any options deactivated? Record your observations in your lab journal or in a word-processed document.

6. What options are available to define the group type? Record your observations.

7. Click **Domain local**. Also, make sure that **Security** is selected.

8. Click **OK**.

9. Leave the Active Directory Users and Computers tool open for the next hands-on project.

To place the new group that you created on a folder's ACL:

1. Double-click **My Computer** on the desktop.

2. Double-click drive **C:**, or whichever drive contains the system files folder \WINNT.

3. Right-click the **Program Files** folder and click **Properties**.

4. Click the **Security** tab.

5. Click **Add**.

6. Scroll to find the domain local group that you created, such as MJPDomainGroup, and double-click that group.

7. What happens when you double-click the group?

8. Click **OK**.

9. Make sure that the group you added is highlighted in the *Name* box. What permissions are automatically granted? How would you give the new group Full Control permissions?

10. Click **OK**.

11. Close **My Computer** (the Local Disk window).

Project 8-2

In this project, you create two global groups and then nest one group in the other. Finally, you make the top-level global group a member of the domain local group that you created in Hands-on Project 8-1.

To create the two global groups and nest one group in the other:

1. Make sure that the Active Directory Users and Computers tool is open, and if not, open it.

2. Click **Users** in the tree.

3. Click the **Create a new group in the current container** icon on the action bar.

4. In the *Group name* box, enter your initials and GlobalTop, such as MJPGlobalTop.

5. Make sure that **Global** is selected as the group scope.

6. Make sure that **Security** is selected as the group type.

7. Click **OK**.

8

8. Click the **Create a new group in the current container** icon on the action bar.

9. Enter your initials plus GlobalNested, such as MJPGlobalNested.

10. Make sure that **Global** is selected as the group scope, and that **Security** is selected as the group type.

11. Click **OK**.

12. How can you make sure that both global groups are now created in the Users folder? Record your observations in your lab journal or in a word-processed document.

13. Right-click the second global group that you created, such as MJPGlobalNested, and click **Properties**.

14. Click the **Member Of** tab.

15. Click **Add**.

16. Scroll to find the top-level global group that you created, such as MJPGlobalTop, and then double-click it. Where does the group appear now in the Select Groups dialog box? (If the top-level global group you created is not displayed, this means that you are in mixed mode. With your instructor's permission, go to Hands-on Project 8-3 to convert to native mode, and then complete this project)

17. Click **OK**.

18. What new information is displayed on the Member Of tab? How would you nest a group under the first nested group, such as under MJPGlobalNested? Now that you have practiced nesting one group under another, consider how nesting groups 10 or 20 levels deep might get confusing. Record your observations.

19. Click **OK**.

To join the top-level group and its nested group to your domain local group:

1. Make sure that the Users folder is open in the tree, and scroll to find the domain local group that you created in Hands-on Project 8-1.

2. Right-click the domain local group, such as MJPDomainGroup, and click **Properties**.

3. Click the **Members** tab, and then click the **Add** button.

4. Scroll to find the top-level global group that you created, such as MJPGlobalTop, and double-click it.

5. Click **OK**.

6. What security access do both global groups that you created have to the Program Files folder? Record your observations.

7. Click **OK**.

8. Leave the Active Directory Users and Computers tool open for the next project.

Project 8-3

In this project, you learn how to convert a domain from mixed mode to native mode. Ask your instructor about what domain to use for this project.

To convert a domain:

1. Make sure that the Active Directory Users and Computers tool is open, and if not, open it.

2. Right-click the domain in the tree that you want to convert, such as TheFirm.com.

3. Click **Properties**.

4. Make sure that the General tab is displayed.

5. What mode is shown in the Domain operation mode box? What type of domain controllers are supported by this mode? Record your observations in your lab journal or in a word-processed document.

6. Look for a button in the bottom right-hand corner of the dialog box on the General tab, but *do not click the button* for this assignment (unless you have permission from your instructor). If you see the Change Mode button, then it is possible to use this button to convert to native mode. If you do not see this button, then the domain is already in native mode.

7. Click **Cancel**.

8. Leave the Active Directory Users and Computers tool open for the next project.

Project 8-4

In this project, you change the scope of a group (note that the domain must be in native mode for this assignment).

To change the scope:

1. Ensure that the Active Directory Users and Computers tool is open, and if not, open it.

2. Make sure that the Users folder is open in the tree, and if it is not, open it.

3. Scroll to find the domain local group that you created in Hands-on Project 8-1, such as MJPDomainGroup, and right-click it. Click **Properties**.

4. Notice the group scope boxed-in area. What group scope is currently selected? Are there any options that are deactivated? Record your observations.

5. Click **Universal**, and then click **OK**.

6. How can you check to make sure that you have changed the group scope?

7. Leave the Active Directory Users and Computers tool open for Hands-on Project 8-6.

8

Project 8-5

In this project, you configure the account policies for the default domain policy.

To configure the default domain policy:

1. Click **Start**, click **Run**, and enter **mmc** in the Open box. Click **OK**.

2. Maximize the console windows.

3. Click MMC's **Console** menu and click **Add/Remove Snap-in**.

4. On the Add/Remove Snap-in dialog box, click **Add**, and then double-click **Group Policy**.

5. When the Select Group Policy Object Wizard starts, click the **Browse** button, and double-click **Default Domain Policy** in the Name box.

6. Click **Finish**.

7. Click **Close** and click **OK**.

8. Click **Default Domain Policy** in the tree to display the child objects under it, if they are not already displayed.

9. Double-click **Windows Settings** in the tree under Computer Configuration.

10. Click **Security Settings** in the tree. What security settings are displayed in the right-hand pane? Record your observations.

11. Double-click **Account Policies** in the right-hand pane. What account policies can be set?

12. Double-click **Password Policy** in the right-hand pane.

13. What parameters are currently set for password policies? Record your observations.

14. Double-click **Enforce password history** in the right-hand pane.

15. Make sure that there is a checkmark in **Define this policy setting**.

16. Set the *passwords remembered* box to **10**. Click **OK**.

17. Double-click **Maximum password age**.

18. Make sure that there is a checkmark in **Define this policy setting**.

19. Set the *Passwords expire in* box to **60** days. Click **OK**.

20. Click **Account Lockout Policy** in the tree.

21. How would you set account lockout so that an account is locked out for one hour after there are seven unsuccessful attempts to log on to it?

22. Close the console and click **No** so that your console settings are not saved (but note that the group policy changes you have made are saved).

Project 8-6

This project enables you to create an OU group policy object to configure IP security and to disable the Control Panel at users' desktops.

To create the group policy:

1. Open the Active Directory Users and Computers tool, if it is not already open.

2. Create an OU that is named with your initials and the word Secure, as in MJPSecure. (Refer to Hands-on Project 7-2 in Chapter 7, if you are unsure about how to create an OU.)

3. Right-click the OU that you created in Step 2, such as MJPSecure, and click **Properties**.

4. Click the **Group Policy** tab.

5. Click the **New** button. Type in a name for the group policy object, such as MJPSecure Group Policy. Press **Enter**.

6. Make sure that the group policy name that you entered is highlighted, and then click **Edit**.

7. Double-click **Windows Settings** in the tree under Computer Configuration.

8. Double-click **Security Settings** in the tree.

9. Click **IP Security Policies on Active Directory**. What options are displayed in the right-hand pane?

10. Right-click **Secure Server (Require Security)** and click **Assign**.

11. How has the Policy Assigned column changed in the right-hand pane?

12. Double-click **Administrative Templates** in the tree under User Configuration.

13. Click **Control Panel** in the tree.

14. Double-click **Disable Control Panel** in the right-hand pane.

15. Make sure that the Policy tab is displayed, and if not, click the tab.

16. What options are available on the Policy tab? Record your observations.

17. Click **Enabled** and click **OK**.

18. How has the Setting column changed in the right-hand pane?

19. Close the Group Policy tool, and close the OU Properties dialog box.

20. Leave the Active Directory Users and Computers tool open for the next project.

Project 8-7

In this project, you learn where to set parameters for optimizing group policy execution.

To optimize group policy performance:

1. Make sure that the Active Directory Users and Computers tool is open, and if not, open it.

8

2. Right-click the OU that you created in Hands-on Project 8-6, and click **Properties**.

3. Click the **Group Policy** tab.

4. Make sure that the group policy you created is selected in the Group Policy Object Links list.

5. Click **Properties**.

6. Make sure that the General tab is displayed, and click the tab if it is not displayed. How would you optimize performance when you have not set up any Computer Configuration settings? How would you optimize performance when you have not set up any User Configuration settings? Record your observations.

7. Click the **Security** tab.

8. Make sure that Authenticated Users is selected. What permissions are granted to this group?

9. Click **Domain Admins**. Make sure that neither the Allow or Deny boxes are checked for Apply Group Policy. Why is it desirable to avoid granting the Apply Group Policy permission to a group for which the group policy does not apply? What other permission should not be granted when the group policy does not apply to a particular group?

10. Click **Cancel**, and then click **Cancel** again.

11. Leave the Active Directory Users and Computers tool open for the next project.

Project 8-8

This project enables you to add the Winnt.adm administrative template for client computers to a group policy.

To add the Winnt.adm template:

1. Ensure that the Active Directory Users and Computers tool is open, and if not, open it.

2. Right-click the OU that you created in Hands-on Project 8-6, such as MJPSecure, and click **Properties**.

3. Click the **Group Policy** tab.

4. Select the group policy in the Group Policy Object Links box, such as MJPSecure Group Policy, and click **Edit**.

5. Under User Configuration in the tree, right-click **Administrative Templates**.

6. Click **Add/Remove Templates**.

7. What templates are already added? Record your observations.

8. Click **Add** in the Add/Remove Templates dialog box.

9. What templates are displayed? Record your observations.

10. Double-click **winnt.adm**. (Click **Yes**, if you see a confirmation box because the template is already installed.) For what clients does this template apply?

11. Click **Close**.

12. Close the Group Policy tool, and then click **OK** in the OU Properties dialog box.

13. Close the Active Directory Users and Computers tool.

CASE PROJECT

Aspen Consulting Project: Planning Groups and Group Policy

Anderson Elevators manufactures elevators for commercial use and is located in Chicago. Your organizational analysis shows that Anderson's board, management, and employees work in the following functional areas:

❑ The board of directors, who make decisions on a broad scale about the company's direction

❑ Marketing and sales, who develop sales programs and who have sales teams that work with builders all over the United States

❑ Accounting, which handles general ledger, accounts receivable, accounts payable, and payroll

❑ Human resources, which handles employee records, hiring practices, promotions, terminations, and other employee related issues

❑ Purchasing, which handles the acquisition of the materials that are used to build elevators

❑ Research and engineering, which designs the elevators and oversees how designs are brought into production

❑ Manufacturing, which makes the elevators

❑ Inventory, which stocks and tracks elevator parts

❑ Delivery, which operates a fleet of trucks that delivers elevator equipment and parts to customer locations

Also, your analysis of the management decision-making structure shows that it is very decentralized, using the project-based approach. Your business process analysis shows that Anderson has business cycles that reflect major construction times, which shows that there is highest demand for elevators between April and November. New models of elevators are introduced in March of every year.

8

You have been assigned to work with Anderson Elevators to help their IT department create security groups and group policy.

1. What recommendations do you have for planning the default domain policy?

2. The IT department has little experience with Windows 2000 Server and needs training about security groups. Explain the types of security groups in Windows 2000 Server and their purpose.

3. Develop a plan for creating security groups, and then develop an alternate plan so that you can present both to Anderson Elevators. Explain which plan you recommend most and why.

4. The employees who engage in research and engineering are in an OU called Engine, and the shared folders that they use are also in that OU. These employees have two urgent requests:

   ◻ To customize their desktops so that there are icons to run a computer-aided design software system, and an icon that accesses data in a research database

   ◻ To establish the strongest possible security for the Engine OU that enables their accounts and shared folders to remain absolutely secure

   What do you recommend to accomplish these requests?

5. Most of the engineers and designers have Windows 2000 Professional workstations, but there are a few who are using Windows 98 or Windows NT. What administrative template(s) should you use in the group policy for their Engine OU? Also, two of the engineers who use Windows 2000 Professional occasionally delete their connections to network printers. How can you prevent this from happening?

OPTIONAL CASE PROJECTS FOR TEAMS

Team Case One

Mark Arnez is curious about comparing the abilities of security groups in Windows 2000 Server to those in Windows NT Server. He asks you to gather together a couple of the consultants and to develop a chart that compares the types of groups and how they are used. Also, he asks you to include your opinions about why there are differences between groups in Windows 2000 Server and Windows NT Server.

Team Case Two

Mark has learned that there are several consultants who are not sure about the ways to effectively plan and deploy a default domain policy compared to deploying group policy objects for OUs. He asks you to form a group that can compare deploying a default domain policy to deploying group policy objects for OUs in a domain.

PLANNING ACTIVE DIRECTORY SECURITY AND COEXISTENCE

After reading this chapter and completing the exercises, you will be able to:

♦ Plan and implement Active Directory object security by using administrative security groups

♦ Plan and implement Active Directory object security for domains, sites, OUs, and group policy

♦ Plan and create group policy filters

♦ Plan for Active Directory coexistence with other directory services

Securing administrative access to Active Directory should be part of every Active Directory design. From the beginning, carefully plan how to implement Active Directory security so that there are no unexpected surprises or "back doors" that compromise security. Active Directory offers many ways to secure essential containers, such as domains and OUs. Along with planning for security, organizations often need to develop secure ways to translate and update data that is shared between Active Directory and other directory services or databases in an enterprise.

In this chapter, you will learn how to use the key administrative security groups in Active Directory. You also will learn how to use permissions to lock vital Active Directory containers so that their security matches the particular administrative goals of an organization. In the second half of the chapter, you will learn how to enable Active Directory to work alongside other directory services, such as Novell Directory Services (NDS) and bindery services.

ACTIVE DIRECTORY OBJECT SECURITY

When you plan an Active Directory structure, make security planning a top priority. There are two interrelated types of security planning: (1) deployment of administrative security groups, such as the Domain Admins and Enterprise Admins groups, and (2) configuring security for principal objects, such as for domains and OUs.

Deploying Administrative Security Groups

There are several default security groups available for controlling access to manage Active Directory objects (see Chapter 8 and try Hands-on Project 9-1). These groups are:

- *Administrators*: A built-in domain local group that has blanket access to the local computer and to the domain

- *DHCP Administrators*: A domain local group that can administer DHCP servers

- *DnsAdmins*: A domain local group that can administer DNS servers

- *DnsUpdateProxy*: A global group of network clients that can dynamically update DNS zones for their own clients. A DHCP server can be configured to update DNS zones for the clients to which it leases IP addresses

- *Domain Admins*: A global group of administrators who can manage the domain

- *Enterprise Admins*: A global (in mixed mode) or a universal (in native mode) group of administrators who can manage all domains in the forest

- *Group Policy Creator Owners*: A global group that can create and modify group policy in a domain

- *Schema Admins*: A global (in mixed mode) or a universal (in native mode) group of administrators who can manage the schema in the forest, including adding new schema objects

When you plan security for a domain, first determine which user accounts should have administrator privileges in addition to the default Administrator account, and make these accounts members of the Domain Admins security group. These accounts are normally those held by the server administrators for a specified domain, such as a main server administrator and her or his backup administrators. Your analysis of the IT organization (see Chapter 3) will help you determine the users who should belong to Domain Admins, such as members of the IT systems development or IT network units within the organization. In Jefferson Philately, for example, candidates for Domain Admins will likely be individuals who belong to the Applications and Systems Programming group, the Operations group, or particular individuals from both groups (in this case, "group" refers to the unit of people in the organization; refer to Figure 3-1). In any of the companies within York Industries, Domain Admins will likely be individuals from the Systems unit in the IT department (refer to Figure 3-4). After the user accounts to be added as Domain Admins are identified, the steps to implement administrative access are:

1. Make sure that the Administrator account is already a member of the Domain Admins group.

2. Add the appropriate user accounts to the Domain Admins group.

3. Make the Domain Admins group a member of the Administrators group (see Figure 9-1).

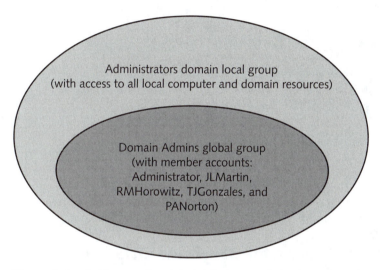

9

Figure 9-1   Setting up the Administrators and the Domain Admins groups

Designing Security Groups for an Enterprise

When you design security for a multiple-domain native mode enterprise, consider the membership for the Enterprise Admins universal group, which has authority to manage all domains in the forest. Membership in this group will be affected by your analysis of the IT organizational structure. In a centralized structure, the Enterprise Admins group may consist of only the server administrators at the headquarters office. For example, if the headquarters administrators are in the Domain Admins group in the root domain, then this group would be made a member of the Enterprise Admins group. In a more decentralized organization, such as York Industries, only certain accounts from each domain might have authority to make forest-wide changes. In this case, you would create special global groups in each domain containing the specified members, and then make each global group a member of the Enterprise Admins group. If there are not enough accounts to merit creating the global groups, then you would make the appropriate accounts members of the Enterprise Admins group and bypass creating the extra global groups. For example, consider York Industries, in which all members of the

Domain Admins group in the york.com domain are to have authority over all domains. Also, one member from each of the other domains—be.york.com, nantes.york.com, kanazawa.york.com, pampas.york.com, sudeten.york.com, and palisades.york.com—would be made a member of Enterprise Admins (see Figure 9-2).

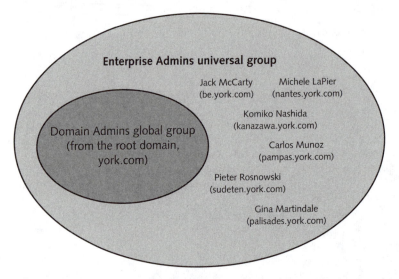

Figure 9-2   Managing forest-wide security at York Industries via the Enterprise Admins group

Designing Security Groups for DHCP and DNS Services

Management of the DHCP leasing and DNS resolution services is secured through the DnsAdmins and DHCP Administrators groups. Often the members of the DHCP Administrators and the DnsAdmins domain local groups will be the same or similar, depending on your analysis of the IT organization. DHCP administration and DNS administration are often performed by the same people because DHCP servers and DHCP clients can be configured in the DHCP services to automatically update DNS zones. However, in any company, it is important to have a unified DNS namespace design, which means that the DNS administrators are often centralized in one location or work in close cooperation.

In a relatively small organization, such as Jefferson Philately, the DHCP and DNS administrators may be the same as the domain administrators. In this situation, you will simply add the Domain Admins global group as a member of both the DHCP Administrators and DnsAdmins domain local groups, as in Figure 9-3. Try Hands-on Project 9-2 to practice configuring the membership of these groups.

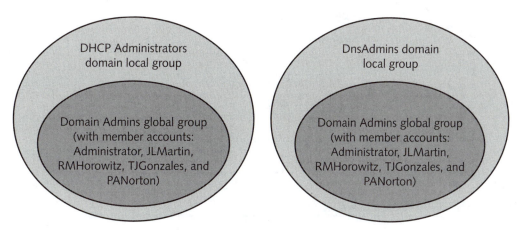

Figure 9-3 DHCP and DNS management security at Jefferson Philately

In larger and more complex organizations, such as York Industries, the DHCP and DNS administrators can also be those who perform domain administration. In this situation, you would:

1. Promote the DHCP Administrators group to be a universal group instead of a domain local group.

2. Promote the DnsAdmins group to be a universal group instead of a domain local group, as in Figure 9-4.

3. Make the Domain Admins global group in the root domain a member of the DHCP Administrators and DnsAdmins universal groups, if Domain Admins is not already a member of each group.

4. Make the selected domain administrators' user accounts from each domain members of the DHCP Administrators and DnsAdmins groups (see Figure 9-5).

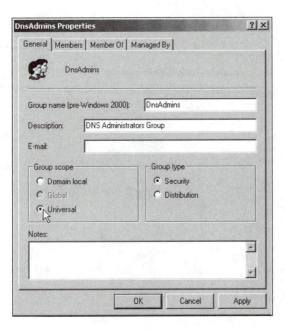

Figure 9-4   Promoting the DnsAdmins group from a domain local to a universal group

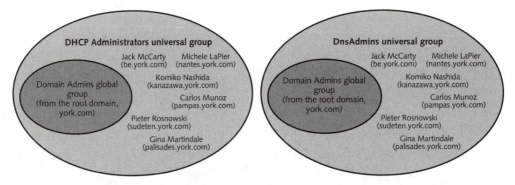

Figure 9-5   DHCP and DNS management security at York Industries

Interstate Security Bank has a relatively decentralized and federated security model (see Chapter 3). It can be considered federated because different departments have their own IT groups. The headquarters office and each regional office maintains its own DNS and DHCP servers. In this organization, there is a global group in each of the tree root and child domains: ISBDnsDHCP, IdahoDnsDHCP, MontDnsDHCP, OregDnsDHCP, WashDnsDHCP, and WyoDnsDHCP. Each global group consists of the DNS administrative members who have been selected for each domain in the DNS and namespace planning (see Chapters 6 and 7). Also, these global groups are members of the DHCP Administrators and DnsAdmins domain local groups in each domain, because these functions are managed independently per domain (see Figure 9-6).

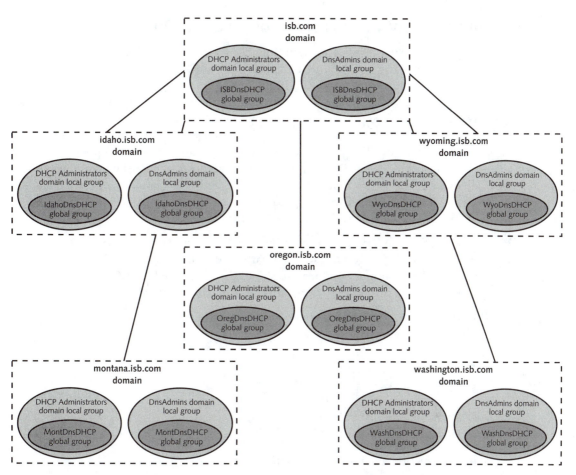

Figure 9-6   DHCP and DNS management security for Interstate Security Bank

In the Interstate Security Bank example, the global groups are all named differently, such as ISBDnsDHCP and IdahoDnsDHCP, so that if there is a future management philosophy change or reorganization, the groups can still be used. In a reorganization, two or more of these global groups could be used simultaneously as members of any domain local or universal groups that are created to manage DHCP and DNS. For example, if all of the DHCP and DNS functions were to be centralized in the isb.com domain under that domain's DHCP Administrators and DnsAdmins groups (which would be converted to universal groups), then some or all of the global groups could be members of the DHCP Administrators and DnsAdmins groups in the isb.com domain.

 When a DHCP server is configured to update IP addresses in DNS on behalf of clients, make that DHCP server a member of the DnsUpdateProxy global group. Also, add the DnsUpdateProxy global group to the DnsAdmins group, so that the DHCP server has authority to update DNS servers.

Designing Security Groups for Group Policy Objects

If the IT and company decision-making functions are centralized, creating group policy for an organization may be a task that is given only to the IT department, such as to the systems or user support units within IT. If the IT and company decision-making functions are decentralized, such as in the case of the federated IT structure used by Interstate Security Bank, then configuring group policy may be delegated. For example, consider Jefferson Philately, which has given group policy management responsibilities to the User Support unit within its IT department. The company wants the User Support unit to be able to customize the client desktops (which they support), such as by assigning the specialized customer service software to the customer service OU. In this case, the members of the Group Policy Creator Owners global group are those members in the User Support unit who are charged with managing group policy objects for OUs.

First Interstate Security Bank has a more decentralized approach, so it has a Group Policy Creator Owners global group in the headquarters root domain and in the regional office child domains. For example, your analysis shows that there are the following departments and business units in the headquarters office and in each regional office:

- Auditors
- Board
- Executive
- Loans department
- Marketing department
- Business department
- Information Technology department
- Investments department
- Customer Service department

Because Interstate Security Bank operates using a decentralized, federated IT organizational structure, there is a computer professional from each department who belongs to the Group Policy Creator Owners global group. Interstate Security Bank has decided to create OUs that reflect the department and unit structure, so each computer professional is given responsibility for creating the group policy for his or her department or business unit. For example, there is an OU called CS for the Customer Service department (refer to Figure 7-5) in each domain (one for each of the headquarters and regional offices), and there is a corresponding computer professional in each of the Customer Service departments who belongs to the Group Policy Creator Owners global group in each domain. Figure 9-7 illustrates the membership of the Group Policy Creator Owners global group for the idaho.isb.com domain, which consists of computer professionals from each department or business unit.

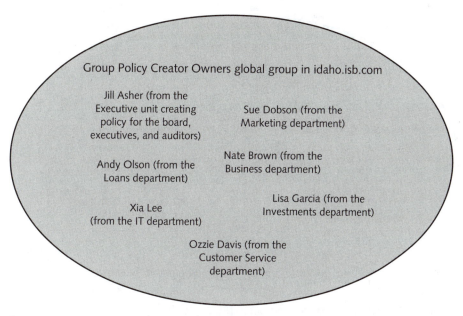

Figure 9-7   Group policy administrators for the idaho.isb.com domain

Designing Security Groups for Schema Security

A last security group that can be configured is the Schema Admins universal group in a native mode enterprise. The membership of this group should be carefully controlled, because members can make schema changes that will affect all trees and domains in a forest. Typically, organizations will restrict schema change authority to a handful of individuals in the IT department and usually to administrators of tree root domains.

The Schema Admins group is one example of the exception to the rule of using mainly global groups as members of universal groups. In many organizations, there are user accounts from the top-level domain that are administrators and members of the Schema Admins group. For example, the tree root domain for Interstate Security Bank is isb.com, and the Schema Admins group contains two user accounts of administrative users who are the designated schema administrators and who work in the IT department at the bank headquarters. Another approach is to make the Domain Admins group from each domain (or each tree root domain) in a forest a member of Schema Admins, and to be very selective about who belongs to the Domain Admins group. This is the practice at York Industries, which carefully limits the users who belong to the Domain Admins groups in each domain, as shown in Figure 9-8.

In a mixed mode domain, the Schema Admins group is a global group, but is automatically converted to a universal group when the domain is converted to native mode. If you are starting in a mixed mode domain, add the appropriate administrators accounts, the Domain Admins group, or both to the Schema Admins group.

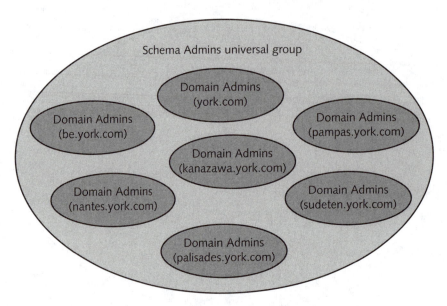

Figure 9-8   Schema Admins membership for York Industries

Regularly and carefully monitor the membership of the Schema Admins group and ensure that only authorized administrators belong to this group. This is critical because giving access to change the schema to an inexperienced administrator could result in serious or disastrous problems for all domains in a forest.

USING SECURITY FEATURES TO PROTECT KEY ACTIVE DIRECTORY OBJECTS

Domains, OUs, sites, and group policies can be protected by using the security measures that are associated with them. Several important security measures are:

- Delegating authority over a domain
- Setting permissions on domains, sites, and OUs
- Establishing permission security for group policy objects
- Establishing filters for group policy objects

Each of these security configuration options is discussed in the next sections.

Delegating Authority over a Domain

Just as you can delegate authority over an OU, you can also delegate authority over a domain. By default, authority for a domain is generally granted to the Administrators built-in domain local group, and the Domain Admins and Enterprise Admins groups are default members of the Administrators group. The Enterprise Admins group is also granted Full Control permission by default for a domain. On the basis of your analysis of the IT department in an organization, all tasks or particular tasks in domain administration can be delegated to other groups or to individual user accounts. For example, York Industries has an active set of network administrators who work in the IT departments at each geographical location. The York Industries' network administrators often adjust or reconfigure subnets to achieve increased network efficiency. The managers of the York Industries IT departments have decided that the network administrators should have access to manage site and subnet parameters in their own domains. Customized delegation of control of a domain enables the company (via a member of the Domain Admins group) to give them authority to manage the following domain objects:

- Site objects

- Site Link objects

- Site Link Bridge objects (two or more sites that are bridged, see Chapter 11)

- Site Settings objects

- Sites Container objects

- Subnet objects

- Subnets Container objects

In another example, Jefferson Philately has designated a group of server operators within their IT operations unit to create groups, publish shared folders, and publish shared printers in the domain. Jefferson can create a global operators group, make this group a member of the built-in domain local Server Operators group, and then delegate authority in the domain over group objects, shared folder objects, and printer objects.

When you delegate authority, there are two general options (see Figure 9-9):

- *Delegate the following common tasks*: This option contains two selections. One selection is to *Join a computer to the domain*, which is the ability to join a server or workstation to the domain. The other selection is to *Manage Group Policy links,* which is the ability to associate a group policy object with a particular domain object, such as an OU.

- *Create a custom task to delegate*: When you select this option, it leads to two more options, shown in Figure 9-10. The first option, *Delegate control of: This folder, existing objects in this folder, and creation of new objects in this folder*, enables you to delegate control of the entire domain, including all existing objects in the domain, and to delegate the ability to create new objects. The second option, *Delegate control of: Only the following objects in the folder*, enables you to select from a list of objects to delegate, which are presented in Table 9-1. Try Hands-on Project 9-3 to use the Delegation of Control Wizard for a domain.

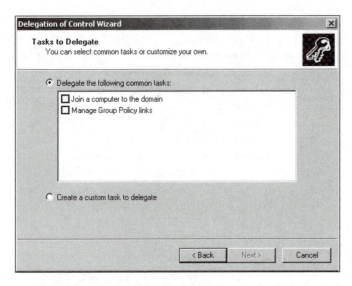

Figure 9-9   Basic options for delegating authority over a domain

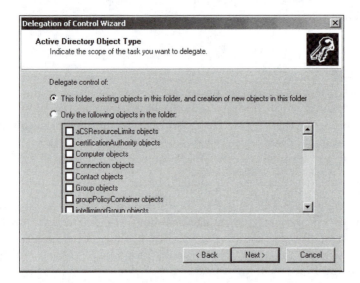

Figure 9-10   Customizing task delegation for a domain

Table 9-1   Domain Objects That Can Be Delegated

Domain Object	Description
aCSResourceLimits objects	Managing the Kerberos connection (client/server exchange) options, such as ticket expiration
certificationAuthority objects	Configuring computers (certificate authority objects) that have authority to issue certificates or public keys for security
Computer objects	Creating and managing computer accounts in the domain
Connection objects	Creating and managing connection objects, such as the replication connection between domain controllers and connections between different directory services, such as those between Active Directory and Novell Directory Services (NDS)
Contact objects	Creating and managing contacts (users or entities that can be contacted over a network or Internet connection), such as a user in an OU
Group objects	Creating and managing security and distribution groups in the domain
groupPolicyContainer objects	Creating and managing group policies
intellimirrorGroup objects	Creating and managing Intellimirror objects in group policy (that apply to Windows 2000 clients)
intellimirrorSCP objects	Creating and managing the use of Service Connection Point (SCP) objects for publishing and locating services via Intellimirror (such as providing site information in the configuration container)
MSMQ Configuration objects	Managing message queuing (communication services for applications) and routing services for Windows 95, Windows 98, Windows ME, Windows NT 4.0, and Windows 2000 computers
Organizational Unit objects	Creating and managing organizational units
Printer objects	Managing published printers
Shared Folder objects	Managing shared folders
Site objects	Creating and managing sites
Site Link objects	Creating and managing site link (WAN connection) objects
Site Link Bridge objects	Creating and managing site link bridges (bridges that combine sites for efficient replication, see Chapter 11)
Site Settings objects	Configuring site settings
Sites Container objects	Configuring containers within sites
Subnet objects	Creating and managing subnets
Subnets Container objects	Creating and managing subnets within subnets
Trusted Domain objects	Configuring domains as trusted and trusting (enabling a trusted domain to access the resources in a trusting domain)
User objects	Creating and managing user accounts

9

Depending on the software that you have installed, there can be additional domain objects that can be delegated. For example, if Microsoft Exchange Server 2000 is installed, then there are several objects that begin with MsExch, such as MsExchMailStorage objects.

Setting Permissions on Domains, Sites, and OUs

Always review the permissions associated with a domain, site, or OU after it is created, to ensure that the permissions correspond to the organization's planning documents and change management plans. As is true for a folder, you can set up permissions (see Figure 9-11), special permissions, auditing, and ownership for a domain (see Figure 9-12), OU, or site.

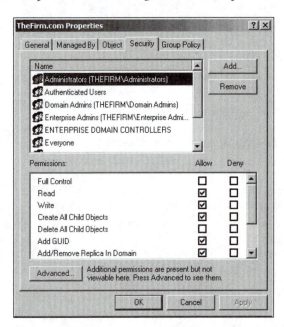

Figure 9-11   Permissions associated with a domain

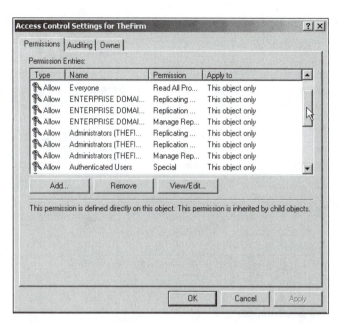

Figure 9-12   Special permissions, auditing, and ownership options for a domain

To configure permissions for a domain or an OU, open the Active Directory Users and Computers tool, click the View menu, and make sure that a check mark appears in front of Advanced Features. If there is no check mark, click Advanced Features to activate this option. Next, right-click the domain or OU in the tree, click Properties, click the Security tab, and set the permissions. Click the Advanced button to set special permissions, auditing, and ownership.

The Security tab for a domain's or OU's properties is not displayed unless the View menu Advanced Features option is selected in the Active Directory Users and Computers tool.

Table 9-2 shows the permissions for a domain, including the default groups that are set to *Allow* for those permissions.

Table 9-2 Domain Permissions and Default Settings

Domain Permission	Description	Default Settings with *Allow* Checked
Full Control	Complete authority over the domain	Enterprise Admins, System (Windows 2000 Server system)
Read	Authority to view the domain contents	Administrators, Authenticated Users, Domain Admins, Enterprise Admins, System
Write	Authority to write to the domain contents	Administrators, Domain Admins, Enterprise Admins, System
Create All Child Objects	Authority to create child objects, such as OUs, in a domain	Administrators, Domain Admins, Enterprise Admins, System
Delete All Child Objects	Authority to delete child objects, such as OUs	Enterprise Admins, System
Add GUID	Authority to assign a new globally unique identifier (GUID) to a domain object	Administrators, Domain Admins, Enterprise Admins, System
Add/Remove Replica In Domain	Authority to create or delete a replica of Active Directory on a domain controller	Administrators, Domain Admins, Enterprise Admins, System
Change PDC	Authority to use dcpromo to designate a domain controller, or to change a domain controller to a standalone PC	Administrators, Domain Admins, Enterprise Admins, System
Manage Replication Topology	Authority to set up the replication parameters for domain controllers and the site topology in the configuration container	Administrators, Domain Admins, Enterprise Admins, Enterprise Domain Controllers, System
Replicating Directory Changes	Authority to reconfigure Active Directory replication	Administrators, Domain Admins, Enterprise Admins, Enterprise Domain Controllers, System
Replication Synchronization	Authority to change Active Directory synchronization parameters and to perform manual synchronization	Administrators, Domain Admins, Enterprise Admins, Enterprise Domain Controllers, System

Dcpromo is the Windows 2000 Server tool that is used to promote a stand-alone Windows 2000 server to a domain controller, or that can be used to demote a domain controller to a standalone server. To use dcpromo click Start, click Run, enter *dcpromo* in the Open box, and click OK.

These permissions enable you to customize domain management security to the particular requirements of an organization. For example, consider a university that has a decentralized and federated IT structure in which there are three autonomous IT groups: one for administrative and business computing, one for academic computing, and one for the university's foundation (fund raising). Each of the three groups manages its own domain, but within the same forest. Your analysis of the three IT organizations shows that they do not trust one another and want total control over their own domains. In this situation, you would remove the Enterprise Admins group as a member of the Administrators built-in domain local group for each domain. Also, you would reconfigure the permissions on each domain so that *Allow* is checked only on the Read permission for the Enterprise Admins group. Or if the concern about autonomy is strong enough, you might check Deny for all of the domain permissions associated with the Enterprise Admins group. Try Hands-on Project 9-4 to practice setting domain permissions.

There are not as many permissions for an OU as there are for a domain, because there are not as many functions that can be performed related to an OU. Table 9-3 shows the permissions that can be configured for an OU and their default configurations.

Table 9-3   OU Permissions and Default Settings

OU Permission	Description	Default Setting with *Allow* Checked
Full Control	Complete authority to manage the OU	Domain Admins, Enterprise Admins, System
Read	Access authority to read the contents of the OU	Administrators, Authenticated Users, Domain Admins, Enterprise Admins, System
Write	Access to modify OU properties and change permissions	Administrators, Domain Admins, Enterprise Admins, System
Create All Child Objects	Authority to create objects within the OU, such as nesting an OU or creating an account	Administrators, Domain Admins, Enterprise Admins, System
Delete All Child Objects	Authority to delete objects within the OU, such as OUs or accounts	Domain Admins, Enterprise Admins, System

Some of the OU default permissions are checked in a shaded box, such as those for the Administrators group (see Figure 9-13). The shaded box means that these permissions are inherited from the parent object, such as from the domain or from an OU that is one level higher. Permissions are inherited when the *Allow inheritable permissions from parent to propagate to this object* box is checked (which is the default). To turn off inheritance, remove the check mark and then click the Remove button on the Security information dialog box.

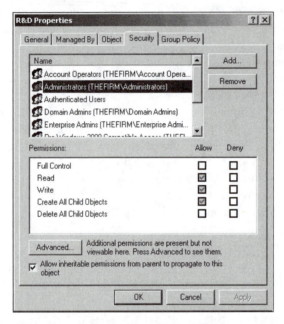

Figure 9-13   Inherited OU permissions

Permissions for a site are configured by using the Active Directory Sites and Services tool. To configure permissions for a site:

1. Click Start, point to Programs, point to Administrative Tools, and click Active Directory Sites and Services (or alternately open the Active Directory Sites and Services MMC snap-in).

2. Double-click Sites in the tree, if no child objects (sites) appear under it.

3. Right-click the site for which you want to configure security.

4. Click Properties.

5. Click the Security tab.

As Table 9-4 shows, the permissions for a site are similar to those for an OU, with the addition of the Open Connector Queue permission. Also, site permissions are, by default, inherited from their parent objects, such as from a domain. Site permission inheritance is turned off in the same way as it is for OU permissions inheritance.

Table 9-4   Site Permissions and Default Settings

Site Permission	Description	Default Settings with *Allow* Checked
Full Control	Complete authority to manage the site	Enterprise Admins, System
Read	Access authority to read the contents of the site	Authenticated Users, Domain Admins, Enterprise Admins, System
Write	Access authority to modify properties and change permissions	Domain Admins, Enterprise Admins, System
Create All Child Objects	Access authority to create child objects in a site	Domain Admins, Enterprise Admins, System
Delete All Child Objects	Access authority to delete child objects in a site	Enterprise Admins, System
Open Connector Queue	Access to manage how messages are exchanged with other computers, such as determining which server is closest to a client	Domain Admins, Enterprise Admins, System

9

Establishing Permission Security for Group Policy Objects

A site, domain, or OU can have a group policy object linked to it, and you can secure that group policy object by adjusting the group policy object's permissions. For example, York Industries prefers to have only its domain administrators manage the default domain group policy in each domain. At Interstate Security Bank, group policy objects that are associated with OUs are managed by computer professionals in specific departments. One way to set up group policy object security is through delegating authority, as discussed earlier in this chapter. Another way is to set the permissions associated with a group policy object. The general steps for setting group policy object permissions associated with a domain or OU are to (try Hands-on Project 9-5 to set the security on the default domain policy):

1. Open the Active Directory Users and Computers tool, right-click the domain or OU that you want to configure, click Properties, and open the Group Policy tab.

2. Select the group policy object and click the Properties button.

3. Access the Security tab.

4. Set up the group policy object's security.

5. Click OK in the group policy object's Properties dialog box, click OK in the domain or OU Properties dialog box, and exit the Active Directory Users and Computers tool.

The general steps for configuring the group policy object associated with a site are (try Hands-on Project 9-6):

1. Open the Active Directory Sites and Services tool, right-click the site that you want to configure, and click Properties.

2. Access the Group Policy tab and select the group policy object that you want to configure. Click the Properties button.

3. Access the Security tab.

4. Set up the group policy object's security.

5. Click OK in the group policy object's Properties dialog box, click OK in the site's Properties dialog box, and exit the Active Directory Sites and Services tool.

The permissions for a group policy are presented in Table 9-5.

Table 9-5   Group Policy Permissions and the Default Setup

Group Policy Permission	Description	Default Settings with *Allow* Checked
Full Control	Complete authority to manage the group policy object	(Not granted to any group by default)
Read	Access authority to read the group policy object	Authenticated Users, Domain Admins, Enterprise Admins, System
Write	Access authority to write to and modify the group policy object	Domain Admins, Enterprise Admins, System
Create All Child Objects	Access authority to add extensions	Domain Admins, Enterprise Admins, System
Delete All Child Objects	Access authority to delete extensions	Domain Admins, Enterprise Admins, System
Apply Group Policy	Access authority to apply the group policy object to a user account, computer, or members of a group	Authenticated Users

If management of group policy is distributed among different departments:

1. Plan to add the user accounts that manage group policy to the Group Policy Creator Owners global group.

2. Create a domain local group, such as Group Policy.

3. Add the Group Policy Creator Owners global group to the Group Policy domain local group. Give the Group Policy domain local group Full Control permissions or Read, Write, Create All Child Objects, and Delete All Child Objects permissions for the group policy object.

For instance, you would set these permissions in the earlier example of Jefferson Philately, in which the User Support unit in the IT department configures group policy. Another example of distributing group policy management would be Interstate Security Bank, in which management of group policy is delegated to individuals in different departments.

Establishing Filters for Group Policy

The security features of a group policy have an added benefit in that they enable management of whether a particular policy applies to a particular group. When you control the application of a group policy through the group policy object's permissions, this is known as creating a **group policy filter**.

Consider Interstate Security Bank, which wants to establish a group policy that manages the desktops of its tellers in the branch offices so that all of the combined computer and cash drawer systems have identical icons and program setups. To accomplish this they would give the domain local Tellers group both Read and Apply Group Policy permissions. Here are the general steps that Interstate Security Bank would follow to set up the filter:

1. Create a global group in the Tellers OU called GlobalTellers and make the local teller user accounts members of this group. Also make the computers used by the tellers members of this group.

2. Create a domain local group in the Tellers OU called Tellers and make GlobalTellers a member of this group.

3. Create a group policy object for the Tellers OU, to manage the desktop settings associated with the domain local Tellers group.

4. Edit the permissions of the Tellers group policy object so that the Authenticated Users group has neither the Allow nor the Deny boxes checked for the Read and Apply Group Policy permissions, as shown in Figure 9-14.

5. Add the Tellers domain local group to the list of groups for the group policy object's permission security and check the Allow boxes associated with the Read and Apply Group Policy permissions for the Tellers group (see Figure 9-15).

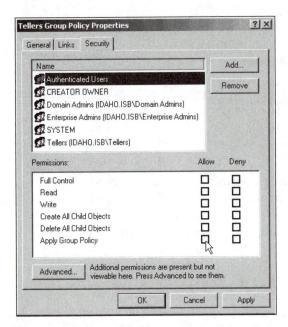

Figure 9-14   Removing permissions for Authenticated Users

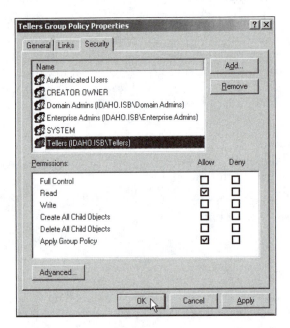

Figure 9-15   Adding permissions for Tellers

In this example, if you click Deny for the Read and Apply Group Policy permissions for the Authenticated Users group, then there would be a security conflict for the members of the Tellers group (and therefore also members of the GlobalTellers group), because the same user accounts and computers are part of Authenticated Users by default. Removing the checks for all of the Deny and Allow boxes in the Authenticated Users group means that the permissions apply to members of Authenticated Users *only if* they are also members of the Tellers group (which has GlobalTellers as a member).

In summary, the following rules apply to setting up a group policy filter:

- To apply a group policy object to a particular group, click Allow for the Read and for the Apply Group Policy permissions for that group.

- To ensure that a group policy does not apply to a particular group, click Deny for the Read and for the Apply Group Policy permissions for that group.

- When a user account belongs to two groups that are on a group policy object's security list, and neither Allow nor Deny is checked for permissions on one group, then permissions apply only to that account if they are checked in the other group. This feature is included to help prevent security conflicts.

Try Hands-on Project 9-7 to practice creating a group policy filter.

ACTIVE DIRECTORY CONNECTORS AND COEXISTENCE WITH OTHER DIRECTORY SERVICES

Part of planning Active Directory security and functionality is planning how to translate identity data between Active Directory and other database or directory services, such as Novell Directory Services (NDS). In an enterprise, identity data is stored in many ways and for many kinds of applications or server operating systems. **Identity data** is the data foundation of a network and consists of:

- User information

- Computer information

- Network information

- Application information

- E-mail client and server information

In a single enterprise, portions of the identity data are stored in many places. Some of it is stored in directory services, such as Active Directory and NDS. Other information, such as Lotus Notes or Microsoft Exchange Server (excluding version 2000) e-mail account data, is stored in a separate database. Network information is stored in specialized databases, such as the Management Information Base (MIB). Each of these storehouses of information uses a different format, which often means that the same information is entered multiple times, once for one directory service, once for another directory service, once for an e-mail service, and so on. The problem with having so many different data storehouses is that they require lots of repetitive data entry, and in a short time information is out of synchronization. For example, when a particular user leaves, his or her account may be removed from NDS, but not from Active Directory or Exchange Server. If a user is promoted, his or her access privileges in Active Directory may be updated immediately, but access privileges in NDS may not be updated for another week or two. When data from different storehouses is out of synchronization, there is inconvenience to the user and there are potential security risks to the organization.

Consider for example, a situation in which a user leaves to work for a competitive organization. His user account and access are terminated in Active Directory, but his account and access are inadvertently left active in NDS. This means that the user retains access to NetWare files, and sensitive company data can be compromised.

As discussed in Chapter 7, an initial planning step to enable different directory services to coexist is to focus on using software that implements basic standards, such as LDAP. Another planning step is to implement **brokering technologies**, which provide ways to reduce repetitive data entry by automating the sharing or synchronization of data among different data storehouses. One of the goals of brokering technologies is to ensure the accuracy of data as it is synchronized between storehouses, which also helps to guarantee user productivity and data security. Microsoft's approach to brokering technologies is to:

- Detect changes in basic Active Directory structures, such as when OUs are changed and accounts are moved because a company is reorganizing

- Develop automated methods to update all related data storehouses when changes are detected

- Eventually develop a **meta-directory** that surpasses Active Directory as a single, comprehensive storehouse of all identity data for all types of operating systems, networks, and applications

When you plan Active Directory, include in your planning the brokering technologies that exist currently and those that are being developed by Microsoft. Three brokering technologies are available as of this writing: Active Directory Service Interfaces (ADSIs), Active Directory Connector (ADC), and Microsoft Directory Synchronization Services (MSDSS). Also, three brokering technologies are under development by Microsoft and third-party vendors at this writing: directory consolidation, meta-directory, and LDAP Proxy interfaces.

Using Active Directory Service Interfaces

Using **Active Directory Service Interfaces (ADSIs)** is like adding a set of small locked doors into regions of Active Directory. Programmers can "unlock" those doors and access or update specific Active Directory data (with appropriate permissions) using ADSIs combined with special programs written to open the ADSI doorways. An ADSI is an interface that is constructed using the **Component Object Model (COM)**. COM consists of standards that enable a software object, such as a graphic, to be linked from one software component to another. ADSIs are extensible by creating programs using popular programming languages such as C, C++, Visual Basic, VBScript, and JavaScript. These programming languages can be used to write specialized programs that access an ADSI to accomplish a specific purpose, such as to rename all user accounts in an OU. Current systems that use ADSIs are Active Directory, NDS, BIND (see Chapter 7), LDAP, and Windows NT SAM. Through ADSIs, an organization can create programs or scripts to translate data between Active Directory and another directory service, such as NDS, and between Active Directory and an e-mail service, such as Microsoft Exchange.

As an example to help you understand an ADSI, begin by considering it as a doorway that can be opened by a key that is programmed into a specialized C++ application. Besides containing lines of code that can open the ADSI doorway, the C++ program also contains coding that is intended to export user accounts from NDS. After the C++ program extracts user account data from NDS, it opens a different ADSI door into Active Directory, and uses that ADSI door to import the NDS account data into a particular Active Directory OU (see Figure 9-16).

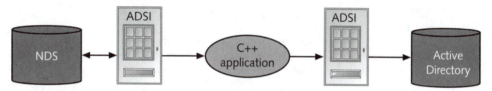

Figure 9-16 Using ADSIs

Using Active Directory Connectors

More generally called a **synchronization connector**, an **Active Directory connector (ADC)** is used to automatically update one database or directory service when the information in another has changed. Its primary function is to ensure that both data storehouses contain the same information about an object, so that if the information about an object changes in one directory service, the same information is updated in an identical way in the other directory service. A synchronization connector is usually written to synchronize two specific databases, e-mail services, or directory services. For example, there are different ADCs that can be used to synchronize Active Directory with Microsoft Exchange Server, one for Microsoft Exchange Server version 5.0 and another one for version 5.5 and higher. Both ADCs synchronize mailboxes, mail recipients, and distribution lists with data for user accounts, contacts, and groups. Figure 9-17 illustrates how an ADC works.

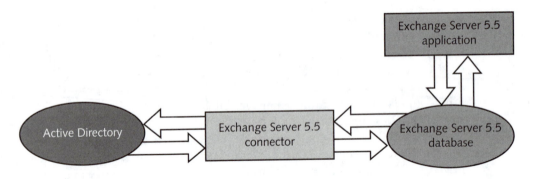

Figure 9-17   Using an ADC

The advantage of ADCs is that Microsoft has already developed some for applications such as Microsoft Exchange Server, and will be developing more. Another advantage is that an ADC works well when the synchronization between two data storehouses is a simple one-to-one relationship. An ADC is not efficient when it is necessary to apply more complex rules in the data translation, such as business or security rules. An example of a security rule is that Active Directory may be set up to require a 12-character password on user accounts, whereas NDS may require only a 7-character password for accounts. Try Hands-on Project 9-8 to install the Microsoft Exchange 5.5 ADC and the ADC Manager.

 The setup files for the Microsoft Exchange ADC are located on the Windows 2000 Server (or Advanced Server or Datacenter) CD-ROM in the folder \Valueadd\Msft\Mgmt\Adc.

Using Microsoft Directory Synchronization Services

Microsoft Directory Synchronization Services (MSDSS) is a set of connector services that is used to synchronize Active Directory data with data in either NDS (for NetWare version 4 and higher) or binderies in NetWare 3.x (see Figure 9-18). The synchronization is one-way from the NetWare 3.x binderies to Active Directory, or two-way between Active Directory and NDS. MSDSS is intended for two purposes: (1) to enable the coexistence of Active Directory and NetWare NDS or binderies on the same network, or (2) to enable migration from NetWare to Windows 2000 Server. MSDSS is a tool from Microsoft that is included in the NetWare interoperability and migration tools, which are purchased separately from Microsoft in the Services for NetWare (SFNW) package. SFNW includes MSDSS, Directory Service Manager for NetWare, the File Migration Utility, and File and Print Services for NetWare (FPNW). For directory services' coexistence, the primary tools you will use from SFNW are MSDSS, Directory Service Manager for NetWare, and FPNW. The Directory Service Manager for NetWare enables you to administer NetWare binderies and NDS from a Windows 2000 domain. FPNW enables Windows 2000 server clients to access NetWare files and printers configured through NetWare.

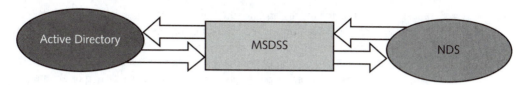

Figure 9-18   Using MSDSS for two-way synchronization

The general steps involved in setting up MSDSS for synchronization between Active Directory and NDS or NetWare 3.x binderies are:

1. Set up Active Directory in Windows 2000 Server (or Advanced Server or Datacenter).

2. Install the NetWare Client 32 redirector in Windows 2000 Server to enable NetWare Core Protocol over IP transmissions.

3. Make sure that you have the necessary rights and permissions to modify the Active Directory schema and the NDS schema.

4. Install and set up MSDSS.

5. Install the Active Directory schema extension for two-way directory synchronization, which is a selection offered when you set up MSDSS.

 The schema extension can be performed at the time you set up MSDSS or via the Command Prompt command: msiexec /a dirsync.msi SCHEMAUPDATE = 1.

6. Install the NDS schema extensions for one- or two-way synchronization (depending on the version of NetWare that is in use), which is a selection offered when you set up MSDSS.

7. Set the appropriate MSDSS synchronization option: create initial synchronization sessions, perform reverse synchronization, one-way synchronization, two-way synchronization, or migration.

 In your planning for using MSDSS, recognize that two-way synchronization results in more network traffic than one-way synchronization.

MSDSS enables you to build filters for the types of objects to synchronize, such as user accounts, groups, and OUs. The synchronization interval is every five minutes, but can be adjusted to meet the needs of an organization. Not all attributes can be mapped for synchronization through MSDSS, but essential attributes can be mapped, such as the members of groups or passwords for accounts.

In terms of saving money on computer support in an organization, synchronizing passwords ranks high on the list. Computer support personnel in organizations that support two or more server systems, such as NetWare and Windows 2000, spend a significant portion of their time resetting passwords for users who have forgotten them or need help resetting a password on one system or another.

Developing a Synchronization Plan

When you plan to set up an ADSI, ADC, or MSDSS, develop an implementation plan, because you should decide in advance on the details of how to synchronize the database of a directory service or application to Active Directory. For example, not every object in Exchange Server 5.5 should be synchronized in Active Directory, or vice versa. Here are the planning steps that you should follow:

- Create an AD design team that includes members of the unit within the organization who manage an application or directory services, such as Exchange Server or NDS. Also, make sure that the team includes an Active Directory schema administrator.

- Determine how the data in the application or directory service is the same as and how it differs from Active Directory data. This analysis will help you determine how objects need to be translated from one side to the other. An example of how objects differ is that the Exchange Server 5.5 object *Mailbox* is translated into the Active Directory object *Mailbox-enabled user*. In another example, the objects may be the same, such as the Exchange Server 5.5 object *Public Folder*, which translates into the Active Directory object *Public Folder*.

- Determine the management strategy of objects, such as which objects to manage from Active Directory and which objects to manage from the application database or directory service that you are synchronizing with Active Directory. Create a goal to manage as much as possible from Active Directory.

- Determine which objects to include in the synchronization. For example, in Active Directory include specific object classes and attributes.

- Determine what portions of the Active Directory schema must be modified and who will modify them. Link this determination to your schema design and change management plan.

- Determine how to synchronize and how often. For example, if your organization has NetWare servers using NDS and Windows 2000 servers, then you will typically use two-way synchronization and schedule the synchronization to occur each time there is an change in the NDS or Active Directory data.

- Determine how to deploy the servers you are synchronizing in terms of network traffic and connection reliability. For example, if you are synchronizing Microsoft Exchange Server 5.5 with Active Directory, consider placing the Exchange server on the same subnet as a DC or the bridgehead DC (in a multilocation network) for fast synchronization and to minimize network traffic.

- Test to ensure that the synchronization is working properly before you make it live on the network.

- Before you go live, back up Active Directory and the database or directory service with which it is synchronizing so that you can restore either side in case there is a problem.

- Create a regular backup strategy to guard against possible problems during synchronization, such as unexpected network outages in the middle of a synchronization.

Using Directory Consolidation

Directory consolidation is the process of developing new applications or new versions of applications so that they store information in Active Directory instead of in a separate database. This is an approach to coexistence that is currently underway at Microsoft and at third-party vendors. Microsoft Exchange 2000 is one example of directory consolidation, because it does not maintain its own database of information, but instead uses Active Directory. Directory consolidation has many advantages, such as:

- Creating one place from which to manage directory service and application data

- Eliminating the need to synchronize data and to translate data to match different business rules

- Eliminating network traffic from synchronization across sites and site links

 When you are planning the deployment of an application, check to determine if that application is compatible with Active Directory. Vendors can now obtain from Microsoft an Active Directory certification for their applications. Also, when you prepare a request for proposal (RFP) or request for information (RFI) to be sent to vendors, include compatibility with Active Directory as one of the specifications for operating systems and applications.

Using a Meta-Directory

A meta-directory is a single directory or data storehouse that holds data from all kinds of software applications, operating systems, and directory services. Using a meta-directory, Windows 2000, NetWare, UNIX, e-mail applications, human resources applications, and other data-generating applications use a pool of common directory services objects and store data in one large database engine (see Figure 9-19). The features built into the database engine might include:

- Storing data in one data storehouse, which means that data is entered one time, yielding stronger data integrity than is possible even through synchronization connectors

- A single place from which to obtain data for queries and for creating reports

- Centralized management of data for lower TCO

- Better network performance because there is controlled traffic from data replication, instead of traffic from both data replication and data synchronization

- Consistency in applying business rules so that all data equally conforms to business and security requirements

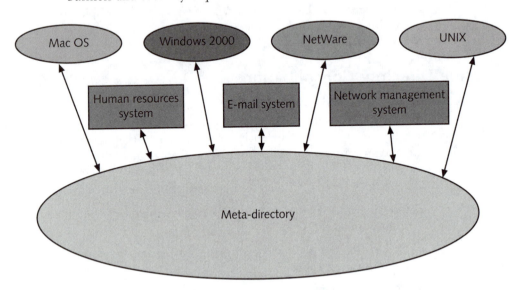

Figure 9-19   Using a meta-directory

When you plan directory service coexistence, consider that Microsoft is working to develop a meta-directory structure using a *hub-and-spoke meta-directory architecture*. The hub is a central set of elements that includes Active Directory, Microsoft Metadirectory Services (MMS), and a Meta-Data database. The spokes consist of all directory services, network operating systems, and applications that will contribute data to the hub elements.

In Microsoft's design approach, Windows 2000 applications will use directory consolidation to store data in Active Directory. The MMS will act as an intermediary between all data storehouses—Active Directory, non-Active-Directory-compliant applications, and other directory services—and the Meta-Data database (see Figure 9-20). For example, when a new OU is created in Active Directory, the MMS will automatically update the Meta-Data database. Or, if a new account is created in NDS, MMS will update the Meta-Data database. The Meta-Data database will be the central data storehouse from which all directory services and databases are updated. Also, all queries for information will be made to the Meta-Data database, instead of requiring a search of all directory service databases. This implementation recognizes that it will take some time for vendors to standardize on a single meta-directory structure. In the meantime, Microsoft-based networks can use this modified meta-directory approach to simplify directory service coexistence.

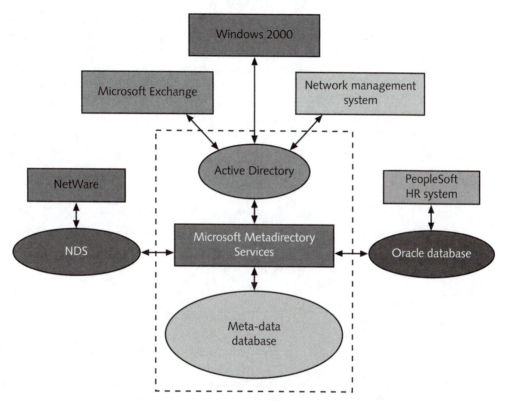

Figure 9-20   Using the hub-and-spoke meta-directory architecture

 Microsoft has purchased the Zoomit Corporation, which offers a rudimentary meta-directory technology. At this writing, you can obtain the Zoomit meta-directory engine, and assistance in setting it up (which is a complex process) through the Microsoft Consultant Services.

Using LDAP Proxy Interfaces

An alternative to using a meta-directory is to implement an LDAP proxy interface. An **LDAP proxy interface** is an interface that uses LDAP standards to access and update data in multiple LDAP-compatible data storehouses. An LDAP proxy interface can connect to any of the directory services or databases for which it is designed. When there is a query for information, such as about a user account, the LDAP proxy interface connects to any or all of its data storehouses. It then takes information about the account from two different directory services and an e-mail database, for example, and combines the information so that it appears to be from one source.

Some third-party vendors are developing LDAP proxy interfaces for Active Directory, NDS, and other directory services. When you are planning for directory service coexistence, it is important to recognize that there are some significant advantages and disadvantages to LDAP proxy interfaces. The most important advantage is that an LDAP proxy interface can simultaneously work with multiple directory services and databases. A disadvantage is that because it connects to multiple databases in real time, the LDAP proxy interface can create significant network traffic, particularly over site links. The traffic affects not only other applications, but it also can slow the response of the LDAP proxy interface. Another disadvantage is that LDAP interfaces typically use administrator accounts to access directory services and databases, which increases the security risks. Finally, LDAP interfaces sometimes do not work with many of the applications that are used to update directory services. This means that there are directory service updates that the LDAP proxy interface does not synchronize to all other directory services, because it is unaware of the updates.

 At this writing Microsoft is assisting LDAP proxy vendors with compliance with Active Directory services, but does not recognize this direction to be as promising as developing meta-directory solutions.

CHAPTER SUMMARY

- ❏ There are many default security groups included in Active Directory to help you control who can administer which resources. Plan how to use the administrative security groups so that you match the correct people with the intended access to the intended Active Directory resources. Never assume that the default composition of administrative security groups is adequate for your organization's security needs. Plan to manage who can administer Active Directory resources as carefully as you manage who can use those resources.

- ❏ There are many ways to delegate authority and to set permissions on Active Directory elements, such as domains, OUs, sites, and group policy objects. Create a plan for using delegation and permissions that matches the way your organization does business. For example, you can use permission access to govern which administrative security groups can manage a domain and which cannot, so that you enforce the particular IT administrative decision structure of your organization.

- ❏ Group policy filters can be important in your planning to fine-tune the way in which a group policy object is used. For instance, you can create an OU, link a group policy object to the OU, and then apply that group policy object only to a specific group of users rather than to all members of the OU or domain.

- ❏ Many complex enterprise networks use multiple directory services and databases. There are several emerging solutions that you can use in your planning to enable the coexistence and synchronization of different directory services and databases. Some of the tools that are already available include Active Directory Service Interfaces and Active Directory connectors. Other tools are in development, such as the use of meta-directories. In your planning, consider the current and long-range solutions for coexistence, because what you choose to use now will affect what you can implement later as brokering technologies mature.

In the next chapter, you will learn how to place global catalog servers and operations masters in design topologies for small to large networks.

KEY TERMS

Active Directory connector (ADC) — A synchronization connector designed for Active Directory; an interface that is used to automatically update or synchronize data in Active Directory with the data in another database or directory service. ADC is a brokering technology for Active Directory.

Active Directory Service Interface (ADSI) — An interface between a software application and a directory service, such as Active Directory, which enables data to be accessed, modified, imported, and exported. Programs written in programming languages such as C++ and Visual Basic can be used with an ADSI and use that ADSI to interface with a directory service. ADSI is an example of a brokering technology.

brokering technology — A technology, such as a synchronization connector, that automates the sharing and synchronization of data between applications, databases, and directory services.

Component Object Model (COM) — Standards that enable a software object, such as a graphic, to be linked from one software component to another one.

dcpromo — A Windows 2000 Server tool that is used to promote a standalone Windows 2000 server (no domain management) to a domain controller, or that can be used to demote a domain controller to a standalone server.

directory consolidation — Developing new applications so that they store information in Active Directory instead of in a separate database.

group policy filter — A set of permissions on the ACL of a group policy object (GPO) that controls to whom the group policy object applies.

identity data — Important data cumulatively stored in server and network databases, such as information about users, computers, the network, software applications, e-mail clients, and e-mail servers.

LDAP proxy interface — A brokering interface that uses LDAP standards to access and update data in multiple LDAP-compatible data storehouses.

meta-directory — A comprehensive storehouse of all identity data for all types of operating systems, networks, databases, applications, and e-mail services. A meta-directory is a very sophisticated brokering technology.

Microsoft Directory Synchronization Services (MSDSS) — A set of connector services used to synchronize Active Directory data with data in either NDS (for NetWare 4 and higher) or binderies in NetWare 3.x.

synchronization connector — An interface between two directory services, two databases, or a directory service and a database that updates data in one when data in the other is added or changed. See Active Directory connector (ADC).

9

REVIEW QUESTIONS

Answer questions 1–9 using this case information:

Weiss Electronics manufactures speakers for stereo systems. The company has one plant with an adjoining business building. It has two domains: weisseletronics.com and specialty.weisseletronics.com. The management style for weisselectronics is very centralized, particularly in the IT department.

1. Weiss Electronics has five individuals who share responsibility for managing both domains. Which of the following security groups is the best choice for housing the accounts of these five people?

    a. Administrators

    b. Domain Admins

    c. DAdmins

    d. Authenticated Users

    e. none of the above

2. Weiss Electronics uses NetWare 3.1 as well as Windows 2000 Server. They are planning to broker data between the NetWare bindery and Active Directory. Which of the following is true?

    a. They can use an existing ADC to carry over business and security rules from the NetWare bindery.

    b. They must use the NetBEUI protocol for data synchronization.

    c. They can use Microsoft Directory Synchronization Services (MSDSS), synchronizing data one way.

    d. They can use Microsoft's BIND proxy service.

    e. all of the above

    f. only a and b

    g. only a and c

    h. only a, c, and d

3. The domain administrators want to set permissions on the domain to ensure its security. Which of the following are permissions that they can set on the two domains?

    a. Full Control

    b. Write

    c. Manage Replication Topology

    d. Add GUID

    e. all of the above

    f. only a and b

g. only a and c

h. only a, b, and c

4. The speaker cabinet workers all need to have a very specialized desktop setup on their workstations in the manufacturing area. Which of the following steps should the IT department take to make sure that this group, and only this group, has the specialized setup?

   a. Create a new Windows 2000 server that is only used by this group.

   b. Create a new domain for the cabinet workers.

   c. Create an OU for the cabinet workers and link a group policy object to it.

   d. Create a group policy filter.

   e. all of the above

   f. only a and b

   g. only c and d

   h. only b, c, and d

5. Weiss Electronics wants to set up a DHCP server to enable automatic updates of DNS. Which of the following groups should have that DHCP server as a member?

   a. Domain Admins

   b. Administrators

   c. DnsUpdateProxy

   d. Enterprise Admins

   e. all of the above

   f. none of the above

   g. only a and d

6. Weiss Electronics is doing some long-range planning for brokering their NetWare and Windows 2000 Server identity data. Which of the following should they plan for in the future?

   a. LDAP proxy interfaces

   b. directory consolidation

   c. meta–directory services

   d. directory services filters

   e. only a and b

   f. only b and c

   g. only a, b, and c

9

7. Weiss has selected two schema administrators. To which of the following groups should they belong in order to make schema changes?

   a. Schema Admins

   b. Group Policy Creator Owners

   c. DnsAdmins

   d. DHCP Administrators

   e. all of the above

   f. only a and b

   g. only b and c

8. The IT department at Weiss Electronics has hired a computer professional to manage the published printers in the weisselectronics.com domain. How can they give the computer professional authority to set up and publish the printers?

   a. The computer professional must be given Administrator privileges in that domain.

   b. The computer professional must be a member of the Enterprise Admins group.

   c. The computer professional should be given permissions to set up public printers from her or his own workstation, and manage them from that workstation instead of through a server.

   d. The computer professional should be delegated authority in that domain over printer objects.

   e. none of the above

9. Weiss Electronics has set up two sites. What tool(s) can they use to set the permissions on those sites?

   a. Group Policy tool

   b. Active Directory Sites and Services tool

   c. Active Directory Users and Computers tool

   d. System icon in the Control Panel

   e. either a or b

   f. either c and d

Answer questions 10–19 using this case information:

Gordon Community College is planning to have four domains: gordoncc.edu, admin.gordoncc.edu, students.gordoncc.edu, and athletics.gordoncc.edu. The college has over 7000 students, 1500 faculty (full- and part-time), and 800 staff members.

10. Currently, all of the personal user accounts of the domain administrators for each domain are members of the Enterprise Admins group. However, the department heads at the college want only the domain administrators in the gordoncc.com

domain to have management authority over the resources in all domains—leaving the other domain administrators to have authority over only their own domains. What should be done to accomplish this?

a. Remove all personal user accounts from the Enterprise Admins group.

b. Place the personal user accounts of the gordoncc.com domain administrators in the Domain Admins group for the gordoncc.com domain, and make the Domain Admins group a member of Enterprise Admins.

c. Delete the Administrators groups in each domain.

d. Disable domain delegation in each domain.

e. all of the above

f. only a and b

g. only a and c

h. only a, c, and d

11. The college is planning to have a customized desktop setup that is the same for each student computer lab. Which of the following permissions should be set to *Allow* for all lab computers or a group containing all lab computers on the group policy object used for that lab?

a. Full Control

b. Write

c. Read

d. Apply Group Policy

e. all of the above

f. only a and d

g. only b and c

h. only c and d

12. The college has human resources databases, e-mail systems, NetWare 5.0 servers, and Windows 2000 Server systems. Which of the following brokering technologies should they explore to broker the data in these systems?

a. Active Directory connectors

b. directory consolidation in new or upgraded applications

c. Active Directory Service Interfaces

d. all of the above

e. only a and b

f. only b and c

9

13. The administrators for the athletics.gordoncc.edu domain are unsure about the term *identity data*. Which of the following are examples of identity data?

    a. computer information

    b. user information

    c. network information

    d. application information

    e. all of the above

    f. only a and b

    g. only a, b, and d

    h. only b and d

14. The domain administrators in the admin.gordoncc.edu domain want to be absolutely certain that only the members of the Cashiers OU can access the group policy for that OU. They have already set up a global group, called GlobalCashiers, containing the cashier's user accounts and a domain local group, called Cashiers, that has the GlobalCashiers group as a member. What should they do next?

    a. Give the Cashiers group Full Control permissions for the Cashiers OU.

    b. Give the Cashiers group Read and Apply Group Policy Allow permissions for the group policy.

    c. Remove the Read and Apply Group Policy Allow permissions from the Authenticated Users group.

    d. Delete the Authenticated Users group from the list of groups with permissions to the OU.

    e. all of the above

    f. only a and b

    g. only b and c

    h. only a, c, and d

15. The college is migrating everyone from Pegasus Mail to Microsoft Exchange Server 2000. In terms of Active Directory integration, Exchange Server 2000 has an advantage over Pegasus Mail because:

    a. There is an Active Directory connector for Exchange Server 2000.

    b. Exchange Server 2000 already uses directory consolidation with Active Directory.

    c. The LDAP proxy service for Exchange Server 2000 is faster than the same service for Pegasus Mail.

    d. Windows 2000 Server already comes with Exchange Server 2000 built in.

16. The college is setting up MSDSS synchronization between Active Directory and NDS. What do they need to install on the Windows 2000 servers that will participate in the synchronization?

    a. Client 32

    b. SMTP

    c. IPv6

    d. proxy server

    e. all of the above

    f. only a and b

    g. only b and c

    h. only a, b, and d

17. The college is planning to nest OUs. What should they take into account when they do this?

    a. OUs can only be nested five levels deep.

    b. A child OU that is nested under a parent OU by default inherits the permissions of the parent OU.

    c. Members of the Authenticated Users group do not by default have permissions to access an OU.

    d. Only members of the Server Admins group have, by default, permissions to manage an OU.

    e. only a and b

    f. only c and d

    g. only a, b, and d

18. The college is researching Microsoft's approach to creating a meta-directory. Which of the following are components of Microsoft's approach?

    a. using the NDS database structure for all data

    b. using multiple LDAP proxy services

    c. using four principal bindery files for operating system data

    d. using Excel spreadsheets for data translations

    e. all of the above

    f. none of the above

    g. only a and b

    h. only c and d

9

19. The User Support unit in the college needs the ability to manage the group policy object used for the computer labs. Which of the following is the best way to give them authority to manage the group policy object?

    a. Make them members of the Group Policy Creator Owners group, join that group to a GP domain local group, and give the GP group Full Control of the group policy object.

    b. Make them members of the Domain Admins group.

    c. Make them members of the Server Admins group.

    d. Delegate control of the default domain group policy to the members of the User Support unit.

    e. None of the above is possible in Active Directory.

Answer questions 20–25 using this case information:

McGreagor Limited is an international company that manufactures glassware in Scotland, Ireland, England, Germany, and Austria. The company employs 4800 people in all five countries. However, it has consolidated all operations under one domain, mcgreagorltd.com. Each country location is represented in the domain by one OU per country, and there are OUs nested in each parent OU. Also, the domain is divided into five sites.

20. After creating the sites, how should McGreagor Limited protect each one?

    a. Establish an OU under each site.

    b. Allow only one subnet per site.

    c. Examine and configure the permissions associated with each site.

    d. Synchronize each site by using Active Directory connectors.

    e. all of the above

    f. only a and b

    g. only a and c

    h. only a, b, and c

21. McGreagor Limited is using Exchange Server 5.5. What tool can they use to synchronize its data with Active Directory?

    a. Directory Replication Services

    b. the e-mail API

    c. an Active Directory connector

    d. No tool is necessary because Exchange Server 5.5 data is automatically integrated with Active Directory data.

    e. none of the above

22. McGreagor Limited is using NDS, UNIX, human resources applications, and other databases. Which of the following promises to offer the ability to translate business rules when synchronizing the data from these sources with Active Directory?

    a. global synchronization connectors

    b. meta-directory services

    c. LDAP synchronization connectors

    d. There is no technology that promises to translate business rules.

23. McGreagor Limited is using two specialized applications, and the company has an immediate need to synchronize key data in the databases of those applications with Active Directory data. What can they use to do this?

    a. Microsoft has many existing Active Directory connectors that McGreagor Limited can adapt for the data from these two applications.

    b. Most applications, including these two, are likely to come with the ability to synchronize data with Active Directory.

    c. The company can use Active Directory Service Interfaces (ADSIs) along with a programming language, such as Visual Basic, to create its own synchronization tools.

    d. If the software application vendor does not already use directory consolidation, then McGreagor Limited is out of luck in terms of synchronization.

24. After the mcgreagorltd.com domain is set up, which of the following permissions does Domain Admins have by default?

    a. Write

    b. Create All Child Objects

    c. Delete All Child Objects

    d. Change PDC

    e. all of the above

    f. only a and b

    g. only b and d

    h. only a, b, and d

9

25. McGreagor Limited has decided to create a special group of site administrators. Which of the following are site management responsibilities that can be delegated to this group?

    a. Site Link objects

    b. Site Settings objects

    c. Subnet objects

    d. Sites Container objects

    e. all of the above

    f. only a and c

    g. only a and d

    h. only a, b, and d

HANDS-ON PROJECTS

Project 9-1

In this project, you examine the location of the key administrative security groups.

To view the administrative security groups:

1. Click **Start**, point to **Programs**, point to **Administrative Tools**, and click **Active Directory Users and Computers**.

2. Double-click **Users** in the tree, if the folder is not already open.

3. Scroll to find the Domain Admins group in the right-hand pane.

4. Double-click **Domain Admins**. What is the group scope? Can you change the group scope? Record your observations in your lab journal or in a word-processed document.

5. Click the **Members** tab. What groups or accounts are members of Domain Admins? How can you add members to this group, and would you add user accounts or other groups as members? Record your findings.

6. Click the **Member Of** tab. For what groups is Domain Admins a member?

7. Click **Cancel**.

8. Double-click **Schema Admins**. What is the group scope? How would you determine the membership of this group? How would you determine the groups to which Schema Admins belongs? Click **Cancel**.

9. What other important administrative groups are listed in the right-hand pane of the console? Record your observations.

10. How can you locate the Administrators group and determine its membership? Record your observations.

11. Leave the Active Directory Users and Computers tool open for the next hands-on project.

Project 9-2

In this project, you make the Domain Admins group a member of the DHCP Administrators and DnsAdmins groups (DHCP and DNS must be installed already).

To configure the Domain Admins, DHCP Administrators, and DnsAdmins groups:

1. Make sure that the Active Directory Users and Computers tool is open, and if it is not, open it.
2. Double-click **Users** in the tree, if the folder is not already open.
3. Double-click **Domain Admins**.
4. Click the **Member Of** tab.
5. Click the **Add** button.
6. What are some examples of groups that Domain Admins can join? Record your observations.
7. Double-click **DHCP Administrators**. What happens next after you double-click it?
8. Double-click **DnsAdmins**.
9. Click **OK**.
10. How can you verify that Domain Admins is now a member of DHCP Administrators and DnsAdmins?
11. Click **OK**.
12. Leave the Active Directory Users and Computers tool open for the next project.

Project 9-3

This project enables you to delegate authority to create and manage OUs and groups in a domain to the Server Operators built-in domain local group.

To delegate authority in a domain for managing OUs and groups:

1. Open the Active Directory Users and Computers tool, if it is not already open.
2. Right-click the domain in the tree for which you want to delegate authority, such as TheFirm.com.
3. Click **Delegate Control**. What happens right after you click this option? Record your observations.
4. Click **Next**.
5. Click the **Add** button.
6. Double-click **Server Operators**.

7. Click **OK**, and then click **Next**.

8. What options are shown on the Tasks to Delegate dialog box?

9. Click **Create a custom task to delegate** and click **Next**.

10. What options are shown in the Active Directory Object Type dialog box? How would you grant blanket authority over the domain management to the Server Operators group?

11. Click **Only the following objects in the folder**. Use the scroll bar to examine the objects that you can select.

12. Click the box for **Group objects**.

13. Click the box for **Organizational Unit objects**.

14. Click **Next**.

15. Click the **General** box, if it is not already selected (see Figure 9-21).

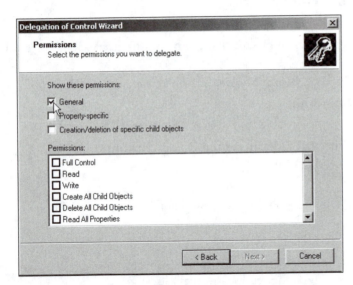

Figure 9-21   Setting permissions

16. Click **Full Control**. What permissions are now checked?

17. Click **Next**.

18. Use the scroll bar to review the parameters that you have selected. What information is provided that enables you to review your actions?

19. Click **Finish**.

20. Leave the Active Directory Users and Computers tool open for the next project.

Project 9-4

This project enables you to set the permissions on a domain. You also verify the delegation of control that you configured in Hands-on Project 9-3

To set the permissions for a domain:

1. Open the Active Directory Users and Computers tool, if it is not already is open.

2. Click the **View** menu and click **Advanced Features**, if there is no check mark in front of the option.

3. Right-click the same domain that you configured in the last hands-on project, such as TheFirm.com.

4. Click **Properties**.

5. Click the **Security** tab. What groups already have security assignments?

6. Click **Enterprise Admins**. What permissions are given to this group? Record your observations.

7. Remove the checks from all of the *Allow* boxes other than for **Read**.

8. Click **Apply**.

9. Click the **Advanced** button.

10. Scroll through the Permission Entries box. What permissions are set up for Server Operators, and how do these correspond to the delegation of control that you configured in Hands-on Project 9-3?

11. Click **Enterprise Admins** in the scroll box, and then click **View/Edit**. What special permissions are granted for Enterprise Admins? Record your observations.

12. Click **Cancel**.

13. What tabs, other than the Permissions tab, are available in the Access Control Settings dialog box for the domain? Record your observations.

14. Click **Cancel**.

15. Click **OK**.

16. Leave the Active Directory Users and Computers tool open for the next project.

Project 9-5

This project enables you to set up security on the default domain policy. You will need access as a member of the Domain Admins or Enterprise Admins group.

To set the security on a default domain policy:

1. Open the Active Directory Users and Computers tool, if it is not already open (or alternately open the Active Directory Users and Computers tool as an MMC snap-in).

2. Right-click a domain in the tree, such as TheFirm.com.

9

3. Click **Properties**.

4. Click the **Group Policy** tab.

5. Click the **Default Domain Policy**, under Group Policy Object Links, if it is not already highlighted.

6. Click **Properties** (see Figure 9-22).

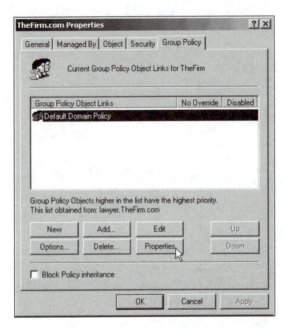

Figure 9-22   Accessing the properties of the default domain policy

7. What tabs are displayed and what is their purpose? Record your observations.

8. Click the **Security** tab.

9. Click the **Domain Admins** group in the Name text box.

10. What permissions are granted for Domain Admins? Record your observations.

11. With Domain Admins selected, click **Allow** for the **Full Control** permission.

12. How would you set special permissions for Domain Admins, so that you can further customize the permissions? Record your answer in your lab journal or in a word-processed document.

13. Click **OK**, and click **OK** again.

14. Leave the Active Directory Users and Computers tool open for Hands-on Project 9-7.

Project 9-6

This project enables you to set up the security on a site's group policy object. You will need access as a member of the Domain Admins or Enterprise Admins group.

To configure security on a site's GPO:

1. Click **Start**, point to **Programs**, point to **Administrative Tools**, and click **Active Directory Sites** and **Services** (or alternately open the Active Directory Sites and Services tool as an MMC snap-in).

2. In either the tree or the right-hand pane, right-click the site for which to configure the group policy permissions.

3. Click **Properties**. What tabs are displayed for the site's properties?

4. Click the **Group Policy** tab. (If no group policy object exists, click the New button, type a name for the group policy, such as the name of the site with your initials appended, and press Enter).

5. Click the group policy object under Group Policy Object Links, if the group policy object is not already highlighted.

6. Click **Properties**. What tabs do you see? Record your observations.

7. Click the **Security** tab.

8. What permissions are set up for Authenticated Users?

9. Click the **Enterprise Admins** group. What permissions are already set for this group?

10. With Enterprise Admins selected, click **Allow** for the **Full Control** permission. How would you set special permissions for Enterprise Admins?

11. Click **OK**, and click **OK** again.

12. Close the Active Directory Sites and Services tool.

Project 9-7

In this project, you create a filter for a group policy object.

To create the group policy filter:

1. Make sure that the Active Directory Users and Computers tool is open, and if not, open it.

2. Create a domain local group, or use the same domain local group that you created in the last chapter for Hands-on Project 8-1.

3. Create an OU and a new group, policy for your domain local group, or use the OU and group policy that you created in the last chapter for Hands-on Project 8-6.

4. Right-click the OU that you created, such as MJPSecure (refer to Hands-on Project 8-6).

5. Click **Properties**.

6. Click the **Group Policy** tab.

7. Make sure that the group policy you created is selected under Group Policy Object Links, and click **Properties**.

8. What tabs do you see for the group policy's properties? Record your answers.

9. Click the **Security** tab.

10. What groups are already listed in the Name box? What permissions are granted to Authenticated Users by default? Record your observations.

11. Remove the check marks from **Read** and **Apply Group Policy**.

12. Click the **Add** button. Double-click the domain local group that you created, and then click **OK**.

13. Click the group that you just added to the list to ensure that it is selected on the Security tab. What permissions are granted to this group by default?

14. Click the **Allow** box for Apply Group Policy.

15. Click **OK**.

16. Click **OK** again.

17. Close the Active Directory Users and Computers tool.

Project 9-8

In this project, you install the ADC for Microsoft Exchange 5.5 and the ADC management tool. You will need the Windows 2000 Server CD-ROM for the project.

To install the ADC for Microsoft Exchange 5.5:

1. Insert the Windows 2000 Server CD-ROM.

2. Wait for the autorun program to display the Microsoft Windows 2000 CD dialog box and then click **Browse This CD**.

3. Double-click each of the following folders as they are displayed, **VALUEADD**, **MSFT**, **MGMT**, and **ADC**.

4. Scroll to find the setup program and then double-click **SETUP** (see Figure 9-23).

5. Click **Next** after the Active Directory Connector Installation Wizard starts.

6. Click the boxes for **Microsoft Active Directory Connector Service component** and **Microsoft Active Directory Connector Management components**.

7. Click **Next**.

8. Use the default folder location for the files, or use the Browse button to put the files in a different location that is specified by your instructor. Click **Next**.

9. Keep the Administrator account as the account under which to run the services, or use a different account as specified by your instructor. Also, enter the password for the account. Click **Next**.

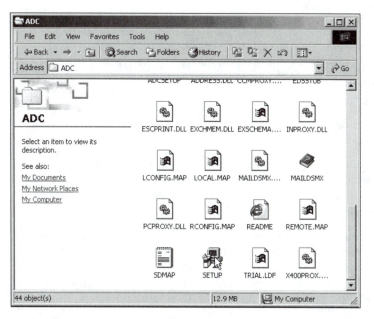

Figure 9-23   Starting the ADC installation

10. Click **Finish**.

11. Close the ADC window.

12. Click **Exit** to close the Microsoft Windows 2000 CD window.

13. Click **Start**, point to **Programs**, point to **Administrative Tools**, and click **Active Directory Connector Management**.

14. Right-click **Active Directory Connector** (*servername*).

15. Point to **New**.

16. Click **Connection Agreement**.

17. What replication directions can be set up? Record your observations.

18. Enter your initials and **Test**, such as MJPTest, in the Name box so that you can later access the other tabs in the dialog box (the name is a required entry). What tabs are available? Record your observations.

19. Click each tab to view its parameters, but make sure that you click the Connections tab last (because it has a required entry). Record your observations about the parameters that can be set via the tabs.

20. Click **Cancel**.

21. Close the Active Directory Connector Management tool.

CASE PROJECT

Aspen Consulting Project: Planning Active Directory Security and Coexistence

Pharmacopia is an international pharmaceutical company that has offices and plants in Canada, Italy, Australia, France, and Sweden. Your analysis of this company reveals the following information:

❑ There is a tree root domain associated with each site, and from two to five child domains under each tree root. The tree roots are: pharmacopia.com (the headquarters domain in Canada), pharmacopia.it, pharmacopia.au, pharmacopia.fr, and pharmacopia.se.

❑ Each of the country locations has its own autonomous IT organization. Within each IT organization, there is a Systems unit that is responsible for management of the trees and domains. However, there is also a User Support unit in each IT department that manages the OUs in each domain and the group policy objects associated with the OUs.

❑ Overall forest management is in the hands of the Systems unit in the IT department at the Canadian location.

❑ In general, the management style of the IT departments at each location is centralized. The exception is the Italian location, which is decentralized and which uses a project-based approach.

❑ All sites have agreed that schema administration for the forest is to be handled only by a small group of schema administrators, who are located at the Canadian site.

❑ The Canadian, Australian, and Swedish sites use primarily Windows NT and Windows 2000 servers. One of their projects is to upgrade all of their Windows NT servers to Windows 2000 within the next eight months.

❑ The Italian and French sites use primarily NetWare 5.x servers, but each site also has at least three Windows 2000 servers.

Pharmacopia has just been placed in the hands of a new CEO, and the French and Australian sites are likely to have new managing vice presidents soon. The CEO is warning that there will be a reorganization at all company locations after he has studied the current workings of the company for about six months. You are assigned to work with the company to help them develop Active Directory security features, and to enable existing directory services and databases to coexist on the enterprise network.

1. The Australian IT department has two units of different people who handle domains, DHCP, and DNS servers in their tree. The tree consists of two domains under the parent pharmacopia.au domain: admin&research.pharmacopia.au and manufacturing.pharmacopia.au. One unit manages the domains, and one unit manages the DHCP and DNS servers. Develop a design plan to show how you would configure administrative security groups for the Australian location. Include in the plan how you would set up permission security on the three domains.

2. Create a design plan to show how you would set up administrative security for schema management for the forest.

3. At the Italian location, the default domain policy is managed by the domain administrators. Further, each OU and the group policy associated with each OU is set up by the IT department's User Support unit. Develop a plan for creating security groups to help manage OUs and the group policies that are linked to the OUs. Also, discuss in general how to set up permission security on the OUs.

4. Your analysis shows that the IT department at each site does not fully trust the IT departments at the other sites. As a result, they want to ensure that no one from another department can manage their parent and child domains. Create a plan that enables each department to configure administrative security groups and domain permissions to ensure the management autonomy that each department wants.

5. One of the current problems is that the company does not have a way to enable the NetWare NDS and Windows 2000 Active Directory directory services to coexist. Create a general review of the tools that are available to enable coexistence. In your review, provide a recommendation for the company to implement in the next six months, and then discuss how to plan for coexistence technologies over the next two to three years.

OPTIONAL CASE PROJECTS FOR TEAMS

Team Case One

Mark Arnez wants examples of connectors that can be used right now for Windows 2000 Server. He asks you to develop a team and to research the Microsoft Web site for connectors. Prepare a report of your results for Mark.

Team Case Two

Mark is interested in the LDAP proxy interfaces that are currently on the market. Use the same group that you formed for Team Case One and research via the Internet, for example, what LDAP proxy interfaces are available. Create a report for Mark that describes the directory services and databases that are compatible with the interfaces that you find.

DESIGNING FOR OPERATIONS MASTERS AND GLOBAL CATALOG SERVERS

After reading this chapter and completing the exercises, you will be able to:

♦ Explain the operations master roles in Active Directory

♦ Transfer and seize the roles of operations masters

♦ Explain the role of the global catalog server in Active Directory

♦ Create an operations master and global catalog server design topology for a basic Active Directory installation

♦ Create operations master and global catalog server design topologies for regional, national, and international geographic models

For most of us, there are key people who play an important role in shaping who we are, including parents, teachers, mentors, and friends. These people work behind the scenes, but provide a foundation for what we accomplish. Similarly, Active Directory relies on operations master servers that play key roles behind the scenes to enable schema changes, the creation of new domains, the creation of new accounts, and logon access. Another type of server that plays a behind-the-scenes role is the global catalog server, which provides forest-wide access to the resources in all domains. When you set up Active Directory, one of the most important design steps is to carefully plan the location and management of these key servers.

In this chapter, you will learn how the operations masters work and why they are important to effective Active Directory design. You will learn to maintain the operations masters by transferring the operations master roles from one server to another. Also, you will learn what to do when an operations master fails or is taken out of service, so that network functions continue without interruption. Finally, you will learn how to carefully design the placement of operations masters and global catalog servers to match your analysis of an organization, particularly on the basis of geographic and decision-making models. Understanding these design topologies enables you to create a network that is easier to manage and that is more efficient for users.

UNDERSTANDING THE PURPOSE OF OPERATIONS MASTERS

The relationship of Active Directory to its domain controllers is generally built on a multimaster model (see Chapter 1) to ensure that:

- There is a copy of all of the Active Directory objects for a domain, which is the entire domain partition, on each of the domain controllers in that domain.

- Any domain controller can update the contents of Active Directory.

- In a domain that has two or more domain controllers, users can log on to the domain even when the domain controller that is nearest to them is down.

The multimaster model is designed to enable fast, efficient access to a domain combined with fault tolerance so that users will never notice when a domain controller has failed. It is also designed to allow information that is updated frequently, such as the creation of a new shared printer object or an update to a user account, to be performed on any domain controller.

Even if two or more users update the same information at the same time, but on different domain controllers, Active Directory can handle the situation. This might occur when a server administrator changes a user's password at the same time that the user is changing his or her password, for example. Active Directory uses a conflict resolution technique that enables it to determine which update to accept. In the conflicting password situation, the password with the latest timestamp is the one that is finally used by Active Directory and is the one that is replicated to all domain controllers.

For the most frequently used Active Directory data, using a conflict resolution technique does not create significant or permanent damage if the result is an inappropriate choice. Consider, for instance, the conflicting password situation. It may occur because a user sets a new password so complex that he forgets it, calls the server administrator, and leaves a voice mail message requesting the administrator to reset the password. After hanging up the telephone, the user remembers the password, logs on, and decides to set a new, simpler password, which is different from the one the server administrator is planning to use. At the same time, the server administrator resets the password. The server administrator finishes just a second after the user finishes, which means that the server administrator's version is used by Active Directory. The harm in this situation is relatively minor, because the user can call the server administrator for the password or to work out a solution.

Consider another situation in which there are two server administrators who make schema changes at the same time, but on different domain controllers. Using a conflict resolution technique in this situation is risky, because it could result in accepting mismatched updates and corrupting the schema throughout the forest. Consider another situation in which two server administrators are confused about who is assigned to create a new domain so that both administrators attempt to create the same domain at the same time. Conflict resolution in this situation also can be risky, because creating a domain starts a process that establishes a new partition in Active Directory.

For updating schema data and for creating or deleting domains, using the multimaster model for conflict resolution creates an unnecessary risk. Also, there is less need for multimaster operations in these situations, because these updates occur far less frequently than changing passwords, for example. To accommodate this situation, Microsoft has created a specialized role, called **flexible single-master operations (FSMO)**. FSMO (pronounced *fizmo*) means that Active Directory accepts changes to specific objects, such as schema object classes, from only one domain controller in a forest or domain.

10

 In the event that a server in the FSMO role fails or must be taken offline, Active Directory services include a mechanism to transfer the role to another server, as you will learn later in this chapter.

An **operations master** is a domain controller that is assigned one or more critical functions needed by Active Directory, such as generating a unique pool of numbers from which to create security identifiers for new accounts or the ability to create new domains. *Three operations masters are set up within each domain in a forest* and function in the FSMO role, as illustrated in the telecommunications company example shown in Figure 10-1:

- Relative identifier (ID) master

- Infrastructure master

- Primary domain controller (PDC) emulator master

Two additional operations masters are created, *one each for every forest*, that operate in the FSMO role (see Figure 10-1):

- Domain naming master

- Schema master

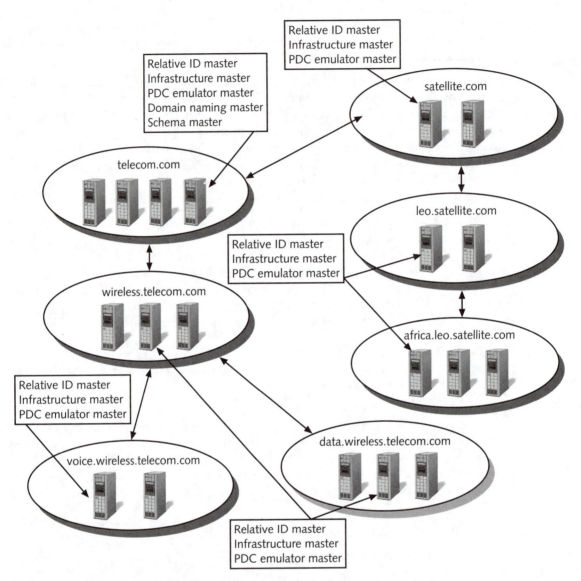

Figure 10-1   Forest and domain operations masters

When you create an Active Directory domain for the first time in an enterprise, the first domain controller that is created is assigned all five roles by default. As more forests, trees, and domains are created, you will assign operations master roles to specific domain controllers in the enterprise to achieve top performance and redundancy. Each of the operations masters is discussed in the sections that follow. After you learn the operations master roles, you will learn how to assign and place operations masters in an enterprise.

In a small business that has only one domain and one domain controller, that domain controller, called the **operations master domain controller**, plays the roles of all five operations masters. For fault tolerance, it is recommended that a second domain controller be established so that it not only contains a copy of Active Directory information, but also so that the operations master roles can be moved to it, if necessary. The second domain controller is the **standby operations master domain controller.**

Relative Identifier Master

The **relative ID master** is an operations master that generates a pool of **relative identifier (RID)** numbers from which to create security identifiers for new user accounts, groups, and computers. A **security identifier (SID)** is a unique number, in addition to the GUID (see Chapter 1), that is assigned to a security principal object, such as a user account, computer, or security group. Each SID contains two important elements:

- A number that identifies the domain in which the user account, computer, security group, or other security principal object resides (this number is the same for all security principal objects in that domain, just as the network ID portion of an IP address is the same for all clients in the same network)

- A RID number, which is a variable length number and is unique to each security principal object, so that the object it identifies cannot be confused with any other object (every security principal object has a different RID, just as the host ID portion of an IP address is different for each client in the same network)

When you assign permissions and other security levels, Active Directory uses the SID to identify the object with the security level. For example, when you create a security group called Accountants, Active Directory generates a unique SID for that group. Each time you give permissions for the Accountants security group to access a shared folder, for example, the SID and not the group's name is placed on the shared folder's access control list.

When there are two or more domain controllers in a domain, one domain controller is assigned the role of relative ID master. There can be only one relative ID master per domain. The relative ID master creates a pool of consecutive RIDs for any domain controller that is out of its supply of RIDs (see Figure 10-2). If a domain controller is out of RIDs, it cannot be used to create new user accounts, computers, groups, or other security principal objects until it contacts the relative ID master for a new supply. Should the relative ID master be down, or if it cannot be reached because there is a network problem, then a domain controller that has used up its RID supply cannot create new security principal objects. Other domain controllers that still have a supply of RIDs can continue to create security principal objects. The administrator creating a new account via Active Directory Users and Computers, for example, will see a message that says the pool of relative identifiers is used up. The situation is corrected as soon as the relative

ID master is back online or can be reached through the network. The temporary absence of the relative ID master does not cause problems for users, computers, or security groups that have been previously created, such as interfering with their ability to access the network or resources. But it may cause a delay in the ability to create new user accounts, computers, or groups in Active Directory on a specific domain controller.

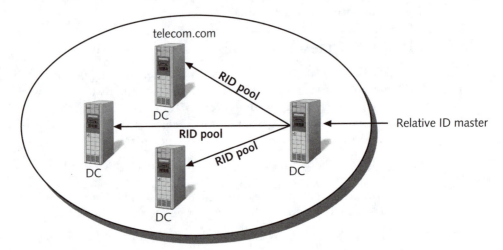

Figure 10-2   Relative ID master in a domain

 When you are creating a large number of user accounts, computers, or groups in Active Directory, make sure that the relative ID master is online so there is no interruption in your work.

 Windows 2000 Server includes a command called Movetree (Movetree.exe) that can be used from the command prompt to move objects from one domain to another. To successfully move a user principal object with Movetree, you must log on to the relative ID master in the source domain (the domain in which the object currently exists). Movetree and other Active Directory support tools are available on the Windows 2000 Server (or higher) CD-ROM located either in \Support\Tools (to install all of the tools) or \Support\Tools\Support (to install individual tools such as Movetree). Try Hands-on Project 10-1 to find out how to install a single support tool, such as Movetree, and to view the Movetree commands. Also, Hands-on Project 10-2 shows you how to determine which domain controller is the relative ID master.

Infrastructure Master

The **infrastructure master** is a domain controller that replicates to other domains changes to an SID, DN (distinguished name), or both, for example, changes to the user account members in a group. When an object is referenced between domains, such as when an account in a global group in one domain accesses resources in another domain, the other domain checks the GUID, SID, and DN of that account. In the case of a global group, the GUIDs, SIDs, and DNs of the global group and of its member user accounts are checked before access to resources is granted in another domain. This is an example of *cross-domain object references*.

For example, if an account is renamed or is moved to another domain, the SID and DN of that account changes, but not the GUID. Other domains must be notified of the change, or the account will lose access to some resources in other domains, even though it still belongs to a group that has access. When changes to accounts in a group contained in one domain are replicated to all other domains in the forest, this is called updating the *cross-domain group-to-user references*.

There is only one infrastructure master designated for a domain. When it detects a change, such as an account that has been renamed, it replicates the changed SID and DN information to the infrastructure masters in all other domains with which it has one- or two-way trust relationships.

Consider York Industries using the domain model: york.com, be.com, nantes.com, kanazawa.com, pampas.com, sudeten.com, and palisades.com. Next, consider a global security group called Inventory in be.com in which the user Janet Vasquez, who is a member of the Inventory group, is recently married and decides to change her name to Janet Marcum-Vasquez. She also wishes to change her user account name from VasquezJ to MarVasquezJ. In this situation, her account's SID remains the same, but the DN is changed. After the account is renamed, the infrastructure master in be.com replicates this change to the infrastructure masters in each of the other domains. Of course, the replication takes a short period of time to complete, which means that if a server administrator in pampas.com looks for the change just after it is made, the administrator will not immediately see Janet Marcum-Vasquez in the Inventory group.

 Make sure that you do not assign the infrastructure master role to a domain controller that is also a global catalog server. If you do, the infrastructure master will not update group-to-user references to other domains. The unique way in which the global catalog handles the SIDs of user accounts between domains causes the infrastructure master to fail to detect group-to-user changes when both run on the same computer.

Because security group composition affects who can access what resources in a domain or forest, it is important that the infrastructure master always be available to all points on a network. If it is down or cannot be reached, some users may be unable to access the resources that they need.

10

Primary Domain Controller Emulator Master

The **primary domain controller (PDC) emulator master** simulates a Windows NT Server 4.0 **primary domain controller** to provide backward compatibility for Windows NT servers in a mixed-mode domain. A mixed-mode domain is one that has Windows 2000 servers, uses Active Directory, and has Windows NT 4.0 or earlier **backup domain controllers** (**BDCs**, see Chapter 1). A BDC is a Windows NT 4.0 or earlier server that acts as a backup to the primary domain controller in a Windows NT 4.0 or earlier domain. There is only one PDC emulator master in an Active Directory-based domain and it fulfills the following roles:

- Handling password changes for non-Windows 2000 operating systems

- Resolving failed password attempts for Windows 2000 operating systems

- Copying specific Active Directory changes, such as the addition of new accounts or groups, to the Security Accounts Manager (SAM) in Windows NT 4.0 and earlier backup domain controllers in the same domain

- Resetting an account's lockout count to zero in Active Directory and replicating this information to all other domain controllers

- Operating as the master browser for non-Windows 2000 operating systems

Server and workstation operating systems that are not running Windows 2000 and that do not have the Directory Service Client software installed (DSClient, see Chapters 1 and 4) must be able to reach a PDC emulator master to change their passwords. Without DSClient, these systems do not directly communicate with Active Directory. The requirement for a PDC emulator master for these systems applies to password changes for user and for computer accounts in the domain. The operating systems that are affected include:

- MS-DOS

- Windows 3.x

- Windows 95

- Windows 98

- Windows NT 3.5, 3.51, 4.0

 If a user is attempting to change her or his password and sees a message that states the system is unable to change the password on the account, this means that the PDC emulator master cannot be reached or is down. Also, when the PDC emulator master cannot be accessed, Windows NT 3.5, Windows NT 3.51, and Windows NT 4.0 server (BDC) administrators will see a message that reports that the domain is not available. A similar message will be displayed when an administrator is creating an account using the *net user /add* command on Windows NT 4.0 and earlier servers.

When DSClient is installed on computers running Windows 95 and Windows 98, these systems are able to communicate directly with Active Directory so that user account and computer passwords can be changed at any domain controller and participate in multimaster operations. Also, the Active Directory Client can be installed in Windows NT 4.0 by implementing service pack 3 or higher.

For all Active Directory clients in a domain, the PDC emulator master acts as the final authority for password issues. For example, when a password is changed for any user or computer account, including for those on Windows 2000 systems, the domain controller that processes the change sends that change to the PDC emulator master. After the PDC emulator master receives the password change, it replicates the change to all other domain controllers in that domain, because the PDC emulator master is responsible for replicating password changes to all domain controllers. Also, if a user logs on by entering a password that is not accepted by the domain controller nearest to the user, the password authentication is next tried at the PDC emulator master. If it fails at the PDC emulator master, then the user cannot log on. This process is used because a changed password may be known to the PDC emulator master, but not yet replicated to all domain controllers.

In a mixed-mode domain, the PDC emulator master replicates Active Directory data to the Security Accounts Manager (SAM) databases on Windows NT 4.0 and earlier servers functioning as BDCs (see Figure 10-3). After all Windows NT servers are upgraded to Windows 2000 and the domain is converted to native mode, the PDC emulator master is no longer in the SAM replication role, because regular Windows 2000 multimaster Active Directory replication is used.

10

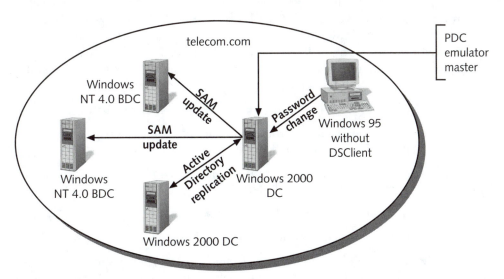

Figure 10-3   PDC emulator master in a mixed-mode domain

In the design of a Windows NT 4.0 or earlier domain, the **Security Accounts Manager (SAM)** is a database, located in the Registry, that stores information about user accounts, groups, and access privileges. The master copy of this database is kept on the primary domain controller (PDC) and backed up to one or more backup domain controllers (BDCs).

Windows NT 4.0 and earlier servers record system log event errors when the PDC emulator master cannot be accessed.

Another role that the PDC emulator master has for all clients in a domain is to coordinate account lockout information. **Account lockout** is a security measure in the account policies (set up as a group policy) that prohibits logging on to an account after a specified number of unsuccessful logon attempts. The account lockout can be set so that an account cannot be accessed for a specified time after a designated number of unsuccessful attempts within a given period of time. For example, if a user unsuccessfully enters her or his password five times within one hour, Windows 2000 Server might be set up to lock out that account for 30 minutes. After 30 minutes, the account can be accessed. In this example, the PDC emulator master notifies all other domain controllers that an account is locked out, and 30 minutes later it notifies all other domain controllers that the account is again available for access.

A last role given to the PDC emulator master is to act as the master browser for non-Windows 2000 clients that do not have the Directory Service Client software. Formerly, in Windows NT 4.0 and earlier domains, one Windows NT server was designated as the **master browser**, keeping the main list of logged-on computers. Other computers were selected as backup browsers, maintaining a copy of the list of logged-on users in case the master browser went offline. For pre-Windows 2000 clients that do not run the Directory Service Client, the PDC emulator master provides the ability to locate resources, such as networked computers and shared printers.

The primary problems that occur when the PDC emulator master is not available are:

- Some non-Windows 2000 users cannot change their passwords, and others of these users may not be able to browse for network resources.

- Accounts and groups cannot be managed on Windows NT 4.0 and earlier servers in a mixed-mode domain.

- Access to an account after it has been locked out may be delayed.

- SAM information is not updated on Windows NT 4.0 and earlier servers.

- Users who have just changed their passwords, logged off the domain, and then logged on again, may be able to access only the local computer on which they changed their password, but no other network resources.

As you can determine from the list, a situation in which the PDC emulator master is unavailable can prevent some users from accessing their accounts or finding network resources, making those users unproductive and costing the organization money.

Domain Naming Master

In every forest, there must be one and only one domain controller that is also the designated domain naming master. The **domain naming master** is a single domain controller in a forest that has the authority to create new domains and delete domains. A second and less recognized ability of the domain naming master is to create **cross-reference objects**, which are objects in Active Directory that reference a domain partition or a directory service other than Active Directory, such as NDS.

When an administrator creates a new domain, the domain naming master examines Active Directory to make sure that a domain of the same name does not already exist. Because there is only one domain naming master, it is not possible for two different administrators to simultaneously create two domains that have the same name, but different GUIDs.

 A new domain is created by a member of the Enterprise Admins security group using either the Active Directory Installation Wizard or the *ntdsutil* command-line utility. Both return an error message when the domain naming master cannot be accessed.

A cross-reference object can only be added or deleted from Active Directory by the domain naming master. This is one reason why the domain naming master must be available to create or delete a domain, because only it can add or remove the cross-reference object that represents that domain in Active Directory. Also, the domain naming master must be available when you set up a link between Active Directory and another directory service by using a synchronization connector or an LDAP proxy interface (see Chapter 9).

If the domain naming master is down or is unavailable because of network difficulties, the main problem is that administrators cannot add or delete a domain. When there are multiple directory services, the synchronization of services may also be delayed. Both of these situations are unlikely to cause many problems for users, unless the domain naming master is unavailable for an extended time. Try Hands-on Project 10-3 to determine the domain naming master in a forest.

Schema Master

The **schema master** is responsible for making additions and changes to the forest-wide schema. There is only one schema master per forest. Whenever an object class or attribute is changed in the Active Directory schema, it is the schema master's job to make sure that the change is replicated to all domains in the forest (see Figure 10-4). The schema

10

master plays a vital role, because as an FSMO, it is able to ensure that schema changes are carefully orchestrated to prevent a disastrous conflict. Even though the role of this domain controller is vital, the schema master can be down or unavailable without immediately affecting the performance of anyone but those who need to make a schema change. Try Hands-on Project 10-4 to determine the schema master in a forest.

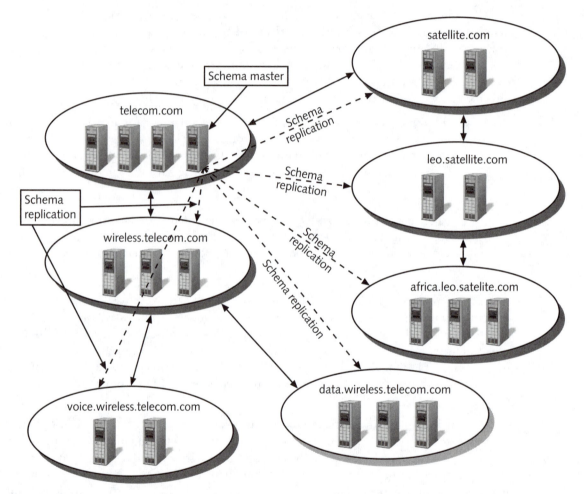

Figure 10-4   Schema master in a forest

Maintaining Operations Masters

Sometimes it is necessary to transfer or seize the role of an operations master. *Transferring the role* of one or more operations masters is the process of changing the role from one domain controller to another, with the assistance of the domain controller that currently holds the role. For example, it might be necessary to transfer the role because you want to place a particular operations master in a different location or on a different domain controller from the one that is set up by default. Another reason for transferring the role of an operations master is because the network topology has changed, as happens when two companies merge and the schema and domain naming masters are to be moved to a new high-level tree root domain. Try Hands-on Project 10-5 to transfer the role of an operations master.

Seizing the role of an operations master is performed without the assistance of the currently designated operations master. Typically, the role of an operations master is seized because the current operations master has failed or is on a portion of the network that cannot be accessed because of a network failure. Usually an operations master's role is seized only when you anticipate that the operations master will be unavailable for a relatively long time. Determining whether to seize an operations master also depends on which operations master cannot be reached, because some operations masters are vital to providing uninterrupted service to users, and some are not. The general guidelines about how long to wait before seizing an operations master are:

- *For the relative ID master, domain naming master, and schema master:* Wait longest, such as several days or a week, for these operations masters to become available before you seize their roles. Usually you would not seize the role of one of these operations masters unless you were certain that the services of their host computer will be offline permanently. The temporary absence of one of these operations masters is generally not experienced as an immediate problem for users or administrators. If you must seize the role of one of these operations masters, then the computer that formerly had the role should not be brought back into service on the network until you restore it offline without the operations master role that was seized.

- *For the infrastructure master:* How long you wait for the return of the infrastructure master depends on how soon changes to the contents of security groups are needed. In some cases, you can wait several days, and in other cases you may need to seize the infrastructure master role within a few hours instead of asking users to wait for access privilege changes. If you do need to seize the infrastructure master role, make sure that the new infrastructure master is not also a global catalog server.

- *For the PDC emulator master:* You can afford to wait the least time for the availability of the PDC emulator master, particularly if your network clients are using MS-DOS, Windows 3.x, Windows 95, Windows 98, or Windows NT and do not use DSClient. You also can afford to wait less time if the domain is running in mixed mode. If this is your situation, then consider seizing the PDC emulator master role without delay. If this is not your situation because the domain is in native mode and because clients use Windows 2000 operating systems, then it is more appropriate to wait for several hours or more before deciding to seize the PDC emulator master role.

10

> If you seize the role of any operations master, it is safest to physically discon-
> nect that computer from the network so that it does not attempt to function
> in its operations master role, and reattach it only after you have restored the
> computer to functionality.

An operations master is seized by using the *ntdsutil* command from the command
prompt, as shown in Figure 10-5. Try Hands-on Project 10-6 to seize the role of an
operations master.

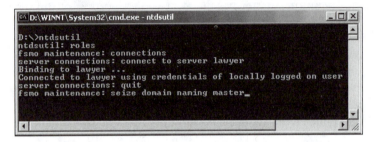

Figure 10-5   Seizing the role of an operations master

To transfer or seize the role of an operations master, you must access the domain or forest using an account or group that has the appropriate privileges. Table 10-1 shows which
security groups have the privileges needed to transfer or seize operations master roles.

Table 10-1   Security Groups with Privileges to Change Operations Master Roles

Operations Master	Security Group Membership with Transfer and Seize Authority
Relative ID master	Domain Admins security group
Infrastructure master	Domain Admins security group
PDC emulator master	Domain Admins security group
Domain naming master	Enterprise Admins security group
Schema master	Schema Admins security group

UNDERSTANDING THE PURPOSE OF THE GLOBAL CATALOG SERVER

The **global catalog** is the catalog service that is part of the directory services built into
Active Directory. As a directory service, Active Directory partitions information into
domains. The problem with partitioning information is that it is distributed across domain
controllers in different domains on a network. For example, if there are five domains in
a forest, then there are five partitions of information. Domain 1 is a partition that contains primarily information for that domain, Domain 2 contains mainly its information,
and so on. The purpose of a **catalog service** is to compile information about each separate partition into one central data storehouse. The global catalog provides this function

for Active Directory, because it is a storehouse of information about every object in every domain within a forest. This means that every object class and objects within each class in the forest's schema are contained in the global catalog. The global catalog, though, is not a full replication of object information in all domains, because it contains only a copy of the most-used attributes for each object. If it contained all attributes of all objects, the global catalog would be too immense to store and to replicate across LANs and WANs. For example, the global catalog contains the user account object class, and it contains a copy of all user account objects in all domains. Also, for each user account, it contains commonly used attributes, such as the passwords of user accounts and group membership information.

 The global catalog in a particular domain contains a complete image (all objects and attributes) of that domain's objects, a partial image (all objects, but not all attributes) of the objects in all other domains in the same forest, plus the schema namespace and the configuration container namespace for the forest.

As a comprehensive storehouse of data for a forest, the global catalog fulfills these functions:

- Authenticating users to the forest when they log on
- Providing fast searches for any object within a forest
- Providing fast access to objects in a forest
- Replicating objects and specific attributes in a forest
- Keeping a copy of the most-used attributes for each object for quick access

One of the most important functions provided by a global catalog server is assisting in the logon process. When a user or computer account logs on to the nearest domain controller in a native-mode domain, the global catalog server provides that domain controller with information about the universal group memberships of the account. The universal group membership information gives that account access to forest-wide resources to which the account is authorized. In a mixed-mode domain, the global catalog server provides a combination of information about global security group memberships in that domain and in other mixed-mode domains in the same forest. If the global catalog server is not accessible, then the account can only log on to the nearest domain controller, treating it as a local computer and accessing only the resources on that domain controller and on no other server in the domain or forest. For this reason, if your analysis shows that a company's risk tolerance is low in terms of user access, you can address this by configuring two or more global catalog servers in a domain for the sake of redundancy.

10

Try Hands-on Project 10-7 to enable a domain controller as a global catalog server.

Because administrators must be able to access the forest-wide resources in the event of the failure of the global catalog server, their membership in the Domain Admins security group enables them to access forest-wide resources even when a global catalog server is not available.

Also, in the first revision to Active Directory (Windows XP) Microsoft is planning to eliminate the requirement for logon authentication through a global catalog server, because global catalog data can be cached locally in domain controllers that are not global catalog servers.

In some cases it may be necessary to turn off the requirement for global catalog server authentication for the forest-wide enterprise. This might be necessary, for example, when users are at a small remote site that has a domain controller, no global catalog server, a slow site link, and where universal groups are not used. To turn off the requirement for global catalog logon authorization, you would change a Registry entry in the domain controller to: HKEY_LOCAL_MACHINE\System\CurrentControlSet\Control Lsa\IgnoreGCFailures.

TOPOLOGY AND GEOGRAPHIC MODELS

Designing the topology and location for the operations masters and global catalog servers is dependent on several factors in an organization, such as:

- Number of servers
- Number of domains
- Tree structure of domains
- Geographic organization
- IT decision-making structures

A small organization that has only one server will have a different design topology than an organization that has 10 servers in a single domain. An organization that is spread over many locations will use a different design topology than one that has a single location. In the sections that follow, you learn how to craft a design topology to match the particular circumstances of an organization.

Designing for the Simplest Topology

The simplest design topology is used in a small organization that has only one domain controller and one domain. A small eight-person law office or an independent retail store that has 22 employees are examples of a simple design topology. In this situation, the single domain controller has all operations master roles by default. The domain controller also is the global catalog server (see Figure 10-6).

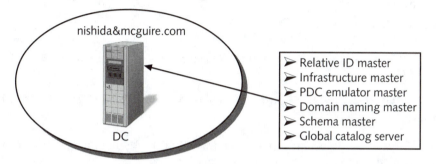

Figure 10-6   Using a single domain controller in a single domain

A main design issue for a small office is determining when to add another domain controller for more efficient network access and for multimaster replication. A small office might add a second domain controller when it reaches the point at which server operations must run without interruption—for example, when an organization relies on the server to take customer orders or to respond to client queries. Another reason for adding a second domain controller is to balance the load. Consider, for example, an office in which large database queries cause a server to respond slowly, and users often have to wait. This situation signals the need to add a server and to spread out access to resources—for example, by using the Distributed File System (Dfs, see Chapters 3, 4, and 11) to distribute access to commonly used files.

When load balancing is the reason for adding a second server, then it is also appropriate to consider spreading the load of the operations masters. The infrastructure master and the PDC emulator master roles, for example, can be transferred to the second server. By transferring these roles you accomplish several goals. One reason for transferring the roles is that traffic is likely to be highest going to the global catalog and PDC emulator master servers, thus transferring the role of the PDC emulator master to the second computer divides the traffic more evenly. Another reason for transferring the role of the PDC emulator master is to separate it from the relative ID master, so that access to the PDC emulator master is not hindered when the relative ID master is processing and sending a pool of RIDs. Also, moving the infrastructure master to the second DC eliminates the group-to-user updating conflict with the global catalog server, as mentioned earlier in this chapter. Figure 10-7 illustrates how the operations master and global catalog server roles can be divided between two DCs in one domain.

10

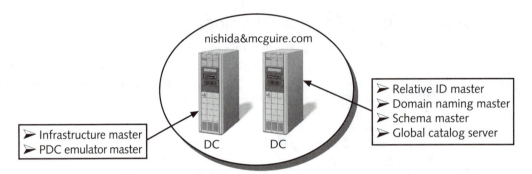

Figure 10-7   Dividing operations master and global catalog server roles between two DCs

Designing for a Regional Geographic Organization with Plans for Growth

Jefferson Philately is an example of a company that currently has one geographic location, one domain, and multiple domain controllers. The company has a centralized business management model, which applies to the organization as a whole and to the IT department specifically. Because the IT department uses a centralized decision and management model and stresses centralizing its servers, all servers are located in a secure machine room next to the IT department's offices. The machine room offers fast and reliable connectivity to the network backbone, and the servers are connected via 1 Gbps links. The analysis of the company also shows that the customer service operations are a vital business process that requires fast response from the servers that house customer service information. The workstations used by the company run Windows 2000 Professional, Windows NT 4.0, and Windows 98. Because the company currently has only one location, there is only one Active Directory site.

The analysis of growth plans reveals that Jefferson Philately is planning to construct a new manufacturing facility either in a building that is close to its current location in Cincinnati or in Cambridge, Ohio, which is 180 miles from the main Cincinnati location. If Jefferson Philately builds the new facility next door in Cincinnati, the two locations will be connected by a 155 Mbps ATM backbone link. If it builds the facility in Cambridge, the two locations will be connected by a 256 Kbps frame relay WAN link. The design for Jefferson Philately requires creating an operations masters topology that meets the current single location needs and that can be expanded to accommodate growth into the new building.

In any design situation, the following factors should be considered:

- The infrastructure master should not be on the same domain controller as a global catalog server.

- The infrastructure master should be on a network link that provides fast and reliable access to a global catalog server.

- The link on which users rely to access a global catalog server should be fast and reliable.

- The fastest logon access for users translates into placing a DC and a global catalog server at each LAN or at each Active Directory site joined by a site link.

- Network traffic to the operations masters is reduced when you place the PDC emulator master on a different DC from the relative ID master.

A design topology that can be used for the present single location at Jefferson Philately is (see Figure 10-8):

- Place the global catalog server role on two separate DCs for better performance and for redundancy.

- Place the relative ID master, infrastructure master, domain naming master, and schema master on one DC.

- Place the PDC emulator master on one DC.

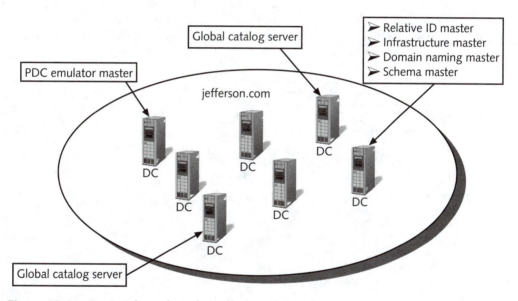

10

Figure 10-8   Regional topology for Jefferson Philately

This design topology accomplishes several purposes. First, all of the operations masters and the global catalog server are on fast and reliable links because they are located in the machine room. This gives users fast access to DCs, and it provides fast access for users to a global catalog server and the PDC emulator master for logons, password changes, password verification, and master browser access (for the Windows NT and Windows 98 clients). Separating the PDC emulator master and the relative ID master ensures faster network and user response, particularly when the relative ID master is busy preparing and transferring a new pool of RIDs. Placing the global catalog servers on their own DCs further reduces this kind of traffic to a single server and ensures the fastest access for users, because user logon activity does not have to compete with any of the activity of the operations masters. Also, neither global catalog server is on the same DC as the infrastructure master server, which means that the infrastructure master server is able to perform its job accurately. The global catalog servers and the infrastructure master have fast and reliable connections because they are both in the machine room with 1 Gbps links and fast access to the network backbone. Finally, by having two global catalog servers, there is redundancy for logon authorization, in case one of these servers fails.

If Jefferson Philately goes with the plan to build a manufacturing facility next to its main headquarters building in Cincinnati, then it can use the same operations master and global catalog design topology without making changes. This decision would be based on verification that the 155 Mbps ATM link between the buildings remains fast and reliable. If usage in the manufacturing facility grows and traffic across the ATM link is relatively high, such as 50 percent or more network utilization, then an improved design would be to place an additional DC and global catalog server in the manufacturing building (see Figure 10-9). Another step would be to make the networks in the manufacturing building and in the main building separate sites, to help reduce replication traffic across the ATM link.

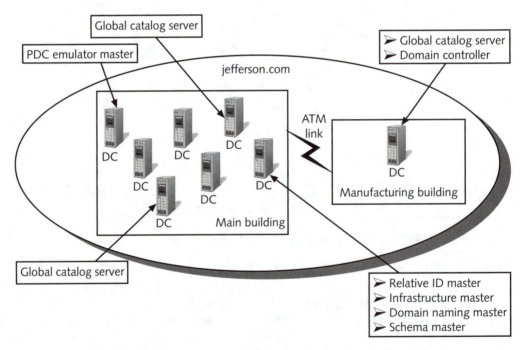

Figure 10-9   Expanding the Jefferson Philately topology to two locations in the same city

If Jefferson Philately builds the new manufacturing facility in Cambridge and makes the Cambridge network an Active Directory site, then at least one DC and global catalog server would be placed at that site. This would give users fast access to the network and enable the company to control the replication traffic over the frame relay site link. Another option would be to set up a child domain, such as manufact.jefferson.com, and to establish at least two DCs for redundancy in the new manufacturing facility. The child domain would be set up using the model shown in Figure 10-7, so that the infrastructure master and PDC emulator master are on one DC, and the relative ID master and the global catalog server are on another DC. The design topology to accommodate Jefferson Philately's expansion into Cambridge is shown in Figure 10-10.

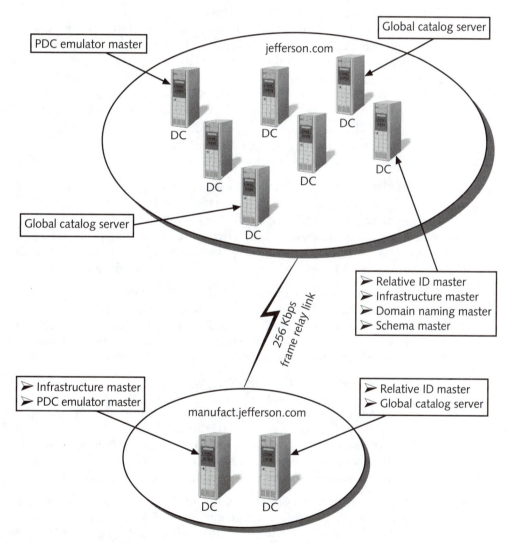

Figure 10-10   Expanding the topology to Cambridge for Jefferson Philately

There are several advantages to the design in Figure 10-10. First, the two domains enable the company to have a security boundary around the networks at each site, which makes the networks at each site as well as communications across the frame relay link more secure. Another advantage is that the speed of user access is maximized at each geographic location, while the replication traffic over the site link is minimal (such as that for schema changes). By having two or more DCs, each site also enjoys multimaster replication for fault tolerance.

Designing for a National Organization with Plans for Growth

The national organizational model of Interstate Security Bank consists of geographic locations in Idaho, Montana, Oregon, Washington, and Wyoming. Also, Interstate Security Bank follows a business unit organization that consists of the main headquarters, regional offices, and branch offices, each of which can be broken down further into departments, such as Customer Service, Loans, Business, and IT. The management decision-making model in the IT department is decentralized. The analysis of the WAN links between the headquarters in Seattle and each regional office shows that all are relatively high-speed reliable connections at speeds of from 1.544 Mbps to 44.736 Mbps. The links between the regional and branch offices vary widely. For example, the link between the branch office in Jackson, Wyoming and the regional office in Cheyenne is 64 Kbps. The link between the Casper branch and the Cheyenne office is faster, at 1.544 Mbps.

One proposed tree and domain design plan, illustrated in Chapter 6, is to create a tree root domain at the headquarters office in Seattle, called isb.com. There would be five child domains under the tree, called idaho.isb.com, montana.isb.com, oregon.isb.com, washington.isb.com, and wyoming.isb.com. In designing the operations master and global catalog server topology for Interstate Security Bank, you can follow several techniques that you have already learned, applying them to the tree root domain and to each child domain:

- Use a model similar to the one shown in Figure 10-8 for locating the operations masters and global catalog servers in the tree root domain, isb.com, which is located in the headquarters office. This model places the PDC emulator master on one domain controller, the global catalog servers on two other domain controllers, and the remaining operations masters on a third domain controller.

- Place at least one DC, housing one PDC emulator master, one infrastructure master, one relative ID master, and a global catalog server, in each of the child domains located at each regional office. Putting more than one DC at each regional office is even better, so that the infrastructure master and global catalog server can be separated and to separate the PDC emulator master from the relative ID master and global catalog servers. Also, having at least two DCs ensures redundancy.

- Place at least one domain controller and a global catalog server in each branch office, using a design similar to the setup for the manufacturing building, shown earlier in Figure 10-9. If there is money to have two servers at branch offices, then make both DCs, and make one or both global catalog servers.

The resulting design topology make both DCs, and for the headquarters and regional offices is shown in Figure 10-11, and has these advantages:

- The domain naming master and the schema master are located in the tree root domain for coordinating schema maintenance and the creation of new domains from one location. This topology follows the rule that there can be only one domain naming master and one schema master in a forest.

- The tree root domain and each child domain contains a PDC emulator master, an infrastructure master, and a relative ID master, following the rule that there should be one of these per domain in a forest.

- Each geographic location contains one or more domain controllers and global catalog servers to provide faster user access to the network and for Active Directory redundancy.

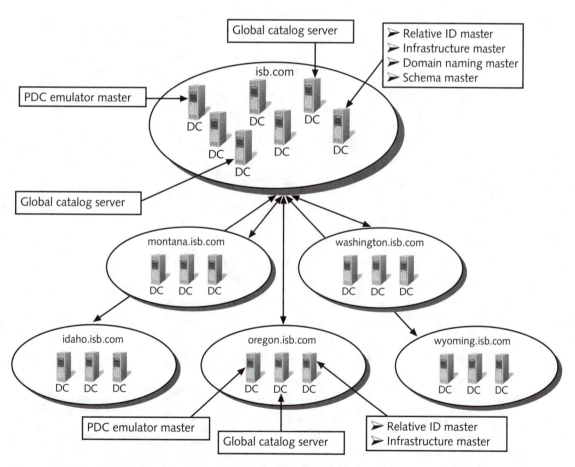

Figure 10-11   National topology for Interstate Security Bank

If there is a need to have redundant global catalog servers at the regional offices in Figure 10-11, then you would set up the DCs so that one would have the PDC emulator and infrastructure masters, one would be only a global catalog server, and one would have the relative ID master and global catalog server roles.

If one or more of the Interstate Security Bank regional offices were to have only two Windows 2000 servers, another way to design this topology would be to combine the PDC emulator master and the infrastructure master on one domain controller, and combine the relative ID master and global catalog server on the other domain controller. This would be the best alternative because it separates the global catalog server and the infrastructure master so that the infrastructure master works properly. Also, it separates the PDC emulator master and the relative ID master for better separation of the load from these operations masters. Figure 10-12 illustrates this scenario.

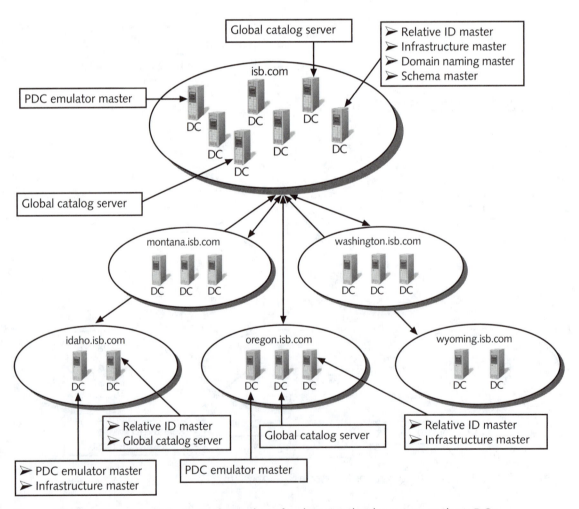

Figure 10-12 Interstate Security Bank topology for domains that have two or three DCs

The design topology for the branch offices consists of placing at least one DC and global catalog server in each location, as shown in Figure 10-13, which illustrates this design in two Oregon branch offices, a large branch in Portland, and a small branch in Cottage Grove. This strategy ensures that users will have fast access to the network. Each branch that has two or more DCs also has the advantage of Active Directory redundancy.

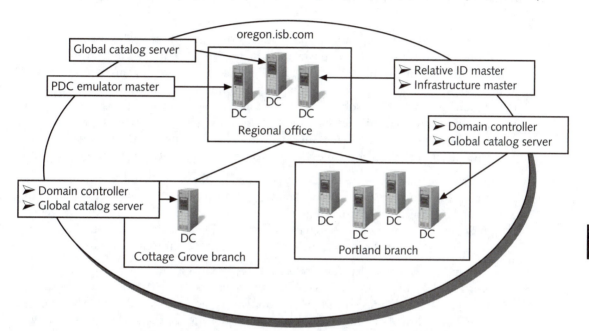

Figure 10-13   Interstate Security Bank topology for the Oregon regional office and two of its branches

 If global catalog redundancy is also important at the locations shown in Figure 10-13, then you would set up the regional office so that one DC would serve the PDC emulator and infrastructure master roles, one would be only a global catalog server, and one would have the relative ID master and global catalog server roles. Also, you would set up two or more global catalog servers at the Portland branch.

One area in which Interstate Security Bank is growing is its payroll clearinghouse service. The bank is planning to create a separate child domain to have a security boundary around the payroll clearinghouse service to separate it from the other bank services and the Internet, through which customers access the clearinghouse service. The new domain will be called clearinghouse.isb.com. When the bank creates the new child domain, there will be only two Windows 2000 servers at the start. The design topology in this situation is the same as for the existing child domains, such as idaho.isb.com, that have only two Windows 2000 domain controllers (refer to Figure 10-12). One domain controller will be the combined PDC emulator master and infrastructure master; the other domain controller will combine the functions of the relative ID master and the global catalog server.

Designing for an International Organization with Plans for Growth

York Industries is an example of an international organization that also uses the project-based organizational model. The business management style at York industries is decentralized throughout the organization. The IT departments are organized under a CIO who is at the headquarters office, but each subsidiary has its own decentralized IT department and staff. Each subsidiary also has an independent set of goals and strategies that include individual mission statements, business objectives, and strategic, operating, and project plans. Although each subsidiary is relatively independent, there is mutual trust among all of them that enables them to operate in a single forest using one schema.

Some of the site links are relatively fast, such as the 10 Mbps SMDS link between the headquarters in Toronto and Palisades Corporation in Buffalo, New York. The slowest site links, at 64 Kbps, are from the headquarters site to Pampas Fixtures in Buenos Aires, Argentina, and to Sudeten Motors in Szczecin, Poland (refer to Figure 6-18 in Chapter 6). Some of the site links have been unreliable, such as the link between Toronto and Szczecin.

The tree and domain plan that York Industries is currently considering is to create tree root domains for each subsidiary: york.com, be.com, nantes.com, kanazawa.com, pampas.com, sudeten.com, and palisades.com. The first domain to be created will be york.com, with the others to follow. After each tree root is created, some of the subsidiaries will eventually create child domains.

Using this tree and domain plan, the design topology for York Industries is similar to the one for Interstate Security Bank, except that there is no single parent domain, so it is necessary to select one of the tree root domains to house the domain naming and schema masters:

- The york.com domain is selected as home to the domain naming and schema masters, because it is housed at the headquarters location, which is the best location from which to coordinate these functions.

- Each tree root domain will have one PDC emulator master, one infrastructure master, and one relative ID master.

- Each tree root domain will have at least one global catalog server (more are desirable for logon authorization redundancy).

- Each child domain under a tree root domain will have one PDC emulator master, one infrastructure master, and one relative ID master.

- Each child domain will have at least one global catalog server (more are desirable for logon authorization redundancy).

Figure 10-14 illustrates the tree root domain topology for the York Industries headquarters and subsidiaries. The topology is intended to satisfy the following factors revealed in the analysis of York Industries:

- The IT departments are decentralized, and so each has its own tree root domain to manage. The child domains under each tree root domain can be created in coordination with the Toronto headquarters location. Schema changes also can be coordinated with the headquarters location. This structure also enables each subsidiary to set its own independent business strategies.

- Having at least one global catalog server in each domain enables fast logon and Active Directory searches for users.

- Having one PDC emulator master, one infrastructure master, and one relative ID master in each tree root domain (and later in each child domain) ensures uninterrupted access for users, even when a WAN link is down. Also, slow WAN links will not affect logon access and Active Directory access for users.

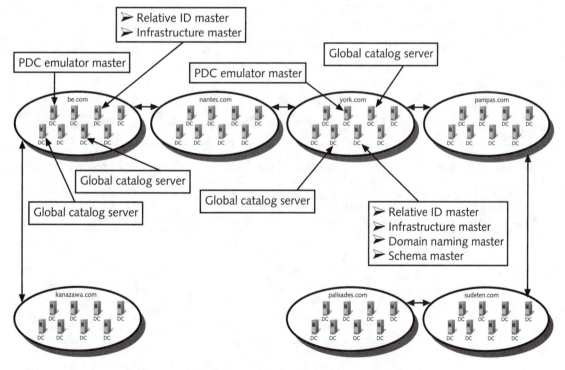

Figure 10-14   International topology for York Industries

The proposed design is suitable for growth because a new company can be purchased by York Industries and added into the structure as another tree root domain, containing a PDC emulator master, infrastructure master, relative ID master, and at least one global catalog server. Also, any of the subsidiary companies can add child domains as necessary, with each child domain having a PDC emulator master, infrastructure master, relative ID master, and at least one global catalog server.

Consider another scenario in which the subsidiaries of York Industries are distrustful of one another, and each wants to be able to maintain its own schema and retain control over creating child domains. In this scenario, a separate forest could be created for each subsidiary. There would be a tree root domain in each forest and the option to have child domains under each tree root domain. The tree root domains would still have the names as proposed earlier, but also represent a separate forest model: york.com, be.com, nantes.com, kanazawa.com, pampas.com, sudeten.com, and palisades.com.

In this scenario, every tree root domain would have all five operations masters plus at least one global catalog server. Changes to the schema would be made via each separate tree root domain, and new domains would be created from the same place, giving each subsidiary complete autonomy from every other one. The design topology in this scenario is shown in Figure 10-15. The dotted lines between each separate forest show that they are connected to one another through network connections, but not through complete two-way transitive trusts. Instead, access among forests is accommodated by different arrays of rights and permissions.

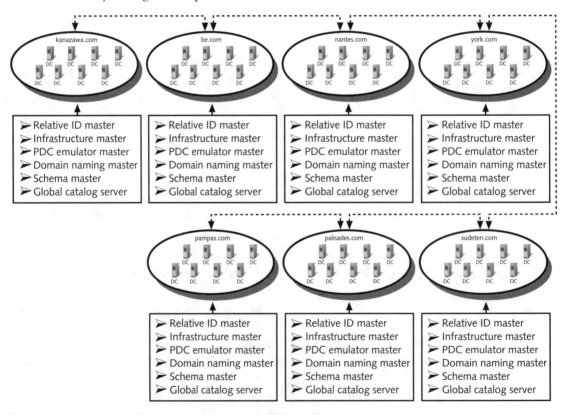

Figure 10-15   Using a separate forest topology for the York Industries subsidiaries

Try Hands-on Project 10-8 to create a design topology for operations masters and global catalog servers.

Chapter Summary

❑ When you create an Active Directory design, take into account the roles of the operations masters. The relative ID master dispenses RIDs to domain controllers so that they can create unique user and computer accounts. The infrastructure master tracks changes to group memberships and plays a role in network resource access for users. The PDC emulator master provides backward compatibility for Windows NT servers and for clients that rely on the master browser, such as Windows 98. The domain naming master is used to create or delete domains, while the schema master is used to manage schema changes.

❑ The global catalog server also plays a key role in Active Directory, because it authenticates logons and enables users to quickly find network resources beyond their immediate domain, such as published folders and printers. When you design a network, it is important to plan the locations of global catalog servers so that there are no conflicts with the infrastructure master, and so that users can quickly access network resources.

❑ After you fully understand the roles of the operations masters and the global catalog servers, you are ready to apply your understanding to different design topologies. For example, understanding the role of the schema master enables you to place it in a network location that matches the needs of a company, and that takes into account the geographical organization of that company. How you locate operations masters determines how effectively your network operates.

In the next chapter, you will learn how Active Directory is replicated on a network and how to place domain controllers to provide the best replication service, uninterrupted user access, and disaster recovery.

10

Key Terms

account lockout — A security measure in Active Directory account policies that prohibits logging on to an account after a specified number of unsuccessful logon attempts within a specified time.

backup domain controller (BDC) — A Windows NT 4.0 or earlier server that acts as a backup to the primary domain controller (PDC), and has a copy of the Security Accounts Manager (SAM) database containing user account and access privilege information.

catalog service — A service within a directory service that compiles information about each separate partition in the directory service, and that stores the information in a single data storehouse for centralized queries.

cross-reference object — An object in Active Directory that references a domain partition in the same forest or in a different forest, or that references a directory service other than Active Directory, such as NDS. It is used by one domain or directory service to obtain specific information about another domain or directory service.

domain naming master — The single domain controller in a forest that has the authority to create new domains or delete existing domains. It is also used to manage cross-reference objects to other directory services.

flexible single-master operations (FSMO) — A role allocated to one domain controller in which Active Directory accepts changes for only specific objects, such as for schema object classes, from that domain controller. The schema master and the domain naming master each function in the FSMO role in a forest, and the relative ID master, infrastructure master, and PDC emulator master have FSMO roles in a domain. The pronunciation of FSMO is *fizmo*.

global catalog — A single storehouse of information about every object in every domain within a forest. As a storehouse, the global catalog contains a copy of the most-used attributes for each object, such as the actual user's name that is associated with a user account. The global catalog also provides services to users, such as the ability to find an object or information about an object, without already knowing the domain or OU in which the object is held.

infrastructure master — A domain controller that replicates to other domains changes to an object's SID, DN, or both, and that is particularly important for reflecting changes to members of groups—for example, when an account already in a group is renamed or is moved to another domain in the same forest.

master browser — In a pre-Windows 2000 server domain, a mixed-mode Windows 2000 server domain, and in domains that have clients that cannot communicate with Active Directory, a server that is designated to keep the main list of logged-on computers.

operations master — A domain controller that plays one or more critical domain-wide or forest-wide roles for Active Directory, such as generating a unique pool of numbers from which to create unique security identifiers (SIDs) for new objects or creating new domains. The operations master roles are: relative ID master, infrastructure master, primary domain controller (PDC) emulator master, domain naming master, and schema master.

operations master domain controller — A domain controller that plays all five operations master roles when there is only one domain and only one or two domain controllers.

primary domain controller (PDC) — A Windows NT 4.0 or earlier server that acts as the master server when there are two or more Windows NT servers on a pre-Windows 2000 server network. There is only one PDC in a Windows NT 4.0 or earlier domain, and it holds the master database (called the SAM) of user accounts and access privileges.

primary domain controller (PDC) emulator master — A domain controller that duplicates the role of a Windows NT 4.0 primary domain controller (PDC) when Active Directory is operating in mixed mode, because there are Windows 4.0 NT or earlier backup domain controllers in a domain. Two important roles of the PDC emulator master are to enable password changes for computers running non-Windows 2000 operating systems, and to replicate specific Active Directory information to Windows NT 4.0 or earlier backup domain controllers.

relative ID master — A domain controller that assigns a pool of relative ID numbers to every DC in the same domain, including to the domain controller designated as the relative ID master. Creating pools of relative ID numbers enables the other DCs to assign security identifier numbers to newly created security principal objects, such as accounts, computers, and groups. There is only one relative identifier master per domain.

relative identifier (RID) — A unique number that is used as a portion of a security identifier. Each domain creates a pool of RIDs that is used for creating unique security identifiers for user accounts, computers, and groups.

schema master — The single or unique domain controller in a forest that is able to make additions and changes to the forest-wide schema. When a schema modification is made, the schema master copies that modification to every domain controller in the same forest.

Security Accounts Manager (SAM) — Located in the Windows NT 4.0 or earlier server Registry, a database that stores information about user accounts, groups, and access privileges for a domain. The master copy of this database is kept on the primary domain controller (PDC) in the domain, and backed up to one or more backup domain controllers (BDCs). The SAM is also used in a Windows 2000 server to store local computer account information, such as that for a standalone computer that does not have Active Directory installed.

security identifier (SID) — A unique identification number that is created each time a new security principal object is created, such as a user account, computer, or group. A portion of the SID is a number that identifies the domain, and that is the same in all SIDs generated for that domain. Another portion of the SID is a relative identifier (see *relative identifier*), which is a unique number used only in that SID.

standby operations master domain controller — A domain controller that can be designated as the operations master domain controller in the event that the main operations master domain controller fails. An operations master domain controller and a standby operations master domain controller are used in a small organization that has only one domain and two domain controllers.

10

REVIEW QUESTIONS

Answer questions 1–9 using this case information:

Alvarez Travel Center is a national travel agency with headquarters in Denver, Colorado, and regional offices in Omaha, Nebraska; Albuquerque, New Mexico; Fargo, North Dakota; Sioux Falls, South Dakota; and Dallas, Texas. There are branch offices under each of the regional offices. Alvarez Travel uses a decentralized management mode, giving each regional and branch office freedom to create special promotions and trips. The domain structure is alvareztravel.com, neb.alvareztravel.com, nd.alvareztravel.com, sd.alvareztravel.com, nm.alvareztravel.com, and tx.alvareztravel.com.

1. In which of the following domains would you most likely locate the schema master?

   a. neb.alvareztravel.com, because it is most geographically central

   b. alvareztravel.com, because it is the tree root domain

   c. tx.alvareztravel.com, because it has the most branch offices

   d. nd.alvareztravel.com, because it has the fewest branch offices

   e. all of the above, because all domains require a schema master

   f. only a and b

   g. only a, b, and c

2. Three of the domains, alvareztravel.com, neb.alvareztravel.com, and tx.alvarez-travel.com, have a combination of Windows 95, Windows 98, Windows NT 4.0 Workstation, and Windows 2000 Professional clients. The Windows 95 and Windows 98 client computers do not have DSClient. The Windows NT clients all have service pack 5 or higher. Which of these clients can search Active Directory for printers?

   a. Windows 95

   b. Windows 98

   c. Windows NT 4.0 Workstation

   d. Windows 2000 Professional

   e. all of the above

   f. none of the above

   g. only a and b

   h. only c and d

3. Referring to the information in Question 2, which of the following would strictly rely on using the master browser to locate a computer on the network?

   a. Windows 95

   b. Windows 98

   c. Windows NT 4.0 Workstation

    d. Windows 2000 Professional

    e. all of the above

    f. none of the above

    g. only a and b

    h. only a, b, and c

4. Which of the following domains would contain an infrastructure master?

    a. alvareztravel.com

    b. neb.alvareztravel.com

    c. nm.alvareztravel.com

    d. tx.alvareztravel.com

    e. all of the above

    f. none of the above

    g. only a and b

    h. only b, c, and d

5. Which of the following would most likely be placed in a branch office in Texas that has 42 users?

    a. PDC emulator master

    b. DC

    c. global catalog server

    d. domain naming master

    e. all of the above

    f. only a and b

    g. only b and c

    h. only b, c, and d

6. In the nd.alvareztravel.com domain, a server administrator is attempting to move several accounts of travel agents to the sd.alvareztravel.com domain, because those agents have been transferred to branch offices in South Dakota. The server administrator is not able to move the accounts using the Movetree command. Which of the following might be the problem?

    a. The server administrator is not logged on to the relative ID master.

    b. The server administrator is not a member of the Account Admins security group in the nd.alvareztravel.com domain.

    c. The infrastructure master has not finished synchronizing security group membership updates with the nearest global catalog server.

    d. none of the above

10

e. only a and c

f. only b and c

7. Which of the following should not be combined on the same domain controller?

a. PDC emulator master and infrastructure master

b. infrastructure master and relative ID master

c. global catalog server and infrastructure master

d. global catalog server and schema master

e. all of the above

f. only a and b

g. only b and c

8. You have just changed your password on a client running Windows 2000 Professional. You log off, and then decide to quickly log back on. Behind the scenes, the first domain controller that you reach does not yet know your new password. Which of the following does it contact to verify that you have a new password?

a. domain naming master

b. PDC emulator master

c. infrastructure master

d. relative ID master

e. none of the above

9. In creating a design topology, which of the following would you place in the nm.alvareztravel.com domain?

a. relative ID master

b. PDC emulator master

c. infrastructure master

d. all of the above

e. only a and b

f. only b and c

Answer questions 10–19 using this case information:

Extreme Gear (extreme.com) is an international company that makes gear for specialty outdoor sports. The company headquarters is in Lansing, Michigan, where they make parachutes and hang gliders. In Vancouver, Canada, a subsidiary called Subzero (bags.com), manufactures sleeping bags for surviving subzero temperatures. FastWater (fastwater.com) is a subsidiary in Mexico City, Mexico that makes rubber rafts for floating whitewater rapids. Another subsidiary in Lima, Peru (climbers.com) manufactures rock and ice climbing gear, such as ice picks. All of the domains are in one forest. Extreme Gear and its subsidiaries have a decentralized management structure in relation to one another.

10. Which locations would have a global catalog server?

    a. climbers.com in Lima

    b. bags.com in Vancouver

    c. fastwater.com in Mexico City

    d. extreme.com in Lansing

    e. all of the above

    f. none of the above

    g. only b and c

    h. only a, b, and c

11. How many domains will contain a domain naming master?

    a. none

    b. one

    c. two

    d. three

    e. four

12. In the extreme.com domain, what is contained in the security identifier that is created to identify a new account?

    a. a number that identifies the extreme.com domain

    b. unique numbers that identify the domains bags.com, fastwater.com, and climbers.com

    c. a unique RID

    d. the device ID of the NIC in the domain controller on which the account is first created

    e. all of the above

    f. only a and b

    g. only a and c

    h. only a, b, and d

13. An Active Directory administrator in the extreme.com domain wants to move the role of the PDC emulator master. What security group membership gives her privileges to make the role transfer?

    a. Schema Admins

    b. Account Admins

    c. Domain Admins

    d. Master Admins

    e. none of the above, because the ability to transfer a role is only granted through a Windows 2000 Server right set in a group policy

10

14. Extreme Gear has NetWare servers and Windows 2000 servers, and uses an LDAP proxy interface to synchronize NDS and Active Directory data. Which of the following enables them to create a reference in Active Directory to help perform the synchronization?

   a. domain naming master

   b. relative ID master

   c. PDC emulator master

   d. infrastructure master

   e. all of the above

   f. only a and b

   g. only a and c

   h. only b, c, and d

15. The climbers.com domain in Lima runs in mixed mode, because it has four remaining Windows NT 4.0 servers along with the eight newly upgraded Windows 2000 servers. All of the Windows NT servers have copies of the SAM. What kind of servers are they, and what operations master is needed because of their presence?

   a. The Windows NT servers are domain controllers, and the relative ID master is needed to accommodate them.

   b. The Windows NT servers are backup domain controllers, and the PDC emulator master is needed to accommodate them.

   c. The Windows NT servers are global catalog servers, and the PDC emulator master is needed by them.

   d. The Windows NT servers are primary domain controllers, and they synchronize partitions with the domain naming master.

16. Which of the following would you design into the climbers.com domain?

   a. infrastructure master

   b. global catalog server

   c. relative ID master

   d. PDC emulator master

   e. all of the above

   f. only a and b

   g. only b and c

   h. only a, c, and d

17. Several users in the bags.com domain have called because they have been locked out of their accounts today, and even though they have waited for over 30 minutes, which is the specified wait time, they are still unable to access their accounts. Which of the following servers is likely to be down in the bags.com domain?

   a. schema master

   b. relative ID master

   c. PDC emulator master

   d. domain naming master

   e. none of the above

   f. either a or b could be down

   g. either b or d could be down

18. The employees of FastWater have just purchased the company and have negotiated an agreement to go on their own without ties to the Extreme Gear company. However, FastWater does still plan to use the fastwater.com domain. Which of the following should FastWater plan to do?

   a. create a separate forest and schema

   b. set up a domain naming master in the fastwater.com domain

   c. set up a schema master in the fastwater.com domain

   d. all of the above

   e. none of the above

   f. only a and b

   g. only b and c

   h. only c and d

19. Subzero has lost the server that functions as its relative ID master, because a water pipe broke in the machine room where that server is located and permanently damaged the server. What can they do to move the role of the relative ID master to another server?

   a. transfer the role

   b. seize the role

   c. wait for 90 minutes, after which time Active Directory automatically reassigns the role to another server

   d. not worry, because the relative ID master in the nearest domain automatically takes ownership of that role for the bags.com (Subzero) domain

   e. None of the above is possible in Active Directory.

10

Answer questions 20–25 using this case information:

Dermatologists, LLC is a physicians group that employs 220 people in 18 locations within the same state. The main office has 32 employees and eight Windows 2000 servers. The domain name is skindocs.com. There are 17 branch offices that each have one or two servers, which are part of the skindocs.com domain.

20. Why would it be a good idea to add one more servers to those branch offices that have only one?

   a. One server is not large enough to hold a domain partition.

   b. A global catalog server cannot also be a DC.

   c. This would provide fault tolerance for the Active Directory contents at each branch.

   d. This would enable each branch office to have a domain naming master.

   e. all of the above

   f. only a and b

   g. only b and d

   h. only a, b, and c

21. Which of the following design topologies would provide an efficient design for the skindocs.com domain?

   a. Put the relative ID master and infrastructure master on servers in different branch offices.

   b. Use only one global catalog server and locate it at the main office.

   c. Move the PDC emulator master and domain naming master to one of the branch offices.

   d. all of the above

   e. none of the above

   f. only a and b

   g. only a and c

22. One of the server administrators is attempting to create user accounts, but she is unable to create the accounts because there is an error message from Active Directory. She verifies that she has the correct permissions to create the accounts. What might be the problem?

   a. A global catalog server is down.

   b. The domain naming master is down.

   c. The relative ID master is down.

   d. The schema naming master is down.

   e. none of the above

23. Each branch office should have which of the following for the most efficient operation?

    a. global catalog server

    b. backup domain controller

    c. PDC emulator master

    d. backup browser

    e. all of the above

    f. none of the above

    g. only a and b

    h. only c and d

    i. only b, c, and d

24. You have been working to make several changes to user accounts, including removing some from particular security groups, renaming some accounts, and adding new accounts to security groups. Which of the following operations masters is most affected by the changes you are making?

    a. relative ID master

    b. infrastructure master

    c. schema master

    d. PDC emulator master

    e. none of the above are affected

25. Which of the following would you expect to find in flexible single-master operations (FSMO) roles in skindocs.com?

    a. schema master

    b. domain naming master

    c. infrastructure master

    d. relative ID master

    e. all of the above

    f. none of the above

    g. only b and c

    h. only b, c, and d

10

HANDS-ON PROJECTS

Project 10-1

In this project, you find out how to install and run a specific support tool, such as the Movetree support tool. You will need access to the Windows 2000 Server (or higher) CD-ROM, and to log on using an account with Administrator privileges.

To install and run a specific support tool, such as Movetree:

1. Insert the Windows 2000 Server CD-ROM.
2. Click **Browse This CD**.
3. Double-click the **SUPPORT** folder.
4. Double-click the **TOOLS** folder.
5. Double-click the **SUPPORT** cabinet file.
6. Scroll to find the movetree.exe file.
7. What other tools are shown? Record three or four examples in your lab journal or in a word-processed document.
8. Double-click **movetree**.
9. Double-click the drive that contains the %SystemRoot% or \Winnt folder (the system files), such as Local Disk (C:). Double-click the %SystemRoot% folder, and then double-click the **system32** folder.
10. Click **OK**. (Click Yes if you are asked to replace an existing copy of the file.)
11. Double-click **movetree.dll**.
12. Double-click the drive that contains the %SystemRoot% or \Winnt folder (the system files), such as Local Disk (C:). Double-click the %SystemRoot% folder, and then double-click the **system32** folder.
13. Click **OK**. (Click Yes if you are asked to replace an existing copy of the file.)
14. Close the SUPPORT window.
15. Click **Exit** to close the Microsoft Windows 2000 CD window.
16. Click **Start**, point to **Programs**, point to **Accessories**, and click **Command Prompt**.
17. In the Command Prompt window, type **movetree /?**. Press **Enter**.
18. Maximize the Command Prompt window, if necessary, and scroll to view the Movetree switches and examples. Record three or four examples in your lab journal or in a word-processed document.
19. In the Command Prompt window, type **exit** and then press **Enter**.

If you want to install all of the Active Directory Support Tools as a group, refer to Hands-on Project 6-4 in Chapter 6.

Project 10-2

In this project, you determine the relative ID master in a domain. You will need access to a domain controller via an account that has Administrator privileges.

To determine the relative ID master:

1. Click **Start**, point to **Programs**, point to **Administrative Tools**, and click **Active Directory Users and Computers**.

2. Right-click a domain, such as TheFirm.com.

3. Click **Operations Masters**.

4. Ensure that the RID tab is displayed.

5. What computer is the relative ID master, and what is its domain?

6. How would you determine the infrastructure master and the PDC emulator master for the domain? How would you determine these for another domain?

7. Click **Cancel**.

8. Close the Active Directory Users and Computers tool.

Project 10-3

This project enables you to determine the current domain naming master in a forest. You will need an account that has Administrator privileges, and the account should be a member of the Domain Admins group.

To determine the domain naming master:

1. Click **Start**, point to **Programs**, point to **Administrative Tools**, and click **Active Directory Domains and Trusts**.

2. Right-click **Active Directory Domains and Trusts** in the tree.

3. Click **Operations Master**.

4. What is the name of the server that is the domain naming master? In what domain is the server? Record your observations.

5. What else can you do in the Change Operations Master dialog box?

6. Click **Close**.

7. Close the Active Directory Domains and Trusts tool.

10

Project 10-4

In this project, you determine the schema master in a forest. You will need an account that has Administrator privileges, and the account should be a member of the Schema Admins group. Also, the Active Directory Schema MMC snap-in must already be installed as one of the Windows 2000 Administration Tools (see Hands-on Project 6-6 to install the Administration Tools).

To determine the schema master:

1. Click **Start**, click **Run**, enter **mmc** in the Open box, and click **OK**.

2. Maximize the console windows.

3. Click the **Console** menu and click **Add/Remove Snap-in**.

4. Click the **Add** button.

5. Double-click **Active Directory Schema** and click **Close**.

6. Click **OK**.

7. Double-click **Active Directory Schema** in the tree, to make sure that you connect to the schema master (you should see folders for Classes and Attributes appear in the tree).

8. Right-click **Active Directory Schema** in the tree.

9. Click **Operations Master**.

10. What is the name of the computer that is the schema master? In what domain is the computer? Record your observations.

11. What else can you do in the Change Schema Master dialog box?

12. Click **Cancel**.

13. Close the console and click **No** so that your settings are not saved.

Project 10-5

In this project, you practice transferring the role of the PDC emulator master. You will need access to an account that is a member of the Domain Admins security group. Ask your instructor for the name of the domain controller that is in the role of the PDC emulator master, or refer to Hands-on Project 10-2 to determine it for yourself. Also, ask your instructor to which computer to transfer the role.

To transfer the role of the PDC emulator master:

1. Click **Start**, point to **Programs**, point to **Administrative Tools**, and click **Active Directory Users and Computers**.

2. Click **Active Directory Users and Computers** in the tree, or click a domain in the tree.

3. Click the **Action** menu and click **Connect to Domain**. Use the Browse button, if necessary, to select the domain in which to perform the transfer (click Browse, click the domain, and click OK). Click **OK** after selecting the domain via the Browse button or to accept the domain that is displayed by default.

4. Click the **Action** menu and click **Connect to Domain Controller**. What domain controllers are in the domain, and are they associated with any sites? Record your observations.

5. In the *Available controllers in (domain)* box, click the domain controller that you will transfer the PDC emulator master role to, such as lawyer.TheFirm.com.

6. Click **OK**.

7. Right-click the domain in tree, such as TheFirm.com, and click **Operations Masters**. What tabs are displayed? Record your observations.

8. Click the **PDC** tab.

9. Click the **Change** button. (If you are transferring the role to the server that already has that role, you will see a message to this effect. Click OK in the message box.)

10. Click **OK**.

11. How would you transfer the role of the infrastructure master? Record your answer in your lab journal or in a word-processed document.

12. Close the Active Directory Users and Computers tool.

Project 10-6

10

In this project, you learn how to seize the role of the relative ID master. You will need to be logged on using an account that is a member of the Domain Admins security group. *Before starting, make sure that the current relative ID master is disconnected from the network* (or you can stop before actually seizing the role).

To seize the role of the relative ID master:

1. Click **Start**, point to **Programs**, point to **Accessories**, and click **Command Prompt**. (Another way to access the command prompt is to click Start, click Run, enter cmd, and click OK.)

2. Enter **ntdsutil** and press **Enter**.

3. Enter **?** and press **Enter**. What commands are displayed? Do you see a command for roles? Record your observations.

4. At the next prompt, type **roles** and press **Enter**.

5. Type **connections** and press **Enter**.

6. Type **connect to server**, press the **spacebar**, and enter the name of the server that will be the new relative ID master, such as lawyer, and press **Enter**.

7. Type **quit** and press **Enter**.

8. Type **seize RID master** and press **Enter**. (If you do not have permission to actually seize the RID master, type quit instead of pressing Enter and then type quit on each subsequent command line until you exit the ntdsutil tool. Next, type exit to close the Command Prompt window.)

9. What message do you see displayed? Record your observation.

10. Type **quit** and press **Enter**.

11. Type **quit** again and press **Enter**.

12. Type **exit** and press **Enter** to close the Command Prompt window.

Project 10-7

In this project, you enable a domain controller as a global catalog server. Ask your instructor for the name of a server to use and for the site in which the server resides (or use a default site). You will need to access an account that has Administrator privileges and that belongs to the Domain Admins or Enterprise Admins security groups.

To enable a domain controller as a global catalog server:

1. Click **Start**, point to **Programs**, point to **Administrative Tools**, and click **Active Directory Sites and Services**.

2. Double-click the **Sites** folder in the tree, if the sites are not already displayed in the folder.

3. In the tree, double-click the site specified by your instructor, or double-click the default site.

4. In the tree, double-click the **Servers** folder, if the domain controllers in this folder are not already displayed.

5. What servers are displayed? Which of these servers are domain controllers? Record your observations.

6. In the tree, click the server specified by your instructor, or click the first server in the list.

7. What information is displayed in the right-hand pane?

8. Right-click **NTDS Settings**. What options are displayed in the shortcut menu?

9. Click **Properties**.

10. Make sure that the **General** tab is displayed.

11. Check the box for **Global Catalog**, if it is not already checked.

12. How would you disable a domain controller as a global catalog server?

13. Click **OK**.

14. Close the Active Directory Sites and Services tool.

Project 10-8

This project enables you practice creating a design topology for operations masters and global catalog servers.

To create the design topology:

1. Refer to Figure 10-16, which shows the tree and domain plan for a single forest.

2. In your lab journal or in a word-processed document, describe where, both in terms of domains and on individual DCs, you would locate the following:

- PDC emulator masters
- Infrastructure masters
- Relative ID masters
- Domain naming masters
- Schema masters
- Global catalog servers

3. Record comments about the benefits of your design plan.
4. Record how the plan might be improved by adding domain controllers in specific domains.

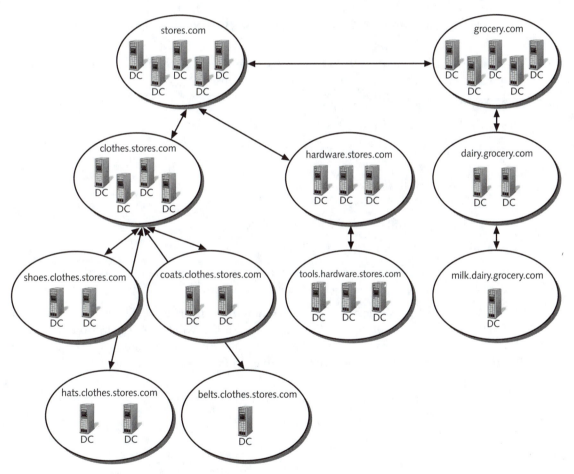

Figure 10-16   Design topology example

CASE PROJECT

Aspen Consulting Project: Designing the Operations Masters Topology

International Integrated Circuits (IIC) makes specialized circuits and power chips for cell phones, portable computers, handheld computers, CD players, and other popular electronic devices. The headquarters of IIC are in Bonn, Germany, along with one of the company's manufacturing plants. There are additional manufacturing locations in Austin, Texas; Mountain View, California; Ontario, Canada; Tokyo, Japan; Stockholm, Sweden; Brisbane, Australia; and Cambridge, England. Your analysis of the company shows that the manufacturing operations at each location are carefully coordinated through the headquarters offices in Bonn, using a centralized decision-making model. The IT department in each location is run by an IT director who reports to the CIO in Bonn. The IT operations also use the centralized model.

When you diagram the WAN connectivity between each site and the headquarters office, you find the following types of connections:

◻ Austin to Bonn: 2 Mbps frame relay

◻ Mountain View to Bonn: 2 Mbps frame relay

◻ Ontario to Bonn: 10 Mbps SMDS

◻ Tokyo to Bonn: 4 Mbps SMDS

◻ Stockholm to Bonn: 2.048 Mbps X.25

◻ Brisbane to Bonn: 4 Mbps wireless satellite

◻ Cambridge to Bonn: 25 Mbps SMDS

All of these WAN connections are generally reliable, but every one of them has gone down two or three times a year, for one hour to two days at a time.

IIC has developed a plan for its forest, tree, and domain structure. The plan is to have one forest with one tree root domain. The tree root domain will be located in Bonn and called iic.com. Each of the manufacturing locations, including the separate manufacturing location in Bonn, will have a child domain under the tree root, using the domain names:

◻ bonn.iic.com

◻ austin.iic.com

◻ mtnview.iic.com

◻ ontario.iic.com

◻ tokyo.iic.com

❑ stockholm.iic.com

❑ brisbane.iic.com

❑ cambridge.iic.com

Currently, each of the domains at IIC are mixed-mode domains that include one or more Windows NT 4.0 servers, along with Windows 2000 servers. Also, there is a mix of Windows 98, Windows NT 4.0 Workstation, and Windows 2000 Professional clients on every network in the company.

Because IIC already makes electronic parts for cell phones, the company is currently negotiating to purchase a speech simulation and recognition software company, SpeechDynamics, that is designing software to fit in a specialized chip. The headquarters of SpeechDynamics is in Raleigh, North Carolina, and the company has a small manufacturing location in Rocky Mount, North Carolina. They already have a tree root domain on the network in Raleigh that is called talk.com, and a separate child domain in Rocky Mount that is called manufact.talk.com.

1. The server administrators at IIC do not have much experience with Active Directory. To help educate them, the CIO has arranged for a teleconference to all of the sites so that you can make a presentation explaining the operations masters. Create a written presentation or a PowerPoint slide presentation that can be used for the teleconference. Also, for your presentation, explain why the PDC emulator master might play a particularly important role on IIC's network.

2. Before the slide presentation, the CIO asks about global catalog servers. He asks you to include a segment in your teleconference presentation to explain the function of global catalog servers.

3. Using the analysis of IIC, create a design topology including each of the following:

❑ Relative ID master

❑ Infrastructure master

❑ PDC emulator master

❑ Domain naming master

❑ Schema master

❑ Global catalog server

Illustrate your design topology by creating a basic network diagram. Explain how your design proposal is compatible with the possibility that IIC may purchase SpeechDynamics.

4. After you create your design topology, the CIO informs you that IIC has completed the purchase of SpeechDynamics, which will be a subsidiary of IIC. Show how you would expand your design topology to take this new development into account.

10

OPTIONAL CASE PROJECTS FOR TEAMS

Team Case One

IIC is concerned about developing a fail-safe plan in case any location loses an operations master or global catalog server. Mark Arnez asks you to form a team whose first job is to determine the risk tolerance of IIC in relation to the operations master and global catalog server roles. Use your team to develop a list of questions to ask IIC's management and IT staff about IIC's risk tolerance and how it would be affected by the loss of one or more operations masters. Next, develop contingency plans describing what IIC should do in the event of a WAN link failure between the headquarters site and another site.

Team Case Two

Several months after you complete your work at IIC, Mark Arnez calls to inform you that IIC has been purchased by one of its customer companies that makes cell phones. Before assigning you to work on the new design topology for IIC and its new parent company, Mark asks you to form a team for the purpose of creating some design rules. Your team is charged with developing a set of generic rules for placing operations masters and global catalog servers to keep the number of changes or transfers to a minimum in the event of a company takeover or reorganization.

11

DESIGNING REPLICATION AND DISASTER RECOVERY

After reading this chapter and completing the exercises, you will be able to:

♦ Explain how Active Directory replication works, including the use of the Knowledge Consistency Checker

♦ Design the Active Directory replication topology for an organization

♦ Design Dfs for folder and file replication

♦ Plan disaster recovery methods, including backing up and restoring Active Directory and other critical system data

All of us have experienced losing work or valuable information on a computer. Losing Active Directory data multiplies this problem to a large scale and can be disastrous for an organization. Another commonly experienced scenario is waiting for a computer to accomplish work for us, especially over a network. Active Directory replication enables an organization to avoid losing critical data and also to access network resources faster. Active Directory replication makes the multimaster model work, so that users can access any domain controller for logon services without waiting for a specific domain controller to respond. Replication enables other servers to take over when one domain controller is down, and it means that Active Directory data is automatically copied from one site to another for offsite fault tolerance.

In this chapter, you will learn how Active Directory replication works and how to design your network to take full advantage of replication. You will also learn how Dfs can be used to replicate information that is not in Active Directory, for faster access and fault tolerance. Although both Active Directory and Dfs replication are valuable for disaster recovery, this chapter will also show you how to back up and restore critical system data for extra disaster recovery insurance.

USING ACTIVE DIRECTORY REPLICATION

Active Directory **replication** is the process of creating a copy of specific Active Directory data, called a data store, on domain controllers. Through replication, each copy of Active Directory on each domain controller is regularly synchronized to ensure that it is identical to every other copy on domain controllers in the same domain. Key elements are also replicated between domains, such as global catalog data and the schema namespace.

The vital elements in Active Directory that are replicated in the multimaster topology include:

- Domain partition namespace
- Schema namespace
- Configuration container namespace
- Global catalog
- DNS namespace (when DNS is integrated with Active Directory)

The domain partition namespace is regularly synchronized on all domain controllers that are in the same domain. If there are eight domain controllers in one domain, Active Directory replication works to ensure that all of the domain controllers are regularly synchronized so they have exactly the same version of the domain partition namespace data (see Figure 11-1). For the sake of reducing network traffic, not all of the domain partition namespace is updated each time a change is made. Instead, only the specific objects and object attributes that have changed are updated. For example, if a new user account is created along with particular attributes, such as a user name and password, then only the new user account and its attributes are updated to all domain controllers.

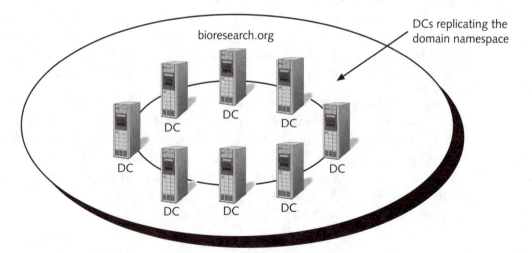

Figure 11-1 Domain partition namespace replication

Identical schema and configuration namespaces (see Chapter 6) are replicated on all domain controllers in a forest. If there are four domains in a forest, then the schema and configuration namespaces are replicated within and between domains (see Figure 11-2). The domain partition namespaces will be different between domains, but the schema and configuration namespaces will be the same. Similar to domain partition namespace replication, only new modifications are replicated, and not the entire schema or configuration container.

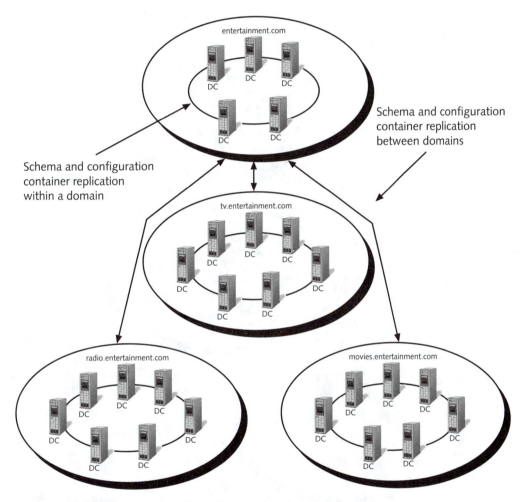

Figure 11-2   Schema and configuration container replication

Schema changes are made on and replicated from the schema master. Configuration container changes can be made on and replicated from any domain controller.

Global catalog servers within the same site and between different sites replicate to one another. Unlike domain partition, schema, and configuration container replication, global catalog server replication does not occur between every domain controller; global catalog server replication occurs only between those domain controllers that are also designated as global catalog servers (see Figure 11-3). The same principle holds true for replication between DNS servers, because DNS server data is replicated only between domain controllers that are also set up as DNS servers that are integrated with Active Directory.

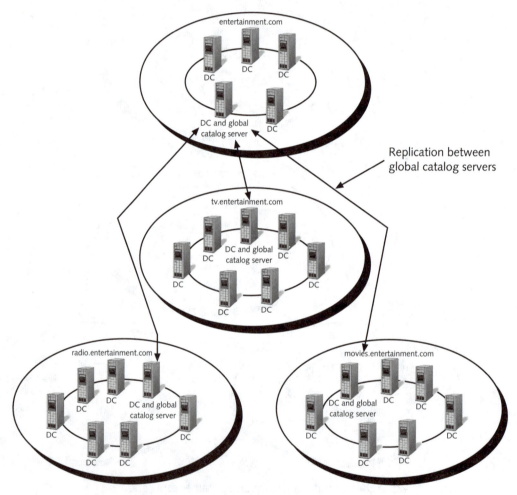

Figure 11-3   Replication between global catalog servers

   DNS servers that are not set up to be integrated with Active Directory and that have standard primary zones or standard secondary zones are not replicated by Active Directory.

Directory replication occurs from domain controller to domain controller. When multiple connections exist between domain controllers on the same LAN and between domain controllers in different sites, Active Directory establishes redundant paths between DCs, so that if one path is down there is a second path that can be used for replication. The connections are created by the **Knowledge Consistency Checker** (**KCC**, see Chapters 1 and 7). Replication occurs in a logical ring format, going from DC to DC around a ring until each DC is replicated. If a DC is down, the KCC sends replication information in the opposite direction around the ring. Whenever a new DC is added or a new site is configured, the KCC reconfigures the ring to make sure there are two replication paths available from each DC. Any two adjoining domain controllers on the ring are called **replication partners**. The KCC determines replication partners by using the following criteria:

- The distance between the domain controllers
- Whether the domain controllers are currently online and connected to the network
- Whether two domain controllers at either end of a site link are bridgehead servers

The Replication Process

Active Directory replication is designed to work efficiently and to ensure the integrity of the data through several processes:

- Tracking Active Directory changes
- Providing fault tolerance
- Packaging changes to match the site topology

Every domain controller is able to track Active Directory changes by using several methods. One method is that every change is tracked in sequence. Each time a sequential change is made, a counter, called the *Originating Write* property, is incremented for the object that is changed. For example, consider a change to the password associated with a user's account at a business. When the account is first created, the password is set by an account administrator as "newaccount," which is tracked as the first password entry by associating it with a "1" in the Originating Write property. As soon as the user logs on, she changes the password to "sheep!dog," which is the second change in the sequence, and the Originating Write property for the password attribute is incremented to "2." Five weeks later, the user changes her password to "downhill%skiingis#1," which is third in the sequence, and the Originating Write property is incremented to "3."

Another method for tracking changes is to place a timestamp on each change. In the case of the user account that has three password changes, each change is given a *timestamp*, which means that it is associated with the date and time of the change. The combination of tracking changes by sequence, by the contents of the Originating Write counter, and

11

with the timestamp all help to ensure the integrity of Active Directory data on each domain controller and to provide fault tolerance.

Consider, for example, that site links are down for several hours between the Interstate Security Bank regional office and all of its branch sites. While the site link is down, users change their passwords, account administrators create new accounts, and the domain administrator makes changes to the default domain policy. When the links are restored, the domain controllers at each site compare Active Directory changes with their replication partners. When they detect changes, they first compare values in the Originating Write counters for each change, to determine which change is sequentially most recent. They also check the timestamps of each change. These checks enable the domain controllers to determine the most recent changes and whether or not they have already implemented the changes. For example, consider a user account password change that has been made at a branch office and for which the Originating Write counter for that attribute has been incremented to 4. When the site link to the regional office is restored, the bridgehead domain controller at the regional office detects the change, because its Originating Write counter is only 3 for that account's password, compared to the counter of 4 for that password on the branch office's bridgehead server (bridgehead servers are discussed later in this chapter). The comparison enables the regional office domain controller to determine that it needs to update the password. Once the regional office DC updates the password, it increments its Originating Write counter to 4; however, it also signals to its replication partner, the bridgehead server at the branch office, that it has made a change. The replication partner is able to detect that it already has updated this particular change by comparing its Originating Write counter, which is 4, to the same Originating Write counter for the password attribute that it has received from the regional office domain controller. In this situation, the Originating Write counter keeps the integrity of the data intact in two ways:

- It enables the DC on which the change is made to show other DCs that a change was made and to show what change is most recent.

- It enables the DC on which the change is made to reject making the same change again, when it is notified of a change by a replication partner, so that changes do not become circular and result in unnecessary work on the part of domain controllers.

In another situation, the value in the Originating Write counter may not be enough to ensure the integrity of the data. Consider the situation mentioned in Chapter 10 in which two administrators make a change to a user account's password at nearly the same time, but on different domain controllers. In both changes, the Originating Write counter is incremented to the same number. However, the timestamps will be slightly different on the basis of seconds. The timestamp is used to determine which password change is the most recent and should be used for the final entry in Active Directory. In this case, the use of timestamps enables Active Directory to resolve a data conflict.

Consider another situation in which two administrators create the same account on two different DCs at exactly the same time and with the same timestamp. In this case, the Originating Write counters and the timestamps are of no value in determining which account entry to accept into Active Directory. Fortunately, there will be two different GUIDs for these accounts, and the account that is finally used is the one that has the highest GUID number.

In all of the cases that have been described, the ability of Active Directory to track changes ensures the integrity of data and provides fault tolerance. Even if a network or site link is broken, Active Directory is accurately replicated and preserved when the link is restored. If users add a new object or change the same attribute at the same time, Active Directory can use its tracking information to determine which change to use.

Another important Active Directory process is the ability to tailor how data is replicated on the basis of the characteristics of network links. By definition, data transfer within a site is relatively fast. Active Directory takes this into account by replicating data in an uncompressed format between DCs in the same site. By not compressing the data, there is less demand placed on each DC's CPU. When replication occurs over a site link, such as over a relatively slow WAN link, it is compressed so it goes over the link more quickly and creates less interference with other WAN communications. The data compression that is used over a site link is in a ratio of up to 10 to 1.

How the KCC Works Within a Site

The purpose of the Knowledge Consistency Checker (KCC), which is a system process, is to guarantee that Active Directory replication takes place. The KCC establishes connections between domain controllers and polls those connections every 15 minutes to determine if a connection needs to be reestablished, if a new DC needs to be added for replication, or if a DC has been removed from the network. The KCC ensures efficient replication and establishes the replication ring by using information about sites and site links that it obtains from the configuration container.

When a site is created out of one or more subnets, that information is defined in the configuration container namespace and is used to provide vital information to the KCC about how to replicate Active Directory data along the most efficient paths. After a site is created, the KCC determines which DCs are located in the same site. The subnet information tells the KCC which DCs are located closest to one another. This means that replication partners are selected on the basis of the site and then the subnet locations. Two DCs on the same subnet are considered closer than two DCs on two different subnets in the same site. For example, consider a site that consists of three subnets: 129.70.1, 129.70.2, and 129.70.3. The subnet 129.70.1 houses three DCs, 129.70.2 houses two DCs, and 129.70.3 houses two DCs. With this information, the KCC can determine that replication is fastest and creates less network traffic when it occurs between the three DCs in subnet 129.70.1, with one of those DCs replicating to a target DC in subnet 129.70.2 (see Figure 11-4). This is more effective and creates less network traffic than if DCs in one subnet randomly replicated to DCs in the other subnets, as in Figure 11-5.

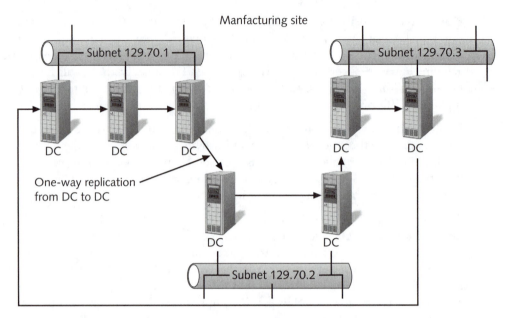

Figure 11-4 Optimized DC replication using subnet information within a single site

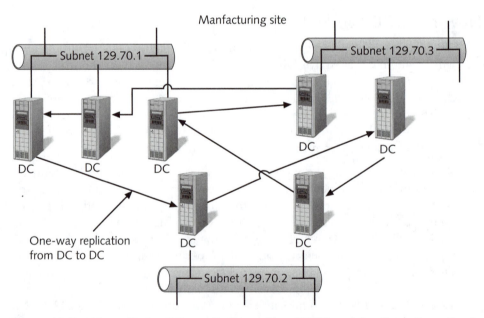

Figure 11-5 Nonoptimized site replication without KCC coordination using subnet information

By using the subnet and site information, the KCC also determines that it does not need to compress replicated data that is sent within the same site, because it assumes that all links within that site are relatively fast. When there are two or more sites connected through site links, the KCC determines that the site links are likely to be slower than links within a site, so it sends data over site links in a compressed format.

The replication within a site automatically occurs each time a new object is added or modified and whenever an object's attribute, such as a password, is modified. This practice ensures that new and modified Active Directory information is replicated to all DCs as soon as possible. Immediate replication within a site is considered particularly important because users on the same site are most likely to be affected by a change.

The information about all of the replicating DCs in a site, including global catalog servers, is contained in an Active Directory child object under a site called *NTDS Site Settings* (see Figure 11-6). The NTDS Site Settings container has information about all replicating partner DCs, including connection objects. A *connection object* is the one-way linkup between a source DC and a target DC. Information about how often to perform replication, such as every three hours, is also housed in the NTDS Site Settings container.

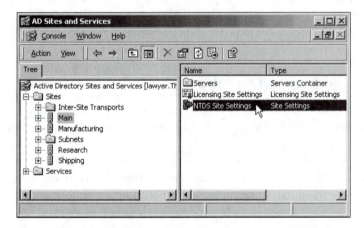

Figure 11-6 NTDS Site Settings container

Also shown in Figure 11-6 is a folder within each site that is labeled Servers. The child objects in this folder are the DCs in the site, and each DC has a child object that is called *NTDS Settings*. The NTDS Settings container for a particular DC holds information about which other DC provides it with the replicated data. For example, consider a site in which there are four domain controllers: Accounting, Marketing, Manufacturing, and Research. In this configuration, the Accounting server replicates to the Marketing server, Marketing replicates to Manufacturing, Manufacturing replicates to Research, and Research replicates to Accounting (see Figure 11-7). The NTDS Settings for the Accounting server contain data that indicates that the Research server is the Accounting server's source for Active Directory replication data.

11

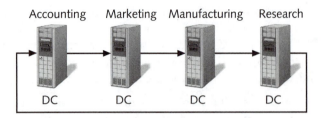

Accounting   Marketing   Manufacturing   Research

DC   DC   DC   DC

Figure 11-7   Replication partners

You can view the Active Directory containers associated with a site, including the NTDS Site Settings and NTDS Settings containers, by using the Active Directory Sites and Services tool or the ADSI Edit tool (see Chapter 6).

The replication process within a site uses a transport protocol called the **remote procedure call (RPC) protocol** (see Chapter 7). RPC is carried over another transport protocol, TCP/IP, and enables one computer to run a program process or procedure called a remote procedure call on another computer. For Active Directory replication, the source DC sends a remote procedure call to its target DC to start replication. The target DC is able to verify which DC is authorized to update it by checking that information in its NTDS Settings container.

How the KCC Works over Site Links

When there are two or more sites, the KCC works by establishing one bridgehead server at each site. As you learned in Chapter 7, a **bridgehead server** is a domain controller on one site that replicates to another bridgehead server at a different site. Only one bridgehead server is designated by the KCC per site, so that site link traffic is kept to a minimum. Also, each bridgehead server is established automatically, unless you override the automatic process and specify a preferred bridgehead server. The practice of establishing only one bridgehead server per site is designed to ensure that there are not multiple DCs replicating with partners across a site link and using up valuable bandwidth. Each bridgehead server replicates Active Directory to other DCs on the same site using the ring-based replication topology. Try Hands-on Project 11-1 to override the automatic designation and to establish a particular preferred bridgehead server.

If you do not create site links between two sites, then those two sites do not engage in Active Directory replication with one another. The KCC does not automatically configure connections or designate bridgehead servers in this situation. Also, if you select a preferred bridgehead server, keep in mind that you have disabled the KCC from automatically designating a bridgehead server. If the preferred bridgehead server goes offline, replication does not occur until you manually designate another preferred bridgehead server. The system log will report whenever a preferred bridgehead server is offline.

If there are two or more site links between the same two sites, the source bridgehead server automatically chooses the site link that is assigned the lowest cost by a network administrator. Usually the slowest or least expensive link is assigned the lowest cost. For example, Interstate Security Bank plans to set up two site links between the headquarters office and each regional office. There is currently a 25 Mbps SMDS site link to each regional office, and the bank is planning to establish a 2 Mbps frame relay backup site link. They have also decided to use the frame relay link for Active Directory replication traffic, which will be configured to occur every 90 minutes. Try Hands-on Project 11-2 to assign a cost to a site link.

The cost for a link is set at 100 by default. When there are two or more links between two sites, plan to change the cost on each link to reflect how critical the site link traffic is to the organization, so that replication traffic goes over the least critical link. The KCC will send traffic over the link assigned the lowest cost. For example, if there are two links between two sites, one a critical link assigned a cost of 2 and the other a backup link assigned a cost of 1, then replication traffic will be sent over the link assigned a cost of 1 (unless that link is down).

Besides establishing a cost with a site link, you can determine the replication frequency so that you can tailor the replication interval to reduce the total site link traffic. On Windows NT Server 4.0 and other network operating systems, one of the greatest sources of traffic over WAN links is replication traffic, such as the PDC replicating to BDCs (see Chapter 1). In Windows 2000, you can control DC and global catalog server replication traffic so that it occurs less frequently, such as only every six hours. Another way to customize replication traffic over a site link is to have it occur during off-hours for a business, such as only between 6 pm and 6 am. In the case of Interstate Security Bank, for example, Active Directory replication over the site links to the branch offices occurs only after the regional and branch offices close at 5:30 pm. The default replication frequency is set at 180 minutes. You can configure the replication frequency in minutes, by the day of the week, and by the time of day. Figure 11-8 shows how to set the day of the week and time of day. Try the second part of Hands-on Project 11-2 to learn how to set the replication interval.

11

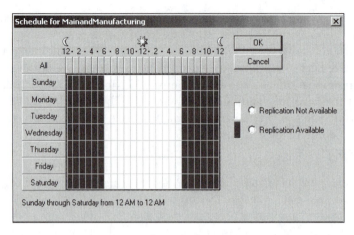

Figure 11-8   Setting replication frequency over a site link

The RPC protocol is also used for replication between sites. RPC is carried over TCP/IP when replication occurs through non-mail-based communications, such as through direct network links. **Simple Mail Transport Protocol (SMTP)** is used to transport the RPC protocol when the replication is performed through an e-mail connection, such as over the Internet. Replication through SMTP has some significant limitations compared to replication over TCP/IP. The most significant is that only the global catalog server, configuration container namespace, and schema namespace are replicated. This is because SMTP-based replication can be used only across site links that join two different domains.

Although replication is only one-way within a site, it is desirable to have multiple-way replication between two or more sites so that the shortest replication routes can be taken and so that replication can go in any direction. This is called **transitive replication**. Transitive replication is made possible by establishing a site link bridge. A **site link bridge** is two or more site links that transitively replicate to one another through the same host transport protocol, either TCP/IP or SMTP. The transitive replication means that they can replicate in any direction because each site link is like a two-way bridge, instead of going in just one direction. Also, replication only occurs over the site links configured into the site link bridge.

To create a site link bridge, all site links within the same bridge must use the same protocol, IP or SMTP. For example, consider the York Industries subsidiary of B & E Electronics, which has five manufacturing locations in London. Three sites, called A, B, and C, have three combined site links that use IP. Three sites C, D, and E have two site links that are Internet links using SMTP. Three of the site links use IP for replication, and the other two use SMTP over Internet connections. Also, Sites D and E are in different domains than sites A, B, and C, which are all in the same domain. In this situation, you would configure the three IP-based site links as one site link bridge and the two SMTP-based site links as a separate site link bridge (see Figure 11-9).

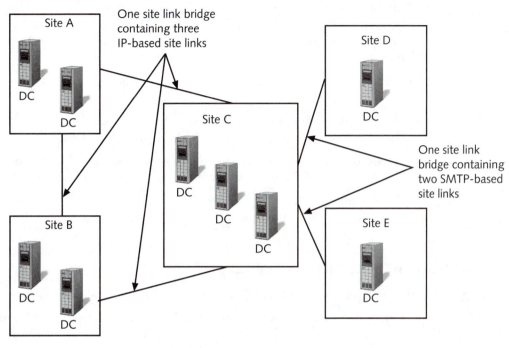

Figure 11-9 Using site link bridges

11

On many networks, all site links use IP for replication communications. When this is the case, you can use the option to *bridge all site links* to combine all site links into one bridge that allows multiple replication routes throughout the network. This is a good option when you are working with small and medium-sized networks. On large networks, you may decide to avoid this option, because it can result in unanticipated network traffic over some links. When you configure a large network, it is wiser to monitor the network traffic across each network link; for example, by using Network Monitor or another network monitoring tool. Once you understand the traffic flow across links, you can create individual site link bridges that enable you to control the traffic flow on the basis of the traffic patterns that emerge from your analysis. Try Hands-on Project 11-3 to learn where to configure all site links into a bridge and how to enable or disable this setting. Next, try Hands-on Project 11-4 to create an individual site link bridge consisting of two site links.

Before you plan a replication topology, keep the following review of replication factors in mind:

- The KCC checks every 15 minutes for changes to the site topology.

- Intrasite replication occurs when a change is made to Active Directory, such as adding a new user account.

- Intersite replication (over a site link) occurs by default every 180 minutes, 24 hours a day and seven days a week, but the replication interval can be manually configured at intervals that include minutes, hours of the day, and days of the week.

- Replication between two sites occurs only if a site link is configured between them.

- If two or more site links exist between the same site, configure each site link with a cost. Replication goes over the link with the lowest cost.

- Replication between sites is performed by one bridgehead server designated (automatically by the KCC or manually by the server administrator) per site.

- Configuring site link bridges enables two or more sites to replicate transitively (in multiple directions).

DESIGNING A REPLICATION TOPOLOGY

When you design a replication topology, use the following guidelines:

- On a small network, use two or more domain controllers so that replication can take place.

- When you divide a single domain network into two or more sites, locate at least one domain controller and global catalog server at each site, which provides automated offsite backup for the domain partition, global catalog, schema namespace, and configuration container (if you configure site links between the sites). Also, consider placing a DNS server that is integrated with Active Directory at each site.

- When you set up a multiple domain network that has two or more sites, locate two or more DCs in each domain, at least one DC in each site, and at least one global catalog server at each site. Place a DNS server integrated with Active Directory in each domain and, if possible, at each site.

- When there are two or more site links between two adjoining sites, configure the cost of each site link so that the KCC will direct replication traffic over the site link that has the lowest cost.

- For each site link, configure the replication frequency, including times of day and days of the week so that the replication does not interfere with the regular business use of the site link.

- For small and medium-sized networks, configure site links that use the same protocol so that all site links are in the same site link bridge.

- For some medium-sized and large networks, disable the setting to link all site links into a single bridge. Instead, configure individual site link bridges on the basis of your analysis of network traffic over the site links.

- Use TCP/IP as the main RPC host transport protocol for site links within and between domains, whenever possible.

- Use SMTP as the main RPC host protocol when replicating between two different domains over an e-mail and Internet-based site link.

Jefferson Philately provides one example of how these design guidelines can be applied. Consider the Jefferson Philately model described in Chapter 7, in which two sites are configured, one for the main location and one for the manufacturing plant located in the same city near the main location. In this situation, Jefferson Philately can have off-site Active Directory backup by locating at least one DC at each site, with each DC also doubling as a global catalog server, as shown in Figure 11-10. Further, because the network design calls for a 155 Mbps ATM link between the sites, Jefferson Philately would use the RPC protocol over TCP/IP for replication. In this context, the KCC would automatically designate one DC at the Main site and one DC at the Manufacturing site as a bridgehead server. To minimize the replication traffic, the company can set the replication frequency to occur every 4 or 5 hours.

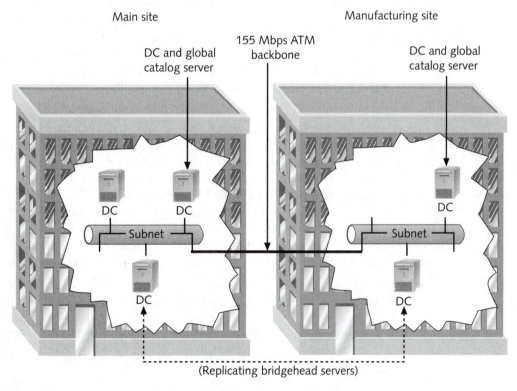

Figure 11-10   Jefferson Philately sample replication topology

The advantages of this design are:

- There is offsite replication of the domain partition, configuration container, schema, and global catalog, in case there is a disaster that damages servers in one of the buildings.

- Replication over the site link is compressed to reduce traffic.

- Replication traffic over the site link can be scheduled so that it does not interfere with regular business operations over the site link.

If Jefferson Philately decides to build the manufacturing plant in Cambridge, Ohio instead of in Cleveland, the company can use the same design. But in the case of the Cambridge plan, the site link would be slower, using frame relay at 256 Kbps. In this situation, the company might set up replication to occur in the evenings after regular work hours.

Consider another example, which is the Pampas Fixtures subsidiary of York Industries. Pampas operates out of five different buildings that are in different locations around Buenos Aires. All of the buildings are connected through 128 Kbps X.25 connections. Three of the connections are reliable and two are unreliable. The networks in all of the buildings are in the same domain. The best replication topology for Pampas is to configure each location into a separate site with its own combined domain controller and global catalog server, as shown in Figure 11-11. Because the site links are slow and congested during normal work hours, Pampas plans to schedule replication across the site links to occur every 120 minutes between midnight and 4 am. So that replication can occur in any direction across the site links, Pampas is using the *bridge all site links* option in Active Directory.

In the near future, because two of the sites have unreliable links, Pampas Fixtures plans to install an additional link at those two sites, and eventually at all five sites. In this plan, all of the sites will have two links within the next six months. The new links will be DSL, which is a new service offered by the local telecommunications company. After the DSL links are installed, Pampas plans to designate a cost of 1 to the X.25 link and a cost of 2 to the DSL link at each site, so that Active Directory replication goes over the slower X.25 link, which will be used for lower-priority business functions. Also, they will reconfigure each site link so that replication occurs every three hours, 24 hours a day, seven days a week. The advantages of the Pampas replication topology after the DSL links are installed include:

- There is offsite replication at five different sites, so that if one or more sites is damaged, there is a greater chance of continued operations at the remaining sites. At each site there is replication of the domain partition, configuration container, schema, and global catalog.

- The *bridge all site links* option ensures that replication occurs in any direction among the sites.

- By assigning the lowest cost to the X.25 links, the company ensures that replication goes over the links that have the least important network traffic. There is additional redundancy built in, because if one of the X.25 links is down, replication traffic will go over the DSL link at the corresponding site.

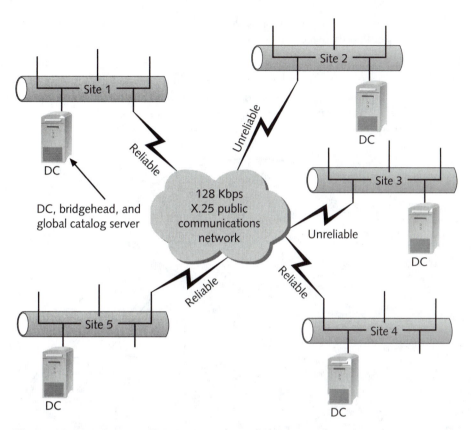

Figure 11-11 Pampas Fixtures sample replication topology

 If the budget allows, another way to improve the design in Figure 11-11 is to add DCs to each site so that there are two or more DCs per site for intrasite replication and fault tolerance.

The more general plan for providing a replication topology in all seven of the domains in York Industries includes the following features:

- Multiple domain controllers and at least one global catalog server in each company's domain for redundancy within domains

- Two or more domain controllers and at least one global catalog server in each child domain

- At least one domain controller and global catalog server at each site, for domains that are divided into multiple sites

- Use of multiple site link bridges to manage replication traffic so that it does not interfere with other business traffic over site links

- Scheduling replication traffic over each site link to match the differing business demands placed on each link

Figure 11-12 illustrates the general replication topology for York Industries, using the original domain plan described in Chapter 6, which consists of a tree root domain for the parent company and child domains for the other companies. Although not shown, this model also gives each company the option to add new child domains under its main child domain.

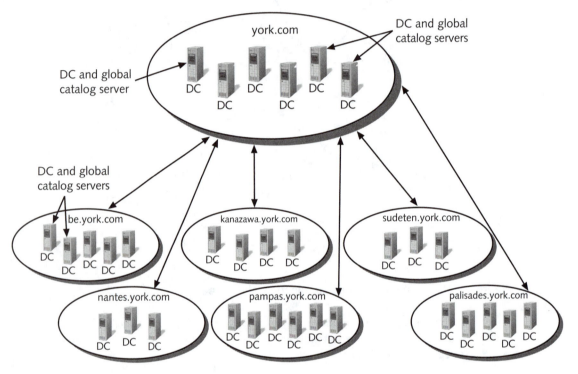

Figure 11-12   York Industries sample replication topology

The advantages of the York Industries topology are:

- Domain partition replication occurs across multiple servers within the same domain.

- Offsite domain partition replication is set up for sites in the same domain that are in different physical locations, as is true of Pampas Fixtures (refer to Figure 11-11).

- Global catalog server replication occurs between all domains, providing offsite replication of global catalog server information, such as all objects in all domain partitions, selected attributes, the forest schema, and the forest configuration container.

Using Dfs for File Replication and Disaster Recovery

Active Directory replication can be used to protect the Active Directory contents, but what about protecting critical user files, such as the customer service files used by Interstate Security Bank? Regular files can be replicated by using the Distributed File System. The **Distributed File System (Dfs)** enables you to simplify access to the shared folders on a network, replicate shared folder information to multiple DCs on a network, and load balance access to shared folders. First, access to shared folders is simplified because Dfs enables you to set up folders to appear as though they are accessed from only one place. If the network, for example, has eight Windows 2000 servers that make a variety of shared folders available to network users, Dfs can be set up so that users do not have to know what server offers which shared folder. All of the folders can be set up to appear as though they are on one server and under one broad folder structure. Dfs also makes managing folder access easier for server administrators.

When Dfs is used in a domain, then shared folder contents can be replicated to one or more DCs or member servers, which means that if the original server goes offline its shared folders are still available to users through the replica servers. When the replica servers are located offsite, such as at a remote site or location, then Dfs also provides disaster recovery. **Disaster recovery** involves taking steps to prepare for extreme situations that involve loss of services or data loss. If, for example, the servers at one site are damaged because of a natural disaster, the Dfs shared folder contents will still be intact at another site.

A third advantage of using Dfs is that when multiple users need to access the contents of a shared folder, Dfs spreads the load among multiple Dfs designated servers. One server is not inundated by traffic, which can paralyze that server and its local network. The advantages of using Dfs include:

- Shared folders can be set up so that they appear in one hierarchy of folders, enabling users to save time when searching for information.

- NTFS access permissions fully apply to Dfs on NTFS-formatted volumes.

- Fault tolerance can be enhanced by replicating shared folders on multiple servers, resulting in uninterrupted access for users, file replication that protects files from being inadvertently deleted, and disaster recovery of precious data.

- Access to shared folders can be distributed across many servers, resulting in the ability to perform **load balancing**, so that one server does not experience more load than others.

- Access is improved to resources for Web-based Internet and intranet sites.

- Vital shared folders on multiple computers can be backed up from one set of master folders.

11

Besides enabling users to be more productive, server administrators are also immediately more productive because Dfs reduces the number of calls to server administrators asking where to find a particular resource. Another advantage of Dfs in a domain is that folders can be replicated automatically or manually through Microsoft Replication Services. Shared folders in Dfs are copied to each designated replica computer, which yields two significant advantages: (1) important information is not lost when a disk drive on one server fails, and (2) users always have access to shared folders even in the event of a disk failure.

In the pre-Dfs model of sharing, in Windows NT Server for instance, one or two servers might bear the brunt of most network activity due to heavy access to their shared folders. For example, consider a busy college network in which student registration information is housed in shared folders on one server. During registration that server experiences extremely heavy access, delaying registration and causing students to wait in lines or to be placed on hold when registering by telephone or through the Internet. If Dfs is implemented, the critical registration folders are replicated to multiple servers, which leads to access being equally distributed among those servers. The result is faster registration and fewer headaches for students and the registrar's office. The same load balancing features can be used to improve Web access by distributing the load among many servers. This is especially important, for example, to companies that rely on e-commerce for much of their business, because the companies can handle higher volumes of customer traffic, and at the same their customers are happier because they do not have to wait to transact business.

 In a mixed-mode domain that has a combination of Windows 2000 and Windows NT 4.0 servers, Dfs can be fully implemented on the Windows NT 4.0 servers as long as Service Pack 3 or above is installed.

Dfs Models

There are two models for implementing Dfs: standalone and domain-based. The standalone Dfs model offers more limited capabilities than the domain-based model. In the standalone model there is no Active Directory implementation to help manage the shared folders, and there is only a single or flat-level share, which means that the main Dfs shared folder does not contain a hierarchy of other shared folders. Also, the standalone model does not have Dfs folders that are linked to other computers through a Dfs container that has a main root and a deep, multilevel hierarchical structure.

The domain-based model of Dfs has more features than the standalone approach. Most importantly, the domain-based model takes full advantage of Active Directory and is available only to servers and workstations that are members of a domain. The domain-based model enables a deep root-based hierarchical arrangement of shared folders that is published in Active Directory. Dfs shared folders in the domain-based model are replicated for fault tolerance and load balancing, whereas the standalone Dfs model does not implement these features.

Dfs Topology

The hierarchical structure of Dfs in the domain-based model is called the **Dfs topology**. There are three elements to the Dfs topology:

- The Dfs root
- The Dfs links
- Servers on which the Dfs shared folders are replicated as replica sets

A **Dfs root** is a main container in Active Directory that holds links to shared folders that can be accessed from the root. The server that maintains the Dfs root is called the host server. When a network client views the shared folders in the Dfs root, all of the folders appear as though they are in one main folder on the same computer, which is the Windows 2000 server containing the Dfs root—even though the folders may actually reside on many different computers in the domain.

 There can be only one Dfs root per server.

A **Dfs link** is a designated access path between the Dfs root and shared folders that are defined to the root. For example, a Dfs root might be set up to contain all shared research folders for a plant biology research group that has folders on four different servers. Those folders can be shared via links drawn from them to the Dfs root so that all of the folders appear as though they are available from one place through the published information in Active Directory. Dfs links can also be made to another Dfs root on a different computer or to an entire shared volume on a server (see Figure 11-13).

A **replica set** is a set of shared folders that is replicated or copied to one or more servers in a domain. In the plant biology example, the replica set would consist of all shared folders under the Dfs root that are designated to be replicated to other network servers. Part of this process means that links are established to each server that participates in the replication. Another part of the process is to set up synchronization so that replication takes place among all servers at a specified interval, such as every 30 minutes.

11

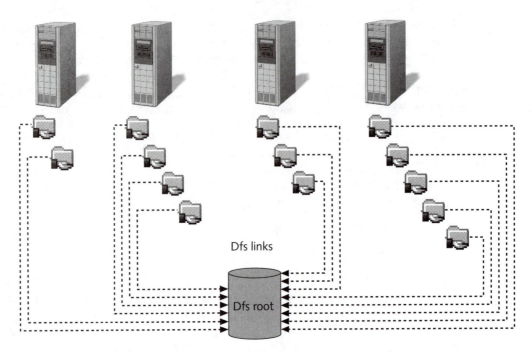

Figure 11-13   Dfs links in the Dfs root container

Creating a Dfs Implementation Plan

A Dfs implementation is most successful when it is well planned. There are several factors that Microsoft recommends you consider before installing and setting up Dfs:

- When Active Directory is installed, plan to use the domain-based model because it provides the most options and enables you to manage the resulting network traffic.

- Place Dfs shared folders on disks that are formatted using NTFS to ensure that there are strong security options.

- Use more than one Dfs root to reflect the particular needs of an organization; for instance, to reflect its geographic organization. For example, the Wyoming regional office of Interstate Security Bank might configure a separate root for each of its branch offices, resulting in a Dfs root structure, as shown in Figure 11-14.

wyoming.isb.com

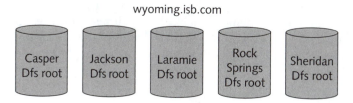

Figure 11-14   Sample Dfs root topology for the Wyoming regional and branch offices

■ Use upper-level subfolders under a root to reflect other elements of an organization, such as its organization by department or division. For example, the analysis of the Interstate Security Bank headquarters office shows that there are several departments and special groups: federal auditors, external auditors, the board of directors, executives, the Loans department, the Marketing department, the Business department, the Information Technology department, the Investments department, and the Customer Service department. In the isb.com domain for the headquarters office, there might be one Dfs root and a subfolder under the root for each of the special groups and departments, as shown in Figure 11-15.

11

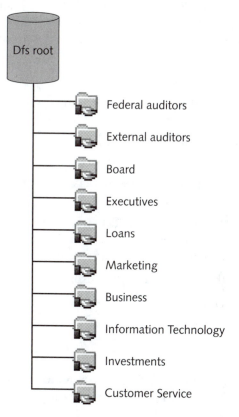

Figure 11-15   Sample Dfs subfolder topology for the Interstate Security Bank headquarters

- Determine the impact that Dfs will have on network traffic. Use the domain-based model with load balancing to help equally disperse network traffic. When you use load balancing in the domain-based model, Dfs is able to work with a Microsoft DNS server to connect each user to the closest server providing Dfs services.

- When designing a domain-based model, create the first Dfs root and links to that root before creating additional Dfs roots.

- In the domain-based model, develop a synchronization schedule that will take into account the existing network traffic along different routes (segments) on which synchronization will occur. For example, synchronize more frequently on routes that have high-speed links, such as 100 Mbps, and less frequently on lower-speed routes that operate at 10 Mbps.

- Review all Dfs shared folders on a regular basis so that you can purge folders that are no longer in use.

Setting up Dfs

Dfs is configured using the Distributed File System tool in the Administrative Tools menu (click Start, point to Programs, point to Administrative Tools, and click Distributed File System) or the Distributed file system MMC snap-in. The general steps for setting up Dfs are:

1. Plan the Dfs implementation before you set up Dfs.

2. Use the Distributed File System tool to set up the Dfs root (try Hands-on Project 11-5).

3. Locate all of the shared folders on all of the servers that you want to incorporate into Dfs.

4. Create the Dfs links in the Dfs root to the shared folders (try Hands-on Project 11-6).

5. Create a Dfs root replica to replicate all of the folders in the Dfs root, or create particular Dfs replica sets for the folders that you want to replicate for load balancing, fault tolerance, and disaster recovery (try Hands-on Project 11-7).

6. Set up permission security on the Dfs root and the Dfs links.

7. Publish the Dfs root in Active Directory.

PLANNING DISASTER RECOVERY

Carefully planning Active Directory replication and Dfs are two ways to plan for disaster recovery. In addition to these steps, plan for disaster recovery through the following means:

- Develop a backup strategy and perform regular backups.

- Back up system state data and the system protected files.
- Create boot disks.
- Create and regularly update emergency repair disks.

Each of these steps is described in the following sections.

Developing a Backup Strategy

One of the best disaster recovery methods is to back up all servers on a regular schedule, such as once each day. Windows 2000 Server offers five backup methods: normal, incremental, differential, copy, and daily. Each of these methods was described in Chapter 4 and are summarized in Table 11-1 (review Hands-on Project 4-7 to practice using the Backup tool).

Table 11-1   Windows 2000 Server Backup Options

Backup Option	Description
Normal	A full file-by-file backup, such as that used for backing up one or more volumes
Incremental	Only backs up files that have the archive attribute, and removes the archive bit after each file is backed up
Differential	Only backs up files that have the archive attribute, but does not remove the archive bit after a file is backed up
Copy	Backs up specific files and folders that have been selected, but does not remove the archive bit
Daily	Only backs up files that have been changed or added on the day of the backup, but does not remove the archive bit

If there is time, perform a normal backup of all Windows 2000 servers each evening. When servers store so much information that normal backups take more than an evening to complete, (1) use a combination of normal, incremental, and differential backups; for example, performing a normal backup on Friday night and incremental or differential backups on all other nights, or (2) use a combination of incremental and differential backups every night to ensure that all data is regularly backed up.

Develop a backup media rotation plan that includes:

- *At least two complete sets of media:* For example, use one set of tapes one week and another set the next week. If one tape or the entire set is damaged, there is another set that can be used for a restore. Using this method, some data will be lost in a restore when one or more tapes is damaged, depending on how you have set up normal, incremental, and differential backups—but you will still have recent data that *can* be restored.

11

- *Use a media rotation method:* Media rotation involves backing up more frequently to some media than to others in a set. For example, some tapes in a tape set might be used four times in a month, while other tapes are only used once each month. If one of the frequently used tapes is damaged or wears out sooner than expected, one of the less used tapes is likely to remain intact. Deploying media rotation combined with using two or more complete sets of media enables you to minimize possible data loss to one day or less of new data.

- *Store backup media offsite:* Certain media can be regularly stored offsite, such as in a bank vault. If you use two or more sets of media, you can store the set that is temporarily not used offsite. Offsite storage is good protection against fire, flood, and other disasters.

 Windows 2000 Server has a scheduler that can be used to ensure that back-ups start automatically at a particular time of day and day of the week.

Disaster Recovery for System State Data and System Protected Files

To protect against a disaster and to provide a way to recover system information, regularly back up the Windows 2000 Server system state data and the system protected files (also see Chapter 4). In Windows 2000 Server the system state data consists of several critical elements:

- System and boot files
- Active Directory
- SYSVOL folder
- Registry
- COM+ Class Registration information
- DNS zones (when DNS is installed)
- Certificate information (when certificate services are installed)
- Server cluster data (when server clustering is used)

The system state data is backed up as a group because many of these entities are interrelated. To back up the system state data, insert the backup medium, click Start, point to Programs, point to Accessories, point to System Tools, and click Backup. Next, click the Backup tab, click the System State box under My Computer, and click Start Backup. Each time you back up this information—for example, to tape—a duplicate copy is also created in \%SystemRoot%\repair\regback (refer to Hands-on Project 4-7 in Chapter 4).

When you back up the system state data, keep in mind that you can back it up only from the local computer, which means that the backup medium, such as a tape drive, must be physically attached to that computer.

If you need to restore the system state data, remember that all of the data must be restored, and not just selected portions, such as the Registry. The general steps for restoring the system state data are:

1. Shut down the server and reboot (press F8) into the Directory Services Restore mode.

2. Open the Backup tool from the System Tools menu and click the Restore tab.

3. Insert the medium from which to perform the restore, such as a tape, and in the left-hand pane, double-click the medium name from which to perform the restore, such as Travan or DAT (for a tape drive). In the right-hand pane (or on the left-hand pane under the medium), find the label of the backup that you want to restore and double-click it.

4. Click the System State box.

5. In the *Restore files to* box, select the location to which to restore the files and folders, such as to the *Original location*.

6. Click the Start Restore button.

7. Click OK to start the restore.

8. Click Close and close the Backup tool.

The system protected files are:

- *Ntldr:* A boot program that initiates the startup process, operating system selection, and hardware detection

- *Bootsect.dos:* A file that is used for dual-boot systems

- *Boot.ini:* An initialization file that is used by Ntldr to obtain startup information, such as which operating systems are available and their locations

- *Ntdetect.com:* A program that detects the computer's hardware

- *Ntbootdd.sys:* A driver for SCSI adapters

- *Ntoskrnl.exe:* A program that is the Windows 2000 kernel

- *Hal.dll:* The hardware abstraction layer (a driver for CPUs)

These files are vital for booting a server. If you have them backed up, you can restore one or more files, if damaged. These files are backed up by following the steps to back up the system state files plus selecting *Automatically backup System Protected Files with the System State* in the advanced options for backing up server files (see Figure 11-16 and refer to Hands-on Project 4-7).

11

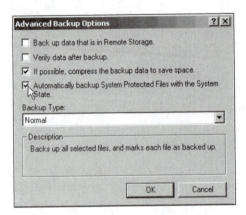

Figure 11-16   Backing up system protected files

You can restore one or more protected system files by using the Windows 2000 Server recovery console, which provides the ability to boot into a command-line mode. The command-line mode includes a *copy* command with which to copy files.

The recovery console also offers two important utilities to repair boot problems. One utility is the *fixmbr* command, which is used to fix the Master Boot Record. The second utility is the *fixboot* command, which is used to fix the boot sector on the system boot partition.

Creating Boot Disks

Make a set of floppy boot disks that will enable you to boot a server. This set of disks can be vital if you cannot boot from a hard drive or a CD-ROM drive. The boot disks are also needed so that you can boot the computer and use the emergency repair disk (see the next section).

The general steps to make a set of boot disks are:

1. Format four floppy disks.

2. Insert the Windows 2000 Server CD-ROM.

3. Click Start and then click Run.

4. In the Open box, enter the drive letter of the CD-ROM, plus the path \bootdisk\makeboot a:.

5. Click OK.

6. Follow the on-screen instructions.

Creating and Using an Emergency Repair Disk

After Windows 2000 Server is installed, create an **emergency repair disk (ERD)** for each server. The ERD enables you to fix several kinds of problems, such as repairing the Windows 2000 Server system files. Plan to create a new ERD each time you install software, make a server configuration change, install a new adapter, add a NIC, restructure a partition, or upgrade the operating system. You can create or update the ERD at any time after Windows 2000 Server is installed by starting the Backup utility and clicking the Emergency Repair Disk button (try Hands-on Project 11-8).

To use the emergency repair disk, follow these steps:

1. Power off the computer.

2. If your computer supports booting from the Windows 2000 Server CD-ROM, insert it in the CD-ROM drive. If not, insert the Windows 2000 floppy disk labeled Setup Disk 1 (the first of the boot disks you created in the last section). Power on the computer, enabling it to boot from the CD-ROM or floppy disk. If you boot from floppy disk, follow the instructions to insert Setup Disk 2.

3. On the Welcome to Setup screen, press R for repair (see Figure 11-17).

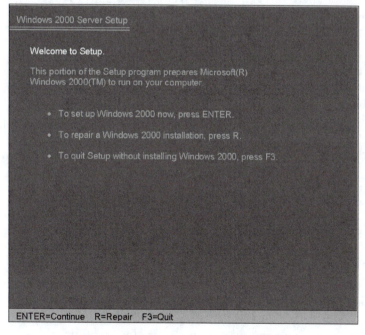

Figure 11-17   Starting the emergency repair disk

4. On the next screen, press R again to use the emergency repair disk to perform the recovery. Also note that there is an option to start the recovery console by pressing C.

5. Insert the emergency repair disk.

6. There are two options that you can choose: one is to press M so that you can choose from a manual list of repair options, and the other is to press F to perform all repair options. If you select the manual option, you can select any or all of the following: inspect startup environment, verify Windows 2000 system files, and inspect boot sector. If you select F, then all of these functions are performed.

7. After you make your selection, follow the instructions on the screen to repair the problem.

8. Reboot the computer.

CHAPTER SUMMARY

❑ Active Directory replication accomplishes several tasks. It makes multimaster replication work so that users can access the nearest domain controller for fast access to accounts and resources. Because each DC in a domain has the same domain partition information, there is automatic fault tolerance. Also, when domain controllers are on separate sites, there is offsite disaster recovery for Active Directory data. Replication not only provides a copy of the domain partition, but it also provides redundancy for the schema, configuration container, global catalog, and DNS server information.

❑ Replication can be customized within sites and over site links so that network traffic is controlled. For example, because site links are normally slower than communications within a site, replication can be adjusted to occur less frequently.

❑ Dfs provides a way to automatically replicate vital information in shared folders. Using Dfs enables you to provide automatic backup of folders and files, to simplify access to shared folders, and to spread the work among multiple servers. Similar to Active Directory replication, Dfs can be a source of disaster recovery when there are multiple sites in a network.

❑ Besides using Active Directory replication and Dfs, there are at least four more steps you can take in designing disaster recovery: develop a media-based backup strategy, back up system state and system protected files, create boot disks, and create emergency repair disks. Plan to include all of these backup techniques to provide versatile disaster recovery options for solving all kind of problems.

In the next chapter, you will find a review of many of the topics discussed in this book, such as analyzing an organization and designing Active Directory services. Plan to use the chapter to review specific concepts and to prepare for certification.

KEY TERMS

bridgehead server — A domain controller at each site and with access to a site link, which is designated by the KCC to exchange replication information. There is only one bridgehead server per site.

disaster recovery — Taking steps to prepare for extreme situations that involve the loss of computer services or data loss.

Distributed File System (Dfs) — A system that enables folders shared on multiple computers to appear as though they exist in one centralized hierarchy of folders instead of on many different computers. Dfs enables fault tolerance, disaster recovery, and server load balancing.

Dfs link — A path that is established between a shared folder in a domain and a Dfs root.

Dfs root — The main Active Directory container that holds Dfs links to shared folders in a domain.

Dfs topology — Applies to a domain-based Dfs model and encompasses the Dfs root, Dfs links to the root, and servers on which the Dfs structure is replicated.

emergency repair disk (ERD) — A disk that contains repair, diagnostic, and backup information for use in case there is a problem with Windows 2000 Server.

Knowledge Consistency Checker (KCC) — A process run by Active Directory to establish network connections between DCs and to ensure that replication services take place. It obtains site and site link information from the configuration container and assesses the locations of DCs, site link costs, and the replication strategy of server administrators.

load balancing — On a single server, distributing resources across multiple server disk drives and paths for better server response; on multiple network servers, distributing resources across two or more servers for better server and network performance.

remote procedure call (RPC) protocol — A transport protocol that enables an initiating or source computer to run a program process on a target computer.

replica set — A grouping of shared folders in a Dfs root that is replicated, or copied, to all servers that participate in Dfs replication. When changes are made to Dfs shared folders, all of the participating servers are automatically or manually synchronized so that they have the same copy.

replication — A process that, when used by Active Directory, creates a copy of specific Active Directory contents, called a data store, on domain controllers. For example, every domain controller in the same domain contains a regularly synchronized copy of the domain data store (the domain partition data) because of replication.

replication partners — Two domain controllers that directly replicate Active Directory data, one with the other.

Simple Mail Transfer Protocol (SMTP) — An e-mail protocol used by systems that have TCP/IP network communications.

11

site link bridge — Two or more site links that transitively replicate to the connected sites through the same host transport protocol, either TCP/IP or SMTP. Physically, a site link bridge is often a network device, such as a router or brouter. The site link bridge enables replication to go in any direction, along any site link within the site link bridge.

transitive replication — Active Directory replication that can go in any direction through a site link bridge.

REVIEW QUESTIONS

Answer questions 1–9 using this case information:

Watson Furnace manufactures forced air furnaces for homes and small businesses. They are a national company that has four main locations: Houston, Texas; Beaumont, Texas; Kansas City, Kansas; and Cedar Rapids, Iowa. The main headquarters is in Houston, which has a branch location in Beaumont. Both of these locations are in the watson.com domain. There are two network connections between Houston and Beaumont, one at 2 Mbps and another at 10 Mbps. Also, the Kansas City, Kansas location is part of the watson.com domain and is connected to Houston with a 1.544 Mbps connection. The Cedar Rapids, Iowa location is in a child domain, called thermostats.watson.com, and is connected to the Houston location using a 1.544 Mbps connection, and to the Kansas City location at 128 Kbps.

1. When Watson Furnace sets up replication over the two site links between Houston and Beaumont, which of the following should they do?

   a. Disable replication over the 2 Mbps link, because it is slower than the other link.

   b. Designate a cost of 2 to the 10 Mbps link, and a cost of 1 to the 2 Mbps link.

   c. Designate a cost of 2 to the 2 Mbps link, and a cost of 1 to the 10 Mbps link.

   d. Set up replication to occur every 15 minutes over the faster 10 Mbps link.

   e. none of the above

   f. only a and d

   g. only b and d

   h. only a, c, and d

2. How many bridgehead servers will the KCC establish at the Houston site, which has 18 Windows 2000 domain controllers?

   a. only one

   b. two; one for each site link

   c. four; two for each site link for fault tolerance

   d. All of the domain controllers are automatically set up as bridgehead servers.

   e. There will be no bridgehead servers at the Houston location, but at least one is needed at every other location.

3. How many sites should Watson establish?

    a. at least four sites, one for each geographic location

    b. only one site for all of the locations, for faster access to DCs

    c. three sites; one combined site for Houston and Beaumont, one for Kansas City, and one for Cedar Rapids

    d. two sites; one for Houston and Beaumont, and one for Kansas City and Cedar Rapids

    e. no sites, so that all Active Directory replication will be uncompressed

    f. none of the above

4. None of the replication between sites is accomplished via e-mail or the Internet. This means that replication occurs using:

    a. RPC protocol

    b. SMTP protocol

    c. TCP/IP protocol

    d. IPX/SPX protocol

    e. all of the above

    f. none of the above

    g. only a and b

    h. only a and c

    i. only a, b, and d

5. On the basis of the information you have from Question 4, which of the following would be a good idea?

    a. Disable site links and use com links.

    b. Increase the number of communication lines between all locations to four.

    c. Bridge all site links.

    d. Convert to NetBEUI because it is more easily routed.

    e. all of the above

    f. only a and b

    g. only c and d

    h. only b, c, and d

11

6. The chief information officer has learned that she must cut the IT budget by 20 percent. She is thinking about deploying a single large Windows 2000 server in Houston and eliminating all other servers company-wide. What is your reaction?

   a. This is a good plan, because only one server will save money; for example, by reducing maintenance costs.

   b. This is almost a viable plan, but it would be better to place a second server that has a fast 1 Gbps NIC at the Beaumont location to take advantage of the 10 Mbps connection.

   c. This is not a good plan, because the same server cannot act as both a global catalog server and a DNS server.

   d. This is not a good plan because it does not take advantage of Active Directory replication, and users at the three other sites will experience slower access, resulting in more expense to the company.

7. Watson is considering the use of Dfs. What elements are part of the Dfs topology?

   a. Dfs root

   b. Dfs replica sets

   c. Dfs links

   d. Dfs bridges

   e. all of the above

   f. only a and b

   g. only b and c

   h. only a, b, and c

8. Your assistant wants to establish bridgehead servers manually for better control. If you go with this plan, how can you find out when a bridgehead server is down?

   a. Check for error messages in the Distributed File System tool.

   b. Check for error messages in the system log.

   c. You must purchase RMON network monitoring software to detect this problem.

   d. Only the domain naming master will display a console message that the bridgehead server is down.

   e. All of the above methods can be used.

   f. only a and c

   g. only a, b, and d

9. What type of Active Directory replication occurs between watson.com and thermostats.watson.com?

   a. domain partition

   b. global catalog

   c. schema

    d. configuration container

    e. all of the above

    f. a and b

    g. only b, c, and d

Answer questions 10–19 using this case information:

Thomasborough Community College has six campuses: a main campus, two branch campuses in the same city, and three satellite campuses in neighboring cities. The main campus and its branches are in the same domain, which is thomasboroughcc.edu. Each of the three satellite campuses has its own child domain under the main domain and over 5000 students at each location. Neither of the branch campuses has a server, even though each has a staff of 50 and registers over 2000 students. Both branch campuses rely on the main campus for server services. Each of the three satellite campuses has one Windows 2000 domain controller, and each domain controller offers vital student and registration information. The links between the main campus and all other locations are each 1.544 Mbps.

10. The server administrators at all of the campus locations have never backed up Active Directory to tape. What should they back up to accomplish this?

    a. the system state data

    b. the Registry

    c. the SAM

    d. the Exchange engine

    e. none of the above

11. In terms of providing users with fast access to accounts and resources at the branch campuses, which would you recommend?

    a. Place at least one DC at each location.

    b. Place at least one global catalog server at each location.

    c. Place a schema master at each location.

    d. Place a domain naming master at each location.

    e. all of the above

    f. only a and b

    g. only c and d

    h. only b, c, and d

11

12. In terms of replication for the thomasboroughcc.edu domain partition, which would be wise?

   a. Place domain controllers only on the main campus to keep the Active Directory data from being intercepted over the WANs.

   b. Place a global catalog server, but not a domain controller, at each of the branch campus locations.

   c. Place at least one domain controller at one of the branch campus locations for offsite Active Directory replication for disaster recovery.

   d. Place a secure Windows 2000 Professional workstation at each of the branch campuses and replicate the schema and configuration container to that workstation.

13. At least how many domain controllers would you recommend for each of the satellite campuses in terms of replication?

   a. only one because the domain partition at each can be replicated to the domain at the main campus

   b. three domain controllers, one to hold the domain partition, one to hold the configuration container, and one to hold the schema

   c. four domain controllers, one for the domain partition, one for the configuration container, one for the schema, and one for the global catalog

   d. two domain controllers to replicate the domain partition and other Active Directory information to one another

14. The IT manager at the main campus, which has multiple domain controllers, has heard that new accounts cannot be replicated to all domain controllers in the same site, except at three-hour intervals. What is your answer when he asks you if this is true?

   a. Replication occurs every 90 minutes, not every 180 minutes.

   b. Replication occurs as soon as an account is added.

   c. His information is correct, replication does occur every three hours.

   d. Replication occurs every 15 minutes when the KCC runs.

   e. Replication only occurs after midnight, unless the server administrator runs it manually.

15. Active Directory replication over the site links between the main campus and the satellite campuses seems to be congesting these links, which are needed for vital school communications. Which of the following would be sensible alternatives?

   a. Turn off replication over these links, because it is not necessary.

   b. Configure the site links so that replication occurs only between 10 pm and 6 am, when there is not much school-related activity over the links.

   c. Establish two links between each site, with the second link at each location operating more inexpensively at 128 Kbps, then configure a cost for the site links.

    d. Use a bridge instead of a router between each location for faster network transmissions.

    e. all of the above

    f. only a and d

    g. only b and c

    h. only a, c, and d

16. The college has a new president who has asked two different account administrators to create an account for him as soon as possible. Ironically, both administrators create the account at exactly the same time. Which of the following does Active Directory use as the final authority for which account to accept for its permanent data?

    a. Originating Write counter

    b. GUID

    c. timestamp

    d. datestamp

17. In the main domain, a domain controller can determine its replication partner through information in the:

    a. replication container in the configuration container

    b. NTDS Settings container associated with that domain controller

    c. server's parent OU or folder

    d. pooling parameter using the RPC protocol

    e. all of the above

    f. only a or c

    g. only a, b, and c

    h. only a, c, and d

18. In the college's main domain, a replication partner is determined by:

    a. the KCC

    b. a replication partner program that the server administrator must run each time a new domain controller is added to the network

    c. the schema master

    d. the domain naming master

    e. all of the above

    f. only a and b

    g. only a and c

    h. only b, c, and d

11

19. Which of the following would you include in a disaster recovery plan for the college?

    a. Perform regular backups using tape rotation and offsite storage.

    b. Create and update emergency repair disks.

    c. Create boot disks.

    d. Disable Dfs for better security.

    e. all of the above

    f. only a and b

    g. only b and c

    h. only a, b, and c

Answer questions 20–25 using this case information:

Chen Brassworks is a small regional company that is established at a single location. The company makes brass fixtures and trim, such as house numbers and porch lights to decorate homes. Their business relies on one Windows 2000 server that is configured to use Active Directory. They have 442 employees who work in shifts around the clock. The name of the company's domain is brassworks.biz.

20. Which of the following roles does the company's server play?

    a. domain partition

    b. domain naming master

    c. schema master

    d. DNS server

    e. all of the above

    f. only a and b

    g. only a and c

    h. only a, b, and c

21. The IT manager for the company insists that they do not need any more servers, because the single server has a fast CPU and creates little network congestion. What is your response?

    a. Adding at least one more server would enable Active Directory replication.

    b. Adding another server would enable faster response, because there would be two domain partitions instead of one.

    c. One server is enough, because the company regularly backs up information to tape.

    d. The company should use dcpromo to remove Active Directory, because it creates extra network traffic.

    e. only a and b

    f. only a and d

22. Chen Brassworks is planning to purchase another company with which it has worked in the past to fulfill orders. The two companies have a trusted relationship and similar management styles. They also use accounting, manufacturing, and inventory systems from the same software vendor. However, they do want to retain some autonomy from one another in terms of operations. Also, each company, which is in a different city, wants to make sure its network and network resources are secure. Which of the following do you recommend?

a. House both companies' network resources in one forest.

b. Enable each company to retain its current domain name.

c. Make each company a separate site.

d. Disable replication so that each company retains its autonomy.

e. all of the above

f. only a and d

g. only c and d

h. only a, b, and c

23. Chen Brassworks' server will not boot because Active Directory is damaged, and so is the Ntdetect.com file as the result of a severe power surge. Which of the following must be restored?

a. system protected files

b. Registry

c. system state data

d. SAM

e. all of the above

f. only a and b

g. only a and c

h. only a, c, and d

24. Chen Brassworks has decided to immediately purchase an additional server so that they can move their inventory database onto that server and keep the server in the manufacturing area. What should they do to implement Active Directory replication when they set up this server?

a. manually start the KCC

b. make the server a bridgehead server

c. use dcpromo to install Active Directory on the new server

d. configure a site link bridge

e. all of the above

f. only a and b

g. only a and d

h. only a, b, and c

11

25. In planning for the merger between the two companies (see Question 22), the IT manager becomes curious about how Active Directory replication works. Which of the following is true?

   a. Replication within the same site is one-way.

   b. Replication over a site link bridge is one-way.

   c. Replication over a site link is uncompressed.

   d. Replication over a site link can be managed according to intervals, based on minutes, hours of the day, and days of the week.

   e. all of the above

   f. only a and b

   g. only a and c

   h. only a and d

   i. only a, b, and c

HANDS-ON PROJECTS

Project 11-1

This project enables you to establish a preferred bridgehead server for a site. The process overrides the KCC's automatic selection of a bridgehead server. You will need an account with Administrator privileges for the project. Before you begin, ask your instructor for a site to use, or use the default site (called Default-First-Site-Name) that is created when you install Active Directory.

To establish a preferred bridgehead server:

1. Click **Start**, point to **Programs**, point to **Administrative Tools**, and click **Active Directory Sites and Services**.

2. Double-click **Sites** in the tree, if the child objects under Sites are not displayed.

3. In the tree, double-click the site provided by your instructor or double-click **Default-First-Site-Name**.

4. Double-click the **Servers** folder in the tree.

5. What servers are child objects in the Servers folder? Which of these servers are domain controllers?

6. Right-click a server in the tree or in the right-hand pane.

7. What options are displayed on the menu? How would you move a server to another site?

8. Click **Properties**.

9. Ensure that the Server tab is displayed.

10. What transports are shown for the site communications?

11. Click **IP**.

12. Click the **Add** button.

13. What happens after you click the Add button? Record your observations.

14. Click **OK**.

15. Leave the Active Directory Sites and Services tool open for the next project.

Project 11-2

In this project, you assign a cost to a site link. Next, you configure the replication parameters over that site link. A site link must already be established before you start (ask your instructor which site link to use), or refer to Hands-on Project 7-7 in Chapter 7 to create a site link.

To assign a cost to a site link:

1. Open the Active Directory Sites and Services tool, if it is not already open.

2. Double-click **Sites** in the tree, if the child objects under the folder are not already displayed.

3. Double-click **Inter-Site Transports** in the tree, if the child objects for this folder are not displayed.

4. What folders are child objects of Inter-Site Transports? Record your observations.

5. In the tree, double-click the folder that contains the site link, such as IP.

6. What site links are shown in the right-hand pane? Record your observations.

7. Right-click the site link specified by your instructor or the one that you have created.

8. Click **Properties**.

9. Make sure that the General tab is displayed. What other tabs are available? Record your observations.

10. How would you add additional sites to this site link?

11. What is the current value in the Cost box?

12. Set the value in the Cost box to **1**.

13. Leave the site link Properties dialog box open for the next set of steps.

To set the replication parameters for the site link:

1. With the site link Properties dialog box still open, what is the current setting for the replication interval? What is the default?

2. Enter **360** in the *Replicate every___ minutes* box.

3. Click the **Change Schedule** button.

11

4. How would you set up the replication schedule so that replication can occur all day on Saturday and Sunday, but only between 6 pm and 6 am Monday through Friday? Set up this schedule in the *Schedule for* [*Site Name*] dialog box.

5. Click **OK**.

6. Click **OK** in the site link Properties dialog box.

7. Leave the Active Directory Sites and Services tool open for the next project.

Project 11-3

This project enables you to determine where to bridge all site links in Active Directory. For this and Hands-on Project 11-4, it is desirable to have at least three site links configured (you can configure hypothetical site links without actually having the physical links). Determine from your instructor what site links are available, or create your own using Hands-on Project 7-7 for guidance. Also, for this project you should use an account that has Administrator privileges or that is a member of the Enterprise Admins group.

To determine where to bridge all site links:

1. Make sure that the Active Directory Sites and Services tool is open, and if not, open it.

2. Double-click **Sites** in the tree, if the child objects under Sites are not displayed.

3. Double-click **Inter-Site Transports** in the tree, if its child objects are not displayed.

4. Right-click the **IP** folder in the tree.

5. Click **Properties**.

6. What tabs are displayed? Record your observations in your lab journal or in a word-processed document.

7. Ensure that the General tab is displayed.

8. What boxes can you check on the General tab, and what is their purpose?

9. Notice that the *Bridge all site links* box is checked by default, unless the checkmark is purposely removed.

10. To prepare for the next project, remove the checkmark from in front of **Bridge all site links**, if this option is checked.

11. Click **OK** in the IP Properties dialog box.

12. Leave the Active Directory Sites and Services tool open for the next project.

Project 11-4

In this project you bridge two site links. Complete Hands-on Project 11-3 before you start.

To bridge two site links:

1. Open the Active Directory Sites and Services tool, if it is not already open.

2. Double-click **Sites** in the tree, if this container's child objects are not already displayed.

3. Double-click **Inter-Site Transports** in the tree, if its child objects are not displayed.

4. Right-click the **IP** folder in the tree.

5. Observe the menu options and record your observations.

6. Click **New Site Link Bridge**.

7. Enter a name for the site link bridge, consisting of your initials and Bridge, such as MJPBridge.

8. Click one of the site links in the *Site links not in this site link bridge* box.

9. Click the **Add** button (see Figure 11-18).

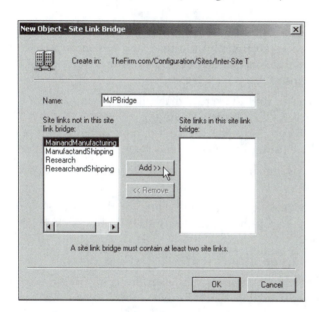

Figure 11-18   Creating a site link bridge

10. Click one other site link in the *Site links not in this site link bridge* box.

11. Click **Add**.

12. How would you configure additional site links into the bridge?

13. Click **OK**.

14. How can you verify that the site link bridge is created?

15. How can you add more site links to the bridge after it is created?

16. Close the Active Directory Sites and Services tool.

Project 11-5

In this project, you create a Dfs root folder that will hold a Dfs link, which you will create later in Hands-on Project 11-6. Make sure that the server on which you create the root has no other Dfs root. Before you start, check with your instructor about which domain and server to use for the Dfs root. You will need access using an account that has Administrator privileges.

To create the Dfs root:

1. Click **Start**, point to **Programs**, point to **Administrative Tools**, and click **Distributed File System**.
2. Click **Distributed File System** in the console tree, if it is not already selected.
3. Click the **Action** menu, click **New Dfs Root**, and click **Next** after the New Dfs Root Wizard starts.
4. Click **Create a domain Dfs root**, if it is not already selected. Click **Next**.
5. What domain is displayed as trusting? Ensure that the domain displayed in the Domain name box is the domain that is specified by your instructor, or use a different domain per your instructor. Click **Next**.
6. Click the **Browse** button to find the server that will house the Dfs root. Double-click the appropriate server. Click **Next**. (If you see a message that says "This server already hosts a Dfs root," ask your instructor for a different server or obtain permission to delete the existing Dfs root.)
7. How can you turn an existing shared folder into a Dfs root? Record your observations.
8. Click **Create a new share**. Enter a path and name for the Dfs root, such as C:\TestDfsRoot. Enter the share name, such as TestDfsRoot. Click **Next**, and then click **Yes**.
9. Use the default Dfs root name, such as TestDfsRoot. Click **Next**.
10. Review the summary of information for the Dfs root creation. Can you go back and change any of this information? Click **Finish**.
11. How can you confirm that the Dfs root has been created?
12. Leave the Distributed File System tool open for the next project.

Project 11-6

In this project, you create a Dfs link to the Dfs root that you set up in Hands-on Project 11-5.

To create the new Dfs link:

1. Start by opening **My Computer** to create a shared folder to use for the link.
2. Double-click the drive on which to create the shared folder, such as Local Disk (C:).
3. Click the **File** menu, point to **New**, and click **Folder**.

4. Type a name for the folder, consisting of your initials and Share, such as MJPShare. Press **Enter**.

5. Right-click the new folder and click **Sharing**.

6. Click **Share this folder**. Click **OK**.

7. Open the Distributed File System tool, if it is not already open.

8. Right-click the Dfs root that you created, such as TestDfsRoot, under Distributed File System in the tree.

9. Click **New Dfs Link**.

10. Click the **Browse** button. Double-click **Entire Network**. Double-click **Microsoft Windows Network**. Double-click the domain that houses the shared folder that you created. Double-click the computer that houses the shared folder. What shared folders do you see? Click the shared folder you created, such as MJPShare. Click **OK**. What is now entered in the Create a New Dfs Link dialog box?

11. Enter the name of the shared folder that you created, such as MJPShare, in the Link name box (see Figure 11-19). Could you enter a different name in this box?

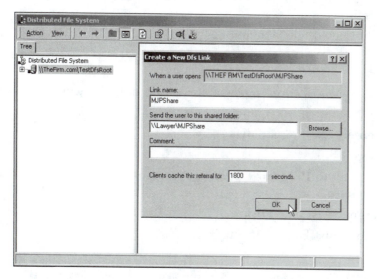

Figure 11-19   Configuring a Dfs link

12. What else can be configured in the Create a New Dfs Link dialog box?

13. Click **OK**.

14. How can you make sure that your Dfs link has been created?

15. Leave the Distributed File System tool open for the next project.

Project 11-7

In this project, you view where to create a Dfs root replica and a replica of a Dfs link.

To view where to create a Dfs root replica and a Dfs link replica:

1. Make sure that the Distributed File System tool is open, and if it is not, open it.
2. Right-click the Dfs root that you created in Hands-on Project 11-5.
3. Click **New Root Replica**.
4. Click the **Browse** button to view the servers on the network.
5. How would you enter the name of a server for the root replica? What qualifications should the server meet? How would you find a server, if you did not already know its name? Close the Find Computers dialog box.
6. Click **Cancel**.
7. Right-click the Dfs link that you created in Hands-on Project 11-6.
8. How would you create a replica set of only that Dfs link?
9. Move the pointer to a blank area on the screen and click it to close the shortcut menu.
10. Close the Distributed File System tool.

Project 11-8

This project enables you to create an emergency repair disk. You will need a blank, formatted floppy disk.

To create an emergency repair disk:

1. Insert the floppy disk.
2. Click **Start**, point to **Programs**, point to **Accessories**, point to **System Tools**, and click **Backup**.
3. Click **Emergency Repair Disk**.
4. Check the box to backup the registry.
5. Click **OK**.
6. Click **OK** when the copying process is complete, and then close the Backup utility.
7. Click **Start**, point to **Programs**, point to **Accessories**, and click **Windows Explorer**.
8. Use Windows Explorer to view the files created on the emergency repair disk in drive A. Open the setup.log file using Notepad and examine its contents. Record your findings in a lab journal or in a word-processed document.
9. Close Notepad.
10. Close Windows Explorer.

CASE PROJECT

Aspen Consulting Project: Designing a Replication Topology

Sunray Motor Company manufactures automobiles, SUVs, and light trucks that run on a combination of solar batteries and gasoline. The headquarters offices are in Detroit, Michigan. There are vehicle manufacturing plants in Chicago, Toronto, Baltimore, and Atlanta. Two additional plants, one in Seattle and one in Portland, make parts and small equipment, such as starters and voltage regulators. In the Active Directory design, the company has one forest, one tree, and multiple domains:

- *sunray.com*, which is in Detroit
- *trucks.sunray*.com, which is in Chicago
- *autos.sunray.com*, which encompasses both Toronto and Baltimore
- *suvs.sunray.com*, which is in Atlanta
- *parts.sunray.com*, which includes Portland and Seattle

There are WAN connections between the locations as follows:

- Detroit to Chicago is 10 Mbps frame relay and 2 Mbps frame relay (two lines).
- Detroit to Toronto is 155.52 Mbps SONET.
- Detroit to Baltimore is 10 Mbps frame relay and 2 Mbps (two lines).
- Detroit to Atlanta is 10 Mbps frame relay.
- Detroit to Portland is 4 Mbps SMDS and 256 Kbps (two lines).
- Detroit to Seattle is 4 Mbps SMDS.
- Portland to Seattle is 4 Mbps SMDS and 256 Kbps frame relay (two lines).
- Toronto to Baltimore is 256 Kbps frame relay.

Each location has a mixture of Windows 2000, NetWare, and UNIX servers, but the company is slowly migrating to a primarily Windows 2000 Server-based network. Currently, there are the following numbers of Windows 2000 servers at each location:

- Detroit has 30 computers running Windows 2000 Server, Advanced Server, and Datacenter.
- Toronto has 15 computers running Windows 2000 Server.
- Chicago has seven Windows 2000 servers.
- Baltimore has one Windows 2000 server.
- Atlanta has 20 Windows 2000 servers.
- Portland has one Windows 2000 server.
- Seattle has one Windows 2000 server.

Sunray operates using a decentralized mode of management, and it uses project-based teams. All of the Windows 2000 servers contain vital data and must be able to operate seven days a week and 24 hours a day.

1. Begin by creating a diagram of the network.

2. Develop a written site plan for this network and show the sites in your network diagram.

3. Create an Active Directory replication plan for the entire company and outline the plan in a written document for Sunray Motors. Include in the plan:

   ◻ Where to place domain controllers

   ◻ Where to place global catalog servers

   ◻ How directory partitions, the schema, and configuration container will be replicated

4. Use your network diagram to illustrate the replication plan.

5. Explain how you would configure site links, including setting up cost and replication parameters.

6. The Toronto location uses its Windows 2000 servers for administrative computing. They keep information on different servers in shared folders called:

   ◻ Human resources

   ◻ Payroll

   ◻ Accounting

   ◻ Sales

   ◻ Budget

   ◻ Inventory

   ◻ Purchasing

   ◻ Physical Plant

   Explain how they can use Dfs to replicate the information in these shared folders, and to provide disaster recovery for the folders.

7. The IT operations manager in Detroit is not certain about how to compose a disaster recovery plan. Explain what should go into the plan.

OPTIONAL CASE PROJECTS FOR TEAMS

Team Case One

Mark Arnez is aware that clients often must weigh the cost of purchasing equipment against the cost of providing redundancy for fault tolerance. He asks you to form a team to develop a document that describes the advantages of purchasing extra domain controllers for Active Directory and file replication, as compared to the costs of possible loss because there is not enough redundancy on a network. Develop one or two hypothetical examples, such as those of a regional and of a national organization to compare these extra equipment costs to costs due to lost data. For example, the equipment costs might include extra servers and operating system licenses. The losses might include lost data and lost work time. Consider finding research via the Internet to supplement your findings.

Team Case Two

As a consultant, you sometimes make presentations to IT teams about disaster recovery. One question that is often asked in these presentations is: "What disaster recovery methods are most important?" To help you prepare for this question, form a small team and develop a brief document that addresses this question and that provides a sample disaster recovery plan for an organization.

11

12

ANALYSIS AND DESIGN REVIEW

After reading this chapter and completing the exercises, you will be able to:

♦ Explain Active Directory containers

♦ Discuss organizational analysis techniques

♦ Discuss Active Directory design techniques

♦ Discuss planning for an Active Directory implementation

The Active Directory designer has many elements to consider in the process of analyzing an organization and then applying that analysis to a directory services design. This chapter provides a quick review of the concepts and design principles that you have learned so that:

- You have an instant reference when you are involved in an Active Directory design project.

- You have a quick study guide when you are preparing for the MCSE certification examination #70-219, Designing a Microsoft Windows 2000 Directory Services Infrastructure.

The chapter begins with a review of the principal Active Directory containers, followed by a review of the concepts for analyzing the business and technical requirements of an organization. Next, you will review concepts for designing a directory services architecture and for planning server locations. An additional review is provided for developing an Active Directory implementation plan. At the end of the chapter there are two capstone hands-on projects, one for the analysis of an organization, and another to practice creating a directory services design.

ACTIVE DIRECTORY CONTAINER REVIEW

The principal container objects used for Active Directory services design are:

- *Forest:* A grouping of one or more trees that each have contiguous name-spaces within their own domain structure, but that have disjointed name-spaces between trees. The trees and domains in a forest use the same schema and global catalog, and are related through transitive trusts.

- *Tree:* Related domains that use a contiguous namespace, share the same schema, and have two-way, transitive trust relationships. The domains in a tree, in general, have a common configuration and employ the same global catalog.

- *Domain:* A grouping of resource objects—computers, printers, network devices, user accounts, and user groups, for example—that can be managed as a unit in Active Directory in Windows 2000 Server. A domain usually is a higher-level representation of how a business, government, or school is organized; for example, reflecting a geographical site or major division of that organization. An important function of a domain is to create a security boundary around the objects held within it.

- *Organizational unit (OU):* A grouping of objects, usually within a domain, as a means to establish specific policies for governing those objects and to enable object management to be delegated. An OU contains objects such as user accounts, computers, printers, groups, shared folders, and nested OUs—and is the smallest container to which you can delegate authority and apply a GPO.

- *Site:* One or more TCP/IP-based subnets that are aggregated into a logical Active Directory container object (a site). The links between subnets in a site are relatively fast (512 Kbps or faster) and reliable.

- *Group policy object (GPO):* An Active Directory object that contains group policy settings for a site, domain, OU, or local computer. Each GPO has a unique name and globally unique identifier.

ORGANIZATIONAL ANALYSIS REVIEW

Organizations come in many flavors. When you analyze an organization so that you can match Active Directory services to the organization's needs, analyze the following:

- Business models
- Organizational models
- Company strategies
- IT management structures

- Technical environment
- Desktop management needs

Each of these analysis approaches is reviewed in the sections that follow.

Business Model Review

When you analyze a business, look for the following business structures:

- *Organization by geography*, which includes *regional* (all network and computer resources are located in relatively close proximity), *national* (covers multiple states, provinces, or other major boundaries within the same country), and *international* (spans multiple countries and can span different continents)

- *Organization by function*, such as by the work performed by a group or unit of employees (management, accounting, sales, research, and so on)

- *Organization by department, division, or business unit*—check the organization chart to identify these, such as the Accounting department, IT department, and others

- *Organization by product or service*, such as a company that manufactures cars and trucks and that is divided into two separate product divisions

- *Organization by project teams*, which are groups of employees who are organized to accomplish a specific task or goal and often have a project leader

- *Organization by cost center*, which usually is combined with one of the other organizational models to determine the cost of doing business, such as the cost to run IT servers or to manufacture a specific product

Organization by geography particularly influences domain and site design. Organization by function, department, project teams, and cost center particularly applies to the design of OUs and the application of group policy objects. Any of these organizational models are also influenced by the presence of subsidiaries and branch offices. A *subsidiary* is a portion of an organization that is owned by a parent company or organization, but that has relative decision-making autonomy and often does business under a different name than the parent. A *branch* is a portion of an organization that is relatively dependent on a higher-level office or corporate headquarters, because it is not an autonomous organizational entity, such as a branch bank in a community.

Part of the business model includes analyzing factors that influence how the company operates, which are:

- Business processes, such as hiring an employee, generating a payroll, or developing a budget

- Information and communication flow, such as top-down from managers to line staff in centralized organizations, or peer-to-peer for project-based and decentralized organizations

12

- Business cycles, such as those defined by the fiscal year or printing statements for customers
- Product and service life cycles, such as the introduction of a new product
- Decision-making model, such as centralized versus decentralized decision making (see the next section)

The factors that influence how a company operates particularly influence the structure of OUs and the application of group policies. However, special circumstances, such as distrust between company divisions and the need for security, can also influence the forest, tree, and domain structure.

Organizational Model Review

The typical management models in an organization are:

- *Centralized*, in which decision making is performed by those in the top levels of an organization, such as by managers and supervisors
- *Decentralized*, in which decision making is spread among different layers in an organization, including among project teams for project-based organizations
- *Formal and informal*, in which either the formally designated decision makers make the decisions, or the decisions are really made by others who are the unofficially designated or informal decision makers
- *Path-goal*, in which decisions are made on the basis of the goals to be met and the path to those goals; often used by project-based organizations
- *Situational,* in which decision making is influenced by a continuum of factors: loyalty, trust in management, management authority, and the complexity of the work

The organizational models are usually linked to the business models. For example, centralized organizations may be linked with functional or department-based business models. Decentralized and path-goal organizations are often linked to project-based business models. These factors particularly influence the design of forests, trees, domains, and OUs.

When you analyze the organizational model, also look for:

- Relationships with vendors, such as those with equipment and parts suppliers
- Relationships with partner companies, such as those between computer hardware and software companies
- Relationships with customers, such as those maintained via Web sites
- Plans to purchase other companies, as in mergers

The relationships that you find often influence the scope of the Active Directory design, such as whether it affects only the immediate company or the immediate company plus other companies with which it works. Relationships with vendors may require the creation of special OUs or domains. Merger plans emphasize the need to use more flexible containers, such as OUs and groups, instead of containers that are difficult to restructure, such as trees and domains.

Company Strategies Review

The analysis of company strategies should include:

- *The mission statement* of an organization, which is a broad-brush overview of the organization's purpose

- *Goals and objectives*, which are statements of specific tasks or programs that are to be accomplished

- *The strategic or long-range plan* that is used to outline what will be accomplished over the next several years

- *The operating plan*, which is a short-range plan usually encompassing one year and that often contains the budget or operating expenses

- *Cost of operations*, which is often combined with the operating plan and budget, and can be analyzed in companies that have a cost-centered organization

- *Projected growth*, which can be determined from the strategic plan, the operating plan, and the cost of operations

- *Project plans*, which are short-term plans for each project the company wants to undertake; project plans are often linked to specific business goals or objectives

- *Legal requirements and company policies*, such as federal tax laws for payroll and the policies in the employee handbook

- *Tolerance of risk*, which can influence how quickly a company is able to make changes or implement new computer systems

These factors often can be combined with the analysis of the business and organizational models. For example, companies that have a project-based organization will also have project plans as part of the company strategies. Many of the elements described in this section influence the design of domains, OUs, group policy objects, and security.

IT Management Structure Review

IT departments are typically set up using the same structures that are used in the overall analysis of a business:

- Centralized organization
- Decentralized organization

12

- Organization by function
- Organization by department
- Organization by project
- Organization by cost center
- Organization by federation

One IT management model that does not correspond to a previously defined business management model is organization by federation, which is a set of IT groups or departments that have their own separate areas of responsibility, that exist to perform specific business functions, and that have different objectives, but that all exist within one parent organization. A college in which each academic and administrative department has its own IT group is an example of organization by federation.

The IT management structures often are the same as those for the entire organization, but this is not always the case. For example, an organization that is project-based may have a centralized IT management structure. Most IT departments have a budget that describes funding, which you can find in the operating plan for the parent organization. Also, some IT departments outsource specific tasks, such as applications development.

The IT management structure plays a significant role in Active Directory design for forests, trees, domains, OUs, group policy objects, and the delegation of authority. For instance, a centralized IT organization may not delegate authority over OUs to anyone outside the IT department. In another example, an IT department that outsources some tasks will have special security, OU, group, and group policy creation needs.

Technical Environment Review

Begin the technical environment analysis by assessing:

- The size of the organization in terms of the numbers of users and the locations of those users; for example, by using worksheets and network monitoring tools, including Network Monitor and System Monitor

- The type of connectivity that exists within sites (LANs) and between sites (WANs) that are in different geographic locations, including these factors:
  - Transport methods and protocols, such as Ethernet, token ring, FDDI, TCP/IP, IPX/SPX, NetBEUI, AppleTalk, DLC, and SNA
  - LAN bandwidth, such as 10 Mbps and higher for Ethernet
  - WAN bandwidth, which can range from 56 Kbps for a modem connection to 2.488 Gbps for SONET
  - WAN connectivity options, which include: modem, X.25, frame relay, ISDN, SMDS, DSL, ATM, SONET, and others

- Performance, using a network analysis tool, such as Network Monitor

- Network data and access by assessing the numbers and types of operating systems and the software in use

- Network security, such as the locations of routers and the use of authentication, encryption, and folder permissions

Analyze the software environment for possible interaction with Active Directory:

- Determine what client operating systems are in use, such as Windows 98 or Windows 2000 Professional.

- Determine what application software is in use, such as accounting systems.

- Determine what database software is in use, such as Oracle or Microsoft SQL Server.

- Determine the user base for the different types of software.

- Determine how users are supported, such as by a group of user consultants.

- Determine how networks are managed, such as through SNMP.

The analysis of the technical environment affects many design issues, including the locations of operations masters, global catalog servers, DNS servers, and the creation of sites. The analysis of existing software also affects the schema design and group policies, such as publishing and assigning software.

Desktop Management Analysis Review

Users' desktops and access to software can be managed through Active Directory using group policies. In your analysis, determine the following:

- The types of operating systems that are in use and which ones can be supported through Intellimirror and group policies

- How network clients use their computers to access the network and software

- The organization's goals for computer use by employees, including change management to ensure that users (1) are employing similar software, (2) have standardized desktop setups, and (3) cannot inadvertently disable software access or operating system files

- How to use Active Directory features to provide automated support to users

The analysis of users' desktops and software access particularly affects the design of OUs, groups, and group policy objects. Try Hands-on Project 12-1 to practice analyzing a company.

ACTIVE DIRECTORY DESIGN REVIEW

Designing Active Directory and ensuring Active Directory replication is a complex undertaking. As you work on an Active Directory infrastructure design, start by reviewing a set of general guidelines for each stage of the design. The first guideline is to start by keeping the Active Directory design simple and easy to expand. Other guidelines affect (1) forest, tree, domain, OU, and site design, (2) DC placement, (3) DNS server placement, (4) namespace design, (5) operations master placement, (6) global catalog server placement, and (7) replication design.

Forest, Tree, Domain, OU, and Site Design Review

When you design forests, trees, domains, OUs, and sites, consider the following general guidelines:

- Use one forest, if Active Directory can be set up to use one schema, as in organizations that have subsidiaries that operate in an environment of mutual trust.

- Use separate forests when it is necessary to establish separate schemas, as when subsidiaries in an organization do not operate in an environment of mutual trust.

- Use the minimum number of domains and trees possible, to keep Active Directory design simple and to reduce management costs.

- Domains are partitions within a forest and are typically used when a large security boundary is needed around a set of resources and accounts, such as for resources that are geographically separated (particularly for companies with national and international organizational structures) or for different companies. Do not use domains to reflect company groupings, such as departments, that are subject to reorganization.

- Trees are built around the domain plan to reflect parent and child domain naming. Determine the number and types of domains that are needed and then build these into trees. Often, but not always, tree root domains are used as management centers for tree administration, such as for operations masters.

- When there are three or more domains and when there are two or more trees, create cross-link trusts to enable faster access to particular resources. Cross-link trusts speed access among domains that are not directly related, such as tree root domains and non-tree-root domains that are in different trees.

- OUs can be used to reflect company structures, such as departments, and are more easily reconfigured for company restructuring than are domains.

- OUs are particularly useful as a means to delegate authority over a set of accounts and resources, and as a way to associate a group policy object with specific accounts and resources.

- Avoid nesting OUs too deeply, because nested OUs increase the demand on the servers' CPUs. Keep OU nesting to three or four layers and avoid nesting more than 10 layers deep.

- Use sites to enable user and computer accounts to more quickly access resources for organizations that have locations separated by geography and WAN links. Also, use sites for offsite Active Directory replication and to manage replication traffic.

Domain Controller Placement Review

As you plan the number of domain controllers and where to place them, consider these guidelines:

- Each domain controller in the same domain contains that domain's partition in Active Directory. Implement at least two domain controllers per domain for Active Directory replication and fault tolerance.

- Place a domain controller at each site, for faster user access to accounts and resources.

- Place a domain controller at each site to achieve offsite Active Directory replication for fault tolerance and disaster recovery.

DNS Server Placement Review

The guidelines for DNS server placement include:

- Implement Microsoft Windows 2000 DNS server to take advantage of integration with Active Directory and of dynamic DNS (DDNS) updating.

- Place a DNS server at each site.

- Create two or more DNS servers per domain for load balancing, multimaster replication, and fault tolerance.

- Use DNS forwarding to offsite domains to reduce traffic over WAN links.

Namespace Review

There are several namespaces contained in Active Directory:

- DNS namespace

- Domain partition namespace

- Configuration container namespace

- Schema namespace

12

The DNS namespace is a naming system representing a hierarchy of domains, and is correlated to a dotted decimal notation system. When you design the DNS namespace, consider:

- What naming structures to use, such as the top-level domain name
- What naming structures to use based on the number and types of trees and domains that are deployed
- Developing names that can be used internationally
- Protecting names by registering them
- Following naming standards

When you plan the other namespaces, keep these ideas in mind:

- The domain partition namespace contains objects, such as OUs, accounts, and shared folders that are associated with a particular domain. A domain namespace is used to provide a security boundary around the objects within it, and a default domain policy can be linked to a domain.
- The configuration container namespace contains information about sites, site links, site link configuration parameters (cost and replication interval), and subnets. It is used, for example, by the KCC to determine how to set up replication between domain controllers.
- The schema namespace defines all of the object classes and attributes in Active Directory. You can add new object classes and attributes, such as those for specialized software—but carefully plan schema modifications before implementing them. When you add a new object, generally it is better to create it as a new object class under an existing object class, instead of adding it as an attribute to an existing object class.

Operations Master Placement Review

Use these general guidelines as you consider where to place operations masters:

- The operations masters include the domain naming master, schema master, relative ID master, infrastructure master, and PDC emulator master.
- Place one domain naming master and one schema master in each forest (no more than one per forest).
- The domain naming master and schema master roles are automatically allocated to the first domain created in a forest, but can be moved to another domain to accommodate the administrative plans of a company.
- Place one relative ID master, one infrastructure master, and one PDC emulator master in each domain in a forest (no more than one of each per domain). Each of these master roles can be moved to different domain controllers in the same domain.

- If there are two or more domain controllers in a domain, spread the load of the operations masters between the domain controllers for more efficient operation. For example, consider placing the PDC emulator master on a different domain controller than the relative ID master.

Global Catalog Server Placement Review

When you are planning where to locate global catalog servers, consider these guidelines:

- Place at least one global catalog server in each domain in a forest to enable fast logon and resource access for accounts.

- Place at least one global catalog server in each site and geographic location to enable fast logon and resource access for accounts. Also, having a global catalog server at each site enables offsite replication for fault tolerance.

- Place global catalog servers on fast links to users for faster user logon access and access to resources.

- Avoid setting up the same domain controller in the dual roles of global catalog server and infrastructure master.

Replication Design Review

Some of the following replication design guidelines are covered in the previous review sections, but they merit listing separately for replication review:

- Place two or more domain controllers in each domain for replication.

- Place at least one domain controller on each site for offsite replication and disaster recovery.

- Place at least one global catalog server in each domain and site for replication.

- Configure the replication interval and cost parameters on each site to manage replication traffic.

Try Hands-on Project 12-2 to practice using these Active Directory design guidelines.

12

ACTIVE DIRECTORY IMPLEMENTATION REVIEW

As you move from the design to the implementation phase, use the following guidelines for planning the implementation:

- Create the following plans as described in Chapters 6 through 11:
  - Forest plan
  - Domain and tree plan
  - Schema plan
  - DNS plan

- OU plan
- Site plan
- Group and group policy plan
- Security plan
- Operations masters and global catalog servers location plan
- Replication plan

■ Start simply and progress gradually, so that you do not make multiple changes at once. Simple and methodical progression is easier on users and makes it easier to troubleshoot design problems. You can accomplish this by using project management and by implementing each plan in stages.

■ Determine which Active Directory brokering technologies to implement for coexistence with server operating systems that will remain, such as UNIX and NetWare.

■ Create a timetable for migrating other server operating systems to Windows 2000 Server, such as Windows NT, UNIX, and NetWare, so that the impact to users is minimized. Also, migrate systems one at a time to make pinpointing problems easier.

■ Create a timetable for client operating system upgrades, such as upgrading from Windows 98 to Windows 2000 Professional, to maximize the effectiveness of Active Directory and minimize the impact on users.

■ Plan the timing to convert from running in mixed mode to running in native mode, so that the impact to users is minimized.

■ Establish implementation teams and determine what security to provide to team members.

■ Create implementation scenarios and scripts that technical professionals on the implementation teams can follow for each stage of the implementation.

■ Monitor the implementation at every stage so that the implementation teams can modify the design plans and implementation scenarios as needed to fit the realities of the network impact and company politics.

■ Establish testing methods for each stage before you bring the implementation live to users.

■ Create change management plans and contingency plans so that there are existing methods to quickly implement change and updates to match the evolving needs of an organization.

CHAPTER SUMMARY

❑ When you begin designing Active Directory for an organization, use this chapter to review the analysis and design guidelines.

❑ When you are studying to take the Microsoft certification examination, Designing a Microsoft Windows 2000 Directory Services Infrastructure (#70-219), use this chapter to help you in last-minute review.

HANDS-ON PROJECTS

Project 12-1

This project enables you to practice an analysis of a company.

To perform the analysis:

1. Study the following information about the company you will analyze:

   Maplewood Lumber is a conglomerate of seven companies: Maplewood Lumber, Carlson Lumber, Joyner Tools, Handy Tools, Goldman Plumbing, Jason's Unfinished Furniture, and Fairbanks Electrical Supply House. These companies are suppliers to hardware stores and lumberyards throughout the United States. The company's headquarters is Maplewood Lumber, located in New Hampshire. The other companies are located in different states, and these companies are connected to one another through WAN links, as shown in Figure 12-1.

   Maplewood Lumber is set up so that each company has the same management and functional structure. The management consists of a CEO over all of the companies, who maintains a tight rein and who believes that managers should be benevolent dictators over their employees. Also, he believes in creating standardization of company policies throughout all of the companies. The CEO reports to a board of directors. Each company has a president, vice president of finance, vice president of operations, and vice president of marketing. Under the vice president of finance there are managers of the Accounting department and the Information Technology department. The three managers who report to the vice president of operations supervise the Manufacturing, Warehouse, and Shipping departments. The marketing vice president oversees the managers of the Marketing, Sales, and Customer Service departments. Each of these managers is encouraged to rule her or his department with a tight rein, following the model of the CEO. Every vice president is required to prepare a set of departmental objectives, a yearly budget, and a three-year plan for her or his division.

12

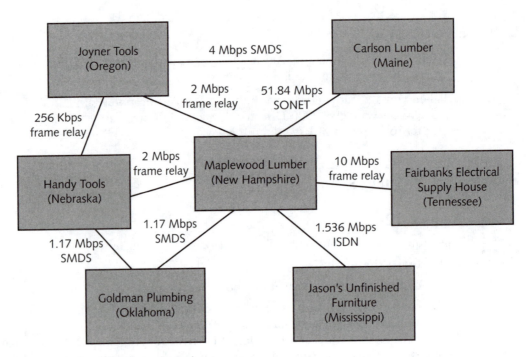

Figure 12-1   Maplewood Lumber

All of the companies have Ethernet networks that transport TCP/IP and IPX/SPX, but no Web sites are set up at this time. The networks are 10 Mbps to the desktop and either 100 Mbps or 1 Gbps on the network backbones. Maplewood Lumber plans to build a Web site for each company after the Active Directory services design is completed. Currently, each company uses a combination of Windows NT 4.0, Windows 2000, and NetWare 4.1 servers. Three companies—Maplewood Lumber, Handy Tools, and Jason's Unfinished Furniture—have UNIX servers. The users in all of the companies operate Windows 98 and Windows NT Workstation 4.0 client operating systems, but the companies are planning to upgrade all of these to Windows 2000 Professional during the next three months. Besides these client operating systems, Fairbanks Electrical uses some older Apple Macintosh computers, which support only AppleTalk.

The CEO believes that desktop computer use is fundamental to staying ahead of the competition, because it is a vital tool for each employee. Through Active Directory, he wants to set up all employee client computers to have the same desktop of selected programs and shared folders, which will include e-mail, product information shared folders, accounting shared folders, word-processing shared folders, and shared spreadsheet folders.

2. What type of business model can be applied to Maplewood Lumber? How might this business model affect Active Directory design? Record your answers in your lab journal or in a word-processed document.

3. How would you describe the organizational model? How does it influence Active Directory design? Record your answers.

4. Create a sample forest, tree, domain and site design for Maplewood Lumber.

5. Explain how the CEO's requirement to have standardized desktops can be accomplished through Active Directory.

6. Why is information about the LAN and WAN links important for your analysis? Record your answer.

7. How would you develop an Active Directory design for coexistence with the Windows NT, UNIX, and NetWare servers?

Project 12-2

This project gives you a diagram of one company so that you can apply the general Active Directory design guidelines reviewed in the chapter.

To apply the guidelines:

1. Study the diagram in Figure 12-2 and answer the following questions in your lab journal or in a word-processed document. As you answer the questions, take into account that this is one company that originally started in Richmond, Virginia, and that has purchased four subsidiaries. All of the computers pictured are Windows 2000 Server DCs. This company uses a decentralized business decision model, giving each subsidiary wide latitude for its own decision making. The main company and each subsidiary has its own IT department, all of which use a centralized decision model. All of the domains are in one forest.

   ❑ Where would you create sites? Where would you create site links?

   ❑ Where would you locate the operations masters?

   ❑ Where would you locate global catalog servers?

   ❑ Where would you place Windows 2000 DNS servers?

   ❑ Would you recommend more DCs at any sites for replication?

   ❑ How would you create a replication topology, including setting up site link bridges and controlling replication between sites?

   ❑ Would you change the forest or domain structure in any way?

12

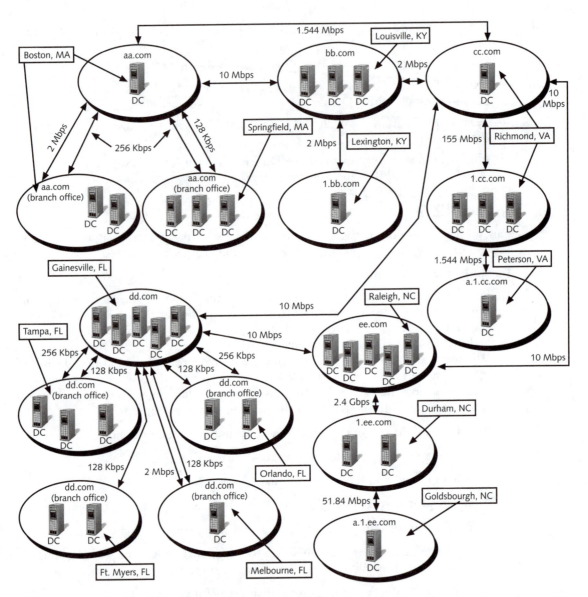

Figure 12-2   Network architecture of a company

EXAM OBJECTIVES TRACKING FOR MCSE CERTIFICATION EXAM #70-219: DESIGNING A MICROSOFT WINDOWS 2000 DIRECTORY SERVICES INFRASTRUCTURE

ANALYZING BUSINESS REQUIREMENTS

Objective	Chapter: Section
Analyze the existing and planned business models. ■ Analyze the company model and the geographical scope. Models include regional, national, international, subsidiary, and branch offices. ■ Analyze company processes. Processes include information flow, communication flow, service and product life cycles, and decision-making.	**Chapter 2: Analyzing Organizational Models, Analyzing Business Management Models, Analyzing Business Flow and Business Processes** Chapter 3: IT Organization, IT Decision Flow, Company and IT Relationships, Matching Business Goals and Strategies to IT Strategies Chapter 12: Organizational Analysis Review (see particularly the section Business Model Review)
Analyze the existing and planned organizational structures. Considerations include management model; company organization; vendor, partner, and customer relationships; and acquisition plans.	**Chapter 2: Analyzing Organizational Models, Analyzing Business Management Models, Analyzing Outside Relationships, Analyzing Acquisition Plans** Chapter 3: IT Organization, Company and IT Relationships, Outsourcing **Chapter 4: Analyzing the Existing Corporate Culture and Software Implementation** Chapter 12: Organizational Analysis Review (see particularly the section Organizational Model Review)

Note: Primary Chapter/section references are bolded.

Objective	Chapter: Section
Analyze factors that influence company strategies. ■ Identify company priorities. ■ Identify the projected growth and growth strategy. ■ Identify relevant laws and regulations. ■ Identify the company's tolerance for risk. ■ Identify the total cost of operations.	**Chapter 2: Analyzing Business Goals and Strategies, Analyzing Legal Requirements and Company Policies, Analyzing Acquisition Plans, Analyzing Risk Tolerance** **Chapter 3: Company and IT Relationships, Matching Business Goals and Strategies to IT Strategies, Funding and Cost Issues, Change Management and User Productivity** Chapter 4: Analyzing the Existing Corporate Culture and Software Implementation Chapter 12: Organizational Analysis Review (see particularly the section Company Strategies Review)
Analyze the structure of IT management. Considerations include type of administration, such as centralized or decentralized; funding model; outsourcing; decision-making process; and change-management process.	**Chapter 3: All of Chapter 3 and in particular see sections IT Organization, IT Decision Flow, Funding and Cost Issues, Change Management and User Productivity, Outsourcing** Chapter 12: Organizational Analysis Review (see particularly the section IT Management Structure Review)

ANALYZING TECHNICAL REQUIREMENTS

Objective	Chapter: Section
Evaluate the company's existing and planned technical environment. ■ Analyze company size and user and resource distribution. ■ Assess the available connectivity between the geographic location of worksites and remote sites. ■ Assess the net available bandwidth. ■ Analyze performance requirements. ■ Analyze data and system access patterns. ■ Analyze network roles and responsibilities.	Chapter 1: Security Management of Objects, Hierarchical Elements of Microsoft Active Directory (see the section, Domain), and An Overview of TCP/IP and Active Directory Chapter 2: Analyzing Organizational Models **Chapter 4: Evaluating the Company User Base and Resources, Analyzing User Access and Productivity, Analyzing Databases and Data Structures, Analyzing Software System Performance Issues, Analyzing Backup and Disaster Recovery Methods, Analyzing Software Security Issues**

Objective	Chapter: Section
■ Analyze security considerations.	**Chapter 5: All of the chapter, but see in particular Local Area Network Systems and Bandwidth; Wide Area Network Systems and Bandwidth; Analyzing Network Management; Analyzing User Access, Productivity and Performance Issues; Analyzing Network and Internet Security** Chapter 12: Organizational Analysis Review (see particularly the section Technical Environment Review)
Analyze the impact of Active Directory on the existing and planned technical environment. ■ Assess existing systems and applications. ■ Identify existing and planned upgrades and rollouts. ■ Analyze technical support structure. ■ Analyze existing and planned network and systems management.	**Chapter 4: Evaluating the Company User Base and Resources; Evaluating Existing Software and Software Systems; Analyzing Databases and Data Structures; Analyzing Backup and Disaster Recovery Methods; Analyzing Technical Support, User Help, and Training** **Chapter 5: All of the chapter, but see in particular Analyzing Hardware Systems; Local Area Network Systems and Bandwidth; Wide Area Network Systems and Bandwidth; Analyzing Network Management; Analyzing User Access, Productivity, and Performance Issues** Chapter 12: Organizational Analysis Review (see particularly the section Technical Environment Review)
Analyze the business requirements for client computer desktop management. ■ Analyze end-user work needs. ■ Identify technical support needs for end-users. ■ Establish the required client computer environment.	Chapter 3: Company and IT Relationships, **Change Management and User Productivity** **Chapter 4: Evaluating the Company User Base and Resources; Analyzing User Access and Productivity; Analyzing the Existing Corporate Culture and Software Implementation; Analyzing Software System Performance Issues; Analyzing Technical Support, User Help, and Training** **Chapter 5: Analyzing Hardware Systems; Analyzing User Access, Productivity, and Performance Issues** Chapter 12: Organizational Analysis Review (see particularly the section Desktop Management Analysis Review)

DESIGNING A DIRECTORY SERVICE ARCHITECTURE

Objective	Chapter: Section
Design an Active Directory forest and domain structure. ■ Design a forest and schema structure. ■ Design a domain structure. ■ Analyze and optimize trust relationships.	Chapter 1: Hierarchical Elements of Microsoft Active Directory (all sections) **Chapter 6: All of the chapter, but see in particular General Design Issues, Creating a Forest Plan, Developing a Forest Modification Policy, Creating a Domain and Tree Plan, Schema Design and Modification, Active Directory Design Examples: Organizational and Business Management Models, Active Directory Design Examples: Network Model** Chapter 9: Active Directory Object Security (particularly see the sections Deploying Administrative Security Groups and Using Security Features to Protect Key Active Directory Objects—especially the sections Delegating Authority over a Domain and Setting Permissions on Domains, Sites, and OUs) Chapter 12: Active Directory Design Review (particularly see the section Forest, Tree, Domain, OU, and Site Design Review)
Design an Active Directory naming strategy. ■ Establish the scope of the Active Directory. ■ Design the namespace. ■ Plan DNS strategy.	Chapter 1: Windows 2000 Directory Services (see the section Directory Service Standards and Name Formats) **Chapter 6: Creating a Forest Plan, Creating a Domain and Tree Plan (see the sections Determining How Many Domains and Trees to Create, Determining a Root Domain in a Forest, Determining the Namespace for DNS Naming of Domains), Active Directory Design Examples: Organizational and Business Management Models, Active Directory Design Examples: Network Model** **Chapter 7: Planning DNS Implementation (see all sections, including Additional DNS Server Roles, Creating a DNS Implementation Plan, Creating a DNS Change Management Plan, DNS Implementation Examples)** Chapter 12: Active Directory Design Review (see particularly the sections DNS Server Placement Review and Namespace Review)

A

Objective	Chapter: Section
Design and plan the structure of organizational units (OUs). Considerations include administration control, existing resource domains, administrative policy, and geographic and company structure. ■ Develop an OU delegation plan. ■ Plan Group Policy object management. ■ Plan policy management for client computers.	Chapter 1: Windows 2000 Directory Services (see the section Delegating Management of Objects), Hierarchical Elements of Microsoft Active Directory (see the section Organizational Unit), and An Overview of Group Policies
	Chapter 7: Creating an OU Plan (see all sections including Reasons to Create OUs, Managing OUs, and Creating an OU Change Management Plan)
	Chapter 8: All of Chapter 8 but see in particular Using Group Policy (see all sections including Planning Group Policy, Planning and Using Group Policy Objects, Configuring and Planning Default Domain Policy, Creating and Planning a New Group Policy for a Site, Creating and Planning a New Group Policy for an OU, Planning Group Policy Management for Client Computers, and Creating Group Policy Using the Security Templates Tool)
	Chapter 9: Active Directory Object Security (particularly see the sections Deploying Administrative Security Groups, Designing Security Groups for an Enterprise, and Designing Security Groups for Group Policy Objects), Using Security Features to Protect Key Active Directory Objects (especially see the sections Setting Permissions on Domains, Sites, and OUs; Establishing Permission Security for Group Policy Objects; and Establishing Filters for Group Policy)
	Chapter 12: Active Directory Design Review (particularly see the section Forest, Tree, Domain, OU, and Site Design Review)
Plan for the coexistence of Active Directory and other directory services.	Chapter 1: Windows 2000 Directory Services (see the sections Directory Service Standards and Name Formats, and LDAP URL Naming Used in Active Directory)
	Chapter 7: An Introduction to Planning for Coexistence with Other Directory Services

Objective	Chapter: Section
	Chapter 9: Active Directory Connectors and Coexistence with Other Directory Services (see all of the sections: Using Active Directory Service Interfaces, Using Active Directory Connectors, Using Microsoft Directory Synchronization Services, Developing a Synchronization Plan, Using Directory Consolidation, and Using a Meta-Directory, Using LDAP Proxy Interfaces)
	Chapter 12: Active Directory Design Review (particularly see the section Active Directory Implementation Review)
Design an Active Directory site topology. ■ Design a replication strategy. ■ Define site boundaries.	Chapter 1: Hierarchical Elements of Microsoft Active Directory (see the section, Site)
	Chapter 4: Determining the User Base, Analyzing User Access and Productivity, Evaluating Existing Software and Software Systems, and Analyzing Backup and Disaster Recovery Methods
	Chapter 5: Local Area Network Systems and Bandwidth, Wide Area Network Systems and Bandwidth
	Chapter 7: Creating a Site Plan (see all sections, including Factoring in Active Directory Replication, Starting the Planning Process, Creating a Site Change Management Plan, and Sample Site Designs)
	Chapter 8: Using Group Policy (see the section Creating and Planning a New Group Policy for a Site)
	Chapter 9: Using Security Features to Protect Key Active Directory Objects (see the section Setting Permissions on Domains, Sites, and OUs)
	Chapter 11: Using Active Directory Replication (all sections); Designing a Replication Topology
	Chapter 12: Active Directory Design Review (particularly see the sections Forest, Tree, Domain, OU, and Site Design Review; Domain Controller Placement Review; DNS Server Placement Review; Global Catalog Server Placement Review; and Replication Design Review)

Objective	Chapter: Section
Design a schema modification policy.	Chapter 1: Windows 2000 Directory Services (see the section, Active Directory Schema)
	Chapter 6: Schema Design and Modification (see the sections Designing a Schema Structure, and Designing a Schema Modification Policy
Design an Active Directory implementation plan.	Chapter 6: General Design Issues, Creating a Forest Plan, Developing a Forest Modification Policy, Creating a Domain and Tree Plan, Schema Design and Modification (see the section, Designing a Schema Modification Policy)
	Chapter 7: Creating an OU Plan, Creating a Site Plan, Planning DNS Implementation
	Chapter 8: Windows 2000 Groups (all sections), Using Group Policy (see in particular Configuring and Planning Default Domain Policy, Creating and Planning a New Group Policy for a Site, Creating and Planning a New Group Policy for an OU, Planning Group Policy Management for Client Computers, and Creating Group Policy Using the Security Templates Tool)
	Chapter 9: Active Directory Object Security (see all sections), Using Security Features to Protect Key Active Directory Objects (see all sections), Active Directory Connectors, and Coexistence with Other Directory Services (particularly see the subsection, Developing a Synchronization Plan)
	Chapter 10: Topology and Geographic Models (see all of the sections)
	Chapter 11: Using Active Directory Replication, Designing a Replication Topology
	Chapter 12: Active Directory Design Review (particularly see the section, Active Directory Implementation Review)

DESIGNING SERVICE LOCATIONS

Objective	Chapter:Section
Design the placement of operations masters. ■ Considerations include performance, fault tolerance, functionality, and manageability.	**Chapter 6: Creating a Domain and Tree Plan, and Schema Design and Modification (see the section, Schema Structure)** **Chapter 10: Understanding the Purpose of Operations Masters (see the sections Relative Identifier Master, Infrastructure Master, Primary Domain Controller Emulator Master, Domain Naming Master, Schema Master, and Maintaining Operations Masters), Topology and Geographic Models (see the sections Designing for the Simplest Topology, Designing for a Regional Geographic Organization with Plans for Growth, Designing for a National Organization with Plans for Growth, and Designing for an International Organization with Plans for Growth)** Chapter 12: Active Directory Design Review (particularly see the section, Operations Master Placement Review)
Design the placement of global catalog servers. ■ Considerations include performance, fault tolerance, functionality, and manageability.	Chapter 1: Hierarchical Elements of Microsoft Active Directory (see the section, Tree) Chapter 6: Creating a Forest Plan, Creating a Domain and Tree Plan (see the sections Beginning Domain and Tree Design Considerations, and Establishing the Best Methods for Fast User Authentication) **Chapter 7: Creating a Site Plan (see particularly the beginning section and the Site Designs section, Sample)** **Chapter 10: Understanding the Purpose of the Global Catalog Server, Topology and Geographic Models (see the sections Designing for the Simplest Topology, Designing for a Regional Geographic Organization with Plans for Growth, Designing for a National Organization with Plans for Growth, and Designing for an International Organization with Plans for Growth)**

Objective	Chapter: Section
	Chapter 11: Using Active Directory Replication (see all sections), Designing a Replication Topology
	Chapter 12: Active Directory Design Review (particularly see the sections Global Catalog Server Placement Review, and Replication Design Review)
Design the placement of domain controllers. ■ Considerations include performance, fault tolerance, functionality, and manageability.	Chapter 1: Windows 2000 Directory Services (see the section Distributing Active Directory Services)
	Chapter 6: Creating a Domain and Tree Plan (all sections), Schema Design and Modification
	Chapter 7: Creating a Site Plan (see particularly the beginning section and the subsection, Example Site Designs)
	Chapter 10: Understanding the Purpose of Operations Masters, Topology, and Geographic Models (see the sections Designing for the Simplest Topology, Designing for a Regional Geographic Organization with Plans for Growth, Designing for a National Organization with Plans for Growth, and Designing for an International Organization with Plans for Growth)
	Chapter 11: Using Active Directory Replication, Designing a Replication Topology
	Chapter 12: Active Directory Design Review (particularly see the sections Domain Controller Placement Review, and Replication Design Review)
Design the placement of DNS servers. ■ Considerations include performance, fault tolerance, functionality, and manageability. ■ Plan for interoperability with the existing DNS	**Chapter 7: Planning DNS Implementation (see all sections, including Additional DNS Server Roles, Creating a DNS Implementation Plan, Creating a DNS Change Management Plan, and DNS Implementation Examples)**
	Chapter 11: Using Active Directory Replication, Designing a Replication Topology
	Chapter 12: Active Directory Design Review (particularly see the section DNS Server Placement Review)

B

ACTIVE DIRECTORY
MANAGEMENT TOOLS

This appendix lists the main Active Directory management tools and summarizes what you can accomplish with them. There are two general types of tools for managing Active Directory: (1) Windows-based GUI tools, and (2) tools that you access through the Command Prompt window.

GUI MANAGEMENT TOOLS

Most of the graphical management tools can be accessed from the Start menu and MMC snap-ins. Use these tools for management activities such as creating accounts, managing security and distribution groups, establishing trusts, modifying the schema, establishing sites, managing group policies, and configuring security.

Domain Partition Object Management

Use the Active Directory Users and Computers tool to manage objects in a domain partition (see Figure B-1). Open this tool by clicking Start, pointing to Programs, pointing to Administrative Tools, and clicking Active Directory Users and Computers; or open it as an MMC snap-in. With this tool you can:

- Connect to a specific domain

- Delegate control over a domain

- Connect to a specific domain controller

- View the child objects in a domain

- Manage the relative ID, primary domain controller emulator, and infrastructure operations masters

- Manage OUs, such as creating, deleting, and delegating control over OUs

- Create and manage computer and user accounts

- Create and manage groups

- Create and manage contacts

- Publish shared folders and printers

- Create and manage group policy objects for the domain and for OUs

- Move and restructure domain child objects

- Establish security on a domain, OU, and other child objects in a domain

- Convert a mixed mode domain to a native mode domain

- Find objects in a domain partition namespace

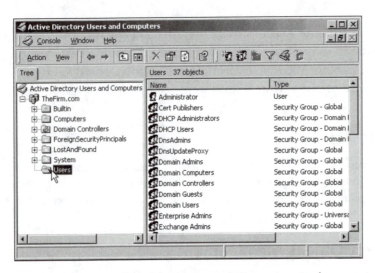

Figure B-1   Active Directory Users and Computers tool

Large-Scale Domain Management

The Active Directory Domains and Trusts tool can be used to manage trusts and other domain properties (see Figure B-2). Open this tool by clicking Start, pointing to Programs, pointing to Administrative Tools, and clicking Active Directory Domains and Trusts; or open the Active Directory Domains and Trusts snap-in. You can use this tool to:

- Connect to a specific domain controller

- Manage the domain naming master

- Set up an explicit one-way nontransitive trust

- Designate trusted and trusting relationships with other domains

- Convert a mixed mode domain to a native mode domain

- Open the Active Directory Users and Computers tool

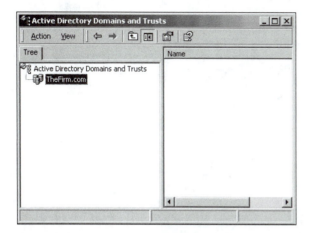

Figure B-2   Active Directory Domains and Trusts tool

Schema Management

The Active Directory Schema tool is used to manage object classes and attributes in the schema (see Figure B-3). To open the tool click Start, point to Programs, point to Administrative Tools, and click Schema; or open the Active Directory Schema snap-in. The Active Directory Schema tool is used to:

- Access a specific domain controller
- Manage the schema master
- Establish security for the schema
- Reload the schema
- View the object classes and attributes
- Create a new object class
- Create a new attribute
- Establish hierarchical relationships between object classes

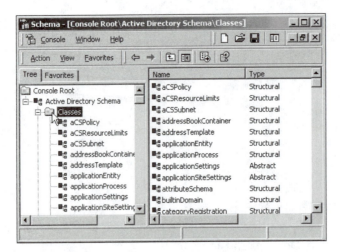

Figure B-3   Active Directory Schema tool

Site Management

A site is managed by using the Active Directory Sites and Services tool (see Figure B-4), which is opened by clicking Start, pointing to Programs, pointing to Administrative Tools, and clicking Active Directory Sites and Services (or you can access this tool as an MMC snap-in). With this tool you can:

- Connect to a forest
- Connect to a specific domain controller
- Create, delete, and manage sites
- Delegate control over sites
- Define and manage subnets
- Create, delete, and manage site links (including managing cost and replication interval)
- Associate a site link with a particular site
- Create, delete, and manage site link bridges
- Manage security for sites, site links, and subnets
- Create a group policy object and link it to a site
- Add a server to a site or delete a server from a site
- Establish a preferred bridgehead server

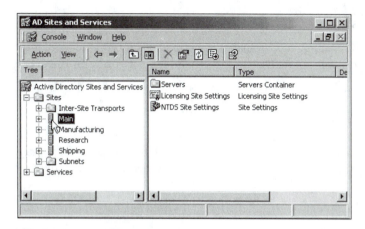

Figure B-4   Active Directory Sites and Services tool

Group Policy Object Management

Besides managing group policy objects from the Active Directory Users and Computers and Active Directory Sites and Services tools, you can manage GPOs from the Group Policy MMC snap-in (see Figure B-5). The Group Policy tool is used to:

- Access any group policy object
- Manage multiple group policy objects from one console window
- Manage computer configuration and user configuration group policies
- Determine the sites, domains, and OUs to which a group policy is linked
- Establish group policy object security
- Create a group policy object filter
- Export a group policy object

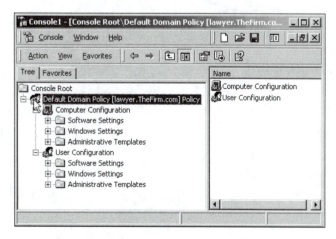

Figure B-5   Group Policy MMC snap-in

Configuring and Analyzing Security

Accessed as an MMC snap-in, the Security Configuration and Analysis tool is used to configure security settings and to analyze security (see Figure B-6). With this tool you can:

- Create a database of security information

- Apply a security database (security settings) to a local computer

- Configure security settings for areas such as account policies and local computer policies, configure event log settings, define members of restricted security groups, establish security on system services, establish security on the Registry, and establish file system security

- Analyze the security settings associated with a security database

- Import a security template created through the Security Templates tool

- Export a security template so that it can be accessed through the Security Templates tool

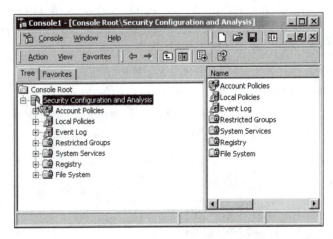

Figure B-6   Security Configuration and Analysis tool

Security Policies Management

Security policies can be configured using the Security Templates MMC snap-in (see Figure B-7), and then applied to a specific group policy object. Use this tool to:

- Access any of the default security templates that are provided with Active Directory

- Create a new security template

- Configure or modify a security template, including the default templates

- Configure security settings for areas such as account policies, local computer policies, and event log settings

- Define members of restricted security groups

- Establish security on system services and on the Registry

- Set up file system security

- Delete a security template

- Export a security template so that it can be applied to a group policy object using the Security Configuration and Analysis tool

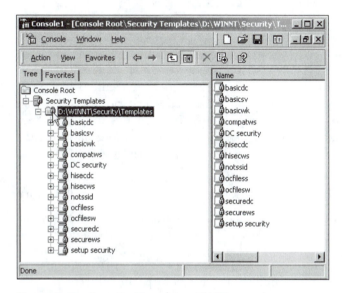

Figure B-7   Security Templates MMC snap-in

Active Directory Connector Management

The Active Directory Connector Management tool is used to manage Active Directory connectors (ADCs), such as the ADC for Microsoft Exchange version 5.5, and is installed when you install an ADC. To access this tool, click Start, point to Programs, point to Administrative Tools, and click Active Directory Connector Management; or open the tool as an MMC snap-in (see Figure B-8). The Active Directory Connector Management tool is used to:

- View the ADCs that are installed on specific servers

- Set up a connection agreement

- Set up diagnostic logging of ADC activity

- Configure ADC security

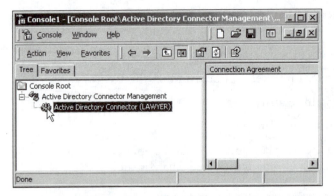

Figure B-8 Active Directory Connector Management MMC snap-in

Low-Level Active Directory Editing

The ADSI (Active Directory Service Interface) Edit tool (see Figure B-9) is used to edit and manage Active Directory namespaces, and is installed when you install the Windows 2000 Support Tools (refer to Hands-on Project 6-4). To open this tool, click Start, point to Programs, point to Windows 2000 Support Tools, point to Tools, and click ADSI Edit; or open the tool as an MMC snap-in. The ADSI Edit tool enables you to:

- Access the domain partition namespace, configuration container namespace, and schema namespace to perform basic editing of Active Directory

- Add, delete, move, or rename an Active Directory object, such as an OU in the domain partition or a site in the configuration container

- Modify and delete attributes associated with an object

- Query the contents of Active Directory for specific objects

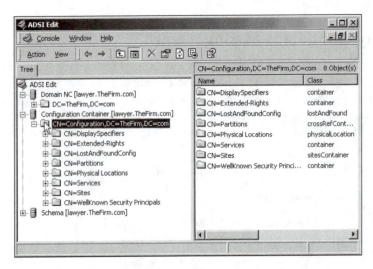

Figure B-9 ADSI Edit tool

Monitoring Active Directory Replication

The Active Directory Replication Monitor is included in the Windows 2000 Support Tools, and is used to monitor replicating DCs (see Figure B-10). This tool is opened by clicking Start, pointing to Programs, pointing to Windows 2000 Support Tools, pointing to Tools, and clicking Active Directory Replication Monitor. The Active Directory Replication Monitor enables you to:

- Specify which domain controllers to monitor by site location
- Determine and display the replication topology for multiple sites
- Monitor the active status of domain controllers
- Manually synchronize the domain partition namespace
- Manually synchronize the schema namespace
- Manually synchronize the configuration container namespace
- Show directory partition, schema, and configuration container change notifications sent by domain controllers

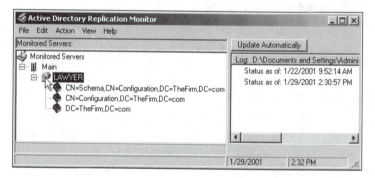

Figure B-10 Active Directory Replication Monitor

COMMAND-LINE SUPPORT TOOLS

The Windows 2000 Support Tools contain a variety of Active Directory tools th~ accessed by using commands in the Command Prompt window (see Figu~~, and can determine the specific parameters associated with one of the~~ing ing the command followed by /? in the Command P~ Command Prompt window, click Start, point to click Command Prompt.

Many of these commands rec an account name and passw

The following is a summary of the commands:

- *acldiag:* Used to check the ACL security entries for a group or user, and to reset an ACL to have the default entries

- *dcdiag:* Tests the operability of domain controllers, such as IP address information, intersite connectivity, and the existence of operations masters

- *dsacls:* Manages the permissions and special permissions on an object's ACL

- *dsastat:* Used to determine if the Active Directory contents on two domain controllers are the same

- *dommap:* Manages DNS servers, such as viewing zone information or creating a new zone

- *ldap:* Starts a Windows interface that enables you to access Active Directory using LDAP communications

- *movetree:* Moves objects, such as OUs and user accounts, between domains and also offers the ability to check object hierarchies in a domain prior to a move

- *netdom:* Used to add, remove, query, move, rename, and verify domains. The command also provides trust management for domains

- *nltest:* Used to make sure that the netlogon service is working on a server, to synchronize Windows NT server BDCs with Active Directory, to determine if BDCs are replicating, to determine the status of security channels, to generate a list of domain controllers, to determine user information on a server, to determine domain trusts, and to determine parent domains for servers

- *ntdsutil:* Enables you to fix data problems in the Active Directory database, restore Active Directory, restore the schema, manage the assignments of operations masters, establish LDAP policies, clean out unused Active Directory data, and create a domain

- *repadmin:* Used to manually force the KCC (Knowledge Consistency Checker) to perform specific Active Directory replication tasks, and to verify replication

- *replmon:* Starts the Windows-based Active Directory Replication Monitor to monitor replicating domain controllers, and to offer the ability to manually synchronize domain controllers

- *sdcheck:* Verifies that ACLs (security descriptors) are accurately replicated on all domain controllers, and that security inheritance is working properly

- *showaccs:* Used to show ACL information in the Registry and on specific ~cts, such as shared folders and shared printers

- ~ed to manage and clean up security identifier (SID) references

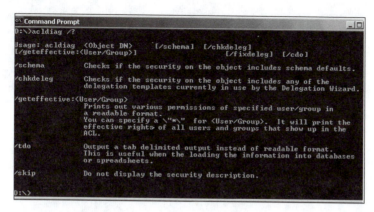

Figure B-11   Acldiag Command Prompt command

Glossary

access control list (ACL) — A list of all security properties that have been set up for a particular object, such as for a shared folder or a shared printer.

access server — A network device that links a network to telecommunications lines, for example by offering modem banks, T-carrier connectivity, and ISDN connectivity.

account lockout — A security measure in Active Directory account policies that prohibits logging on to an account after a specified number of unsuccessful logon attempts within a specified time.

Active Directory connector (ADC) — A synchronization connector designed for Active Directory; an interface that is used to automatically update or synchronize data in Active Directory with the data in another database or directory service. ADC is a brokering technology for Active Directory.

Active Directory Service Interface (ADSI) — An interface between a software application and a directory service, such as Active Directory, which enables data to be accessed, modified, imported, and exported. Programs written in programming languages such as C++ and Visual Basic can be used with an ADSI and use that ADSI to interface with a directory service. ADSI is an example of a brokering technology.

active hub — A network transmission device that connects nodes in a star topology, regenerating, retiming, and amplifying the data signal each time it passes through the hub.

AppleTalk — A peer-to-peer protocol used on networks for communication between Macintosh computers.

assigning applications — Also called assigning software, an IntelliMirror feature that enables the setting up of a group policy so that a particular version of software is automatically started through a desktop shortcut, through a menu selection, or by clicking a file that has a specific file extension.

asynchronous transfer mode (ATM) — A transport method that uses cells, multiple channels, and switching to send voice, video, and data transmissions on the same network.

attribute — A characteristic, quality, or property associated with an Active Directory object class, such as the name of the object and a security list of who can access that object.

backup — Making a copy of software and data so that they can be restored in the event of a system failure or accidental data deletion.

backup domain controller (BDC) — A Windows NT 4.0 or earlier server that acts as a backup to the primary domain controller (PDC), and has a copy of the Security Accounts Manager (SAM) database containing user account and access privilege information.

bandwidth — The transmission capacity of a communications medium, which is typically measured in bits per second (for data transmissions) or hertz (for data, voice, and video transmissions), and which is determined by the maximum minus the minimum transmission capacity.

base DIT attribute listing — The original set of schema attributes (attributeSchema objects) that are set up when Active Directory is installed.

base DIT class listing — The original set of schema object classes (classSchema objects) that are set up when Active Directory is installed.

basic input/output system (BIOS) — A program on a computer's read-only or flash memory chip that establishes basic communications with components such as the monitor and disk drives. The advantage of a flash chip is that you can update the BIOS.

benchmark — A measurement standard for hardware or software used to establish performance baselines under varying loads or circumstances. Also called a baseline.

Berkeley Internet Name Domain (BIND) — A standardized version of Domain Name System that is specified by the Internet Software Consortium (ISC).

branch office — A portion of an organization that is relatively dependent on a higher level office or corporate headquarters because it is not an autonomous organizational entity, such as a branch bank in a community.

bridge — A network transmission device that connects different LAN segments using the same access method, for example connecting one Ethernet LAN to another Ethernet LAN, or a token ring LAN to another token ring LAN.

bridgehead server — A domain controller at each site and with access to a site link, which is designated by the KCC to exchange replication information. There is only one bridgehead server per site.

broadcast — A transmission that sends one copy of each frame to all points on a network, regardless of whether or not a recipient has requested to communicate with the sender.

brokering technology — A technology, such as a synchronization connector, that automates the sharing and synchronization of data between applications, databases, and directory services.

brouter — A network device that acts as a bridge or a router, depending on how it is set up to forward a given protocol.

catalog service — A service within a directory service that compiles information about each separate partition in the directory service, and that stores the information in a single data storehouse for centralized queries.

CD-ROM array — Multiple CD-ROM drives connected into a single unit or device for access through a network or through a network server.

centralized decision model — A decision-making management model in which the locus of decision making is held in the top positions of an organization. When applied to network and computer resources, the centralized decision model often means that management of those resources is performed by a limited group of people in a central location.

change management — The implementation of processes and capabilities that enables organizations to control how changes are made and whom they affect.

channel service unit (CSU) — A device that is a physical interface between a network device, such as a router, and a telecommunications line.

child object — In the hierarchical structure of Active Directory, an object that is layered under a higher-level object, such as the server Accounting, that is a domain controller (child object) in the Domain Controllers parent object container. A child object is an object that is contained in another object.

Classless Interdomain Routing (CIDR) — A new IP addressing method that ignores address class designations and that uses a slash at the end of the dotted decimal address to show the total number of available addresses.

Common Management Interface Protocol (CMIP) — A protocol that is a standard for network management, that gathers network performance data, and that is primarily used on networks that deploy IBM devices.

common name (CN) — The most basic name of an object in Active Directory, such as the name of a printer.

Component Object Model (COM) — Standards that enable a software object, such as a graphic, to be linked from one software component to another one.

configuration container — A master container in a forest that holds information used or stored by some applications, such as the site topology that is used by the DC replication process.

configuration namespace — See *configuration container.*

container — An element of Active Directory that holds a grouping of related objects, such as the Domain Controllers container, which holds all of the computers that are set up as domain controllers.

contiguous namespace — A namespace in which every child object contains the name of its parent object.

cost centers — Areas or groups in an organization that are connected with the cost of operations. Cost center analysis enables an organization to understand the cost of producing a product or providing a service, such as computer operations. To help determine the cost of operations, one group, department, division, or unit may charge others within the organization for its services.

cross-link trust — A manually created trust that provides a one- or two-way trust between two specific domains, and that provides a short-cut through the normal transitive trust verification process.

cross-reference object — An object in Active Directory that references a domain partition in the same forest or in a different forest, or that references a directory service other than Active Directory, such as NDS. It is used by one domain or directory service to obtain specific information about another domain or directory service.

Data Link Control (DLC) protocol — A protocol that is designed for communication with an IBM mainframe or minicomputer, and that is set up to use SNA communications.

data service unit (DSU) — A device used with a channel service unit (CSU) for communications over a telecommunications line. The DSU converts data to be sent over the line and converts data received from the line into a format for the receiving network.

dcpromo — A Windows 2000 Server tool that is used to promote a standalone Windows 2000 server (no domain management) to a domain controller, or that can be used to demote a domain controller to a standalone server.

decentralized decision model — A decision-making model in which the decision-making responsibilities are spread through more than traditional top-level managers—for example, to midlevel managers, nonmanagerial staff, and project teams. When compared to the centralized decision management model, the decentralized model stresses placing management and decision making in hands that are closer to those who make the products or provide the services.

default domain policy — Automatically set up when a domain is created, this is the group policy object that is used for a domain, that is inherited by child domains, and that can be modified to match the particular needs of an organization.

Dfs link — A path that is established between a shared folder in a domain and a Dfs root.

Dfs root — The main Active Directory container that holds Dfs links to shared folders in a domain.

Dfs topology — Applies to a domain-based Dfs model and encompasses the Dfs root, Dfs links to the root, and servers on which the Dfs structure is replicated.

digital subscriber line (DSL) — A technology that uses advanced modulation techniques on existing telecommunications networks for high-speed networking between a subscriber and a telecommunications company, and that has communication speeds up to 55 Mbps.

directory consolidation — Developing new applications so that they store information in Active Directory instead of in a separate database.

directory information tree (DIT) — Another name for the schema, which contains object classes and their associated attributes for defining all objects in Active Directory, such as organizational units, domains, computers, printers, user accounts, ACLs, and other resources.

directory service — A large container of network data and resources, such as computers, printers, user accounts, and user groups that (1) provides a central listing of resources and ways to quickly find specific resources and (2) provides a way to access and manage network resources.

Directory Service Client (DSClient) — Microsoft software for non-Windows 2000 clients that connects to Windows 2000 Server and that enables those clients to use Kerberos authentication security, and to view information published in Windows 2000 Active Directory, such as all network printers.

directory system agent — A server, such as one running Windows 2000 Server, that houses a directory service's database, has directory service APIs, and communicates with clients and other directory system agents.

disaster recovery plan — Creating a plan to continue computer operations after a disaster such as a fire, flood, or earthquake.

discretionary access control list (DACL) — A portion of an access control list (ACL) of users, groups, and computers that are granted or denied some form of permission for an object, such as to a group policy or a shared folder.

disjointed namespace — A namespace in which the child object name does not resemble the name of its parent object.

distinguished name (DN) — A name in Active Directory that contains all hierarchical components of an object, such as that object's organizational unit and domain, in addition to the object's common name. The distinguished name

is used by an Active Directory client to access a particular object, such as a printer.

Distributed File System (Dfs) — A system that enables folders shared on multiple computers to appear as though they exist in one centralized hierarchy of folders instead of on many different computers. Dfs enables fault tolerance, disaster recovery, and server load balancing.

distribution group — A list of Windows 2000 users that enables one e-mail message to be sent to all users on the list. A distribution group is not used for security and thus cannot appear in an ACL.

DNS Dynamic Update protocol — A TCP/IP-based protocol that enables information in a DNS server to be automatically updated; for example, when a Windows 2000 Professional workstation updates its leased DHCP IP address.

DNS naming — A naming system that is based on a dotted notation and that can reflect a hierarchy of domains.

domain — A grouping of resource objects, computers, printers, network devices, user accounts, and user groups, for example, that can be managed as a unit or partition in Active Directory in Windows 2000 Server. A domain usually is a higher-level representation of how a business, government, or school is organized—for example, reflecting a geographical site or major division of that organization. An important function of a domain is to create a security boundary around the objects held within it.

domain controller (DC) — A Windows 2000 server that contains a copy of Active Directory domain information (an Active Directory partition), that is used to add a new object to Active Directory and to modify an object, and that replicates all changes made to Active Directory so those changes are updated on every DC in the same domain. Domain controllers also help manage user account and computer account access to a domain, including logon access and access to resources such as shared folders.

domain local security group — A security group that typically is placed on the access control lists of resources in a domain and that has global security groups as members.

Domain Name System (DNS) — A TCP/IP application service that resolves domain and computer names to IP addresses, or IP addresses to domain and computer names. In Active Directory implementations, DNS is also used to enable clients to find domain controllers.

domain naming master — The single domain controller in a forest that has the authority to create new domains or delete existing domains. It is also used to manage cross-reference objects to other directory services.

domain partition namespace — A database of the objects, such as user accounts, computers, and printers, contained in a single domain.

driver signing — A digital signature that Microsoft incorporates into driver and system files as a way to verify the files and to ensure that they are not inappropriately overwritten.

Dynamic DNS (DDNS) — A modern DNS application that enables client computers to automatically register their IP addresses without intervention by a user or network administrator.

Dynamic Host Configuration Protocol (DHCP) — A TCP/IP-based network protocol that provides a way for a server running DHCP services to automatically assign (through a lease) an IP address to a workstation or client computer on its network.

emergency repair disk (ERD) — A disk that contains repair, diagnostic, and backup information for use in case there is a problem with Windows 2000 Server.

Ethernet — A transport system that uses the CSMA/CD access method for data transmission on a network. Ethernet typically is implemented in a bus or bus-star topology.

explicit one-way nontransitive trust — One of two types of trust relationships used in Windows 2000. This type of trust is different from a two-way transitive trust because (1) the trust relationship does not go beyond the two domains specified in the trust, and (2) the trust relationship is one-way. An explicit one-way nontransitive trust is typically used between two domains in two different trees in the same forest.

Extensible Storage Engine (ESE) — The database engine that stores Active Directory object information in a database system.

federated IT organization — A set of IT groups or departments that have their own separate areas of responsibility, that exist to perform specific business functions, and that have different objectives, but that all exist within one parent organization.

Fiber Distributed Data Interface (FDDI) — A fiber-optic data transport method capable of a 100 Mbps transfer rate using a dual-ring topology.

file lock — Flagging a file so that it cannot be updated by more than one user at a time, giving only the first user to access it the ability to perform an update.

flat file database — A database in which data is stored sequentially in regular files in the same directory on a first-in basis.

flexible single-master operations (FSMO) — A role allocated to one domain controller in which Active Directory accepts changes for only specific objects, such as for schema object classes, from that domain controller. The schema master and the domain naming master each function in the FSMO role in a forest, and the relative ID master, infrastructure master, and PDC emulator master have FSMO roles in a domain. The pronunciation of FSMO is *fizmo*.

forest — A grouping of trees that each have contiguous namespaces within their own domain structure, but that have disjointed namespaces between trees. The trees and domains in a forest use the same schema and global catalog, and are related through transitive trusts.

formal decision making — A decision-making model in which decisions follow the formally defined management lines.

forward lookup zone — A DNS zone or table that maps computer or domain names to IP addresses.

frame — A unit of data that is transmitted on a network that contains control and address information (OSI Layer 2), but not routing information.

frame relay — A communications protocol that relies on packet switching and virtual connection technology to transmit data packets, and that achieves higher transmission rates by leaving extensive error checking functions to intermediate nodes.

full backup — A backup of an entire system, including all system files, programs, and data files. In many Windows-based and other file systems, the archive bit (or equivalent) is removed on each file after the backup is complete.

global catalog — A single storehouse of information about every object in every domain within a tree or forest. As a storehouse, the global catalog contains a copy of the most-used attributes for each object, such as the actual user's name that is associated with a user account. The global catalog also provides services to users, such as the ability to find an object or information about an object, without already knowing the domain or OU in which the object is held.

global security group — A security group that typically contains user accounts and other global groups from its home domain—and that is a member of domain local groups in the same or other domains as a way to give that global group's member accounts access to the resources defined to the domain local groups.

globally unique identifier (GUID) — A unique number, up to 16 characters long (128 bits), that is associated with an Active Directory object.

goals — Specific and quantifiable tasks that an organization plans to accomplish, particularly within a certain time. Goals are also referred to as objectives or business objectives.

grandchild domain — A domain that is more than one level removed from an upper-level

domain. For example, voice.wireless.telecom.com is a grandchild of the telecom.com domain.

group policy — A Windows 2000 Server concept that enables a server administrator to standardize the working environment of clients and servers. A group policy is applied to specific users or computers in an Active Directory site, domain, or OU container, such as requiring that logon passwords be over a certain length or removing the My Network Places icon from the desktop of specific users. Group policies cover areas such as account security, network security, logon and logoff scripts, folder redirection, software installation, and desktop settings.

group policy filter — A set of permissions on the ACL of a group policy object (GPO) that controls to whom the group policy object applies.

group policy object (GPO) — An Active Directory object that contains group policy settings for a site, domain, OU, or local computer. Each GPO has a unique name and a globally unique identifier.

host address (A) resource record — A record in a DNS forward lookup zone that consists of a computer or domain name correlated to an IP version 4 (or 32-bit) address.

Hypertext Transfer Protocol (HTTP) — A protocol in the TCP/IP suite that transports HTML documents over the Internet (and over intranets) for access by Web-compliant browsers.

identity data — Important data cumulatively stored in server and network databases, such as information about users, computers, the network, software applications, e-mail clients, and e-mail servers.

implicit two-way transitive trust — See *transitive trust*.

incremental backup — A backup of new or changed files. In Windows NT and Windows 2000, an incremental backup removes the archive bit after backing up the files.

informal decision making — A decision-making model in which decisions follow the informal lines of authority—for example, when an administrative assistant really makes the decisions for a manager.

infrastructure master — A domain controller that replicates to other domains changes to the user accounts in a group, such as when an account is added to the group or an account already in a group is renamed. It is also needed to ensure that the group membership remains intact when a group is renamed or is moved to another domain in the same forest.

Integrated Services Digital Network (ISDN) — A telecommunications standard for delivering data services over digital telephone lines with a current practical limit of 1.536 Mbps, and a theoretical limit of 622 Mbps.

international geographic organization — An organization that spans multiple countries and that can also span different continents.

Internet Packet Exchange (IPX) — A protocol developed by Novell for use with its NetWare file server operating system.

IP security (IPSec) — A set of IP-based secure communications and encryption standards created through the Internet Engineering Task Force (IETF).

IPv6 host address (AAAA) resource record — A record in a DNS forward lookup zone that consists of a computer or domain name mapped to an IP version 6 (or 128-bit) address.

Kerberos — The main logon security for Windows 2000 Server; a security system developed by the Massachusetts Institute of Technology to enable two parties on an open network to communicate without interception by an intruder, by creating a unique encryption key per each communication session. Kerberos enables the authentication of a user or computer. At this writing, Active Directory uses Kerberos version 5 (v5), which is supported by all Windows 2000 operating systems, including Windows 2000 Professional.

Knowledge Consistency Checker (KCC) — A Windows 2000 service that runs by default on all domain controllers. It sets up domain controller replication connections within and between sites and determines the most efficient replication routes between domain controllers.

LDAP proxy interface — A brokering interface that uses LDAP standards to access and update data in multiple LDAP-compatible data storehouses.

Lightweight Directory Access Protocol (LDAP) — A standard directory access protocol that is used to help access and manage objects in a directory service.

load balancing — On a single server, distributing resources across multiple server disk drives and paths for better server response; on multiple network servers, distributing resources across two or more servers for better server and network performance.

local security group — A group of user accounts that is used to manage resources on a standalone Windows 2000 server that is not part of a domain.

master browser — In a pre-Windows 2000 server domain, a mixed-mode Windows 2000 server domain, and in domains that have clients that cannot communicate with Active Directory, a server that is designated to keep the main list of logged-on computers.

media access control (MAC) sublayer — A network communications function that examines physical address information in frames and controls the way devices share communications on a network.

meta-directory — A comprehensive storehouse of all identity data for all types of operating systems, networks, databases, applications, and e-mail services. A meta-directory is a very sophisticated brokering technology.

Microsoft Directory Synchronization Services (MSDSS) — A set of connector services used to synchronize Active Directory data with data in either NDS (for NetWare 4 and higher) or binderies in NetWare 3.x.

mission statement — A general statement from an organization that describes its purpose, such as the products it makes and the constituents or customers that are reached.

mixed mode — When Active Directory has Windows NT 4.0 domain controllers (BDCs) and Windows 2000 Server domain controllers (DCs) that coexist in the same domain.

multicast — A transmission method in which a server divides recipients of an application, such as a multimedia application, into groups. Each data stream is a one-time transmission that goes to one group of multiple addresses, instead of sending a separate transmission to each address for each data stream. The result is less network traffic.

multimaster replication — In Windows 2000 Server, there can be multiple servers, called domain controllers (DCs), that store the Active Directory contents for the domain, including all objects, and replicate the contents to one another. Because each DC acts as a master, replication does not stop when one is down and updates to Active Directory continue, for example, when new accounts are created.

multiplexer — A switch that divides a communication medium into multiple channels so several nodes can communicate at the same time. When a signal is multiplexed, it must be demultiplexed at the other end.

multistation access unit (MAU) — A central hub that links token ring nodes into a topology that physically resembles a star, but in which packets are transmitted in a logical ring pattern.

named pipe — A communication link between two processes, which may be local to the server or remote, such as between the server and a workstation.

namespace — A logical area on a network that contains directory services and named objects, and that has the ability to perform name resolution.

national geographic organization — An organization that covers multiple states, provinces, or other major boundaries within the same country.

NetBIOS Extended User Interface (NetBEUI) — Developed by IBM in the mid-1980s, this protocol incorporates NetBIOS for communications across a network and is used on early, small Microsoft-based networks.

NetBIOS name system (NBNS) — A domain name that is recognized by NetBIOS and that consists of a single name. NBNS names cannot be scaled in the same way as DNS names.

Network Basic Input/Output System (NetBIOS) — Used on many Microsoft networks, a method for interfacing software with network services; it provides network object naming services.

network database — A flat file database that uses a simple table structure.

Network File System (NFS) — A TCP/IP file transfer protocol that transfers information in record streams instead of in bulk file streams, and that is typically used by UNIX systems.

Network Monitor — A Windows NT and Windows 2000 network monitoring tool that can capture and display network performance data.

Network Monitor Driver — Enables a Microsoft-based server or workstation NIC to gather network performance data for assessment by Microsoft Network Monitor.

NTFS permissions — In Windows 2000, privileges set up via NTFS to access and manipulate resource objects, such as folders and printers; for example, privilege to read a file, or to create a new file.

object — A network resource, such as a server or a user account, that has distinct attributes or properties, that is usually defined in a forest, tree, domain, OU, or site, and that exists in the Windows 2000 Active Directory.

object class — A type or grouping of network resources that is tracked by Active Directory. User accounts, groups, and computers are examples of different object classes. Each object class has attributes associated with it.

object identifier (OID) — Assigned to each object class and attribute in a schema, an OID is a unique dotted number as defined by the X.500 standard.

objectives — Also called business objectives, see *goals*.

one-time costs — Costs that an organization pays initially for specific items, such as the cost of purchasing a new server or network router.

ongoing costs — Continuous expenditures that involve costs for items such as staffing, user support, equipment and software leases, and hardware and software vendor support agreements.

Open Database Connectivity (ODBC) — A set of rules and an application programming interface developed by Microsoft for accessing databases and providing a standard doorway to database data. An ODBC driver is used between an application and a database to enable data to be queried and manipulated.

operating plan — A plan that is written approximately once a year to reflect relatively short-term actions, and that normally includes an organization's immediate budget projections.

operations master — A domain controller that plays one or more critical domain-wide or forest-wide roles for Active Directory, such as generating a unique pool of numbers from which to create unique security identifiers (SIDs) for new objects or creating new domains. The operations master roles are: relative ID master, infrastructure master, primary domain controller (PDC) emulator master, domain naming master, and schema master.

operations master domain controller — A domain controller that plays all five operations master roles when there is only one domain and only one or two domain controllers.

organizational unit (OU) — A grouping of objects within a domain, used as a means to establish specific policies for governing those objects and to enable object management to be delegated. An OU contains objects such as user accounts, computers, printers, groups, shared folders, and nested OUs, and it is the smallest container for which to delegate authority or to apply a GPO.

outsourcing — When a separate individual or company performs specific tasks for an organization—for example, IT tasks that are not provided by a department or employee in that organization, such as supporting that company's payroll software applications or network implementation.

packet assembler/disassembler (PAD) — A device that encapsulates a packet into X.25 format and adds X.25 address information. The PAD removes the X.25 format information when the packet reaches its destination LAN.

parent object — A hierarchical Active Directory container that holds objects under it.

passive hub — A network transmission device that connects nodes in a star topology, performing no signal enhancement as the data signal moves from one node to the next through the hub.

path-goal decision model — A decision-making model that focuses on defining the goal that is to be achieved and the steps that must be completed along the path to achieve the goal.

permission — In Windows 2000, privilege to access and manipulate resource objects, such as folders and printers; for example, the privilege to read a file, or to create a new file.

pointer (PTR) resource record — A record in a DNS reverse lookup zone that consists of an IP (version 4 or 6) address correlated to a computer or domain name.

primary DNS server — A DNS server that is used as the main server from which to administer a zone, such as for updating records in a forward lookup zone for a domain. A primary DNS server is also called the authoritative server for that zone.

primary domain controller (PDC) — A Windows NT 4.0 or earlier server that acts as the master server when there are two or more Windows NT servers on a pre-Windows 2000 server network. There is only one PDC in a Windows NT 4.0 or earlier domain, and it holds the master database (called the SAM) of user accounts and access privileges.

primary domain controller (PDC) emulator master — A domain controller that duplicates the role of a Windows NT 4.0 primary domain controller (PDC) when Active Directory is operating in mixed mode, because there are Windows NT 4.0 or earlier backup domain controllers in a domain. Two important roles of the PDC emulator are to enable password changes for computers running non-Windows 2000 operating systems and to replicate specific Active Directory information to Windows NT 4.0 or earlier backup domain controllers.

print server — A network computer or server device that connects printers to the network for sharing and that receives and processes print requests from print clients.

project plan — A specific-purpose plan that describes in detail a new project, such as a plan that outlines the addition of a new wing on a hospital.

publish — To make an object, such as a printer or shared folder, available for users to access when they view Active Directory contents, and to allow the data associated with the object to be replicated.

publishing applications — Also called publishing software, setting up software through Active Directory services so that users install the software from a central place using the Add/Remove Programs applet in Control Panel.

redundant array of inexpensive (or **independent**) **disks (RAID)** — A set of disks in arrays that are used to store data and provide fault tolerance.

regional geographic organization — An organization in which company sites and resources are located in relatively close proximity, such as in a single building, on a business or school campus, in multiple locations within the same city, or in different cities that are relatively close—a large city and its suburbs, for example.

relational database — A database in which data is stored in tables that can be designed with optimized relationships to one another for fast data access.

relative distinguished name (RDN) — An object name in Active Directory that has two or more related components, such as the RDN of a user account name that consists of User and the first and last name of the actual user. In an RDN, part of the DN name is a reference to another part of the object's name.

relative identifier (RID) — A unique number that is used as a portion of a security identifier. Each domain creates a pool of RIDs that is used for creating unique security identifiers for user accounts, computers, and groups.

relative identifier (RID) master — A domain controller that assigns a pool of relative ID numbers to every DC in the same domain. Creating pools of relative ID numbers enables the other DCs to assign security identifier numbers to newly created security principal objects, such as accounts, computers, and groups. There is only one relative identifier master per domain.

remote procedure call (RPC) protocol — A transport protocol that enables an initiating or source computer to run a program process on a target computer.

repeater — A network transmission device that amplifies and retimes a packet- or cell-carrying signal so that it can be sent along all outgoing cable segments attached to that repeater.

replica set — A grouping of shared folders in a Dfs root that are replicated, or copied, to all servers that participate in Dfs replication. When changes are made to Dfs shared folders, all of the participating servers are automatically or manually synchronized so that they have the same copy.

replication — A process that, when used by Active Directory, creates a copy of specific Active Directory contents, called a data store, on domain controllers. For example, every domain controller in the same domain contains a regularly synchronized copy of the domain data store (the domain partition data) because of replication.

replication partners — Two domain controllers that directly replicate Active Directory data, one with the other.

resource record (RR) — A record that is used to provide data in a DNS zone or lookup table. The information in a DNS server is built from resource records.

reverse lookup zone — A DNS server zone or table that maps IP addresses to computer or domain names.

right — In Windows 2000, an access privilege for high-level activities such as logging on to a server from the network, shutting down a server, and logging on locally.

roaming profile — Desktop and other settings that are associated with an account so that the same settings are employed no matter what computer is used to access the account (the profile is downloaded to the client from a server). Also called a roaming user profile.

router — A network device that connects networks having the same or different access methods and media, such as Ethernet to token ring. It forwards packets to networks by using a decision-making process based on routing table data, discovery of the most efficient routes, and preprogrammed information from the network administrator.

schema — A database that consists of the definitions of all objects in Active Directory, and that reflects the skeletal structure and rules of Active Directory. The principal elements of the Active Directory schema are object classes and object attributes.

schema master — The single or unique domain controller in a forest that is able to make additions and changes to the forest-wide schema. When a schema modification is made, the schema master copies that modification to every domain controller in the same forest.

schema namespace — An Active Directory namespace that holds object classes and the attributes associated with each object class. See *schema*.

scope of influence — The reach of a type of group, such as access to resources in a single domain or access to all resources in all domains in a forest (see domain local, global, and universal groups).

secondary DNS server — A DNS server that is a backup to a primary DNS server and therefore is not authoritative.

Security Accounts Manager (SAM) — Located in the Windows NT 4.0 or earlier server Registry, a database that stores information about user accounts, groups, and access privileges for a domain. The master copy of this database is kept on the primary domain controller (PDC) in the domain, and backed up to one or more backup domain controllers (BDCs). The SAM is also used in a Windows 2000 server to store local computer account information, such as that for a standalone computer that does not have Active Directory installed.

security descriptor — A collection of security properties that are associated with an Active Directory object, such as granting permission for the Managers group of user accounts to read the contents of a folder and auditing that group each time one of its members accesses the folder.

security group — A grouping of Windows 2000 user accounts, computers, and other security groups that is used to assign access privileges— rights and permissions—to objects and services. Security groups appear in ACLs. Although not technically a distribution group, a security group can also be used to send an e-mail message to all members of the group.

security identifier (SID) — A unique identification number that is created each time a new security principal object is created, such as a user account, computer, or group. A portion of the SID is a number that identifies the domain, and that is the same in all SIDs generated for that domain. Another portion of the SID is a relative identifier (see *relative identifier*), which is a unique number used only in that SID.

security principal object — A main security object in a domain, such as a group, user account, or computer name, that enables users to access the domain and that enables verification of access to domain resources. The Everyone security group is an example of a security principal object.

security template — A file that contains preconfigured group policy settings for security, which can be imported into a group policy object linked to a domain or OU.

separate forest — An Active Directory model that links two or more forests in a partnership; however, the forests do not have Kerberos two-way transitive trusts and do not use the same schema.

Sequence Packet Exchange (SPX) — A Novell protocol that is used for network transport for application software where there is a particular need for data reliability.

service resource record (SRV RR) — A record in a DNS zone that is created to locate commonly used TCP/IP services. The SRV record is formatted to include information about the service that is provided by a server, the domain that is serviced by a server, and the protocol used by the server.

share permissions — Permissions that apply to a particular shared object, such as a shared folder or printer and that control access to that object over a network.

Simple Mail Transfer Protocol (SMTP) — An e-mail protocol used by systems that have TCP/IP network communications.

Simple Network Management Protocol (SNMP) — A TCP/IP-based protocol that enables servers, workstations, and network devices to gather standardized data about network performance and identify problems. SNMP also provides a means to manage specific network services and devices.

single forest — An Active Directory model in which there is only one forest, with interconnected trees and domains that use the same schema and global catalog.

site — Set up to enable efficient Active Directory operations on a network, one or more TCP/IP-based subnets that are aggregated into a logical Active Directory container object (a site). The links between subnets within a site are relatively fast (512 Kbps or faster) and reliable.

site link — A WAN link that is often slower and less dependable relative to the LANs or sites that it connects. Active Directory replication can be enabled and scheduled over site links.

site link bridge — Two or more site links that transitively replicate to the connected sites through the same host transport protocol, either TCP/IP or SMTP. Physically, a site link bridge is often a network device, such as a router or brouter. The site link bridge enables replication to go in any direction, along any site link within the site link bridge.

situational decision model — A model in which decision making is related to specific sociological factors or situations that exist in an organization.

standalone server — A server that is not a member of a domain, but that is a member of an existing workgroup or that establishes its own workgroup, as in peer-to-peer networking.

standby operations master domain controller — A domain controller that can be designated as the operations master domain controller in the event that the main operations master domain controller fails. An operations master domain controller and a standby operations master domain controller are used in a small organization that has only one domain and two domain controllers.

strategic plan — A long-range planning document that is usually linked to the mission statement of an organization.

subnet mask — A subnet mask is a designated portion of an IP address that is used to indicate the class of addressing on a network and to divide a network into subnetworks as a way to manage traffic patterns.

subsidiary office — A portion of an organization that is owned by a parent company or organization, but that has relative decision-making autonomy and often does business under a different name from the parent.

switch — A network device that has incoming and outgoing circuits and that can direct network traffic along a specific path using a process of filtering and forwarding data frames. On Ethernet networks, modern switches have replaced hubs in popularity because they support the use of the star topology and can direct frames and packets to a specific device or IP addresses, enabling fast communication.

switched megabit data service (SMDS) — Also called switched multimegabit data service, this is a transport method developed by regional telephone companies to provide cell-based, high-speed communication over WANs.

synchronization connector — An interface between two directory services, two databases, or a directory service and a database that updates data in one when data in the other is added or changed. See *Active Directory connector (ADC)*.

synchronous optical network (SONET) — A fiber-optic communications technology that is capable of high-speed (over one gigabit per second) data transmission. Networks based on SONET can deliver voice, data, and video communications.

system access control list (SACL) — A portion of an access control list that determines which events associated with an object are to be audited for user and user group activity.

system policy — A set of basic user account and computer parameters that can be configured in Windows NT 4.0 (and is contained in Windows 2000 for backward compatibility) to control the desktop environment and specific client configuration settings.

system policy editor — An editor, Poledit.exe, that is used to configure system policy parameters in Windows NT 4.0 and that is also available in Windows 2000 Server.

Systems Network Architecture (SNA) — A layered communications protocol used by IBM for communication between IBM mainframe computers and terminals.

terminal — A device that consists of a monitor and keyboard, and is used to communicate with host computers that run the programs. The terminal does not have a processor to use for running programs locally.

thin client — A specialized personal computer or terminal device that has a minimal Windows-based or GUI-based operating system. A thin client is designed to connect to a host computer that does most or all of the processing. The thin client is mainly responsible for providing a graphical user interface and network connectivity.

token ring — An access method developed by IBM in the 1970s and which remains a primary LAN technology. This transport method uses a physical star topology along with the logic of a ring topology. Although each node is connected to a central hub, the packet travels from node to node as though there were no starting or ending point.

total cost of ownership (TCO) — The cost of installing and maintaining computers and equipment on a network, which includes hardware, software, maintenance, and support costs.

transitive replication — Active Directory replication that can go in any direction through a site link bridge.

transitive trust — A trust relationship between two or more domains in a tree, between domains and a tree, or between two or more trees in the same forest, in which each domain or tree has access to objects in the others. When a new domain or tree is created in a forest, a transitive trust is automatically established. In Active Directory, a transitive trust is also called an *implicit two-way transitive trust.*

Transmission Control Protocol (TCP)/Internet Protocol (IP) — The key protocols used for network and Internet communications. TCP is a transport protocol that establishes communication sessions between networked software application processes and that provides for reliable end-to-end delivery of data by controlling data flow. IP is a protocol that is used in combination with TCP or UDP to enable packets to reach a destination on a local or remote network by using dotted decimal addressing.

tree — Related domains that use a contiguous namespace, share the same schema, and have two-way, transitive trust relationships. The domains in a tree, in general, have a common configuration and employ the same global catalog.

tree root domain — The highest-level parent domain in a tree. The tree root domain has no higher-level parent domain.

trusted domain — A domain that has been granted security access to resources in another domain.

trusting domain — A domain that allows another domain security access to its resources and objects, such as to servers.

two-way trust — A domain relationship in which both domains are trusted and trusting, enabling one to have access to objects in the other.

unicast — A transmission method in which one copy of each packet is sent to each targeted destination.

universal security group — A group that is used to provide access to resources in any domain within a forest. A common implementation is to make global groups that contain accounts members of a universal group that has access to resources. The universal security group is only available in native mode domains.

virtual private network (VPN) — A private network that is like a tunnel through a larger network—such as the Internet, an enterprise network, or both—that is restricted only to designated member clients.

Windows Internet Naming Service (WINS) — A Windows 2000 Server service that enables the server to convert IP addresses to NetBIOS computer names for network and Internet communications. WINS is needed to provide naming services for Windows NT, Windows 98, and earlier Windows operating systems.

X.25 — An older, very reliable packet-switching protocol for connecting remote networks at speeds up to 2.048 Mbps.

zone — A partition or subtree in a DNS server that contains specific kinds of records in a lookup table, such as a forward lookup zone that contains records in a table for looking up computer and domain names in order to find their associated IP addresses.

Index